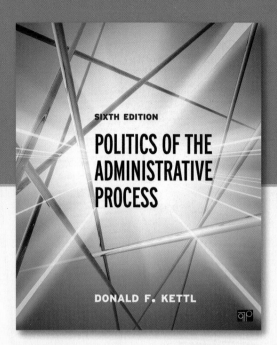

SIXTH EDITION

POLITICS OF THE ADMINISTRATIVE PROCESS

DONALD F. KETTL

Three overarching themes of politics, accountability, and performance

Today's public administrators struggle to remain efficient in the face of political polarization and gridlock, while at the same time, they must maintain their performance despite shifting demographics and challenging economic and budgetary conditions. Kettl hones in on three overarching themes of politics, accountability, and performance to give students a realistic, relevant, and well-researched view of the field.

Understanding the need to balance theory with practice, chapter discussions provide the foundational concepts necessary to understand how the administrative process works, while case studies apply those concepts at the federal, state, and local levels.

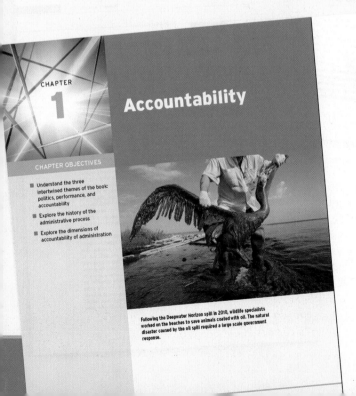

CHAPTER 1

Accountability

CHAPTER OBJECTIVES

- Understand the three intertwined themes of the book: politics, performance, and accountability
- Explore the history of the administrative process
- Explore the dimensions of accountability of administration

Following the Deepwater Horizon spill in 2010, wildlife specialists worked on the beaches to save animals coated with oil. The natural disaster caused by the oil spill required a large scale government response.

AMERICANS HAVE ALWAYS HAD AN UNEASY RELATIONSHIP with their government. The nation was born in revolution, a very long time ago, and to a truly remarkable degree that shadow of the American Revolution continues to hang over our views toward government and the rules we use to guide it. We have very high expectations. Our founding documents are always worth rereading, not as sacred texts but as political statements, and they are full of soaring aspirations. Our Declaration of Independence asserts that "We hold these truths to be self-evident, that all men are created equal, that they are endowed by their Creator with certain unalienable Rights, that among these are Life, Liberty, and the pursuit of Happiness." Stop and think—the revolutionaries who founded our government wanted to protect their liberty—and they wanted a government that would allow them to be happy. When was the last time you thought about "happiness" and "government" in the same sentence? Then there's our basic framework, captured in the Constitution. It starts with a foundation in "We the People" and pledges justice, domestic tranquility, defense, the general welfare—and "The Blessings of Liberty to ourselves and our Posterity."

We're the "posterity," living and walking today, but we're often not feeling especially happy about our government. The revolutionary DNA is still in our body politic. We have tea parties trying to shrink government's size and power and activists pushing hard for a strong governmental role in climate change. We quite deliberately put opposing forces into office to get anything done. We are often a marvel to people in other parts of the world, who admire our freedom and our vast progress since our founding—and we are a puzzle to people who are amazed at the battles we wage in governing ourselves. Those who view us from afar struggle to capture what we know intuitively: both our progress and our battles flow from our uneasy relationship with government, from our simultaneous efforts to empower and control it, and from our ceaseless struggles to figure out how to secure justice, defense, and the general welfare while seeking tranquility and happiness. We struggle to balance our lofty expectations for government with our deep distrust of it.

That struggle becomes most real in the politics of our administrative process. It's one thing to argue the case for justice, but it's another to make our state prisons secure without abusing inmates. It's one thing to argue for domestic tranquility, but it's another to determine how much force local police should use in fighting neighborhood crime. It's one thing to pursue defense, but it's another to find just the right balance of weapons to protect the country without bankrupting it. It's one thing to advance the general welfare, but it's quite another to decide which citizens whose homes are destroyed by a superstorm should get federal aid. The basic administrative questions, on the front lines of government, are how we really set the balance and define what government is. No matter how bold or simple our policies, very little in government has any meaning until we seek to administer them.

For example, we have a clear national policy about the many oil drilling platforms in the Gulf of Mexico. When companies extract the oil, our laws and regulations say, they should keep their workers safe and ensure that their practices don't pollute. But on the evening of April 20, 2010, everything went tragically wrong. Workers on the Deepwater Horizon, a highly specialized drilling platform—part boat, part oil rig—noticed a highly explosive burst of methane gas moving up the pipes. One crew member raced to trigger the blowout preventer, a massive device on the ocean floor a mile below designed to seal the drilling pipe in

Covering *contemporary, real-world topics,* each chapter features *three case studies*—with one always focused on a state and local issue—giving students the opportunity to see concepts in action.

Questions to Consider encourage critical analysis and help students apply concepts.

With this new edition, every chapter features one brand new case

CASE 1.1

Do NOT Read This Case! The NSA's Surveillance Program

In July 2013, U.S. Department of Homeland Security employees received a message warning them not to use their home computers or personal smartphones to look at an article on the *Washington Post* website. The website, it turns out, contained a "top-secret" slide leaked by former intelligence analyst Edward Snowden. If an agency employee viewed the top-secret material from an unclassified computer, it would constitute "classified data spillage," which had to be reported to supervisors like a toxic chemical spill.

Here's the email, as the *Post* reported it:

From: [REDACTED]

Sent: Friday, July 1...

hq.dhs.gov<mailto:Opssecurity@hq.dhs.gov>   <mailto:Opssecurity@hq.dhs.gov> <mailto:Opssecurity@hq.dhs.gov> >).

Again, please exercise good judgment when visiting these webpages and clicking on such links. You may be violating your Non-Disclosure Agreement in which you sign that you will protect Classified National Security Information. You may be subject to any administrative or legal action from the Government.[1]

What caused all the fuss was a PowerPoint slide revealing the basic structure of the federal government's PRISM program.[2] No one but highly placed insiders had previously even [heard] about the program. Through PRISM, the [National] Security Agency (NSA) worked with a [variety] of information technology compa[nies including] Apple, Google, Skype, Yahoo, and [others] to collect information on the commu[nications] of individuals that the NSA wanted to [monitor]. The companies shared the informa[tion with the] NSA, which then put its analysts to [work to deter]mine whether any of the communi[cations consti]tuted a threat to national security. [Who the] "targets" was NSA investigating? At [Snow]den's leak, there were 117,675 [Americans, however, might have] [commu]nications shared with NSA "inci[dent as a] result of the agency's work.

[If you have] a top-secret security clearance [and, in] this case, you must immediately [tell your super]visor to report a "classified data [spillage.] don't have a top-secret clear[ance, you] read something you weren't

supposed to see to begin with. Either way: Do NOT read this case!

Questions to Consider

1. What do you think about this government surveillance program, which allows the NSA to work with popular service providers like Facebook, Google, and Skype to collect personal information without the user's knowledge? On the one hand, terrorists frequently use the Internet to plan attacks. On the other hand, such surveillance is clearly an invasion of individual privacy.

2. The memo to employees might seem silly to some. But the government has a broad policy on not allowing users to look at classified information on unclassified computers. Why? Unclassified computers can be infiltrated by viruses and spyware, which

allow others to capture anything that goes across the screen. (The CIA and the NSA do not allow cell phones inside their buildings' secure zones.) If you were a manager, how would you handle this situation?

3. Perhaps nothing more sharply frames the problem of accountability in modern government than determining how to safeguard the personal communications of individual Americans while preserving national security. What kind of accountability system would you design to find the balance?

NOTES

1. Josh Hicks, "DHS Warns Employees not to Read Leaked NSA Information," *Washington Post* (July 15, 2013), http://www.washingtonpost.com/blogs/ federal-eye/wp/2013/07/15/dhs-warns-employees-not-to-read-leaked-nsa-information.

2. To view the slide, go to http://www.washington-post.com/business/economy/the-nsa-slide-you-ha vent-seen/2013/07/30/32801426-e8e6-11e2-aa9f-c03a72e2d342_story.html

CASE 1.2

Snow Removal i[...] Who Gets Plow[...]

Throughout much of the East Coast, the winter o[f] 2010 was painfully burned into everyone's mem[ory]. Children looking forward to snow days ha[d] their dreams fulfilled—and then some. By mi[d-] February, the Washington, D.C., area had alrea[dy] shattered the all-time record for snow, with [...] inches of accumulation. Even Baltim[ore,] Maryland, had more snow than Buffalo, [New] York. Many football fans found themselves s[...] at home instead of partying with friends fo[r the] Super Bowl. Some local universities were [closed] down for a week as the snow removal crews [strug]gled to dig out the sidewalks and parking l[...]

CASE 1.3

Google Earth versus Privacy in Riverhead, New York

In Riverhead, New York, town officials launched an aggressive campaign to find backyard swimming pools whose owners hadn't obtained the required permits to build them. As the town's chief building inspector, Leroy Barnes Jr., explained, "It's a safety issue more than anything else." Faulty plumbing could cause water damage to neighboring properties. If electrical wiring for lights or filters were installed improperly, someone could be electrocuted. In addition, the town's ordinance required pool owners to install a fence around the pool to prevent small children from wandering in and accidentally drowning. The campaign, in this small town near the tip of Long Island, found 250 pools that had been constructed but whose owners had not received the requisite permits. In addition, the aggressive inspection program produced $75,000 in fees from violators.[1]

Barnes, however, quickly found himself under fierce attack, from the American Civil Liberties Union (ACLU) and scores of angry townspeople. It wasn't because of the campaign to find violators, at least on the surface. Rather, it was because Barnes had cleverly used the Google Earth search program to find the pools. He used the program's online satellite feature to find pools, identify the address, check the address against the town's database of permits, and find pools that did not have the permits required by law. Town officials wondered what all the fuss was about. After all, Google Earth is available to any user, on any computer. It doesn't show anything that anyone anywhere can't see. Why can't the town use publicly available information to enforce its laws?

"Technically it may be lawful," replied Donna Lieberman of New York's ACLU, "but in the gut it

does not feel like a free society kind of operation."[2] Some local residents complained that it felt creepy to know that the town was peeking into their lives via satellite. Critics pointed out that the Fourth Amendment to the Constitution prevents government officials from conducting unlawful searches. Using remote satellites without a search warrant crossed the line, they argued.

Just how far should government go in combining emerging technology with its soft power? In Greece, as well as New York, government officials are using Google Earth to track down pools without permits to collect fines. Enterprising private citizens are also making innovative use of satellite surveillance. Thieves in the United Kingdom are using the technology to identify backyard ponds stocked with exotic fish, which they steal and sell for large sums. A private company is already using private satellites to photograph the parking lots of Wal-Mart stores. Counting the cars tells analysts which communities have the fastest-growing economies. If private companies are doing it, should government be handcuffed in using the same readily available technology to enforce its laws?

It's easy to see even bigger issues in the future. If governments pass aggressive energy-saving laws to restrict backyard barbeques (too many hydrocarbons being released) and to require better insulation of homes (to prevent energy from being wasted), should the government be able to use remote-sensing devices to detect heat emissions? Private companies are now trying to sell special vans to local police that provide a comprehensive scan of every car passing by. It can detect illegal items onboard without a search warrant. Should local police

Ripped from the Headlines boxes connect the themes of politics, accountability, and performance to current issues recently in the news.

ACCOUNTABILITY

A Bad Week for the IRS

It had been one of the worst weeks ever for the Internal Revenue Service, perhaps the least-loved bureaucracy in government. Senior official Lois Lerner disclosed that the IRS had singled out dozens of organizations for extra review to see if they were violating their nonprofit status, on the grounds of their political affiliation. Putting "patriot" or "tea party" in the application triggered extra attention and, Lerner acknowledged that this was wrong. Then, speaking words no one could recall ever coming from an IRS official, she apologized for the agency's actions.

In trying to insulate the White House from the fallout, President Obama said that the IRS is an independent agency. His press secretary Jay Carney reinforced the message by telling reporters that the IRS was an independent agency with only a pair of political appointees at the top.

The White House reaction raises a very tough question. If the IRS is "independent," to whom is it accountable? Everyone, including the manager in charge of the operation, acknowledges that using politics to enforce the tax code was wrong. What does accountability mean if an agency and its employees are "independent"?

Elements that help students read, review, research, and study

CHAPTER 6

CHAPTER OBJECTIVES

- Understand the sources of organizational performance problems
- Examine the strategies to improve coordination
- Chart the advantages and disadvantages of structural reorganization to solve organizational problems

Chapter-opening Key Objectives

Part II Organizational Theory and the Role of Government's Structure

Administrative Implications

Six basic propositions flow from the view of public administration as a structuring of authority

1. *Principals and agents.* In a democracy, the **principals** are the elected officials who make policy on behalf of the people and delegate responsibility to **agents**, who are the administrators charged with carrying out the law. This, in fact, is where the concept of agencies comes from—agencies are the agents established to do the principals' work.
2. *Narrow, defined specialization.* An agency is assigned by law to a particular field of activity and a set of responsibilities.
3. *Internal specialized structure.* The agency has an internal structure that divides responsibilities among bureaus (or whatever its principal units are called) and, further down, among individual positions.

Bolded Key Concepts

---

134   **Part II** Organizational Theory and the Role of Government's Structure

KEY CONCEPTS

areal, or prefectoral, system 117
bureaus 116
cabinet 112
function 112
government corporations 115

independent agencies 114
National Security Council 122
Office of Management and Budget 122
regulatory commissions 114

FOR FURTHER READING

Arnold, Peri E. *Making the Managerial Presidency: Comprehensive Reorganization Planning, 1905–1980.* Princeton, N.J.: Princeton University Press, 1986.
Campbell, Colin. *Managing the Presidency: Carter, Reagan, and the Search for Executive Harmony.* Pittsburgh: University of Pittsburgh Press, 1986.
Fesler, James W. *Area and Administration.* Tuscaloosa: University of Alabama Press, 2008.
Fountain, Jane E. *Building the Virtual State: Information Technology and Institutional Change.* Washington, D.C.: Brookings Institution, 2001.

Heclo, Hugh. *A Government of Strangers: Executive Politics in Washington.* Washington, D.C.: Brookings Institution, 1977.
Hess, Stephen, and James Pfiffner. *Organizing the Presidency.* Washington, D.C.: Brookings Institution, 2003.
Nathan, Richard P. *The Administrative Presidency.* New York: Wiley, 1983.
Perri 6. *E-Governance: Styles of Political Judgment in the Information Age Polity.* New York: Palgrave, 2004.
Seidman, Harold. *Politics, Position, and Power: The Dynamics of Federal Organization.* 5th ed. New York: Oxford University Press, 1998.

SUGGESTED WEBSITES

The National Academy of Public Administration conducts excellent research on the management of the executive branch and of management problems within individual agencies, making its reports available on its website, www.napawash.org. In addition, the Government Accountability Office, www.gao.gov, is an invaluable source for analysis of both management and policy issues.

For information about employment trends in the federal government, see the Office of

Personnel Management's Federal Employment Statistics webpage, www.opm.gov/feddata.

There is an enormous amount of information about e-government available on the web. An excellent foundation for exploring the federal government's websites is the federal portal www.usa.gov. Most state and local governments have webpages and portals as well; among the very good ones are those for the Commonwealth of Virginia, www.virginia.gov, and for the city of Phoenix, http://phoenix.gov.

End-of-chapter Lists: Key concepts, for further reading, and suggested websites

---

Key Concepts Glossary

480   Politics of the Administrative Process

economic regulation: the portion of public sector rulemaking that affects the behavior of private markets (compare social regulation).

efficiency: a measure of the level of inputs required to produce a given level of outputs.

e-government: a strategy of using information technology, especially the Internet and the World Wide Web, to make it easier for citizens to interact with government.

entitlements: governmental programs through which an individual is automatically guaranteed services—typically, a payment—because the individual meets requirements set in law.

ethical behavior: the adherence to moral standards and avoidance of even the appearance of unethical actions.

executive leadership: strategic direction provided by the top officials of an organization.

executive privilege: the claim by presidents that communication with aides is protected from outside scrutiny, including investigation by Congress.

exit: the decision by members of an organization to leave, especially because they disagree with

fiscal year: the government's ing October 1 for the fe July 1 for many state and

formal approach: a theory relies on a rigorous mode between actors, especial and agents.

formula-based program grant programs in whi grant is determined by

function: the specific role a part of an organizatio

fungibility: the ability transfer the proceeds the expenses of anoth

furloughs: days off wi employees.

G

government by proxy: use of indirect tools ing contracts, grant tax provisions) to p

government-by-proxy

A new full-color interior grabs students' attention and improves data analysis skills

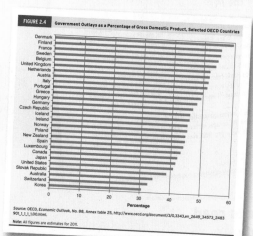

FIGURE 2.4 Government Outlays as a Percentage of Gross Domestic Product, Selected OECD Countries

Source: OECD, *Economic Outlook*, No. 88, Annex table 25, http://www.oecd.org/document/3/0,3343,en_2649_34573_2483
901_1_1_1,00.html.

Note: All figures are estimates for 2011.

TABLE 2.1	**Number of Governments in the United States**							
Type of government	1952	1962	1972	1982	1992	2002	2007	2012
Federal	1	1	1	1	1	1	1	1
State	50	50	50	50	50	50	50	50
Local	116,756	91,186	78,218	81,780	84,955	87,525	89,476	89,004
Total units	116,807	91,237	78,269	81,831	85,006	87,576	89,527	89,055
Type of local government								
County	3,052	3,043	3,044	3,041	3,043	3,034	3,033	3,031
Municipal	16,807	18,000	18,517	19,076	19,279	19,429	19,492	19,522
Township and town	17,202	17,142	16,991	16,734	16,656	16,504	16,519	16,364
School district	67,355	34,678	15,781	14,851	14,422	13,506	13,051	12,884
Special district	12,340	18,323	23,885	28,078	31,555	35,052	37,381	37,203

Source: U.S. Census Bureau, *2012 Census of Governments*, http://www.census.gov/govs/cog2012.

FIGURE 2.5   License Plate Data Retention Policies for Selected States

MILPITAS, CA
Population: 67,000
Data policy: None
Stored plate reads: 4.7 million
(as of 8/2/12)

MINNESOTA STATE PATROL
Population: 5.3 million
Data policy: Delete after 48 hours
Stored plate reads: Less than 20,000

GRAPEVINE, TX
Population: 47,000
Data policy: None
Stored plate reads: 2 million
(as of 8/29/12)

JERSEY CITY, NJ
Population: 250,000
Data policy: Delete after 5 years
Stored plate reads: 10 million (estimated)
(as of 8/2/12)

Source: American Civil Liberties Union, *You Are Being Tracked: How License Plate Readers Are Being Used To Record Americans' Movements* (New York: July 2013), p. 17, at http://www.aclu.org/files/assets/071613-aclu alprreport-opt-v05.pdf.

that they were the focus of administration decisions that, in Jindal's view, represented the wrong political decisions. Of course, Jindal's attack was itself political. In these cases, as well as in so much of what government does, political decisions take their meaning in the ways public administrators carry them out. Government's power takes its form through public administration.

These themes also capture the inevitable tradeoffs at the core of government power. More steps to increase accountability, including more rules to restrict administrators' power, can reduce efficiency by multiplying red tape. Streamlining government to make it more efficient can risk making administrators less accountable. At every stage, these basic questions frame the size and role of government, and there's nothing more fundamental to politics than that.

Public administration is about everything that's important about government, and everything that's important about government touches on or flows through public administration. Those twists and turns are often hidden, and the issues can be subtle. If we care about government—especially if we care about making government work better—we need to pay very careful attention to the politics of the administrative process. And that's the mission of this book.

For example, consider the mundane problem of plowing snow from city streets. Could it possibly be about politics? Just ask former New York Mayor John Lindsay. Following a blizzard in February 1969, much of the city was impassable for days. Almost 40 percent of his snow removal equipment was sidelined because of poor maintenance, and the borough of Queens was especially isolated. When he used a four-wheel-drive vehicle to make his way to the snowbound residents, they booed him and called him a bum. He managed to win reelection, but the story haunted him for the rest of his career and undermined his 1972 presidential campaign.

A 1979 storm in Chicago torpedoed the campaign of Chicago Mayor Michael A. Bilandic. Washington Mayor Marion S. Barry Jr. suffered for years after a blizzard hit his city while he was enjoying sunny weather in Southern California, where he was attending the Super Bowl.[4] A senior official in a Midwest city once confided in me that there was a special snow removal plan for election day, to ensure that the precincts most likely to vote for the mayor got plowed out first. It's not especially surprising to discover that officials use government power to advance political purposes—or that administrative failures have political consequences. This is an echo of a great scene in the movie *Casablanca*, which might well be the best film of all time. Police Captain Louis Renault loves Casablanca's nightlife

A 2010 blizzard blanketed Washington, shut down the government, and created a massive job for these National Park Service employees struggling to dig out the Lincoln Memorial. History has shown that snow clearing can be a surprisingly political matter.

FIGURE 4.1   Hierarchical Bureaucracy

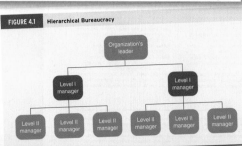

Organization's leader
Level I manager
Level I manager
Level II manager
Level II manager
Level II manager
Level II manager
Level II manager
Level II manager

Teachers in Chicago's public schools, the third-largest district in the country, went on strike at the beginning of the 2012 school year for better compensation and job security.

POLITICS OF THE ADMINISTRATIVE PROCESS

SIXTH EDITION

POLITICS OF THE ADMINISTRATIVE PROCESS

SIXTH EDITION

Donald F. Kettl
University of Maryland

Los Angeles | London | New Delhi
Singapore | Washington DC

Los Angeles | London | New Delhi
Singapore | Washington DC

FOR INFORMATION:

CQ Press
An Imprint of SAGE Publications, Inc.
2455 Teller Road
Thousand Oaks, California 91320
E-mail: order@sagepub.com

SAGE Publications Ltd.
1 Oliver's Yard
55 City Road
London EC1Y 1SP
United Kingdom

SAGE Publications India Pvt. Ltd.
B 1/I 1 Mohan Cooperative Industrial Area
Mathura Road, New Delhi 110 044
India

SAGE Publications Asia-Pacific Pte. Ltd.
3 Church Street
#10-04 Samsung Hub
Singapore 049483

Acquisitions Editor: Charisse Kiino
Associate Editor: Nancy Loh
Production Editor: Laura Barrett
Copy Editor: Sarah J. Duffy
Typesetter: C&M Digitals (P) Ltd.
Proofreader: Dennis W. Webb
Indexer: Judy Hunt
Cover Designer: Auburn Associates, Inc.
Marketing Manager: Amy Whitaker

Printed in Canada

Library of Congress Cataloging-in-Publication Data

Kettl, Donald F.

Politics of the administrative process/Donald F. Kettl, University of Maryland. — Sixth edition.

pages cm
Includes bibliographical references and index.

ISBN 978-1-4833-3293-2 (pbk. : alk. paper)

1. Public administration—United States—Textbooks. I. Title.

JK421.K4817 2015
351.73—dc23   2013039292

This book is printed on acid-free paper.

13 14 15 16 17 10 9 8 7 6 5 4 3 2 1

Brief Contents

Contents

Figures, Tables, and Boxes

Figures

Tables

Boxes

Boxes

Preface

I wrote this sixth edition of *Politics of the Administrative Process* at an especially difficult moment for American government. A Republican Congress and a Democratic Congress had negotiated what they thought would be an inescapable deadline for dealing with the federal deficit, through a deal that imposed consequences too crazy to happen. Come up with a plan to cut the deficit by the end of 2012, or across-the-board cuts would savage government programs. But they found a way to escape the deadline, the unthinkable became unavoidable, the cuts occurred, and then Congress and the president stumbled into an extended shutdown of the federal government.

Federal law, as Chapter 1 of this book explains, forbids the federal government from spending money not appropriated by Congress, except for matters of the highest national interest. That meant the federal government closed down most of its offices that serve the public and shut down national monuments and parks. That led Rep. Randy Neugebauer (R-Texas) to confront a National Park Ranger, who was doing her duty at Washington D.C.'s closed World War II memorial. Pointing to veterans who had traveled many miles to see the memorial, Rep. Neugebauer demanded, "How do you look at them and... deny them access?" The ranger sadly replied, "It's difficult." The congressman shot back, "The Park Service should be ashamed of themselves," and the ranger replied, "I'm not ashamed." At that point, a bystander stepped in and went face-to-face with the congressman. "This woman is doing her job, just like me," he said. "I'm a 30-year federal veteran—I'm out of work." The conversation soon ended, with the congressman walking in one direction, the long-time fed heading in another, and the Park Service ranger remaining on duty, even though she was not being paid.[1]

It's hard to escape the sense that we're in a fundamental battle over government, what it should do, and how it should work. Many Americans believe that government is too big and intrusive. Others demand it do more. Few Americans believe that government is doing a good job, and almost no one trusts Congress. Through it all, though, millions of workers come to their jobs every day to do their very best to make government work—and some, like the ranger, even show up in uniform, without pay and often without respect.

Despite this loud and sometimes nasty debate, the federal government shutdown in 2013, and the many public services and facilities that were suspended or closed as a result, showed us just how much we all rely on government. We might not all agree on what it ought to do but, when it's charged with doing something we care deeply about, we want it to be done well. This challenge is the core of the book: deciding which public problems are governmental problems, and then equipping government—federal, state, and local—to solve them. Given our vast public debate about the role of government, it's little wonder that these puzzles are enmeshed in politics. Of course, nothing lies more at the core of politics than figuring out what government ought to do. That, in turn, means the work of turning policy into results—public administration—is itself full of politics. Forces that lose in the "what government should do?" battle often come back to continue the fight in the "how should government do it?" issues.

For generations, we've had a fierce debate about whether we can—and should—separate the "what" from the "how"—to suggest that politics should focus on the "what" and that the "how" should be a matter for technical steps. In reality, that division is impossible, because every administrative act has a political consequence, from which street gets plowed first after a big snowstorm to which forms the tax authorities process first. That's why this is a book about the *politics* of the administrative process. It's also why the central problems at the core of this book are more important today than ever.

ORGANIZATION OF THE BOOK

Following this careful look at politics and administration in chapter 1, *Politics of the Administrative Process* explores the issues in five parts. Part 1 considers what government does and how it does it. Chapter 2 lays out government's strategies and tactics, as well as the growth of government's reliance on nongovernmental partners to do its work. Chapter 3 examines the basic issues of administrative responsibility and the meaning of the "administrative state."

Part 2 moves on to probe the theories underlying organizations and their structure. Chapter 4 charts the basics of organizational theory. Chapters 5 and 6 analyze the structure of the executive branch and the problems that periodically hamper good organizational performance. Chapter 7 examines the enduring instinct of policymakers and administrators alike to reform organizational structure.

Part 3 addresses the role of people inside these organizational structures, and looks at the challenge of recruiting younger employees to public service, as the wave of Baby Boomers begin retiring. Civil service systems have long defined the basic rules and procedures for hiring and firing government workers, and that constitutes the focus of chapter 8. Chapter 9 asks how government can make the most of the intellectual capital its employees bring to the job.

Part 4 carefully examines how administrative agencies accomplish their missions. Administration is about making decisions, and chapter 10 analyzes the theories about this process. Chapter 11 applies these theories to budgeting, which is the most important administrative decision and which drives much of administrative action. Chapter 12 explores how implementers transform decisions into practice.

Part 5 takes on the theme of government accountability, with chapter 13 probing the strategies of regulation and the courts. Chapter 14 concludes the book by returning to the central overarching themes of executive power, politics, and accountability and examines, in particular, the control of administration by legislatures.

KEY FEATURES

This new edition contains significant changes from the fifth edition. First off, the most noticeable change is the beautiful full-color design! The book's graphics program has benefitted enormously from this change and I think students will really enjoy the experience of using this new edition. The photos jump off the page now and offer additional visual interest and the tables, figures, maps, and charts more effectively display data, concepts, and processes. I should also note that all supporting data and examples have been extensively revised and updated.

The book explores three big themes and how they affect public administration—politics, performance, and accountability—and there is a special "Ripped from the Headlines" box in each chapter to examine how one of the themes connects with the topic of the chapter. For example, a box on the IRS's targeting of conservative non-profit organizations to be audited raises the issue accountability in our government – we are all accountable to the IRS, but isn't it important that the IRS be held accountable for its actions as well? A box on the leak of top-secret documents by a former employee of the National Security Agency frames a tough puzzle on the role of politics in national security—a special judicial panel is responsible for overseeing electronic spying, but are government officials interfering with an impartial review of the oversight process? Then there are the efforts in New York City to improve accountability of the police department—can an in-depth real-time data collection system transform the way police do their jobs? New learning objectives open each chapter. Readers will also find key concepts bolded within the text and listed at the end of each chapter for ease of review, and a comprehensive glossary at the back of the book defines all the key concepts. Each chapter concludes with a list of suggested readings and a discussion of websites to aid further study.

The cases, 3 in each chapter, have been thoroughly revised. The cases play a crucial role in bringing home the key points in the chapter text. The issues and situations presented in each case bring the chapter material to life—they show how these concepts actually play out in the real world. For example, in chapter 12, on implementation, I discuss the complications arising in the rollout of President Obama's health insurance program, a major reform initiative that proved to be a tremendously complicated undertaking. This was the signature program in the president's agenda, but the launch of its website not only undermined the president's promises but weakened his credibility. For thousands and thousands of health insurance hopefuls, negotiating the website proved painful or impossible. The case provided one more example of why management matters—no policy idea can be good if it fails in execution, and failed execution itself can become a point of enormous political contention.

I've kept the content fresh by including at least one new case in each chapter, and each chapter also has at least on chapter on state and local government issues. In addition, each case ends with a "Questions to Consider" section, which challenges students to think critically about the big issues at play, to connect the ideas in the chapter with real-world examples, and to foster discussion among students about how *they* would solve the problems. The new case topics include:

- The challenges in implementing President Obama's signature health insurance program
- The coordination of government services following the 2013 Boston Marathon bombing
- An order forbidding government employees to read documents—that were printed in the newspaper for all to see
- Challenges to local government in managing water shortages

- High-tech scanning of license plates as part of government's surveillance
- Challenges to local governments' police power, including the use of a squad car to stage a prank during a marriage proposal
- The recruitment of millennials into government service
- The management of the furlough process for federal workers
- The issues posed by the coming retirement of baby boomers from government jobs
- Baltimore's battle with international bankers over municipal investments
- The hidden reaches of the federal government's security apparatus, buried in the "black budget"
- Public health challenges in managing whooping cough
- The issues faced by Seattle's police department following legalization of marijuana
- Consideration of "expectation management" in government
- President Obama's management reform agenda

PUBLIC ADMINISTRATION RESOURCE CENTER

Working with CQ Press, we have created a new **Public Administration Resource Center** (**http://college.cqpress.com/adminprocess**) to accompany my text which offers a robust array of tools and resources to help students review and study, and to help instructors prep for class. But the truly innovative elements of this new resource center feature a new online case archive, data-based exercises, and access to SAGE journal articles focused on public administration research and scholarship. I am thankful to the work of Michael Stewart Keeney and of Eric Zeemering, who revised or authored many of the resources listed below.

Students can benefit from a variety of open-access resources for reviewing, self-testing, and exploration:

- **Chapter summaries** with **learning objectives**
- Mobile-friendly **eflashcards**
- Mobile-friendly **practice quizzes**
- Annotated **multimedia** links that support and add depth to the book's case studies

With purchase of a new printed text, students will have free access to premium content on the resource center:

- A **case study archive** with additional online-only cases written by me. I will be writing 6 new cases that will be posted every semester, helping to keep my book up-to-date and to give students access to very current case topics happening in between editions. We will also be posting cases that appeared in previous editions of the book but are no longer in the current edition.
- Access to a selection of annotated full-text **journal articles**, from such SAGE journals as *Public Personnel Management, Public Policy and Administration, The American Review of Public Administration, Administration and Society*, among others. Each article comes with **Critical Analysis** questions help students link this scholarship to discussion in the text.

- **Data-based exercises** offer students the opportunity to use publicly available federal data, from sources such as OMB and GAO, to apply concepts learned in the text.

For instructors, there are resources to support your teaching and instruction. Go to the website (**http://college.cqpress.com/adminprocess**), click on "Instructor's Resources," and you can register and download the following:

- A complete **test bank** of more than 700 multiple-choice, true-or-false, and essay questions has been crafted specifically for the book and is available with *Respondus* test-generation software.
- An **instructor's manual** with chapter overviews, lecture starters, ideas for class activities, and discussion questions.
- PowerPoint **lecture slides** for each chapter outline key concepts
- **Graphics from the book** available in PowerPoint, .pdf, and .jpg formats.
- Sample syllabi.

ACKNOWLEDGMENTS

This sixth edition is the product of more than 70 years of intellectual capital. James W. Fesler published the first version of the text in 1980, and it represented the insights he had gained in more than 40 years of work in the field.[2] I was Jim Fesler's last graduate student and, in 1991 we joined in the first edition of *The Politics of the Administrative Process,* with the outstanding support of distinguished publisher Ed Artinian. Since his death in 2005, at age 94, I've continued the tradition. Jim was an exceptionally wise observer of administration and politics, and he had a keen instinct for finding the right question at the bottom of every big issue. He also had a taste for history. Worried about the problem of connecting the dots between organizations that share the same policy space? Consider the problem that England's Queen Victoria had in keeping the windows of her palace clean in the 1800s. Different agencies were in charge of cleaning the inside and the outside of the windows, as Chapter 6 explains, and even the queen could not get the agencies in sync. Jim's instinct was for uncovering the tough problems that go back generations—and, in many cases—millennia.

He would be the first to remind us that the problems we're struggling with—determining what government should do and how best to do it—have roots stretching to the very meaning of government. Moreover, Jim found great reassurance in discovering those roots. That did not lessen the huge conflicts over big issues, but it did help explain why the battles were worth fighting—and which fundamental issues will continue to shape the enduring issues about government and its administration. Jim's great contribution lays in explaining which fight we can win, which will endure, and why the battles matter.

In preparing this new edition, I'm especially grateful to Brenda Carter, executive editorial director; Charisse Kiino, publisher; Nancy Loh, associate editor; Laura Barrett, production editor, and Allison Hughes, assistant editor. Sarah J. Duffy did an outstanding job of copy editing the manuscript. In addition, I want to thank Michael Abels, University of Central Florida; Neal Buckwalter, Indiana University; Nelson Dometrius, Texas Tech University; Kurt Fenske, Northern Arizona University; Patricia Freeland, University of Tennessee; John

Klemanski, Oakland University; and Mark Morris, Miami University, who provided invaluable comments on the last edition. Finally, let me thank the instructors who have taught from this book and the students who have used it. You are joining the growing intellectual community that builds on Jim Fesler's tradition—and you are expanding the search for ever-better ways of making our government work.

NOTES

1   Mark Segraves, "Congressman Confronts Park Ranger Over Closed WWII Memorial," NBC4 Washington (October 3, 2013), at http://www.nbcwashington.com/news/local/Congressman-Confronts-Park-Ranger-Over-Closed-WWII-Memorial-226209781.html
2   James W. Fesler, *Public Administration: Theory and Practice* (Englewood Cliffs, N.J.: Prentice-Hall, 1978).

Abbreviations and Acronyms

AEC	Atomic Energy Commission
AFGE	American Federation of Government Employees
AFSCME	American Federation of State, County, and Municipal Employees
AIDS	Acquired Immune Deficiency Syndrome
APA	Administrative Procedure Act of 1946
BIA	Bureau of Indian Affairs
BOB	Bureau of the Budget
CBO	Congressional Budget Office
CDC	Centers for Disease Control and Prevention
CEQ	Council on Environmental Quality
CFR	Code of Federal Regulations
CIA	Central Intelligence Agency
CPSC	Consumer Product Safety Commission
DHS	Department of Homeland Security
DIA	Defense Intelligence Agency
DOD	Department of Defense
EDA	Economic Development Administration
EOP	Executive Office of the President
EPA	Environmental Protection Agency
FAA	Federal Aviation Administration
FBI	Federal Bureau of Investigation
FCC	Federal Communications Commission
FDA	Food and Drug Administration
FDIC	Federal Deposit Insurance Corporation
Fed	Federal Reserve Board
FEMA	Federal Emergency Management Agency
FHA	Federal Highway Administration
FLRA	Federal Labor Relations Authority
FTC	Federal Trade Commission
GAO	Government Accountability Office (formerly General Accounting Office)
GDP	Gross domestic product
GIS	Geographic Information System
GPP	Government Performance Project
GPRA	Government Performance and Results Act
GS	General Schedule of Classification and Pay

GSA	General Services Administration
HEW	Department of Health, Education, and Welfare
HHS	Department of Health and Human Services
HR	Human resources
HUD	Department of Housing and Urban Development
ICC	Interstate Commerce Commission
INS	Immigration and Naturalization Service
IRS	Internal Revenue Service
JCS	Joint Chiefs of Staff
LGA	Local Government Association (UK)
MBO	Management by objectives
MIL-SPECS	Military specifications
MSPB	Merit Systems Protection Board
NAPA	National Academy of Public Administration
NASA	National Aeronautics and Space Administration
NHTSA	National Highway Traffic Safety Administration
NIH	National Institutes of Health
NIMBY	"Not in my backyard"
NMA	National Motorists Association
NPR	National Performance Review
NSC	National Security Council
NYPD	New York Police Department
OECD	Organization for Economic Co-operation and Development
OGE	Office of Government Ethics
OMB	Office of Management and Budget
OPA	Office of Price Administration
OPM	Office of Personnel Management
OSD	Office of the Secretary of Defense
OSHA	Occupational Safety and Health Administration
PART	Program Assessment Rating Tool
PPBS	Planning-Programming-Budgeting System
RIF	Reductions in force
SEC	Securities and Exchange Commission
SEPTA	Southeastern Pennsylvania Transportation Authority
SES	Senior Executive Service
SSA	Social Security Administration
TABOR	Taxpayer Bill of Rights
Taser	Thomas A. Swift Electric Rifle
TQM	Total quality management
TSA	Transportation Security Administration
TVA	Tennessee Valley Authority
USDA	U.S. Department of Agriculture
ZBB	Zero-base budgeting

About the Author

Donald F. Kettl is dean of the School of Public Policy at the University of Maryland and a nonresident senior fellow at the Brookings Institution. Prior to his appointment at the University of Maryland, he was the Robert A. Fox Leadership Professor at the University of Pennsylvania, where he also served as professor of Political Science. Kettl is the author of numerous books, including *The Politics of the Administrative Process, The Next Government of the United States: Why Our Institutions Fail Us and How to Fix Them, The Global Public Management Revolution,* and *Leadership at the Fed.* Kettl has twice won the Louis Brownlow Award for the best book in public administration for *The Transformation of Governance: Public Administration for Twenty-first Century America* in 2003 and *System under Stress: Homeland Security and American Politics* in 2005. In 2008, he received the John Gaus Award of The American Political Science Association for lifetime contributions to the scholarship in the joint tradition of political science and public administration. Kettl has consulted broadly for government organizations and is a regular columnist for *Governing* magazine.

Accountability

- Understand the three intertwined themes of the book: politics, performance, and accountability

- Explore the history of the administrative process

- Explore the dimensions of accountability of administration

Following the Deepwater Horizon spill in 2010, wildlife specialists worked on the beaches to save animals coated with oil. The natural disaster caused by the oil spill required a large scale government response.

AMERICANS HAVE ALWAYS HAD AN UNEASY RELATIONSHIP with their government. The nation was born in revolution, a very long time ago, and to a truly remarkable degree that shadow of the American Revolution continues to hang over our views toward government and the rules we use to guide it. We have very high expectations. Our founding documents are always worth rereading, not as sacred texts but as political statements, and they are full of soaring aspirations. Our Declaration of Independence asserts that "We hold these truths to be self-evident, that all men are created equal, that they are endowed by their Creator with certain unalienable Rights, that among these are Life, Liberty, and the pursuit of Happiness." Stop and think—the revolutionaries who founded our government wanted to protect their liberty—and they wanted a government that would allow them to be happy. When was the last time you thought about "happiness" and "government" in the same sentence? Then there's our basic framework, captured in the Constitution. It starts with a foundation in "We the People" and pledges justice, domestic tranquility, defense, the general welfare—and "the Blessings of Liberty to ourselves and our Posterity."

We're the "posterity," living and walking today, but we're often not feeling especially happy about our government. The revolutionary DNA is still in our body politic. We have tea parties trying to shrink government's size and power and activists pushing hard for a strong governmental role in climate change. We quite deliberately put opposing forces into office to balance power and then complain very strongly about government's ability to get anything done. We are often a marvel to people in other parts of the world, who admire our freedom and our vast progress since our founding—and we are a puzzle to people who are amazed at the battles we wage in governing ourselves. Those who view us from afar struggle to capture what we know intuitively: both our progress and our battles flow from our uneasy relationship with government, from our simultaneous efforts to empower and control it, and from our ceaseless struggles to figure out how to secure justice, defense, and the general welfare while seeking tranquility and happiness. We struggle to balance our lofty expectations for government with our deep distrust of it.

That struggle becomes most real in the politics of our administrative process. It's one thing to argue the case for justice, but it's another to make our state prisons secure without abusing inmates. It's one thing to argue for domestic tranquility, but it's another to determine how much force local police should use in fighting neighborhood crime. It's one thing to pursue defense, but it's another to find just the right balance of weapons to protect the country without bankrupting it. It's one thing to advance the general welfare, but it's quite another to decide which citizens whose homes are destroyed by a superstorm should get federal aid. The basic administrative questions, on the front lines of government, are how we really set the balance and define what government is. No matter how bold or simple our policies, very little in government has any meaning until we seek to administer them.

For example, we have a clear national policy about the many oil drilling platforms in the Gulf of Mexico. When companies extract the oil, our laws and regulations say, they should keep their workers safe and ensure that their practices don't pollute. But on the evening of April 20, 2010, everything went tragically wrong. Workers on the Deepwater Horizon, a highly specialized drilling platform—part boat, part oil rig—noticed a highly explosive burst of methane gas moving up the pipes. One crew member raced to trigger the blowout preventer, a massive device on the ocean floor a mile below designed to seal the drilling pipe in case of trouble, but it failed. Explosions rocked the rig and the decks became sheets of flame. Some workers scrambled for the lifeboats. Other workers, facing a choice between the flaming cauldron and the dark sea 75 feet below, took the seven-story dive into the inky water. Rescuers fished some of the crew out of the water, but the Deepwater Horizon's accident cost the lives of eleven crew members. The massive fire burned for a day and a half until the rig sank to the bottom, leaving oil gushing from the broken pipes. More than 4 million barrels of oil flowed into the Gulf, contaminating beaches, marshes, and wetlands in the largest oil spill in history.

One worker later reported, "There was no chain of command. Nobody in charge."[1] It quickly became clear that BP was in the midst of an epic disaster. No one really knew what was happening on the floor of the Gulf of Mexico, so deep that only unmanned submarines could reach the source of the spewing oil, so dark that submarines had to bring their own lights to see anything, and pressure so great that awkward remote-control arms proved the only way workers could work to contain the spewing oil.

At first, BP assured everyone that it would get the spill under control and that it would deal with the environmental damage. At every step, though, television coverage undermined the corporation's pledge of quick, effective relief. Video of the out-of-control fire gave way to new shots of oil slicks on the water's surface and sludge-coated birds on the shoreline. Exasperated by the intense news coverage, BP's chief executive, Tony Hayward, told reporters, "I would like my life back." That only infuriated Gulf residents. Tom Young, a Louisiana fisherman devastated by the fishing ban imposed after the explosion, told a reporter, "Our way of life is over. It's the end, the apocalypse and no one outside of these few parishes really cares. They say they do, but they don't do nothing but talk. . . . Where's the person who says these are real people, real people with families, and they are hurting?"[2] BP didn't seem to know how much oil was flowing out of its well, and state and local governments pleaded for help.

BP called the spill "a well control event" that "allowed hydrocarbons to escape." In plain English, the spill was the result of a blowout caused by the failure of private companies to manage their operations safely—BP and its two major contractors: Transocean, the world's largest ocean drilling company and the operator of the Deepwater Horizon, and Halliburton, a company that supplies a wide range of support services including, in this case, cementing the well on the floor of the Gulf. It was a private sector failure—but congressional investigators began asking whether the federal government was doing enough. President Barack Obama appointed Coast Guard Commandant Admiral Thad Allen as the "national incident commander" to coordinate the response. A tough and burly commander who had distinguished himself in leading the government's response to Hurricane Katrina five years earlier, Allen had become the federal government's go-to leader for impossible jobs. In the months that followed, Admiral Allen struggled to pull together the many players—and the thousands of workers—who were involved in the response effort. Complicating the damage control process was simply determining how much oil was flowing from the well.

In short order, a failure by a private company to manage its drilling operations became an inescapable demand for a government response. The government response, in turn, became not just a program to be managed but a vast, complex, interconnected web across many government agencies, levels of government, and public-private connections that all had to unite to overcome the spreading ooze. It was a tale of enormous political pressure, as fishermen fearful of going out of business and a Republican governor with political ambitions, Louisiana's Bobby Jindal, had to join with the Democrats in the Obama administration. BP worked hard to contain the oil, repair its image, and fend off the inevitable lawsuits. Residents along the Gulf just wanted the assault on their lives and their beaches to stop.

The story of the BP spill is the essence of modern government: We the people identify problems that we expect the government will solve, to promote the general welfare. How does it do so? Government, on behalf of us all, sets goals, and then it creates complex organizations to meet those goals. In short, it creates *public administration*. And running throughout public administration are three enduring themes.

The first theme is *politics*. Many people often see administration as the business of the detail, which can't possibly be interesting. In reality, because no decision—especially no political decision—has any value except in the way it's implemented, public administration inevitably shapes and is shaped by politics. *Politics (and, therefore, public administration) is about the choices among values*, including which values get emphasis and which don't. That is the very fabric of public administration. Which neighborhoods get extra police protection? Who gets the preferred line through airport screening? When it snows, which highways are plowed first? Each of these is a matter of detail richly wrapped in politics.

The second theme is *performance*. Public administration exists to get things done. How well does it work? How long does it take to respond to a house fire or report of a mugging? Do Social Security recipients get their checks on time and in the right amounts? Do state prisons keep prisoners inside, protecting citizens outside without abusing inmates inside? We expect *public administration to work well, delivering effectiveness (high-quality goods and services) and efficiency (goods and services at the lowest cost to taxpayers)*.

The third theme is *accountability*. The prospect of a powerful bureaucracy out of control rightly terrifies citizens. The fear of a despotic government, after all, drove colonial Americans to revolution against the king. It brought down the Nixon administration in 1974. Worries that Obamacare will unleash a powerful, out-of-control bureaucracy have plagued the administration throughout Obama's time in office. Accountability is a *relationship*. It is about *answerability to whom, for what*. When we debate whether public administration is accountable, we are asking to whom individual administrators must answer (legislative bodies like the city council, state legislature, and congressional committees, as well as administrative superiors up the chain of command) and for what activities they must answer (including the value judgments they make and the performance they demonstrate).

These three themes shape the big debates about public administration, because they all frame the big debates about the *power* of government. In 2013, for example, Louisiana Governor Bobby Jindal attacked the Obama administration for what he labeled the "two central philosophies of the Obama administration—the massive expansion of the size and power of the federal government and a lack of trust in the American people." What evidence did he present? Conflicting stories he said that the administration had presented about the attack on the American mission in Benghazi, Libya; mismanagement within the Internal Revenue Service; and "disastrous attempts to enforce Obamacare," the administration's health care reform.[3] And what does this evidence have in common? The use of administrative agencies to exercise power on behalf of government. Jindal suggested that the agencies were unaccountable to the people, that they were not performing on behalf on the public interest, and that they were the focus of administration decisions that, in Jindal's view, represented the wrong political decisions. Of course, Jindal's attack was itself political. In these cases, as well as in so much of what government does, political decisions take their meaning in the ways public administrators carry them out. Government's power takes its form through public administration.

These themes also capture the inevitable tradeoffs at the core of government power. More steps to increase accountability, including more rules to restrict administrators' power, can reduce efficiency by multiplying red tape. Streamlining government to make it more efficient can risk making administrators less accountable. At every stage, these basic questions frame the size and role of government, and there's nothing more fundamental to politics than that.

Public administration is about everything that's important about government, and everything that's important about government touches on or flows through public administration. Those twists and turns are often hidden, and the issues can be subtle. If we care about government—especially if we care about making government work better—we need to pay very careful attention to the politics of the administrative process. And that's the mission of this book.

For example, consider the mundane problem of plowing snow from city streets. Could it possibly be about politics? Just ask former New York Mayor John Lindsay. Following a blizzard in February 1969, much of the city was impassable for days. Almost 40 percent of his snow removal equipment was sidelined because of poor maintenance, and the borough of Queens was especially isolated. When he used a four-wheel-drive vehicle to make his way to the snowbound residents, they booed him and called him a bum. He managed to win reelection, but the story haunted him for the rest of his career and undermined his 1972 presidential campaign.

A 1979 storm in Chicago torpedoed the campaign of Chicago Mayor Michael A. Bilandic. Washington Mayor Marion S. Barry Jr. suffered for years after a blizzard hit his city while he was enjoying sunny weather in Southern California, where he was attending the Super Bowl.[4] A senior official in a Midwest city once confided in me that there was a special snow removal plan for election day, to ensure that the precincts most likely to vote for the mayor got plowed out first. It's not especially surprising to discover that officials use government power to advance political purposes—or that administrative failures have political consequences. This is an echo of a great scene in the movie *Casablanca*, which might well be the best film of all time. Police Captain Louis Renault loves Casablanca's nightlife

A 2010 blizzard blanketed Washington, shut down the government, and created a massive job for these National Park Service employees struggling to dig out the Lincoln Memorial. History has shown that snow clearing can be a surprisingly political matter.

but the Nazis who occupy the city expect him to enforce public order. When the Nazis insist he crack down on his friend Rick's casino, he picks an ironic pretense. "I'm shocked, shocked to find that gambling is going on in here!" he tells everyone—just before his favorite dealer hands him his own winnings. We should be no more shocked to discover that politics surrounds the exercise of public power through public administration.

HISTORICAL ROOTS

These tensions and tradeoffs have deep roots in American history. We don't much like politics or government, but we like bureaucracy even less. The United States is a country born of revolution. Our founders rebelled against King George III, but the prime complaints were against his administrators. The Boston Tea Party was a public act of rebellion against the king's tax collectors. (For a small historical tidbit, check the modern heritage of colonial brewer Sam Adams, who was a ringleader of the Tea Party.) The Declaration of Independence specifically condemns King George III, saying, "He has erected a multitude of New Offices, and sent hither swarms of Officers to harass our people and eat out their substance." Signing the document required tremendous bravery on the part of the signatories, but declaring independence was the easy part. First they had to win the war against the world's most powerful army, and then they had to make independence stick by learning how to govern. The new government, in fact, failed an early test of governing, when it stumbled in putting down a rebellion in 1786, led by Daniel Shays in western Massachusetts. The founders concluded that protecting their hard-won democracy required a stronger government. That led in 1787 to another major Philadelphia conference, this time to write a constitution.

Determining the role of administrators in the new constitutional system, however, proved difficult. No one wanted to recreate the tyranny against which the Founders had rebelled, but a weak government risked inviting invasion and conquest. The Founders famously and delicately balanced government's power through the legislative, judicial, and executive powers. They finessed the tough question about how to exercise those powers, especially the administrative powers. Article II of the Constitution vests "the executive power" in the president, but the definition of executive power is fuzzy and the founders carefully balanced the exercise of this power through the powers given to the other two branches. Trying to define executive power further risked fracturing the fragile coalition that brought the new country together. What they left out couldn't draw political fire, and they left to future leaders how to administer the nation they worked so hard to create.

There is profound irony here. The Founders were determined to prevent a recurrence of the abuse of power that prompted the revolution, but when they had the chance to define the power of the new government, they sidestepped the question. From its first moments, American public administration was grounded in politics—the political battle against the king, followed by the delicate political balance to get the Constitution ratified. The political issues about public administration colored Washington's two presidential terms, as John Adams and other Federalists battled with Thomas Jefferson and his Democratic-Republican colleagues about how far the government's power should go. Defining the nature of executive power produced the first big divisions in the new nation, fueled a feud that cost the life of the Secretary of the Treasury in a duel, and fed the creation of political parties with very different views on how that power ought to be exercised. The discovery that government power was about public administration and that public administration was about politics was about as surprising as Captain Renault's discovery that there was gambling—gambling!—going on in the casino where he did his betting.

The struggles change with the times, but the basic issues are as old as the United States: creating an administration strong enough to do the public's work but accountable enough to prevent the tyranny that the nation's Founders sought to guard against. That leads us to a more detailed examination of the puzzle of *accountability*.

THE MEANING OF ACCOUNTABILITY

We use the word **accountability** a great deal, but we rarely stop to ask ourselves what it means, how it works, what we seek to control, or who controls whom. Let us examine these issues in turn.

What Is Accountability?

Accountability is a relationship between people (who is accountable to whom?) about actions (what are they accountable for?). It is the foundation of bureaucracy in a democracy, because accountability depends on the ability of policymakers to *control* administrators' actions. Control, in turn, can be either *positive* (requiring an agency to do something it ought to do) or *negative* (seeking to prevent an agency from doing something it should not do). Sins of omission as well as acts of commission are subject to investigation, criticism, instructions, and sanctions. The principal focus of control is on discovering bureaucratic errors and requiring their correction—a largely negative approach that tends to become dominant for several reasons. First, it is easier to see—and to criticize—sins of commission, for they tend to be the stories that attract media attention; the more intense the news coverage, the stronger the policymakers' reaction is likely to be. In 2004 the abuse of Iraqi prisoners by a small group of American soldiers drew media coverage for months, while the effective military service—and considerable suffering—of other American troops in Iraq got little attention in comparison. Second, an external control body (such as Congress or a state legislature or a city council) can more easily identify specific problems to be solved than it can devise a broader strategy to be followed. Oversight hearings promptly focused on the behavior of that handful of troops, but Congress struggled to sort out the far more complex issues underlying American policy in the region. Our discussion focuses on efforts of policymakers to shape administrative behavior. It therefore focuses primarily on the negative aspects of external control: correcting bureaucratic behavior that policymakers believe is not in the public interest. But we must explore that issue also in the context of the often confusing dynamics of the underlying policy.

But do policymakers actually *want* to control administrators? Often they do not. If policymakers specify policy goals very carefully, that would in turn make them more directly responsible for the results. Policymakers often like to keep some distance between the decisions they make and the consequences that flow from them. When problems occur—from accidents in the space program to slow response time of fire trucks—reporters and top officials like to prowl for someone to blame. If control were an unbroken chain from policymakers to administrators, the links of accountability would lead directly to the top and blame would land in the laps of elected officials. Top officials certainly do not want to encourage problems, but they also do not want the finger of blame pointing directly at them when problems inevitably occur. When the independent commission investigating the September 11, 2001, al Qaeda attacks set out to identify those responsible for preventing the attacks, its members discovered that the patterns of responsibility were so unclear that it was impossible to fix the blame. Despite heavy pressure to hold someone accountable for failures in intelligence and security, no one was fired. When Hurricane Katrina in 2005 produced the worst administrative failure in American history, only the administrator of the Federal Emergency Management Agency, Michael Brown, lost his job, despite manifest problems throughout the federal, state, and local policy system.

Members of Congress subjected former FEMA Administrator Michael Brown to tough questions about the agency's performance following Hurricane Katrina's assault.

Even if elected officials actually wanted a clear chain of accountability, it would create a "gotcha" effect: if administrators knew they would have to answer for every problem, they would have to work in a demoralizing climate of distrust. In many cases, good administration requires the exercise of professional judgment. How likely is it that some drugs will cause deformities in humans, or that landing an airplane in a thunderstorm is likely to be unsafe? How can a dangerous chemical dump best be cleaned? When a storm wobbles between snow, ice, and rain, when is it best to plow the roads, and how many chemicals should be applied to keep them clear (and what damage to the environment and to the roadway might the chemicals cause)? If we create a climate that punishes risk-taking, we are likely to get too-safe decisions that interfere with getting government's job done. Excessive controls increase red tape and delay action. Finger pointing leads to administrators digging deep foxholes instead of taking risks to achieve high performance. So much energy can be spent attempting to control administrative activities—and filing the paperwork to document that the control standards have been met—that there may be little money or time left to do the job. Controls that are too tight, therefore, may actually *reduce* administration's responsiveness to its public. Indeed, as British scholar Peter Self put it, "The tensions between the requirements of responsibility or 'accountability' and those of effective executive action can reasonably be described as *the* classic dilemma of public administration."[5]

Discretion is inevitable—and desirable—in administrative action. The process of filling in the gap between broad policy at the top and specific actions on the front line requires the constant exercise of judgment. Legislators can never specify all the factors that administrators must weigh in making decisions; even if they could, the necessity of reaching legislative compromise typically produces vague, sometimes even conflicting guidance. Not all circumstances are the same, and good administration requires adapting general policies to special needs. When first responders arrive on the scene of a serious traffic accident or a building collapse, what should they do first? Every accident is different, and effective response depends on good training and professional judgment. That always requires discretion. We want to give administrators enough room to make the right decisions, yet we want to hold them accountable. Administrators must follow the law and meet the goals of public policy—at the same time.

Who ultimately is accountable for what? That, in fact, is a question that stretches back centuries. The Roman satirist Juvenal asked two millennia ago: *"Quis custodiet ipsos custodes?"*—"Who is to watch the watchers?"[6] Who will control the controllers, to ensure that they get the balance right? We all want accountability, but there is no absolute standard for accountability, and a large number of hands tussle over what it ought to look like. Accountability thus is not only a relationship. It is also an uneasy one, with the balance among competing forces constantly in flux.[7]

Underlying the accountability debate is the responsibility of individual administrators. Can—should—must administrators follow the orders of top officials? Or: can—should—must they become "whistleblowers," divulging to the public activities that they believe are wrong? On one hand, the answer seems clear. The post–World War II war crimes trials established that following orders was no defense against administrators who committed heinous acts. It's clear that administrators must exercise their own judgment. On the other hand, if administrators each exercised their own individual judgment as they went about their daily work, coordination would evaporate, the work wouldn't get done, and there would be little meaning to accountability.

Over the years we've had a very mixed view of **whistleblowers**—individuals who take it on themselves to disclose activities they believe are wrong. In a fascinating background story, *Wall Street Journal* reporter Ben Zimmer explains that the phrase "blowing the whistle" seems to have entered American language in the early part of the twentieth century, when fans expected sports officials to blow their whistles to stop play. If a football player committed a penalty or a boxer had beaten his opponent, fans called on referees to blow the whistle. A few decades later, during the 1930s, a new meaning crept in. "Blowing the whistle" took on the meaning of someone revealing a dramatic secret, often breaking a code of silence to authorities as a "snitch" or a "rat."

In the 1970s, consumer advocate Ralph Nader deliberately changed the meaning. He challenged those with important information on misconduct, in either private companies or the government, to stand forward, even if that meant "blowing the whistle against the system."[8]

This raises a fundamental question about accountability. How much obedience do government officials owe to organizational superiors and elected officials—and how much discretion should officials exercise on their own? Because there is no firm answer to that question, there is no single, clear approach to accountability. Accountability is, at once, the bedrock on which administrative power in a democracy builds and a puzzle that requires endless work in search of solutions.

Ripped
from the Headlines...

ACCOUNTABILITY

A Bad Week for the IRS

It had been one of the worst weeks ever for the Internal Revenue Service, perhaps the least-loved bureaucracy in government. Senior official Lois Lerner disclosed that the IRS had singled out dozens of organizations for extra review to see if they were violating their nonprofit status, on the grounds of their political affiliation. Putting "patriot" or "tea party" in the application triggered extra attention and, Lerner acknowledged that this was wrong. Then, speaking words no one could recall ever coming from an IRS official, she apologized for the agency's actions.

In trying to insulate the White House from the fallout, President Obama said that the IRS is an independent agency. His press secretary Jay Carney reinforced the message by telling reporters that the IRS was an independent agency with only a pair of political appointees at the top.

The White House reaction raises a very tough question. If the IRS is "independent," to whom is it accountable? Everyone, including the manager in charge of the operation, acknowledges that using politics to enforce the tax code was wrong. What does accountability mean if an agency and its employees are "independent"?

Approaches to Accountability

In the United States, the effort to resolve this dilemma has focused on three big issues: the search for *legal boundaries* to constrain and channel administrative action, what we call the **rule of law**; the *political challenges* that have surfaced when administrative realities stretch those legal boundaries; and *evolving policy problems* that increasingly confound the strategies and tactics to hold governmental power accountable and to ensure that administration serves the public interest.

Legal Boundaries

The problem of balancing governmental power with individual freedom, of course, is nothing new. When King John met England's nobles in 1215, they pledged him fealty—but only after the king agreed to limits on his power. For generations, historians have worked to disentangle the long roots and lasting impact of the Magna Carta, but two things are clear. One is that the uneasy pact forged at Runnymede helped establish the basis for the modern state.[9] The other is that the rule of law emerged as the guide for setting the balance between governmental power and individual liberty. Kings (and later queens) found power useful to work their will. Citizens sometimes found the exercise of that power overbearing and expensive.

Across a wide range of issues, King John and his successors agreed to accept legal limits on their power, even though the British monarchs claimed that their power flowed from divine right.

The *rule of law* thus became enshrined in English common law. In practice, the rule of the sword often pushed aside written agreements, and it took centuries for kings to realize that modern government required real accountability to the people. It's not surprising, therefore, that the story of the rule of law is the story of struggle and conflict.[10] The rule of law seeks to define and protect the basic rights of citizens against a too-powerful government, even though claims for its historical impact have been much exaggerated.[11] It helps frame a system where everyone knows the rules and where the rules apply to everyone. Finally, the rule of law creates the foundation for administrative accountability. Since government in action is often the action of administrators, the rule of law provides the mechanism for constraining how administrators exercise their power. It tells them what they can do and what will happen to them if they step beyond their boundaries.[12]

This basic outline, of course, is far clearer in theory than it ever was in practice, but the rule of law provided at least a basic blueprint for the Founders of the United States. In *Common Sense*, Thomas Paine wrote that "a government of our own is a natural right," with that right protected by the law, because

> in America the law is king. For as in absolute governments the king is law, so in free countries the law ought to be king; and there ought to be no other. But lest any ill use should afterwards arise, let the crown at the conclusion of the ceremony be demolished, and scattered among the people whose right it is. (1791)

The rule of law was central to the colonial Founders as they tried to create their new government. Paine, and others, argued that citizens could establish that government because they would also bind its power.

The Articles of Confederation, the principles that guided the nation in the uneasy days between independence from the British crown and the adoption of the 1787 Constitution, proved a clumsy first effort. But the Constitution that followed is a web of crosscutting restraints on government and the basic strategy for administrative accountability in American government: give the government power but set legal bounds to limit the dangers of its use. In the United States, the Founders did not trust a single check. Multiple backstops, through separated institutions sharing authority, provided the extra insurance that the wary Founders wanted. But this balance of powers was an unsteady deal. In the nation's first decades, officials created a national bank only to close it; they tried a second time and closed it again. Hamilton's powerful argument for government's help in promoting the economy repeatedly encountered a hurricane of citizen opposition.

The conflict became razor sharp during the Progressive Era, toward the end of the nineteenth century. In tackling the problems of rising corporate power and the enormous potential of the industrial age, the **Progressives** faced a dilemma. They were convinced that stronger government, with new programs and stronger agencies, was necessary to drive the country forward and to constrain the giant private companies. But they also knew that citizens would be nervous about a more powerful government, for the American Revolution against King George III's tyranny remained in the country's collective consciousness. How could the government grow without creating bureaucratic tyrants? For the Progressives, the answer lay in the rule of law. Before being elected president, Woodrow Wilson, then a political scientist at Princeton University, famously sketched a solution:

> If I see a murderous fellow sharpening a knife cleverly, I can borrow his way of sharpening the knife without borrowing his probable intention to commit murder with it; and so, if I see a monarchist dyed in the wool managing a public bureau well, I can learn his business methods without changing one of my republican spots.[13]

Wilson, along with his fellow Progressives, contended that government administrators could be empowered to do government's work without threatening individual rights because the rule of law would hold them accountable. Delegation of power to administrators from elected officials and hierarchical control through authority controlled the use of power within administrative agencies. Separating politics from administration, in what became known as the **politics-administration dichotomy**, was their strategy for an effective administrative state in a modern democracy: politicians would determine policy, and administrators would carry out that policy within the bounds set by elected officials.[14]

The Progressives' reliance on the rule of law was an elegant solution to a very tough problem. As they contemplated the twentieth century, they concluded that government would have to become far stronger. Caught between the growing corporate power of the railroad barons and captains of industry and the limitless opportunities of industrial and territorial expansion, the reformers found in the rule of law a way to fit old theories to the new prospects. The rule-of-law formulation was not the last word for the Progressive movement, any more than it was for King John, but it licensed the expansion of government in the twentieth century while holding it accountable.

Political Challenges

Of course, big problems soon strained this neat formula. Herbert Hoover and his advisers fumbled in their response to the 1929 stock market crash. When Franklin D. Roosevelt launched the New Deal to attack these problems, critics complained it was a vast and unconstitutional overreach of power. The rule of law had real appeal, both because of its common law and historical roots and because it provided a logical answer to the nation's pragmatic problems. But the theory inevitably collided with politics, as John M. Gaus reminded everyone: "A theory of public administration means in our time a theory of politics also."[15] Not only did the rule of law fit uneasily between governmental power and individual liberty, it rested on the inescapable reality, captured so well by Gaus, that administration has always been about politics. Political pressures maneuvered King John into putting his seal on the Magna Carta, and they have swirled around the rule of law since.

In his 1936 essay "The Responsibility of Public Administration," Gaus noted that cracks had appeared in the rule of law from the earliest times. He described a replica of a Babylonian monolith, which displayed a carving of the Code of Hammurabi from 2000 B.C. Above the code is a relief of Hammurabi receiving the command to establish a just law from the sun-god, Shamash. That, Gaus pointed out, established the "earliest conception of political responsibility": "Somewhere in the wisdom of God was to be found the absolute code, the fixed standard, which the ruler was to follow." However, he continued,

> the inadequacy of such a conception of responsibility is obvious. Responsibility is accountability, but who, under such conditions, could call power to account? Is God's will always so clear? Should not, then, His vicar interpret him? But can one be sure that the vicar is correct in his interpretation?[16]

Therein lies the core conundrum of administrative accountability and the rule of law. It's hard to beat an accountability system coming directly from God. But it's also impossible to translate, with complete transparency and total predictability, the rule of law into administrative action. As administrators interpret the rule of law to bring the law to life, the law slips in its hold on their rule. Gaus concluded in his essay that "neither the electorate nor the legislature can express in concrete detail the specific policy which it desires the administrative organization to enforce,"[17] so administrative discretion is the inevitable result of any administrative act. Indeed, the dilemma of building sufficient capacity to allow Congress to oversee executive branch actions is a puzzle that has echoed through the American Political Science Association lectures given in Gaus's name.[18]

What solution does Gaus offer? If forces external to the administrator cannot adequately shape the exercise of discretion, then democracy must necessarily rely on the administrators' professional norms. Gaus's argument set the stage for one of the most trenchant battles of public administration theory, the 1940 debate between Herman Finer and Carl J. Friedrich on whether professional training or external controls could best hold administrators accountable.[19] The battleground was the rule of law, as Finer made the case for the long tradition of administration held accountable by legal standards. But Friedrich echoed Gaus in making an inescapable point: if the law cannot fully control administrative action, then how can administrators be held accountable? For Gaus and Friedrich, the case for relying on professional norms was the inescapable conclusion. They argued that government had to rely on what it had at its disposal. That, in turn, not only makes public administration about politics, since it brings the value judgments of administrators squarely into the process; it also brings in the question of *whose* political values shape administrative action.

Evolving Policy Problems

Resorting to pragmatism beyond the law was perhaps inevitable, but it also set the stage for a fierce debate about administrative theory and practice. The Magna Carta was important because it established the premise that law could limit the king's power, but the Runnymede meeting did not erase the enormous pressures on the exercise of political power that came before or after. The United States relied on the rule of law to define and protect individual rights, but few rights have ever been absolute and the debate over how to shape them has always involved substantial cross-pressures. As governmental programs became more complex in the first half of the twentieth century, and especially as more public programs involved partnerships with the multiple levels of government and with the private sector, strains on the rule of law hit the breaking point. Gaus argued:

> In a state in which the powers of government intermesh widely with those of industry, commerce, and finance the traditional restraints upon the discretion of the administrator through making him responsible to the electorate, the courts, and the legislators are inadequate.[20]

Although Gaus wrote this in 1936, he could easily have been describing BP: big problems that blur the legal boundaries in ways that make it hard to define who is responsible for what action.

Those changes in the complexity of governmental programs accelerated during the 1930s. Franklin D. Roosevelt's New Deal programs, in particular, not only reinforced the challenge of politics in accountability and pushed more reliance onto the professional norms of administrators, they also brought more players from a wider variety of organizations into the pursuit of public policy. World War II, as it spawned a massive network of private contractors to help the war effort, accelerated the trend. These steps, in turn, had two effects.

First, it became far more difficult to rely on any single rule-of-law standard to guide administrative action. There was a theoretical simplicity in the basic model—policymakers could track the exercise of discretion by administrators through the hierarchy and through the rule of law. Complicating that chain through new partnerships, where each member operated inside its own traditions, made it much harder to define and enforce a single rule of law to guide that partnership.

Second, different governments—and different government agencies—have very different cultures, and that makes it hard to ensure that any single set of professional norms can shape administrative behavior. The federal government has a different culture than its state and local partners, and the cultures of each government agency often have surprising variations. Professionals in the government's private and nonprofit partners often live by far different cultures that stretch far beyond the typical profit-making or public good motives presumed to be at the core of their missions. Community-based organizations are very different than

In 1933, President Franklin D. Roosevelt signed a law creating the Tennessee Valley Authority, which for the first time brought inexpensive electric power to many in the nation's South.

international environmental protection organizations, and they differ tremendously from defense contractors and road builders. There have even been famous squabbles at the scene of local incidents, where police officers and firefighters have thrown punches over who was in control. In fact, when Tony Hayward complained in the BP case that he wanted to "get my life back," he demonstrated the frustration of a private-sector executive operating within the realm of public policy, in harsh public light. Combining private actors and public expectations created a very nasty mix.

The rule of law, of course, was always more powerful in theory than in practice. But the rise of such mixed federal-state-local-public-private actions further undermines the theory's applicability. Since no single model of accountability is likely to work, how can government can be effective, efficient, responsive, and accountable in the world of twenty-first century politics?

Elements of Accountability

When we look at how well government works, we focus on three elements of account-ability: fiscal, process, and program.[21] In **fiscal accountability**, we seek to ensure that agency officials spend money on the programs they are charged with managing—and only on those programs. This issue cuts both ways. On the one hand, we want to make sure that, in fact, the money is spent. A recurring complaint in the early 2000s was that the Department of Homeland Security failed to distribute quickly enough to state and local governments the funds that Congress had appropriated to support their security efforts. On the other hand, we want to make sure that the money is spent according to the law and is not wasted. In 2011, for example, Fox News pundit Bill O'Reilly and *The Daily Show* host Jon Stewart tangled over charges that the U.S. Department of Justice paid $16 for each muffin served at a Washington conference. A vast number of very senior Obama administration officials spent a huge amount of time tracking down the story, which turned out to be "mostly untrue," according to a later Politifact analysis. In reality, the $16 muffin included beverages, some fruit, a fee for the meeting space—and the muffin. Not cheap, but certainly not a vastly overpriced baked good.[22] But the tale underlines the fact that there's nothing like a headline on wasted government money to stir political conflict.

Process accountability is concerned with *how* agencies perform their tasks. While we often argue about the meaning of procedural fairness, government agencies regularly find themselves charged with unfair treatment. Massive problems in the 2000 presidential election focused national attention on the voting machines that many state and local governments used and whether problems with those machines had prevented some votes from being counted. Those complaints about process led to a massive investment in new machinery for future elections. Despite the investment, however, many voters waited hours after closing time in the 2012 presidential election to cast their ballots.

Program accountability is the newest and most difficult objective of control systems. Is a public program achieving its purpose, as defined in law? The U.S. Government Accountability Office (GAO), the investigative arm of Congress, has increasingly conducted program analyses to measure how well federal agencies answer this question. At the local, state, and federal level, governments have developed sophisticated performance-measurement systems to gauge how well programs met their goals. These new systems increasingly try to put hard numbers on the tough question of whether programs actually work.

Everyone agrees that citizens deserve accountability for their hard-earned tax dollars. But we tend to measure accountability in these three different ways—sometimes relying more on one standard than another and rarely trying to reconcile all three into an overall picture of an agency's performance.

Holding Administration Accountable

The related problems of making administration work efficiently and ensuring it is democratically accountable are deep and lasting. Administrators can follow the basic doctrine of accountability, through the hierarchical system of delegated authority. When that leaves gaps, they can use their best judgment to discover the intent of the policy, rely on their professional judgment to determine how best to achieve that intent, and consult with the controllers to resolve uncertainties.[23]

But this is certainly not a magic solution. Administrators may face multiple controllers, and these controllers may not always agree on an agency's priorities. A congressional statute may suggest a set of priorities that conflicts with the president's, leaving agency heads, appointed by the president, to choose which to obey; appointees who choose the legislature's course could find themselves replaced by appointees more willing to follow the president's wishes. Moreover, when an agency head seeks clarification of Congress's priorities, there is no "Congress" to talk to—only a congressional committee or its chair, whose interpretation may not conform to the view of Congress as a whole. And with many agency heads answering to multiple committee and subcommittee chairs, uncertainty often multiplies, and Congress often does not speak clearly to begin with. At the state and local levels of government, of course, the same problems ripple through the system.

These real-world conflicts leave administrators responsible for resolving many uncertainties, for which they must rely heavily on their own internal compasses—their personal character, professional training, devotion to the public service, and respect for faithful execution of the law. When controllers give conflicting directions or confusing signals, administrators face a conflict of loyalties. In the classic collection of options, they can choose **voice**: remaining in their positions and fighting for what they think is right, even if that risks dismissal. Or they can choose **exit**: resigning, possibly with a public attack on the controller whose mandate they condemn.[24] But they know that the exit option may put the policies they care about at even greater risk, for they can be replaced by people who will bend more easily to the very pressures they have battled against. In fact, the idea of a conscience-driven exit from government is more popular in the press than in reality, because civil servants often have families to support, college tuition to pay, and relatively few available job options. In contrast, most high-level political appointees, cushioned by established reputations and extensive contacts outside government, can often exit to private-sector jobs at higher salaries. Furthermore, an attack by a resigning official is

The detention of Iraqi prisoners at Abu Grahib prison outside Baghdad created security worries, as well as international outrage at the treatment of the prisoners held there.

usually only a one-day media event, so anyone deciding to resign in protest must weigh the short-term political effect against the long-term personal impact.

In the end, the solution to the problem of accountability hinges on the balance between forces that come from outside administrators, including efforts by outside controllers, and forces that emerge from administrators themselves, including their character, background, and training. Theorists for generations have debated which forces are—and should be—more important. Should we assume that external controllers can never know enough about an administrator's actions and that setting the administrator's internal compass is most important? Or should we insist on extensive external controls to compensate for the tendency of administrators sometimes to stray off course?

Friedrich and Finer were unable to resolve this debate in the 1940s. Subsequent scholars and practitioners have not done any better. Accountability, in the final analysis, is a fine balance between external and internal controls. This balance, in turn, depends ultimately on ethical behavior by administrators.

GOVERNMENTAL POWER AND ADMINISTRATIVE ETHICS

Citizens and elected officials alike demand a higher standard of ethics than typically prevails in the private sector. Indeed, that ethical upgrade often comes as a shock for political appointees who come to government from the private sector.[25] As Calvin Mackenzie writes,

> At one time or another in their work lives, most business leaders have found jobs in their own companies for family members or friends, have entered into contracts with firms in which they had a financial interest, or have accepted substantial gifts from people with whom they regularly do business. . . . When public officials engage in similar activities, however, they break the law.[26]

The pursuit of high **ethical behavior** in government raises a different tradeoff. On the one hand, we want skilled employees who can ensure that government's work is done well.

In particular, we don't want to make the process of screening and hiring officials to be so burdensome, in the pursuit of high ethical standards, that we drive away good people. On the other hand, the public expects that those who exercise the public's trust will meet high standards and that, in particular, they will not use their power to line their own pockets, advantage their friends, or trade in the future on the relationships they developed in public service.

The issue crosses all governmental boundaries. Philadelphia Mayor Michael A. Nutter emphatically made the point in his January 2008 inaugural address. "There is nothing government does that cannot be done ethically and transparently," he said. His goal, he told Philadelphians, was "a government that serves all of us, not a few."[27] Nutter's speech underlined the recurring central themes of public administration: creating governmental power to serve citizens; holding that power accountable to elected officials and ultimately to voters; exercising power ethically, according to high standards of public service; and ensuring accountability through transparency.

THE PUBLIC SERVICE

In the end, the quality of government's work depends on the quality of the individuals recruited and retained in the public service, on their respect for bureaucratic accountability and ethical behavior, and especially on their commitment to the constitutional, democratic system. Instilling such values is a societal task; it depends on communication by family, schools, and peers. It also depends on creating a system that is accountable within our political system—especially since, in so many ways, the politics of the administrative process shapes the performance of American government.

Those capabilities encompass much more than they did in the past. Public administration is no longer primarily the direct execution of governmental programs. Much of it now is administration by proxy, with complex partnerships among government agencies, for-profit companies, and nonprofit organizations responsible for the implementation of government programs. That, in turn, multiplies the problem of public ethics, since many private and nonprofit employees find themselves doing the public's work, during at least part of their time, but often without a clear signal that they are entering the public realm.

An ethical government begins with ethical public servants—public servants devoted to the fundamental challenge of helping "to form a more perfect union, establish justice, insure domestic tranquility, provide for the common defense, and secure the blessings of liberty to ourselves and our posterity."[28] Encouraged by such possibilities, they will recognize that the public service, as President George H. W. Bush said, is "the highest and noblest calling."[29] In running for the presidency in 2008, Barack Obama was more direct. His goal, he said, was "to make government and public service cool again."[30] Few vocations offer greater promise for improving the lives of so many of the world's citizens. Charting the course is the fundamental challenge of this book.

CASE 1.1

Do NOT Read This Case! The NSA's Surveillance Program

In July 2013, U.S. Department of Homeland Security employees received a message warning them not to use their home computers or personal smartphones to look at an article on the *Washington Post* website. The website, it turns out, contained a "top-secret" slide leaked by former intelligence analyst Edward Snowden. If an agency employee viewed the top-secret material from an unclassified computer, it would constitute "classified data spillage," which had to be reported to supervisors like a toxic chemical spill.

Here's the email, as the *Post* reported it:

From: [REDACTED]

Sent: Friday, July 12, 2013 9:50 AM

Subject: SECURITY ALERT ***Washington Post Article***

Importance: High

FYSA . . . From DHS HQ

Per the National Cybersecurity Communications Integration Center:

There is a recent article on the Washington Post's Website that has a clickable link titled "The NSA Slide you never seen" that must not be opened on an Unclassified government workstation. This link opens up a classified document which will raise the classification level of your Unclassified workstation to the classification of the slide which is reported to be TS/NF.

If opened on an Unclassified system, you are obligated to report this to the SSO as a Classified Data Spillage (Opssecurity@

hq.dhs.gov<mailto:Opssecurity@hq.dhs.gov> <mailto:Opssecurity@hq.dhs.gov <mailto:Opssecurity@hq.dhs.gov> >).

Again, please exercise good judgment when visiting these webpages and clicking on such links. You may be violating your Non-Disclosure Agreement in which you sign that you will protect Classified National Security Information. You may be subject to any administrative or legal action from the Government.[1]

What caused all the fuss was a PowerPoint slide revealing the basic structure of the federal government's PRISM program.[2] No one but highly placed insiders had previously even known about the program. Through PRISM, the National Security Agency (NSA) worked with a wide variety of information technology companies, including Apple, Google, Skype, Yahoo, and Facebook, to collect information on the communications of individuals that the NSA wanted to investigate. The companies shared the information with NSA, which then put its analysts to work to determine whether any of the communications constituted a threat to national security. How many "targets" was NSA investigating? At the time of Snowden's leak, there were 117,675 targets. Other Americans, however, might have had their communications shared with NSA "incidentally," as a result of the agency's work.

So if you have a top-secret security clearance and if you read this case, you must immediately go to your supervisor to report a "classified data spillage." If you don't have a top-secret clearance, you've just read something you weren't supposed to see to begin with. Either way: Do NOT read this case!

Questions to Consider

1. What do you think about this government surveillance program, which allows the NSA to work with popular service providers like Facebook, Google, and Skype to collect personal information without the user's knowledge? On the one hand, terrorists frequently use the Internet to plan attacks. On the other hand, such surveillance is clearly an invasion of individual privacy.

2. The memo to employees might seem silly to some. But the government has a broad policy on not allowing users to look at classified information on unclassified computers. Why? Unclassified computers can be infiltrated by viruses and spyware, which allow others to capture anything that goes across the screen. (The CIA and the NSA do not allow cell phones inside their buildings' secure zones.) If you were a manager, how would you handle this situation?

3. Perhaps nothing more sharply frames the problem of accountability in modern government than determining how to safeguard the personal communications of individual Americans while preserving national security. What kind of accountability system would you design to find the balance?

NOTES

1. Josh Hicks, "DHS Warns Employees not to Read Leaked NSA Information," *Washington Post* (July 15, 2013), http://www.washingtonpost.com/blogs/federal-eye/wp/2013/07/15/dhs-warns-employees-not-to-read-leaked-nsa-information.

2. To view the slide, go to http://www.washingtonpost.com/business/economy/the-nsa-slide-you-havent-seen/2013/07/10/32801426-e8e6-11e2-aa9f-c03a72e2d342_story.html

CASE 1.2

Snow Removal in the Blizzard of 2010: Who Gets Plowed First?

Throughout much of the East Coast, the winter of 2010 was painfully burned into everyone's memory. Children looking forward to snow days had their dreams fulfilled—and then some. By mid-February, the Washington, D.C., area had already shattered the all-time record for snow, with 55 inches of accumulation. For a time, Baltimore, Maryland, had more snow than Buffalo, New York. Many football fans found themselves stuck at home instead of partying with friends for the Super Bowl. Some local universities were shut down for a week as the snow removal crews struggled to dig out the sidewalks and parking lots.

Most people in the area tried to bring good humor to the onslaught, but in some neighborhoods snow plow drivers were threatened by angry residents. Stuck for days and watching the plows drive by without dropping their blades, some residents of a neighborhood in Prince George's County, a Washington, D.C., suburb, told several snow plow drivers that they were going to "throw them out of their trucks and beat them up" if they didn't stop to plow their streets. Other drivers called 911 for reinforcements when angry taxpayers made threats. A county spokesperson said that the drivers "are working as hard as they possibly can." She explained, "I understand people are frustrated. . . . Obviously we know we have work to do and we're trying . . . just as hard as we can. We want to go home."[1]

In nearby Arlington County, across the Potomac River, county officials pointed to their snow removal priority plan with a sophisticated map that charted which streets the plows worked on first. Plowing starts when the snow becomes two to four inches deep. The snow crews focus on priority areas: snow emergency routes marked with bright signs, main arteries, roads leading to hospitals and fire stations, and the areas around subway stations and police stations. Crews work twelve-hour shifts, get twelve hours off for food and sleep, and then come back to work again.[2] Even that effort struggled to keep up with 2010's blizzards of the century, and for months afterward residents complained about being marooned. Why, they asked, couldn't the government plow them out faster?

Questions to Consider

1. Assume you are the head of the department of public works of your county. You're in charge of snow removal. What streets would you plow first?

2. What would you say to residents whose streets end up at the bottom of the plowing priority list? After all, they will tell you: they pay taxes, too!

3. Following the blizzard, Arlington County considered an ordinance that would require local residents to join with the county in the snow removal effort. In particular, "the ordinance first would require all property owners to remove snow and ice adjacent to their property,

creating a path that is a minimum of thirty-six inches wide (to accommodate wheelchairs, strollers, and adults with children in hand) within twenty-four hours after the snow stops falling, when accumulations are less than six inches, and within thirty-six hours when six or more inches of snow accumulate. Failure to comply with the ordinance could result in a civil penalty." Would you favor the passage of such an ordinance, which brings individual citizens into a partnership with government in providing public services? What would you do for older and disabled residents, who might not have the physical strength to shovel their sidewalks? Just how far should a government's reach into an individual's property go?

4. One official of a Midwest town once admitted that the town had a special snow removal plan for election day. If it snowed, he said, there was a plan to make sure that the "right" neighborhoods— those most likely to vote for the mayor—were plowed first. The other neighborhoods— those most likely to vote for the mayor's opponent—would have to wait much longer. Do you think that this is a proper use of government's power, of the way that administrative decisions shape values in society?

NOTES

1. Johnny Mummolo, "Snow Removal Workers Threatened in Prince George's, Official Says," *Washington Post* (February 11, 2010), http://voices .washingtonpost.com/annapolis/2010/02/snow_ removal_workers_threatene.html.

2. "Snow Removal in Arlington County," http://www .arlingtonva.us/departments/Environmental Services/uepd/snow/EnvironmentalServicesSnow .aspx.

CASE 1.3

Google Earth versus Privacy in Riverhead, New York

In Riverhead, New York, town officials launched an aggressive campaign to find backyard swimming pools whose owners hadn't obtained the required permits to build them. As the town's chief building inspector, Leroy Barnes Jr., explained, "It's a safety issue more than anything else." Faulty plumbing could cause water damage to neighboring properties. If electrical wiring for lights or filters were installed improperly, someone could be electrocuted. In addition, the town's ordinance required pool owners to install a fence around the pool to prevent small children from wandering in and accidentally drowning. The campaign, in this small town near the tip of Long Island, found 250 pools that had been constructed but whose owners had not received the requisite permits. In addition, the aggressive inspection program produced $75,000 in fees from violators.[1]

Barnes, however, quickly found himself under fierce attack, from the American Civil Liberties Union (ACLU) and scores of angry townspeople. It wasn't because of the campaign to find violators, at least on the surface. Rather, it was because Barnes had cleverly used the Google Earth search program to find the pools. He used the program's online satellite feature to find pools, identify the address, check the address against the town's database of permits, and find pools that did not have the permits required by law. Town officials wondered what all the fuss was about. After all, Google Earth is available to any user, on any computer. It doesn't show anything that anyone anywhere can't see. Why can't the town use publicly available information to enforce its laws?

"Technically it may be lawful," replied Donna Lieberman of New York's ACLU, "but in the gut it

does not feel like a free society kind of operation."[2] Some local residents complained that it felt creepy to know that the town was peeking into their lives via satellite. Critics pointed out that the Fourth Amendment to the Constitution prevents government officials from conducting unlawful searches. Using remote satellites without a search warrant crossed the line, they argued.

Just how far should government go in combining emerging technology with its vast power? In Greece, as well as New York, government officials are using Google Earth to track down pools without permits to collect fines. Enterprising private citizens are also making innovative use of satellite surveillance. Thieves in the United Kingdom are using the technology to identify backyard ponds stocked with exotic fish, which they steal and sell for large sums. A private company is already using private satellites to photograph the parking lots of Wal-Mart stores. Counting the cars tells analysts which communities have the fastest-growing economies. If private companies are doing it, should government be handcuffed in using the same readily available technology to enforce its laws?

It's easy to see even bigger issues in the future. If governments pass aggressive energy-saving laws to restrict backyard barbeques (too many hydrocarbons being released) and to require better insulation of homes (to prevent energy from being wasted), should the government be able to use remote-sensing devices to detect heat emissions? Private companies are now trying to sell special vans to local police that provide a comprehensive scan of every car passing by. It can detect illegal items onboard without a search warrant. Should local police buy these disguised vans to locate contraband and possible terrorist threats—and deploy them without search warrants? What about anti-terrorism forces in the FBI? The federal government's Transportation Security Administration is deploying new scanners that can look through an airplane passenger's clothing to see, well, just about everything. Passengers boarding planes know that they are subject to searches, though there's always a debate about just how intrusive those searches ought to be. But should drivers steering their cars past a van parked at the side of the road have any expectation of privacy, even if they are carrying something under the seat or in the trunk that is illegal?

Public complaints in Riverhead forced town officials to end the Google Earth project, even though the information was available to everyone on the web and it was used to find people who had broken local ordinances. But it raised very tough questions about how government officials should exercise discretion in doing their jobs—and how they should wield their power.

Questions to Consider

1. Do you think there was anything wrong with the town's decision to use Google Earth to detect individuals who had broken local laws by installing pools without obtaining the required permits?
2. How should local officials, like Leroy Barnes, be held accountable for their actions?
3. Sam Adams, in addition to brewing beer, also helped lead the revolt that culminated in the Boston Tea Party, during which colonists tossed tea into the harbor to protest the power of the English king. What do you think he and his fellow revolutionaries would think about the use of Google Earth to detect lawbreakers?

NOTES

1. Russell Nichols, "Is Google Earth Eyeing Your Pool?" *Government Technology* (August 17, 2010), http://www.govtech.com/policy-management/Is-Google-Earth-Eyeing-Your-Pool.html?topic=117688#.
2. Ibid.

KEY CONCEPTS

accountability 6

ethical behavior 16

exit 15

fiscal accountability 14

politics-administration dichotomy 11

process accountability 14

program accountability 14

Progressives 10

rule of law 9

voice 15

whistleblowers 8

FOR FURTHER READING

Burke, John P. *Bureaucratic Responsibility.* Baltimore: Johns Hopkins University Press, 1986.

Finer, Herman. "Administrative Responsibility in Democratic Government." *Public Administration Review* 1 (Summer 1941): 335-350.

Friedrich, Carl J. "Public Policy and the Nature of Administrative Responsibility." In *Public Policy,* edited by Carl J. Friedrich and E. S. Mason, 3-24. Cambridge, Mass.: Harvard University Press, 1940.

Gruber, Judith E. *Controlling Bureaucracies: Dilemmas in Democratic Governance.* Berkeley: University of California Press, 1987.

Hirschman, Albert O. *Exit, Voice, and Loyalty: Responses to Decline in Firms,* *Organizations, and States.* Cambridge, Mass.: Harvard University Press, 1970.

Landau, Martin. "Redundancy, Rationality, and the Problem of Duplication and Overlap." *Public Administration Review* 29 (July-August 1969): 346-358.

Rohr, John A. *Ethics for Bureaucrats: An Essay on Law and Values.* 2d ed. New York: Marcel Dekker, 1989.

SUGGESTED WEBSITES

Extensive discussion on federal ethics laws and policies can be found on the website of the U.S. Office of Government Ethics, **www.usoge.gov**.

More broadly, the Council on Governmental Ethics Laws, **www.cogel.org**, tracks policies on ethics. In addition, many state and local governments have their own sites—which search engines can readily locate—detailing laws and regulations on ethics.

THE JOB OF GOVERNMENT

Public administration does not exist as an abstract concept. It gets its meaning from how public administrators do their jobs, as they give life to policy decision. But not all administration or administrators are the same. At different levels of government, the process can look very different, ranging from the distant and hush-hush world of the Central Intelligence Agency to the front-line work of police officers and fire fighters whom we see every day.

So if we want to understand what public administration really is, we must begin by looking at the tasks that public administrators seek to do. Even more fundamentally, we must understand the connections between citizens, the officials they elect, the administrators they empower—and how all this combines to shape what government actually does. That, in turn, is the key for holding public administrators accountable for *what* they do and *how* they do it.

CHAPTER OBJECTIVES

- Understand where government has grown in recent years—and where it hasn't

- Examine the variations in government's programs and tools

- Explore how these variations affect the study and practice of public administration

What Government Does—and How It Does It

Washington's subway was just one part of the adventure through many different organizations on the trip from Philadelphia to the nation's capital.

ONE VERY EARLY MORNING NOT LONG AGO, I STRUGGLED out of bed for an early-morning trip to Washington, D.C. From my Philadelphia apartment, I rode an elevator down to the lobby and caught a trolley to the 30th Street train station. I emerged from the underground tunnel at the station just as the sun was coming up and just in time to scoot across the street as the "Don't Walk" signal began flashing. As I waited for the Amtrak train, the barking of a bomb-sniffing dog echoed throughout the concourse. The dog had not spotted a suspicious package—he was a pup in training and was struggling to focus on the job instead of all the fascinating people and their breakfast snacks milling around the platforms. The train, fortunately, was on time, and it was a pretty ride, with the rising sun shining on the Chesapeake Bay, before rolling into Union Station at the foot of Capitol Hill. A quick trip on Washington's Metro subway got me to a meeting in a nearby federal office building.

This tale, of course, is about more than the trip of a sometime road warrior and textbook author. It is also a map of government—and government administration—in action. The Philadelphia elevator had an inspection sticker certifying that the Pennsylvania Department of Labor and Industry had found the elevator safe, for which I was grateful (since it would have been a long fall down the shaft to the basement). The inspection might have been performed by a private company licensed by the state, but the state government stood behind the certificate pasted on the elevator's wall. The Southeastern Pennsylvania Transportation Authority (SEPTA), a regional organization stretching across a collection of local governments and three states, ran the trolley. The city of Philadelphia's Traffic Engineering Division managed the "Walk/Don't Walk" signal, and the excited puppy was an employee of Amtrak's own police department. Amtrak is really the National Railroad Passenger Corporation, a quasi-governmental corporation that operates like a private company but is controlled by government officials and subsidized by public money. Maryland's Chesapeake Bay is more scenic because of the efforts of Pennsylvania, Virginia, and Maryland, in concert with the U.S. Environmental Protection Agency, to ensure the waterway is clean. Like SEPTA, Washington's Metro system is a regional transportation authority, involving two states and the District of Columbia. Its stations contain hidden security devices to detect terrorist threats, with security provided by a complicated network of federal, state, regional, and local law enforcement agencies. Before I had fully awakened, I had encountered the vast reach of public administration.

None of us can even start our days without bumping into government. The water we drink, the cars we drive, the bicycles we pedal, the streets we walk—all are the products of government bureaucracy in action. We take it all for granted, but we expect the highest levels of service. Indeed, over the years, public administration's role in society has become so pervasive that we often speak of the rise of the **administrative state**.[1] In fact, political scientist Dwight Waldo wrote a doctoral dissertation by this title and published it in 1948. Since then, bureaucratic power has been the focus of huge debate. Some critics have condemned the growth of government and its power. More sympathetic observers have seen it as part of an inevitable—even desirable—reaction to the growing complexity of social problems and Americans' demands to solve them. Some fear that the growth of government has empowered nameless, faceless bureaucrats with greater control over our lives. Others point to government's help in solving big problems. Some plead for making government work more like a business. Others argue that government and business are so fundamentally different that corporations can't teach public organizations very much. But one thing seems certain: when trouble strikes, whether it's a giant superstorm that savages the East Coast or a tornado that pulverizes an Oklahoma city, Americans look to their government for help.

These debates have produced a wide array of approaches to the study of public administration, but one issue dominates: **administrative responsibility.** Americans expect, indeed insist, that the nation's bureaucracy be held accountable to elected officials and, through these officials, to the people. Critics sometimes complain that government bureaucracy has no bottom line. In fact, government does have a bottom line: administrative responsibility, not only for administering programs efficiently but also for ensuring that both the process and its results are accountable to elected officials and, ultimately, to the people. Americans care deeply about what government does—whether its agencies pick up the trash promptly and regularly or prevent dangerous food products from being sold in stores—and about how it does it, including making sure that people are treated fairly and that government officials do not abuse their power. How government works is key to the politics of the administrative process. And nothing is more central to these politics than the ongoing, often fierce debate about the size of government.

THE SIZE OF GOVERNMENT

Especially since the end of World War II, citizens have demanded far more services from government—better roads, a stronger safety net, safer food, better mass transit, more effective schools, and even better public colleges and universities. New programs and more ambition led to the creation of more government agencies, more government workers, and more government spending. As Waldo pointed out, this not only led to a bigger bureaucracy; it also created demand for ensuring that a bigger bureaucracy did not threaten our strong and vibrant democracy.[2]

Government Employment and Spending

Just how big is government? As Paul C. Light showed in his masterful *The True Size of Government*, getting a good measure of government's size is surprisingly difficult.[3] But consider perhaps the most common yardstick: the number of government employees. The absolute number of federal employees grew rapidly in the last century, from just 231,000 in 1901 to 2.1 million in 2014.[4] That's more than a ninefold increase. However, over the same period of time, the U.S. population has grown as well. As a share of the population, as Figure 2.1 reveals, the number of federal employees isn't much larger now than it was in 1920. The federal employment grew rapidly during World War II, increased during the expansion of government programs through the Great Society of the 1960s, and then began tapering off. However big we think "big government" is, it's not because of an explosive growth of federal employees. The real growth in government employment has come at the state and, especially, local levels—more than 50 percent from 1982 to 2009 (see Figure 2.2)—and that growth came to provide services to a larger number of citizens. Total government employment has grown in proportion to the growth of the population.

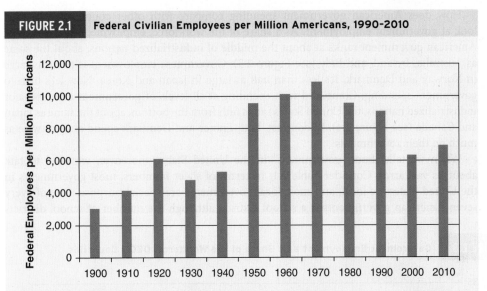

FIGURE 2.1   **Federal Civilian Employees per Million Americans, 1990-2010**

Source: U.S. Bureau of the Census; U.S. Office of Management and Budget, *Budget of the United States Government: Historical Tables.*

Note: Federal employees includes all executive branch civilian employees but excludes the postal service.

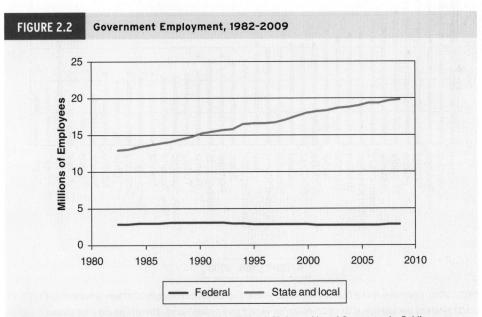

FIGURE 2.2   **Government Employment, 1982-2009**

Source: U.S. Census Bureau, Governments Division, "Federal, State, and Local Governments, Public Employment and Payroll Data," May 2011.

How does American government spending compare with other countries? Let's first look at government employment. As a share of the workforce, employment at all levels of American government ranks at about the middle of industrialized nations, about the same as Australia, Ireland, and Italy (see Figure 2.3). Government employment is twice as large in Norway and Denmark. It's less than half as large in Japan and Korea. Now let's turn to government spending. Compared with spending at all levels of government among major industrialized nations, the United States ranks fifth from the bottom, about the same as Japan and Canada (see Figure 2.4). In contrast, both France and Denmark spend almost twice as much on their governments.

When we talk about "government" in the United States, moreover, we need to talk about its vast array. Consider Table 2.1. In terms of sheer numbers, most governments in the United States are local, and most local governments are special purpose. One of every seven American governments is a school district, although the number of school districts

| FIGURE 2.3 | Government Employment as a Share of the Workforce, OECD Countries |

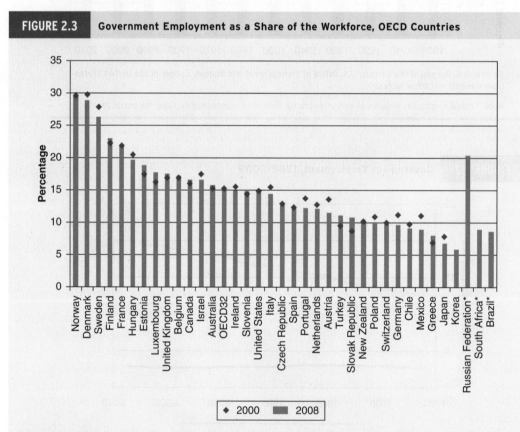

Source: OECD (2011), *Government at a Glance 2011*, OECD Publishing. http://dx.doi.org/10.1787/gov_glance-2011-en.

Note: OECD32 refers to the average of all OECD countries except Iceland and Korea. There is no data for Iceland.

*The Russian Federation, South Africa, and Brazil are not members of the OECD.

FIGURE 2.4	Government Outlays as a Percentage of Gross Domestic Product, Selected OECD Countries

Source: OECD, *Economic Outlook*, No. 88, Annex table 25, http://www.oecd.org/document/3/0,3343,en_2649_34573_2483 901_1_1_1,00.html.

Note: All figures are estimates for 2011.

has dramatically decreased in the last sixty years. Two of every five governments is a special district—for water, sewer, and mass transit, among other functions—and these districts have dramatically increased in the last sixty years, growing by a factor of three. We have a lot of government, but most of it is local; most Americans are served by multiple governments, but most of these deal with narrow purposes. That is a direct product of the rich texture of American federalism, and it makes the United States unique in the world.

How does this add up? It's scarcely a portrait of explosive big government. The number of employees has grown, but only in proportion to the growth of the population, and mostly at the state and local government levels. There hasn't been a big growth in the number of feds. On the international stage, American government is about average in the number of

TABLE 2.1	Number of Governments in the United States							
Type of government	1952	1962	1972	1982	1992	2002	2007	2012
Federal	1	1	1	1	1	1	1	1
State	50	50	50	50	50	50	50	50
Local	116,756	91,186	78,218	81,780	84,955	87,525	89,476	89,004
Total units	116,807	91,237	78,269	81,831	85,006	87,576	89,527	89,055
Type of local government								
County	3,052	3,043	3,044	3,041	3,043	3,034	3,033	3,031
Municipal	16,807	18,000	18,517	19,076	19,279	19,429	19,492	19,522
Township and town	17,202	17,142	16,991	16,734	16,656	16,504	16,519	16,364
School district	67,355	34,678	15,781	14,851	14,422	13,506	13,051	12,884
Special district	12,340	18,323	23,885	28,078	31,555	35,052	37,381	37,203

Source: U.S. Census Bureau, *2012 Census of Governments*, http://www.census.gov//govs/cog2012.

employees, and it's relatively small in spending. The number of American governments has grown, but mainly to serve special purposes that have accompanied the growth of the nation's populations. These conclusions certainly don't match popular perception, but they're the underlying bedrock of public administration.

WHAT GOVERNMENT DOES

Consider these snapshots of government in action:

- The Social Security Administration distributed 58 million monthly payments, totaling $821 billion in benefits, in 2013. The benefits amount to nearly 40 percent of the income of the elderly. Among the elderly, more than one in five married couples and two in five unmarried persons rely on Social Security for 90 percent or more of their income. The program has been a major force in dramatically reducing the poverty of older Americans.[5]
- In 1989 the Federal Deposit Insurance Corporation (FDIC), best known for its bank-window stickers promising $100,000 insurance for each account, took over the management of two hundred financially troubled savings and loan institutions. As part of this process, the FDIC found itself the temporary owner of 12 percent of the Dallas Cowboys football team. Even fans in other parts of the nation had to grudgingly admit that, for a time, the Cowboys were America's team.[6]
- Inspectors for the Food and Drug Administration, alerted in March 1989 to the possibility that terrorists might attempt to poison imported fruit, managed to find two grapes—in a shipment of 364,000 crates of grapes—that had been injected with cyanide.[7]

- In 2012, the City of New York Fire Department responded to 25,612 structural fires, with an average response time of just four minutes and four seconds. For almost 218,329 medical emergencies, help arrived in four minutes and twelve seconds, even in the city's famously snarled traffic.[8]
- The Port of Los Angeles is the nation's busiest port. Managed as a department of the City of Los Angeles, its facilities handle more than $283 billion in cargo per year, including more than 200,000 imported cars.[9]
- Ohio State University enrolls more than 56,000 students, making it the largest campus in the country. The University of Michigan, of course, would counter that it has the largest football stadium in the country. The "Big House" seats almost 110,000 people, and every seat is filled for the game with Ohio State. Since these two Big Ten schools are state universities, they're part of the state bureaucracy. Engineers promised a big increase in noise on the field following renovations, in the hope of rattling opposing players.

The scope of the American government's activities is nothing short of remarkable. From controlling drug safety to researching AIDS, from protecting the food supply to protecting the nation's finances, from arresting criminals to protecting waterfalls, government agencies oversee an amazing variety of services. Public administration is central to all these operations.

Not surprisingly, the functions of government are different at each level of government. As Table 2.2 shows, the federal government has primary responsibility for national defense, although the states run the National Guard. The federal government also runs the postal service and conducts space exploration, and it spends more than the other two levels of government put together on veterans' services, protection of natural resources, and entitlement programs like Social Security. State governments have primary responsibility for higher education, welfare, highways, and prisons and jails. In some states, liquor stores are government-owned monopolies. In Pennsylvania, for example, a former liquor control board commissioner was also a wine aficionado, and his state liquor stores featured his "chairman's selections"—a government official was also serving as the state's quasi-official wine steward. Finally, local governments carry primary responsibility for basic services such as fire protection, police, and elementary and secondary education. For a few services, including health and hospitals, governmental responsibilities are balanced among the levels of government.

Although most government functions are concentrated in one level of government, there's almost no area in which a level of government has exclusive responsibility for any major function. Federal and state governments provide aid to local schools and set broad policies. Local governments pass resolutions on foreign policy questions. In short, America's public administration system is part of the nation's system of federalism, and that system is a world of blended functions. On any issue that matters, many Americans want a voice, and there are few barriers to governments getting involved in important questions. This blended system is a logical product of America's politics and rich history, but it also creates many of its administrative cross-pressures. Political imperatives lead to shared policymaking; shared policymaking means that no single level of government has full responsibility for anything. This fundamental political reality muddies accountability and vastly complicates performance.

TABLE 2.2	Concentration of Government Spending		
Level of Government with Primary Responsibility			
Federal	**State**	**Local**	**Mixed responsibility**
Defense	Higher education	Elementary education	Health
Postal service	Welfare	Libraries	Hospitals
Space	Highways	Police	
Veterans' services	Corrections	Fire	
Natural resources and environment	Inspections	Parks	
	Liquor stores	Housing and community development	
Social Security		Sanitation	
Homeland security		Utilities	

Note: "Primary responsibility" means accounting for more than 50 percent of direct government spending for the function.

HOW GOVERNMENT DOES IT

This story of mixed policymaking and policy administration is the cornerstone of American public administration. It explains how government could extend its reach without expanding its workforce. And it explains why accountability and performance so often seem difficult, since rarely is anyone fully in charge of anything and many hands share responsibility for results.

One helpful way of understanding the work of government is to see public administration not just as a collection of departments, bureaus, and agencies but as a collection of basic tools, which organizations and their leaders operate. As Christopher C. Hood puts it:

> We can imagine government as a set of administrative tools—such as tools for carpentry or gardening, or anything else you like. Government administration is about social control, not carpentry or gardening. But there is a toolkit for that, just like anything else. What government does to us—its subjects or citizens—is to try to shape our lives by applying a set of administrative tools, in many different combinations and contexts, to suit a variety of purposes.[10]

Some of these tools are **direct tools**—including the provision of goods and services, such as police and fire protection; income support, such as Social Security; and the cost of doing business, such as basic organizational management and the payment of interest on the national debt. As we move from the federal to the state and then to local governments, the administrative tools are more likely to be direct: from local ambulances to libraries, schools to criminal justice, local administration is most likely to be **direct administration**. This is the approach we most often think of when we think of government, and it matches the model that citizens and policymakers alike carry around in their heads. Government is a vending machine into which policymakers load programs, insert money, and wait for goods and services to pop out. When the wrong things come out of the machine, the answer is to tinker with its mechanisms. If the price goes up, then the machine can be reset to take more money. As long as government was direct, the vending machine fit the popular model, and improving public administration remained a matter of adjusting its parts.[11]

But government has also undergone a quiet revolution—the development of a government by proxy through **indirect tools** of action.[12] Such indirect tools include contracting out governmental programs to nongovernmental partners; disbursing grants to encourage other levels of government to do things they might not otherwise have done; regulating behavior to change private-sector actions; handing out vouchers to allow citizens to purchase services from private organizations; and administering loan programs to enhance the ability of individuals and private organizations to borrow private money to pursue public goals. We will return to a detailed examination of these issues when we examine policy implementation in Chapter 12, but a brief excursion through these tools now will help set the stage for the discussions to follow.

Contracts

While governments have always relied on **contracts**—to feed and supply armies, for example—their use has increased markedly since World War II. The growing complexity of government has led to greater reliance on private-sector experts and outside organizations. In a contract, government administrators sign a formal agreement with private parties: the government agrees to pay a certain amount of money in exchange for a good or a service.

The reach of contracts is long and sweeping. Consider America's long and painful war in Afghanistan. Just a month after the terrorist attacks of September 11, 2001, the United States and a collection of allies launched a major counterattack to root out the al Qaeda organization that had planned the September 11 attack, to disrupt any future attacks, and to get al Qaeda's leader, Osama bin Laden. The Obama administration finally did get bin Laden, in a daring 2011 raid by Navy Seals in neighboring Pakistan, but the war dragged on for years afterward. From the beginning, the Pentagon strategy was to keep the size of deployed forces as small as possible. Following a surge of troops in 2011, for example, there were nearly 100,000 soldiers in the country. But supporting the troops was a vast army of civilian contractors. At the end of 2008, for example, there were 2.2 contractors for every U.S. soldier, including American and international workers, as well as tens of thousands of local contractors hired to support the war effort. For most of the war, American troops accounted for less than half—and sometimes only a third—of the force sent to root out al Qaeda.[13] Recruiting enough soldiers to fight the war would have been very difficult, and the contracting strategy allowed the military extra flexibility. But relying on so many contractors vastly complicated the war-fighting effort and the problem of ensuring accountability for the use and support of force.

Contract administration thus requires the government to employ officials to set the standards for contracts, to negotiate effective programs at low prices, and to oversee the results that contractors produce. While newspaper stories about Pentagon contracting scandals remind us about both the scope of federal contracting and how difficult it can be to administer contracts well, they disguise the degree to which government at all levels relies on contracting. From the management of cafeterias in federal office buildings to the construction of roads by local governments, contractors play an important role in many governmental activities. The effective management of contracts poses a growing challenge for public administrators.

Ripped
from the Headlines...

PERFORMANCE

North Carolina Upgrades Medicaid

In 2012, North Carolina faced the daunting task of updating its Medicaid computer system, which had to track 88 million claims every year. CSC, a high-tech company from Northern Virginia, won the contract, but the project quickly fell behind schedule and far over budget. CSC promised a "state of the art" system, but the company decided to use COBOL as the programming language, a language from the 1950s so rare that the company had to fly workers from India to finish the work in Raleigh. State auditors found that the state's Department of Health and Human Services had done a poor job of designing and overseeing the contract, especially in tracking the objectives and controlling the costs.

News coverage of the continually delayed project repeated a very familiar problem: a government agency struggling to manage a very complicated program, deciding to contract out the technical parts of the job to a private company that promised higher performance at a lower cost, and then struggling to keep the project on time and under budget. It was hardly the case that the state's DHHS wasn't trying. But managing an extraordinarily complex contract requires equally extraordinary skills, and state managers struggled to keep up. For the millions of low-income Americans who relied on Medicaid to obtain health care, the consequences could be very serious. How can governments ensure that they can provide important and necessary services to their constituents?

Source: Joseph Neff, "Costs Soar for Updating NC's Medicaid Computer System," *News & Observer* (June 17, 2012), http://www.newsobserver.com/2012/06/17/2142627/state-contract-for-updating-computer.html.

Grants

Much governmental activity occurs *between* levels of government. Sometimes one level of government wishes to provide financial assistance to another level—often to encourage other governments to do what they could not otherwise afford or might not otherwise choose to do. Sometimes one level of government wants to induce another level to perform a certain service in a particular way. For example, the federal government created the interstate highway system to encourage state governments to build modern high-speed roads; it provided 90 cents of every construction dollar, and the states naturally found the funds irresistible. In fact, the use of this tool dates from the Ordinance of 1787—before the drafting of the Constitution—which provided land grants to the states for education. Since then, **federal grants** have been used for everything from supporting land-grant colleges to helping states provide medical care for the poor. Many state governments provide a large share of the support for local schools, to help improve the quality of education and to level out the financial disparities among local governments. As Donald Haider argues, "federal grants are the oldest, most widely used, and probably the best-understood tool that the federal government has available to carry out public policy."[14]

The administration of grants differs significantly from direct administration and from administration through contracts. Administrators at one level must supervise administrators at another, but they cannot command actions or write contracts. Most often, grants work by providing incentives for state and local governments to act, but also to use their own judgment on how to administer programs. This creates another complex front on which to weigh the issues of politics, performance, and accountability, and it incorporates new challenges for administration.

Regulations

As the beginning of this chapter makes clear, we can't even get out of bed in the morning without encountering government regulation, for it dictates the disclosures about the content of the bed on which we sleep, the strength of the floors on which we walk, the safety of the electricity that powers our alarm clocks, the labels on our orange juice, and almost everything else we touch before we even leave our homes. We often refer to this as the world of **red tape**. The term has long historical roots; it comes from the brightly colored ribbon used to tie up documents presented to the English king in centuries past. After the American Civil War, veterans had to show proof of their service to receive their pensions. The war records were bound in red ribbon, so government officials had to "cut the red tape" to get to the papers. Since then, "red tape" has captured the image of a government tied up in its own rules. We often complain bitterly about red tape and look for someone with a sharp knife to cut through complications. This is one more way that government can increase its reach into our lives without increasing its size. A relatively small number of government administrators can write rules that affect us all. But we often want this to happen—we expect government to ensure our elevators and cars are safe, that companies don't pollute our drinking water, and that we get a fair shake at tax time. We might hate the process, but we also insist that it work well. Regulation is one more way that the government increases its reach into our lives without increasing its size.

Regulatory programs can significantly expand government's power while spending relatively little money. A mere handful of government regulators can promulgate extensive and costly rules that apply to entire industries or large segments of the population. Even the volume of **regulations**—there are more than two hundred volumes in the *Code of Federal Regulations,* the federal government's compendium of rules—does not provide a really good gauge of the size or scope of federal regulations. The rules are wide ranging: there are twenty volumes of rules on agriculture, eighteen covering the Internal Revenue Service's tax regulations, and one on the Panama Canal. A casual look around us shows the breadth and importance of regulation by all levels of government. Federal food experts found the tainted grapes. State regulators check the management of many banks and insurance companies. Local inspectors ensure the accuracy of the scales grocery stores use to measure and charge for our food. Everything from the cars we drive, the gas we put in them, the bicycles we peddle, the clothes we wear, the banks we use, the air we breathe, the food we eat, and the airplanes

Funds provided by the American Recovery and Reinvestment Act in 2010 helped put people back to work and funded projects across the country, including this one in Summerhaven, Arizona.

in which we fly is covered by regulations—and by public administrators who write and enforce these rules.

Tax Expenditures

Governments at all levels include a wide variety of features in their tax codes to give individuals and taxpayers special advantages in paying their taxes. These features do more than ease taxpayers' burdens. They serve as incentives to promote many different social and economic policies to encourage taxpayers to do some things and avoid doing others. Such tax advantages are called by a variety of names—tax breaks, tax loopholes, and **tax expenditures** (which is the term we use, to emphasize their relationship to regular spending). Tax expenditures reduce the cost of homeownership and thus encourage taxpayers to buy rather than rent their homes, for example. The federal tax deduction for mortgage interest and local property taxes, which makes family homes much cheaper to own, will cost the federal government $157 billion by 2018.[15] Other tax expenditures exempt from income taxes the interest taxpayers earn on state and local government bonds and thereby reduce the cost of state and local government borrowing. The special tax breaks for oil and gas exploration encourage more exploration for these resources.

Most state income taxes use federal tax law to structure their systems, so federal tax expenditures spill over into the state level as well. Moreover, many local governments have devised their own special tax preferences, especially those designed to promote economic development. Many local economic growth programs, including enterprise zones and tax increment financing zones, create special tax abatements to encourage investment in economically depressed areas. For many economic development projects, the tax breaks can provide incentives. State and local governments view them as investments in the future.

Proponents of tax expenditures often promote them as "free" programs. The government does not have to budget or spend any money on these programs, which hides their cost. In fact, of course, they are scarcely free: tax expenditures cost the government money, by taking away from current and future revenues instead of adding to the pool of money for spending. Moreover, because their cost is relatively hidden—estimates for federal tax expenditures are buried deep inside the budget in a place only real tax policy wonks can find them—once tax expenditures are created, there usually is no process for renewing them or for assessing their effectiveness. But they can be very complex to administer. Tax expenditures require tax administrators to write and enforce rules, which can be, as anyone who has encountered the Internal Revenue Service can testify, a very difficult process. Those problems constantly embroil the IRS in controversy and political conflict.[16]

Loan Programs

The federal government has become the largest lender in the country. From guaranteeing student loans to extending credit to farmers, the federal government provides financial assistance through a broad range of **loan programs.** (Other levels of government have their own programs as well, but the federal government plays the most important role in this area.) Federal lending began during the Great Depression, but it grew dramatically during the late 1970s and early 1980s. As budget deficits swelled, members of Congress seeking new ways of funding federal programs found that loans provided an easy answer. As Rep. Willis D. Gradison Jr. (R-Ohio) put it, federal loans are "a technique used during a period of budget stringency to do good things where the cost doesn't show up until later." The result is a huge but hidden support of the lending markets—more than $800 million per year in direct loans and federal guarantees of nearly $2 trillion in additional loans.

Although the federal government dominates government credit policy, lending programs are administered in a highly decentralized fashion. Loans for college students and home mortgages, for example, are administered by local banks under the supervision of state and federal agencies. Government loan programs, thus, are part of the subtle and complex public-private mixture of administrative strategies that have grown in the American system, especially since 1945.

IMPLICATIONS FOR PUBLIC ADMINISTRATION

The many threads in this discussion of what the government does and how it does it suggest three broad implications.

1. *The job of government varies by level.* Local governments tend to concentrate on direct provision of goods and services. State governments provide many goods and services directly as well, but they also play a crucial intermediary role in the American federal system by transferring money to local governments (especially for public schools) and administering grants from the federal government (especially for welfare and Medicaid). The federal government, by contrast, devotes most of its administrative energy to national defense and the transfer function. Different levels of American government tend to do different things. That means public administration in America also varies by the level of government.

2. *The job of government varies by function.* The growth of transfer functions emphasizes that different kinds of governmental programs require different administrative approaches. Providing goods and services, from education to national defense, requires sharp technical skills. For example, education administrators work to develop the best techniques: the best way to train teachers, the right kind of audiovisual aids, textbooks that do not promote stereotypes or advance the "wrong" values, tests that most appropriately measure students' achievements. In direct provision of goods and services, most administrative action is internal to the government's bureaucracy. By contrast, administering transfer programs involves extensive action external to the government

An investigator from FDA's San Francisco field office (left) worked with an investigator from the California Department of Health Services to collect soil samples. They were tracking the source of a 2006 E. coli outbreak in spinach, which originated in California farms and sickened people throughout the United States and Canada.

bureaucracy. Instead of mailing checks for welfare and Social Security, government could directly provide such services as government-run shelters for those who could not afford their own homes, government-run kitchens for those who could not afford food, and so on. Transfer payments serve both to make the government's administrative task easier and to preserve dignity and free choice for the recipients. They also fundamentally change the administrative task: instead of providing the necessary services, the government seeks to determine the size of the check to which the law entitles a recipient. That is a very different kind of government-citizen interaction than would be involved in direct services, and it requires a different collection of administrative skills. Thus, the job of government varies with the job it does.

3. *The job of government varies by who finally provides the goods and services.* Even services that formerly were offered directly by government are now being provided instead through contracts, intergovernmental grants, tax expenditures, and loan programs. Just as in transfer programs, much of the administrative work is external to the government bureaucracy. When contractors manufacture weapons for defense or collect local garbage, government officials are "in the uncomfortable position of being held responsible for programs they do not really control."[17] There is, in short, a difference between who *provides* a service, by creating a program and paying for it, and who *produces* it by actually administering the service.[18] As government has grown bigger, more and more of its growth has come about through providing more services but relying on nongovernmental agents and organizations—or sometimes governments at other levels—to produce them.

Such **government by proxy**—the use of third-party agents to deliver programs that the government funds—is different from transfer programs because the responsibility of government officials extends far beyond simply ensuring that checks are mailed out correctly, and different from directly administered programs because government officials do not control those who finally provide the service. Each kind of program requires a different approach to administration, tailored to the special problems and needs that the program presents. We explore this problem in more depth in Chapter 12. For now, it's important to note that the job of government varies with who ultimately delivers the service.

This complexity, in turn, is part of the problem of trust in government, because it's hard to trust a government in which no one seems clearly in charge. The growing problem of trust in government is inescapable. In 1958, 73 percent of Americans said they trusted government "just about always" or "most of the time." By 2013, it was 26 percent, bouncing along the bottom for a decade.[19] Even worse, by early 2013 the share of Americans who said they were "angry" about Washington hit 30 percent.[20] Of course, Americans have always been ambivalent about their government. After all, one of the things that distinguishes the United States of America from many of the world's other nations is that it was founded through a revolution. Its citizens rejected their king, fought off the world's most powerful army, and dedicated themselves to the idea that they would never again permit such concentrated governmental power to rob them of their liberty.

On the other hand, Americans have always expected government to protect them. The Marine Corps hymn celebrates the Marines' role in protecting the nation "from the halls of Montezuma" (the site of a famous battle in the Mexican-American War, in 1847) "to the shores of Tripoli" (a battle against North African pirates in 1805). From these early battles to the effort to stop and clean up the BP oil spill, Americans expect their government to work for them—but they never like the governmental power that goes along with its job. As one Republican strategist told *The Washington Post*, "Americans don't want government to work." Why is that so? "They want it to stop working because they suspect every time it does work, they pay a price."[21] There's a deep paradox here—a fear of a government so powerful it could erode their liberty and the insistence on a government powerful enough to solve almost any problem. That's a tall order, if not an impossible job, and public administrators find themselves always squeezed in this paradox.

CONCLUSION

If there truly is a crisis of confidence in American government, its roots are not necessarily in "big government." While government unquestionably has gotten bigger, it has not become more concentrated. Its growth has come through **entitlements** and loan guarantees and contracts, as well as through an expansion of services that citizens expect—and demand. In fact, the "size of government" issue is really a reflection of government's growing complexity. More and more, governmental programs rely on intricate relationships among levels of government or between government and private contractors or other agents. That web, in turn, has disconnected decisions about raising money from the ways we spend it. Those responsible for the performance of governmental programs are not always within the same level of government, and often they are not within government itself.

That complicates the task of accountability. Traditional approaches to accountability, as we see in the next chapter, depend on a direct link between government policymakers and the administrators executing governmental decisions. When the chain of implementation stretches beyond a government agency to another level of government—or even to nongovernmental partners—traditional approaches to government are strained. This certainly does not mean that the growth of government's reliance on indirect tools makes accountability impossible. Nor does it necessarily make it more difficult, although holding government's partners accountable often requires different and more complex approaches. But it does mean that today's accountability is often different from the accountability system that government has been used to in the past, and that raises new challenges for government accountability.

Indeed, from filling out income tax forms to borrowing money through student loans to working as government contractors, all citizens have become more involved in the performance of governmental programs. Public functions are more intricately interwoven with the private sector, and this interweaving brings new complexities into the administration of government. If government depends both on public and private values, whose values are to prevail in the inevitable conflicts, and who will work out solutions to these conflicts?

These fundamental issues, which underline the crucial problems of accountability and performance in public administration, will follow us through the book as we explore the value of traditional theories of management, both public and private, and as we examine the challenges of the new approaches, both to existing notions of public administration and to lasting values of American democracy.

CASE 2.1

Pennsylvania: Who Is in Charge of Homeland Security?

In late 2010, investigative journalists at the ProPublica nonprofit website got their hands on a copy of "Pennsylvania Intelligence Bulletin No. 131," a twelve-page newsletter distributed to law enforcement officials and managers of some private-sector operations by the state's Office of Homeland Security. In the coming weeks, the newsletter warned, officials in Cranberry Township would be holding a hearing on drilling for natural gas in a shale formation. Near the Delaware River in Philadelphia, a group had scheduled a screening of the movie *Gasland,* a documentary that explored whether new natural gas wells risked contaminating the nation's water supply. The movie, the bulletin warned, was controversial and might pose a threat to homeland security.[1] How controversial was the film? The movie won a documentary award at the Sundance Film Festival and was later broadcast on PBS.

But the bulletin didn't stop there. Antiwar activists planned a short car caravan through a small town to stop at a defense contractor's facility. The newsletter listed other looming dates: Eid, the end of the Ramadan month of fasting for Muslims, and the Jewish high holidays, which "may present additional risk factors"

because there would be "very high attendance at Jewish houses of worship and public gatherings." A few days later, an animal rights group planned to protest against a rodeo. Gay and lesbian activists planned a PrideFest event.

All of this information came from the state's Office of Homeland Security, through the Institute of Terrorism Research and Response, a private contractor hired with $125,000 of grant money. The source of the grant money? A federal program designed to help state and local governments identify threats to "critical infrastructure"—power plants, bridges, water systems, and other facilities that, if attacked by terrorists, might cause big disruptions.

Governor Ed Rendell, a Democrat winding down his term, was furious. "Tell me," he wondered out loud, "what critical infrastructure does the gay and lesbian PrideFest threaten?" He went on, "How in the Lord's name can we consider them to be terrorists?" An anti-drilling activist asked, "I remember when Iran, Iraq, and North Korea were enemies of the state." He went on, "When did Lassie, Mother Nature, and vegetarians become the Axis of Evil?"

Embarrassed supporters of the newsletter quietly told reporters that the natural gas industry had suffered some acts of vandalism, and that environmental activists were "beginning to morph—transitioning to more criminal, extremist measures." The newsletter, a spokesperson for the state office overseeing the Homeland Security agency said, helps "increase situational awareness for public safety officials."[2]

Reporters discovered that an organization, Good Schools Pennsylvania, which was founded by the governor's own policy adviser, previously appeared in a warning. Rendell said he was "deeply embarrassed" and promised to terminate the contract. He said he wouldn't fire the head of the Homeland Security office, however, because "there's shared responsibility here." It turns out that some members of Rendell's staff knew that the contractor had been tracking innocent activities around the state for several months.[3]

Just what was the Institute of Terrorism Research and Response? Its website says that it is an "American and Israeli nonprofit corporation created to help organizations succeed and prosper in a world threatened by terrorism," with offices in Philadelphia, Washington, London, and Jerusalem. Its head was a former police officer from York, a small town in south-central Pennsylvania who had worked in military and counter-terrorism operations in Israel.

Tom Ridge, the Republican former Pennsylvania governor, founding director of the Office of Homeland Security, and adviser to the shale oil company that was the object of some of the demonstrators, said he found the program "rather bizarre." Had he had any role in the contract, Ridge was asked? "Hell, no," he replied.[4]

Questions to Consider

1. After the September 11, 2001, terrorist attacks, experts worried that a new round of small but carefully targeted terror attacks against "critical infrastructure" could cripple American cities by shutting off power, poisoning water, or blocking traffic. Does the broader strategy to identify possible threats to this critical infrastructure strike you as a wise idea?

2. Who is accountable for this action? The money flowed from the U.S. Department of Homeland Security to the Pennsylvania Office of Homeland Security to a private contractor. If you wanted to fire someone, who would you fire? The federal official who awarded the grant? The state official who managed the contract? The contractor? Would you fire the official in charge at each step—or the higher-level officials who were in charge of the agencies? Or would you just terminate the contract?

3. What steps do you think government ought to take to control the actions of contractors who spend taxpayers' dollars in the government's name?

4. More generally, is the analysis of possible threats to homeland security something that can—and should—be contracted in part to private organizations, which might have more expertise than government agencies? Or is it an activity, full of implications for individual freedom, that the government ought to keep within its own organizations?

NOTES

1. See Pennsylvania Intelligence Bulletin, no. 131 (2010), http://www.propublica.org/documents/item/pennsylvania-intelligence-bulletin-no.-131-aug.-30-2010.

2. Angela Couloumbis, "Rendell 'Appalled' by State's Tracking of Activists," *Philly.com* (September 15, 2010), http://articles.philly.com/2010-09-15/news/24975314_1_rendell-peace-activists-bulletin.

3. Donald Gilliland, "Gov. Ed Rendell's Top Staffers Knew of Homeland Security Tracking Protesters in July," *Patriot-News* (September 15, 2010), http://www.penlive.com/midstate/index.ssf/2010/09/rendells_top_staffers_knew_of.html.

4. Joe Smydo, "Shale Adviser Ridge Calls Anti-Terror Pact 'Bizarre,'" *Pittsburgh Post-Gazette* (September 16, 2010), http://www.post-gazette.com/stories/local/state/shale-adviser-ridge-calls-anti-terror-pact-bizarre-264195.

CASE 2.2

Reading License Plates: Collecting Data on American Citizens

If there's any part of government that citizens seem to take for granted, it's the license plate. They're everywhere. Some states just have one, at the rear of the car. Some have both. Some states take fierce pride in the slogans on the plates. "Live free or die" has been on New Hampshire license plates for years. Since 2000, Washington, D.C., has put "Taxation without representation" on its plates to protest the lack of full congressional representation for its citizens. DC plates with the phrase have gone on the presidential limousine during the Clinton administration, off during the Bush administration, and back on for the Obama administration. Wisconsin is proud of its "America's Dairyland" plates, and Maryland residents have a choice of plates that proclaim "Treasure the Chesapeake."

Whatever plate might be on your car, though, you might not know that police around the country are keeping a close eye on it—and you. Technological advances have made it possible for police to mount relatively inexpensive cameras on road signs, overpasses, police cars, and buildings around the country. The cameras have amazing resolution. They can capture the license plate number as well as the location, date, and time of the scan; pour it into an enormous database; and compare the information with "most wanted" information in national databases. These systems around the nation collect thousands of license plate numbers every minute.

The data systems are tremendously valuable for tracking the movement of suspects, but in the process they also collect enormous amounts of information on everyone else. As a report by the American Civil Liberties Union found,

"enormous databases of innocent motorists' location information are growing rapidly. This information is often retained for years or even indefinitely, with few or no restrictions to protect privacy rights."[1]

Police officials not only like the ability to scan enormous numbers of license plates in the hunt for suspects, ranging from individuals who have abducted children to possible terrorists. They also like the ability to keep a long-running database. As David J. Roberts, a senior program manager for the International Association of Chiefs of Police, put it, "We'd like to be able to keep the data as long as possible, but it does provide a rich and enduring data set for investigations down the line."[2] An individual whom police identify as part of one crime might be connected with others by tracking license plate numbers back through the system. Camera systems are even used on many campuses, with college police departments quietly tracking every car that enters the campus.

ACLU worried that the systems collected vast amounts of information about completely innocent citizens. In Maryland, for example, it discovered that the license plate readers scanned 29 million plates, but only 0.2 percent (1 in 500) were "hits," that is, associated with any wrongdoing.[3] In many jurisdictions, the information remains in storage for a long time, as Figure 2.5 shows.

Three communities in the ACLU survey— Grapevine, TX; Mesquite, TX; and Yonkers, NY— kept the information indefinitely. To safeguard citizens' privacy, ACLU recommended a five-step policy (see Table 2.3).

FIGURE 2.5   License Plate Data Retention Policies for Selected States

MILPITAS, CA
Population: 67,000
Data policy: None
Stored plate reads: 4.7 million
(as of 8/2/12)

MINNESOTA STATE PATROL
Population: 5.3 million
Data policy: Delete after 48 hours
Stored plate reads: Less than 20,000

GRAPEVINE, TX
Population: 47,000
Data policy: None
Stored plate reads: 2 million
(as of 8/29/12)

JERSEY CITY, NJ
Population: 250,000
Data policy: Delete after 5 years
Stored plate reads: 10 million (estimated)
(as of 8/2/12)

Source: American Civil Liberties Union, *You Are Being Tracked: How License Plate Readers Are Being Used To Record Americans' Movements* (New York: July 2013), p. 17, at http://www.aclu.org/files/assets/071613-aclu alprreport-opt-v05.pdf.

TABLE 2.3	ACLU Recommendations on License Plate Cameras

License plate readers may be used by law enforcement agencies only to investigate hits and in other circumstances in which law enforcement agents reasonably believe that the plate data are relevant to an ongoing criminal investigation.

The government must not store data about innocent people for any lengthy period. Unless plate data has been flagged, retention periods should be measured in days or weeks, not months and certainly not years.

People should be able to find out if plate data of vehicles registered to them are contained in a law enforcement agency's database.

Law enforcement agencies should not share license plate reader data with third parties that do not follow proper retention and access principles. They should also be transparent regarding with whom they share license plate reader data.

Any entity that uses license plate readers should be required to report its usage publicly on at least an annual basis.

Source: American Civil Liberties Union, "YOU ARE BEING TRACKED: How License Plate Readers Are Being Used to Record Americans' Movements" (2013), http://www.aclu.org/alpr.

Questions to Consider

1. Are you surprised by the findings of the ACLU report? Does the license plate camera system worry you?
2. Would you recommend adopting ACLU's proposals on license plate cameras?
3. If you were the chief of police of your community, and if you were using such a system, how would you respond to a reporter's questions about the system?

NOTES

1. American Civil Liberties Union, "You Are Being Tracked" (2013), http://www.aclu.org/alpr.
2. Craig Timberg, "License Place Cameras Track Millions of Americans," *Washington Post* (July 17, 2013), http://www.washingtonpost.com/business/techno logy/license-plate-cameras-track-millions-of-ameri cans/2013/07/17/40410cd0-ee47-11e2-bed3-b9b6 fe264871_story.html.
3. American Civil Liberties Union, *You Are Being Tracked: How License Plate Readers Are Being Used To Record Americans' Movements* (2013), 13, http://www.aclu .org/files/assets/071613-aclu-alprreport-opt-v05 .pdf.

CASE 2.3

Wasting Away? Fifty Examples of Government Waste[1]

In late 2009, the conservative Heritage Foundation released a list of fifty examples of government waste. The examples fell into six categories, according to the foundation's analysts:

1. Programs that should be devolved to state and local governments
2. Programs that could be better performed by the private sector

3. Mistargeted programs whose recipients should not be entitled to government benefits

4. Outdated and unnecessary programs

5. Duplicative programs

6. Inefficiency, mismanagement, and fraud

And here's their list:

1. The federal government made at least $72 billion in improper payments in 2008.

2. Washington spends $92 billion on corporate welfare (excluding expenditures under the Troubled Assets Relief Program [TARP]) versus $71 billion on homeland security.

3. Washington spends $25 billion annually maintaining unused or vacant federal properties.

4. Government auditors spent the past five years examining all federal programs and found that 22 percent of them—costing taxpayers a total of $123 billion annually—fail to show any positive impact on the populations they serve.

5. The Congressional Budget Office published a "Budget Options" series identifying more than $100 billion in potential spending cuts.

6. Examples from multiple Government Accountability Office (GAO) reports of wasteful duplication include 342 economic development programs; 130 programs serving the disabled; 130 programs serving at-risk youth; 90 early childhood development programs; 75 programs funding international education, cultural, and training exchange activities; and 72 safe water programs.

7. Washington will spend $2.6 million training Chinese prostitutes to drink more responsibly on the job.

8. A GAO audit classified nearly half of all purchases on government credit cards as improper, fraudulent, or embezzled. Examples of taxpayer-funded purchases include gambling, mortgage payments, liquor, lingerie, iPods, Xboxes, jewelry, Internet dating services, and Hawaiian vacations. In one extraordinary example, the Postal Service spent $13,500 on one dinner at a Ruth's Chris Steakhouse, including "over 200 appetizers and over $3,000 of alcohol, including more than 40 bottles of wine costing more than $50 each and brand-name liquor such as Courvoisier, Belvedere, and Johnny Walker Gold." The 81 guests consumed an average of $167 worth of food and drink apiece.

9. Federal agencies are delinquent on nearly 20 percent of employee travel charge cards, costing taxpayers hundreds of millions of dollars annually.

10. The Securities and Exchange Commission spent $3.9 million rearranging desks and offices at its Washington, D.C., headquarters.

11. The Pentagon recently spent $998,798 shipping two 19-cent washers from South Carolina to Texas and $293,451 sending an 89-cent washer from South Carolina to Florida.

12. Over half of all farm subsidies go to commercial farms, which report average household incomes of $200,000.

13. Health care fraud is estimated to cost taxpayers more than $60 billion annually.

14. A GAO audit found that 95 Pentagon weapons systems suffered from a combined $295 billion in cost overruns.

15. The refusal of many federal employees to fly coach costs taxpayers $146 million annually in flight upgrades.

16. Washington will spend $126 million in 2009 to enhance the Kennedy family legacy in Massachusetts. Additionally, Senator John Kerry (D-Mass.) diverted $20 million from the 2010 defense budget to subsidize a new Edward M. Kennedy Institute.

17. Federal investigators have launched more than 20 criminal fraud investigations related to the TARP financial bailout.

18. Despite trillion-dollar deficits, last year's 10,160 earmarks included $200,000 for a tattoo removal program in Mission Hills, California; $190,000 for the Buffalo Bill Historical Center in Cody, Wyoming; and $75,000 for the Totally Teen Zone in Albany, Georgia.

19. The federal government owns more than 50,000 vacant homes.

20. The Federal Communications Commission spent $350,000 to sponsor NASCAR driver David Gilliland.

21. Members of Congress have spent hundreds of thousands of taxpayer dollars supplying their offices with popcorn machines, plasma televisions, DVD equipment, ionic air fresheners, camcorders, and signature machines—plus $24,730 leasing a Lexus, $1,434 on a digital camera, and $84,000 on personalized calendars.

22. More than $13 billion in Iraq aid has been classified as wasted or stolen. Another $7.8 billion cannot be accounted for.

23. Fraud related to Hurricane Katrina spending is estimated to top $2 billion. In addition, debit cards provided to hurricane victims were used to pay for Caribbean vacations, NFL tickets, Dom Perignon champagne, "Girls Gone Wild" videos, and at least one sex change operation.

24. Auditors discovered that 900,000 of the 2.5 million recipients of emergency Katrina assistance provided false names, addresses, or Social Security numbers or submitted multiple applications.

25. Congress recently gave Alaska Airlines $500,000 to paint a Chinook salmon on a Boeing 737.

26. The Transportation Department will subsidize up to $2,000 per flight for direct flights between Washington, D.C., and the small hometown of Congressman Hal Rogers (R-KY)—but only on Monday mornings and Friday evenings, when lawmakers, staff, and lobbyists usually fly. Rogers is a member of the Appropriations Committee, which writes the Transportation Department's budget.

27. Washington has spent $3 billion resanding beaches—even as this new sand washes back into the ocean.

28. A Department of Agriculture report concedes that much of the $2.5 billion in "stimulus" funding for broadband Internet will be wasted.

29. The Defense Department wasted $100 million on unused flight tickets and never bothered to collect refunds even though the tickets were refundable.

30. Washington spends $60,000 per hour shooting Air Force One photo-ops in front of national landmarks.

31. Over one recent 18-month period, Air Force and Navy personnel used government-funded credit cards to charge at least $102,400 on admission to entertainment events, $48,250 on gambling, $69,300 on cruises, and $73,950 on exotic dance clubs and prostitutes.

32. Members of Congress are set to pay themselves $90 million to increase their franked mailings for the 2010 election year.

33. Congress has ignored efficiency recommendations from the Department of Health and Human Services that would save $9 billion annually.

34. Taxpayers are funding paintings of high-ranking government officials at a cost of up to $50,000 apiece.

35. The state of Washington sent $1 food stamp checks to 250,000 households in order to raise state caseload figures and trigger $43 million in additional federal funds.

36. Suburban families are receiving large farm subsidies for the grass in their backyards—subsidies that many of these families never requested and do not want.

37. Congress appropriated $20 million for "commemoration of success" celebrations related to Iraq and Afghanistan.

38. Homeland Security employee purchases include 63-inch plasma TVs, iPods, and $230 for a beer brewing kit.

39. Two drafting errors in the 2005 Deficit Reduction Act resulted in a $2 billion taxpayer cost.

40. North Ridgeville, Ohio, received $800,000 in "stimulus" funds for a project that its mayor described as "a long way from the top priority."

41. The National Institutes of Health spends $1.3 million per month to rent a lab that it cannot use.

42. Congress recently spent $2.4 billion on 10 new jets that the Pentagon insists it does not need and will not use.

43. Lawmakers diverted $13 million from Hurricane Katrina relief spending to build a museum celebrating the Army Corps of Engineers—the agency partially responsible for the failed levees that flooded New Orleans.

44. Medicare officials recently mailed $50 million in erroneous refunds to 230,000 Medicare recipients.

45. Audits showed $34 billion worth of Department of Homeland Security contracts contained significant waste, fraud, and abuse.

46. Washington recently spent $1.8 million to help build a private golf course in Atlanta, Georgia.

47. The Advanced Technology Program spends $150 million annually subsidizing private businesses; 40 percent of this funding goes to Fortune 500 companies.

48. Congressional investigators were able to receive $55,000 in federal student loan funding for a fictional college they created to test the Department of Education.

49. The Conservation Reserve program pays farmers $2 billion annually not to farm their land.

50. The Commerce Department has lost 1,137 computers since 2001, many containing Americans' personal data.

Questions to Consider

1. Look over the list. Which examples do you think are the most serious? Are there programs on the list that you think are, in fact, not wasteful?

2. Assume that in at least some of these cases, someone thought there was a good reason to fund the programs. Can you identify five such programs and craft an argument that could be used to support the programs?

3. Pick five programs you think are simply bad ideas. They are likely to be decisions made by elected officials. What steps would you take to end them?

4. Responding to some of these problems might require administrative changes. Can you pick one program on this list that you think you could improve through better public administration? What steps would you take to strengthen its administration to reduce waste?

NOTE

1. Excerpt from Brian Reidl, *50 Examples of Government Waste*, Heritage Foundation (October 6, 2009), http://www.heritage.org/research/reports/2009/10/50-examples-of-government-waste. The citations to the original sources can be found at the Heritage Foundation website. Emphasis is in the original.

KEY CONCEPTS

FOR FURTHER READING

Hood, Christopher C. *The Tools of Government.* Chatham, N.J.: Chatham House, 1983.

Kerwin, Cornelius. *Rulemaking: How Government Agencies Make Law and Write Policy.* Washington, D.C.: CQ Press, 2003.

Kettl, Donald F. *Government by Proxy: (Mis?) Managing Federal Programs.* Washington, D.C.: CQ Press, 1988.

Kettl, Donald F. *The Next Government of the United States: Why Our Institutions Fail Us and How to Fix Them.* New York: Norton, 2009.

Salamon, Lester M., ed. *The Tools of Government: A Guide to the New Governance.* New York: Oxford University Press, 2002.

SUGGESTED WEBSITES

For research on how the federal government spends its money, the basic source is the federal budget, published by the Office of Management and Budget **(www.whitehouse.gov/omb)**. OMB annually publishes two useful reports: *Analytical Perspectives*, which provides background information on issues such as federal taxing, spending, and lending programs, and *Historical Tables*, which provides long-term data on federal budget trends. Many of the key budget tables are available for download in Excel format.

In addition, the Congressional Budget Office **(www.cbo.gov)** assembles federal budget data and is especially useful for tracking trends in entitlement and discretionary spending and in federal government revenue.

The best source of information about trends in state and local government finances is the U.S. Census Bureau **(www.census.gov)**. For international comparisons, the "statistics" portal at the Organization for Economic Co-operation and Development **(www.oecd .org)** is valuable. OECD is an international organization that tracks the policy and financial issues facing nations around the world.

CHAPTER

3

CHAPTER OBJECTIVES

- Understand what makes public administration "public"

- Discuss what public administration is

- Look at the deep historical debates that have shaped the study of public administration

What Is Public Administration?

The government's response to the enormous devastation of Superstorm Sandy in November 2012 was a huge change from the problems that surrounded Hurricane Katrina's assault on the Gulf Coast in 2005. As with the case of Loretta Abruscato here, aided by New York National Guard troops, government at all levels responded far more effectively to citizens' needs, thanks to the careful analysis that happened in response to the failures seven years earlier.

THE BIG QUESTIONS OF PUBLIC ADMINISTRATION LEAD directly to ageless debates about *bureaucracy*. The term has deep roots going back to fourteenth century France. At the Chamber of Accounts, field administrators placed their financial records on a brown woolen cloth, *la bure*, which covered the table where they faced the king's auditors. The room thus came to be called "the bureau," and the way these officials did their work became known as "bureaucracy." It didn't take long for the term to take on a negative meaning. In an 1836 novel, French author Honoré de Balzac characterized the bureaucracy as "a gigantic power manipulated by dwarfs" and as "that heavy curtain hung between the good to be done and him who commands it."[1] Trashing bureaucracy and those who work in it, of course, is nothing new. In the New Testament, Jesus was criticized for naming a government tax collector, Matthew, as one of his apostles. Bureaucracy is something we all love to hate—and something we can't live without. And the tensions go back thousands of years.

There is a deep contradiction buried in this ageless debate.[2] On one hand, red-tape-bound civil servants are viewed as inefficient, unresponsive, negative, bored, impolite, and unhelpful to citizens seeking services. On the other hand, bureaucracy is feared for housing all-too-efficient officials who have amassed tremendous power and who arbitrarily decide matters without due process. How can both be true: a bureaucracy as too inefficient to accomplish much of anything but also so powerful that it threatens our liberty? This is the central problem of bureaucracy in modern life.

In the study of public administration, the term *bureaucracy* has a neutral meaning. Indeed, bureaucracy is not even a public-sector term—it's a basic description for the organization and structure of complex organizations, and private companies have bureaucracies, too. Apple and Microsoft, the American Red Cross and the American Cancer Society, the power company and the Internet service provider all are bureaucracies. The oldest continuously functioning bureaucracy in the world is the Roman Catholic Church. (The New Testament records that after the ascension of Jesus, the new church immediately created a formal organization to carry on the work of its charismatic founder.) In this book, we will use *bureaucracy* to refer to complex public organizations: the formal, rational system of relations among persons vested with administrative authority to carry out public programs. In Chapter 4 we examine this interpretation of bureaucracy—and some of its alternatives—more fully.

Even though the term bureaucracy itself is neutral, the negative meanings are never far away. The often contradictory images of bureaucracy point to very real problems of large-scale administration. They also shape the politics of public administration. As presidential candidates, both Jimmy Carter and Ronald Reagan campaigned on bureaucracy-bashing themes; Bill Clinton dealt with calls to shrink the bureaucracy; both Presidents Bush campaigned on a conservative agenda to reduce government (even though they both actually increased it); and John McCain and Barack Obama sparred over who could best promote change in the way Washington does business. Obama and Mitt Romney replayed many of the same themes.

The negative image of bureaucracy is universal and crosses national boundaries. A foreign prime minister once complained, "Creating the appearance of work, taking cover behind hollow rhetoric, bureaucracy may hold back the improvement of the economic mechanism, dampen independence and initiative, and erect barriers to innovation." A second said, "Bureaucratism remains a serious problem in the political life of our party and state. The overstaffing, overlapping and unwieldiness of Government organs, confusion of their responsibilities and buck-passing are . . . major causes of bureaucratism. We must therefore reform these organs from top to bottom." The first speaker was prime minister of the former Soviet Union, the second, an acting prime minister of the People's Republic of China.[3] The impulse to reform the bureaucracy is a common aim of government officials around the world.[4]

If almost everyone hates bureaucracy and red tape, why don't we abolish the system? The answer is that government officials can't get their work done any other way—and citizens expect that the work will get done, no matter how much they complain. Complexity and red tape are inherent in large organizations, especially in government, where public policy embraces a broad array of complex goals.[5] Politicians have tried to shred the red tape, but the fundamental patterns have endured. We might not much like paying taxes or dealing with rules, but we often demonstrate that we like much of the government we get. Americans want bureaucracy cut—except for *their* bureaucracy and the programs that serve *them*. That is a central puzzle in the search for the meaning of public administration.

THE MEANING OF PUBLIC ADMINISTRATION

So how should we define **public administration**? Analysts and scholars have never agreed on a common definition.[6] In a system that includes delivering mail, collecting trash, and licensing motor vehicles to launching cameras and spacecraft on Mars, dispatching Peace Corps volunteers all over the world, helping citizens recover from hurricanes, and precisely mapping dangerous storms through satellite images, a concise definition is impossible. For scholars of public administration, the problem has sometimes seemed so difficult that experts sometimes point to a crisis of identity.

We might consider breaking public administration in half, defining *administration* and then *public*. That approach fails, however. Scholars have sometimes used phrases like *administration is executing*, but that phrase needs further definition. Other writers characterize administration as cooperative human action that has a high degree of rationality, which maximizes the realization of certain goals.[7] But this formulation could include people who use text messages to create a flash mob. Still other writers, operating at a less abstract level, say that administration is concerned with "how, not what," with "means, not ends," with "process, not substance," with "efficiency, not other values"—sets of dichotomies that provoke debate rather than provide definition.

A better starting point for understanding the meaning of *public* administration is to distinguish it from *private* administration. We begin by evaluating the argument that administration is administration wherever it exists, whether in the public or the private sector. Next we examine policy execution versus **policymaking** (or policy formulation). This separates the administrative processes, in which government administration shares similarities with private administration, from the distinctly public nature of governmental decisions. Finally, we emphasize the ways that administrative responsibility in public administration differs in both form and content from its analog in private enterprises. Of central importance to public bureaucracies, administrative responsibility defines the very essence of our puzzle—and of this book.

Public versus Private Administration

Public administration is *public:* it is the administration of governmental affairs. Yet it is also *administration,* an activity essential to all large organizations. For years, experts have debated the questions: Are its basic features the same as other types of administration? Is it simply a subset of more generic management issues? Or does it have special, distinctly public elements that require separate attention? Several schools of thought seek to answer these questions.

Leading the movement toward a generic approach to administration are sociologists who specialize in **organizational theory** and many business school students of management. At the broadest level, some organizational theorists contend that administration is administration, whatever its setting, and that the problems of organizing people, leading them, and supplying them with resources to do their jobs are always the same.[8] More practically oriented thinkers have argued that politics is about conflict and that "political conflict is at the center of management life;" management is always fundamentally about managing that conflict, regardless of its organizational setting.[9] Most broadly, Barry Bozeman has argued that "all organizations are public because public authority affects some of the behavior or processes of all organizations." Thus, organizations are neither purely public nor purely private, but all organizations, Bozeman contends, share public and private features independent of their legal or formal status.[10] In fact, a leading British political scientist, William A. Robson, has noted that "modern American theory is heavily committed to the view that one can discuss every kind of administration in a generalized manner." This effort, Robson explains, is like "an effort to produce a treatise on ball games, as distinct from studies of golf, or tennis, or football, or polo, or baseball."[11]

Indeed, the distinction between the public and private sectors has gradually become more blurred. As Dwight Waldo pointed out in 1980, "In the United States—and I believe much more widely—there is a movement away from a sharp distinction between *public* and *private,* and *toward* a blurring and mingling of the two."[12] As government becomes more involved in business, and as more business organizations are incorporated into the provision of public services, such blurring is inevitable. But our central question remains: is there something distinctly *public* about public administration?

The response of private-sector managers who move into top public-sector positions is a solid yes. They have universally underlined crucial differences between the two sectors.[13] Scholars have emphasized other differences as well.[14] One can distinguish public agencies in two ways: First, and most crucially, public organizations do the public's business—they administer law. Second, there are important differences of character—public organizations have fundamentally different processes from those of private organizations and work in a different environment.

The Critical Role of Public Authority

The most fundamental distinction between public and private organizations is the rule of law. Public organizations exist to administer the law and every element of their design—their structure, staffing, budget, and purpose—is the product of legal authority. Every action taken by a public administrator ultimately "must be traceable to a legal grant of authority; those of private firms need not be," as Harold F. Gortner, Julianne Mahler, and Jeanne Bell Nicholson argue.

> Managers of private firms can generally take any action, establish any policy, or use any means of operation not specifically prohibited. Public managers, in contrast, may not do so in the absence of specific grants of authority. Private organizations can act unless proscribed or forbidden; public ones may act *only* if the authority is granted. As a veteran public manager remarked . . . "For the private organization, it is a matter of 'go until I say stop'; but to the public manager the message is 'don't go unless I tell you to.'"[15]

Public administration exists to implement the law, and the constitutional system charts the path of authority. In the American system, authority flows from the people to those they elect to govern them. But when a legislature passes a law and an executive signs it, the law does not implement itself. That is the task the legislature delegates to an administrator, and it is this chain of authority, flowing from the people through elected institutions to the public administrator, that makes public administration distinctively public. Faithful execution of these laws is the highest calling of public administrators. It is the core of administrative responsibility.

Public management scholar Steven Kelman points to a fundamental difference between public and private management. All organizations, he says, must balance goals and constraints. Goals are the good things organizations try to do—the value they produce, the objectives they seek to accomplish. Constraints are the negative forces they must work around and the rules they must obey in pursuing their goals. Ideally, organizations would find the right balance that ensures good results and strong accountability. For private organizations, the balance leans toward the goals. With fewer constraints, private organizations sometimes encounter "the Enron problem," christened after the energy management company whose free-wheeling tactics caused it to collapse in 2001, leaving both shareholders and employees financially devastated. For public organizations, the balance leans toward the constraints. With additional constraints, government sometimes struggles to accomplish the objectives that policymakers set for it. This, Kelman says, is "the Katrina problem"—red tape that restrains the ability of government to do its job. Public and private organizations both share the need to balance goals

Public libraries are an important government-funded service. In many communities, like this one in Wilmington, North Carolina, public libraries are not only repositories of books—they are increasingly gateways to the information age.

and constraints, but the forces underlying their operations tend to push them in different directions. That dynamic, in turn, frames very different problems for their leaders and for the people they serve.[16]

Processes that Make Public Administration Public

Although these differences are not fixed in law, there typically are important distinctions between public and private organizational processes.[17] Here are the most fundamental differences:

- *Career service.* Whereas private-sector organizations tend to be led by individuals who devote their careers to the organization, American public bureaucracies tend to be headed by relative amateurs whose tenure is of short duration. Assistant secretaries in federal departments, for example, typically serve only eighteen months and spend much of their time in office simply learning their jobs.
- **Performance measures.** The private sector has the market in which to test its performance. Few public-sector organizations, by contrast, have any "direct way of evaluating their outputs in relation to the cost of the inputs used to make them," as Anthony Downs puts it.[18] For public administrators, compliance with the law is the ultimate measure of performance, but laws often are vague and give little guidance.
- *Competing standards.* Whereas efficiency is the ultimate private standard, public administrators are expected to manage both efficiently and equitably. These two standards often compete: what is fair often is not the most efficient, and vice versa. As economist Arthur Okun notes, the balance between equality and efficiency is "the big tradeoff."[19]
- *Public scrutiny.* Far more than in the private sector, public administrators work under public scrutiny. Public administrators labor under laws whose very titles, such as "Government in the Sunshine," underline the role of public **oversight,** covering both internal and external operations. This "goldfish-bowl effect" is in stark contrast with the much more limited public scrutiny that private organizations receive. Dealing with the media has long been a feature of public administrative activity.[20]
- *Persuasion.* In the private sector, managers tend to manage by authority. They give orders and expect them to be obeyed. In the public sector, by contrast, administration depends far more on persuasion and the balancing of conflicting political demands.
- *Scope of authority.* Government officials are legally required to administer the law— and the federal **Antideficiency Act** explicitly forbids officials from spending money on any purpose not explicitly *authorized* by law.[21] In the private sector, by contrast, officials are allowed to do anything not explicitly *forbidden* by law.[22]
- *Oversight.* Public administrators must answer not only to their superiors but also to legislators and the courts. Administrators must appear before legislative committees to explain their activities and must answer complaints raised in court. If the private sector has one bottom line—the annual or quarterly financial statement—the public sector has several: accountability to higher-level administrative officials, to the chief executive, to legislators, to the courts, and ultimately to the public.

We tend sometimes to separate public and private activities by the profit motive. To be sure, this is an important difference, but it does not clearly distinguish the two sectors. Private organizations sometimes put other goals before profitmaking. Some nongovernmental organizations are **nonprofit**; they exist to advance social agendas. Furthermore, some public organizations, such as the U.S. Postal Service, simulate the market by imposing fees and charges. In fact, as reformers try to make public organizations more efficient, these strategies are on the rise.

Most fundamentally, however, public organizations are public because they administer the law and because their existence springs from the law. Moreover, public organizations typically operate in a different environment from that of private organizations. Wallace Sayre once wryly suggested that "business and public administration are alike only in all unimportant respects."[23] The basic challenge of *public* service distinguishes public from private administration.

Policy Execution versus Policy Formation

Public administration shares with private administration many basic features of policy execution. From managing computer systems to processing forms, the basic work often is similar. But public-sector execution differs fundamentally in the goals to be served and the standards by which its achievements are judged. Indeed, part of what makes public administration public is its execution of the will of the people as defined by governmental institutions. Because public administration contributes to the shaping and execution of policies, it is often very different indeed from private administration. We look first at the more familiar function—policy execution.

Policy Execution

Consider what it means when we say that the government has "adopted" a policy. In our system, this normally means that the elected policymakers have enacted a law forbidding, directing, or permitting members of the society to behave in specified ways. Then what happens? The law is merely a text printed on paper. The task of public administration is to translate the print from statute books into changed behavior by members of society—individuals, groups, organizations, and businesses—in other words, to convert words into action, form into substance.

Execution of policy is a complex task. It means expanding some individuals' opportunities by extending governmental services and protections to them. It means regulating some individuals' freedom by drawing taxes from them, discovering and prosecuting those who engage in forbidden behaviors, granting or denying permission to engage in certain activities (for example, licensing radio and television stations and selling prescription drugs), and manipulating the environment of subsidies and interest rates. The government administers some enterprises itself, either as monopolies or as competitors of private enterprises: local libraries and the Social Security Administration function largely as monopolies; the U.S. Postal Service and the Tennessee Valley Authority compete with private companies. Reformers have increasingly sought to bring private competition into local schools, and public schools increasingly have to compete with private schools and parents schooling their children at home. The government also administers the defense establishment and foreign affairs, including hundreds of outposts over the world. The range is immense, and the pattern mixes old and new concerns.

Authorizing these governmental activities, as well as giving policy direction, and providing the necessary resources are among the central tasks of the elective legislature and chief executive. But all this initiative merely permits something to happen; it does not *make* something happen. Administration translates paper declarations of intent into reality. It shapes the behavior of citizens to match policy goals and delivers the benefits promised in legislation.

Administration as execution cannot be taken for granted. Weak or unresponsive administration will enfeeble the political system. For example, in many developing countries the critical problem is not so much the government's political instability as it is the government's incapacity to carry out its decisions. Public policies, no matter how bold or innovative, are worthless if government cannot carry them out. When Hurricane Katrina submerged New Orleans in 2005, official governmental policy was to provide help quickly, but the government failed, not because its officials did not want to help but because executing the policy proved tremendously complex. Five years later, much of the Gulf Coast was under assault from BP's oil spill. Everyone wanted it to stop—that was the clear governmental policy—but it took months to figure out how. Making policy does not ensure that results happen.

Policy Formation

Administration's second role is to help form policy. Its role plays out at two stages: (1) before the legislature and chief executive have made the policy decisions for which they're responsible under the Constitution and (2) after these actors have enacted statutes or issued executive orders, and then delegated to administrators the job of interpreting these actions. In the first stage, proposals for new laws flow from many sources, and the special expertise of administrative agencies makes them prime players. Government agencies possess much factual information about their specific field, retain an expert staff to analyze data, discover the defects in existing statutes after applying them, and exhibit devotion to the program's objectives. Often, though not always, the agency is trusted as a less biased source of information than other available sources, such as organized interest groups.

In recent years, two developments have enhanced administrators' role in this early stage of policymaking. As policy has become ever more technical, so has the specialized competence of administrative staffs. Regulating oil wells and building bridges, for example, must be guided by sophisticated information, analysis, and advice from engineers. Expert knowledge and advice are essential to policy development for national defense weaponry, space exploration, public health, research and development, education, poverty, urban renewal, energy, air and water pollution, and a host of other program areas. Within government, most experts are in the administrative agencies. The preferences and political judgments of the president and members of Congress weigh in as well. The other development is the expansion of the chief executive's role as a major agenda setter for governmental policymaking. The chief executive—president, governor, mayor, county executive—initiates most of the proposals that legislatures review. Typically the executive shapes this program through consultation with the agency-based experts of the executive branch. Although they are not the only sources of the executive's ideas, agency experts are strategically situated to initiate and counsel on policy proposals in the search for the executive's support. And to complete the circle, the executive's need for expert help has grown as public policy problems have become increasingly technical.

The second stage of the policy formation process occurs after the laws are on the books. In most cases, the statutes are not clear enough so that what happens afterward can be regarded as execution in the narrow sense. Legislative behavior sometimes produces highly detailed statutes and other times results in only a fuzzy identification of a problem that administrators must wrestle with. In effect, administrators make policy by trying to decide what the legislators meant and acting on it.

There are several reasons for delegating such extensive policymaking power. In a new policy field in which there is little experience to build on, the legislature may only be able to make a vague gesture in the direction that action should take. In a field in which  technology or other features change rapidly, the statute must permit flexible action by the agency, rather than requiring frequent returns to the legislature for enactment of new language. Congress, for example, could never possibly anticipate all the steps of putting satellites into space. (There was a time when the computer code for a rocket launch was the most complicated on earth.) Some subjects, such as licensing liquor stores and operating taxis, simply do not lend themselves to the specification of criteria that would confine administrative discretion. Statutes often do specify some conditions (for example, requirements that liquor store owners must not have criminal records and that liquor stores not be located near schools), but they offer few guidelines about how to choose among the numerous applicants who meet these simple criteria. In addition, ingenious entrepreneurs can often generate clever ways of evading any highly specific prohibitions in a statute. Congress broadly forbids "unfair methods of competition . . . and unfair or deceptive acts in commerce," leaving the administrative agency and the courts to refine those vague terms "unfair" and "deceptive."

At times, the legislative process is so stormy and full of crosscurrents that the resulting statutes incorporate contradictory policy guidelines, leaving agency managers to use their own judgment in reconciling the contradictions. Sometimes, too, a compromise leads to legislative language that papers over disagreement, but that gives administrators a wide range for interpretation. Most agencies, furthermore, administer many statutes passed at different times and mirroring different legislative preferences, leaving administrators to reconcile the accumulated instructions. Finally, the legislature may not appropriate sufficient funds to enable an agency to carry out a program as enacted. Unless the legislature itself gives specific direction, the agency must then decide whether to spread the money thinly or choose which of its objectives it will pursue with vigor and which it will slight.

In short, public administration shapes policy on the way up, executes policy after it has been made, and exercises discretion about policy matters on the way down.

Ripped from the Headlines...

POLITICS

Bill Gates's Warning

In his amazing career, Bill Gates evolved from the founder of Microsoft to one of the world's great philanthropists. Along the way, he developed a deep criticism of government. During a visit to Washington, he looked around sadly and observed that no businessperson would run his or her organization the way government works. He insisted that good performance metrics, like customer satisfaction, drove the success of private-sector organizations and that government badly needed to do the same.

In a democracy, citizens connect to administration through their elected officials as well as directly to the administrators who make government work. Gates's argument was powerful and echoes the refrain heard often in governments around the country: run government more like a private company! Companies, however, can simply decide on a course of action that is most profitable; they do not need to operate in a world where political considerations must be taken into account and political compromise is necessary. What would running the government like a private company look like for public administration, where politics shapes what administrators do and how they do it? What is the bottom line for public administration?

The Politics-Administration Dichotomy

As scholars studied public administration early in the twentieth century, they separated policy—the political work of shaping public decisions—from administration—the detailed work of carrying them out. As we saw in Chapter 1, this dichotomy came from the need to identify a distinctive field of study and, even more so, from the efforts to reform city, state, and national governments in the late nineteenth and early twentieth centuries. Establishing a neutral realm for administration, protected by civil service laws and governed by a drive for efficiency, would dry up the patronage resources of political machines and leave policymaking organs of government more directly accountable to the people.

Today the dual goals of assuring a nonpartisan body of civil servants remain unchanged: loyal service to officials from different political parties and the achievement of efficient administration. The obvious fact that administrative staffs share in policy formation—as well as the fuzzy line between policy and administration—has led many students to reject the policy-administration dichotomy. Analysts have tried to reestablish the distinction by forbidding administrators from participating in political activities, but that line may waver. Civil servants need to be respectful of the policy goals of elected officials and sensitive to the political implications of their policy suggestions. But civil servants have other obligations as well—to long-range policy goals, continuity and consistency, effective administration, and resistance to corruption. Furthermore, they must balance an administration's preferences against legislative and judicial mandates.

Civil servants have responsibilities different from those of politically elected officials. Policy and administration are certainly intertwined, but the motivations and behaviors of policy-makers and public administrators are very different. Separating them is a core issue of public administration.

Administrative Responsibility

Every well-developed organization has some system for holding subordinates accountable to their superiors. Nowhere is the system so complex and confining as in government.[24] Statutes and regulations specify elaborate procedures that seriously limit administrators' discretionary authority. Legislative committees call administrators to testify about complaints that have arisen on the programs they manage. Members of legislative staffs closely monitor administrative actions in agencies of interest to their superiors. Budget offices typically review proposed regulations and information-gathering proposals in addition to reviewing financial requests and setting personnel ceilings.

From the career administrators' perspective, this is a formidable control system. Yet as we suggested earlier, administrative responsibility goes beyond these external controls on behavior. There are also norms for behavior that are internalized by administrators themselves. First, knowing that they serve in government, they must be sensitive to the legitimate roles of other parts of the government, including institutions charged with legal control of their behavior. Second, they have a loyalty to their agencies and the programs entrusted to them. Third, in a civil service now populated by professional experts, they have absorbed their professional standards and are motivated to be recognized by their fellow professionals outside the government. All these commitments shape administrative responsibility, even though at times they may not all point in the same direction.[25]

That leads to a fundamental problem of accountability. External controls on bureaucracy often lead to red tape. External controls can replace external oversight, but that requires enhanced trust between the political and the civil service strata of government. And that, in turn, sets up some of the most fundamental debates about the study of public administration.

THE STUDY OF PUBLIC ADMINISTRATION

How, then, should we think about public administration?[26] Dwight Waldo suggests that we face a difficult task. He points out that public administration has roots deep in historic crosscurrents, including the political ideas of the small Greek city-state (the *polis*) and the large-scale administration of the Roman Empire, both of which helped shape the American system.[27] One way of addressing this task is claiming that administration and policy (or politics) are separate spheres. Woodrow Wilson and Frank J. Goodnow, writing in the late nineteenth and early twentieth centuries, took this view.[28] Nicholas Henry identifies 1900–1926 as the period when the politics-administration dichotomy reigned. He then traces later periods: 1927–1937, when students affirmed the existence of clear principles of public administration; 1938–1950, marked by rejection of the politics-administration dichotomy and loss of confidence in principles; the reaction of 1950–1970, years of reorientation to public administration as political science; overlapping and contradicting that reorientation, a 1956–1970 emphasis on management, often borrowing from business management, together with the rise of public policy studies (focused on effective achievement of policy objectives); and, finally, the post-1970 reversion to a specific focus on public administration. That work is often lodged in distinct schools of public administration that are hospitable to management methods but are sensitive to the public-interest commitment of administrators of governmental affairs.[29]

In our study, we need to confront three questions. First, does public administration have meaning apart from its historical context? Second, does it have meaning regardless of place, circumstance, and level of government? Third, if we make even limited generalizations, how shall we proceed? To such fundamental questions, we must offer perplexing answers:

A congressional investigation into a conference sponsored by the federal General Services Administration brought tough congressional questions about events featuring a professional mind reader, a clown, and a team-building exercise for building bicycles. Inspector General Brian Miller (left) produced a report on the conference, which led agency administrator Martha Johnson (center) to resign. Jeff Neely, regional commissioner (right), organized the conference.

1. Public administration is timeless but is time-bound.[30]
2. Public administration is universal but is also culture-bound and varies with situations.
3. Public administration is complex but is intelligible only by a simplified model or a step-by-step combination of such models.

We consider the first two puzzling answers together, because time and space are related variables.

Public Administration in Time

Public administration has a longer history and a wider geographic range than almost any other aspect of government. It is far older than American government—it has been the instrument of ancient empires, monarchies, democracies, and dictatorships, in both developed and developing countries. Carl J. Friedrich has cogently argued that the achievement of representative government in Western Europe depended on the prior development of effective bureaucracies by undemocratic regimes.[31] Indeed, revolutions that seek to transform the structure of political authority also struggle to control the bureaucracy.

In the United States, public administration received scant discussion from the nation's Founders for decades after the writing of the Constitution. As he traveled the United States in 1835, Alexis de Tocqueville was amazed at the neglect of the subject in the young nation, compared with experience in his native France:

> The public administration is, so to speak, oral and traditional. But little is committed to writing and that little is soon wafted away forever, like the leaves of the Sibyl, by the smallest breeze. . . . The instability of administration has penetrated into the habits of the people . . . and no one cares for what occurred before his time: no methodical system is pursued, no archives are formed, and no documents are brought together when it would be very easy to do so. . . . Nevertheless, the art of administration is undoubtedly a science, and no science can be improved if the discoveries and observations of successive generations are not connected together in the order in which they occur. . . . But the persons who conduct the administration in America can seldom afford any instruction to one another. . . . Democracy, pushed to its furthest limits, is therefore prejudicial to the art of government; and for this reason it is better adapted to a people already versed in the conduct of administration than to a nation that is uninitiated in public affairs.[32]

To deal with these issues, Woodrow Wilson wrote that "the poisonous atmosphere of city government, the crooked secrets of state administration, the confusion, sinecurism, and corruption ever and again discovered in the bureau at Washington forbid us to believe that any clear conceptions of what constitutes good administration are as yet very widely current in the United States."[33] Noting that "the functions of government are every day becoming more complex and difficult" and "are also vastly multiplying in number," Wilson pleaded in his 1887 essay for "a science of administration which shall seek to straighten the paths of government, to make its business less unbusinesslike, to strengthen and purify its organization, and to crown its duties with dutifulness." Such a science, he noted, existed on the European continent, especially in Prussian and French practice. He anticipated that comparative study would yield "one rule of good administration for all governments alike. So far as administrative functions are concerned, all governments have a strong structural likeness; more than that, if they are to be uniformly useful and efficient, they must have a strong structural likeness."

From one point of view, then, public administration has universal elements, independent of time, place, and political system. Those who serve in any **public bureaucracy** must be selected, paid, given specific assignments, controlled, disciplined when necessary, and so on. To pay them and to support other governmental activities (minimally, provision for military forces and construction of roads), a revenue system must be devised, the receipts allocated by some kind of budgetary system, and accounting and other recordkeeping methods worked out.

To say that there are such universal elements implies that governments everywhere can accumulate experience, and that this constitutes a reservoir on which governments can draw to avoid repeating mistakes. As Wilson stated, "the object of administrative study is to rescue executive methods from the confusion and costliness of empirical experiment and set them upon foundations laid deep in stable principle." However, despite expectations that more than one hundred years of public administration study should by now have yielded stable principles, that has not yet happened. Wilson based his analysis on a perception of administration as a neutral instrument, distinct from policy, politics, and particular regimes. Such a perception seemed essential to define a distinct field of study, separate from the study of policy and politics. It may also have sprung from the **neutrality doctrine** of civil service reformers, who had succeeded in getting the Pendleton Civil Service Act passed just four years before Wilson's essay appeared in the *Political Science Quarterly*. But it was an especially critical assumption for Wilson's thesis that "nowhere else in the whole field of politics, it would seem, can we make use of the historical, comparative method more safely than in this province of administration." That is, we can learn administration from the Prussian and French (Napoleonic) autocracies without being infected by their anti-democratic political principles.

Wilson's line of argument framed two contradictory themes. One was that administration must be fitted to the particular nation's political ideas and constitutional system. The science of administration, Wilson wrote,

> is not of our making; it is a foreign science, speaking very little of the language of English or American principles. . . . It has been developed by French and German professors, and is consequently in all parts adapted to the needs of a compact state, and made to fit highly centralized forms of government. . . . If we would employ it, we must Americanize it, and that not formally, in language merely, but radically, in thought, principle, and aim as well. It must learn our constitutions by heart; must get the bureaucratic fever out of its veins; must inhale much free American air.

Wilson advanced a second theme that blurs the distinction he made elsewhere between policy and administration. He contended that the

> lines of demarcation, setting apart administrative from nonadministrative functions . . . run up hill and down dale, over dizzy heights of distinction and through dense jungles of statutory enactment, hither and thither around "ifs" and "buts," "whens," and "however," until they become altogether lost to the common eye.

Wilson suggested "some roughly definite criteria": "public administration is detailed and systematic execution of public law," "every particular application of general law," "the detailed execution" of "the broad plans of governmental action," the "special means" as distinguished from the "general plans." Yet he went on to plead for the vesting of "large powers and unhampered discretion" as the indispensable conditions of administrative responsibility.

Here, then, are Wilson's basic contradictions: He contends that public administration needs to be interpreted in the light of a particular country's political ideas and form of government, but at the same time he sees it as a neutral instrument. He seeks a goal of "one rule of good administration for all governments alike," but he notes that different settings can produce different problems. He explains that administrators have large powers and great discretion, but he says that the administrative cannot readily be distinguished from the non-administrative aspects of government.

Much of the literature on administration since Wilson's time has been troubled by the same contradictions that he inadvertently set forth. The reason is that each of the positions he embraced has just a piece of the whole truth. A number of problems are common to all or most public bureaucracies. Most of these issues flow from a simple question, which Wilson laid out: how can government do things "with the utmost possible efficiency and at the least possible cost either of money or of energy"? Yet there are also problems, some of them among the most critical for administration, that require different criteria and different answers in dissimilar social and political systems, at the several stages of national development, and even in the individual agencies of a single government.

The experiences of Western experts asked to advise developing countries have demonstrated how difficult these dilemmas are. Western models have not proved very suitable for understanding the role of the bureaucracy in non-Western political systems. And when developing countries have looked to the West for models, they have struggled to choose which ones to follow. A substantial comparative administration movement appeared in the 1960s, but the movement virtually evaporated until the global public management revolution that began in the late 1980s helped to rejuvenate it. Time and space are interlinked in the recent and growing literature on the history of governmental administration.[34] Moreover, as Christopher Pollitt argues, the deep traditions of behavior and culture have a powerful influence over administrative action. The pace of social change has accelerated around the world, and "this makes considerations of time and of the past even *more* important, not less so."[35] We need to understand where administration comes from to understand how the past shapes the way we think about the present and future.

Complexity and Simplicity

Any real organizational system is extremely complex, and it is therefore impossible to describe any such system fully. It might appear to be a reasonable assumption that the main features of the system can be described—for example, by a single model that simplifies *total* reality in order to clarify *essential* reality. Even this assumption is wrong, however, for three reasons.

First, the complexity of any large-scale organization is not a puzzle that a single key will unlock. Instead, there are so many ways of looking at an organization that no single model can suffice as a model, as can be seen from the following list of complicating factors:[36]

- *Interconnections of Policymaking and Execution:* An organization (as we have seen) both shapes policy and executes it, and they intertwine in ways that are sometimes both supportive and awkward.
- *Coordination:* An organization is a way of both dividing up and coordinating work.
- *Relationships and Power:* An organization is both a formal, prescribed structure of relationships among offices and organization units and an arena in which ambitious persons and units work to expand or at least maintain their status and power.

- *Floating in the Seas of Time*: An organization both persists over time despite changes in its personnel (complete change in the case of long-lived organizations) and at any single point in time contains a particular group of individuals, each with a special set of psychological needs and frustrations.
- *Top-Down and Bottom-Up*: An organization is both a top-down system of authority, conformity, and compliance and a bottom-up system for the flow to the top of innovative ideas, proposed solutions to problems, claims on resources, and reports of trouble signs in program execution and content.
- *Information*: An organization is an information generation system, a storage and retrieval file, and a communication network, subject to overloads of information, misreading of signals, and supplementations and wire crossing by informal grapevines.
- *Headquarters and Field*: An organization usually includes both a headquarters staff and a far-flung field service, the former organized by functions and the latter by geographical areas—a feature that hinders their effective linkage.
- *Values*: An organization's decision-making process must embrace the broad choices in which the personal value preferences and educated guesses of officials play a large part. It must provide for other major choices for which quantified data and other scientific evidence can clarify the options and reduce the role of mere hunches, and it must program the narrow choices capable of routine handling by clerks and automatic data-processing machines.
- *Inside and Outside:* An organization looks both inward and outward, having to maintain internal effectiveness and adapt to the external environment in which it encounters the pressures of other organizations, temporary crises of the society and the economy, occasional wrenching change, and the often poorly articulated needs of the customers of its service.
- *Physical and Organic Models*: An organization is sometimes compared to a physical system such as a machine, and sometimes to an organic biological system such as that of an animal or a living plant.
- *Success:* It can be judged successful if it simply survives, or it can be so judged only if it achieves the purpose that justifies its existence.

Second, it is hard to produce a single model because most writers on organizations have sought to describe organization in the abstract. Realities are often far more complex, and theorizing has often become disconnected from concrete experience.[37]

Third, organizational theorists do not agree on a single theory or model. Theories and models of organization abound. Each one usually seeks to define, in its own way, the essence of organizations, but in fact each theory tends to focus on a limited number of organizational characteristics. The complexity of an organization can be accurately portrayed only by a combination of the partial truths that most models have expressed. We can imagine each model's bit of truth being mapped on a transparent sheet of paper; when one is placed on top of another, the series of overlays comes closer to the real organization than any single sheet does.[38]

In Chapter 4, we move from this foundation—the nature of public administration—to explore the basic building blocks of organization theory.

The Administrative State: Enforcement of Speeding Laws and Police Discretion

Attention, motorists! Driving through the East Coast? You might want to check out a website sponsored by the National Motorists Association (NMA), called the National Speed Trap Exchange, at www.speedtrap.org. Here's what their writers have to say about a particularly notorious stretch of the Interstate 83 highway near York, Pennsylvania:

> The Interstate goes from 65 to 55 mph but with absolutely no change in the highway construction, condition, or population densities as it's out in the country. It just so happens that just off the Loganville exit is a state police barracks which makes it awful convenient for them to work this stretch of road.[1]

A reader chimes in with her two cents below that entry:

> My mother lives in PA, and I have seen troopers measuring speed in that area—especially where that little cut-out is on the southbound hill of I-83. Troopers in PA have to use stationary radar, so they have learned to be quite creative with their hiding places.

Even if we'd like to spare this person a ticket on her way to her mother's house, doesn't it seem a little, well, *dishonest* to share this kind of information? Isn't the speed limit the speed limit—in other words, the law—after all?

Ethically challenged? Maybe. But, in fact, the idea that the speed limit is whatever the officially posted limit sign says it is misses the point. The posted limit may be the official maximum, but everyone knows that these posted limits often have little meaning in reality, a fact that the NMA apparently both recognizes and embraces.

Sometimes, traffic moves along at barely a crawl. Congestion, poor road engineering, and the unpredictable behavior of drivers can limit speeds. On clogged roads, the posted limit can seem a distant dream instead of a realistic limit.

On wide-open roads, in contrast, many drivers have discovered that if they drive at the posted limit, most other traffic goes flying past them.

So what is the real speed limit? It's the speed at which one can safely drive without being pulled over by the police or a state trooper and issued a citation. On an interstate highway, the conventional wisdom is that a driver can drive at 5, or perhaps 7, miles per hour over the posted limit with little fear of being stopped and ticketed.

Does that mean that if the posted speed is 65 mph, the speed limit is *really* about 72 mph? Not quite. If a driver is clocked by radar at going 71 in a 65 mph zone, the fact that the driver's speed is under the conventional-wisdom limit would be no defense in traffic court. Police officers can—and do—issue citations for driving at that speed. But if the police stopped everyone going just a bit over the posted limit, they would spend all their days and nights stopping just about everyone. Aggressive speeders might then get a free pass, because the police would be so busy stopping people driving just a few miles over the limit that they might not catch the super-speeders, drunk drivers, and others who are reckless on the road. As a result, the highway death toll might shoot up. In short, the real speed limit is determined less by what the posted limit is than by how the police choose to enforce it.

It is one thing for elected officials to pass a law, create a policy—such as a speed limit—and post it for all to see. It is quite another to translate that policy into action. When it comes to the speed limit, how that process works depends on the discretion that police officers and state troopers exercise as they patrol the nation's highways. The police invest a great deal of time in deciding how best to exercise that discretion: where most effectively to concentrate their energy, according to their best judgment about how to save the most lives, improve traffic flow, and (sometimes) increase the flow of cash to the local government.

Governmental policy on the control of speeding depends not only on how the police translate the official limits into their operating plans but also on how individual police officers, often operating alone in cars with no supervision, decide to exercise their own discretion. Should a police officer ticket a husband who is driving fast to get his wife to the hospital because she is in labor? Should the officer just issue a warning to someone who says, "Gee, officer, this is my first ticket"? Should the officer concentrate on easy pickings—drivers with out-of-state licenses who will most likely want to settle quickly so they can get on their way? And should the officers' commanders—and the elected officials who set policy—worry if different officers make these decisions in different ways, so that the real speed limit depends ultimately on the subjective discretion of the individual officer operating the radar in the police car?

The work of government bureaucrats (for that is what police officers are) extends far beyond enforcement, reaching into policy planning, development, and research. Some of the world's leading experts on traffic safety work for the U.S. Department of Transportation's Federal Highway Administration (FHA). A fascinating study conducted by the FHA in 1992 found that changes in the speed limit—lowering it by as much as 20 mph or raising it by as much as 15 mph—had little actual effect on drivers' speed. Moreover, the FHA found, *most* drivers regularly exceed the speed limit. Lowering the speed limit below the 50th percentile (that is, to a speed lower than that at which half the drivers drive) did not reduce accidents—but it did increase the number of violations.

Where should state and local governments set the speed limit? The FHA determined that it should be set at the 85th percentile (the speed on any given road at which 85 percent of the drivers drive slower and 15 percent drive faster). Because most accidents are caused by people who drive *very* fast, setting the limit at the 85th percentile would allow most drivers to drive as fast as is reasonable and safe, and it would allow the police to focus their attention on those drivers who are most likely to cause accidents.[2]

Having that FHA data in hand isn't the end of the story, however. Policymakers often resist such seemingly sound advice on setting the speed limit as different constituents weigh in on the ramifications of raising or lowering the limit. Higher speeds burn more gasoline, so environmentalists often favor lower limits. In many western states, drivers chafe at even high limits and press for even higher limits—as high as possible—and enforcement as loose as possible. A string of accidents on a stretch of road can create enormous pressure on policymakers and police officers for a crackdown. Citizens demand that governments respond to their preferences. When it comes to speed limits, policymakers need—and want—administrators to be accountable, because if lax enforcement of speeding laws causes accidents, the political costs for politicians can be very high. But when it comes to setting and enforcing speed limits, that's a tough trade-off. In the end, one thing is clear: the posted speed limit is one thing, but the government's actual policy against speeding may be quite another.

Questions to Consider

1. The announced policy on speeding usually does not match the policy as the police actually enforce it. Why? What forces are at work?
2. Should citizens worry that there seems to be such a gap between policy and administration?
3. Where the speed limit policy posted on traffic signs and the actual enforcement behavior of the police differ, what issues are potentially the most difficult to resolve?
4. Police are bureaucrats—but so are the technical experts who have conducted published studies on the speed limits. What impact can—and should—government's bureaucratic experts have on its policy?
5. Who is responsible for what in this surprisingly complex system: framing policy options, setting overall policy, setting patrol strategies, and enforcing the policy on the roads? What does this tell us about the politics of the administrative process?

NOTES

1. See National Speed Trap Exchange, http://www.speedtrap.org/speedtraps/comments.asp?state=PA&city=York&st=18369.
2. Federal Highway Administration, U.S. Department of Transportation, *Effects of Raising and Lowering Speed Limits,* Report FHWA-RD-92-084 (October 1992). See also Elizabeth Alicandri and Davey L. Warren, "Managing Speed," *Public Roads* (January–February 2003), http://www.tfhrc.gov/pubrds/03jan/10.htm.

CASE 3.2

Should Private Contractors Be Guarding Government Buildings?

Vernon Hunter and his wife Valerie both worked for the Internal Revenue Service in Austin, Texas. They both loved their jobs, but Vernon, age 67, was thinking about leaving the government and spending some quiet years in retirement. For Vernon, a Vietnam War vet, those thoughts ended abruptly in February 2010. Joseph Stack, a man with a long grudge against the IRS, posted a hate-filled diatribe on the web, set fire to his own home, drove to an airport, and took off in his plane. He seemed to have aimed it directly at the portion of the building occupied by the IRS. Valerie heard the explosion, and when she couldn't find Vernon right away, she assumed he was helping others out of the fire. Only later did she discover that Vernon died in the explosion caused by the plane's fuel tank.

Attacks on government buildings have worried security officials even more since the September 11, 2001, terrorist attacks. Timothy McVeigh's 1995 assault on the Alfred P. Murrah Federal Building, an Oklahoma City federal government building, with a truck bomb that killed 168 people showed how vulnerable government facilities could be. Other attacks, including Russell Eugene Weston Jr.'s 1998 attempt to shoot his way into the U.S. Capitol and James W. von Brunn's 2009 attack on Washington D.C.'s Holocaust Museum, showed the risk. But just how vulnerable are government buildings to such attacks?

Government investigators decided to find out. The Government Accountability Office, Congress's investigatory agency, sent undercover operatives into federal buildings with guns, knives, and fake bombs. In eighteen tests, the guards detected the weapons—but they missed them thirty-five times, for a two-thirds failure rate. At one facility, an investigator put a bag containing a fake bomb onto a belt for an x-ray check. The guard missed it and the investigator was able to pick up the bag and carry it into the building. In another test, an inspector put a bag holding a fake gun on the belt. The guard caught this one, and held the inspector off in a corner—but without a further search or handcuffs, as the rules required. As the guards concentrated on the first decoy, a second inspector walked right through the checkpoint with two knives—and without being stopped. In a broader check, investigators were able to get into ten different facilities with the materials they needed to build a bomb.[1]

Is this a failure of government security? The answer to that is clear. But is it a failure of government security guards? That, as it turns out, is a far tougher question. The agency responsible for security in federal buildings, the Federal Protective Service (FPS), employs 1,225 persons—but is responsible for 2,360 federal facilities. How does it plug this gap? With 15,000 private security guards, working under contract to FPS. In fact, though most visitors never notice it, the shoulder patches on the arms of most guards protecting the majority of most federal buildings show they work for private companies. The Secret Service guards the White House. But for many years, the guards charged with preventing terrorists from storming the facilities manufacturing parts for nuclear weapons—including sites stocked with plutonium, perhaps the most dangerous substance on the planet—were from private companies. On a visit to one such plant, I talked with a guard who proudly told me he was trained on twenty-one different weapons. He worked for Wackenhut, one of the world's largest private security companies.

But the combination of rising threats and the government's high reliance on private guards has made many members of Congress uneasy. Rep. Sheila Jackson Lee (D-Tex.) has argued that FPS ought to be required to shift more of its guards from private contractors to federal employees. She pointed to the decision to federalize airport inspectors after the September 11, 2001, terrorist attacks. "Many of us believe that it may be time to un-privatize the contractors of the Federal Protective Service or at least put in higher requirements," she said.[2]

Questions to Consider

1. Do you think that it matters *who* provides security at government facilities? Why? Fans of contracting say that whoever can do the job for the lowest cost ought to get the work. Opponents counter that protection is an inherently governmental activity that ought to be performed by government employees.

2. Do you like the idea of arming private employees and allowing them to shoot to kill, in the interest of protecting government buildings and their employees? Or should lethal force be a power given only to government guards doing the government's work?

3. More generally, how would you sort out the work that you think government ought to perform? And who ought to perform that work on behalf of government?

NOTES

1. U.S. Government Accountability Office, *Homeland Security: Federal Protective Service's Contract Guard Program Requires More Oversight and Reassessment of Use of Contract Guards*, GAO-10-341 (April 2010), http://www.gao.gov/new.items/d10341.pdf.
2. Ed O'Keefe, "Legislation Would Federalize Private Guards Who Protect U.S. Government Buildings," *Washington Post* (September 14, 2010), http://www.washingtonpost.com/wp-dyn/content/article/2010/09/13/AR2010091306355.html.

CASE 3.3

Crisis of Water in Maryland

What could be worse than days of temperatures in the mid-90s with steamy humidity, thought residents of Prince George's County, Maryland, than the announcement by their local water district that all water would be turned off for days? Residents scrambled to buy cases of bottled water in neighborhood stores. Many filled their bathtubs to the brim. Others scrambled for anything they could find that could hold water, from recycling bins to trash cans. With oppressive temperatures in the forecast for days, residents feared they were in for a very tough time.

The source of the problem was a 48-year-old valve, 4-1/2 feet in diameter, that threatened to burst not far from the Washington Beltway. Just a few weeks before, the Washington Sanitary Sewer Commission (WSSC), a special-district government that supplies water and waste treatment to the region, had installed a new acoustic cable through the water pipe to detect problems before they exploded suddenly in a massive water-line break. Just a few months before, a water main burst on the other side of the city, creating a 20-foot deep crater and sending a geyser 40 feet into the air. Problems with a main water-supply line are never good, but they're worst when they happen by surprise and cause blast-like damage in the process.

Officials from WSSC were proud that their new equipment had caught the problem before it ruptured. Their plan was to shut off the water, repair the valve before it blew, and then get the system back on line as soon as they could. The valve was at an especially hard-to-reach spot, and they had to begin by building a road to the site to bring in equipment before they could start repairs, all the while hoping that the pipe wouldn't burst before they could fix it.

WSSC recommended that residents stockpile at least 2 gallons of water per person per day, and that set off the scramble. Supermarkets called their suppliers for extra truckloads of bottled water. Restaurants inside the affected area shut down, since there would be no water for cooking or dishwashing. A major resort hotel sent all of its guests home, since there would be no water for laundries, restaurants, sinks, or toilets. Firefighters made plans to respond to alarms with big tanker trucks, since fire hydrants wouldn't work. Scott Peterson, the county executive's spokesman, told reporters that the "economic impact of this event will be the equivalent of a natural disaster hitting the county."[1] The shutdown story made news around the country and worried residents prepared for a long siege.

But hours into the repairs, workers managed a minor miracle. Two workers, exposed to miserable heat and working 4 feet below ground level, found a way to repair the valve without having to shut down the pipe, and the water never stopped flowing. They managed to get the valve unstuck and to make the 400 turns required to put it back in operation. "No one thought these guys were going to pull this off," the WSSC spokesperson happily explained.

County Executive Rushern Baker III, however, was in no mood to celebrate. He was stunned to discover that his county had gone through such wrenching preparations, only to have no interruption in service. "When did they first know about this other option, and how soon were they able to tell us other than this morning?" Baker wondered. "We are going to ask some very tough questions. We are going to have a very long and lengthy discussion about how we can make sure this doesn't happen again." Jim Neustadt, speaking on behalf of WSSC, explained, "The bottom line is our experts make the best decisions they can with all the information we have available. We have to protect the public, and that's what we felt we were doing."[2]

There wasn't a soul in the county who wasn't immensely relieved that their water continued to flow. But after the catastrophic explosion several months before, followed by what local officials viewed as warnings of risk without transparency, tough questions lay ahead for WSSC's leaders.

Questions to Consider

1. Suppose you were an administrator charged with the public health and safety of your community, and you learned that your water, within hours, would be shut off for days. What would you do? How would you communicate with citizens? How would you protect essential services?

2. Consider the situation that WSSC faced. Its top officials did not believe that its team was likely to be able to repair the water line without shutting it off—and if it had to shut it off, service would be out for days. Officials did not tell the public or Prince George's County government officials that there was a chance that its workers could make the repairs without shutting off the water. Do you believe that WSSC handled the situation properly? If they told everyone that there was a chance that a shutoff might not be necessary, they risked having thousands of citizens who failed to make preparations if the shutoff happened, at a time of extreme heat. They did not share the word, but then received harsh criticism from the county executive.

3. County Executive Baker was in a difficult situation. WSSC is a special-district government, providing water and sewage service to his county and to a neighboring county. It was not under the political or operational control of either. WSSC was making decisions that affected his constituents, but he had no control over WSSC's actions. What strategies could—and should—Baker use in this case?

NOTES

1. Katherine Shaver and Ashley Halsey III, "Prince George's Residents Brace for Water Shut-off," *Washington Post* (July 16, 2013), http://www.washingtonpost.com/local/prince-georges-residents-brace-for-water-shut-off/2013/07/16/abdaa72c-ee05-11e2-9008-61e94a7ea20d_story.html.

2. Ashley Halsey III and Katherine Shaver, "Prince George's Water Shut-off Averted," *Washington Post* (July 17, 2013), http://www.washingtonpost.com/local/prince-georges-copes-with-water-restrictions/2013/07/17/12c44bcc-eed4-11e2-9008-61e94a7ea20d_story.html.

KEY CONCEPTS

Antideficiency Act   57

neutrality doctrine   65

nonprofit   58

organizational theory   55

oversight   57

performance measures   57

policymaking   54

public administration   54

public bureaucracy   64

FOR FURTHER READING

Fry, Brian R. *Mastering Public Administration: From Max Weber to Dwight Waldo.* 3rd ed. Washington, D.C.: CQ Press, 2013.

Goodsell, Charles T. *The Case for Bureaucracy: A Public Administration Polemic.* 4th ed. Washington, D.C.: CQ Press, 2004.

Pollitt, Christopher. *Time, Policy, Management: Governing with the Past.* Oxford: Oxford University Press, 2008.

Okun, Arthur. *Equality and Efficiency: The Big Tradeoff.* Washington, D.C.: Brookings Institution, 1975.

Waldo, Dwight. *The Administrative State: A Study of the Political Theory of American Public Administration.* New York: Ronald Press, 1948.

Wilson, Woodrow. "The Study of Administration." *Political Science Quarterly* 2 (June 1887). Reprinted in *Political Science Quarterly* 56 (December 1941): 481–506.

SUGGESTED WEBSITES

The Internet contains a vast reservoir of information about public administration and public organizations. A good place to explore the subject is with the associations that focus most on the field: the American Society for Public Administration (**www.aspanet.org**) and the National Academy of Public Administration (**www.napawash.org**).

Moreover, the federal government has an excellent search engine that provides easy access to the huge amount of data, reports, and programs produced by the government: **www.usa.gov**. In addition, **www.searchgov.org** is another valuable source for information about the federal government's activities. Most state and local governments have their own websites as well, and **www.state localgov.net** provides an easy index of them.

PART

II

ORGANIZATIONAL THEORY AND THE ROLE OF GOVERNMENT'S STRUCTURE

The organization is the basic building block of public administration. Done badly, the work of complex organizations can create all of the pathologies that make bureaucracies appear "bureaucratic." Done well, bureaucracies make it possible to accomplish the complex tasks that society wishes to pursue—and often, it's the only way to make these programs work. There is a long intellectual history of thinking about how best to structure bureaucratic organizations—and, given the problems of such organizations, there is also an equally long history of efforts to reform bureaucracy.

Every choice about how to build bureaucracy or how to fix it is inevitably a political choice that emphasizes some values over others. Because these are political decisions, and the political decisions require tradeoffs among competing values, no choice has proven very stable for very long. The values of individuals shift and change, so do the ways they arrange organizational structure. In the chapters that follow, we examine the basic foundations of organizational theory, the strategies to reform it, how organizational structure affects the behavior of political executives, and how efforts to reorganize bureaucracy can improve the way it functions.

CHAPTER

4

Organizational Theory

- Understand the central role that structure plays in the work of bureaucracy

- Grasp the range of competing theories that shape the study of bureaucracy

- Note the importance of hierarchy in theories—and their critiques

- Explore the challenges to existing organizational theories

Some management experts use team-building exercises, like this rope exercise that demands cooperative problem solving, to promote collaboration in the workplace.

IN ANY LARGE-SCALE ADMINISTRATION, THE BASIC BUILDING is **structure**—a formal arrangement among the people engaged in the organization's mission. In the traditional model, organizational theory begins with officials at the top, connected to individuals at the bottom through **hierarchy**, the top-down delegation of authority from higher officials to lower ones. The top official sets policy for the organization and then delegates responsibility for pieces of that policy to subordinates, who answer to the top official through channels of authority. The pattern cascades throughout the organization, as subordinates become superiors to the workers on the next lower level. The chain of authority ensures accountability all the way through the organization. The result is the familiar organizational chart that dominates both the abstract model and the operating reality of complex organizations (see Figure 4.1). In the traditional approach to organizations, hierarchy defines the basic shape, and authority shapes the fundamental relationships.

This hierarchical model is the dominant approach to organizing complex work. Over time, however, four major challenges to its basic premises have arisen. The **humanist approach**, rooted in the dynamics of human relations, condemns the impersonality of bureaucratic hierarchies and so pleads for the humanizing of organizations. The **pluralist approach**, emphasizing the realities of political life, posits a less orderly model of organizational interactions. The **government-by-proxy approach,** introduced in Chapter 2, notes that government shares power with other governments, private organizations, and mixed public-private enterprises, as well as within its own **organizational structure**, and so develops a mixed model. The **formal approach** returns to a structural perspective but adds a very different theoretical twist.

A variety of approaches describes how organizations in general work, but there is little agreement on which theoretical approach works best. Neither is there any consensus on which approach best fits the public sector. This chapter examines the competing theories and explores their implications.[1]

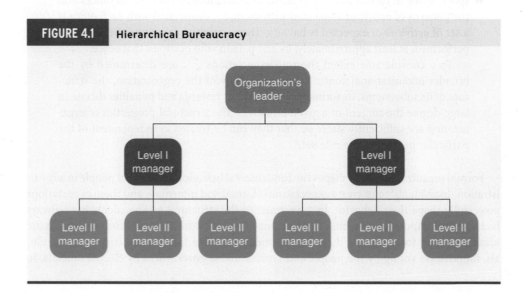

FIGURE 4.1   **Hierarchical Bureaucracy**

THE STRUCTURAL APPROACH TO LARGE ORGANIZATIONS

For a very long time, *structure* has been the basic building block of large, complex organizations. When the structure doesn't seem to work, reformers become convinced that rearranging boxes will improve the organization's function. Critics often condemn restructuring as "just moving boxes around on the organizational chart." For better or worse, structure is the fundamental element of organizational theory. People matter, but *positions* are clearly distinct from the persons who occupy them. The structural approach certainly considers the personal relations among the chief executive, the department heads, the bureau chiefs, the division directors, and the section chiefs. But anyone who has carefully studied bureaucratic behavior knows that patterns of behavior persist regardless of who holds a position. Although no one in the U.S. government puts a personal stamp on a position as much as does the person who is the president, use of the terms the "presidency" or the "president" describes an office with certain powers and a reasonably determinate scope of expected behavior, independent of the identity of the incumbent. Students of administration tend to focus on bureaucratic positions—and the patterns of behavior in them—more than on the people who hold the jobs, especially when seeking a long-term perspective on how organizations work.

The concept of an administrative position separated from its human occupant is closely connected to the concept of *role* in sociology and psychology. Although in these scholarly disciplines, a person's role is defined by the expectations of adjacent fellow workers (including peers, superiors, and subordinates), those expectations in turn derive substantially from the person's formal position in the organization. The relation of role to organizational position is captured by the social psychologists Daniel Katz and Robert L. Kahn, who write:

> In any organization we can locate each individual in the total set of ongoing relationships and behaviors that make up the organization. The key concept for this is *office* [i.e., position], by which is meant a particular point in organizational space; space in turn is defined in terms of a structure of interrelated offices and the patterns of activities associated with them. . . . Associated with each office is a set of *activities* or expected behaviors. These activities constitute the *role* to be performed, at least approximately, by any person who occupies that office. . . .
>
> To a considerable extent the role expectations . . . are determined by the broader organizational context. The technology of the organization, the structure of its subsystems, its formal policies, and its rewards and penalties dictate in large degree the content of a given office. . . . The structural properties of organization are sufficiently stable so that they can be treated as independent of the particular persons in the role-set.[2]

Formal organization, then, shapes the fundamental behavioral pattern of people in administration. Individuals' roles create expectations (formal and informal), and these expectations powerfully shape their behavior. In governments, the structural arrangements have always had a special importance, because these arrangements flow from the political society's basic ideas. We need to appreciate these arrangements to make the leap from democratic ideals, founded on voting by the people and representative government by elected officials, to the complex job of carrying out governmental policy through a large, powerful, unelected bureaucracy. To those following the structural approach, that is no great leap, as explained in the following section. To those who object to the structural approach, the problem can be significant. This chapter and the next more fully explore that issue.

Authority and Hierarchy

This sets the stage for the role of politics and power in the theory of public organizations. The central issue of politics is power: who has it and how they use it. In constitutional systems, the government is accorded power that, within the stated limits, is legitimate—that is, power is conferred through the constitution, rather than seized from the people. Because this approach builds on the notion that governmental power flows from the people, the government expects citizens to comply with its decisions. Most citizens do so voluntarily, regardless of their personal agreement or disagreement with the specific content of those decisions and regardless of how severe is the punishment for noncompliance. In sum, a legitimate government is said to have **authority**—that is, the rightful power to make decisions within constitutionally defined limits, with the expectation of widespread compliance.[3]

A government's authority is exercised through institutions and the people who occupy institutional positions. The constitution vests authority in designated major bodies (e.g., legislature, courts, chief executive, government agencies). The constitution also limits who has authority over which purposes. The legitimacy of the authority of these institutions depends on their compliance with the conditions prescribed in the constitution. And because, in democratic theory, the constitution flows from the people's support, the authority exercised by public institutions ultimately flows from the people's grant of power.

This is the short-form explanation for the legitimacy of governmental power. Administrative authority further extends this concept. Administrators have legitimacy because their power is authorized by higher-level officials, especially elected officials. Thus, administrative authority is delegated authority. Note, though, that the idea of delegated authority has two applications. First, an administrative agency can expect most citizens to comply with its decisions because, within its field of activity, the government agency is vested with the government's legitimacy. Second, the legislature, the courts, and the chief executive expect administrators to comply with *their* decisions because they bear a higher legitimacy, through the popular vote of the people and the nature of constitutional government. Now, put these two applications together: citizens owe obedience to an administrative agency, but their obligation extends only as long as the agency's demands comply with the relevant constitutional, legislative, judicial, and executive limitations and instructions.

Thus, the structuring of authority in administration, with its emphasis on linking power and legitimacy, has theoretical and historical roots in such great political questions as the nature of "the State," the legitimacy of governments themselves, the limits to their powers, and the rights of revolution and civil disobedience. The answers form elaborate bodies of doctrine about the delegation of power, the legal liability of government executives and their agencies for wrongs done private citizens, and the right of public servants individually to expose wrongdoing and collectively to strike. Public administration, as government in action, cannot be understood without understanding its relationships to these great political, doctrinal, and moral issues.

Administrative Implications

Six basic propositions flow from the view of public administration as a structuring of authority:

1. *Principals and agents.* In a democracy, the **principals** are the elected officials who make policy on behalf of the people and delegate responsibility to **agents**, who are the administrators charged with carrying out the law. This, in fact, is where the concept of **agencies** comes from—agencies are the agents established to do the principals' work.
2. *Narrow, defined specialization.* An agency is assigned by law to a particular field of activity and a set of responsibilities.
3. *Internal specialized structure.* The agency has an internal structure that divides responsibilities among bureaus (or whatever its principal units are called) and, further down, among individual positions.
4. *Rules of the game.* The agency has a set of procedures that identify which units and position holders do what, and in what sequence, as business flows through the agency.
5. *Staff of experts.* The agency has a staff of officials and employees who are expected to contribute to performance of the kind of activity and the specific responsibilities assigned to the agency. Although the staff is constantly losing and gaining members, this by itself does not alter the stable expectations about the nature of the members' contributions. Principals hire agents because they expect the agents to be expert in the work to be done.
6. *Outside definition of roles and responsibilities.* Other parts of the government—such as the legislature, chief executive, and judiciary—have authority to abolish the agency; to continue, add to, or contract the scope of its field of activity and its responsibilities; to fix the amount of funds it can use; to appoint some staff members and specify how others shall be chosen; and to impose structural and procedural requirements on its organization and operation.

The government agency does not spontaneously spring into being. Rather, it is formally created by a constitutionally legitimate body or official. The agency cannot choose its own objectives. Rather, citizens and constitutional officials expect it to operate in a limited range of subject matter and to fulfill responsibilities assigned to it by an outside authority. The agency is not simply a social pattern developed out of who likes whom or who can seize and hold power. Rather, it has a formal organizational structure intended to specify who is meant to do what and who is meant to have authority over whom. Its officials and employees are not supposed to serve private groups' interests that are incompatible with their official responsibilities, to mobilize colleagues to subvert the agency's objectives, or to use their power for personal gain. Rather, they are judged by their service to the agency and its objectives. The agency is not set up and left to proceed on its own as an autonomous "closed organization" or to wrestle with a vague set of forces called "the environment." Rather, it remains part of a very specific environment—the government—whose major legitimate power holders have authority to appraise its performance, determine the input of its resources, and alter its mission and activities.

These propositions, based on the structure of authority, do not guarantee that public administrators will always work without problems. The lawmaking body may create an agency that is not needed. The assignment of responsibilities may be vague, and they may overlap those of other agencies. The internal structure of an agency may be poorly designed. Any feature of the legitimate power model may be subverted by developments not taken into account by the model itself. Aggressive individuals or groups in an agency may seize or gradually accumulate power and, in the process, undermine the formal structure of authority. An agency may generate such internal dynamics and so powerful a set of allies that superior holders of authority will hesitate to challenge its independent actions. Or a superior holder of authority may induce an agency to make decisions that serve private economic, political, or personal interests that are incompatible with the larger public purpose. Despite these issues, organizational structures—and the theories connected with them—are the basic building blocks of public administration. Organizational structures also emphasize the fundamental role of hierarchical authority in structuring the legitimacy of bureaucratic power, and the structures point to the ways in which power can be misused or redirected.

Two Models: Classical and Bureaucratic

The premise that legitimate power is the starting point for developing the structure of public administration is also the premise of two schools of administrative thought that developed in the first half of the twentieth century. These schools, the classical and bureaucratic, assume a higher source of authority for the agency's existence and powers. They see the fundamental organizational problem as one of setting up internal units and subunits, each charged with a specified portion of the agency's activities. The approach is top-down. Critics have often labeled the approach of these two schools as authoritarian because it makes lower units subordinate to higher units—often called a **chain of command**.

Both the classical and the bureaucratic schools rely on values in addition to legitimacy that are based in power. Among these values, rationality is the most important, partly because both schools view organizations simply as neutral instruments for achieving whatever policy objectives (that is, political values) the state's rulers may choose. The models are therefore meant to be politically neutral; they are designed to be rational, which is equated with efficiency.

The Classical Model

The **classical theory** of organization begins at the top of the organization, with clear, bounded jurisdictions of authority and responsibility. The theory further subdivides these jurisdictions among the positions immediately under the top positions, and it continues through all administrative levels. Its prime value is **efficiency**, which focuses on *differentiation* (sometimes labeled specialization) of functions and *coordination* of responsibilities. The theory reached its peak in the 1930s, when organizational theorist Luther Gulick published its most persuasive exposition.[4] The classical theory still has wide currency, both as a theory in itself and as the foundation for other approaches. Gulick identified objective principles of organization to shape organizations.

The classical school builds on six specific doctrines:

1. *Bases of organization.* Organizations can be structured according to four different strategies:
   a. Purpose (e.g., defense, education, crime control)
   b. Process (e.g., accounting, engineering, typing, purchasing)
   c. Clientele (e.g., Indians, children, veterans, the elderly)
   d. Place (e.g., the Tennessee Valley, New England, Mississippi, Latin America)

2. *Mutually exclusive alternatives.* When policymakers design an organization, they must recognize that the four bases of organization are mutually exclusive and that one basis must be given precedence over the others. It is impossible to give equal weight, for example, to organization by both purpose and place. However, that does not mean that only one base of organization must be used throughout the organization. As Gulick pointed out, if an organization is erected on one base, "it becomes immediately necessary to recognize the other[s] in constructing the secondary and tertiary divisions of work."[5]

3. *Focus on purpose at the top.* Although organizational designers have four alternatives, the doctrine holds that the executive branch of a government should usually be organized at its top level by major purposes (not by any of the other three bases or by a mixture). Each department should include all activities that contribute to its purpose.

4. *Span of control.* Any executive can effectively oversee only a limited number of immediate subordinates. Therefore, the number of departments under the chief executive, the number of bureaus under a department head, and so on should not exceed the executive's span of control—the number of subordinates he or she can effectively supervise.

5. *Single head for agencies.* Administrative authority and responsibility should be vested in single administrators, not in plural-membership ("collegial") bodies such as boards and commissions, because under such arrangements, the fixing of individual responsibility for mistakes is difficult, and clear-cut decisions are less likely than fuzzy compromises among the members. This leads to the principle of *unity of command,* with one person responsible for those in subordinate positions.

6. *Separate line and staff.* Line activities and staff activities should be sharply distinguished. Line activities are those operations *directly* related to the major purpose of the agency—that is, the achievement of a public objective through service to or regulation of the whole public or particular segments of it. Staff activities, in contrast, are *assisting* functions to facilitate the work of the line officials—for example, research, policy, and program analysis; planning; budgeting; personnel administration; and procurement of supplies. Essentially, line executives exercise powers of decision and command, whereas staff officials are—or should be—restricted to advising and providing raw materials. Although we often use *staff* as a generic term for agency employees, in the formal sense staff refers to those individuals in support positions.

The classical model has been closely associated with the pursuit of efficiency, as well as closely related ideas such as a commitment to a civil service of qualified persons selected by merit and a single-budget system for the whole executive branch. The classical model also anticipates a rational decision-making process, through which higher officials draw on the specialized knowledge at lower levels and decision makers at lower levels are furnished criteria and subjected to controls that assure conformity with higher policy. It has attracted a large collection of critics over the years, but in public administration its principles remain important in creating the basic building blocks of the field.

Ripped from the Headlines...

PERFORMANCE

What's the Best Place to Work?

The Partnership for Public Service, based in Washington, DC, has been conducting regular surveys on "the best places to work" in the federal government. You've seen the argument—that happy workers do better work. Which are the best places to work? Check out NASA, the intelligence community, and the State Department. Consider the Federal Deposit Insurance Corporation, the Government Accountability Office, and the Nuclear Regulatory Commission. Among small agencies, there's the Surface Transportation Board, the Congressional Budget Office, the Federal Mediation and Conciliation Service, and the Peace Corps. How about the worst places to work? At the bottom of the survey was the Department of Homeland Security, the National Archives, and the Office of the U.S. Trade Representative.

And what separates the best from the rest? It's the senior leadership, which focuses on making communication a two-way street and on signaling respect for the people who do the agency's work.

Do happy workers perform better? The Partnership for Public Service says it found that most government workers want to be innovative and do their jobs better, but too often they don't feel their leaders support them or reward them for their efforts. But that raises the biggest question of all: with tight budgets and declining trust in government, can leaders lead their employees and motivate them to better performance? Is making workers happier the best route to better administration?

Source: "The Best Places to Work in the Federal Government," http://bestplacestowork.org/BPTW/index.php; Jason Miller, " Highest Ranked Agencies Distinguished by Strong Leadership," http://www.federalnewsradio.com/204/3156902/Highest-ranked-agencies-distinguished-by-strong-leadership.

The Bureaucratic Model

Max Weber, a German sociologist, is the intellectual father of the **bureaucratic model**, and sociologists are its contemporary exponents and refiners. Bureaucratic theory is similar to classical theory, although it arose through a different path of study. Moreover, it gained prominence in the United States only after World War II. Weber originally wrote in German, and his views did not become widely accessible to American readers until the English translation appeared in 1946, long after Weber's death in 1920.[6]

Weber focused an important part of his work on why people feel obligated to obey commands without asking whether they agree with each one. He suggested that a stable system of authority cannot depend purely on appeals to subordinates' sense of self-interest, nor on their liking or admiration of their superior, nor on their sense of the ideal. Instead, a stable pattern of obedience rests on the subordinates' belief in the legitimacy of the system of authority. That leads them to defer to superiors and, ultimately, to the source of command in that system.

German social scientist Max Weber not only championed economic reform but also produced an analysis of "ideal types" of bureaucracy, which continues to influence the way scholars and practitioners think about theories of organizing complex work.

Weber found it useful to think in terms of three "pure" models of legitimate authority: traditional, charismatic, and rational-legal. **Traditional authority** rests on the belief in the sacredness of immemorial traditions ("what actually, allegedly, or presumably has always existed"); it thus depends on the loyalty of individuals to someone who has become "chief" in a traditional way. **Charismatic authority** rests on personal devotion to an individual because of the exceptional sanctity, heroism, or exemplary character of this person. Both of these types of authority may be exercised in an arbitrary way or through revelations and inspirations. The bureaucratic model holds, therefore, that both types of authority lack rationality.

By contrast, **rational-legal authority** (Weber used both terms interchangeably in characterizing this model) rests in "the legally established impersonal order." He found it useful to describe this as an "ideal type" of bureaucracy, by which he meant not "something to be desired" but rather the "basic characteristics" of a bureaucratic system. Obedience is due to "the persons exercising the authority of office under it only by virtue of the formal legality of their commands and only within the scope of authority of the office."[7] Weber describes how the "official duty . . . is fixed by *rationally established* norms, by enactments, decrees, and regulations, in such a manner that the legitimacy of the authority becomes the legality of the general rule, which is purposely thought out, enacted, and announced with formal correctness."[8] Weber also describes the basis of why obedience is owed to the person in authority: persons in a corporate body, "in so far as they obey a person in authority, do not owe this obedience to him as an individual, but to the impersonal order."[9] Weber's rational-legal approach establishes the basic structure for accountability, because it describes the flow of power and responsibility from top officials to those at the bottom of the organization.

To Weber, such a bureaucratic structure leads to efficiency. He wrote:

> Experience tends universally to show that the purely bureaucratic type of administrative organization . . . is . . . from a purely technical point of view, capable of attaining the highest degree of efficiency and is in this sense formally the most rational known means of carrying out imperative control over human beings. It is superior to any other form in precision, in stability, in the stringency of its discipline, and in its reliability. It thus makes possible a particularly high degree of calculability of results for the heads of the organization and for those acting in relation to it.[10]

To achieve such rational efficiency, Weber explains, the organization requires two conditions (which are similar to those in the classical approach). First, laws and administrative regulations establish "fixed and official jurisdictional areas" as part of a systematic division of labor, each area being assigned "regular activities . . . as official duties" and "the authority to give the commands required for the discharge of these duties" (subject to rules delimiting the use of coercive means for obtaining compliance). Members of the bureaucracy can be efficient only if the scope of their responsibilities is sharply defined. Second, "the principles of office hierarchy and of levels of graded authority mean a firmly ordered system of super- and subordination in which there is supervision of the lower offices by the higher ones." Efficiency also depends on clear patterns of hierarchy and authority, from the top to the bottom of the organization.[11]

Weber, like the classical theorists, complements the organizational requisites with other characteristics of a full-fledged rational bureaucracy. He specifies particularly that officials should be full-time, salaried, and selected on the basis of technical qualifications. But, again as with the classical theory, the human beings who constitute "the bureaucratic machine" seem stripped of their human differences:

> The individual cannot squirm out of the apparatus in which he is harnessed . . . the professional bureaucrat is chained to his activity by his entire material and ideal existence. In the great majority of cases he is only a single cog in an ever-moving mechanism which prescribes to him an essentially fixed route of march.[12]

Weber's image of the individual as a cog in a machine has long been one of the principal criticisms of bureaucracy and the object of parody—from Charlie Chaplin's famous silent movie *Modern Times* to the satire on the Korean War, *M.A.S.H.*, which led to a long-running television comedy.

It is an oddity of the history of organization theory that, despite the similarities of the two theories, many modern students of administration have scathingly attacked classical theory, while bureaucratic organizational theory continues to command their profound respect. Classical theory has, to some theorists, seemed impersonal and autocratic. Weber's bureaucratic theory, on the other hand, seemed to paint a richer canvas. To be sure, Weber has attracted much criticism. For example, critics have pointed out that he both emphasizes the importance of hierarchical authority and recognizes that bureaucracy builds on specialized, professional knowledge and technical competence among subordinates, expertise that gives subordinates a kind of authority that can conflict with the top-down patterns of organizational authority.[13] Despite these criticisms, however, Weber's concepts remain central to modern sociological analyses of bureaucratic organization.

SYSTEMS THEORY

Systems theory has arisen as a major alternative to the hierarchical approach. It is the most ambitious effort to generalize about *all* organizations, public and private, large and small. Indeed, the theory has an enormous scope. A system can be any set of related parts—from the universe to a molecule. Its application to organizations, therefore, draws on analogies to both physical and biological phenomena.[14]

A system can be either closed or open. **Closed-system theorists** analogize an organization to a physical system, such as a machine, whose own operation is substantially unaffected by its environment. A common example is the heating system of a house: the thermostat is set for a given room temperature; when the temperature falls below the set point, the thermostat triggers the furnace, and when the temperature rises again to the level set on the thermostat, the thermostat turns off the furnace. (Room temperature is an environmental factor affecting the timing of the thermostatic system's activity, but the system's operation is self-contained—once set, it reads the temperature changes and performs its function, without the need for anyone to intervene.)

Open-system theorists see an organization as something akin to a biological organism, such as an animal or a plant living in the environment. A common example is the human body's normal temperature of 98.6 degrees Fahrenheit: when an individual contracts a disease from outside the system (that is, from outside the body), the body's temperature rises in response and the body's own system—sometimes with help from a physician—tries to kill the disease and restore the temperature to normal. Systems theorists have tended to be fascinated with nature's processes for restoring normalcy. Their tendency to look at both the nature of the system and that of the forces that pull the system back to equilibrium has often led system theorists to produce static, rather than dynamic, models of organizations.

Most systems approaches to organizational theory treat an organization as an open system—that is, one that interacts with its environment. The essential elements are these: an organization is a system that receives **inputs** of resources (equipment, supplies, the energies of employees), which it **throughputs** and transforms to yield **outputs** (products or services). (Some of the input resources, however, go for use in maintaining the organization itself as a system—that is, for overhead costs.) Such a system also operates a **feedback loop:** Some feedback can be negative, in flagging problems that must be corrected. Some feedback can be positive, in identifying things that work well. In either case, this information can help adjust the inputs and the system so that the system produces better outputs at a lower cost. The usual graphic representation is shown in Figure 4.2.

Even though open-systems models dominate, the closed system remains important. Many large organizations have tried to reduce their dependence on an uncertain environment by bringing much of that environment within their own systems—sometimes by manufacturing their own component parts instead of relying on outside suppliers, sometimes by attempting

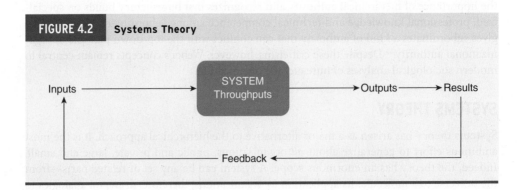

FIGURE 4.2   Systems Theory

to buy out their competitors. In recent years, however, some corporations have moved in precisely the opposite direction, toward a more open system, by relying on "just-in-time" delivery of supplies and equipment from outside suppliers. This practice, some corporations believe, makes their own systems more lean and efficient, and it gives them greater flexibility in getting the material they need. Government agencies seek autonomy in selecting employees, purchasing supplies, and evaluating their own program outputs. In sum, open systems often try to reduce risks by evolving toward closed systems. Sometimes they are willing to take extra risks in exchange for greater flexibility. In an increasingly globalized and interconnected economy, however, it is increasingly hard to embrace the closed-system model even in the abstract.

Two important elements in the classical and bureaucratic theories of organizational structure come into sharp focus in systems theory: agency jurisdictions, which define **system boundaries**, and agency missions, which define **system purpose.**

System Boundaries

For both classical and bureaucratic theories, boundaries are essential, so that the authority and responsibility of each department and each bureau will be clear. A system, too, must have boundaries, so that one can tell what is within the system and what is outside it. This inside-outside distinction is vital for two reasons. First, systems theorists need to identify inputs to the system from the environment (the outside) and the system's outputs to the environment. These transactions occur at the system's boundaries. Second, the theory distinguishes two requisites for the survival of a system: its capacity to manipulate or adapt to its external environment and its capacity to suppress or moderate internal threats.

It is often difficult to see a business corporation as a neatly bounded organizational system, and the problems are even greater in the public sector. One can formally assert, of course, that the Department of Agriculture is a distinct system with precise boundaries, with everything else merely the department's environment. More broadly, one can treat the department, its pressure groups, and Congress's agricultural committees as a system. Nevertheless, legal, political, and organizational realities allow the department far less autonomy and clarity of boundaries than the corporate analogy would require. The Department of Agriculture is a part of the executive branch, so many of its important decisions require the concurrence of other departments, the president, and central agencies (such as the Office of Management and Budget). Indeed, decisions directly affecting agriculture may actually lie with other agencies or with the president. These active sharers of decision-making authority cannot realistically be analogized to a business corporation's competitors, suppliers, and customers. To be sure, the Department of Agriculture does have a distinctive identity within the executive branch, but its identity rests in its core of concerns, not in the sharpness of its boundaries. The same holds true for government agencies at other levels of government, from state highway departments to local fire departments.

System Purpose

Classical theory proposes that the executive branch should be organized at the top by major purpose. Systems theory goes much further. It asserts that every organizational system has a purpose, goal, or objective—its translation of inputs into outputs.

Systems theory also borrows heavily from the idea of a biological system. Living organisms, of course, are systems. They take in inputs (nutrients) from the environment, process the inputs, and turn them into outputs (activities or behaviors that characterize the organism's way of living). Of course, the first imperative of all organisms is simply to survive.[15] Systems theorists conclude that the same is true for organizations as well. Business corporations must take in more money than they spend or they cannot stay in business; according to systems theory, a corporation's long life is, therefore, a sign of the success of its system.

Systems theorists then extend the basic argument to sociologists' views about human beings. Unlike most organisms, humans are moral beings, and they seek a purpose beyond themselves. When they join in complex organizations, these organizations likewise seek to serve broader purposes. As Lord Ashby explained long ago in writing about universities as organizations:

> Among living organisms it is assumed that the prime function is to survive. . . .
> Among social institutions one cannot make so simple an assumption. The biological analogy breaks down. It is not enough to say that the function of a university is to survive. It has functions over and above survival: in other words, it has purpose. . . . Unlike the biologist, the university administrator cannot eschew teleology; he must squarely face the fact that universities do not exist simply for their own sakes, as daffodils and sparrows and mice do; they have a purpose.[16]

Thus, systems theory focuses on an organization's purpose and how best to achieve it—how best to translate inputs into outputs. Systems theorists conclude that organizations need to be understood in terms of their purposes and that those purposes define the nature of organizations. However, this process of definition through purpose is often difficult to identify in practice, because—especially in the case of government agencies—organizational purposes often multiply and sometimes conflict.

Let's return to the Department of Agriculture. Is it the department's purpose to advocate the American farmer's interests? Or is it to assure that the agricultural sector contributes to the stability and growth of the national economy, serves consumer needs, adjusts to world trade conditions and American foreign policy, and forgoes products and practices that endanger public health? Is its purpose to serve the interests of large-scale, commercial farm corporations? Or is it to reduce the poverty of small-scale farmers and migratory farm workers? Or is it all of the above and, if so, in what proportions? Congress does not provide the answers, for Congress has assigned the department multiple and conflicting purposes without conveying a sense of which are more important. The president, as chief executive, does not provide the answers either. President Nixon said in 1971 that he wanted his secretary of agriculture "to speak for the farmers to the president" rather than "for the president to the farmers"[17] and, contrarily, that "when any department or agency begins to represent a parochial interest, then its advice and support inevitably become less useful to the man who must serve *all* of the people as their president."[18] Nothing has changed in the generations since.

Nor can a department's own definition of its mission help to solve this problem. The 1973 official statement of purpose and functions (since revised) was ridiculously vague:

The Department of Agriculture (USDA) is directed by law to acquire and diffuse useful information on agricultural subjects in the most general and comprehensive sense. *To accomplish this purpose,* the Department functions in the areas of research, education, conservation, marketing, regulatory work, agricultural adjustment, surplus disposal, and rural development.[19]

Rather than stating a useful declaration of goals, such rhetorical flourishes are instead a part of the department's performance—they are carefully designed to enlist external and internal support. Systems theory needs a clear statement of an organization's objectives so that the organization's performance can be measured against the stated objectives; such circular reasoning will not help. In its 2003 annual report, the USDA defined its mission: "to provide leadership on food, agriculture, natural resources and related issues based on sound public policy, the best-available science and efficient management."[20] That hazy statement did little to advance on the department's goal statement from thirty years before. Specific mission statements are very difficult for agency officials to write, usually because legislators have layered, multiple, and often conflicting goals on their desks—and new events often challenge what's written before the ink dries.

Government agencies certainly do not fade away because their goals are vague. Indeed, the fuzzy nature of their boundaries provides extra flexibility in coping with the complex policy and political environments in which they operate. (That is, in a systems sense, they have more flexibility in responding to external stimuli because they can decide which stimuli to respond to more.) What we know is that an agency operates in a field of activity, such as agriculture, national defense, education, transportation, public health, public safety, or sanitation. The agency may not monopolize the field, and the field's boundaries may be imprecise. The objectives pursued by the agency, and the priorities among them, may shift with changes in political control of the executive and legislative branches (to name only the most obvious of many factors). These features of the real world help explain how government agencies actually operate. But they require relaxation of system theory's demand that every organizational system have precisely described boundaries and purposes.

CHALLENGES TO THE DOMINANT THEORIES

The models and theories described so far have much in common. Each offers a rather formal, abstract view of an organization with clear goals and sharply defined boundaries. Systems theory views an organization as a "black box" that translates inputs into outputs. The classical model looks inside the black box and sees organizational units and subunits as clearly bounded and arranged to provide a hierarchical structuring of authority that is often pictured as a pyramid.[21]

These approaches focus on the organization's basic structure and on the relationship among its elements. Over time, they have drawn fire from three directions. Humanists charge that the various structural approaches are authoritarian—that their focus on boundaries stifles the creativity of the human beings who are the organization's lifeblood. Pluralists charge that the classical and bureaucratic models ignore the political system, give an unreal portrayal of the executive branch, and conflict with democratic values. Other critics from the government-by-proxy perspective contend that government agencies rely increasingly on other levels of government and on private and nonprofit organizations to administer public functions. To the degree that governments in fact do depend on such indirect administration, traditional patterns of hierarchy and authority are uprooted and displaced. All three approaches, therefore, raise fundamental challenges to the structuralist perspectives embodied by Weber, Gulick, and systems theory. We discuss each of these approaches in detail below.

THE HUMANIST CHALLENGE

The humanist challenge to the structural models looks inside the bureaucracy, focusing on the life of individual workers within the organization. Most of this challenge arises from research in industry and large corporations.

Jobs, Productivity, and Happiness

Industrial managers have long recognized that the business organization's performance depends on the productivity of individual workers. Among the major factors in a worker's productivity are the design of the job and the procedures that all workers follow. The **scientific management movement**, which developed the profession of industrial engineering, dates back to the early 1900s, when Frederick W. Taylor began to study how long it took workers to accomplish specified tasks. The movement used time-and-motion studies to find the most efficient way of completing these tasks, which led, in turn, to patterns for specialization and standardization of jobs and designed procedures to guide the flow of work from job to job.[22] This single-minded pursuit of efficiency was, even then, perceived as dehumanizing. Taylor unfortunately wrote that because of "the grinding monotony" of the work, "one of the first requirements for a man who is fit to handle pig iron as a regular occupation is that he shall be so stupid and so phlegmatic that he more nearly resembles in his mental make-up the ox than any other type."[23]

Such views reinforced the concern that bureaucratic work wrung the humanity out of individuals. Organizational reformers sought to make the work more rewarding and, therefore, to help the organizations perform better. The humanist challenge built on basic questions of motivation: why an individual joins a particular organization, stays with it, performs well, leaves.[24] Money helps, but it does not adequately explain variations among companies or among a single company's work groups. Important research in the late 1920s and 1930s at the Hawthorne Works of the Western Electric Company showed how variations in working conditions could affect the motivation and productivity of workers.[25] Researchers concluded they had found a "Hawthorne effect"—paying attention to workers as individuals increased their productivity. This research helped establish that human behavior matters to organization. That left questions about how, how much, and how it connected with authority and hierarchy.

The **human relations movement**, which peaked in the 1950s and again in the antiestablishment mood of the late 1960s, sought to answer these questions and to establish a link to the managerial approach. Both were concerned with workers' productivity and such related matters as absenteeism and turnover. The humanists argued that happy workers were more productive, and their early research studies confirmed this. Happiness—or satisfaction, as it was usually called—was not a matter of monetary and promotional rewards but of the interpersonal relations in the small face-to-face group of fellow workers and their immediate supervisor. According to the humanists, an atmosphere that generates satisfaction, and presumably productivity, does not flow from bureaucratic structure but from a commitment to participation by the workers in reaching decisions for the group. In such a system, the supervisor is not autocratic and directive, but informal, consultative, trusting, and concerned for the team members' welfare.

Although such arguments seemed promising, researchers found that (1) these conditions make some workers happy and some unhappy—some workers like to participate in decision making but others resist having to share the risk and responsibility for big decisions—and (2) happy workers are not necessarily more productive workers.[26] Though many research studies consistently showed that "job satisfaction is related to absences and turnover; they have been equally consistent in showing negligible relationships between satisfaction and level of performance or productivity."[27] That complicated the puzzle of connecting motivation to results, but the power of the argument lives on. In fact, California's dairy industry waged a campaign arguing that "happy cows make better milk" and implied that their cows were happier than those in the "dairy state," Wisconsin. The campaign was powerful because it resonated with the way many people *think* motivation works.

Ideology

After these findings, what remained was a normative commitment to the individual's opportunity for "self-actualization" (creativity, self-direction, the realization of one's full potential as a human being) and to the equality of persons (and thus minimal subordination to a leader's direction and maximal participation in decision making). Members of the human relations movement insisted that large, formal organizations, with their hierarchical authority structure, are repressive. Chris Argyris wrote that organizational planners

> assume that efficiency is increased by a fixed hierarchy of authority. The man at the top is given formal power to hire and fire, reward and penalize, so that employees will work for the organization's objectives.
>
> The impact of this design-feature on human personality is clearly to make the individuals dependent on, passive and subordinate to the leader. The results are obviously to lessen their self-control and shorten their time-perspective . . . pushing individuals back from active toward passive, from being aware of long time-perspectives toward having only a short time-perspective. In all these four ways, the result is to move employees back from adulthood toward immaturity.[28]

The human relations school has been severely attacked, through four lines of argument.[29] First, most of the early research presenting empirical proof of the doctrines was conducted by "true believers," and other scholars found the research seriously flawed. Those who rejected the traditional hierarchical approach embraced the human relations school; those devoted to the traditional approach tended to immediately reject the human relations movement.

Second, the sweeping contrast of the bad hierarchical organization with the ideal humanist organization was overdrawn, resting on assertion rather than scientific study of organizations. Many writers simply adopted Douglas McGregor's distinction between two different approaches to organization and management: Theory X, which relied on hierarchical authority, and Theory Y, which relied on motivation. McGregor advocated Theory Y.[30] (See Box 4.1 for a summary of McGregor's theory.) The simplicity of his argument made it persuasive to those seeking to capture the human relations approach, but it provided scant guidance to those trying to think more carefully and systematically about organizational management. Recent studies have rejected this simple contrast. Instead, the theory leads to prescriptions for tailoring leadership and participatory styles to the particular circumstances.[31] However, this call to adapt strategies to specific situations thwarts the search for general propositions, which is the essence of theory.

Third, although the human relations school was committed to development of "the whole person," the job was treated as if it were the worker's whole life. Critics made the obvious point that in societies with limited workdays and workweeks, most people obtain important satisfactions off the job. A high overall level of happiness often comes despite only moderate satisfaction with the job's sociopsychological attributes.

BOX 4.1   McGregor's Theory X and Theory Y

Theory X

1. The average human being has an inherent dislike for work and will avoid it if he or she can.
2. Because of this human characteristic of dislike of work, most people must be coerced, controlled, directed, threatened with punishment to get them to put forth adequate effort toward the achievement of organizational objectives.
3. The average human being prefers to be directed, wishes to avoid responsibility, has relatively little ambition, and wants security above all.

Theory Y

1. The expenditure of physical and mental effort in work is as natural as play or rest.
2. External control and the threat of punishment are not the only means for bringing about effort toward organizational objectives.
3. Commitment to objectives is a function of the rewards associated with their achievement.
4. The average human being learns, under proper conditions, not only to seek but to accept responsibility.
5. The capacity to exercise a relatively high degree of imagination, ingenuity, and creativity in the solution of organizational problems is widely, not narrowly, distributed in the population.
6. Under the conditions of modern industrial life, the intellectual potentialities of the average human being are only partially utilized.

Source: Douglas McGregor, *The Human Side of Enterprise* (New York: McGraw-Hill, 1960), 33–49.

Fourth, the school's normative commitments tended to ignore the fact that leaders need to lead. Abraham Maslow, a psychologist much admired by humanists, made the point most sharply:

> The writers on the new style of management have a tendency to indulge in certain pieties and dogmas of democratic management that are sometimes in striking contrast to the realities of the situation.
>
> With dogma occupying this front-rank position, it is not surprising that human relations theory has evaded the problem of the very superior boss. The participative kind of management, where subordinates work toward a good solution to a problem, is often an inappropriate setting for the superior boss. He is apt to get restless and irritated. . . . The less intelligent subordinates are also affected adversely. Why should they sweat for three days to work toward the solution of a particular problem when they know all the time that the superior can see the solution in three minutes. . . .
>
> The relationship of the boss to the people whom he might have to order around or fire or punish is, if we are realistic about it, not a friendly relation among equals. . . . This hard reality ought to have some impact on the theories of participative, democratic management.[32]

Sensitivity Training and Organization Development

Many members of the human relations school concluded that large organizations would work better only if their top officials changed their behavior. If higher executives were more "authentic" in their own interpersonal relations—deemphasizing their competitive, hierarchical positions and developing instead their own identities as human beings interacting with other human beings—the psychological atmosphere of the whole organization would be transformed. To achieve this behavioral modification, the executives needed to be trained in new attitudes, the leaders of the human relations school contended. Business corporations embraced the approach, and selected executives were sent off to participate in "team-building" or **sensitivity training** activities. The movement began in the 1960s and has continued into the twenty-first century. Newer approaches have brought managers together for exercises that focus on interpersonal skills and the development of effective teams. Some approaches have even used nature-based challenges, such as developing a team to build a bridge across a river or relying on teammates to catch blindfolded employees as they fell backward. Outdoor-based leadership training programs have continued to flourish.

Objective assessments of the human relations approach do not report much reliable evidence to support its claims.[33] Although many participants value the experience on these experiential retreats and alter their behavior back on the job, the new behavior may either improve or lessen their effectiveness in their organizations. The effects of the experience usually fade after a few months; the organizations often are left unchanged, and underlying organizational problems sometimes continue to fester.

Despite its uneven impact on organizational performance, the antibureaucratic school has had a profound effect on the study of organizations. It has become a rallying point for those seeking to move the study and practice of organizations past the structural approaches to new ones founded on interpersonal relationships. Improving those relationships, human relations theorists have long argued, has been the foundation for improving organizational performance.

THE PLURALIST CHALLENGE

The pluralist challenge to the formal, structural model is externally oriented and empha-sizes the responsiveness of a governmental organization to society's politically active interest groups. It focuses on the ability of these outside groups to shape a bureaucracy's behavior.

The pluralist model assumes a society characterized by the political interplay of groups, each seeking to have its interests prevail. The pluralist model regards administration as a set of battlegrounds to which the interest groups carry their struggles from the electoral and legislative arenas.[34] Adherents of this model perceive a fragmented administrative structure linked with a fragmented Congress. Overhead direction is weak: the president is so occupied with policy and political leadership, international affairs, and other demands on his energies that he can give only partial and periodic attention to administrative responsibilities, and the department heads he appoints, birds of passage as they are, only rarely achieve effective control of the bureaus in their charge. Far from being a symmetrical pyramid, the executive branch is a jumble of structures, each pushed around by political crosscurrents. The task of administration, at least at its highest levels, is the same as the task of politics—to facilitate the peaceful resolution of conflicts, according to the distribution of power among groups in our society, and to use the interplay of these groups to seek the public interest.

Administrative organizations, according to the pluralistic model, are the products of this conflict and accommodation of interests.[35] Their survival as individual agencies depends on their command of sufficient outside support to withstand assault by disadvantaged interests. Their top officials can retain their power only as they adjust their use of power to the prefer-ences of the supporting groups—or if they succeed in winning sufficient support from other groups to break free from the original supporters. The president appears in this model as the spokesperson not for the nation in the sense of "all the people," but for the specific combina-tion of forces that enables him to attain power and that makes it possible for him to retain and exercise power. He is, in a sense, just another player—more a man with influence than a man with effective authority. To survive, administrative agencies must be responsive to Congress, and especially to congressional committees and their leaders, for both substantive power and appropriations derive from Congress. This has a sobering influence on administrators inclined to look to the president for their sole guidance.

Organizational Culture

A variant of the pluralistic approach emphasizes the variety of **organizational cultures**.[36] Agencies differ in many ways, which makes suspect any generalizations about the structure of authority. Some have such strong interest group support that they enjoy substantial auton-omy within the executive branch; some enjoy such support without creating and mobilizing it; others foster the birth of sympathetic organizations. Some have such records of devotion to the public interest or to professional standards that they can resist interest group pressure and politically motivated efforts to intervene; others are orphans in the storm, the easy victims of unsympathetic interest groups, politicians, and sister agencies. An agency physically consolidated in one building differs from one whose headquarters units and staff members are scattered among many buildings or among capital, suburbs, and distant cities.[37]

The concept of organizational culture stresses these and many other differences among agencies. One can enter a state liquor-control agency or an athletics-regulating agency and sense a different atmosphere from that in, say, a banking or insurance department or a labor department. In Washington, "one has only to walk into the ancient Treasury Department building . . . to sense the atmosphere of a conservative financial institution."[38] Even more is this the case with the independent Federal Reserve, which additionally illustrates the possibility of a culture in which one "subordinate" (the New York Federal Reserve Bank) at various times dominates the system.[39] The Forest Service and the National Park Service, located in different departments, will probably never be merged because they cannot forget a bitter controversy early in the twentieth century. The Forest Service, too, has a professional esprit de corps, a decentralization practice, and a systematic socialization of its rangers to the agency's norms that all substitute for centralization.[40] Other agencies often have difficulty maintaining morale and effective control of their field-office employees.

Critics have sometimes dismissed the organizational culture approach as being too fuzzy to guide either theory or practice. However, after the space shuttle *Columbia* disintegrated on reentry from orbit on February 1, 2003, killing all seven astronauts on board, the National Aeronautics and Space Administration (NASA) went through a deep soul-searching investigation about how the accident had happened. Subsequent investigation revealed that the accident had been caused by hot gases pouring through a hole in the leading edge of the right wing and eating away at the internal support, until the wing gave way and the *Columbia* broke up; the hole, in turn, had been caused by the impact of a piece of insulation at launch. NASA's cameras had caught the impact, but meetings held while the shuttle was in orbit had concluded that it posed little risk. Investigators later determined that NASA had developed a culture that was unreceptive to airing and resolving problems. In fact, an extensive survey of NASA employees a year after the disaster found that "there appear to be pockets

Hal Gehman, who headed the NASA-convened board that investigated the February 1, 2003, *Columbia* space shuttle accident, asked a question during a public hearing six weeks after the disaster. The board found that NASA had slipped back into many of the same problems that had contributed to the *Challenger* disaster years before.

[within NASA] where the management chain has (possibly unintentionally) sent signals that the raising of issues is not welcome. This is inconsistent with an organization that truly values integrity." How should NASA solve the problem? NASA's report concluded, "There is an opportunity and need to become an organization whose espoused values are fully integrated into its culture—an organization that 'lives the values' by fostering cultural integrity."[41]

Critics may wonder whether the idea of organizational culture has any real bite, but NASA's top officials concluded that NASA's organizational culture lay at the center of the factors that had caused the *Columbia* disaster. NASA administrator Sean O'Keefe said bluntly, "We need to create a climate where open communications is not only permissible, but is encouraged."[42] Together with outside experts brought in to help prevent future disasters, NASA's leader concluded that organizational culture was real, that NASA's culture had contributed to the accident, and that with hard work it could be changed.

Assessment

The hierarchical and pluralistic models perform different functions. The pluralistic model yields a more realistic description and explanation of what goes on in administration and politics, but the fragmentation it describes and even celebrates as part of the genius of the American political system affords little or no guidance as to what direction we should move in if we have the opportunity to express a preference or to exert influence. This model slides across the line dividing description from prescription—what *is* from what *ought to be*—but it does not tell reformers how to change organizations. The organizational culture variation of pluralist theory even suggests that change may be fleeting, because cultures are deep-seated, rooted in particular functions and histories that alter only slowly and incrementally.

The hierarchical model, in contrast, draws strength from the wide support it has long enjoyed. It is the pattern advocated by every reorganization commission that surveys the whole sweep of federal administration. After the September 11, 2001, attacks, reformers argued for the need to "connect the dots" among related government agencies that failed to coordinate their information and operations. Congress created a new Department of Homeland Security designed to bring related agencies together under the same bureaucratic umbrella. It was, in short, a classic case of pursuing the hierarchic model and its prescriptions for clarifying missions and responsibilities. A decade of internal struggles made progress, but investigations into the failed terrorist car bomb attack in New York's Times Square in 2010 showed many dots remained unconnected.

Much of what are widely regarded as administrative improvements in the past several decades can best be understood as attempts to impart hierarchical arrangements to a pluralistic government, a process that creates the fundamental dilemma—administration is inevitably part of politics, a search for hierarchical control and efficiency within a pluralistic system. We need administrative institutions and processes that contribute rationality and order rather than happenstance and confusion; that are designed to seek the general interest rather than merely to reflect particular private, often selfish, interests; and that take the long view of policy goals rather than the short view of tactical maneuvers. The role of government in a democracy has always been to combine energies for widely shared objectives, whether for national security against foreign enemies, for maintenance of the legal system, or for the affirmative promotion of economic and social welfare. We should therefore not be surprised that efforts to improve government and its administration often emphasize the coordination, rationality, and legitimacy found in the hierarchic model—and that such efforts need to be accommodated to the variety of interest groups, legislative committees, and government agencies whose competing interests are the central fact of the pluralistic model. Embedded in politics, administration always has a heavy political flavor.

THE CHALLENGE OF GOVERNMENT BY PROXY

All of these theories assume that a government's programs are carried out by the government's own employees through the government's own bureaucracies. As we saw in Chapter 2, much of the government's work is farmed out to other governments and to private organizations, or to entities whose mix of public and private control puts them outside the administrative hierarchy. Because government relies on a wide variety of tools, the strains with the traditional hierarchical approach have grown.[43]

The more government administration relies on third-party tools—government by proxy—the less it fits the classical and bureaucratic models. Authority does not work well if the work is not conducted through hierarchies. Hiring, firing, and direct management of work are hierarchical powers that work poorly, if at all, when dealing with grants and contracts. To manage the programs effectively, government must seek other forms of leverage, especially through negotiation, contract law, and performance measurement. The vast spread of these tools makes it difficult for government to monitor all these outside agents. It cannot easily cancel large grants and contracts for violation of the prescribed conditions without damaging its programs and the public they serve.

Some scholars have suggested that an approach built on organizational networks might help to explain these problems better.[44] Such networks, Eugene Bardach explains, consist of "a set of working relationships among actors such that any relationship has the potential both to elicit action and to communicate information in an efficient manner."[45] Pragmatic in its exploration of how organizations share

THIS HIDDEN SITE HAS BEEN SEIZED
by the Federal Bureau of Investigation,
in conjunction with the IRS Criminal Investigation Division,
ICE Homeland Security Investigations, and the Drug Enforcement Administration,
in accordance with a seizure warrant obtained by the
United States Attorney's Office for the Southern District of New York
and issued pursuant to 18 U.S.C. § 983(j) by the
United States District Court for the Southern District of New York

In October 2013, the U.S. Department of Justice shut down an underground web business that specialized in peddling illegal drugs, including heroin and cocaine, called "Silk Road." The site was doing millions of dollars of business before a multi-agency investigation arrested the dealer, who went by the alias "Dread Pirate Roberts," a fictional character in the movie *The Princess Bride*.

common ground—missions, clients, and goals—and coordinate their work, this approach has been developed by administrative scholars who sought to explain the management of public programs but found existing theories lacking. For example, they have discovered that most social service programs work through complex networks: a chain of federal grant money, frequently supplemented by state grant funds, that is passed on to local governments and administered through governmental organizations, as well as for-profit and nonprofit contractors. These programs, in turn, connect with local schools, police departments, anti-drug programs, programs managed through churches, and volunteer organizations, among others. The growth of this movement has given rise to extensive research into "collaborative governance," including a 2007 special issue of *Public Administration Review* that examined the rise of networked strategies for government action.[46]

Network analysis is distinguished from other approaches by two characteristics. Scholars debate whether networks constitute an approach, a theory, a method, or a prescription, but there is rising recognition of the power of collaborative approaches to public administration. On one level, the network approach is important for what it is not: the approach is based neither on traditional hierarchical control of organizations nor on market-based transactions among them. Organizations help one another because they discover that collaboration advances their own goals as well. On another level, such interdependence has come to define more governmental programs. Whereas traditional administration begins by assuming that the legislature delegates to government agencies the job of managing programs, network analysis begins with the discovery that the management of programs depends on the interconnections among those who actually implement programs and that links of the implementation process often lie outside the bureaucratic chain of command. Some networks connect different agencies within a single department; the performance of a state's human services department typically depends on the network connecting its child welfare, health, and social service agencies. Some networks, especially those for federal grant programs, connect different departments at different levels of government. The performance of governmental programs depends on how well these networks function.

Compared with traditional hierarchical authority, network analysis is in its relative infancy. Its proponents disagree about whether it is a broad-based theory or simply a useful approach. But in moving past the traditional theories of hierarchy and in exploring the pragmatic tactics that managers develop to tackle the problems of government by proxy, network analysis offers fresh insights for government's emerging issues.

FORMAL MODELS OF BUREAUCRACY

By the 1980s, many theorists were unhappy with the development of the various theories of public bureaucracy. They liked the fundamental simplicity of the hierarchical model, but they found that it did not yield enough clear propositions about how best to organize bureaucracy. They did not believe that the systems model produced enough insight, and they found the human relations approach too imprecise. As the government-by-proxy model emerged, they believed that it moved too far from the hierarchical approach, which in their view still provided the best foundation for bureaucratic theory. So they adapted economic propositions to produce new, formal models of bureaucracy.[47]

The formal approach to organizational theory fundamentally transformed public administration. Theorists began with elemental questions. Identifying individuals as the basic building blocks of economic systems, they asked: What motivates them? How do these motivations shape their behavior? How does their behavior shift as they come together in formal organizations? Traditional public administration assumed that authority relationships between superiors and subordinates shaped the basic relationships within an organization: individuals did what they did because superiors asked them to do it. The formal approach, by contrast, began with the proposition, borrowed from microeconomics, that individuals seek their self-interest: workers agree to work because the work provides them with valued rewards, such as pay and fulfillment; employers agree to pay workers to get the job done, and the market determines how much employers must pay and what employees will agree to accept.

These basic assumptions have led to approaches that view bureaucracies as networks of contracts, built around systems of hierarchies and authority.[48] Each of these networks consists of relationships between superiors and subordinates, and each relationship has a variety of **transaction costs**—especially the cost to the supervisor of supervising the subordinate. As originally developed by Nobel laureate Ronald Coase in 1937, this theory has made several advances.[49] Beginning with the motivations of individuals, it explains how they fit into organizations. It charts the problems that such motivations can cause within organizations and identifies the problems that supervisors have in overseeing subordinates. By building on the concept of a contract between individuals and the organization, the theory links organizational theory to economics and its related ideas.

Principals and Agents

From this foundation, theorists developed **principal-agent theory**, an approach that details the contracts between superiors and subordinates. A top-down alternative to hierarchical authority, this approach stipulates that higher-level officials (principals) initiate the contracts and then hire subordinates (agents) to implement them. It also provides an alternative theory of accountability: workers (agents) are responsible to top-level officials (principals) not because they have been ordered to do so but because they have negotiated contracts in which they agreed to pursue specific actions in exchange for specific rewards. Principal-agent theory thus offers an elegant and theoretically powerful solution to the problems with which traditional public administration struggled for nearly a century. The task of devising the most efficient organizational structure and the best operating processes becomes a matter of constructing the best contracts. In both cases, the measure of "best" is the same: the ability of the organization to produce the most efficient and responsive goods and services possible.

Because principals and agents operate through contracts, results will be only as good as the contracts. Theorists contend that predictable problems grow out of any contractual relationship. To write a good contract requires good information. But principals can never know enough about their agents to make sure they have selected the best ones, and that lack of insight can produce adverse selection problems, in which ill-chosen agents cannot or choose not to do what their principals want. Moreover, principals can never observe their agents' behavior closely enough to be sure that their performance matches the terms of the contract—a lack of knowledge that can produce moral hazard problems, in which agents perform differently than the principals had in mind.

Principal-agent theory thus focuses on information and the incentives for using that information as the critical problems of public administration. Principals need to learn the right things about their agents before hiring them, and they need to improve their monitoring of agents' behavior to learn what results they produce. They can use this improved knowledge to adjust agents' incentives and to redesign organizations to reduce the risks from adverse selection and moral hazard. And because conventional wisdom and formal theory alike predict that bureaucrats resist change, principals can use this analysis to improve performance and oversight.

For public administration, this approach produces a straightforward theory: institutions headed by elected officials, such as the presidency and Congress, create bureaucracies; that is, bureaucracies can be viewed as agents for the principals'—elected officials'—wishes. The principals design bureaucracies' incentives and sanctions to enhance their control, and when the principals detect bureaucratic behavior that does not match their policy preferences, they use these incentives and sanctions to change that behavior. Among the important sanctions are the president's appointment power and the budgetary leverage that the branches share.[50]

Principal-agent theory thus has introduced a simple, precise solution to the enduring puzzle of how principals should manage their relationships with their agents. Since these are market-based relationships, with costs and benefits on both sides, it makes sense to structure the relationship through a basic tool of the market, a contract, which specifies what the principal wants and what the principal will pay. When both the principal and the agent sign it, they thereby resolve the uncertainties that otherwise would surround their relationship—and potentially undermine their work. Moreover, principal-agent analysis has provided an inductive approach to theory-building. Starting with a simple assumption—that individuals seek their self-interest—the theorists have built propositions about why individuals join organizations, how organizations structure their work, and what problems can emerge from such relationships. Those propositions, in turn, have produced hypotheses (for example, that rational bureaucrats seek to maximize their budgets) that seem to explain much commonly observed administrative behavior. Principal-agent theory not only has helped to develop an alternative explanation of bureaucratic behavior but has also identified the pathologies that, especially by the late 1970s, seemed so often to afflict bureaucratic behavior.

The very popularity of principle-agent analysis, however, has stirred heavy criticism, especially from theorists who contend that the search for rationality robs the study of organizations of its very life. Economic theories of organization, Charles Perrow argues, represent "a challenge that resembles the theme of the novel and movie *The Invasion of the Body-Snatchers*, in which human forms are retained but all that we value about human influence, and resentment of domination—has disappeared."[51] Even one of formal theory's strongest voices, Terry M. Moe, agrees, commenting that the inner workings of bureaucracies tend to evaporate from most of these models. Instead, they appear "as black boxes that mysteriously mediate between interests and outcomes. The implicit claim is that institutions do not matter much."[52] Theorists from the structural approaches schools often add that the same goes for the people inside these institutions.

This debate leads to several important conclusions about the formal approaches to bureaucracy. First, although they are intriguing, they are not theoretically mature. Their proponents frankly acknowledge that large holes remain in their arguments and that far more work needs to be done. In particular, even though the approaches build from models of individual behavior, many of the models are peculiarly people-free. Public administration, at the least, has demonstrated that bureaucratic behavior matters, and if they are to be successful, the formal approaches will need to become more sophisticated about modeling that behavior. Second, the approaches lead in different, even contradictory, directions. The theorists have engaged in lively, even heated, arguments among themselves about which formal approach is most useful, and the battles are nowhere close to resolution. Third, the theoretical propositions are far more elegant than their empirical tests. The behaviors they seek to model are extremely complex and not easily reducible to equations and statistics. To conduct empirical tests, the formalists must impose large constraints and look only at pieces of the puzzle. That, they contend, is a natural part of theory building.

Traditional public administration scholars have found the assumptions and models of the formal approach arbitrary and unrealistic; practically inclined researchers and practitioners have found them unpersuasive. Nevertheless, the formal models do provide theoretical elegance and a clear, logical set of propositions that many scholars find extremely powerful in a discipline that has long been searching for an intellectual anchor.

CONCLUSION

How can theorists look at the phenomenon of public organizations and reach such different interpretations?[53] Despite the multiple and contradictory approaches, three broader propositions surface. First, each approach embodies a significant truth about governmental organizations. Each has enjoyed a long life because it has captured at least an important nugget of reality for a large number of analysts.

Second, as a mere matter of common sense, the error of these approaches lies in overgeneralization: not all organizations are the same; not all small groups are the same; not all jobs are the same. Therefore, we need to take situational variables into account. That recognition suggests an agenda for research, but pursuing the variation risks losing the capacity for broader generalization, which of course is the essence of building a theory.

Third, a step away from grand-scale theorizing leads to two more modest points. One is the direct study of reality—a practical understanding of how the context of public agencies can affect their behavior. The other is the formulation of middle-range theories—that is, theories that attempt to explain only a limited range of phenomena. For example, which organizational arrangements appear most likely to save a regulatory agency from being dominated by those it is meant to regulate? Is coordination of the elements of a complex program more likely under a hierarchical authority arrangement or under an interagency committee? What are the major frustrations of government executives, of civil servants, and of clients? Can they be significantly reduced, and if so, how? Does an effective use of networks promise greater effectiveness in public administration?

If, as we have suggested, each of the approaches reviewed in this chapter contributes something that is true, then together they may be viewed as painting a rich portrait of a complex reality:

■ The *formal models* of bureaucracy provide great intellectual power in explaining what bureaucracies are and how they work. The models also furnish a bridge between twenty-first-century concerns and the fundamental issues that defined the field of public administration more than a century before. However, critics have pointed out that the models provide little practical guidance to public administrators, and in the minds of many theorists, they have not been supported by enough research.

■ The growth of *government by proxy* is a fact, one that forces a shift from sole reliance on hierarchical authority to honing of bargaining and negotiation skills. Yet because the execution of farmed-out work by contractors and grant-receiving organizations is susceptible to corruption and other abuses, government officials need to devise incentives for faithful performance, to monitor behavior, and to apply sanctions. It is a clear trend without a clear solution for the management issues it raises.

■ The *pluralist* approach soundly emphasizes the societal and political environment in which powerful interest groups intervene in administration to achieve their objectives. How such groups' often narrow interests can receive due attention without sacrificing the larger public interest is an issue that is difficult to reconcile with hierarchical responsibility.

■ The *humanist* approach, though flawed in several ways, usefully reminds us that individual workers' incentives and teamwork matter in gauging the effectiveness of administration.

■ A *systems* approach, however simple to portray, is in fact very complex in application. As with pluralism, its contribution lies in its emphasis on the interplay between an administrative system and its environment. In addition, its attention to feedback reminds us that organizations learn from experience over time.

■ The *structural* approach, with which we started, goes back to first principles about government, viewing authority—legitimate power—as the heart of the matter. Executive branch departments are agents that hold authority that is delegated and restricted by other elements of the constitutional system—legislatures, executives, and the courts. In turn, each such agency organizes a hierarchy for further delegating and restricting authority and for holding subordinates accountable for their use of such authority. Despite more than a century of criticism and complaint about this approach, it remains the foundation for both the theories and practice of public administration.

That summary of the approaches returns us to the first principles, linked to the concept of *authority*. The concept of authority provides the building blocks for understanding organizational structure, staffing, the making and implementing of decisions, budgeting, and the enforcement of bureaucratic responsibility. The other approaches are complementary to this basic structural orientation. Despite all its difficulties, the concept of authority remains the fundamental building block of organization, in both theory and practice.

We need to tolerate the ambiguities of organizational theory. Physical scientists have long lived with both the wave theory of light and the particle theory of light, despite their contradiction. Our problem is less troublesome than the massive theoretical problems with which physicists must struggle.

Differences in Organizational Culture: Is the FBI from Mars and the CIA from Venus?

Author John Gray has made a global reputation with his best-seller *Men Are from Mars, Women Are from Venus*. His argument: that men expect women to think and talk like men, that women expect men to think and talk like women, and that "our relationships are filled with unnecessary friction and conflict."[1]

Gray must be on to something. His Mars/Venus books have sold more than 30 million copies in forty languages. In fact, thanks to appearances on *Oprah* and *Live with Regis,* his first book was the best-selling book of the 1990s.

Some people think Gray's guide to male-female relationships helps explain the tensions between governments as well. Journalist Siobhan Gorman thinks so. She writes that the key agencies responsible for protecting the United States from terrorist attacks, the Central Intelligence Agency (CIA) and the Federal Bureau of Investigation (FBI), "have such different approaches to life that they remain worlds apart"—and even White House–ordered relationship counseling might not be enough to bring them together.[2]

Prior to the September 11, 2001, attacks, U.S. government intelligence agencies spread across the nation and around the world had collected fragments of information, hints, and warnings about the potential attacks from numerous disparate sources. But the information never came together as a picture of the impending disaster. Even in retrospect, it isn't certain that the picture would ever have been clear enough for the government to stop the attacks. However, the country never found that out because high bureaucratic barriers prevented the flow of information.

In the months after the attacks, critics and reformers universally called on government to "connect the dots"—to do a much better job of interpreting the information collected by the various intelligence agencies. That process, they all concluded, would make America safer by helping top officials identify the greatest threats. Everyone agreed that the intelligence system needed better coordination and reached consensus that bureaucratic battles between the intelligence agencies were undermining the nation's security.

The national commission investigating the September 11, 2001, attacks confirmed that deep divisions between the nation's intelligence agencies had frustrated the government's ability to uncover valuable clues and, perhaps, take steps to prevent the attacks. Commission chairman Thomas Kean declared that the government had not been able to protect its citizens from attack because of "a failure of policy, management, capability and, above all, a failure of imagination." Who or what was to blame? Kean's commission answered, "There's no single individual who is responsible for our failures." The commission's recommendation? Create a new cabinet-level national intelligence director to oversee the nation's network of fifteen different intelligence agencies.[3] A single head of intelligence, the commission argued, would improve coordination and break down the barriers that had prevented the sharing of intelligence before the attacks. This national intelligence director needed to be able to steer the agencies' investigations, coordinate the information they collected, and provide clear advice to the president. That complex assignment, the commission concluded, required a new position at the highest level of the federal government—with the power to hire and fire employees and to control the intelligence budget.

At the center of the organizational battle was a decades-old struggle between the CIA and the FBI. "It's not that [FBI agents and CIA officers] don't like each other, but they're really different people," explained Jim Simon, who had worked as an analyst in the CIA. "They have a hard time communicating."[4]

For years, the two agencies had coexisted uneasily: the CIA focused on digging out information abroad on threats to the United States, while the FBI concentrated on dangers inside the country. A tidy boundary, perhaps, but not one that the nation's enemies respected. In fact, it was one they were able to exploit in carrying out the September 11, 2001, attacks, in which foreign operatives burrowed into American society, only to pop up to stage the biggest assault on American soil since the Japanese attack on Pearl Harbor in December 1941. President Bush, congressional leaders, and the 9/11 Commission issued an inescapable challenge to the agencies: cooperate! "But the organizations' institutional cultures are so different," concluded Gorman, "that real coordination will be very difficult to achieve."[5]

Since its creation in 1947, in the early days of the Cold War, the CIA has focused on building long-term relationships with potential intelligence sources. A field agent may spend long hours in conversation with a subject who is plied with good liquor, swapping tales, and building trust, in the hope that, when things begin to happen, the source may share some important information. Within this clandestine world, where it is always hard to predict what is going to happen where, the CIA—known as "The Company" to insiders—has encouraged a loose, nonhierarchical style of operating.

Success here consists in digging out a critical piece of information and passing it along to top policymakers. Field agents often cut corners to make this possible, and then they melt back into the background.

By contrast, the FBI, founded in 1908, has long had an informal motto: "We always get our man." Dogged police work combined with careful training of its agents has always been the hallmark of the FBI. Knowing that their job is to catch and incarcerate criminals, this agency's operatives scrupulously avoid crossing legal lines so they won't jeopardize prosecutions. Success means putting bad guys behind bars, one case at a time.

FBI agents take up a case, track it to its completion, file it away, and move on; their work is linear. In contrast, CIA agents circle constantly around problems, pick up on leads until they either solidify or evaporate, and work them like a prospector panning for gold.

These different styles of work lead each agency to recruit a different kind of person. John Vincent, a twenty-seven-year FBI veteran, explains, "The type of people that go into the CIA is completely different from the type of people who go into the FBI." In the FBI, most employees "are pretty normal Joes off the street. The CIA guys—they're a different group of people. Most of the CIA guys I've met are very intelligent but wouldn't know how to put a nut on a bolt."[6] FBI agents, in Gorman's analysis, are from Mars.

Sixteen-year CIA veteran Ronald Marks says that's because, in the CIA, judgment is much more important than rules. "You have a source who will tell you X. Your judgment of that source is based on the time you've spent with them. You're dealing pretty much in a murky world." That, Marks concludes, is "the world of judgment."[7] As Gorman puts it, CIA agents are from Venus.

These different operating styles have led to very different antiterrorism strategies. The information-based, judgment-driven world of the CIA has focused on rooting out information about possible attacks in advance, even if the information does not come together in sharp focus. The conviction-based, rule-driven world of the FBI has focused on trying to arrest and convict terrorists, often after the fact.

Nevertheless, the stark realities of the post–9/11 world make it essential for the two agencies to cooperate. As the 9/11 Commission warned, "Countering transnational Islamist terrorism will test whether the U.S. government can fashion more flexible models of management needed to deal with the twenty-first-century world."[8] In fact, toward the end of its report the commission quoted the following stark conclusion, drawn from a study of the Pearl Harbor attack: "Surprise, when it happens to a government, is likely to be a complicated, diffuse, bureaucratic thing. It includes neglect of responsibility, but also responsibility so poorly defined or so ambiguously delegated that action gets lost."[9]

To prevent poorly defined, ambiguously delegated policy in the future—to prevent the government's bureaucratic problems from getting in the way of its war on terror—the commission argued that the nation needed a single, powerful director of national intelligence with the authority to force coordination between the FBI and the CIA, as well as the thirteen other intelligence agencies. That change, the commissioners concluded, was the only way to create a unified homeland security culture from the very different independent organizational cultures that had grown in the vast intelligence community.

But even a new organization, Gorman argued, might not solve the problem. Looking back at Gray's best-seller, Gorman wrote, "Mars and Venus can expect to need couples' counseling for a very long time."

Questions to Consider

1. What are the roots of the different organizational cultures in the FBI and the CIA? How do these cultures affect their work? In both good and bad ways?
2. How likely is it that the two agencies will be able to change their cultures?
3. Do you think that changes in the organizational structure can produce changes in the organizational culture? Is the 9/11 Commission's proposal a good idea? Why or why not? How else might an organization's culture change, if not by changes to its structure?

NOTES

1. John Gray, *Men Are from Mars, Women Are from Venus* (New York: HarperCollins, 1992), 10.
2. Siobhan Gorman, "FBI, CIA Remain Worlds Apart," *GovExec.com* (August 1, 2003), http://www.govexec.com/defense/2003/08/fbi-cia-remain-worlds-apart/14671.
3. Chris Strohm, "9/11 Commission Scolds Government over Attacks, Calls for Major Reforms," *GovExec.com* (July 22, 2004), http://www.govexec.com/defense/2004/07/911-commission-scolds-government-over-attacks-calls-for-major-reforms/17234. See the Commission's report, *The 9/11 Commission Report* (2004), http://www.9-11commission.gov/report/911Report.pdf.
4. Gorman, "FBI, CIA Remain Worlds Apart."
5. Ibid.
6. Ibid.
7. Ibid.
8. *The 9/11 Commission Report*, 406.
9. Thomas Schelling, foreword to Roberta Wohlstetter, *Pearl Harbor: Warning and Decision* (Stanford University Press, 1962), viii.

CASE 4.2

Learning to See in the New York Police Department: How Studying Art Makes You a Better Cop

It was a tough case, and the officers split up into two- or three-person surveillance teams. Their assignment: to study the scene carefully and try to figure out what was going on. The scene was puzzling—a man, with short hair and lots of muscles, was getting rough treatment. A buxom woman ripped the shirt he was wearing. One 52-year-old inspector, a long-time veteran of the New York Police Department (NYPD), quickly concluded it was the end of a trial and the victim was "possibly being led off to be tortured." The woman? Part of a lynch mob, he said.[1]

The case? A close-up examination of a seventeenth-century painting by Italian baroque artist Guercino depicting the biblical hero Samson, after Delilah betrayed Samson to the Philistines. The scene? A gallery in New York's Metropolitan Museum of Art, in art historian Amy Herman's course titled "The Art of Perception." Herman's course was highly focused, designed for NYPD officers ranked as captains or higher. No discussion about brush strokes or light or palettes of color. Just observation.

Herman's course began with instruction for medical students in 2004. One night as they were eating pizza, a friend asked her if she had thought about expanding her audience. Herman visited the New York City Police Academy to explain what she thought her course could accomplish. She remembered one of her early courses. One officer said, on looking at a painting with everyone looking up, that if he drove up on the scene, "I'd figure I had a jumper," someone poised to leap off a ledge. The picture was baroque artist Claude Lorrain's *Sermon on the Mount.*

Officers found great value in not only honing their powers of observation but also talking to their detectives about what to look for. Herman noted in class that one murder victim's body had not been found for more than a year because the commander had issued only fuzzy instructions about how and where to look for it. One of her students said that instead of telling his detectives to "search the block" for evidence like shell casings, he would order them to make their search more systematic, by telling them where to start, where to stop, where to look, and what to search for. A graduate, Lt. Dan Hollywood, said Herman's teaching on perception had helped him snag criminals lurking around Times Square. As coordinator of a twenty-four-person team of plainclothes officers, Hollywood said, "Instead of telling my people that the guy who keeps looking in one parked car after another is dressed in black, I might say he's wearing a black wool hat, a black leather coat with black fur trim, a black hoodie sweatshirt, and Timberlands."

One FBI agent who took Herman's course went undercover for eighteen months as part of a task force trying to break up mob control over the sanitation business in nearby Connecticut. With his powers of observation sharpened, he helped provide the basis for search warrants that produced thirty-four convictions and that busted up $60–$100 million in garbage companies. "Amy taught us that to be successful, you have to think outside the box," said the task force's commander, Bill Reiner. "Don't just look at a picture and see a picture. See what's happening."

Herman follows her own advice, of course. On a subway, she nervously eyed two large men who, in turn, were eyeing her. They hadn't shaved and their clothes were shabby, and she prepared to hop off the train as soon as it stopped.

"Hey," one of the men said, noticing that she was noticing, "we took your course. We're cops."

Questions to Consider

1. In police department culture, could there be many things further removed than the study of art history? Consider how an organization's culture helps the organization accomplish its mission—and how bringing other cultural insights can help hone the ability to achieve results.

2. Choose one or two other local governmental organizations. Assess the culture that operates inside those organizations. How might that culture support the mission—and where do you think that culture might blind the organization to things it ought to know to get its job done? Can you suggest ways of providing the organizations with new insights?

3. Organizational culture is the product of the hierarchy, the informal norms that shape the organization, and the way that individuals approach their jobs. What lessons do the lessons from Herman's course suggest for organization theory?

NOTE

1. The case comes from Neal Hirschfeld, "Teaching Cops to See," *Smithsonian.com* (October 2009), http://www.smithsonianmag.com/arts-culture/Teaching-Cops-to-See.html.

CASE 4.3

Ben Proposes Marriage: Romantic Gesture or Abuse of Police Power?

Ben Vienneau noticed a special offer from Canada's CHSJ Radio 94.1. The station was running a competition for an ultimate "wedding by the sea," featuring a ceremony, limo, reception, flowers, and a honeymoon—all worth $20,000. What did he have to do to win? Create a video, post it on YouTube, and get more people to click and vote than anyone else.

So he came up with a very unusual proposal to his girlfriend, Marcia Belyea. Ben talked his brother-in-law, who was a police officer, into driving up behind Marcia, hitting the siren and lights, and pulling her over. The officer, in full uniform, told her she had over $2,000 in parking tickets, put her in the back of the police car,

and threatened to put her in jail for 30 days. She broke down in tears—until the officer told her, "We've agreed to waive the fine, OK, and let you go, if you take his hand in marriage."[1] Ben got down on his knee, told her "I love you so much. I want to spend the rest of my life with you." Marcia's worries turned into smiles as Ben slipped the ring on her finger—and the police officer asked to see the ring, "just for evidence," he said.

Ben put the video on YouTube, and it went viral. In the United States, television shows like "The View" and "Whoopi" picked it up. The video ran on ABC's "Good Morning America" and Peres Hilton's website. All the publicity pushed them into the finals of the radio station's competition, and Marcia made a Facebook post asking people to vote for them and put them over the top.

The stunt started a wild online chat about whether what Ben—and his brother-in-law—did was OK. Some applauded the couple for being so much in love. Others said it was "a huge waste of taxpayers' money."

But almost no one wondered whether it was right for a police officer to use his government authority to set up the prank. The story echoed against another one from Charlottesville, Virginia, where a twenty-year-old University of Virginia student found herself surrounded by plainclothes police. She had just come out of a store, having purchased some sparkling water. Agents from the state's Alcohol Beverage Control agency mistook the water for a twelve-pack of beer. One agent jumped on the hood of her car. Another drew a gun. They pulled out identification but the woman, Elizabeth Daly, couldn't read it in the dark parking lot, at 10:15 pm. Terrified by the officers—and not knowing that they were officers, because they were not in uniform—she tried to escape by driving out of the parking lot. In the process, she grazed a couple of the officers. A police car with a siren and flashing lights pulled her over a few blocks away.

There was no engagement ring waiting for Elizabeth. The agents charged her with three felonies and put her in jail overnight. They had mistaken her sparkling water for beer; they charged her with assaulting an officer.[2] They later dropped the charges and apologized.

Two women driving cars. Both were pulled over by officers with sirens and flashing lights. Neither had done anything wrong. One was punked as part of an engagement for a radio station competition, by an officer in uniform. The other was a victim of mistaken beverages, by officers not in uniform.

And by the way: Ben and Marcia won their dream $20,000 wedding by the sea in the radio station's Facebook competition.

Questions to Consider

1. Police officers, every day, take enormous personal risks to do their jobs. They often ride alone and have to make snap life-or-death decisions. Citizens count on their hard work to keep them safe. What kind of supervisory issues does that pose for police departments and their leaders?

2. Do you think that Ben's brother-in-law committed a harmless prank in helping Ben surprise Marcia? Or did he abuse his police power?

3. What, if anything, did Virginia's Alcohol Beverage Control agents do wrong? They suspected Elizabeth, who was under age, of buying beer, and they had staked out a store where they believed such purchases were frequent. They were not wearing uniforms, to make it easier to catch suspected lawbreakers. If you were their supervisor, would you make any changes to the procedures to prevent such an occurrence from happening again?

4. Are there any links between these two cases, especially in the trust that citizens must have for the police, and the flexibility that police must have to do their jobs?

NOTES

1. "Fake Arrest Proposal" (July 1, 2013), http://www .youtube.com/watch?v=RAzXRezukdo.

2. K. Burnell Evans, "Bottled-Water Purchase Leads to Night in Jail for UVa Student," Charlottesville *Daily Progress* (June 27, 2013), http://www.dailyprogress .com/news/bottled-water-purchase-leads-to-night-in-jail-for-uva/article_b5ab5f62-df9b-11e2-81c4-0019bb30f31a.html.

KEY CONCEPTS

agencies   80

agents   80

authority   79

bureaucratic model   83

chain of command   81

charismatic authority   84

classical theory   81

closed-system theorists   86

efficiency   81

feedback loop   86

formal approach   77

government-by-proxy approach   77

hierarchy   77

human relations movement   90

humanist approach   77

inputs   86

network analysis   98

open-system theorists   86

organizational cultures   94

organizational structure   77

outputs   86

pluralist approach   77

principal-agent theory   99

principals   80

rational-legal authority   84

scientific management movement   90

sensitivity training   93

structure   77

system boundaries   87

system purpose   87

systems theory   85

throughputs   86

traditional authority   84

transaction costs   99

FOR FURTHER READING

Goldsmith, Stephen, and William D. Eggers. *Governing by Network: The New Shape of Government.* Washington, D.C.: Brookings Institution, 2004.

Goldsmith, Stephen, and Donald F. Kettl, eds. *Unlocking the Power of Networks: Keys to High-Performance Government.* Washington, D.C.: Brookings Institution Press, 2009.

Gulick, Luther. "Notes on the Theory of Organization." In *Papers on the Science of Administration,* edited by Luther Gulick and L. Urwick, 1–45. New York: Institute of Public Administration, 1937.

Katz, Daniel, and Robert L. Kahn. *The Social Psychology of Organizations.* 2nd ed. New York: Wiley, 1978.

Khademian, Anne M. *Working with Culture: The Way the Job Gets Done in Public Programs.* Washington, D.C.: CQ Press, 2002.

McGregor, Douglas. *The Human Side of Enterprise.* New York: McGraw-Hill, 1960.

Moe, Terry M. "The New Economics of Organization." *American Journal of Political Science* 28 (1984): 739-777.

Perrow, Charles. *Complex Organizations.* 3d ed. New York: Random House, 1986.

Simon, Herbert. *Administrative Behavior.* New York: Macmillan, 1947.

Weber, Max. *From Max Weber: Essays in Sociology.* Translated and edited by H. H. Gerth and C. Wright Mills. New York: Oxford University Press, 1958.

SUGGESTED WEBSITES

For an exploration of academic research about organizational theory, see the websites of the Public Management Research Association, **www.pmranet.org**, and of the Academy of Management, **www.aom.org**. Both provide links to cutting-edge research in the field. In addition, the website prepared by Babson College Assistant Professor Keith Krollag, **http://faculty.babson.edu/krollag/org_site/encyclop/encyclo.html**, is a useful encyclopedia of the major terms in the organizational theory literature.

CHAPTER

5

The Executive Branch

In May 2011, President Obama and his senior staff intently tracked the final steps in the hunt for Osama bin Laden, from the White House Situation Room.

A **CAREFUL LOOK AT THE WAY THE EXECUTIVE BRANCH** works begins with a look at structure, from the basic charts that diagram who reports to whom, to the larger questions about organizations as administrative building blocks. Although some theoretical approaches argue that people matter more than structure, there's no doubt that structure sets the basic rules and patterns by which administrators connect, work, and produce public programs.

According to Miles's Law, named after noted Princeton professor Rufus E. Miles, "where you stand depends on where you sit."[1] The organizational setting both defines the way that government officials see their jobs and creates their capacity to do their jobs.

If structure is the building block, coordination is the goal. The point of creating complex structures is to coordinate solutions to complex problems. It's a two-step process. The first step is building great expertise to do hard things, ranging from bringing large jets back safely to cracking a multi-state crime spree. The second is weaving together this expertise to ensure tough problems don't fall through the cracks. "If only we can find the right formula for coordination," Harold Seidman wrote, "we can reconcile the irreconcilable, harmonize competing and wholly divergent interests, overcome irrationalities in our government structures, and make hard policy choices to which no one will disagree."[2] Of course, we have never quite found the magic formula for coordination, but reformers are always searching for the right structure to make it happen.

If getting the right structure is the basic problem, then reorganization is a constant impulse. How can we best ensure security for passengers boarding airplanes? Before September 11, 2001, that was the job of the U.S. Department of Transportation, which often allowed local airports to hire private contractors to screen passengers and their luggage and which coordinated screening with air traffic control and other transportation functions. After the terrorist attacks, Congress decided to make airport screening a government function, with public employees as screeners working for the new Department of Homeland Security.

The debate over the best government structure is universal. In 2004 the California Performance Review declared, "California's government must reorganize to meet the demands of modern California." The report proposed a massive shift in the responsibilities of state agencies that seeks to align "programs by function, consolidates shared services and abolishes outdated entities." Pointing out that California is the fifth largest economy in the world and that the state has a rich tradition of embracing new ideas, the review nevertheless charged that

> California's state government is antiquated and ineffective. It simply does not mirror the innovative and visionary character of our state. Instead of serving the people, it is focused on process and procedure. It is bureaucracy at its worst—costly, inefficient and in many cases unaccountable.

The performance review recommended a fundamental restructuring of the state's eleven agencies, seventy-nine departments, and more than three hundred boards and commissions responsible for carrying out the state's functions.[3] "Form follows function," concluded the California Performance Review's report.

Government's complex mission and intricate structure are closely linked. In this chapter, we will begin by looking at the basic issues. Chapter 6 focuses on critical and persistent organizational problems. Structure matters—a lot. How structure affects organizations and the way they behave, however, is a deceptively complex puzzle.

EXECUTIVE BRANCH COMPONENTS

The first question of structure is how to shape the building blocks. For centuries, organization by **function** has been the foundation, with four functions at the core: (1) managing money, including revenues, spending, and borrowing (as with a Treasury or Finance Ministry); (2) maintaining internal law and order (through the courts and a department for justice); (3) keeping the country safe (through departments for the military and navy); and (4) managing the country's foreign affairs (through a foreign ministry). Soon other functions began appearing, such as a postal service and an engineering construction service (for roads, bridges, waterways, and public buildings). New functions meant new departments. There were departments for agriculture and trade, and later for social welfare, health, housing, and education. With the twentieth century came emphasis on technology, science, energy, the environment, and economic planning. With government's growing scope came new departments.

The top level of organization is usually a "department," but there's no consistent logic about what makes a department a "department." The federal Department of Veterans Affairs had been an independent agency, but became a cabinet department primarily for symbolic reasons, to recognize the contributions of the nation's veterans. The Social Security Administration was spun out of the Department of Health and Human Services to insulate its huge spending from the annual budget battles. NASA and the Environmental Protection Agency both have big missions, but they are agencies independent of any cabinet department, but without "department" status. The head of the EPA has "cabinet rank," in Washington protocol; the head of NASA does not. The reasons are arbitrary; their bases are primarily political. Look around any state or local government, and the same holds true.

Moreover, the structure of the executive branch, at all levels of government, tends to rest on a paradox. We count on the executive (president, governor, or mayor) to serve as chief executive, but the structure this person manages is usually the product of legislative decisions. An executive can propose the creation of a new cabinet-level department, but shaping the structure and funding its budget are both legislative acts. There are occasional exceptions, but executive structure is usually the creature of the legislative branch. That's very different from the private sector, where executives have far greater power to create, abolish, staff, and fund the structures they manage. Nothing symbolizes the difference more than the hideaway office of a recent federal cabinet secretary. This hideaway had a treadmill, and when exercising, the secretary ran long miles looking out a big window at the Capitol dome, which never got any closer.

Cabinet Departments

A careful analysis of executive branch structure is hard because there are so many terms: *bureaus, departments, commissions, offices,* and *agencies.* We typically use *agencies* as the broadest, most generic designation—executive branch units, after all, operate as *agents* of the government. The other terms refer to more specific units of the executive branch.

When agencies are grouped together, we typically refer to them as the **cabinet.** The term dates from the sixteenth century, when the English king began meeting with his closest advisers in a cabinet, or small room. That term, in turn, has its roots in the Old French *cabine,* a gambling room, usually small and private to avoid prying eyes. That made the small, secluded chamber a natural place for the king's advisers to gather. Over time, the meeting of the king's ministers grew into a more formal structure, and the American government incorporated the concept to describe the relationship between the president and department secretaries. *Secretary* comes from Old English and refers to a high-level, confidential officer with the education required to read and write. Its lower-level, clerical meaning emerged much later.

Until the 1950s, the American cabinet structure was remarkably stable. Of the fifteen executive departments now operating at the federal level, three date from 1789 (State, Defense,[4] and Treasury). A fourth agency (Justice) was established then as a separate office, though Justice did not achieve full departmental status until eighty years later. Interior and Agriculture became departments more than a hundred years ago. Commerce and Labor departments date from 1903. Seven newer outer departments have appeared since 1950: Health, Education, and Welfare (HEW) in 1953 (split into separate departments for Health and Human Services [HHS] and Education in 1979), Housing and Urban Development (HUD) in 1965, Transportation in 1966, Energy in 1977, Education in 1979, Veterans Affairs in 1989, and Homeland Security in 2002.[5]

Since 2002, with the creation of the Department of Homeland Security, the federal government has had fifteen cabinet departments (see Table 5.1). They range greatly in size, from

TABLE 5.1	Federal Executive Branch Departments: Estimated Outlays and Employment, FY 2014	
Department	**Outlays (millions of dollars)**	**Employment (thousands of employees)**
Agriculture	$143,642	90.7
Commerce	$9,480	43.0
Defense	$665,815	765.0
Education	$75,394	4.4
Energy	$31,322	15.9
Health and Human Services	$967,196	72.6
Homeland Security	$53,436	191.0
Housing and Urban Development	$49,267	9.2
Interior	$13,497	69.8
Justice	$34,475	117.7
Labor	$86,766	17.5
State	$31,048	33.2
Transportation	$88,247	57.6
Treasury	$507,684	112.7
Veterans Affairs	$147,733	319.3

Source: U.S. Office of Management and Budget, *Budget of the United States Government, Fiscal Year 2014,* Historical Tables, Table 4.1, and *Analytical Perspectives,* Table 10-2.

the Department of Defense, which accounts for a third of all federal civilian employees, to the Department of Education, whose 4,400 employees would make it a small agency within many of the larger cabinet departments. The departments have about 90 percent of the executive branch's civilian employees. (The total does not include the U.S. Postal Service, which is a government corporation separate from regular civilian government employment.)

Independent Agencies

Beyond the cabinet departments lie a large number of **independent agencies**, which account for about one-tenth of the federal government's employees and one-fifth of its spending. The Social Security Administration, which was taken out of HHS in 1995, accounts for much of that spending and most of those employees. But spending and employment figures offer only a rough measure of the size and reach of these independent agencies. They range from the small, such as the American Battle Monuments Commission, to the hugely powerful, such as the Federal Reserve Board. Some are regulatory, such as the Federal Communications Commission, which sets broadcast standards and manages licenses for the nation's broadcasters, while others provide services, such as the Tennessee Valley Authority, which operates flood-control and power-generating dams in the southeastern part of the country. Then there are the super-secret spy agencies, including the Central Intelligence Agency and the National Security Agency.

Congress originally created these agencies as independent bodies to insulate them from presidential control and legislative-executive politics.[6] They have enormous power over important parts of the economy. By various methods (licensing, rate-fixing, cease-and-desist orders, and safety codes, for example), the **regulatory commissions** monitor major features of transportation, communications, power production and distribution, banking, the issuing of corporate securities, commodities and securities exchanges, the prosecution of unfair and deceptive business practices, the safety of consumer products, and labor-management relations. To further complicate the picture, bureaus within many departments—including the Food and Drug Administration (in HHS) and the Occupational Safety and Health Administration (in Labor)—exercise similar regulatory powers. Some analysts rate the chair of the Federal Reserve Board as the second most influential person in the nation, following only the president.[7]

In recent decades, the supposed guarantees of political independence from the

Americans depend on the U.S. Postal Service to deliver their mail, but the rise of the Internet and the changing economics of communication pushed it deeper into the red. In 2012, the USPS ran a record $14 billion deficit and led top officials to searching questions about the future of mail delivery in the country.

president have collapsed.[8] During a president's term, the president can usually appoint a commission's majority, installing members who share similar policy goals and, even more important, designating the chairperson of each commission, who often dominates the commission.[9] The president's Office of Management and Budget reviews commissions' budgets, the Justice Department controls commissions' proposed appeals of cases to the Supreme Court, and the commissions often depend on the president's support in dealing with Congress. On the other hand, political wrangling for years has made it impossible for the Federal Elections Commission to work effectively.

Many of the independent regulatory commissions operate on a case-by-case basis, through steps that often resemble a court proceeding. Other agencies provide goods and services, and their structure represents a high-level commitment to particular missions that neither Congress nor the president wanted to submerge within a larger department. For example, the Tennessee Valley Authority (TVA) dates from President Franklin D. Roosevelt's New Deal and Roosevelt's commitment to create "a corporation clothed with the power of government but possessed of the flexibility and initiative of a private enterprise."[10] The TVA soon brought electric power to a region that had long suffered without an adequate supply and dams to areas that had often been overrun by spring floods. Indeed, over the years it has become more like a private electric utility than a government agency. The Peace Corps, established by President John F. Kennedy, has for decades sent workers to improve the lives of people in foreign lands. The National Science Foundation funds research, and NASA runs the nation's space program.

Concern about increases in terrorist threats has sometimes led the U.S. Transportation Security Administration to supplement its usual screening with pat-downs, much to the dismay of some travelers.

Some of these independent agencies are **government corporations**, mostly engaged in lending, insurance, and other business-type operations.[11] Familiar examples are the Corporation for Public Broadcasting, the Federal Deposit Insurance Corporation, the Legal Services Corporation, the National Railroad Passenger Corporation (Amtrak), the TVA, and the U.S. Postal Service. They vary greatly. Some are wholly government-owned, others are mixed enterprises with both government and private investments, and yet others have only private funding. Some are meant to be profit-making; others are non-profit organizations. Some support themselves from their revenues; others are wholly or partly dependent on government appropriations. Some are integrated into the regular departments; others float freely. And they vary in conformity to standard personnel, budgetary, and auditing practices and controls.

Congress tried to impose some order on this motley collection by passage of the Government Corporation Control Act of 1945, the most important provisions of which included budgetary and auditing controls hitching the corporations to the government that created them. But Congress has often exempted new corporations from various provisions of the act. The debate on the merits turns on a conflict—between the view that every government agency needs to be integrated into the structure of responsibility and accountability of the executive branch and, therefore, needs to be held under tight control, and the counterargument that government agencies ought to be managed by business-style standards of efficiency and, therefore, ought to be allowed substantial autonomy and flexibility. The debate remains unresolved. Indeed, after the financial meltdown of the late 2000s, the debate became even more heated, as critics pointed to mistakes by two government corporations—Fannie Mae and Freddie Mac—for fueling the financial crisis in the housing industry. Proposals surfaced to radically change or even abolish these organizations.

In sum, in contrast to popular impressions, the president has great leverage over federal spending through just a handful of departments. The regulatory commissions' independence of presidential control has largely evaporated. Only government corporations can claim some degree of independence, but they are such a varied lot that making general conclusions is difficult indeed. And all of these organizations share legislative oversight by Congress.

We've been exploring the role of departments and independent agencies in the federal government. At the state and local levels, the same patterns—and underlying issues—hold true, in almost endless variety. The Railroad Commission of Texas, for example, is an independent regulatory commission whose mission grew from its early railroad days to one of the state's most powerful agencies, developing and regulating Texas's vast oil, gas, and other energy resources. North Dakota has an Industrial Commission with great authority over the state's own vast energy resources. Overseeing the commission is a three-member board composed of the governor, attorney general, and agriculture commissioner. The pattern ripples throughout the country, but the same basic question occurs everywhere: who holds the administrators accountable for what they do and how much they spend?

Bureaus

The principal operating organizations of the government are **bureaus**. This general term covers many organizations within the larger departments. Bureaus have a wide variety of titles, such as Bureau of Motor Vehicles, Internal Revenue Service, Geological Survey, Antitrust Division, Federal Highway Administration, Homicide Division, Office of Energy Research, and the famous Federal Bureau of Investigation. These operating units are so important in public administration that they give the field its name: bureaucracy—that is, a government by bureaus.

Bureaus vary dramatically in size and significance. Some of them have long historical roots—longer, often, than those of the departments in which they are currently located. The Public Health Service system traces its origins to 1798, when Congress authorized marine hospitals to care for merchant seamen. Four years later, Congress established the Army Corps of Engineers and soon charged it with improving the navigability of rivers and harbors for civilian as well as military purposes. The Bureau of the Census in the Commerce Department finds its mission in the Constitution's 1789 provision requiring a decennial population census, though the bureau itself dates only from 1902. (Originally, the census was taken by U.S. marshals under supervision of the State Department; after 1850, the Interior Department did the job.) The Bureau of Land Management succeeded the General Land Office (established in 1812), some of whose records bear the signatures of George Washington and Thomas Jefferson.[12] Many other bureaus are old enough to have developed a distinctive culture—a sense of organic institutional life and a doctrine and tradition to which their staffs are dedicated. As we have seen, bureaus do not easily abandon such culture simply at the command of the temporary officials who fill top executive branch positions.

One of the first things that state and local governments did as they became organized was to set up key bureaus to deal with the safety, public health, and transportation of their citizens. At the local level, many such organizations date from before the birth of the nation. Even as he was tinkering with lightning rods and his famous stove, Benjamin Franklin created a lending library, a fire brigade, a night watchmen unit, a hospital, a militia, and a university. In his stimulating biography of Franklin, Walter Isaacson quotes the sage of Pennsylvania as writing, "The good men may do separately is small compared with what they may do collectively."[13]

American state and local governments rely on bureaus as well. Like the federal government, state governments tend to have a collection of cabinet departments and a number of independent agencies. At the local level, however, the number of bureaus is often dizzying. As complex as the organizational structure of the federal government is, the structure of many state and local governments is equally as intricate—or more so, especially given their smaller size but broad reach.

Field Offices

Most discussions about bureaus and bureaucracy focus on the headquarters organization. That is the source of most news, as cabinet secretaries and bureau heads hold press conferences and produce news releases. Headquarters is the center of high-level political conflict, especially when executive branch agencies battle with legislators over programs and money.

The reality, of course, is that most government operations do not happen at headquarters but out in the field. At the federal level, for example, *just 12 percent* of the federal government's civilian employees are located in the Washington, DC, metropolitan area. Seven of eight federal employees work in the field, from airport screeners and air traffic controllers to local Social Security Administration representatives and members of the foreign service in embassies around the world. In fact, in 2012 the federal government hired almost as many new employees in Texas as in Washington, D.C. At the state and local levels, most police officers patrol neighborhoods and rarely visit headquarters. Firefighters staff their trucks at stations around the city. State natural resources workers manage water and sewer permits and oversee hunters. Highway department employees build roads, patch potholes, and plow snow. The headlines tend to focus on big battles in the state capitol building or city hall, but most of government's work happens in the field.

Most bureaus establish their own field organization and procedures. From police precincts to fire stations, from the department of motor vehicles to parks, most field operations are organized by function. There is another strategy, based on area. The **areal, or prefectoral, system** dates from the Roman Empire, where the army commander controlled a region. In such a system, the country is divided into administrative regions, or districts. Each region has a single national official (in some countries called a *prefect*) to oversee all national field agents in the area, regardless of their departmental and bureau affiliations.[14] The French prefectoral system, originated by Napoleon, is the model most widely copied.[15]

The advantage of the area-based prefectoral system is coordination, because all government functions in the area report through a single prefect. The disadvantage is specialization, since the coordinator is by necessity a broad generalist. The United States, at all levels of government, has usually chosen organization by function. The disadvantage here is coordination of activities in the field. As a result, major programs like the war on drugs, organized through functional organizations like the Drug Enforcement Administration (in Justice), the Customs Service (in Homeland Security), the Coast Guard (in Homeland Security), and the State Department, almost always suffer coordination problems.[16] In homeland security, which involves coordination not only among multiple federal agencies but among the federal, state, and local governments as well, the problem has proven even more daunting.[17] Reformers often try to solve coordination problems by creating area-based offices and to replace area-based offices with functional experts. The specialization versus coordination choice is inevitable, and no one has ever figured out an organizational strategy to get the right measure of both at the same time.[18]

LEADERSHIP OF THE EXECUTIVE BRANCH

The chief executive might lead the executive branch, but the pieces of the branch are the creatures of the legislature. The private-sector model of executives often leads us to vastly underestimate the legislature's role in administration. At the same time, it's easy to overestimate the role of executives. The federal government is so vast that the president can never pay attention to more than a handful of public administration issues. The same is true for cabinet secretaries as well, whose biggest nightmare is discovering a major issue about their department for the first time on the front page of *The Washington Post*. At the state and local levels, the executive branch is often little more than a heap of twigs. In most state governments, the governor is only one of five or six popularly elected executive officials, and departments' and agencies' executive heads are often chosen by the legislature or by boards and commissions (whose members have overlapping terms) rather than by the governor. On the average, governors appoint less than half their states' administrative officials (whether with or without legislative confirmation). Some mayors in so-called weak-mayor systems have similar handicaps. More strikingly, even those in strong-mayor systems (and city managers, too) find that many functions are vested in other local governments, including special districts for schools, transportation, and water that are a step removed from their control.

That paints a challenging portrait of the leadership in the executive branch. At the federal level, the president and vice president are the only elected executive officials. The president is vested by the Constitution with "the Executive power," is directed to "take Care that the Laws be faithfully executed," and is authorized to "require the Opinion in writing, of the principal Officer in each of the executive Departments, upon any subject relating to the Duties of their respective Offices." The president is constitutionally empowered to nominate and, by and with the advice and consent of the Senate, to appoint all higher "Officers of the United States" whose appointments are not otherwise constitutionally provided for. Congress can vest appointments of inferior officers only "in the president alone, in the Courts of Law, or in the Heads of Departments." The president can remove executive officers.[19] The president's formal powers, of course, are only the beginning, but they distinguish the president from most chief executives of American governments, to legitimize the president's resistance to excessive congressional incursions, and to guide courts in their interpretations of the president's powers.

At the state and local levels, the tradition of long ballots—with independent races for many key positions—often weakens the leadership of their executives and complicates the problem of coordination. In many states, the attorney general and secretary of state (and sometimes other major positions as well, such as regents for the state university system) are elected independently of the governor. In fact, the state attorney general's election is often a

Ripped
from the Headlines...

PERFORMANCE

Can "Big Data" Make Government Work Better?

"Big data" became the rage in the early 2010s. Big data? Datasets so big and sprawling that usual data management systems and programs can't get their arms around them, so analysts have to devise new techniques to extract the extraordinarily useful information that surrounds us. It's a central mission of Google and all the other big information technology companies.

And big data has come to government as well. State governments are using data mining to make sense of Medicaid. Local governments are tracking a vast array of services through new data systems. As two of America's best observers of state and local politics, Katherine Barrett and Richard Greene, have pointed out, "City and states are awash with data." However, "one obstacle in translating that data into information useful for management is an apples-and-oranges kind of phenomenon: Information in one dataset frequently can't be effectively meshed and analyzed with that in another." New York City discovered that fact. There are 2.5 million trees in the city, and it made sense that pruning them would reduce damage in storms. But the city didn't have information linking pruning with emergency calls—until it found a big data strategy to link pruning activities with hazards and city officials found that good pruning reduced emergency cleanup calls by 22 percent.

That teaches an important lesson, Barrett and Greene concluded. "Big data by itself won't do a bit of good for any government unless it's actually used for management or policy." In fact, one blogger wrote, "You can have all the facts you want but if you can't tell a story, people won't listen." What do you think the lessons are for connecting the rising tide of data, on all sides, with the very real side of making public administration work better? If you were a local official, how would you use data to improve services for your citizens?

Source: Katherine Barrett and Richard Greene, "A Warning for Big Data, 3 Ways to Handle Citizen Feedback, and Why 'Experts' Are Often Wrong," *Governing,* July 11, 2013, http://www.governing.com/topics/mgmt/col-big-data-citizen-feedback-experts-wrong.html.

stepping stone to the race for governor, and that often complicates the governor's job as executive. At the federal level, the president at least has appointment power over the key members of the cabinet; at the state level, that is often not the case. In her political biography of George W. Bush, Texas columnist Molly Ivins wrote, only partly in jest, that the Texas governor is the fifth most powerful person in the state, behind the lieutenant governor, attorney general, comptroller, and land commissioner, all of whom are independently elected.[20] In many local governments, positions such as clerk of courts, coroner, county clerk, district attorney, registrar of deeds, sheriff, and treasurer are often independently elected as well. The fragmentation of administrative organization means that, in many state and local governments, the chief executive may be responsible for the performance of state agencies, but many key officials with whom the executive must work have independent sources of political power.

Problems for Executive Management

The chief job of the chief executive is the faithful execution of the laws. As we know, however, this expectation often falls short. Three facts help explain why.

First, top elected executives are chosen for their electability, not for managerial ability and experience. They rarely have a lively interest in administrative matters, and they must tend to the politics to survive. Before Barack Obama became president, the largest organization he had run was his U.S. Senate office, microscopic in size compared with the executive branch. Presidents quite properly devote much of their energy to making foreign and domestic policy decisions and to resolving crises; they work to influence Congress and to build support with major interest groups and the public. Presidents know that they will not be judged by administrative achievements. Administration captures a president's interest mostly when he perceives its instrumental value for attainment of his policy and power objectives.[21] The same is true for governors, county executives, and mayors. The exception: when the government fails to solve major problems, which can prove fatal at the polls. For George W. Bush, for example, his "negative" ratings exceeded his "positives" following the debacle with Hurricane Katrina, and he never politically recovered.

Second, although top executives appoint cabinet members and their subcabinet officials, too often they discover they cannot count on strong support or good management. Presidential appointees, including department heads, their undersecretaries, and their assistant secretaries, often have brief tenures: two years is the median; a third remain in their positions for eighteen months or less, and only a third stay as long as three years.[22] Many of them have never run a large organization. The door is always revolving at the top of the federal executive branch. In many states and cities, the situation is often the same.

Furthermore, department heads rarely have a free hand in assembling their teams of subordinates. Because the executive appointment system is centralized in the White House, a department's undersecretary, assistant secretaries, and even lesser officials are often appointed independently of the secretary or after intense negotiations. Such negotiations often pit the secretary's need for managerial competence and prior knowledge of the subject matter against the White House's quite different goals, which may include rewarding political service in his presidential campaign, obliging important senators, and consoling defeated candidates for public office. The result is that, despite notable exceptions, secretaries have difficulty in becoming effective executives—and thus in refuting an old charge that they are the weakest links in the chain of authority. The independent base of support enjoyed by many key officials at the state and local level further complicates the problem there. Because top-level administrators can rarely assemble their own team, they must find a way to work with the team that political imperatives assemble for them.

Third, interdepartmental friction points have multiplied. As problems have become more complicated, most agencies find that they must work with others to get their job done, and that complicates the challenge of determining who is in charge of what. Because a department has relatively fewer things to itself, it is more difficult to hold the single department head responsible for results. In New York City's Lower East Side, a September 2005 call for help led to a raging battle among emergency responders. A woman suffering from Alzheimer's disease was threatening to use a knife to cut herself. A fire department ambulance arrived to help. So did a volunteer Jewish ambulance crew. But an argument erupted between a member of the Jewish ambulance crew and a police officer. The police arrested the volunteer ambulance crew member and the battle spilled over into a noisy shouting match pitting the police against friends of the arrested crew member. New York State Assembly Speaker Sheldon Silver, who lived in the neighborhood, personally intervened to cool the tempers, but that only enraged the police. Some officers contended that they had been forced to give the ambulance crew member preferential treatment because of political pressure. Supporters of the volunteer ambulance crew member contended that their volunteers could have given the woman better care, because they were from the neighborhood and spoke Yiddish. The dispute simmered for a long time. Should the city pay attention to the special neighborhood/area-based considerations in the case? Or should the functional specialization of the city's ambulance crew rule?[23]

Reinforcing these trends is the growing size, power, and reach of the executive office itself. Let's take a look at that at the federal level.

The Executive Office and the White House

As long ago as 1937, in transmitting to Congress the report of the President's Committee on Administrative Management (the Brownlow Committee), Franklin D. Roosevelt recognized the enormous burden of trying to manage the executive branch:

> The Committee has not spared me; they say what has been common knowledge for 20 years, that the President cannot adequately handle his responsibilities; that he is overworked; that it is humanly impossible, under the system which we have, for him fully to carry out his constitutional duty as Chief Executive. ... With my predecessors who have said the same thing over and over again, I plead guilty.
>
>
>
> The plain fact is that the present Organization and equipment of the executive branch of the Government defeats the constitutional intent that there be a single responsible Chief Executive to coordinate and manage the departments and activities in accordance with the laws enacted by the Congress.[24]

As a first step, following the passage of the Reorganization Act of 1939, Roosevelt established the Executive Office of the President, transferred to it the Bureau of the Budget (from the Treasury Department), and set up its other units, among them the White House Office. The modern White House establishment was born.

From its relatively modest beginnings, with 570 employees in 1939, the Executive Office had expanded by the year 2010 to include about 1,900 employees.[25] In addition, the White House has long had additional employees detailed to it from executive departments, many of them appointed to department rolls specifically for White House service.[26] "The swelling of the presidency," as Thomas Cronin has called it,[27] was not only quantitative.

Not only has the number of executive office employees increased, but their role has changed as well. In 1937, the Brownlow Committee proposed that six presidential assistants be added to the three White House secretaries (who dealt with Congress, the public, and the media). Contrast the powerful position of recent presidents' aides to the committee's stipulation of the role of the proposed assistants:

These assistants, probably not exceeding six in number . . . would have no power to make decisions or issue instructions in their own right. They would not be interposed between the President and the heads of his departments. They would not be assistant presidents in any sense. . . . They would remain in the background, issue no orders, make no decisions, emit no public statements. . . . They should be men in whom the President has personal confidence and whose character and attitude is such that they would not attempt to exercise power on their own account. They should be possessed of high competence, great physical vigor, and a passion for anonymity.[28]

Surprisingly, eight former chiefs of staff to presidents from Eisenhower to Carter emphatically endorsed this description of the role of presidential assistants.[29] The "passion for anonymity" phrase has proven memorable, but it doesn't have much basis in reality.

The White House staff is now so large, multi-tiered, and specialized that it is increasingly hard to coordinate the coordinators.[30] In fact, says a Carter aide, "even those at the highest levels—assistants, deputy assistants, special assistants—don't see the President once a week or speak to him in any substantive way once a month," and that has become even more pronounced since.[31] Infighting among staff members to gain the president's ear has plagued every modern president. Even the tightly disciplined staff of George W. Bush found itself plagued by books and newspaper stories alleging deep rifts between key advisers. In the Obama administration, a large number of "czars" produced extra White House layers that distanced cabinet officials from the president and created new stovepipes inside the White House apparatus.

A frequent proposal to solve these problems is shrinking the size of the White House staff, but others have seen the staff's growth as the inevitable result of the president's increasing leadership responsibilities, which are attributed to a weakening of congressional leadership and of political parties, the rise of presidential use of public relations technologies, and other factors. "Instead of trying to wish it away," says political scientist Samuel Kernell, "the presence of a large, complex staff must be accepted as a given and its problems addressed forthrightly. . . . The President must give the staff clear direction and vigilantly oversee its performance."[32]

Except for the minor Office of Administration and the office tending to the Executive Residence, the White House office is composed of policy advisers with concerns that cut large swaths across the government. Their role reflects the concept that the Executive Office agencies should provide institutional support to the president by gathering information for him, advising him, monitoring the execution of his decisions by the operating departments, and facilitating interagency coordination. Most of the Executive Office is devoted to providing policy advice and coordination to support the president.

Of the major agencies of the Executive office of the President, two warrant special attention: the **Office of Management and Budget** and the **National Security Council**.

The Office of Management and Budget

Chief executives have always needed help to manage the finances of their governments. At the federal level, that job began in the Bureau of the Budget, established in the Treasury

Department in 1921 and moved to the new Executive Office of the President in 1939. In 1970 President Nixon renamed it the Office of Management and Budget (OMB). His intent was to elevate attention to management, but it's not surprising that the budget has always been the driving core of OMB's mission and culture. It has long been the largest unit of the Executive Office, accounting now for over a third of the executive employees.

At the center of OMB's power is its control of the budget process.[33] OMB analyzes the agencies' budget proposals, makes recommendations to the president for how much money should be provided, and compiles all of the requests into the budget that is formally transmitted to Congress. That gives OMB enormous power. However, because budgeting is virtually the only comprehensive decision-forcing process in the executive branch, the budget review gives OMB great insight into almost everything the federal government does, and that information is power over policy. In addition, OMB is the agency charged with implementing most government-wide policies, ranging from procurement standards to policies about websites, so its role takes it into every nook and cranny of the federal government's operations. Thus, in addition to budgetary review, it has important nonbudgetary functions:

- *Legislative clearance.* Agencies are required to submit to OMB their proposals for new legislation and amendments before transmitting them to Congress. OMB uses this legislative clearance function to ensure that agencies' proposals are "in accord with the president's program."
- *Review of legislation passed by Congress.* OMB is in charge of the time-pressured review of each bill passed by Congress and sent to the president for approval or veto. It rapidly canvasses the views of all concerned agencies about the appropriate action, ensures that the president is aware of those views when the president makes decisions, and often recommends what action the president should take.
- *Review of regulations proposed by agencies.* OMB reviews the principal regulations affecting the public that agencies propose to issue, a recent and powerful policy and management tool (which Chapter 13 discusses).
- *Management review.* OMB's efforts to improve administrative organization, management, and coordination in the executive branch are meant to help meet the president's responsibilities as the chief executive.
- *Intelligence about executive branch operations.* As they perform their jobs, OMB analysts are in constant contact with agency officials, about issues ranging from new rules to budget requests. OMB can therefore be a rich source of intelligence to the president on what is going on in all levels of policy generation and program management.

In the course of its life, the Bureau of the Budget (BOB) and then OMB developed a tradition of serving both the long-term institution of the presidency and the short-term, incumbent president—a difficult balance to keep. Hugh Heclo has described the job as stressing "neutral competence."[34] OMB fills most positions in the agency with career civil servants, attracted by the opportunity for a powerful role and lasting impact. That, in turn, helps provide the White House with a longer-term institutional memory than would be possible in the normal four-year election cycle.[35]

This tradition of service to both the incumbent president and the institution of the presidency has been at the core of OMB's role. Its tradition of neutral competence came under enormous pressure during the Nixon administration, when the president's OMB directors and deputy directors were political activists, making political speeches, advocating the president's policies at congressional hearings, and defending massive impoundments of appropriated funds until a number of courts ruled the impoundments illegal. A new layer of political appointees was inserted between the director and the career civil servants: in 1974 nearly two-thirds of the heads of OMB's major offices and examining divisions had one year's experience or less in their posts (compared to one-tenth in 1960).[36]

In the 1980s OMB enjoyed a resurgence of power. Reagan's first director of the budget, David Stockman, led the administration's top-priority policy of cutting spending on domestic programs; he centralized decision making in the bureau with little input from the agencies.[37] In other functions as well, some of them enhanced by legislation and executive orders, the bureau has become so fully in tune with the president's political objectives that it has recaptured roles earlier yielded to White House staff members. The dozen or so high-level political appointees in OMB, serving for one to three years, ensure that the political orientation will prevail and, as the budget has become even more central to federal policy in the 1990s and 2000s, the bureau's resurgence has continued. During the enormous budget battles of the 2010s, OMB was a central player in the ongoing negotiations.

The management side of OMB has struggled to play the role envisioned when the M was added to the Bureau of the Budget. In one view, "Management has become largely ad hoc, short-term responses to immediate political problems. The management 'initiatives' have been geared principally toward those activities which promise a quick political pay-off or have the potential for a salutary impact on budgetary 'spending.'"[38] Despairing of invigorating OMB's management work, a panel of the National Academy of Public Administration urged transfer of that work to a new Office of Federal Management, in the Executive Office.[39] Opponents argued that such an office would lack the power over agencies that inclusion in OMB confers: when budgeting and management improvement are in a single agency, budgeting is sure to predominate, but putting the management function into a new agency could well weaken the top-level focus on administration even further by separating it from the budgetary muscle that never fails to attract the attention of executive agencies and congressional committees. That logic underlay George W. Bush's management agenda to recouple administrative efforts with budgetary clout (see Chapter 7). This recurring debate demonstrates the sharp dilemmas in which central budget offices such as OMB always find themselves: the tension between long and short term, between management and budgeting, between inputs and performance. It also says a great deal about the role of public administration in a process that is inevitably political.

The National Security Council

The National Security Council (NSC) was established by statute in 1947, "to advise the President with respect to the integration of domestic, foreign, and military policies relating to the national security."[40] Its statutory members are the president, the vice president, the secretary of state, and the secretary of defense; also attending the meetings as statutory advisers are the chair of the Joint Chiefs of Staff and the director of the Central Intelligence Agency, and the president may ask others to attend as well.[41] An elaborate structure of inter-agency committees reviews foreign, defense, international economic, and intelligence policy issues and anticipates and manages crisis situations.[42] Recommendations on policy issues are submitted to the NSC, but its role being advisory, the president retains the decision-making responsibility.

Over time, the NSC has gradually become the focus of presidential foreign policy making. Indeed, that growing power has regularly rankled secretaries of defense and, especially, secretaries of state. It is no wonder that some perceive that the United States has two State Departments.[43]

The director of the NSC staff—more commonly referred to as the national security adviser—has achieved a dominant role for several reasons. The NSC staff is a unit in the Executive Office, but its director is situated inside the White House as assistant to the president.[44] There, she or he has access, briefing the president every morning and being immediately available for counsel in crises. With staff members serving on all NSC interagency committees and monitoring cable traffic from abroad, the national security adviser has a more comprehensive knowledge of developing issues and impending crises than anyone in the departments and agencies. Interagency conflicts, common between the State and Defense Departments, make the national security adviser the only arbiter of disputes short of the president. Free of departmental loyalties, the adviser is well placed to claim primary commitment to the national interest and loyal service to the incumbent president. And with a staff of short-term, personally selected appointees, the adviser can move with greater dispatch and attentiveness to the president's short-term goals than can the State Department, with its experienced foreign service officers and civil servants and its long-term goals of foreign policy.

In addition, the national security adviser enjoys greater freedom of action than the secretary of state because, unlike the secretary, the NSC's head is appointed by the president without Senate confirmation and is normally not subject to reporting to or questioning by congressional committees. In 2013, UN Ambassador Susan Rice became President Barack Obama's national security advisor. Obama had nominated her to serve as secretary of state, but congressional criticism of her involvement in the administration's explanation of terrorist attacks on American diplomats in Benghazi, Libya, made Senate confirmation impossible. Obama instead appointed her to the NSC, which gave him an adviser he trusted without having to negotiate with Congress.

If these factors explain the NSC's rise in power, they do not guarantee its wisdom. In the eight years of the Reagan administration there were only two secretaries of state—the second of whom served over six years—but there were six national security advisers. Such turnover can weaken institutional memory. Indeed, Lt. Col. Oliver North, the major figure in covert operations involving the sale of arms to Iran in exchange for release of hostages (a violation of both a statutory ban on military assistance to Iran and a national policy against dealing with terrorists), found the changing top-level NSC leadership a major advantage in concealing his illegal activities. As North himself became part of the NSC's institutional memory, in the process, he became virtually indispensable.[45]

Proposed strategies for reining in the NSC's power are interlocking. One is to restrict the national security adviser's role to serving as an "honest broker," charged with inviting and coordinating the policy views of the relevant departments and agencies, summing up the areas of consensus and dissension, and presenting the president with the pros and cons of the options, together with indication of the positions of the departments and agencies. This honest broker role would reasonably extend to the monitoring of agencies' progress in implementing presidential decisions. This prescription of the honest broker role excludes direct engagement in operations and conforms to the classic definition of the role of presidential assistants.

A second remedy, consistent with the first, is to reestablish the secretary of state as the principal foreign policy official of the government. Some would do more, in effect substituting that official for the current national security adviser, with oversight of defense, intelligence, and international economics, as well as political affairs. A third proposal, consistent with both of these suggestions, is to shrink the size of the NSC staff, which some reformers hope would lead to greater reliance on the State Department's regional and functional specialists, whose responsibilities are now duplicated by NSC staff members. Finally, most critics of the current setup support the opinion that operational activities belong outside the White House, in the departments and agencies, accountable to Congress as well as to the president. Dissenters are likely to include the president and his entourage, who assume that the president's staff aides will move more speedily and loyally than the departments' "cumbersome" bureaucracies. In the end, it is difficult to separate the president from reliance on a close and trusted White House adviser who can always provide a final look at tough issues before the president makes a final policy decision. It is little surprise that, despite calls for change, presidents from both parties have insisted on a strong national security adviser whom they can trust for unfiltered foreign policy advice.

E-GOVERNMENT

The rise of desktop computers and the Internet in the 1990s led to a radically new approach to some of government's organizational problems. Government officials began recognizing that citizens did not necessarily need to come to government to transact public business. The spread of always-available electronic connections made it possible to build systems to allow citizens to file their taxes, renew their motor vehicle registrations, check on traffic congestion, obtain a police report, pay a traffic ticket, or apply for a job. In almost every government, citizens can connect electronically on a vast array of services.

The Internal Revenue Service (IRS), for example, has increasingly encouraged taxpayers to file their taxes electronically. More than 100 million taxpayers filed online in 2012. The IRS saved money by avoiding the costs of printing, mailing, and then processing millions of paper returns. Electronically filed returns did not have to be hand-keyed into the IRS computer system, and they even proved more accurate than the paper filings, since private-market computer programs such as TurboTax and TaxCut had already double-checked the figures. Taxpayers received their refunds far more quickly, often in just two weeks, by electronic deposits made directly to their bank accounts. In Phoenix, Arizona, citizens can conduct a wide range of transactions with the government without having to leave their keyboards. They can get permits and pay taxes and fines. They can sign up for classes on irrigation and landscaping, get a parking permit or buy surplus city equipment, view city maps, or watch the city's online television channel, all at http://phoenix.gov/eservices. The array of e-government services has vastly expanded since the early 1990s, and it's now universal.

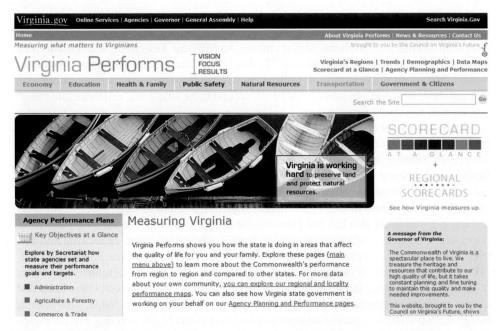

Online services have transformed the way governments communicate with their citizens, and have led to fundamental efforts to measure and report government performance.

The growth of e-government, as the movement is known, has rapidly transformed the operations of many governmental services and has changed the way government connects with citizens.[46] President Obama developed more than 30 million Twitter followers. Newark Mayor Cory Booker had 1.3 million followers and became famous for Tweeting from the cabs of snowplows as workers helped the city recover from storms.

E-government has raised several important implications. First, it has tremendous potential for improving government's performance. It allows government to deliver services on citizens' own schedules, allowing them to determine when they want to conduct transactions. Instead of visiting the motor vehicles or the tax office, citizens can often conduct transactions online. That can make their lives easier—and save the government money. The U.S. Customs and Border Protection agency developed a new series of "trusted traveler" programs, including the Global Entry program that allows air travelers to be screened in advance and then bypass long immigration lines when reentering the country, just by scanning their passport and fingerprints at a handy kiosk.

Second, e-government can enhance the ability of citizens to connect more easily with government. Web portals such as the federal government's USA.gov and the Commonwealth of Virginia's Virginia.gov allow citizens to think in terms of the services they want to access, without necessarily having to determine in advance which government agency provides them. For example, it often takes some time to figure out that in order to obtain a passport one needs to obtain a photograph from a private photographer, visit a post office (run by the U.S. Postal Service), and submit a passport application to the U.S. State Department. On USA.gov, one can simply type in "passport" to find these instructions.

Third, the rise of e-government raises questions of access and equity. By 2012, nearly two-thirds of Americans had high-speed Internet access in their homes, and almost half of all Americans owned a smartphone. Senior citizens, less affluent Americans, and less educated citizens tended to use the Internet less.[47] Technological barriers are falling, but inequities remain. Moreover, the explosion of technology has created new splits, between those who text and those who don't, those who use Facebook and those who don't, and those lured most quickly into new social networks.

Fourth, the advent of e-government also raises significant organizational questions. Freed from dependence on traditional government bureaucracies, e-government can operate in a loose, even invisible network, which offers the chance for creating new virtual strategies for linking governmental organizations. Such technology is unlikely to solve government's eternal coordination problems, but it does offer new strategies and tactics for doing so. However, in attacking the problem through information systems instead of through bureaucratic hierarchies, e-government also has the potential for radically altering the existing patterns of bureaucratic behavior, authority, and power. It raises serious questions of security and privacy, to ensure that sensitive information is kept safe. Moreover, as Jane E. Fountain suggested, the e-government movement "may allow bureaucrats less opportunity to use their accumulated experience and judgment, or tacit knowledge, to consider exceptional cases that do not conform to standardized rule-based systems." Indeed, she concluded, "The state is being reconstructed as organizational actors enact new technologies to reshape relationships in the state and the economy."[48] Public officials have sometimes found themselves surprised by issues that bubble up in blogs, and they sometimes have had to scramble to deal with virtual issues that they never encountered through their traditional communication channels.

Given the tremendous changes in information technology over the past half-generation, it is hard to guess where the next generation will take us. Although, as one study concluded, "E-gov is not yet the 'killer app' among the available tools to contact government,"[49] it is clear that it will continue to develop, with government agencies developing strategies for new applications and other real-time links between citizens and their governments. These technological changes will present deep and fundamental questions for the operation of government—and for the future of democracy.

CONCLUSION

Formal organization is about creating effective strategies for coordinating complex systems. The goal has long been to ensure continuity between policymaking and administration, but the best path is anything but clear. It is impossible to manage complex work without breaking it down into its component parts and then building strong competence in bureaus to carry it out. But any division of complex jobs into bureaus risks creating overlaps for some problems and gaps through which others may fall. Coordination is essential for administration, and organization is perhaps the most basic tool for achieving it. No matter how hard they try, however, government officials can never fully solve the coordination problem, and their efforts to solve some parts of the problem can sometimes create new and unexpected issues. The search for the solution to coordination problems is never-ending, with e-government and web-based technology offering hard-to-predict new opportunities.

This fundamental dilemma of administration points to two other problems. One that afflicts the whole executive branch is the interconnectedness, in the end, of all problems, which means that to solve any of them, top officials need to break the problems down into manageable parts. Top officials then face the challenge of developing enough expertise in their agencies without having the process break down into insulated units that don't talk to each other. The other is the distinction between those who carry out government's work—"line" officials—and those who provide advice—"staff" officials. Staff officials rarely want to stop at giving advice, but top officials don't want to simply follow the counsel of their line managers without careful checking by the staff. These are deep and enduring issues, and we turn to them in the next chapter.

CASE 5.1

The Boston Marathon Bombing: Effective Coordinated Response

In the week between the tragic bombing at the Boston Marathon and the surviving suspect's arraignment in his hospital room, we saw how far homeland security has come since the September 11 terrorist attacks. The message is overwhelmingly good.

We saw tremendous bravery in the moments after the bombs exploded, as citizens and first responders raced toward the victims without regard to whether more bombs were primed to explode. Civilians applied tourniquets to prevent some of the wounded from bleeding to death. The field station, originally set up to treat chilled, dehydrated runners, quickly became a triage station. The city's network of ambulances, police and hospitals responded magnificently, in large part because they had practiced over the years for just such a day.

In the immediate aftermath of the blasts, we learned again the fundamental lessons: all homeland security events are local, beginning with local consequences that require local officials to respond. We learned that effective response depends on robust relationships among people who have learned to work together before events

happen. And we learned that skilled, problem-focused improvisation can fill in the gaps.

Moreover, we've also learned again that good homeland security is intergovernmental, interagency, intersectoral—and enlists ordinary Americans. While the FBI managed the scene, it was a regional Massachusetts Bay Transportation Authority SWAT team that took the suspect down. The first photos of the captured suspect showed federal tactical officers wearing FBI and ATF gear. And don't forget, during the manhunt for the suspect, it was a citizen who found him hiding in a boat. Citizens often worked the front lines, making "Boston Strong" more than a T-shirt message and demonstrating that "if you see something, say something" is far more than a cliché.

The very same week of the alleged bomber's arraignment, the opening of the George W. Bush Presidential Center recalled these same balance-of-responsibility questions. In the center's Decision Points Theater, visitors are asked to relive one of four big moments from the Bush presidency. Listening to briefings from former White House chiefs of staff, participants are immersed in the events as they unfold. In the case of Hurricane Katrina, for example, they're asked what should President Bush do—deploy federal troops or rely on local forces?

The contrast between Boston's lessons and the theater's questions could not be bigger. The Bush administration's initial response to Katrina was anything but successful, with citizens stuck at the Superdome and political support crumbling. During Katrina, the questions about who was in charge and whether to deploy federal troops or rely on local forces preoccupied the Bush White House. In Boston, we learned yet again that this is precisely the wrong question. We've been crippled most when we battle over who's in charge; we succeed best when we send out the best we have to those who need it most.

This is what retired Coast Guard Admiral Thad Allen calls "unity of effort" instead of "unity of command." After the battle between New Orleans, Baton Rouge, and Washington hamstrung the government's Katrina response and cost FEMA Director Michael Brown his job, President Bush sent in Allen. The no-nonsense admiral pushed the bureaucratic squabbling aside, figured out who had which assets to solve which problems, and promised everyone on the front lines that he had their backs. In remarkably short order, Katrina moved from a monument of government failure to a model of effective response.

In Boston, unity of effort drove success in the federal-state-local-private-public-nonprofit-civilian response, just as it eventually did after Katrina when Allen took the helm. The badges on the uniforms didn't matter as much as the capacity to get the job done. And the job got done.

The prevention side remains a huge challenge, and stories continue to trickle out of dots unconnected among federal agencies. But on the response side, we've come light years since the painful days of the 2001 terrorist attacks and the 2005 hurricane. It's heartening to see that we know how to learn, and that we've been able to apply winning strategies to tragedies like Superstorm Sandy and the Boston Marathon bombing.

The Bush Presidential Center poses the big and irresistible "who's in charge" question. The remarkably brave response in Boston shows us why this is the wrong question. Effective response begins with a strong, integrated, practiced-in-advance local response coupled with a nimble problem-solving ability.

More fundamentally, we've learned again that our really important challenges are too big for any one agency, any one level of government, or even government itself to try to control. Someone has to be in charge to make sure that coordination happens. But the job of the field commander isn't barking orders; it's identifying the assets that are needed, who has them, and how to get them to where they're needed. In the end, what works is focusing more on solving that problem than solving who's in charge.

Questions to Consider

1. Consider the questions posed to visitors to the Bush presidential library. What would *you* do in the midst of a crisis like Katrina or the Boston Marathon bombing: deploy federal troops or rely on local agencies?

2. Now step back. Are these cases so different that comparisons make little sense? If so, how would you sort out the question of who ought to respond to which problems? If you think they are alike enough to make comparisons, how would you draw lessons?

3. What lessons do these large-scale events have for organizational theory and effective government operations?

Note: This case comes from my column in *Governing* (June 2013), http://www.governing.com/columns/potomac-chronicle/col-boston-bombing-highlights-homeland-security-done-right.html.

CASE 5.2

Which Way for Cheese? Conflicting Policies at the U.S. Department of Agriculture

Not long ago, Domino's pizza chain was in trouble. Sales were down and even the company's advertisements acknowledged it was not making a very good pizza. But Dairy Management, a nonprofit trade association, came riding to the rescue, with pizza design help and $12 million for a new marketing campaign. The result was a new pizza with 40 percent more cheese, and people loved it. Sales soared and the company began to climb out of the fast-food cellar.

Dairy Management also helped Taco Bell invent a new steak quesadilla, which mixed together pepper jack, mozzarella, and cheddar cheeses, along with a creamy sauce. People loved it, in part because it had eight times more cheese than most other items on the Taco Bell menu.

Dairy Management has become a huge player in the food business.[1] Americans eat an average of 33 pounds of cheese each year, and Dairy Management aims to increase that total. With its $140 million annual budget, it has worked with Pizza Hut to develop its Cheesy Bites pizza, with Wendy's on the Double Melt sandwich, and with Burger King on the Angus Bacon cheeseburger. The organization's goal is to convince Americans to eat more cheese—and to expand the market for cheese producers. In 2007, its efforts increased cheese sales of almost 30 million pounds, and cheese producers love it.[2] The association has been tremendously successful in bringing more cheese to restaurant menus and into supermarkets, and it was behind the wildly successful "Got Milk?" campaign.

Dairy farmers contribute to a fund to help promote the consumption of dairy products. The U.S. Department of Agriculture (USDA) collects the funds and disburses them under a program created by Congress.[3] The program is self-funded, but USDA oversees its operations to ensure the activities are consistent with the law that created the nonprofit corporation designed to encourage dairy production. In addition, USDA regularly reports on its operations to Congress.[4] Is it a governmental organization? No. Is it connected to the federal government? Yes, through the collection and distribution of money and through policy oversight.

In other parts of its operation, USDA is working hard to encourage Americans to make so-called healthier food choices. It's easy to blast past government-recommended levels of saturated fat consumption with a couple of slices of Domino's pizza. USDA's Nutrition.gov program is making an aggressive effort to encourage Americans to reduce their consumption of fatty foods, especially saturated fats. It points out that "a healthy eating plan is one that:

- Emphasizes fruits, vegetables, whole grains, and fat-free or low-fat milk and milk products.
- Includes lean meats, poultry, fish, beans, eggs, and nuts.
- Is low in saturated fats, trans fats, cholesterol, salt (sodium), and added sugars."[5]

First lady Michelle Obama added her own voice to the healthy eating campaign. She told the American Restaurant Association that "One local survey found that 90 percent of those menus includes mac and cheese—our children's favorite; 80 percent includes chicken fingers; 60 includes burgers or cheeseburgers." It's important, she said, to "make a commitment to promote vegetables and fruits and whole grains on every part of every menu. We can make portion sizes smaller and emphasize quality over quantity. And we can help create a culture—imagine this—where our kids ask for healthy options instead of resisting them." She concluded by saying, "I hope that each of you will do your part to give our kids the future that we all know they deserve."[6]

Questions to Consider

1. What do you make of these contradictory policies within a single federal department: one which encourages the consumption of dairy products and another which urges their consumption in moderation?
2. Do you think it makes a difference that the USDA's role in the Dairy Management association is indirect?
3. If you were the leader of USDA, would you have an obligation to reconcile these competing

programs? Or would you view it as an inevitable product of the political battles within American pluralism?

NOTES

1. See Dairy Management Inc's website, http://www.dairyinfo.com.
2. Michael Moss, "While Warning about Fat, U.S. Pushes Cheese Sales," *New York Times,* November 6, 2010, http://www.nytimes.com/2010/11/07/us/07fat.html.
3. See Dairy Today Editors, "Dairy Management, Inc. Answers New York Times Allegations," November 15, 2010, http://www.agweb.com/article/dairy_management_inc._answers_new_york_times_allegations.
4. See *Report to Congress on the National Dairy Promotion and Research Program and the National Fluid Milk Processor Promotion Program* (July 1, 2002), http://www.ams.usda.gov/AMSv1.0/getfile?dDocName=STELDEV3099963.
5. See "Finding Your Way to a Healthier You: Based on the Dietary Guidelines for Americans," http://health.gov/dietaryguidelines/dga2005/document/html/brochure.htm.
6. Michelle Obama, "Remarks by the First Lady in Address to the National Restaurant Association Meeting" (September 13, 2010), http://www.whitehouse.gov/the-press-office/2010/09/13/remarks-first-lady-address-national-restaurant-association-meeting.

CASE 5.3

Partly Cloudy? Wyoming Moves to Google Apps for Government

In October 2010, the state of Wyoming announced it was moving all 10,000 of its employees to Google Apps for Government (http://gov.googleapps.com). The result, Google proudly announced, would save the state $1 million per year and bring all state employees, for the first time, to a common electronic platform. "We welcome Wyoming to the cloud," Google said.[1]

It's always good, of course, to save a lot of money. But what is "the cloud"? In one respect, it's simply another name for the Internet. More

broadly, it's a way of separating the details of computer systems from users—software providers create easy interactions with the key programs that users need, and then manage the back-end Internet systems in ways that are transparent (and therefore unimportant) to users. Web browsers provide the key point of connection to the world. Software and data are stored on servers. Computer analysts have long used cloud-like drawings to depict these connections, and "the cloud" has come to capture the broad approach of web-based computing.

For Google, it was one of a series of agreements it had negotiated with government agencies. Los Angeles and Orlando had both signed up with Google. So did government departments in Colorado, Kansas, and New Mexico. But its mega-competitor, Microsoft, was scarcely standing still. New York City signed a deal to bring 100,000 of its employees to Microsoft's cloud applications. The city built this arrangement into a much broader effort, nicknamed SimpliCity, to streamline the city's work and improve its service to citizens. In its previous system, the city managed forty different software licenses and even more maintenance and support packages. The cloud approach, city officials believed, would allow city officials to collaborate more easily across a single software platform.[2] In addition, New York Mayor Michael Bloomberg and Microsoft CEO Steve Ballmer also agreed that the city would host Microsoft's Imagine Cup 2011 worldwide finals, a global competition bringing high school and college students together to solve problems through technology. As Stephen Goldsmith, New York's deputy mayor for operations, explained, "We took advantage of the competitive moment," in an arrangement that would save $50 million in the next five years.[3]

3. Since the cloud relies on the Internet, the servers provide services that could be located anywhere. For example, some of the leading cloud computing companies are working to expand their operations to China. If you were a government information technology manager, would you be concerned about basing your mission on technologies that rely heavily on elements that aren't transparent to you? Would you use different strategies for different parts of your mission—perhaps maintaining the most confidential work on your own servers and relying on the cloud for the rest of your work—or would you worry that such a divided strategy might compromise the efficiencies you are seeking?

4. Many state and local governments have encountered serious difficulty in managing their information technology resources in recent years. The reason, most often, is that governments have not had sufficient expertise in-house to assess the claims and promises that private companies made. If you were a government official charged with making these decisions, what steps would you take to make sure that you were in the best position to make the best decisions for your government and for the citizens it serves?

Questions to Consider

1. As technology creates new opportunities, how do you think that government can—and should—use technology to increase its efficiency and provide better service to its citizens?

2. Do you think that competition between private companies, such as Google and Microsoft, enhances government's ability to get a good deal? How might this case have worked differently if either Google or Microsoft had been in the game as the sole provider?

NOTES

1. See "Wyoming Is Going Google," October 27, 2010, http://googleenterprise.blogspot.com/2010/10/wyoming-is-going-google.html.
2. See "Mayor Bloomberg Welcomes Students to the First Day of School at Gregorino Luperón High School for Science and Mathematics," http://www.nyc.gov/portal/site/nycgov/menuitem.c0935b9a57bb4ef3daf2f1c789a0/index.jsp?pageID=mayor_press_release&catID=1194&doc_name=http%3A5 2F%2Fwww.nyc.gov%2Fhtml%2Fom%2Fhtml%2F20 10b%2Fpr439-10.html&cc=unused1978&rc=1194&ndi=1.
3. Keven McCaney, "NYC Gets Citywide Deal for Microsoft Cloud," *Microsoft Certified Professional Magazine* (October 20, 2010), http://mcpmag.com/articles/2010/10/21/nyc-gets-citywide-deal-for-microsoft-cloud-apps.aspx.

KEY CONCEPTS

FOR FURTHER READING

Arnold, Peri E. *Making the Managerial Presidency: Comprehensive Reorganization Planning, 1905–1980*. Princeton, N.J.: Princeton University Press, 1986.

Campbell, Colin. *Managing the Presidency: Carter, Reagan, and the Search for Executive Harmony*. Pittsburgh: University of Pittsburgh Press, 1986.

Fesler, James W. *Area and Administration*. Tuscaloosa: University of Alabama Press, 2008.

Fountain, Jane E. *Building the Virtual State: Information Technology and Institutional Change*. Washington, D.C.: Brookings Institution, 2001.

Heclo, Hugh. *A Government of Strangers: Executive Politics in Washington*. Washington, D.C.: Brookings Institution, 1977.

Hess, Stephen, and James Pfiffner. *Organizing the Presidency*. Washington, D.C.: Brookings Institution, 2003.

Nathan, Richard P. *The Administrative Presidency*. New York: Wiley, 1983.

Perri 6. *E-Governance: Styles of Political Judgment in the Information Age Polity*. New York: Palgrave, 2004.

Seidman, Harold. *Politics, Position, and Power: The Dynamics of Federal Organization*. 5th ed. New York: Oxford University Press, 1998.

SUGGESTED WEBSITES

The National Academy of Public Administration conducts excellent research on the management of the executive branch and of management problems within individual agencies, making its reports available on its website, **www.napawash.org**. In addition, the Government Accountability Office, **www.gao. gov,** is an invaluable source for analysis of both management and policy issues.

For information about employment trends in the federal government, see the Office of Personnel Management's Federal Employment Statistics webpage, **www.opm.gov/feddata**.

There is an enormous amount of information about e-government available on the web. An excellent foundation for exploring the federal government's websites is the federal portal **www .usa.gov**. Most state and local governments have webpages and portals as well; among the very good ones are those for the Commonwealth of Virginia, **www.virginia.gov,** and for the city of Phoenix, **http://phoenix.gov**.

CHAPTER

6

CHAPTER OBJECTIVES

- Understand the sources of organizational performance problems

- Examine the strategies to improve coordination

- Chart the advantages and disadvantages of structural reorganization to solve organizational problems

Organization Problems

The response of emergency workers in the aftermath of the Boston Marathon bombing in 2013 proved remarkably effective. A massive manhunt, involving federal, state, and local law enforcement officials, tracked down the two bombers within days of the explosion.

IF THERE'S ANYTHING THAT MOST PEOPLE THINK THEY know about public administration, it's that it just doesn't work well. News reports are full of tales ranging from overpayment for military equipment to excessive delays in responding to fire calls. *Fortune* began a story about city government by saying they "aren't exactly known for innovation. 'Get in line,' 'fill out this form' and 'you need a permit' are the bureaucracy's invariable responses to virtually any question."[1] Cynicism reigns.

In truth, most governmental programs work well most of the time. But Americans are never far from their revolutionary roots, and because their expectations about government are often very (sometimes impossibly) high, anything short of exceptional performance tends to disappoint. Tales of waste, fraud, and abuse only feed the worst fears of angry taxpayers. A sure-fire staple of television newsmagazines is the "can you believe your government did this?" story. There's rarely a story that says "emergency responders risked lives to save citizens."

Of course, private-sector organizations are scarcely immune to waste. The U.S. Environmental Protection Agency, for example, estimates that Americans dispose of 35 million tons of food every year.[2] Behind every business is a collection of tales of mistakes, failed products, and miscalculations. Three U.S. airlines shut down in just one week in 2008: Skybus, ATA, and Aloha Airlines. Several large banks collapsed in the 2008–2009 economic meltdown, and one of the world's proudest, oldest, and largest investment banks, Lehman Brothers, disappeared almost overnight. Smaller miscalculations are simply buried in corporate balance sheets. Success comes to corporations that solve problems and make money. Those that don't go under. In government, however, public administrators don't have the choice of going out of business—their missions exist by law, and the law requires them to administer their programs. The public expects high performance as a matter of routine, and government often ends up with jobs that the private sector will not or cannot do. Problems—and complaints—about how government handles those chores are inevitable, and those problems end up spilled across the headlines for everyone to see.

Many organizational problems have their roots in politics because, as Jack Knott and Gary Miller point out, the very choice of organizational structure itself "is inherently political; we must ask 'who gets what?' from any institutional arrangement."[3] Politics and performance become intertwined in charting what agencies do, how they do it, and how they might work better. These basic puzzles, as Herbert Kaufman recognized in a classic 1956 article, have long revolved around three basic organizational values: **neutral competence, executive leadership,** and **representativeness.**[4] The quest for *neutral competence* calls for the creation of a highly skilled bureaucracy insulated from the political interference that can undermine efficiency. This does not mean that bureaucracy is politically unaccountable or unresponsive, but it does mean that organizational designers must minimize political meddling in issues that deal with the technical parts of administration. The quest for *executive leadership* calls for a strong elected executive—president, governor, mayor—and strong and loyal department heads, all politically chosen. It also calls for a strong hierarchy that ensures the responsiveness of organizational units to the elected executive's policy priorities. The quest for *representativeness* calls for organizational arrangements that respond to legislative interests and to the clienteles most affected by agency decisions.

In American government, we have long professed strong allegiance to each of these values; we seek them all, simultaneously and enthusiastically. But because they obviously conflict, we never quite get from bureaucracy what we want because it can never simultaneously deliver all the contradictory things we ask of it. That, in turn, brings a constant instinct to tinker and reform. Sometimes we do find a better solution, but often we simply substitute one set of values for another. One reform then sets the stage for the next round of political complaint and administrative reform.

THE SEARCH FOR EFFECTIVE ORGANIZATION

Why, despite eternal calls for better administration, do organizational problems recur? Consider the ongoing problem of coordinating emergency response in New York City. In 1988 the New York City police and fire commissioners nearly came to blows in the mayor's presence because of their departments' long rivalry over the handling of emergencies and rescues. In one case, the police blocked fire department scuba divers from joining the search for survivors of a helicopter crash in a river. The police were jealously guarding an image as saviors, not just arresters. The city's firefighters, underemployed by a decade's 40 percent decrease in fires and fearing a loss of jobs, were seeking emergency responsibilities comparable to those of other cities' fire departments and, with time on their hands, promising a faster response to emergencies than that supplied by the police department. It took a detailed peace treaty in 1990, negotiated between commissioners appointed by a new mayor, to bring a peace.[5]

That treaty did not solve the basic problem, however. On the morning of September 11, 2001, the NYPD's helicopter hovering above the World Trade Center towers had a better perspective on the buildings' condition than did the rescuers below, but the police helicopter crew had no way of telling firefighters that the towers were about to collapse. Meanwhile, fire commanders in the lobbies of the two buildings often lost radio and telephone contact with their firefighters in the upper floors. These communication problems, both technical and bureaucratic, had tragic consequences.[6] In the aftermath of the buildings' collapse, everyone promised that the problems would never recur, but years after the terrorist attacks the two departments continued to tussle over who would be in charge of the new integrated command centers. Fire officials explained that they could not risk a command structure that put their forces under the control of other officials who did not really understand firefighting; police officials said the same thing. Each side had a point, but even high-level peace treaties failed to resolve the underlying conflict.

After an explosion rocked 119th Street in New York's Harlem neighborhood in 2007, police, fire, and other emergency officials worked to coordinate their response.

Administrators often find it reassuring to learn that the big issues with which they are struggling are new versions of very old problems. It can sometimes help to know that there are often no easy, good, or lasting solutions. Most often, the problems are new versions of the eternal search for better **coordination**. As is so often the case, the instinct to build strong functional competence creates barriers to coordination across organizational boundaries. That, in turn, often makes elected officials and policy analysts very cynical. Unresolvable problems invite criticism, and their unresolvability invites political interference. Why insist on neutral competence if that seems to produce incompetence? American government tends to sort out these issues through four general approaches: (1) the choice among criteria of good organization, (2) interagency conflict, (3) interagency coordination, and (4) the role of staff in supporting and controlling operating activities.

Organizational Criteria

From the building blocks of organizational theory comes a handy checklist for assessing what makes for a good organization, as a federal task force concluded. The points are ageless; the checklist comes from a 1974 report:

- *Public acceptance:* the amount of trust the public places in the integrity, fairness, and judiciousness of the information and decisions a system generates
- *Adaptability:* the ability of a system to react quickly and positively to changes in (a) technology, (b) major public policies, (c) international developments, (d) state-federal relationships, and (e) economic conditions
- *Consistency of decisions:* the degree to which a system promotes consistent policy decisions
- *Professional competence:* the degree to which a system makes it easy to recruit high-caliber professionals and makes effective use of their talents
- *Participation, representation, and diversity:* the degree to which a system provides for diverse public inputs to governmental decision making
- *Effective database:* the capacity of the system to generate, verify, and use reliable and complete information
- *Cost and timeliness:* the reasonableness of the expense and time required by a system to yield decisions
- *Promotion of private efficiency:* the extent to which a system avoids unintended pressures on private decision makers in their choices of technology, markets . . . , and other decisions
- *Accountability to the president:* the extent to which a system provides clear lines of executive authority
- *Accountability to Congress:* the extent to which a system provides clear data for congressional review and clear charters of responsibility for carrying out congressional mandates
- *Compatibility with state regulation:* the extent to which a system . . . fosters effective state-federal relationships[7]

Most important, the task force concluded,

> Each criterion is important, but all cannot be satisfied at the same time. For example, it is unlikely that a system that yields the fastest decision and also entails the least administrative cost would rank among the best systems with respect to public credibility or public participation. In short, the design of any [organizational] system requires compromises and tradeoffs among desirable attributes.[8]

There is no formula to guide these tradeoffs, so the inevitable battles often prove very frustrating. But it would be foolish to abandon the quest for better answers because no answer works perfectly. Critics often want government to behave more like the private sector, but government often works with different problems, its leaders rarely have the control that private executives have, and private executives rarely have to work within the political constraints facing public executives. That makes resolving interagency conflict a top priority.

Interagency Conflict

The very choice of organizational structure for one agency often creates the foundations for conflict with others. Spotless windows were a rarity in Queen Victoria's nineteenth-century English palace, because their outside cleaning was under the control of the Woods and Forests department, their inside cleaning was the responsibility of the Lord Chamberlain's department, and the work schedules of the two departments often did not match.[9] The queen rarely could view her kingdom through clean windows. Connecting the dots isn't a new problem.

The standard approach for solving coordination problems is to ask the official at the next step above the dispute to work out a solution. The more coordination problems there are, however, the heavier the burden on higher officials. No one wants two different agencies to waste resources doing the same thing—or to risk having important problems fall through the cracks between two agencies, who each assume the other will deal with the problem. Coordination is a basic goal of complex organizations; making it happen is a basic problem. Coordination problems sometimes arise from a mismatch of organizational strategies. Classical organization theory suggests four different strategies: organization by purpose, process, clientele, and place. Agencies organized by one strategy can encounter coordination problems with agencies organized by another. In addition, there are often conflicts among organizations organized by function, when several agencies believe they each are primarily responsible for the same issue.

Purpose versus Clientele

The Department of Health and Human Services (HHS) is a purpose-based organization, and it serves the general population through welfare programs, health research and health system financing, and food and drug regulation, among other functions. The Department of Veterans Affairs and the Interior Department's Bureau of Indian Affairs (BIA) are clientele-based. These single-clientele agencies perform or arrange for many services for their special groups that HHS would otherwise provide for them under its general, national programs. The Department of Veterans Affairs, for example, runs the nation's single largest health and hospital care system, while BIA has its own health clinics—and each operates independently of other health agencies organized by function at the federal, state, and local levels.

The different focus on purpose versus clientele inevitably creates tensions. HHS cannot claim to speak for a truly national health or welfare policy, nor can it assert coordinative authority to ensure equity and consistency in policy execution. Many of the horror stories of administration—two or three agencies building hospitals in a locality that needs only one, agents of the purpose-based Federal Bureau of Investigation (FBI) being killed while serving warrants on an Indian reservation that is under the jurisdiction of the clientele-based BIA—are results of the crisscrossing of jurisdictions of purpose-based agencies and clientele-based agencies.

A reverse situation occurs when a clientele-based agency embraces inconsistent or even contradictory purposes. Many industry-based agencies seek both to promote and to regulate the industry they are assigned to monitor. For instance, the federal agencies regulating both atomic energy and mines tended to emphasize promotion over control in their respective spheres. Congress feared that the Atomic Energy Commission was neglecting protection of the public health and safety, so it moved that function to a new Nuclear Regulatory Commission and placed nuclear energy promotion in the new Department of Energy. The goal of the Interior Department's Bureau of Mines was "to stimulate private industry to produce a substantial share of the nation's mineral needs in ways that best protect the public interest,"[10] but it also was the agency charged with protection of the health and safety of coal miners through mine inspections and enforcement actions. Mine disasters and the resulting public outcry led Congress to transfer the protective function from the Interior Department to a new Mine Safety and Health Administration in the Department of Labor.

In both the nuclear energy case and the coal mining case, a single agency has faced incompatible tasks of fostering an industry while constraining it through health and safety standards. Similarly, state officials have often been criticized for trying both to control and to promote gambling out of a single agency. State environment and parks agencies regularly find themselves caught up in battles between anglers and hunters, who want easy access to the best sporting spots, and environmentalists, who seek to protect scenic parks from snowmobilers and all-wheel-drive vehicles.

Function versus Area

Other conflicts often grow up within departments. Many departments, from local public works agencies to the federal Forest Service, are organized by both function and area. The State Department, for example, manages the nation's foreign policy, and its traditional internal organization is by region and country. But alongside the place-based offices are functional bureaus focused on politico-military affairs (e.g., arms control), human rights and humanitarian affairs, environmental and scientific affairs, economic and business affairs, refugee programs, and international organizations. No functional issue, whether managing the oceans or aiding refugees, stops at any nation's border. However, it is usually difficult to get action on any functional problem without dealing with individual nations, and that requires the department's traditional country-based structure. One of the secretary of state's most difficult internal management jobs is setting the ongoing balance between these conflicting—and inevitable—approaches.

Chapter 5 pointed out that, in contrast to some other countries, the U.S. government has no prefectoral, area-based officials to coordinate the field activities of the various departments and agencies within each of the country's regions. Each functional department has field offices, but coordination among the field offices of different departments in the same region occurs irregularly, at best. For decades, presidents have tried different approaches to this coordination problem, from creating uniform regions to establishing super-regions where high-level officials would have the power to pull related agencies together. The individual departments, not surprisingly, have always resisted the more aggressive efforts. Coordination of federal programs, always difficult in Washington, is often a tougher problem where agency officials face the job of managing programs.

Conflicts among Purpose-Based Agencies

Of course, conflicts also occur among purpose-based departments. The names of departments commonly identify a general field of activity; they do not necessarily convey a sharp sense of purpose. The nation's oldest federal departments—State, Treasury, Defense, and Justice—all have fuzzy missions that have evolved radically since these departments were first created. New issues emerge constantly, from the pressures of the Cold War following World War II, the fall of the Soviet Union, pressures on the dollar along with inflation, the rise of the European Union, and the sudden intrusion of terrorism on American soil. These departments, and many others, have worked to adapt their mission and their work, often with little structural change to match the shifting purposes.

Rather than clear and constant purposes, departments focus on core activities that define the issues that they—as well as their leaders and most important constituencies—pay the most attention to. They do not have clear, constant purposes or firm jurisdictional boundaries. Rather, they tend to focus on general fields of activity.[11] That's one reason why border warfare among departments is so common, because the boundaries cannot be precise. Policymakers are eternally tempted to solve these problems by overhauling organizational structure. Such reorganization can remap the terrain, but it can never put an end to border wars. For the agencies involved, jurisdictional boundaries remain crucial.

For example, the commission investigating the September 11, 2001, attacks found substantial problems in the sharing of information among the nation's intelligence agencies. Indeed, some observers speculated that the attacks might have been prevented if the government had made better use of the information it had collected before the attacks. (Of course, the attacks were on a scale that most officials had not imagined, and the real meaning of much of that information became clear only in hindsight. Indeed, that is why the 9/11 Commission ascribed a large part of the problem to a "failure of imagination.") To reduce the likelihood of future attacks, Congress insisted on creating a new Department of Homeland Security that would answer the constant call to devise a better way of connecting the dots among any pieces of information that might be collected. When the new department emerged from Congress, however, it did not include any of the nation's key intelligence bureaus: the Central Intelligence Agency, the National Security Agency, the Defense Intelligence Agency, or the FBI. Each of them had waged a fierce behind-the-scenes battle to retain its independence—contending that it had critical core activities that would be compromised through a merger—and each one had emerged victorious. So the department that had been prompted by the urgent need to connect the dots ended up leaving most of the dots where they were, with only relatively weak new interagency councils to strengthen information sharing among them.

from the Headlines...

POLITICS

Taking Care of Salmon

In his 2011 State of the Union Address, President Obama posed a challenge. Should the federal government reorganize to better look after salmon? One plan that surfaced was merging the National Marine Fisheries Service into the Fish and Wildlife Service. One agency for all fish—what better way to care for them and to ensure good implementation of important policies like the Endangered Species Act? In addition, with just one agency, officials wouldn't have to spend as much time coordinating the federal government's activities for fish.

What's not to like about a streamlined government, at least when it comes to fish? A study by the Government Accountability Office found that many members of the fish-protection interest groups were worried that consolidating fish policy into the Interior Department would result in a heavier emphasis on conservation policies, and less on the role of fish as an industry. Other observers believed that merging the two agencies wouldn't make much difference, either for the fish or for government efficiency. After GAO's many interviews it concluded, "Overall, officials and stakeholders generally said that the drawbacks of reorganizing the agencies outweigh the benefits." So despite Obama's joke about the salmon and a careful study of the issue, nothing changed.

Some critics suggest that government organizations are immortal, because there are so many entrenched interests that it's impossible to make fundamental changes. Others suggest that the current structure exists for a good reason—it tends to represent the best balance of power in getting things done. Is there really any hope of improving the structure of government with so many political stakeholders at play?

Source: U.S. General Accounting Office, *Government Reorganization: Potential Benefits and Drawbacks of Merging the National Marine Fisheries Service into the Fish and Wildlife Service* (February 2013), http://www.gao.gov/assets/660/652207.pdf.

Interagency Coordination

Conflict among agencies is inevitable. Conflict can undermine coordination, yet coordination is the core of administration. Executives therefore resort to a variety of methods to manage and moderate conflict among agencies.

Coordination is a *horizontal* activity: it seeks to draw related agencies together in common purpose. But because no agency willingly surrenders control over its core activities to another, coordination rarely happens naturally or easily. Coordination requires a coordinator—it rarely happens spontaneously—and that requires a *vertical* activity. So to further complicate the problem, the horizontal and vertical dimensions themselves require coordination.

Horizontal Cooperation

Horizontal cooperation depends on the willingness of agencies to come to agreement with one another. Four methods stand out:

1. Thousands of **interagency agreements** ("treaties") have been negotiated between the concerned agencies to establish specific boundaries and, therefore, to clarify which agency will do what without interference from the other. Most local governments, for examples, have agreements on shared responses to emergency, including who provides which equipment for 911 emergency calls.
2. Hundreds of **interagency committees** at the cabinet, subcabinet, and bureau levels exist to promote collaboration in jointly occupied areas. Officials at all levels complain about spending so much time in meetings, but these meetings provide the foundations for much horizontal cooperation.
3. Under the **lead agency formula**, one agency is designated to lead and attempt to coordinate all other agencies' activities in a particular area. Ironically, even though the lead agency formula does not work well in the federal government, federal agencies often require state and local governments to create lead agencies as a condition of federal grant programs. Most emergency response systems now designate one agency to take the lead when problems develop. After the Boston Marathon bombings in 2013, for example, the FBI became the lead investigative agency.
4. A **clearance procedure** links agencies horizontally by requiring that an agency's proposed decisions in a subject-matter area be reviewed, whether for comment or for formal approval or veto, by other interested agencies.[12]

There is vast experience with these mechanisms. Sometimes, as in the case of the Boston bombings, they worked remarkably well. But often important issues are hard to solve and it's easy to duck the tough decisions.

Narcotics-control efforts illustrate the common situation when neither horizontal cooperation nor vertical coordination seems likely. With the efforts split among many agencies, the Reagan administration's principal recourse in its "war on drugs" was creating multiagency committees.[13] Congress, disenchanted with this weak response, provided in the Anti-Drug Abuse Act of 1988 a "czar" for coordination of narcotics-control efforts, and President George H. W. Bush appointed the first such officer.[14] But if largely voluntary cooperation was no answer, neither, apparently, is a major shift to vertical coordination through a high-level antidrug director. Such directive power as the czar has over bureaus concerned with narcotics conflicts with department heads' authority over the same bureaus. Most such bureaus—including the Customs Service, the Coast Guard, the FBI, the Immigration and Naturalization Service, and the Central Intelligence Agency—have core functions unrelated to narcotics control. Nonetheless, the czar idea is a popular one; it has been advanced, for example, as the cure for the bureaucratic fragmentation that has impeded response to the AIDS crisis.[15] When Congress and President George W. Bush concluded that the White House Office of Homeland Security was not powerful enough to ensure the coordination needed in the area of domestic security, they abandoned the czar approach in favor of a more traditional department, but this arrangement was challenged when the 9/11 Commission countered that a cabinet-level intelligence czar was needed to bring the nation's disparate foreign intelligence together into a coherent picture. Chief executives can't resist naming czars when big problems surface. In the Obama administration, there was a cascading supply of czars for the economy, energy, urban issues, and health care, among others.

Vertical Coordination

A principal function of hierarchy is to provide vertical coordination of units with shared interests. Backed by both authority and structure, vertical coordination is relatively strong when compared with the horizontal approach. The two patterns are very different: in the vertical coordination model, two warring agencies are brought together by the organizational superior of both, who has the formal authority to impose a decision and to monitor the agencies' compliance with it. Although their willingness to use authority may be limited by many influences, superiors have the strong motivation to ensure that the programs under their responsibility proceed effectively.

The vertical dimension involves much more than arbitrating jurisdictional controversies. Superiors constantly must be on guard to protect themselves—their time, energy, and political capital—against the eagerness of subordinates to push up the ladder tough decisions that they do not wish to make themselves. It can often be tempting for officials to pass along these "hot potato" issues, some of which may involve problems of coordination and some of which may hinge on sharp political conflicts. But superiors who allow their subordinates to shirk responsibility in this way can soon find themselves swamped by decisions that they do not need to make. That can make it harder for them to focus on the matters that truly do require their time, and it can make effective coordination more difficult by allowing decisions to rise up above the level at which the issues need to be resolved. If lower-level officials pass the buck instead of working through the problems they encounter, those problems often remain unresolved and the superiors become overwhelmed.

Because the horizontal and vertical dimensions of the hierarchy interact, an eternal question emerges: what is the best number of cabinet-level departments? In brief, how many subordinate units can a superior adequately supervise, a puzzle known as the span of control. If the number is very large, three things are predictable. First, border disputes would multiply beyond the chief executive's capacity to arbitrate. Second, individual department and agency heads' access to the chief executive would be curtailed. Third, cabinet and subcabinet committees would be too large for effective discussion and decision (or advice to the chief executive). If the number is very small, the chief executive can lose contact with front-line operations and can struggle to hold cabinet officials accountable. There are more choke points to block the flow of information up the chain, which creates more potential for distortion; there are also more points at which the flow of instructions down the chain can be drained of clarity and force. A small span of control can also produce delay, because transmission and consideration of messages through a long series of offices take longer than their passage through a short series.

The result is a search for a happy medium, which tends to settle to between ten and thirty.[16] A major exception is the New Zealand government's reforms in the 1980s, which swelled the number of departments to almost forty. However, critics soon began making precisely the point that so many departments hindered the coordination of the government's programs. In searching for the best span of control, we confront a tradeoff for which there is no simple, good solution.

The Role of Staff

So far in this section we have focused mainly on *operating* agencies. That is, we have dealt with people and units responsible for managing programs that directly serve or regulate the public. However, agencies also rely on other units to support their functions. The standard term for these support units is **staff activities**, compared with **line activities**, or operating activities. Of course, we often use the word **staff** to refer to all government employees. Strictly speaking, however, employees who manage the core functions of an agency are *line* officials. Those who support their work are *staff* officials.

There are, in fact, three different staff roles: **core staff**, which provides basic support to the agency's line activities; **auxiliary staff**, which provides a basic housekeeping function; and **control staff**, which helps top officials secure leverage over the organization. The first two roles facilitate operations, and because persons performing these activities assist in the organization's mission, classical theory prescribes that they should have no power to command the line officials. The third activity is quite different, for control necessarily imposes restraints on the freedom of line officials. This intersection of functions often creates deep conflict: staff activities can—and often do—conflict with line activities. We will return to that point shortly.

The Pure-Staff Role

Aides who work in the pure-staff role serve as the top manager's eyes, ears, and auxiliary brain. They assist the manager by originating ideas; gathering, screening, and appraising ideas from others; organizing information for decision making; and keeping track of how quickly relevant agencies execute decisions. In 1975 the Commission on Organization of the Government for the Conduct of Foreign Policy captured the staff function well by listing the appropriate tasks of the president's staff and then strictly defining the scope of the tasks:

- Identify issues likely to require presidential attention
- Structure those issues for efficient presidential understanding and decision—ensuring that the relevant facts are available, a full set of alternatives are presented, agency positions are placed in perspective
- Assure due process, permitting each interested department an opportunity to state its case
- Ensure that affected parties are clearly informed of decisions once taken, and that their own responsibilities respecting those decisions are specified
- Monitor the implementation of presidential decisions
- Assess the results of decisions taken, drawing from those assessments implications for future action

The defining characteristic of these tasks is that they embody staff responsibilities rather than line authority. They provide assistance to the president, not direction to department officials other than to convey presidential instructions. There should be only one official with line responsibility in the White House, and that is the president himself.[17]

All top officials need strong staff assistance. The more complex the organization's mission and structure, the more these officials need help in gathering information, interpreting details, anticipating issues, weighing decisions, and following the process of implementation.

The staff function is so important that it often becomes institutionalized in an organizational unit. For example, in addition to his immediate aides in the White House (the White House staff), the president has a number of staff agencies, all charged with informing, assisting, and advising the president. Department heads and bureau chiefs have not only "assistants to" themselves but also organizational units concerned with program analysis, planning, and research. At least at the departmental level, staff units abound, with such assignments as legislative affairs, international affairs, intergovernmental affairs, public affairs (media relations), civil rights and minority affairs, small business, and consumers. In some departments, all or most of the assistant secretaries have primarily staff roles cutting across the bureaus, instead of, as in other departments, being line officials, each supervising a group of bureaus. At the state and local levels, the pattern is precisely the same.

The Auxiliary Role

Organizations rely heavily on auxiliary activities to assist in accomplishing their mission. For example, most governments have central purchasing offices, building management offices, accounting offices, libraries, public affairs offices, and publications units. These jobs tend to be grouped together under the *administrative support* or housekeeping label. We often tend to ignore the importance of auxiliary staff support—until we try to obtain a job in the agency. Then the important role of the personnel staff becomes very, very clear.

The Control Role

In addition, organizations rely on control activities to monitor performance and enforce compliance with standards and procedures. Federal departments, for example, have inspectors general, who are given broad authority to investigate and report to the secretary and to Congress on suspected fraud, waste, and other mismanagement. In addition, personnel and budget offices enforce civil service laws and regulations as well as appropriations acts and other restrictions on expenditures and programs. Technically, such control activities are not the same as the exercise of line authority. But, technicalities aside, operating officials invariably resent the so-called meddling of controllers, particularly when the controllers divert the operators' energies from what they view as the vigorous implementation of programs to side issues, such as compliance with burdensome red-tape requirements.

Power Building

In practice, staff members often take on very strong power, even compared with line functions.[18] Many staff assistants have regular access to the chief of the unit, and this "face time" can powerfully shape the chief's decisions. Lower-level line officials, therefore, often try to cultivate the staff assistant, to find back doors into the decision-making process. On the other hand, top officials facing a large number of tough problems can be tempted to tell a staff assistant to "just handle it," and staff aides can find themselves slipping into the chair of command. Indeed, cabinet officials regularly complain that the president's staff aides often take it on themselves to issue orders and to filter information to the president.

The problem of power building is aggravated by a tendency for staff, auxiliary, control, and command functions to second-guess operating units. A department's procurement office may be charged not only with supplying the operating units' needs for supplies, an auxiliary activity, but also with the authority to question operating officials' specifications of their requirements, a control and command activity. Line officials, of course, cannot be free to purchase whatever strikes their fancy, but functions is a critical organizational problem. Few events annoy operating officials more than finding that their decisions about what supplies they need have been overruled by purchasing-office employees, who often sit far from the front lines of the agency's activities.

Staff activities thus differ from line (or operating) activities because their role is to assist, not to command, line officials. Although this line is neat, it's often breached in operation, because there is an irresistible temptation to give orders as well as advice. Because staff functions depend so critically on access to information, this can give staff officials a powerful additional source of leverage. It's little wonder that there so often is friction between the line and staff roles.

Solutions?

There are no easy solutions to these deep and lasting dilemmas. For staff officials, there is one obvious solution: a clear sense of the role of staff by those who serve in these positions. Staff persons need to practice self-restraint and resist the temptation to go into business for themselves as decision makers and order givers. Of course, such restraint is often in short supply—it is never easy to fade into the background while others take center stage, and it is hard to push away the temptations of power that the staff role offers. Though the staff-line distinction is not quite as simple as a difference between thinkers and doers, the cultures of most operating organizations tend to put those who "do" into a more valued position than those who "think," and those who think often believe they can do best.

Auxiliary units inevitably exercise specialized control functions, especially because top executives rarely want to invest their scarce time in housekeeping disputes. However, program administrators are often frustrated by the necessity of sharing control over the tools for their jobs with outside auxiliary units that are committed less to program results than to managing the support apparatus, from personnel rules to purchasing standards. As we see in Chapter 8, substantial efforts have been made to give operating managers more control over their personnel systems.

REORGANIZATION

If so many problems are structural, why, some wonder, can't they be solved by reorganizing the structure? To be sure, executive restructuring efforts have regularly sought to rearrange the organizational building blocks to enhance symmetry, improve the logical grouping of activities, reduce the executive's span of control, and strengthen administrative coordination and efficiency. These efforts fall largely within the neutral competence approach to organization, and they have long been an important part of administrative strategy.[19]

Reorganizations have been a never-ending campaign for most government executives. For example, in his 2011 State of the Union Address, President Obama took on the challenge of governmental organizations for salmon:

> There are 12 different agencies that deal with exports. There are at least five different agencies that deal with housing policy. Then there's my favorite example: The Interior Department is in charge of salmon while they're in fresh water, but the Commerce Department handles them when they're in saltwater. (Laughter.) I hear it gets even more complicated once they're smoked.[20]

But like all great stories, this one gets even better the more one pokes into the details. Interior is in charge of protecting natural resources in the nation's interior, which covers fresh water. Commerce seeks to promote business development through fisheries, and that takes the department into the salt water where many salmon swim freely. We've organized the government's policy toward salmon to manage the areas where they swim and the purposes—recreation or commercial fishing—to which those areas are put. We could simplify the situation by creating a "department of salmon," but then commercial fishermen might find the department of salmon's regulations conflicting with those of the departments of cod and haddock. Behind every complaint about governmental organization is a complex puzzle of policy, politics, and efficiency.

Reorganization is always about much more than efficiency, because reorganization is as much a political act as an administrative one. Structure determines which issues get priority. Structure also defines which constituencies get prime attention, strengthens government's ability to serve

In his 2011 State of the Union address, President Obama joked about the multiple government agencies charged with regulating salmon. The quip led to an ongoing debate about how the federal government could improve its efficiency by restructuring its operations. Bears would be unaffected by any of the proposed changes for salmon.

some of these constituencies, and sends a powerful message about who and what matter most. If a program finds itself in an unsympathetic department, it is less likely that the secretary will fight for adequate financing and staffing; as a result, the program will likely be anemic. If a program is placed far down in the hierarchy, the director's access to the secretary will be impeded; recommendations about resources and policy will have to move through a chain of intermediaries, who may block or change them. And when those in immediate charge of a program feel like orphans in their department, they will look elsewhere for support—for funds, staff, and program autonomy that enables them to ease the burdens of abandonment. All of these issues become folded into the value of representativeness that Herbert Kaufman identified as one of the basic approaches to organization.

For much of the past half-century, the president had statutory authority to propose to Congress reorganization plans creating, renaming, consolidating, and transferring whole agencies (other than cabinet departments and independent regulatory commissions) and any of their component units. By means of an ingenious legislative veto arrangement, the president's plans automatically went into effect in sixty days if neither house adopted a resolution of disapproval. In 1983, however, the Supreme Court ruled unconstitutional the legislative veto provisions appearing in hundreds of statutes, including the Reorganization Act.[21] Now, for a president's reorganization plan to be effective, it must be approved by a joint resolution of the two houses passed within ninety days after receipt and signed by the president (or, if vetoed because of amendments, overridden by Congress).[22] The odds were thus significantly altered: before 1983, the congressional engine's idling in neutral gear was to the president's advantage; now it is to his disadvantage, because he needs the House and Senate gears engaged and propelling action in his favor. Even his proposal for a statute would have a better chance of success, as Congress could pass it any time over a two-year session, whereas it would have to approve a reorganization plan within ninety days. As a result, the presidency lost some of its executive power, marking one more major difference in how the executive function differs between the public and private sectors: private executives can change the structure of their organizations whenever and however they like.

The president therefore has a choice of tactics in seeking to restructure. He can seek comprehensive reorganization of the executive branch through an act of Congress. This option is always tempting, but whatever the potential benefits, it always stirs opposition among the interest groups happy with the existing structure—or at least fearful that change might shrink their power and access. Alternatively, the president can focus his reorganization efforts on a small handful of bureaus. Sometimes the opposition to such limited action can be just as fierce, however, and it always has a less sweeping impact. In fact, some bureaus have proven immovable despite long histories of recommendations for restructuring. Reformers have long sought to move the Forest Service and the civil works functions of the Army Corps of Engineers to the Interior Department, in order to bring natural resource functions together in a single department. But both bureaus—and the interest groups supporting them—have fought off every effort to move these groups. At the state and local levels of government, reorganization laws vary, but rarely can chief executives remake the structure of the bureaucracy on their own.

Comprehensive Reorganization

Nearly every one of the presidents from Hoover through George W. Bush has supported some kind of sweeping overhaul of the executive branch. (The exceptions were Kennedy and Ford, because of their short tenures in office, and Reagan, who focused his efficiency efforts on privatization.)[23] Even conservatives like George W. Bush could not resist shuffling the organizational boxes. He championed the largest single government restructuring since the end of World War II with the creation of the Department of Homeland Security. Why, given the odds against them, do presidents bother? Some come into office trailing campaign promises to "straighten out the mess in Washington." Some—such as Hoover and Carter, who were engineers—are personally disposed to fix the machinery of government. Some seek popular credit for trying to improve administration, which may count for more politically than would actual achievement, to which they may devote little energy. Some—including the former senators Truman, Nixon, and Johnson, who knew Washington well—may perceive existing executive branch organization as poorly serving the national interest and propose to invest political capital in structural reform.

But political capital is precious. It can quickly evaporate or shift to urgent policy initiatives. Nixon's ambitious plan (described below) failed to win congressional support, and then the Watergate scandal exhausted his political capital. In 1967–1968 Johnson, losing his political capital because of the Vietnam War, neither allowed publication nor advocated adoption of the recommendations of his Task Force on Government Organization. Of Roosevelt's far-reaching proposals, only two were initially approved by Congress.[24] In fact, no president except Truman has obtained much of what he wanted. Two joint congressional-presidential Commissions on Organization of the Executive Branch of the Government, each chaired by former president Herbert Hoover, reported in 1949 and 1955.[25] Over half of the First Hoover Commission's recommendations were adopted, mostly because of Truman's support and a massive public relations campaign. The Second Hoover Commission focused not on major reorganization but on procedural techniques and policy issues—especially how to reduce the government's competition with and regulation of private enterprise. Nevertheless, "not a single major permanent program resulting from the years of depression, recovery, war, and reform was abolished as a result of this prodigious inquiry."[26]

In 1971 President Nixon proposed a drastic reorganization of the executive branch.[27] The plan would have retained unchanged only the four departments whose heads had sat in George Washington's cabinet. Four departments—Commerce, Labor, Transportation, and Agriculture—would be abolished, most of their work being absorbed by a wholly new Department of Economic Affairs. Three newly named and reconstituted departments— Natural Resources, Human Resources, and Community Development—were to supersede the departments of the Interior; Health, Education, and Welfare; and Housing and Urban Development. But Congress refused to act.[28]

President Carter mounted a heavily staffed reorganization study in the Office of Management and Budget, but the results were modest compared with his ambitions; Carter's successes were establishment of the Department of Education (fulfilling a campaign pledge) and the Department of Energy, partition of the Civil Service Commission into two new agencies, and reorganization of the president's Executive Office.[29] President Reagan then futilely sought abolition of the new Education and Energy Departments he had inherited from Carter but proposed no overhaul of executive branch structure.[30] He relied instead on his cabinet councils for harmonizing interagency concerns, on centralized control of agency behavior, on procedural changes, and on political appointments.[31] Congressional Republicans returned to the battle in 1995 and fought—yet failed—to eliminate the Commerce Department. The creation of the Department of Homeland Security in 2002 moved more agencies (twenty-two) and more employees than any restructuring since the creation of the Department of Defense, but critics continued to battle over the department's effectiveness.

Among state governments, comprehensive reorganizations have come in waves, a recent one centered in the 1965–1978 period when twenty-one states recast their executive branches. Usually the governor initiates the enterprise, and it is achieved through constitutional amendment or statute or both.[32] But the taste for reorganization has scarcely gone away, as shown by the massive 2004 proposal to restructure California's state government. That proposal gave birth to many more—the instinct to reorganize is eternal.

Obstacles to Reorganization

There never is a shortage of reorganization ideas, both because there always are ways of improving government's efficiency and because past reorganizations create the seeds for new ones. However, relatively few of these ideas are translated into action. Those ideas that are adopted tend to be specifically focused in response to perceived performance failures that are seen as products of poor organization. And either the reforms promise enough benefits to command political support or they are so unproblematic as to avoid stirring political opposition. Some reform ideas eventually succeed because they have recurred so often over the years that objections lose credibility.[33]

Indeed, *stability*, not fluidity, characterizes the executive branch's organization.[34] How do we account for this? Most obviously, departments and bureaus resist the loss of functions—they seek to protect their turf. Moreover, although some agencies act imperialistically to expand their realms, protecting what they have tends to be more important.[35] How do agencies attract enough political support to discourage and even defeat reorganization initiatives by presidents and department heads? The answer is that congressional committees and powerful interest groups create powerful counter-pressures. Mustering their forces against a reorganization effort is not difficult; often the opposition springs to arms without much invitation.

Congressional committees have their own jurisdictions to protect. One reason that Congress failed to support Nixon's major reorganization effort was dissatisfaction with the impact it would have had on legislative committees: on average, over nine existing committees would have had fragmentary jurisdiction over each of the four new departments. The alternative would have been a reorganization of the committees' jurisdictions to match those of the departments—not a prospect to warm the hearts of the leading members of committees marked for abolition or loss of jurisdiction.

Interest groups that perceive potential harm to their members throw their lobbying strength against proposed reorganizations, allying themselves with the affected departments or bureaus and with sympathetic congressional committees. The result often is an **iron triangle**, a closely linked network of interest groups, congressional committees, and public administrators that unite to protect their long-term relationships.

Indeed, a major study of government reorganization by Craig W. Thomas teaches several important lessons. First, although we are very long on rhetoric about reorganization, we are very short on evidence. We simply know relatively little about whether changes in government organization do in fact improve efficiency. Second, many efforts to improve the efficiency of government through reorganization have been disappointing: contracting out and creating government corporations can improve efficiency if the changes are well managed, but a common approach—centralizing authority—often does not improve efficiency. Third, despite the constant rhetoric about trying to reorganize government agencies to improve efficiency, "reorganizations are profoundly and unavoidably political and we should accept them as such."[36] If reformers promote reorganization to produce more efficient and more effective government, they cannot be sure of achieving the results they desire. But they can be sure of provoking deep political battles over the structure and symbols of governmental programs.

This strong array of forces against restructuring might be overcome more often if theory and experience pointed to one best way to organize the executive branch or to organize a department or bureau. The difficulty is that when those knowledgeable about administration are asked how to organize, they are likely to answer, "It all depends." This does not mean that anything goes. It does mean, as we have seen, that there are persistent organizational problems, several alternative approaches to them, and in any given situation a set of variables that carry different weights from those they might carry in another situation. It also means that any reorganization's potential for achieving its objectives is contingent on so many factors that neither theory nor experience can ensure that the potential will be fulfilled. Finally, it means that the ultimate choice often depends more on political values than on administrative efficiency.

CONCLUSION

Responses to organization problems usually seek to promote one or another of the values of neutral competence, executive leadership, or representativeness. All such responses may be infused with politics, concerned for "who gets what?" This is true, even of responses in the neutral competence mode, because administrators, including careerists, prefer arrangements that protect their units' powers and that ensure their control of subordinate units.

Organization problems, we have discovered, are not chance or unique occurrences. Instead, they fall into patterns that not only persist or recur but that, more remarkably, also appear at all levels—presidential, departmental, bureau, and field service. The fact that conflict seems structurally embedded, that things go wrong even when neutral competence is the goal, stems from such causes as organizers' failure to take account of the salient criteria: incompatibilities among the organizational structures; the fuzziness of jurisdictional boundaries; the weakness of voluntary, horizontal cooperation; the limits of vertical, hierarchical coordination; and the frustrations that operating officials suffer because of the controls exercised by staff and auxiliary aides and units.

Although organizational structure seems passive, it should now be clear that it both results from and shapes the dynamics of organizational conflict. Those dynamics are political, reflecting the claims of president and Congress to achieve respectively the values of executive leadership and representativeness, and reflecting as well the clash of interest groups.

As later chapters show, public organizations, however passive they appear in the abstract, come to life when perceived as sets of human beings, both civil servants and political appointees, as wrestlers over policy issues and battlers for scarce budgetary resources, as agents attempting to implement service and regulatory programs that have ambitious and contradictory goals, and as bureaucrats adapting to the control efforts of executive, legislative, and judicial overseers. The next chapter turns to those puzzles.

CASE 6.1

Sunset, the Golden Retriever: Governor Schwarzenegger and the Restructuring of California's Executive Branch

For Sunset, a golden retriever, the news from Sacramento wasn't good. Sunset was training to be a guide dog for the blind, and Sunset's instructor, Katryn Webster, was worried about the future of her organization, Guide Dogs of the Desert.[1] The Board of Guide Dogs for the Blind, the state government agency regulating Sunset's training and Webster's organization, was threatened with radical surgery as part of Governor Arnold Schwarzenegger's new reform agenda, the California Performance Review. Webster wasn't sure whether the performance review's recommendations would permanently change the way her organization worked and how effective it could be.

When he took office in January 2004, Schwarzenegger had launched the performance review program to eliminate waste and inefficiency across state government, in part by reducing perceived duplication in "common functions and responsibilities."[2] The "Gubernator," as he quickly became known to fans of his action-hero movies, faced a huge budget deficit and a public tired of taxes. At his inauguration, Schwarzenegger told California's citizens that his

performance review could help slash the state government's costs. "I plan a total review of government—its performance, its practices, its cost," he announced.[3]

Luckily for Sunset, when Schwarzenegger's task force made its recommendations in August 2004, it didn't suggest wiping out the guide dog program and the board that supervised it. Rather, it recommended moving the Board of Guide Dogs for the Blind to a new Department of Education and Workforce Preparation—along with similar changes for more than a hundred other boards and agencies that existed independent of the governor's cabinet agencies. But the board's supporters worried the move would weaken their work.

"Guide dogs take you into situations where it's life and death," explained board member Jane Brackman, "and if a dog isn't properly trained or a student isn't properly trained, people die."[4] Sheila Styron, president of Guide Dog Users, a national support organization, added, "Most people in California are pretty happy with the board." In fact, she said, "We would like it to become stronger."[5]

Eliminating the board, its supporters said, would not even save the state any money—Schwarzenegger's primary goal in launching the performance review—because license fees paid the board's $141,000 annual budget. (Blind persons received the dog and training for free; donations covered the $50,000-per-dog training cost, and the three dog training academies that exist in California paid the state a license fee to be allowed to operate.) The board was scarcely a megabureaucracy soaking up taxpayer dollars; its seven members each received $100 (plus expenses) per day for the board's eight meetings per year.

Tough government rules were necessary, said the board's supporters, because some dog owners were taking unfair advantage of the special rules for guide dogs. Dog lovers with perfectly good eyesight, for example, were pretending their pets were guide dogs to be able to bring them into restaurants. The board performed important advocacy work as well, such as its effort to get an exemption for guide dogs from Hawaii's rule that dogs moving into the state had to be quarantined (to protect Hawaii from importing rabies). Moving the board into the new department, supporters feared, would make it harder to provide dogs for blind citizens. "You put a small entity like the state board into an overarching entity," explained Mitch Pomerantz, a disability law compliance officer for Los Angeles, "and it's going to get lost in the shuffle."[6]

Critics, however, wondered if the California Performance Review had gone far enough. "They did not go to the hard step and say, 'Do we really need to regulate guide dog trainers anymore?'" explained Julie D'Angelo Fellmeth, administrative director of the Center for Public Interest Law at the University of San Diego. "They're not shrinking government. They're just getting rid of multi-member boards and substituting bureaucrats."[7]

The battle over the Board of Guide Dogs for the Blind played itself out hundreds of times over. Schwarzenegger's task force recommended that a third of the state's 339 independent boards and commissions should be moved into executive departments, whose heads would report to the elected governor.

Three months after the California Performance Review issued its report, experts told a public hearing that any kind of reorganization would be difficult to implement. Every board had its own constituency, and every constituency feared its influence over policy would be watered down if the location of its organization was moved lower on the bureaucratic food chain. While searching for billions of dollars of savings, Schwarzenegger and his aides had to decide how far to take a reorganization battle that promised few budgetary savings.

On the other hand, if he were to step back from the reorganization battle, Schwarzenegger risked undermining his credibility. In his 2004 State of the State Address, he had pledged to "blow up boxes" in restructuring the state's bureaucracy—eliminating those boxed entries that are so ubiquitous on organizational charts. Toward the end of his first year in office, however, a *San Francisco Chronicle* editorial said his term so far had mostly been a "victory parade." His performance review offered 1,200 recommendations—ranging from improved electronic government to changing vehicle registration from once a year to once every two years—which would produce $32 billion in predicted savings. "Is he serious about government reform, or is the package for political show?" the newspaper asked.[8]

Schwarzenegger was vastly underrated when he took office. Critics laughed off his campaign as an ego-driven publicity stunt. But they had grossly underestimated the wily Austrian bodybuilder and chess player. In case after case, he proved a far more effective governor than his critics had expected. After a few months, "The only people who are still laughing at Governor Schwarzenegger," explained Jack Pitney, a Claremont McKenna political scientist, "are the people who don't know California."[9]

But his performance review remained a long-running battle. Schwarzenegger had called California's sprawling government bureaucracy "a mastodon frozen in time." He saw the job of restructuring the state bureaucracy—including the Board of Guide Dogs for the Blind—as a symbol to demonstrate his determination to transform the state government. He knew that the reorganization, in itself, would not save billions. But if he could prevail, it would strengthen his hand in controlling the state government apparatus and in enhancing his ability to win on even bigger policy battles later.

The battle had enormous implications, many observers of California politics believed. "To me, the jury's still out on whether he wants real, true structural reform," said Joe Canciamilla, a Democrat from the State Assembly. "If he's not willing to take that step, with the popularity he's had, the independence he's had, the public statements he's made—if this governor isn't willing to go there, it ain't gonna happen for several generations."[10]

The battle hinged on the supervision of Sunset, the golden retriever, and thousands of cases just like Sunset's throughout the state and its government.

Questions to Consider

1. Consider the case for moving independent boards and commissions into executive branch departments. What are the advantages and disadvantages of such a restructuring?

2. Government reformers often lose their appetite for the political battle over restructuring the executive branch when they discover that, in itself, it tends to save little money. Are there other reasons to consider such reorganization? Do these reasons make a strong enough case to make it worth the political fight, even if there are not big savings in tax dollars?

3. Consider the symbolic value of an organization's structure. What roles do such symbols play, on both sides of the reorganization battle?

4. Just how much do you believe that the *structure* of government bureaucracies really matters? If you were an adviser to Governor Schwarzenegger, how much of his political capital would you advise him to invest in the battle over eliminating so many quasi-independent boards and commissions?

NOTES

1. See the organization's website, http://www.guide-dogsofthedesert.org.

2. See the report of the *California Performance Review* (2004), http://cpr.ca.gov/CPR_Report.

3. Ed Mendel, "Optimistic Governor Doesn't Pull Punches," *San Diego Union-Tribune,* January 7, 2004, A1.

4. Jordan Rau, "Guide Dog Board Threatened," *Los Angeles Times,* November 29, 2004, B1.

5. Ibid.

6. Ibid.

7. Ibid.

8. "Now, Governor's Second Act," editorial, *San Francisco Chronicle,* November 17, 2004, B10.

9. Alan Greenblatt, "Strong Governor," *Governing,* July 2004, http://www.governing.com/topics/politics/Strong-Governor.html.

10. Ibid.

CASE 6.2

Obama Launches Management Reform: New—or Recycled—Ideas?

It's become inevitable—every president needs to put his own distinctive mark on the executive branch by launching his own brand of management reform. At least since Truman, presidents have made new management strategies a signature of their administrations. When he succeeded Roosevelt, Truman asked a special commission to find ways of increasing the efficiency of the federal government. Eisenhower followed with a continuation of the effort, this time aimed at restructuring government. Kennedy sought the "best and the brightest" for government service, while Johnson brought "planning programming budgeting" to capture the full cost of a program in decisions about whether to launch or continue it. Nixon expanded that to a "management by objectives" approach. He also proposed a massive reorganization of the federal government, which foundered in the midst of the impeachment battle. Ford stabilized government. Carter brought "zero-base budgeting," which wasn't exactly budgeting from a zero base but a way of bringing tough analysis to packages of spending beyond a specified floor (say, 80 percent of existing spending). Reagan launched broad privatization initiatives to contract out much of the federal government's work. Bush continued it. Clinton sought to "reinvent" government, aimed at making government work better and cost less. Bush (George W., that is) had his own management agenda, with a stoplight set of performance measures to assess the accomplishments of federal programs.

So how did Obama wish to transform the government? In July 2013, after the budget battles simmered down enough to put his second-term budget and personnel team into place, he laid out his three-part plan:[1]

- "Deliver the services that citizens expect in smarter, faster, and better ways." For example, following Hurricane Sandy's assault on the Northeast, citizens could apply for emergency assistance using mobile and web apps. Federal Emergency Management Agency workers, armed with iPads, checked in on citizens.
- Identify "new ways to reduce waste and save taxpayers money." For example, the administration estimated that it saved more than $2.5 billion by eliminating overlapping information technology systems.
- Open "huge amounts of government data to the American people." For example, at Data.gov, it's possible to look through 75,000 government datasets on everything from weather to what different hospitals charge for different procedures.

Obama said he had more he wanted to do. He asked Congress for broader authority to reorganize the federal government. He promised that new information systems would make it easier for citizens to choose the best health care coverage.

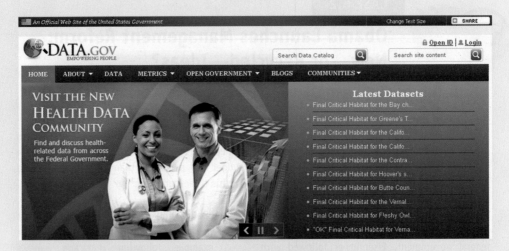

The federal website, Data.gov, became a vast repository of information about the government's operations, as part of an extended commitment to open government.

He told citizens that it would be easier to fill out federal forms because the government's information systems would remember basic information for the next time and that citizens would be able to check the status of their applications for programs through online apps. He concluded by saying, "We've got to have the brightest minds to help solve our biggest challenges," with a simple goal: "deliver on the kind of 21st century government the American people want."

Some analysts were underwhelmed. Writing in *Government Executive,* Tom Shoop wondered if the reforms amounted to much. "Most of the specific recommendations Obama discussed today, such as getting reorganization authority from Congress to restructure agencies, already have been proposed and haven't gotten much traction," he said. Moreover, he wondered if many of the ideas relied on innovation from outside the government. Instead, Shoop argued, "what government needs is to unleash the creativity of its experienced managers and employees, who are the only ones with the savvy to know what can and can't be done within the system of laws, rules and regulations that govern all federal activity—and which aren't going away."[2] For better or worse, in the midst of the titanic battles with Congress, these initiatives represented the Obama administration's best plans for reforming the executive branch.

Questions to Consider

1. What do you think of the Obama administration's reform agenda? Do you agree with the president that it represents a plan for delivering the kind of government that the American people want? Or do you agree with Shoop that the plan represents old ideas and fails to harness the energy of federal workers?

2. Several commentators have noted the administration's heavy reliance on ideas and strategies from the private sector. What role do you think leading practices in the private sector can—and should—play in rethinking the federal government's own management strategy?

3. Suppose you had the responsibility of laying out a management reform agenda for the next four years. What would your plan be?

NOTES

1. "Remarks by the President Presenting New Management Agenda" (July 8, 2013), http://www.whitehouse.gov/the-press-office/2013/07/08/remarks-president-presenting-new-management-agenda.

2. Tom Shoop, "Obama on Management Reform: It's a Private Matter," *Government Executive,* July 8, 2013, http://www.govexec.com/federal-news/fedblog/2013/07/obama-management-reform-its-private-matter/66173.

CASE 6.3

Naughty Aughties: Has American Government Become More Centralized?

What's happened to the balance of power between the federal, state, and local governments in the last fifteen years? Here is my list of the top ten game changers during the Naughty Aughties and beyond.

1. *Census (2000 and 2010).* Take the decennial count, add personal computers equipped with mapping software, and presto—there's a new game where incumbents can create safe legislative districts and permanently lock in their advantage. Reapportionment shrank the number of marginal seats and increased the level of conflict between increasingly polarized political parties. That made it harder for everyone to govern and for newcomers to run in elections.

2. *The September 11 attacks (2001).* Everyone conceded the need to do a far better job connecting the dots, but as the feds fought over who was in charge, state and local governments often found themselves alone on the front lines of first response. The government has done a lot better in pulling the emergency systems together, but too many of the dots remain unconnected.

3. *No Child Left Behind (2002).* The George W. Bush administration's signature domestic initiative had broad support. Who favored leaving children behind? But no one was very happy about the way the initiative worked out. Local school districts complained that the program imposed unfunded mandates. Attacking the program was one of the few things Democratic presidential candidates agreed on in 2008, but finding a fix is proving very hard without pumping in a lot more cash.

4. *John Roberts named chief justice (2005).* The William Rehnquist court left behind a long string of decisions expanding the power of the states at the expense of the feds. Although it's still a bit early to determine the mark of the Roberts court, the Rehnquist "federalism revolution" is ebbing in favor of a much more pragmatic approach. The court, however, is just one vote away from sliding toward a new revolution in states' rights.

5. *Hurricane Katrina (2005).* The storm not only devastated the Gulf States, but also left a major city in near-anarchy and made FEMA a dirty word. The feds concluded that they made a big mistake by trusting state and local officials to deal with really big problems. In the aftermath of the Hurricane Katrina fiasco, the feds have quietly decided they'll be quicker on the trigger with a mega-federal response the next time a big disaster occurs.

6. *Minneapolis bridge collapse (2007).* When the I-35W bridge came down in the Twin Cities, the nation got a stunning reminder of the crumbling state of its infrastructure. Cable failures on the San Francisco-Oakland Bay Bridge, the shutdown of I-95 in Philadelphia to repair a crumbling bridge, and the implosion of a major bridge connecting New York and Vermont underlined the emerging crisis. Great video, but little action.

7. *Ireland rejects European Union reform treaty (2008).* Voters decisively rejected the EU's plan to smooth out battles among its states, create a new president, and strengthen foreign policymaking. Kudos to James Madison and the gang from 1787— this federalism stuff is a lot harder to create and sustain than it looks.

8. *Economic meltdown (2009).* As the rest of the economy staggered back to its feet, state and local governments continue to battle the long-term effects of the Great Recession. At the end of 2009, state and local tax revenues were down 7 percent over the dismal previous year. Almost every state is looking at big deficits. Mayor Scott Smith of Mesa, Arizona, told *The Wall Street Journal* that he wasn't sure if his city's services would ever return to previous levels. "We are redefining what cities are going to be," he says.

9. *New transparency (2009).* What's not to like about tens of billions of dollars in stimulus money? The cash, though, came with lots of strings. Loads of information delivered through Recovery.gov became the new accountability, and it's a safe bet that this "new transparency" will endure long after the stimulus money is gone. Everyone agrees transparency is the answer. No one really knows what it is going to mean.

10. *Health reform (2009).* As the "public option" evaporated from the debate, the states became even bigger players in the national health care reform effort. A close reading of the proposed bills, however, revealed that the feds had taken to writing in state agencies as if they were agents of the federal government. In practice, of course, they long have been. The frantic drafting process of the health care reform bills simply stripped away the old pretense and laid bare the way Congress really thinks about the states.

Where does this leave the country as the new century grows into its teens? The United States has changed a lot since the 1990s, when the states were in the driver's seat of domestic policy and the governor's mansion was the proving ground for presidential candidates. Take away item No. 4— with the balance of the U.S. Supreme Court's views on federalism teetering on the next appointment— and the feds are steering the system.

It's hard to see concerns about terrorism ebbing away, and health care reform is likely to cement the federal government's preeminence. It will be hard for state and local governments to fight back when their coffers are dry and the feds can tip the game with vast infusions of cash borrowed from foreign investors.

Note: This case comes from my column in *Governing,* "Potomac Chronicle," *Governing,* February 2010, http://www.governing.com/columns/potomac-chronicle/A-Decade-To-Remember.html.

Questions to Consider

1. As you assess the balance of centralization and decentralization in American government, what do you think have been the major events of the last fifteen years?

2. Is there a trend in this balance? Do you think we are becoming more centralized or decentralized? What are the forces shaping this trend, if there is one?

3. What difference do you think this makes, both for governance in America and for public administration?

KEY CONCEPTS

auxiliary staff   146

clearance procedure   144

control staff   146

coordination   139

core staff   146

executive leadership   137

interagency agreements   144

interagency committees   144

iron triangle   153

lead agency formula   144

line activities   146

neutral competence   137

representativeness   137

staff   146

staff activities   146

FOR FURTHER READING

Arnold, Peri E. *Making the Managerial Presidency: Comprehensive Reorganization Planning, 1905-1980*. Princeton, N.J.: Princeton University Press, 1986.

Fesler, James W. *Area and Administration*. Tuscaloosa: University of Alabama Press, 2008.

Kaufman, Herbert. "Emerging Doctrines of Public Administration." *American Political Science Review* 50 (December 1956): 1059-1073.

Knott, Jack H., and Gary J. Miller. *Reforming Bureaucracy: The Politics of Institutional Choice.* Englewood Cliffs, N.J.: Prentice Hall, 1987.

Lee, Mordecai. *Nixon's Super-Secretaries: The Last Grand Presidential Reorganization Effort*. College Station: Texas A&M University Press, 2010.

National Commission on Terrorist Attacks upon the United States. *The 9/11 Commission Report*. New York: Norton, 2004.

Thomas, Craig W. "Reorganizing Public Organizations: Alternatives, Objectives, and Evidence." *Journal of Public Administration and Theory* 3 (1993): 457-486.

SUGGESTED WEBSITES

The federal government has moved its extensive guide to its organizational structure, the *U.S. Government Manual*, online to **www.gpoaccess .gov/gmanual**. This is an invaluable resource for understanding the structure and function of government agencies.

The California Performance Review, **http:// cpr.ca.gov**, has assembled thorough background discussions about the organization of the state's government. It is a useful guide for understanding the structural issues faced by the nation's most populous state. Many other state and local governments regularly explore how best to improve their operations, and a web search will uncover the most recent initiatives they are taking.

CHAPTER

7

Administrative Reform

CHAPTER OBJECTIVES

- Explore the competing theories on administrative reform

- Examine the alternative approaches to reform, in both process and structure

- Put the American efforts at reform in a global context

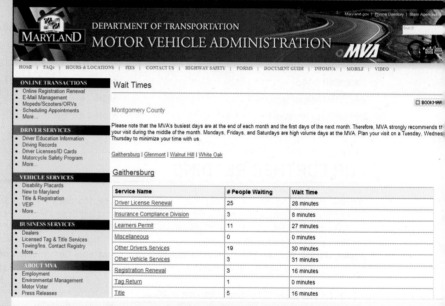

In many states, the Department of Motor Vehicles has used the Internet to connect better with citizens. The website in Maryland provides real-time information about the number of people in line and how long a wait there is to transact business.

IN THE ADMINISTRATIVE WORLD, NOTHING HAS BECOME more constant than change. In fact, administrative reform has become an imperative of modern management, both in the United States and abroad.[1] A 2001 report by the Organization of Economic Co-operation and Development, an association of the world's major industrialized nations, concluded,

> As society continues to change rapidly, the solutions of the past are no longer sufficient. Not only is there no "one size fits all" solution across countries, but countries should also learn to use reform to create institutions that can constantly adapt to changes in their own societies and to changing outside forces.[2]

The institutional reforms attempted across the world have been very different and often have multiple personalities. They have sometimes carried inherent conflicts, usually buried under the frenzy of the tough political realities that provoked the reforms in the first place. But beyond the differences is a remarkably universal movement: virtually every government everywhere is deep in reform, with an irresistible lure to make government work better and cost less. These bold promises, however, are extremely difficult for governments to achieve, because the reform job itself is tough, because the differing personalities of administrative reform often drive it in conflicting directions, and because the reform task seeks a stable solution of nagging tradeoffs to problems that never stay stable for long.

REFORM IN AMERICA

Three important truths characterize public management reform in the United States. First, from the nation's earliest days, America's revolutionary roots have long driven a movement for reform. The country began with a commitment to changing the way that government works, and it hasn't stopped since. Most presidents, governors, and mayors come into office pledging to make public programs work better (better, in particular, than in their predecessor's administration). American public administration revolves around a fundamental paradox: an enduring sense that public bureaucracy is a large, immovable object and that top executives need to produce deep, constant change. Few elected officials champion the cause of public administration per se—over the long haul, making government work better has never been a winning political strategy—but no official can ignore the imperative to make public programs work.

Second, in the United States, the most innovative administrative thinking has often occurred in the private sector. Public managers anxious to save money and improve service delivery have looked for solutions wherever they could find them, and that search has often led them to corporate strategies and tactics. In part, this is because of the recurring, but often wrongheaded, belief that government would be better if it were managed more like the private sector. Private solutions and public problems are not often well matched, but that has scarcely deterred public officials from trying to borrow anything from the private sector that might prove a good idea. Occasionally, as in the Progressive Era of the late nineteenth century, public-sector theorizing has moved in advance of private management, but especially for most of the last century, the "make government work more like the private sector" approach has dominated.

Finally, many American governmental reforms have tended to arise from the experiments of state and local governments, rather than moving from the federal government down; the federal government has often been the last link in the chain. In playing catch-up, however, the federal government has often found that its programs, such as food stamps and Social Security, are poor matches for innovative solutions developed for such state and local programs as garbage collection and park maintenance. Reform often needs a strong hand from the top, but many of the best ideas have bubbled up from the bottom.

American public administration's continued commitment to reform springs from a variety of sources. Some of the commitment to reform reflects a fundamental tension in the American political character between great ideals and forceful pragmatism. Some of it is because many reform ideas are drawn from settings that offer a much different context for the problems they are trying to solve: private-sector strategies applied to government, and state government strategies applied to the federal government. Some of it derives from an ongoing dynamic: government has always tried to do very hard things, and reform has always been a coping strategy when results inevitably fall short of expectations. And some of it simply demonstrates that Americans have always been tinkerers who like tweaking the workings of their governmental institutions.

CONFLICTING THEORIES

Despite the problems that government officials at different levels must tackle, there has been surprising convergence around three basic approaches. Terms such as **downsizing, reengineering,** and **continuous improvement** have quickly entered the administrative vocabulary of managers around the world. The terms themselves are appealing, because they speak to the aspirations of managers and citizens alike. Hardly anyone wants to make the public sector bigger, so reformers resort to downsizing, or shrinking government. When results fail to meet expectations, reformers seek to reengineer organizations. And no one thinks that the incentives in traditional bureaucracy help government bureaucrats adapt easily to a quickly changing world, so continuous improvement seems an attractive solution.

Behind these three basic approaches, however, are deceptively complex ideas. The old bureaucratic orthodoxy, founded on traditional authority and hierarchy, promised a clear, straightforward, and universal set of principles: delegation of authority on the basis of expertise, and

In Garland, Maine, Mary Adams campaigned in 2006 for a "Taxpayer Bill of Rights" to cut taxes and bring down government spending. The 68-year-old grandmother helped advance a movement that had spread from coast to coast.

democratic accountability through hierarchical control. The new ideas driving bureaucratic reform, however, are neither orthodox nor universal. Moreover, at their core are important but often unrecognized contradictions that threaten the success of reform efforts, as recent American experience illustrates.

Downsizing

Arguing that government is too big, conservatives have long battled to shrink its size. In the midst of the white-hot 2010 congressional elections, Republican candidates rolled out their "Pledge to America." They said,

> By cutting Congress' budget, imposing a net hiring freeze on non-security federal employees, and reviewing every current government program to eliminate wasteful and duplicative programs, we can curb Washington's irresponsible spending habits and reduce the size of government, while still fulfilling our necessary obligations.[3]

The principles were clear: government is too big, so one should do whatever is politically possible to make it smaller—set ceilings on taxes, promise big budget cuts, pledge to trim across the board, or pledge to trim the bureaucracy. Angry taxpayers have often proved willing to wield blunt axes in making cuts, even if good programs or key managers are eliminated, if that is what it takes to get their message across. The downsizing movement helped drive the automatic across-the-board cuts that took effect in 2013 when Congress and the president could not agree on a deficit-reduction strategy.

In the United States, such blunt-edge downsizing originated at the state and local levels, especially through cuts imposed to cope with the property-tax reduction movement of the 1970s. New Jersey legislators in 1976 limited the growth of expenditures to the growth of per capita personal income. California voters fired the loudest shot in 1978 by approving an amendment to the state constitution, Proposition 13, which reduced property taxes to 1 percent of market value and limited future property tax growth to a 2 percent annual increase over the amount calculated from the 1975–1976 base. Massachusetts voters followed with Proposition 2½, which reduced property taxes by 15 percent per year until they reached 2½ percent of full market value, where they had to remain (hence the name applied to the proposition).[4] State legislators passed scores of other tax limitations or special tax breaks in the following decade.[5] Between 1976 and 1982, legislators and voters in nineteen states agreed to limit revenues or expenditures.[6]

The movement continued through the 1990s and the 2000s, led by Colorado's passage in 1992 of a constitutional amendment to limit tax increases—christened the **Taxpayer Bill of Rights,** or TABOR for short—which spread to other states as well. The proposal passed with 54 percent of the vote; a decade later, almost three-fourths of Colorado residents favored its tough approach.[7] The Colorado effort sparked a string of copycats over the next decade. Meanwhile, in 1994 Michigan voters agreed to shift a substantial amount of local property tax revenues for education to state taxes, while Wisconsin legislators voted to replace most local property taxes for schools with state aid, to be financed by state government spending cuts.

In both cases, state officials first committed themselves to the broad reform—property tax relief—without deciding how they would produce it, and in both cases, the strategy provoked wild bargaining in the state legislatures to produce the promised aid.

The problem, surveys revealed, was not that citizens were unhappy with the services they were receiving. Instead, they believed that their taxes were too high—that the public sector was fundamentally inefficient and could easily provide the same services for less money.[8] In 2010, the Pew Center on the States and Public Policy surveyed residents of five of the nation's most financially distressed states. The survey found that two-thirds of citizens said that they never trust state government to do what is right, or trust it only some of the time. They want major reforms, but the reforms that they want prove difficult to square with the services that citizens say they want (see Table 7.1).

Elected officials discovered that the mantra of cutting the unholy trinity of "waste, fraud, and abuse" always resonates well with voters. For better or worse, both elected officials and voters have come to believe that government's inefficiency is so great that it's possible to cut spending without hurting the quality of services. E. S. Savas argued that the public, "despairing of the ability or will of its elected government to reduce expenditures, has taken the matter directly into its hands and reduced revenue, like a parent rebuking his spendthrift child by cutting its allowance."[9]

In the mid-1980s, the downsizing movement spilled into the federal government, but with very uneven results. In 1984 the President's **Private Sector Survey on Cost Control** (better known as the Grace Commission, after its chairman, J. Peter Grace) produced 2,478 recommendations that its report said would save $424.4 billion over three years. The commission concluded that the federal government was "suffering from a critical case of inefficient and ineffective management" and that only more businesslike practices and, in particular, huge cuts in governmental programs could reduce the deficit hemorrhage.[10] Academic critics argued that the report was built largely on an ideological, pro-business, anti-government base; that it contained misrepresentations; and that following its recommendations could actually hurt the work of the federal government.[11] Suspicious Democrats, who controlled Congress, saw it as a partisan maneuver by Republican president Ronald Reagan, and the resulting partisan battles doomed almost all of the report's recommendations.

The Grace Commission report did, however, fuel a downsizing movement at the federal level, helping to promote in 1985 the **Balanced Budget and Emergency Deficit Control Act,** better known as the Gramm-Rudman Act, after two of its key sponsors, senators Phil Gramm (R-Tex.) and Warren Rudman (R-N.H.). Among its many important effects, Gramm-Rudman forced both Congress and the president, Democrats and Republicans alike, to begin bringing the burgeoning federal deficit under control; downsizing became an inescapable part of politics at all levels of American government. Even though subsequent efforts nudged Gramm-Rudman aside, it had made downsizing a fundamental part of the strategies used by both political parties. Gramm-Rudman and the TABOR movements intersected and reinforced each other.

Soon after taking office in 1993, President Bill Clinton named Vice President Al Gore to work on **reinventing government,** to make the federal government work better and cost less. The term came from a best-selling 1993 book, *Reinventing Government,* by David Osborne

TABLE 7.1	**Distrust of State Governments: Survey of Residents in Five States**

States surveyed: Arizona, California, Florida, Illinois, and New York

1. **Government Performance Matters:** Residents are more likely to say their elected leaders are wasting their money and could deliver services more efficiently than to complain that state government is too big.

   Reality Check: About two out of three residents say their state government could spend less and still provide the same level of services. Of those, most residents think cuts of 10 percent to 20 percent or even more are possible. But experts who work closely with state budgets say that perception may not be realistic, especially given the steep spending reductions many states already have made since the recession started.

2. **Protect the Essentials:** In all five states, by a range of 63 percent to 71 percent, majorities say they would be willing to pay higher taxes to keep K-12 public schools at current funding levels. Fifty-two percent to 57 percent say they would pay higher taxes to preserve funding for health and human services.

   Reality Check: It will be extremely difficult, given the size of deficits in all five states, to fully protect K-12 education and health and human services, the biggest recipients of state dollars. Doing so would compel deeper cuts everywhere else, and even then may not be enough.

3. **Tax the Other Guy:** Residents would prefer to charge the other guy—particularly corporations, smokers, drinkers, and gamblers.

   Reality Check: The revenue raisers that residents are most widely willing to tolerate—hitting smokers, drinkers, gamblers, and corporations—would tap marginal revenue streams and likely would not be sufficient to address their state's budget shortfalls.

4. **No More Borrowing:** The public is tired of lawmakers borrowing and passing costs to future generations—they'd rather keep cutting and taxing than see states borrow. Given three choices to balance state budgets, more than two-thirds of residents in all five states pick spending cuts first; they prefer tax increases second and borrowing last.

   Reality Check: State and local government borrowing is on the rise. In many cases, debt plays a productive role in providing funding for infrastructure, services, and budget flexibility. Not all debt is bad debt, and borrowing is an important financial tool for state governments. But too much of any kind of debt is problematic.

5. **Lack of Trust—and Desire for Reform:** Across all five states, two-thirds or more of respondents report that they either never trust state government to do what is right or trust it only some of the time. Residents overwhelmingly believe their state should pursue major reforms to their budget processes, and pursue them now.

   Reality Check: Residents across the five states overwhelmingly believe their state should pursue major reforms to their budget processes, and pursue them now.

Source: Excerpt from Pew Center on the States, *Facing the Facts: How Residents in Five States View Fiscal Priorities for State Government* (2010), http://www.pewcenteronthestates.org/report_detail.aspx?id=60803.

and Ted Gaebler.[12] Gore's campaign, the National Performance Review, promised voters $108 billion in savings by fiscal year 1999. Some of the savings were to come from reforms already under way, while others would derive from proposed policy changes and elimination of field offices of federal agencies. Most of the projected savings, however, were to result from reducing the federal workforce by 12 percent over five years—a total cut of 252,000 positions—to leave the workforce at under 2 million for the first time since 1967. The vice president's report promised that the cuts would consist of pruning away unnecessary layers of the federal bureaucracy:

> Most of the personnel reductions will be concentrated in the structures of over-control and micromanagement that now bind the federal government: supervisors, headquarters staffs, personnel specialists, budget analysts, procurement specialists, accountants, and auditors. These central control structures not only stifle the creativity of line managers and workers, they consume billions per year in salary, benefits, and administrative costs. Additional personnel cuts will result as each agency reengineers its basic work processes to achieve higher productivity at lower costs—eliminating unnecessary layers of management and nonessential staff.[13]

The report asserted that the many reforms it proposed—from streamlining the procurement process to giving managers more flexibility to make decisions without endless cross-checking—would improve governmental efficiency, making it possible to eliminate functions and layers of the federal bureaucracy and, therefore, to save billions of dollars. In theory, new efficiencies would produce the savings; in practice, however, the savings were almost totally

separate from the administrative reforms. The report promised that strategic planning within the bureaucracy was to determine where the cuts could be made, but when department heads began working to deliver the promised reductions, the cuts had little if anything to do with the plans. In fact, most departments planned to meet their targets by offering employees buyout packages that included financial inducements for taking early retirement.[14] In the end, by 2001, the number of federal civilian employees had declined by 365,000 (17 percent).

The recurring battles over the size of the government workforce raise important points about the downsizing movement. First, although from time to time the movement has relied on such wildly different theoretical bases as reinventing government[15] and the idea that bureaucrats seek to maximize their power by maximizing their numbers,[16] the movement itself has been largely atheoretical. Pragmatic principle has guided it: the only way to force greater governmental efficiency is to hold a loaded gun—in the form of tax and spending limits—to the heads of public managers. Cynics have called these limits the "starve the beast" strategy: if the beast they see as government cannot be killed in a frontal attack, they suggest it can instead be shrunk by starving it of tax revenue and the employees the money funds. Indeed, as President Bill Clinton struggled to resuscitate his presidency in early 1995 by promising a middle-class tax cut, he promised to fund it by cutting government bureaucracy even further. Fifteen years later, the Tea Party movement pledged more of the same. That ongoing debate provided the foundation for the budget battles of the Obama administration, which produced substantial across-the-board cuts in 2013.

Second, although politicians often boldly talk about cutting away the fat, there typically has been little thought about which fat to cut, and how to avoid slicing into the bone. The usual assumption is that there's so much fat in the budgets that big cuts can be made without hurting core programs. When cuts come, managers struggle to find ways of continuing to deliver desired services with fewer employees. The downsizing movement thus has focused the attention of government officials on coping with immediate pressures instead of charting strategies for lasting performance. Maneuvering through short-term pressure rarely builds

ACCOUNTABILITY

Can Data Change Results?

In 1994, New York City Police Commissioner William J. Bratton brought a new computerized information tracking system to the city's police department. In older days, police analysts identified crime "hot spots" by putting pins in maps—and attacked crime by "putting cops on the dots," as the saying went. Bratton vastly expanded the system, christened CompStat, and brought his police commanders in for regular meetings to track trends in crime and to be held accountable for their efforts to bring crime down in their precincts. Crime, especially violent crimes like murder, came down. Since then, analysts have battled over whether CompStat was responsible, whether aggressive arrests of lower-level offenses took more bad guys off the streets before they could graduate to more violent offenses, or whether the city's improving economic climate helped. But police departments in Washington, Philadelphia, San Francisco, and Los Angeles were convinced, and they adopted the system. HBO's long-running police drama The *Wire* featured Baltimore's CompStat.

One of CompStat's principles, featured in many other administrative reforms, is timely information available to everyone, elected officials as well as citizens. Want to know what's happening with crime or city services? The local "stat" website will have the data. The underlying assumption is that transparency in results will produce pressure for *better* results. But that raises big and unanswered questions: Will elected officials or citizens actually pay attention to the data—or are they more likely to draw their conclusions from newspaper stories or their own observations? Can more and better data change the way that citizens talk about—and talk to—their governments?

the base for long-term productivity. As Congress's watchdog agency, the General Accounting Office (in 2004 it became the Government Accountability Office), concluded in 2002:

> Much of the downsizing was set in motion without sufficient planning for its effects on agencies' performance capacity. Across government, federal employers reduced or froze their hiring efforts for extended periods. . . . This helped reduce their numbers of employees, but it also reduced the influx of new people with new knowledge, new energy, and new ideas—the reservoir of future agency leaders and managers.[17]

Third, while downsizing has in fact limited the growth of government spending and tax revenues in the United States, its effect on the quality of services and the efficiency of administration is anything but clear. American government at all levels has tended to invest relatively little in measuring the quality of what it buys.[18] That has been changing with the rise of the performance management movement in the 2000s and 2010s. State and local governments advanced performance movements (as Chapter 12 discusses).

As attractive as starving the beast might seem, there's a great risk that cutting back on those who manage government programs can drive costs up and performance down. Consider, for example, the federal government's $8 billion program to provide durable medical equipment, like wheelchairs, to older Americans. After years of criticism, the responsible federal agency, the Centers for Medicare and Medicaid Services (CMS), finally achieved progress in controlling the costs of the program. It's a typical case of government by proxy: although CMS manages the program, a large network of private contractors actually provides the services. CMS improved its cost control by managing the contracts better. The federal government isn't likely to cut back on providing wheelchairs to older Americans who need them to get around. Having fewer government employees means less oversight, and as the Government Accountability Office has found over the years, less oversight means higher costs.[19]

The downsizing movement has given officeholders a message that resonates with voters without directly attacking the problem of making government work better. Public officials, both elected and appointed, have turned instead to reengineering and cultural change for that purpose.

Reengineering

Michael Hammer and James Champy's *Reengineering the Corporation*—a tale of corporations faced not only with new challenges but with threats to their very existence—sat on the best-seller list for several months in 1993.[20] To succeed, even to survive, these authors claim, business leaders must move past incremental improvements and instead undertake fundamental reexamination of their operations. Their contention that completely new work processes and organizational structures can produce quantum leaps in performance has proven powerful in the private sector, and its influence has spilled over into government.[21]

Reengineering, Hammer and Champy argue, begins by putting everything on the table. It "means starting all over, starting from scratch," through "discontinuous thinking."[22] Too often, they believe, managers tinker at the edges when they need to start over again. The process begins by having managers consider the "three Cs": customers, competition, and change. The foundation for the new reality builds on customers "who know what they want, what they want to pay for it, and how to get it on the terms that they demand," and the successful companies will be those that build their operations to serve customers' needs. More intense competition means that companies that do not incorporate cutting-edge technology into their operations will not survive. And as change becomes constant, only organizations light on their feet and quick to adapt will prosper. By the 2010s, *disruptive innovation* had become the popular phrase. But the key remained the same: focus on fundamental change to produce big improvements in performance.

Reengineering requires fundamental and radical redesign of work processes. Indeed, *process* is the fundamental building block of reengineering. Effective managers redesign the processes within their organizations to ensure that customers' needs are met. They incorporate the latest technology, especially information technology, to wring extra efficiency out of their operations. Hammer and Champy emphatically argue that reengineering is not the same as downsizing, which is not driven by the need to improve performance; it is not the same as administrative reorganization because reengineers view process as far more important than structure; and it is not the same as **total quality management (TQM)**, which seeks to improve quality within existing processes through continuous improvement. Reengineers, by contrast, search for breakthrough strategies instead of incremental improvements—rather than trying to do a job 10 percent better, reengineers look for strategies that can work ten, or a hundred, times better.[23]

As private managers have popularized reengineering, public managers have found the movement irresistible. Massachusetts, for example, reengineered its child-support collection system. Previously, collection efforts began with complaints by the caregiving spouse against the nonsupporting spouse; caseworkers, through a labor-intensive system, then tried to track down scofflaws and intervene to try to win support. Under the new system, the state instead began relying on computers to find cases with similar characteristics, to search the database for parents who owed support, and to generate letters insisting on payment. After two years, according to one report, 85 percent of collections had occurred without a caseworker's intervention, the number of cases in which payments were collected had increased 30 percent, and the compliance rate had jumped from 59 percent to 76 percent. In Merced County, California, new software designed for individual workstations replaced mainframe-based programs for processing welfare eligibility claims; in the process, the time from initial application to interview decreased from four weeks to three days or less.[24] Texas, meanwhile, launched several major initiatives to improve the state's tax administration system that supporters believed could produce an additional $51 million in revenues per year.[25] The reengineering program recommends focusing on the program's mission, identifying its customers, and rethinking how best to deliver services. The movement argues that more efficient services will follow. The rise of the performance movement of the 2000s has helped fuel the reengineering movement, as governments at all levels have sought to squeeze extra productivity from their operations.

Not all scholars of public administration agree that a government approach founded on customer service is valid. Many leading figures in public administration have attacked reengineering and reinvention. H. George Frederickson, for example, contends that "governments are not markets" and that "citizens are not the customers. They are the owners."[26] Critics add that the broader movement to make government more entrepreneurial is dangerous; even if entrepreneurial behavior were a good idea, they argue, the concept could never be applied to government because there frequently is little private competition in most public functions.[27] Nevertheless, the reinventers counter that energetic, problem-solving managers would perform far better than more traditional bureaucrats rooted in standard operating procedures and organizational structures.

Moreover, even though citizens quite clearly "own" their government, many reformers argue that citizens could be treated far more responsively—as "customers" of governmental programs—without violating the fundamental premises of democratic government. Wisconsin's Department of Motor Vehicles, for example, installed new systems to make it much easier to obtain driver's licenses: take-a-number machines that tell citizens how long they can expect to wait, new strategies to minimize those waits, and satellite offices located in shopping malls and open evenings and weekends to give citizens wider access. The state's Department of Revenue developed a new quick-refund system that got taxpayers their income tax refund checks within two weeks. Maryland's Department of Motor Vehicles has a website that allows citizens to check how long the wait in line is—before they leave their homes. In Oregon, when the state's driver's license bureau surveyed citizens to determine what problem they most wanted solved, it found that the number one problem was the poor quality of the driver's license photographs that embarrassed citizens had to carry around for years. The state installed a new electronic system that allowed citizens to choose the photos that would grace their licenses, making them much happier with the service. As computer programs like TurboTax and TaxCut have made it easier for individuals to prepare their tax returns at home, governments have worked hard to make it easier for taxpayers to file their taxes with a touch of a button. For many Americans, the IRS has an online tax filing service that's free.

Compared with the private sector, government's **customer service movement** is in its relative infancy. Substantial problems need to be worked out, from the difficult task of identifying customers to developing fresh incentives for government employees to serve citizens better. The very strategies and tactics of government further complicate the problem: as we saw in Chapter 2, many governmental programs operate indirectly, through transfers, grants, and contracts; and most government employees are far from the ultimate customers of their programs. That does not mean that a customer service approach is invalid; it does mean, however, that government's managers must work far more creatively to ensure that managers throughout the system remain focused on the ultimate goals of public programs. The growth of **performance management**, in states such as Virginia and at the federal level, has proven important in reshaping incentives throughout the system.

The reengineers aggressively present their arguments as fresh and novel—all the better, of course, to promote book sales and consultancy contracts. In fact, their focus on customers, radical change, nimble organizations, and information technology represents a creative combination. As we saw in the previous chapter, however, organizational theory has traditionally focused on an organization's purpose and how to maximize its efficiency. Process, in fact, was central to much organizational thinking in the 1930s, especially to the work of Henri Fayol.[28] So, too, was information. As Lyndall Urwick argued, "the underlying principle of any form of administration which aims at scientific precision and integrity must be investigation or research yielding information."[29] Indeed, Luther Gulick's famous paper "The Theory of Organization," written for the Brownlow Committee, which advised President Franklin Roosevelt on reorganization of his office, explicitly tackled the issue of "organization by major process." Along the way, Gulick noted the critical problem of process-based organization: "while organization by process thus puts great efficiency within our reach, this efficiency cannot be realized unless the compensating structure of coordination is developed."[30]

In the decades that followed World War II, the interest of organizational theorists—especially *public* organizational theorists—in organizational process diminished considerably. Most discussion of process revolved around *due process* and the guarantee of fair treatment for citizens.[31] James Q. Wilson's brilliant book *Bureaucracy,* however, talks about "procedural organizations" as ones where "managers can observe what their subordinates are doing but not the outcome (if any) that results from those efforts."[32] This limited perspective creates a stark tension: in a situation where they cannot determine what results subordinates produce, Wilson warns, government managers often cannot understand, let alone control, the results of their programs. The reengineers, in contrast, contend that controlling process to improve results is essential to better administration. Indeed, organizational process is implicit in the work of most modern public organization theorists, but it is central to almost nothing (except, as noted earlier, to securing fair treatment).[33] Reengineering seeks to reestablish organizational process in the minds of managers, and to elevate it above even the level it enjoyed in the prewar period.

The single-mindedness of the reengineers is both their greatest virtue and their biggest weakness. Hammer and Champy point to Adam Smith's 1776 classic, *The Wealth of Nations,* as their predecessor. "We believe that the application of the principles of business reengineering will have effects as significant and dramatic as those created by Smith's principles of industrial organization," they write.[34] Like the authors of most reform-minded books, Hammer and Champy are unabashed in their enthusiasm for their idea and unreserved in touting its promise. They strongly argue, moreover, that halfway measures will always prove inadequate—which, of course, provides the perfect excuse, for any failure can be traced to a failure to reengineer thoroughly enough. Such advice, however, provides scant guidance for coping in an environment full of competing expectations. It offers little counsel about what to do when problems emerge except to try even harder, or about how to sustain the revolutionary spirit over the long haul after the revolution has ended and routine has set in.

The pressure on government to reduce costs and improve services is so severe that managers, public and private, are often willing to risk wrestling with the big dilemma of reengineering: overpromising and underdelivering. State governments, including Utah and Virginia, have been aggressively working to improve their management systems for a long time.[35] Although reengineering has barely entered the public administration landscape as more than a slogan, its promise has proved alluring. More important, it has provided a battle flag under which armies of reformers have marched. Most newly elected chief executives push aside the reforms of their predecessors, but new executives now have little choice but to introduce new, bold reforms of their own. They need to squeeze more services from the tax base and to step forward as cutting-edge leaders, and that's made reform an inescapable imperative.

Continuous Improvement

Other administrative reformers have taken a very different tack. In place of the discontinuous, top-down, revolutionary change that the reengineers recommend, the improvers have advocated a more gradual, continuous, bottom-up movement, grounded in the effort to motivate employees to produce better results. Since the late 1980s, this movement has been most strongly associated with TQM, launched by W. Edwards Deming, but its roots in fact go far deeper.[36] Other theorists have adapted TQM to drive a broader movement toward continuous organizational improvement and to develop newer spinoffs of the fundamental preference: the quality of the product matters most, and individuals can be motivated to produce better results.

Deming contends that costs decline as quality increases. "Better quality leads to lower costs and higher productivity," one admirer explains. "The consequences for an individual company are that increasing quality leads to higher productivity, lower costs, higher profits, higher share price, and greater security for everyone in the company—the managers, the workers, and the owners."[37] Instead of looking backward into an organization to determine how to squeeze out more profit, industry should look forward to improve quality, and profit will take care of itself. Employees dominated by the profit motive tend to be unhappy, while employees pursuing quality take more satisfaction in what they do, feel more secure, and work more productively. Thus, according to the TQM movement, a total commitment to continuous effort to achieve quality in everything the organization does is the key to managerial success.

On one level, this may sound little different from the strategy of the reengineers, who also care very deeply about quality. The reengineers, however, believe that fundamental organizational processes too often get in the way of achieving quality and that only radical change in those processes can improve results. TQMers, by contrast, argue the need to "think small," to build from the bottom to the top of an organization.[38] In TQM, whether in government or the private sector, workers themselves are the experts who know best how to solve problems, serve customers, and improve the work.[39]

TQM, moreover, views reengineering as only one part of administrative improvement. Changing the process alone is not enough, in the view of the movement's supporters. One of its foremost advocates, in fact, has argued that process is but one of the five pillars supporting management improvement (along with product, organization, leadership, and commitment). The reengineers contend that only large-scale, fundamental change can work; TQMers, in contrast, urge managers to win big by organizing small and improving continuously.[40]

In part because of its precepts and in part because as an idea it has been around longer than reengineering, TQM has been far more broadly deployed in American government. The Environmental Protection Agency used the technique to improve its management of a program dealing with leaking underground storage tanks, and the Air Force Logistics Command used it to improve the readiness rate of its fighter planes from 40 percent to 76 percent. In the New York City sanitation department, TQM helped to resolve labor union problems. The U.S. Department of Veterans Affairs Philadelphia Regional Office used TQM to improve service to veterans applying for loans.[41] In fact, two students of the process concluded, "quality improvement projects have resulted in significant cost savings, improved services to agency customers and clients, and measurable improvements in employee morale and productivity."[42]

The quality movement has bred a broader range of followers than has reengineering. Some advocates delete "total" from the label to distance themselves from the zealotry that alienated some managers from TQM. Other writers have suggested modifications to the quality improvement approach based on shaping continuous improvement to help organizations learn and on having individuals assume personal responsibility for organizational results. TQM and its successors focus far more on people than on organizations.[43] They tend to be more holistic than reengineering and its cousins, more driven by a concern for operational-level workers than for top leadership, and more convinced of the ability of workers to improve organizational results as they improve their own work.

Indeed, this approach builds on a long tradition of organizational theory rooted in the 1940s, beginning with Mary Parker Follett[44] and Abraham H. Maslow[45] and continuing on to more modern motivation-based theorists. Arguing that personal factors, from motivation to personal satisfaction, matter as much as structure and process in determining organizational results, this tradition has always been influential, but it has never been central to organizational theory. It does not promise quite the same magic in such a short period of time as reengineering. Indeed, its basic precept is that the movement toward quality, once launched, is never finished. No level of quality is ever enough, and only the constant search for quality can keep an organization and its workers sharp.

These ideas, not surprisingly, found deep resonance in American administrative reform, from Vice President Gore's reinventing government task force to state and local government efforts. More than any other set of ideas, the continuous improvement movement drove the Gore report, which promised to "give customers a voice—and a choice" and to "put citizens first," while employees were to be "empowered to get results." Indeed, the footnotes at the end of the report are littered with references to TQM. Similar customer-based, continuous processes have driven reforms at state and local levels as well, from state-based reinvention efforts in Minnesota to sweeping strategic planning in Oregon.[46]

The discussion of continuous improvement, however, proceeds alongside the arguments for downsizing and reengineering. The advocates of continuous improvement argue quite vigorously that managers cannot be expected to take risks when their jobs are on the line. Nor, in their view, can reengineering comprehend the full range of reform needed to make any organization work better. The result, from Gore's task force to other reform efforts around the country, has been an uneasy alliance among competing ideas.

Transparent Performance

When the Obama administration took office, it tackled administrative reform in a profoundly different way. Administration officials knew that they had to come up with some kind of reform, since a reform agenda has become one of the prerequisites for every new presidency. For more than half a century, presidents have felt obliged to demonstrate, to voters and especially to the permanent government, that they take the job of running the government seriously. They worked out of the vending machine model of government: insert cash (a lot of it), push the button, and wait for services to come out. Their goal: figure out how to make the vending machine work better.

Pressed by angry taxpayers, most presidents wanted to squeeze out more services for the same amount of money. Reagan tried to rewire the vending machine by putting the private sector in charge of more of its parts. Clinton's reinventing government was part good cop, in trying to repair government's machinery for federal employees caught in bad systems, and part bad cop, in downsizing the machinery itself. Bush torqued down the machine by forcing managers to say what they were trying to accomplish and to measure how well they did.

But then came Hurricane Katrina. Team Bush recovered from a remarkable collection of crises, but the blow from which it never bounced back was the FEMA fumble. October 2005 was the first time that the president's negative ratings exceeded his positives and did not recover. It was not only a public relations disaster. It was a profound failure of vending-machine government. The administration inserted the cash, pushed the buttons, but the mechanism jammed.

For Team Obama, ever mindful of history, the lesson was clear. The top-down, process-driven, budget-based reforms of the previous fifty years had run out of gas. The vending machine was broken and more presidential tinkering couldn't fix it. Moreover, administration officials decided that a new "big idea" would have to be outlandishly huge even to get the attention of government workers, who have been used to the escalating promises that have come with the regular rising and setting of the reform sun. Moreover, for the first time in a very long time—since the beginning of the Eisenhower administration, in fact—there just wasn't a consensus about what "big idea" ought to drive the next big bang.

Top administration officials also knew, however, that they needed a plan to demonstrate their seriousness about government to make sure their own—inevitable—Hurricane Katrina doesn't do them in as it torpedoed Bush. So they hitched their governance strategy to transparency and to working organically from the bottom-up. The Office of Management and Budget (OMB) remained the center of administrative reform, as it had been during the Bush years. But instead of following the Bush strategy of grading agencies on how well their efforts fit the administration's big policy goals, OMB simply told agencies to develop performance goals that, in agencies' view, best fit the agencies' missions. OMB pushed back when the performance measures seemed not to fit the mission, but it took a far less prescriptive eye to the process. Outcomes mattered, and OMB insisted on performance measures that helped agencies achieve those outcomes. As Shelley Metzenbaum, then OMB's associate director of performance and personnel management, put it, "Our mantra is 'useful, useful, useful,'" she explained. "The word 'why' should be one of [the] most frequent words we talk about in performance management. We're looking for patterns, relationships and anomalies."[47] It was a strategy based on **transparent performance.**

The administration's efforts had several distinctive elements. First, the administration focused on *virtually connecting with citizens.* The Obama staff came to Washington as masters of the new media. The White House was soon on Twitter (even if Twitter is banned inside the West Wing itself) and Tweeting out its own exclusives. Damon Weaver, an eleven-year-old ace reporter from Florida, got an interview with the president. Even though his broadcast news show reaches only 500 students at his Canal Point Elementary School, his Tweeted interview and YouTube video soon hit the broadcast networks and reached millions. Obama staffers are betting that the virtual networking force will be theirs.

Second, the administration sought to *redefine accountability through transparency.* Team Obama quickly concluded that it couldn't steer the government through the usual mechanisms. No one would pay attention to more rules, and traditional authority had broken down. The budget is the usual presidential ace, but with Washington printing money so fast it risked brownouts, the budget was useless. The administration instead has pushed out enormous quantities of information about federal programs, especially on the flow of money through the massive stimulus program passed in 2009 to jump-start the economy. The administration then counted on citizens (and interest groups) to digest the data and figure out what it means. The program's website, www.recovery.gov, provided a staggering collection of information, but that's just part of the enormous avalanche of data pouring out of Obama's Washington.

Instead of the prescriptive approach followed by his predecessors, Obama pushed responsibility down to government's senior managers and focused them on performance. In a September 2010 memorandum, his performance czar wrote,

> We face extraordinary challenges—from growing our economy to transforming our energy supply, improving our children's education, safeguarding our Nation and restoring its fiscal health. There is a distinct role for government in addressing these challenges, but the American people have doubts about the government's capacity to do so effectively and efficiently. According to the Pew Research Center, about two-thirds of Americans believe that "when something is run by government it is usually inefficient and wasteful."[48]

The administration was convinced that focusing on performance, forcing agency managers to set their own goals, and holding the managers accountable for results through transparency would transform the management of the federal government.

Assessing the Reforms

A side-by-side comparison of the defining ideas of these three major administrative reforms—downsizing, reengineering, and continuous improvement—reveals stark differences. Table 7.2 arrays the reforms according to the goals they seek, the directions in which they are implemented, the methods that characterize them, the central focus of managers following them, and the kinds of action that drive them. In brief, they may be described as follows:

■ *Downsizing*, enforced from the outside in by angry citizens, seeks lower government expenditures. Its methods are blunt targets, driven by the assumption that there is ample waste in government to accommodate the cuts. Downsizers seek to shrink the size of government through strategic intervention, indeed, by firing a weapon of sufficient size to signal their fundamental disdain for existing policymakers and managers.

■ *Reengineering* seeks greater organizational efficiency by pursuing a radical change in organizational process. Top leaders, with the broad strategic sense of where the organization needs to go, attempt to harness competition and the urge to serve customers and thereby to transform their organizations.

■ *Continuous improvement* seeks greater responsiveness to the needs of customers by launching an ongoing process to improve the quality of an organization's products. Advocates of continuous improvement believe that workers know best how to solve an organization's problems, so, unlike reengineering, continuous improvement builds from the bottom up. Cooperation among workers replaces the competition imperative, and stronger relations among employees is more important than organizational structure and process.

■ *Transparent performance* seeks a transformation in government by connecting its results to citizens and using outside-in pressure to create pressure for outcomes. It relies heavily on information and the Internet.

TABLE 7.2	Administrative Reform Strategies in the United States			
	Downsizing	**Reengineering**	**Continuous improvement**	**Transparent performance**
Goal	Lower expenditures	Efficiency	Responsiveness	Outcomes
Direction	Outside-in	Top-down	Bottom-up	Top-down/bottom-up
Method	Blunt targets	Competition	Cooperation	Transparency
Central focus	Size	Process	Interpersonal relations	Information
Action	Discontinuous	Discontinuous	Continuous	Virtual, through Internet

The fundamental precepts of each movement directly conflict with the other two. Downsizing begins with the assumption that dramatic action is required to get the attention of public managers and policymakers. Reengineers and continuous improvers, in contrast, believe that greater efficiency and smaller organizations ought to be the result, not the cause, of administrative action. Reengineering seeks to transform the behavior of lower-level workers by dramatic policy change at the top; continuous improvement contends that the job of top managers is to promote the conditions that will allow lower-level workers themselves to define the organization's transformation. Downsizers simply seek smaller government. Reengineers focus on process, while continuous improvers concentrate on people. Reengineers promote competition to drive behavior change, while continuous improvers argue that competition can undercut the interpersonal cooperation required to achieve quality.

Assessing the conflicts among the driving ideas of these administrative reform approaches is itself an important problem. We simply do not know which one works best. Finding out is impossible, not only because governments tend to grossly underinvest in program evaluation but also because no organization adopts any reform in its pure form. Elected officials and managers shop around among the reform ideas, selecting the elements that most attract them. As a result, managers often find themselves attempting to cope with externally imposed

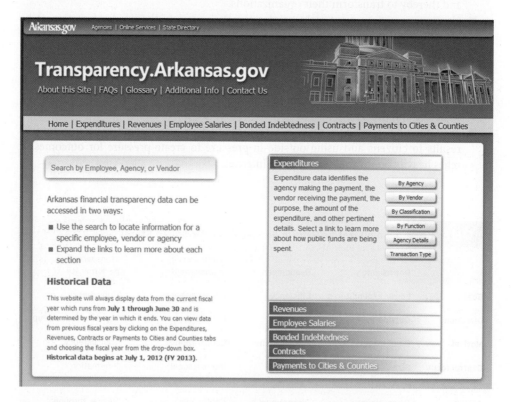

Citizens wanting to track government spending in Arkansas, from employees' salaries to aid to local governments, can easily find the data on a special website devoted to transparency in government.

downsizing targets by reengineering their processes from the top down while encouraging their employees to improve quality from the bottom up. The advocates of each approach often are aghast at such hybrids, because they recognize that ideas for competition and cooperation, for top-down and bottom-up leadership, for process and interpersonal approaches, for discontinuous change and continuous improvement rarely mesh well. The combination of such antithetical reform plans sends out contradictory signals to workers and creates conflicting expectations about results.

These contradictions, however, have scarcely prevented both public managers and policymakers from embracing the basic ideas. The labels themselves have strong symbolic appeal, and the overall goals of each technique are unassailable. Citizens and elected officials alike find alluring the promise of a smaller government, engineered with better processes and devoted to greater responsiveness to citizens and quality. The contradictions of administrative reform ideas are both fundamentally unresolvable and politically unavoidable.

ALL THE WORLD'S A STAGE

Around the globe, two undeniable truths about public administration are evident.[49] One is that administrative reform is a fixture of government everywhere—indeed, it may well be the feature that governments share more than any other. Nations that broke out of a generation of domination by the Soviet Union are struggling to catch up. They face tasks ranging from inventing a system of public law within which a new private sector can grow to revising a tax system in order to fund public programs better. Developing nations are rushing to modernize their economies, and reconstructing their governments is a critical part of that strategy.[50] More developed nations are seeking to reinvent themselves by wringing waste out of the public sector and making governmental programs more efficient. China is a management reform movement in a class by itself, as the country works both to quickly modernize a vast rural population and to sustain world-class technology in other areas.

The other truth is that, despite widespread reform, no single set of ideas is driving it. Reform of public administration is as varied as the nations attempting it. The number of basic ideas at the core of the reform movement is small, but they have come together in a remarkable array of combinations.

Downsizing carries a simple goal: shrink the public sector as much as possible, whether by selling off public enterprises, contracting out services that remain publicly provided, or imposing limits to future growth. However, although downsizing is one of the few government reforms that can produce quick cost savings, it risks pushing government's management capacity out of sync with the job to be done. Downsizing is rarely accompanied by a restructuring of government's workforce, and, as a result, it is very easy to end up with too many of the wrong employees and not enough employees with the skills government needs most. Nevertheless, virtually every major government around the world has tried it, both to signal its determination to cut costs and to produce real savings.

The reengineering approaches employ both procedural and analytical tactics. Many countries have developed new processes to link operating units together better. For example, New Zealand is training top managers to develop new skills in administering programs that cut across agency boundaries. The French decentralization movement aims, in part, to bring together at the local level all those concerned with similar problems. Spain has introduced information technology to link governmental units, and **e-government** has spread around the globe. Meanwhile, a worldwide movement to reduce the number of government regulations, launched in the 1980s, is continuing. Countries are relying as well on information and analysis to increase leverage over administrators' actions. Governments also have spent more than a decade developing performance management systems, in which operating managers are given greater discretion in return for accountability for performance measured against agreed-upon indicators. Many nations are linking such performance measurement with reform of financial management systems to promote planning and cost control. Australia, Finland, Iceland, New Zealand, the United Kingdom, and the United States all have moved (some much further and more eagerly than others) from cost toward accrual accounting to improve accountability. Overall, the result is a widely varied collection of strategies that fly loosely under the reengineering banner.

At the same time, many nations are relying on better measurement and training systems as they seek to change the culture of bureaucrats. Performance measurement systems are designed to focus managers on results and outputs instead of budgets and inputs. Countries are working to change expectations about career paths and to enhance managers' leadership ability. Both the Netherlands and the United States have committed themselves to pushing decisions down to the lowest possible level. Many nations are also working to make public services more "customer-centered." In Canada, for example, public officials are working to "co-locate" related services so that citizens needing public services can come to one place instead of having to run from one government office to another. Japan has launched a major movement to make its programs more consumer-oriented and transparent to citizens. The United Kingdom has championed "joined-up government" to improve service coordination.

All the world unquestionably has become a stage for administrative reform in the public sector. Indeed, the past two decades have seen an unprecedented revolution, in both scale and breadth, in public administration. Not since the immediate post–World War II years have so many governments attempted so dramatic a reshaping of the way they do business. The postwar reforms focused principally on establishing the right structures, organized according to existing administrative orthodoxy to help governments manage their programs most efficiently; those reforms proved remarkably long-lasting. By the 1980s, however, it was clear that the postwar reforms had sowed the seeds of their own undoing. Earlier strategies to create strong bureaucracies for solving postwar problems had evolved into bureaucracies that too often seemed oversized, overbearing, and overcontrolling. Citizens around the world complained that the taxes they paid to governments were far higher than the benefits they received. Meanwhile, governments in less developed countries and in newly independent countries struggled to catch up. A new, global revolution in public administration sprang up, and as it quickly spread around the world, it often echoed many of the same notes.[51]

CONCLUSION

One overarching conclusion stands out sharply in this review of administrative reform in industrialized countries. Even though many different ideas have driven administrative reform and even though these ideas have contradictory ideas built into them, reformers have indiscriminately mixed and matched them with little regard for the contradictions. Moreover, because the mixtures tend to come together in very different forms, patterns rarely repeat themselves. That makes it hard to determine whether the administrative reforms work, whether some ideas work better than others, or which work best where. Reformers can and do take credit for any positive change that happens on their watch. Reform theorists do likewise, quickly pointing to inadequate application of their theories to explain any problems.

It would, in fact, be possible to use this explanation to drive a broader, cynical conclusion that administrative reform is nothing but symbolic politics, cleverly practiced. Is there, under it all, anything real going on? The cynical challenge has merit, for the symbols have proven to have broad and lasting value, in the United States and around the world. Moreover, the reform movement is about vocabulary and prescription: developing a way to capture the unhappiness that so often surrounds government performance and a strategy for solving government's problems.

It would, however, be far too cynical to stop there, for three reasons. First, the reforms have genuinely produced significant effects. American efforts have had a deep, if uneven, impact.[52] In New Zealand, reforms have profoundly transformed the public sector.[53] Indeed, the reform movement has clearly proven that government *can* change, and many of these changes have made government more efficient and effective. Quite simply, management matters. It provides a symbolic language for understanding governmental activity and both strategies and tactics for improving results. This may not seem a very bold claim, but it is one that often is underestimated.

An equally important second conclusion is that management matters only to the degree to which it matters *politically*. It is unrealistic to expect that public administration can live a life independent of politics, or that its most fundamental meaning will be administrative rather than political. The internal theoretical contradictions of most administrative reform efforts matter far less than the fact that the contradictions themselves seem so often to have important political value. It is the politics of the administrative process that matters most.

Third, many of the reforms have created big and sometimes unexpected new problems that demand careful attention. Downsizing has often created imbalances in the workforce. Growing reliance on contracts with the private sector has created problems in supervising those contracts and in ensuring the pursuit of the public interest. More attention to serving the needs of citizens-as-customers has flown directly into the teeth of a basic paradox: most citizens want more public services than they are willing to pay for. If government reforms have solved some problems, they have created new ones. These new issues too often have remained unexplored—and, of course, they thereby plant the seeds of a future round of reforms.

This dynamic suggests a pair of important implications. First, public managers themselves must be ready to accommodate conflicting and contradictory demands. Their lives would unquestionably be far simpler if they were allowed to pursue a single administrative approach. For that matter, their lives would be simpler yet if they were free to follow their own ideas independently of the policies established by elected officials or the needs of citizens. But that was not what they were hired to do. In democratic societies, the fundamental mission of public managers is to reconcile such fundamentally irreconcilable demands. As OMB frankly admitted in 2001:

Though reform is badly needed, the obstacles are daunting—as previous generations of would-be reformers have repeatedly discovered. The work of reform is continually overwhelmed by the constant multiplication of hopeful new government programs, each of whose authors is certain that this particular idea will avoid the managerial problems to which all previous government programs have succumbed. Congress, the Executive Branch, and the media have all shown far greater interest in the launch of new initiatives than in following up to see if anything useful ever occurred.[54]

The job in the twenty-first century has become harder because expectations have grown even as resources have shrunk. That means that the challenges for public managers have never been higher, nor has the need for good public managers ever been greater.

Second, administrative theorists have perhaps an even more daunting challenge. To a significant degree, the central ideas of *public* administration reform have tended to come from *private* managers. Administrative theory has significantly lagged behind these startling changes. The tasks and environment of public administration are so fundamentally different, however, that no matter how suggestive private-sector reforms may be, they are unlikely to provide very sure guides for the public sector. For example, the "customer service" movement has swept the Western world, but there simply has been little careful thought about who government's customers are, how governmental activities can be restructured to advance customer service, how to balance the often conflicting expectations of government's multiple customers, and what other important goals might be sacrificed in the process.

Moreover, administrative theorists face an equally imposing job of reconciling the contradictions that political realities impose on neat organizational theories. Too often, like public managers who complain that their jobs would be much easier if elected officials would stop interfering in their work, theorists complain about elected officials whose contradictory messages muddy neat theories. The problem is far more with the theory than with the practice. And the pace of administrative reform around the world demonstrates just how important tackling these issues is.

CASE 7.1

How Best to Contribute Public Good: Government or Nonprofit?

Cole Ledford was a sophomore at Ohio State and was majoring in political science. He was excited about the internship he got in the Ohio legislature—until he got to the capitol in Columbus. What he learned surprised him.

"I thought I wanted to be one of them," he told a reporter for *USA Today*. After his internship experience, however, he found "it was more that politics was a game they wanted to play, and it wasn't about the constituents." His goal was to "give back and influence the world." He's decided to do that by switching his major to nonprofit management and by focusing instead on working for a charitable organization.

Ledford isn't alone. A 2013 poll showed that Americans want to make a difference, but by a margin of more than two to one, they believe that the best way to do so is through charities and volunteer organizations, not through government. The gap is especially large for those under thirty. Just one in five of those surveyed said they trusted the government to do what's right most of the time. Among those surveyed, it was almost even about whether they saw government as an advocate (42 percent) or an adversary (38 percent) for them and their families.

John F. Kennedy, in his famous 1961 inaugural address, raised a clear call: "Ask not what your country can do for you—ask what you can do for your country." Many of today's Americans want to do something for their country. But as Kelsey Gallagher from Ohio State put it, "Working at a non-profit or doing community service, you get more of a firsthand experience." She concluded, "You get to see the direct effects."

Government's leaders looked carefully at these findings and worried about where they were going to find the talented individuals they needed for the next generation of government leaders. The *USA Today/Bipartisan Policy Center* poll gave them pause.[1]

Questions to Consider

1. Where do you think that a college graduate can make the biggest impact on society—working for government or working in a non-profit organization? Why?
2. Why do you think that the trend has developed toward lower trust in government and a greater tendency to think of government as an "adversary" to families?
3. What steps can be taken to reverse this trend? Is it a trend that can—or should—be reversed?

NOTE

1. The poll and quotes for this case come from Susan Page, "Poll: Public Service Valued; Politics—Not So Much," *USA Today* (July 22, 2013), http://www.usatoday.com/story/news/nation/2013/07/21/public-service-valued-politics--not-so-much/2573743.

CASE 7.2

Poking through the Luggage: At San Francisco Airport, Private Contractors (Not the TSA) Inspect Your Bags

For Samantha and Darrin, it had been a long and grueling trip back home. They finally snagged their luggage from the baggage claim carousel, dragged the bags to the car, and staggered up the stairs. "What a great trip that was!" Samantha told Darrin. "Imagine. Just a day ago—or was it two?—we were standing on top of the Great Wall of China. That's one more item on my bucket list."

Darrin was jet-lagged and found it hard to join the conversation. He unlocked the bags and started pulling out the clothing from their two-week trip. As Samantha started sorting through everything on the bed, she pulled out a paper tag. "What's this?" she asked. Darrin looked more carefully. They found a very polite "Thank you for flying from San Francisco International" printed tag inside—but the next line brought them up short. "Notification of Inspection" the tag continued. "To protect you and your fellow passengers, Covenant Aviation Security (CAS) is required by law to inspect all checked baggage." Who was Covenant? According to the tag, "CAS is a private company under contract with the Transportation Security Administration (TSA) to provide baggage and passenger screening at San Francisco International Airport."

One of Darrin's bags had been singled out for an inspection. He had been using one of the TSA-approved locks. Covenant used a special key, poked through the luggage, left behind the inspection tag, and resealed it. Neither Darrin nor Samantha had been present for the inspection. They had pulled their bags from the carousel in San Francisco, trudged through immigration and customs before reaching the domestic transfer desk, and piled their luggage on top of the growing mountain of bags waiting to be sorted onto connecting flights. At some point after they left their bags in San Francisco, Covenant employees gave the bag and its contents a close look.

Darrin was slightly incredulous that someone had gone through his stuff without his being present. He was too tired to care much that night, but in the next few days he started digging through the Internet.

Soon after the September 11, 2001, terrorist attacks, Congress and the Bush administration decided to federalize airport screeners. Analysts worried that the previous privately operated screening stations had allowed armed terrorists to board the aircraft, and policymakers concluded that the public would feel safer about flying again if federal workers conducted the screening. However, the law also contained a provision allowing individual airports to opt out of the federalized program if they hired private contractors who met tough national standards. San Francisco International Airport decided to go with Covenant.

At SFO, as the airport is known, the company holds an annual tournament where its employees can win big cash prizes for winning competitions. They are challenged to find explosives in carry-on bags, pick locks on luggage, and find disguised terrorists on videos. In one competition, Covenant's

Thank you for flying from San Francisco International, a world-class Airport dedicated to serving the "City by the Bay".

NOTIFICATION OF INSPECTION (NOI)

To protect you and your fellow passengers, Covenant Aviation Security (CAS) is required by law to inspect all checked baggage. CAS is a private company under contract with the Transportation Security Administration (TSA) to provide baggage and passenger screening at San Francisco International Airport.

As part of this process, your bag was identified for physical inspection. If your bag was locked using non-TSA recognized locks, CAS may have had to break the locks. If prohibited items, including Hazardous Materials, were discovered during an inspection, they were turned over to the appropriate authorities.

Furthermore, to ensure the highest quality of service, CAS employees are continuously monitored by either direct supervision or camera surveillance.

We appreciate your understanding and cooperation. For questions and packing tips that may assist you during your next trip, or to learn how to submit a claim, please visit us at _www.covenantclaims.com,_ or call us toll free at 1-800-764-8050.

Screener ID: _1 0 1 3 8_

Flight: _888_

Inspection tag from Covenant Aviation Security LLC.

president, Gerald L. Berry, posed as a dangerous-looking character. Cash prizes range as high as $1,500. "The bonuses are pretty handsome," Berry explained. "We have to be good—equal or better than the feds. So we work at it, and we incentivize."[1]

So the card Darrin found inside his luggage was part of a far larger policy debate: deputizing private companies and their employees to open locked luggage and poke through an individual's private property. The debate grew even more heated toward the end of 2010, when John Tyner, a thirty-one-year-old software programmer, filmed his screening by federal TSA officials at San Diego's airport. He complained about the physical pat-down that one TSA employee gave him. "If you touch my junk," he said, "I'll have you arrested." The story—and his clandestine video—quickly went viral online (see http://johnnyedge.blogspot.com/2010/11/these-events-took-place-roughly-between.html). Rep. John L. Mica (R-Fla.) charged pointedly that TSA "was never intended to be an army of 67,000 employees."[2]

Questions to Consider

1. Would you be concerned if you found a note saying a private security guard had opened a locked piece of luggage and searched it, without you being present and without your knowledge or permission? Or would you assume this action is part of the security procedures you submit yourself to when you fly these days?

2. Do you think there's any difference between using private security guards to check luggage versus having private security guards conduct private pat-downs in the airport security area?

3. What is the proper federal role in airport security? Should the federal government concentrate on setting standards and overseeing those who administer those standards, regardless of whether they are public or private employees? Or do steps like searching luggage and patting down flyers constitute the kind of use of police power that only government officials should be empowered to use?

4. This raises a broader question. Are there functions that are inherently governmental, which only the government should perform? How far should government reform go in turning public power over to the private sector?

NOTES

1. Derek Kravitz, "As Outrage Over Screenings Rise, Sites Consider Replacing TSA," *Washington Post* (December 31, 2010), http://www.washingtonpost.com/wp-dyn/content/article/2010/12/30/AR2010123004986.html.
2. Ibid.

CASE 7.3

StateStat: Performance Management in Maryland State Government

In 2009, *Governing* magazine named Maryland Governor Martin O'Malley one of the nation's "public officials of the year." O'Malley had already made a national reputation as mayor of Baltimore, where he created CitiStat and brought numbers-based performance management to city government. When he was elected governor, he upped the ante with an even broader initiative, christened StateStat. He launched a sweeping website at www.statestat.maryland.gov and used it to chart performance ranging from the state police and corrections to social services and juvenile justice.

He focused especially on efforts to improve the water quality in the Chesapeake Bay. Locals are fond of pointing out that the bay has more shoreline than the entire west coast of the United States, but over the years, pollution has seriously injured the bay and starkly reduced the crabs and oysters for which it has long been famous. The bay is a complicated ecosystem, with water feeding into it from long rivers that flow through Pennsylvania and Virginia as well as Maryland—and with the water picking up large quantities of fertilizer and urban pollution along the way. O'Malley's BayStat program at http://ian.umces.edu/ecocheck/report-cards/chesapeake-bay/2012 produced regular report cards on the bay with grades ranging from an F along the Patapsco River near Baltimore to a B- along the southern stretch of the bay. Overall, its 2012 report card gave the bay a C, with grades determined by water clarity, levels of chlorophyll, the amount of dissolved oxygen, and the amount of plankton in the water.

"We're not going to find the magic factory that allows us to take everything bad that's flowing into the Chesapeake Bay and turn it into clean water," O'Malley told *Governing*. The state charted twenty-seven different core actions required to clean the bay. "So," he explained, "you map those steps out, and they're all connected to one another to create a healthier whole."[1] The underlying reform philosophy was simple: identify outcomes that the state wanted to achieve, develop indicators that measured those outcomes and how much progress the state was making, determine which agency was responsible for which outcome, and hold officials accountable for results.

For O'Malley, however, the process is much more than numbers and outcomes. He built his StateStat and BayStat processes on the belief that these were complex problems that required high levels of coordination among many state agencies to produce results. "Here, the focus is on coming together and on working together," his public safety director, Gary Maynard, told *Governing*, "and there's no question that it's making a difference."[2]

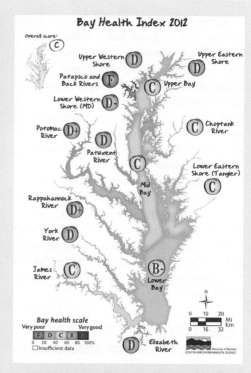

Maryland's online performance system reports on a wide range of state issues, including this report card on the health of the Chesapeake Bay.

Questions to Consider

1. Assess O'Malley's StateStat and BayStat. What positive elements do you think they might bring to state government?

2. An underlying theme of these performance management systems is that, by measuring outcomes, it's possible for state officials to encourage stronger collaboration among state agencies. How might that work? Do you think performance measurement is likely to prove effective as a mechanism for encouraging collaboration?

3. Critics contend that such performance systems won't last long, that they require too much effort in collecting data instead of

investing time and money in delivering programs, and that agency officials quickly discover ways of gaming the system to produce the data top officials are looking for—without really changing anything. What do you think of these criticisms?

4. What steps would you recommend to top officials for improving the coordination of the agencies responsible for managing important programs?

NOTES

1. Jonathan Walters, "Driven by Data," *Governing*, http://www.governing.com/poy/Martin-OMalley .html.
2. Ibid.

KEY CONCEPTS

Balanced Budget and Emergency
  Deficit Control Act   166

continuous improvement   164

customer service movement   172

downsizing   164

e-government   180

performance management   172

Private Sector Survey
  on Cost Control   166

reengineering   164

reinventing government   166

Taxpayer Bill of Rights (TABOR)   165

total quality management (TQM)   170

transparent performance   176

FOR FURTHER READING

Kamarck, Elaine C. *The End of Government as We Know It: Making Public Policy Work.* Boulder, Colo.: Lynne Rienner, 2007.

Kettl, Donald F. *The Global Public Management Revolution: A Report on the Transformation of Governance.* Washington, D.C.: Brookings Institution, 2000.

Niskanen, William. *Bureaucracy and Representative Government.* Chicago: Aldine Atherton, 1971.

Osborne, David, and Ted Gaebler. *Reinventing Government: How the Entrepreneurial Spirit Is Transforming the Public Sector, from Schoolhouse to Statehouse, City Hall to the Pentagon.* Reading, Mass.: Addison-Wesley, 1993.

Osborne, David, and Peter Hutchinson. *The Price of Government: Getting the Results We Need in an Age of Permanent Fiscal Crisis.* New York: Basic Books, 2004.

Pollitt, Christopher, and Geert Bouckaert. *Public Management Reform: A Comparative Analysis–New Public Management, Governance, and the Neo-Weberian State.* Oxford: Oxford University Press, 2011.

Savas, E. S. *Privatizing the Public Sector: How to Shrink Government.* Chatham, N.J.: Chatham House, 1982.

Wilson, James Q. *Bureaucracy: What Government Agencies Do and Why They Do It.* New York: Basic Books, 1989.

SUGGESTED WEBSITES

The Office of Management and Budget website, **www.whitehouse.gov/omb,** contains the administration's most recent management reform initiatives. The congressional Government Accountability Office, **www.gao.gov,** conducts independent assessments of the effectiveness of government management. The best source for tracking government reform initiatives around the world is the Organization for Economic Co-operation and Development, **www.oecd.org**

Reasonable. Effective.
TAXPAYER
BILL OF RIGHTS

PEOPLE IN GOVERNMENT ORGANIZATIONS

The Greek historian Herodotus is credited with the earliest version of the motto the U.S. Postal Service adopted, "Neither snow, nor rain, nor heat, nor gloom of night stays these couriers from the swift completion of their appointed rounds." But Herodotus could not have foreseen the many demands placed upon postal workers or their need to cope with challenges from UPS and FedEx—or the email and texts that shrank traditional written communications. Nor could he have anticipated the rise of anti-government fervor. An organization's structure might provide the system's overall framework, but Herodotus would surely agree that people are the core of public organizations in any century.

Doing the public's work—and doing it well—requires finding, recruiting, and retaining good people; ensuring that they work according to the laws and norms of a democratic society; and creating incentives for the highest levels of performance. This section examines the foundations of the civil service system, the system of political leadership that guides it, and the efforts to reform it. The quality of the system's people determines the quality of the government's work, regardless of whether that work encounters snow, rain, heat, or gloom of night. And, as earlier chapters hinted, the relationship between the work of public administrators and the mission of administrative organizations is the keystone of accountability.

The Civil Service

CHAPTER OBJECTIVES

- Examine the work of public employees

- Understand the basic principles and practices of the civil service system, including strategies for hiring new employees

- Explore the ongoing issues surrounding the civil service

In most communities, police officers, firefighters, and teachers are the front-line public servants. In Albuquerque, New Mexico, high school chemistry teacher Stephen Schum helped his student with an experiment on copper chloride and aluminum.

THE FIRST MAN TO SET FOOT ON THE MOON WAS A CIVIL SERVANT, an employee of the National Aeronautics and Space Administration. The day was one of enormous national celebration, and President Lyndon Johnson designated the day of the moonwalk a holiday for the government's employees. Some employees had jobs that required them to work anyway, but civil servants working on holidays receive premium pay (twice their regular pay). Neil Armstrong's work that day did not qualify, however. He was at the GS-16 level in the federal civil service system, and Congress forbade provision of premium pay for workers above the GS-15 level. So despite the enormous personal risk Armstrong took with that "one small step for mankind," as he put it, providing him holiday pay would have been illegal—even though the eight-year Apollo moon-landing program had spent $25 billion to put him there.[1] He did receive the standard government per diem provided to employees on a travel assignment—$8 per day, although the government made deductions for accommodations, since he was provided a place to sleep in his moon lander (translating to the value of the dollar today, that works out to about $50 per day). His salary was about $17,000 per year.[2]

This unusual case illustrates four basic principles about government civil service systems. First, the government *hires employees by merit.* Armstrong went through a highly competitive process to qualify to be an astronaut. He got the job because of the match between his personal skills and the requirements of the job. Second, government workers receive *pay according to their position,* not their personal characteristics. Astronauts with Armstrong's level of training qualified for the GS-16 level of salary. It was the job, not the person holding the job, that determined the pay. Third, once in the civil service system, workers receive many *protections from political interference and dismissal,* in exchange for their agreement to abide by laws and regulations. This safeguard stems from a long-held belief that there is not a Republican or a Democratic way to do most technical government jobs. Rather, there has long been a belief that there is a best way of doing the government's work—such as flying a moon lander—and the government's workers ought to do what needs to be done in the best way possible. The focus is on effectiveness, separated (in theory) by a wall from politics. Fourth, in doing their work, government's workers have an *obligation to accountability,* to administer the law to the best of their ability regardless of their personal views. For Armstrong and the nation's other government workers, this meant keeping the public interest paramount. There are many variations in details among the federal, state, and local governments, but these four basic principles guide the civil service system throughout American government.

The Pendleton Civil Service Act of 1883 established these principles in law, but within the principles are enduring tensions. The basic standard is to treat all employees the same, but the range of government's work is so vast and the complications so varied that uniform treatment is impossible—and unwise. It's important to motivate individual employees, and being treated as one cog among many, trapped in one wheel among thousands, can extinguish the search for performance. Balancing the system's need for basic rules and the individual's need for motivation is a central problem of the civil service.

And why is this civil service so important? This chapter and the next examine how the quality of the government's performance depends heavily on the skill of the people working in it. Government is large and complex, but the quality of its work hinges on the skill of millions of individual workers. Crime control depends on how police officers on the front lines patrol the streets. Teams of firefighters determine whether fires get put out. One trained emergency medical technician can save your life. Moreover, since so much of government's work happens through third parties, such as private contractors, a very small number of government employees can leverage an enormous amount of government activity. Consider the federal government's Centers for Medicare and Medicaid Services. The agency is responsible for managing the Medicare program, which funds health care for senior citizens, and Medicaid, which funds health care for the poor. Together, these programs account for about 20 percent of all federal spending. There are just over 4,000 federal employees—0.2 percent of all federal employees—responsible for this money. Their job is leverage: a relatively tiny army of feds who work to provide health care through a vast network of for-profit and nonprofit contractors, with the states (in the case of Medicaid) as partners. Individual government employees are tremendously important in the government's system of goods and services. As former Comptroller General David M. Walker told Congress in 2001, "The more skilled and capable our workforce, the more capable our organization will be to perform its mission."[3] The quality of government can only be as good as the quality of the people who work for it.

At the same time, simply trying to understand the civil service system is amazingly complex. "For the unanointed," journalist Jonathan Walters explains, "no topic around public administration is considered more baffling—or stultifying—than civil service."[4] Most students look at the textbook chapter on the civil service with a sense of dread, because they are sure it will be hopelessly boring. They aren't alone. As David Osborne and Ted Gaebler argue in the best-seller *Reinventing Government,* "The only thing more destructive than a line item budget system is a personnel system built around civil service."[5] Some people find the topic so boring that they leave it to others—but that only means they surrender so many of the core questions to insiders who learn enough about the details to steer the course of government. Government's people are its most important resource, but often it's the resource that receives the least attention.

WHAT GOVERNMENT EMPLOYEES DO

Just as government's functions vary by level of government, so too does the work of its employees. We often refer to the work of government employees as "public service," because so many workers are engaged in service to the public (see Table 8.1).

FUNDAMENTAL ELEMENTS OF THE CIVIL SERVICE SYSTEM

Suppose that an individual wants to work for the government. What are the steps? First, of course, there must be an opening, and vacancies can be scarce when the economy turns down or the public mood turns against government spending, as has been the case in recent years. The federal government provides a one-stop website for its vacancies at www.USAjobs .gov. (The well-known private-sector jobs website www.Monster.com provides the technology that supports www.USAjobs.gov.) Many state and local governments have produced their own job-hunting websites. For example, the city of Seattle lists its jobs at www.seattle. gov/personnel/employment. Job hunters seeking a position in the Utah state government can go to http://statejobspostings.utah.gov.

TABLE 8.1	Ten Most Common Jobs in U.S. Federal, State, and Local Government, May 2012
Federal Government Occupation	**Employment (number of employees)**
Postal service mail carriers	305,490
Business operations specialists, all other	171,770
Postal service mail sorters, processors, and processing machine operators	134,230
Information and record clerks, all other	73,820
Computer occupations, all other	73,260
Postal service clerks	69,240
Registered nurses	67,770
Managers, all other	62,900
Management analysts	57,590
Compliance officers	53,910
State Government Occupation	**Employment**
Correctional officers and jailers	237,380
Office clerks, general	183,800
Registered nurses	138,210
Secretaries and administrative assistants, except legal, medical, and executive	128,280
Graduate teaching assistants	91,970
Executive secretaries and executive administrative assistants	87,710
Postsecondary teachers, all other	85,820
Business operations specialists, all other	84,520
Health specialties teachers, postsecondary	79,730
Janitors and cleaners, except maids and housekeeping cleaners	71,310
Local Government Occupation	**Employment**
Elementary school teachers, except special education	1,222,460
Teacher assistants	885,670
Secondary school teachers, except special and career/technical education	845,880
Middle school teachers, except special and career/technical education	564,190
Substitute teachers	550,670
Police and sheriff's patrol officers	545,130
Janitors and cleaners, except maids and housekeeping cleaners	404,920
Secretaries and administrative assistants, except legal, medical, and executive	332,550
Office clerks, general	317,180
Firefighters	270,920
Source: U.S. Bureau of Labor Statistics, "Occupational Employment Statistics," http://bls.gov/oes/2012/may/featured_data.htm.	

But in many civil service systems, the process gets vastly more complex from there. Most web-based systems invite applicants to file their materials online, but because the websites are open, job announcements can attract floods of applications, often far more than personnel officers can review. Many of the individuals trying to work through these systems come away frustrated and disappointed, since applications disappear into an online morass without any feedback. Even for those who successfully navigate the system, the delays and procedural hassles prove discouraging. As the federal government's chief performance officer, Jeffrey Zients, put it in May 2010,

> The current hiring system uses overly complex job descriptions, involves filling out lengthy forms and essays, and is a black hole, providing no feedback to applicants along the way. I know from my business experience that the best talent doesn't wait around for jobs, they find work elsewhere.[6]

One of the biggest challenges in government today is resolving the issue of civil service hiring: preserving the age-old principles of civil service protection while recruiting the top talent that government needs.

There are three fundamental elements of the **civil service system**: rules for position classification, staffing, and compensation. There's a complex chain of issues and actions, for agencies and employees, in filling a government job (see Figure 8.1). Beyond that set of hurdles are policies outlining employee rights and obligations, which make government work so fundamentally different from private-sector jobs.

Position Classification

In civil service systems, as well as in most large corporations, each position is identified in terms of the special knowledge the job requires, its level of difficulty, and the responsibilities (including supervisory duties) that come with it. This process is known as **position classification,** and it is the foundation of the system. Each position is defined according to the occupation (e.g., policy analyst, civil engineer). The degree of difficulty and responsibility are expressed in a grade level. In the federal civil service system, there are fifteen grades in the General Schedule (GS), which governs most employees. Civil service systems at the state and local level generally operate in the same way.

Each position opening is thus described by GS level (or its equivalent in other personnel classification systems) and occupation, which, in turn, define the qualifications an applicant must meet to be considered for the position. Once an individual is hired, the position description details the duties and the salary (see Table 8.2 for the grades and the salary ranges as well as the various roles performed at each level). In the federal GS system, Levels 1 through 8 tend to be clerical positions. College graduates often qualify for entry-level professional positions, beginning at the GS-5 level. With a master's degree, an applicant may qualify for placement at the GS-7 to GS-9 levels, while levels 10 and above tend to be managerial levels that require more experience.

Applicants who want to be considered for a position must demonstrate not only that they have the necessary skills but also that they are better qualified than other applicants. Over

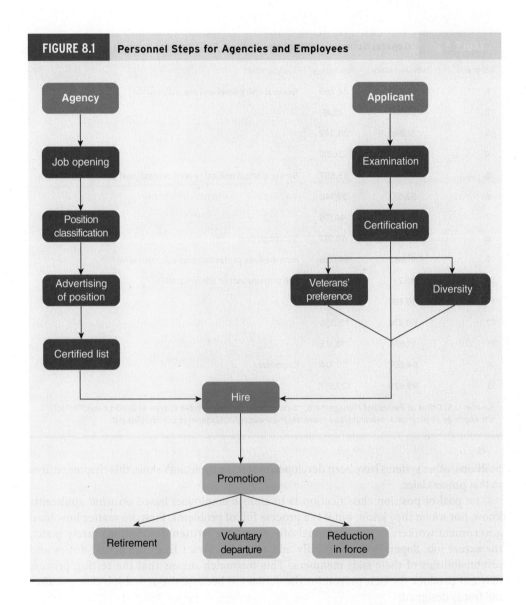

FIGURE 8.1 **Personnel Steps for Agencies and Employees**

time, the government has devised a series of tests to judge an individual's qualifications. The most traditional test is for clerical positions, where applicants are tested for typing accuracy and speed—although with the spread of computers, there are far fewer individuals in this classification. Potential firefighters and police officers must pass both written exams and tests of strength and agility. In some local governments, these traditional tests have been the source of great controversy. As more women sought to move into firefighting positions, for example, critics argued that some strength tests did not match the actual skills required of firefighters and served only to exclude women from the workforce. For professional-level

TABLE 8.2	General Schedule (GS) of the Federal Civil Service System		
GS grade	Bottom salary	Top salary	Typical roles
1	17,803	22,269	General entry-level and preprofessional
2	20,017	25,191	
3	21,840	28,392	
4	24,518	31,871	
5	27,431	35,657	Senior clerical and entry-level professional and administrative
6	30,577	39,748	
7	33,979	44,176	
8	37,631	48,917	Senior clerical
9	41,563	54,028	Intermediate professional or administrative
10	45,771	59,505	Full professional or administrative
11	50,287	65,371	
12	60,274	78,355	
13	71,674	93,175	
14	84,697	110,104	Executive
15	99,628	129,517	

Source: U.S. Office of Personnel Management, "Salary Table 2012-GS: Rates Frozen at 2010 Levels," http://www.opm.gov/policy-data-oversight/pay-leave/salaries-wages/2012/general-schedule/gs.pdf.

positions, other systems have been developed to test the applicant's skills; this chapter returns to that process later.

The goal of position classification is to choose employees based on *what* applicants know, not *whom* they know, but it is a process full of problems. First, no matter how hard government workers in the personnel offices try, the written descriptions rarely match the actual job. Supervisors constantly add to and subtract from the actual duties and responsibilities of their staff members. This mismatch means that the testing process may not produce the best person for the actual job because the actual job changes after the test is designed.

Second, the system creates strong incentives for **grade creep**: a tendency for agencies to multiply the number of high administrative positions, shift professional specialists to administrative roles, or seek higher classifications for existing positions. The higher the classification, the more supervisors can pay their employees, which makes it easier to hire the workers they want and to keep the good ones they have. Government supervisors worry constantly about losing their best employees to better-paying jobs in the private sector, but within the civil service system, it is impossible simply to give the worker a salary increase, because it is the position, not the worker, that determines the salary level. Therefore, in order to increase the salary, the supervisor seeks to upgrade the position. To guard against such grade creep, government personnel offices employ classification specialists, whose job it is to review every request for reclassification, looking carefully at the technical skills required and the number of persons supervised by the employee in question. But the review of reclassification requests only adds to the complexity of the system's rules.

Third, the changing nature of government work makes it hard to keep the system up to date. Not only have information processing experts replaced clerks and typists. Sometimes government needs experts with special skills—not just a mining engineer, but one especially knowledgeable in the shale oil being extracted in many states. The government needs the best experts, for sure—but sometimes agencies define a job so narrowly that only a handful of persons could possibly qualify. That, in turn, makes it tempting for hiring officials to define the job in a way that gives a special advantage to those they know well and, thus, defeats the purposes of competitive hiring. Government managers quickly respond that they want to make sure they get the employees that they need, and they can't afford to be handcuffed by arbitrary testing processes. Central personnel offices, of course, understand both sides of the argument well, and the tension is often a source of controversy in the personnel system.

Staffing

The online job systems have made it much easier to *search* for job openings. However, once an individual finds a job in which he or she is interested, it is usually necessary to qualify for the position through an examination or other means of demonstrating qualifications, and that process often proves extremely difficult to navigate.

The testing process is central to hiring new government employees. The federal government's long-standing regulations require

> open, competitive examinations for testing applicants for appointment in the competitive service which are practical in character and as far as possible relate to matters that fairly test the relative capacity and fitness of the applicants for the appointment sought. . . . An individual may be appointed in the competitive service only if he has passed an examination or is specifically excepted from examination.[7]

For many jobs, of course, there is no good standardized test, but even for these positions the government has had to devise some alternative means of testing a candidate's qualifications to meet both the letter and spirit of the civil service system requirements.

The Hiring Process

In recent years, the Office of Personnel Management (OPM) has given agencies much greater flexibility in devising the best tests for their potential employees, including moves to replace the old tests and Knowledge, Skills, and Abilities (KSAs) with detailed resumes. Through these changes, government agencies have come to rely far less on traditional exams. Over time, exceptions to the exam process have grown, including special provisions for veterans, internships, and flexibility for hiring in high-demand positions like airport screeners.[8] The implications? A dramatic erosion of the long-standing principles that supported the merit system and a risk that the multiple routes of entry could open the door to favoritism in hiring and a workforce that recruits disproportionately from some groups. With many baby boomers certain to retire in the coming years, these cracks in the tradition worried some observers, who feared that the flexibilities would open the door to favoritism and a return to the patronage that the system was created to abolish.[9]

Suppose that an agency wishes to fill a vacant position. It may decide to do so by promoting or transferring a civil servant already in the agency or elsewhere in the government. That individual must meet the qualifications for the new position, and the classification of the new position defines the new salary. But if the agency wishes to consider outsiders, the system generally begins with a request to the personnel agency to certify the names of the top three qualified persons. Sometimes, because the personnel system often operates very slowly, the agency's chosen person may already have accepted another position, and so the system typically provides a process for supplying new names. Sometimes, the agency does not find any of the candidates acceptable, and agency officials may then simply keep the position vacant and hope for a better collection of names on the next try.

Because agencies often find this "rule of three" annoying, many personnel reforms, as we will see in the next chapter, have sought to change it. Still, it remains one of the fundamental principles of most civil service systems. The examination and certification process reduces the hiring flexibility of agencies and can sometimes prove difficult, even incomprehensible, for applicants. College placement officers sometimes wisely suggest that individuals who want to work for the government find someone who would like to hire them—and then allow that person to figure out from the inside how best to ensure that the applicant's name rises to the top of the list. In recent years, however, turmoil in federal internship programs has complicated that strategy. The federal government has created three new "pathways" for entry into service: an internship program; a recent graduates program, to allow those who have just completed their degrees time to find a government position; and a revised Presidential Management Fellows program, which is a highly competitive opportunity to find federal jobs. All of these programs, however, require agencies to advertise open positions, and ongoing budget cuts have made that a difficult road.

Beyond the complexities of the hiring process are two recruitment goals that the government pursues as well: providing favorable treatment for veterans in federal employment and increasing the diversity of the workforce at all levels of government.

Veterans' Preference

There has long been a principle that individuals who serve the nation in the armed forces should get preference in the search for government jobs. In the federal system, veterans earn a five-point bonus; if they are disabled, they get a ten-point bonus. As a result, the names of veterans often rise to the top of the list, above nonveterans with much higher exam ratings. In addition, the system is encumbered with other preferential provisions for veterans. For example, if on the certificate of three names a veteran is listed ahead of a nonveteran, the agency cannot pass over the veteran without stating its reasons and obtaining OPM agreement to the sufficiency of the reasons; both the agency's and OPM's actions are closely monitored by veterans' organizations. More than one-fifth of all federal employees are veterans. Some observers think that the nation's obligation to ensure employment opportunities for those who have fought its wars could be met by granting veterans' preference in governmental appointments during only the first few years after discharge from military service. But veterans' organizations oppose any modification of lifelong preference, and Congress shares their view. The large number of veterans who served in the wars in Iraq and Afghanistan have vastly increased the number of young veterans seeking government employment, and that has squeezed out many other applicants for government service.

Diversity

In many of the world's largest nations, including the United States, diversity among government employees has become increasingly important, to help "achieve political and social government objectives such as social mobility, equity, and quality in service delivery," as a 2009 report by the Organization for Economic Co-operation and Development argued. A more diverse government workforce can also "help to preserve core public service values such as fairness, transparency, impartiality and representativeness," OECD concluded.[10] The diversity argument embraces, in part, the recognition that government is about more than just delivering services but that it is also about defining and promoting values. It is also about the debate between Friedrich and Finer that we saw in Chapter 1: government whose employees mirror the citizens they serve are more likely to be accountable to those citizens.

At a Rutgers University job fair, FBI Special Agent Debra Jean Aros recruited students for careers in the agency. With many senior workers scheduled to retire in the coming years, most government agencies work hard to bring in fresh talent.

Federal statutes protect federal employees (and applicants for employment) against discrimination on grounds of race, color, religion, sex, national origin, age, or physical or mental impairment; some federal statutes apply as well to state and local governments. In addition, since long before the creation of the United States itself, government jobs have been perceived as good and secure positions. That has led government to use its hiring powers toward two social goals: to redress past patterns of discrimination and to make the bureaucracy more representative of the overall population.

Pursuing such diversity requires giving preference in appointment to minority, female, and disabled applicants over equally qualified white males, and that practice naturally provokes dispute over whether such preferences contradict the merit principle. There are two issues here: whether merit is the *only* principle on which the government ought to base its employment and whether the government has such confidence in its system of examination that it should insist on following it to the exclusion of other important objectives. As this chapter later demonstrates, the examination system is imperfect, and that makes it easier to justify balancing merit with other social goals.

At the federal level, these preferences have promoted substantial diversity. Minorities constitute a third of the federal workforce. However, the federal workforce is unbalanced by gender: women comprise a far larger percentage of employees at lower levels, while men have a larger share of the jobs at the upper-level managerial positions. As baby boomers working for the federal government (who are predominantly male) retire, and as the federal government seeks to replace them with younger workers (who come from a pool that is disproportionately female, since more women than men are graduating from college), this will become a far sharper and more important issue.

Promotion

Those already holding career positions advance principally by promotion and transfer. Here the operating agencies have great discretion, subject to the promoted or transferred employee's having at least the minimum educational and experience qualifications for the higher position. The employee need not be put in competition with possibly superior talent outside the government, and the agency does not need to look at all the employees in the government, department, or bureau who might be qualified for the position. Employees can break out of dead-end positions by shopping around to find a unit to which they can be transferred and promoted. The relative ease of transfer, in fact, may encourage individuals to accept a job at a lower level than they might be qualified for, in the hope that in relatively short order they can learn the system to find a better job at a higher salary.

The promotion system rests on the following four premises:

1. *Career service.* The initial recruitment of able candidates for entry to the public service is enhanced by prospects of long, possibly lifetime, careers with advancement by promotion. A mostly closed promotional system, without much lateral entry at higher levels by "outsiders," improves those prospects.
2. *Face-to-face assessment.* Important on-the-job characteristics, such as ability to meet and deal with others, cannot be accurately judged by initial or subsequent formal examinations. They can be accurately judged by an employee's supervisor and an agency promotional board.
3. *Flexibility.* Agency officials need to be accorded much discretion in choosing supervisory personnel and in rewarding demonstrated competence. Effective supervision and high morale depend on finding good matches between people and responsibilities, and the more flexibility managers have to promote from within, the more likely they are to produce high-performing programs.
4. *Chain reaction.* Promotion from within builds staff morale, because each promotion creates a vacancy, which can set off a series of promotions down the line.

Central personnel procedures can still trap managers in cumbersome, time-consuming procedures that do not match the twin goals of choosing the candidate who will do the best job and protecting the system from arbitrary actions tainted by favoritism. Moreover, a closed promotion system, in which most positions are hired from within, can keep new ideas from

POLITICS

Wannabe a Cabinet Member?
Seven Rules to Follow

So you've always wanted to be a cabinet secretary. One of the president's closest political advisers, head of one of the nation's largest public bureaucracies?

Robert M. Simon, staff director for the Committee on Energy and Natural Resources in the U.S. Senate, has seven handy tips.

1. Keep a low profile until you are officially picked. Nothing will kill a cabinet nomination faster than looking like you're hungry for it.
2. You will accomplish perhaps three things as a Cabinet offer—decide on them before you seek the job. Time is short, and everyone will be pulling at your arm for a piece of your power.
3. Don't bash your predecessors. Everyone has friends. Lots of them.
4. Find ways to interact with members of Congress on a personal level. Individual connections can often smooth over tough policy battles.
5. Don't make promises you don't understand. Lots of people will buttonhole you with sales pitches for their favorite ideas. Saying you will "look into" complicated issues will buy you time until you sort out the puzzles.
6. Resist the temptation to reorganize your agency. From the top, most organizations look disorganized, but reorganizing takes more time and energy than you'll have. It's often more important to get the right people into the right jobs.
7. Stay home and mind the store. Rather than cutting ribbons around the country and giving speeches around the world, pay attention to your agency. If you don't, others will step in.

So you've read the rules. Do they make sense? Are you willing to sign up for the job (without, of course, looking too eager for it)? Succeeding in government requires more than just technical expertise—it is important to learn the politics of your environment too.

Source: Robert M. Simon, "Seven Rules for Wannabe Cabinet Members," *Washington Post*, November 16, 2012, http://articles.washingtonpost.com/2012-11-16/opinions/35503240_1_nuclear-waste-nuclear-problems-energy-department.

coming into the system. Some systems, including those for officers of the armed services and in the foreign service, follow a tough up-or-out process: at a certain level, officers either win promotion or must leave the service; at each step up the hierarchy, there are fewer positions at the next level, so the up-or-out process tends to weed out employees along the way. Federal managers sometimes complain that individuals who do not actively seek to get ahead can settle into their positions, produce merely adequate work, be impossible to remove for cause, and lower the overall performance of the organization. Some of the reforms we explore in the next chapter are designed to solve that problem.

Separation

Government employees tend to sustain long careers in civil service: the average length of service of full-time federal employees is about 14 years, although the number has been slowly declining in recent years.[11] Compared with the private sector, turnover of government employees is a bit less than half of turnover in the private sector.[12] Turnover can be good, if it gives government the opportunity to hire freshly trained, highly motivated employees; it can be bad if its most valuable employees leave. Many observers have worried that ongoing attacks on government and its workers, along with restrictions on government employees' pay, have tilted the balance to the negative, making it harder for government to retain its investment in human capital. Nevertheless, a December 2012 survey showed that most Americans believe that public-sector employees are better off than their private-sector counterparts and that 67 percent of those surveyed believe that public-sector employees have better job security.[13] Despite the surveys, however, senior government officials worry that the continuing attacks on government employees, coupled with furloughs and salary freezes, could make it far more difficult to hire the workers the government needs. As former OPM Director John Berry explained, "We cannot recruit and retain a qualified workforce by freezing their pay forever. We cannot do it by changing their retirement plan on an annual basis. We cannot do it by denigrating public service."[14]

Despite the popular perception, all civil service systems make it possible to remove employees for cause. The larger problem is removal of the mediocre. Supervisors are often reluctant to try to remove employees; it is a long and complex process, and if unsuccessful, they may only find themselves saddled with disgruntled employees who can undermine morale. As a result, a supervisor may instead encourage an inferior employee to transfer elsewhere; indeed, the supervisor may be all too willing to provide a glowing recommendation of such an employee's qualifications—for another job.

Governments sometimes find that tight budgets require them to downsize their workforce. In economic downturns, state and local governments have relied on **reductions in force** (**RIFs**, or "riffing," for short). Governments reduced their personnel ceilings, thus triggering elaborate rules about which employees could be retained and which ones had to be riffed first. In general, lowest-seniority employees are the first to go. A higher-seniority employee whose unit shrinks in size generally can "**bump**" a lower-seniority employee, even from a job at a lower level than the one the higher seniority employee originally occupied. That, in turn, can trigger further bumps, until the lowest-seniority employees must leave government service. Needless to say, such RIFs can devastate both an agency's capacity and the morale of its employees. Governments also sometimes use **buyouts**, which provide employees with cash payments in exchange for a decision to leave public service. And when the government needs to reduce its personnel costs because of short-term budget crises, it sometimes will impose a furlough, in which employees are told not to report to work for periods ranging from days to weeks, when they do not receive their pay. As governments navigated through the tough budget problems that followed the 2008 financial crisis—and as the federal government struggled to pass its budget—buyouts and furloughs became more common, to the detriment of employee morale.

Compensation

The government's capacity to attract and keep able people depends heavily on the salaries (and fringe benefits) it offers. Pay, to be sure, is not the only factor that a worker considers in seeking, accepting, or staying in a particular organization.[15] The challenge of the work, the impact one's work can have, the agreeableness of the specific setting (including physical facilities, supervisor's behavior, and stimulus and cooperativeness of one's peers), prospects for promotion, and fringe benefits all weigh on the scales.[16] In the government sector, the sense of working in the public interest is another important motivating force. Still, government must compete in the labor market for competent people, and its employees, current and prospective, naturally weigh their pay in deciding where to work.

At the federal level, the law provides that federal white-collar pay rates shall be comparable with private-enterprise pay rates for the same levels of work. The president therefore annually adjusts the salaries of federal employees to achieve comparability, and the Bureau of Labor Statistics annually surveys private firms to determine how to make the adjustment. Many critics of the federal employment system, however,  have argued that federal employees are substantially overpaid, compared with their private-sector counterparts, especially when fringe benefits like health care, retirement programs, and vacation days are included. A 2012 Congressional Budget Office study found that, on average, federal workers have slightly higher salaries than their private-sector counterparts (by 2 percent). They had substantially higher benefits, by 48 percent, and 16 percent higher overall compensation. The comparisons vary greatly by the education of employees, however. For employees with a high-school education, federal workers had a big edge. Federal employees with a college education still had an advantage. But for employees with advanced degrees, private-sector employees earned 23 percent higher salaries (see Figure 8.2).[17] Moreover, because the federal government tends to employ relatively more workers with advanced degrees, the issue is an important one. However, not everyone agrees that there is a pay gap. An analyst at the Heritage Foundation, for example, contends that Americans are "overtaxed to overpay the civil service."[18] The hotter the issue has become, the harder it has been to determine who is right.

At the core, however, virtually everyone agrees that the federal government's current GS pay system is outdated. In its 2014 budget proposal, the Obama White House argued, "In the past sixty years, the private sector has innovated towards more flexible personnel management systems, but the federal personnel system has not kept up and remains inflexible and outdated."[19] On Capitol Hill, the Republican and Democratic leaders of the House Committee on Oversight and Government Reform asked GAO to take a careful look at the GS pay system, noting that "Much has changed" since the creation of the GS system in 1949, "including the nature of agency work."[20]

Moreover, some officials have argued that the federal government should not try to compete with the private sector for the best employees. Terry Culler, a Reagan administration political appointee, concluded that "the federal government is able to hire the caliber of people it needs at current wage levels and could do so at even lower pay scales. It should be content to hire competent people, not the best and most talented people." The federal government, he wrote, does not "need laboratories full of Nobel laureates, legal offices full of the top graduates

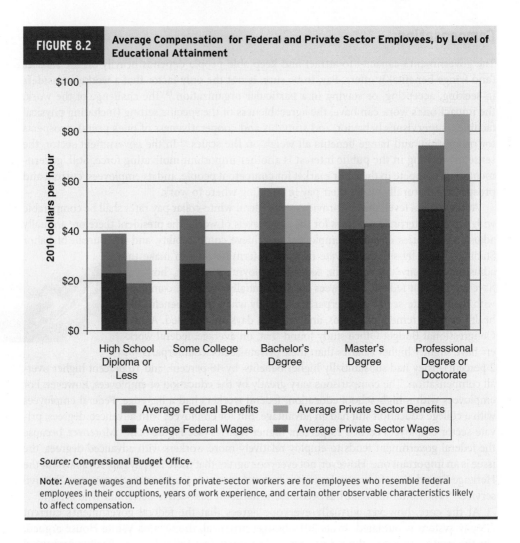

FIGURE 8.2 — **Average Compensation for Federal and Private Sector Employees, by Level of Educational Attainment**

Source: Congressional Budget Office.

Note: Average wages and benefits for private-sector workers are for employees who resemble federal employees in their occuptions, years of work experience, and certain other observable characteristics likely to affect compensation.

of the best schools, administrative offices staffed with MBAs from Wharton, or policy shops full of the brightest whatevers." Indeed, "the brightest and most talented people should work in the private sector."[21] In 2012, however, a U.S. Department of Commerce scientist, David Wineland, *did* win the Nobel Prize in physics, for his work in quantum mechanics. Wineland had worked at the department's National Institute of Standards and Technology for 37 years and made breakthroughs that established the basis for super-fast computers in the future.

Comparable Worth

A core civil service principle is the concept that individuals should receive equal pay for jobs of comparable value. Distinctions in pay should be related to the nature of the job and the level of performance. However, as analysts have pointed out, for many positions traditionally dominated by women (such as secretaries and nurses), the pay in fact has not been equivalent. Moreover, they say, there some-times are few opportunities for promotion, and sex-based discrimination can block opportuni-ties. These critics have pursued reform based on jobs' **comparable worth.** Many state governments have conducted comparable worth or pay equity studies, most of which have found that sex-based wage differences and sex-based occupational seg-regation do exist in their bureaucracies, and some state and local governments have taken remedial action.[22]

Defining what is truly comparable, however, is an extremely difficult problem. To what tra-ditionally male-dominated jobs should tradi-tionally female-dominated jobs be compared? Analysts sometimes note that wages for women can be lower because some women leave the work-force for child-rearing duty and then reenter it later. They suggest as well that some traditionally female-dominated jobs require less work experi-ence and, therefore, do not warrant as high a pay level. Some economists ask why, if women believe that they are underpaid in some jobs, they do not simply switch to other positions; other analysts counter that long-term patterns of discrimination can make that difficult or impossible.[23]

Federal employee David Wineland shared the 2012 Nobel Prize in physics. The award committee recognized Wineland, who worked for the National Institutes of Standards and Technology in Colorado, for his work in quantum physics, "measuring and manipulating individual particles . . . in ways that were previously thought unattainable."

As more women enter the workforce, gain more advanced education and training, and advance up the hierarchy, the comparable worth issue is changing dramatically. Moreover, some men are taking on more responsibility for child-rearing, and more women are return-ing sooner to the workforce after giving birth. These trends are redefining the comparable worth issue, but they are also raising new questions about how best to ensure equity between the sexes in the workplace—and how to accommodate family pressures with career demands. Some governments are adopting more flexible policies for family leave and for telecommut-ing; others are developing child-care programs. As these social trends continue to reshape the government workforce, such issues will become even more important.

Building a Quality Workforce

The public service can attract the ablest persons only by being competitive, which is partly a product of pay, promotional opportunities, and other conditions of work but is also a product of perceptions held by members of the pool of potential recruits. Recruitment of able candi-dates (particularly college seniors and recent graduates) has been most successful in periods when the government is perceived as engaged in interesting, innovative, and exciting pro-grams that promise to have high value for society. The New Deal, World War II, the Kennedy administration, and the Johnson administration (with its Great Society programs) were such periods. At other times, however, particularly in the 1970s and 1980s, successful presidential candidates campaigned against Washington and "the bureaucracy," with predictable effects on the morale of civil servants and on potential recruits' choices among their career options. President George H. W. Bush broke with this negative view, expressing in his 1988 campaign "a very high regard for the overall competence of career civil servants and for the vital role they have in our democratic form of government." And as president he told an assembly of top careerists that he shared their "belief in public service as the highest and noblest calling."[24] President Bill Clinton likewise did not engage in bureaucrat bashing, although his downsizing initiatives made many employees nervous. President George W. Bush, while a conservative, also embraced the positive role that government plays in American society. President Barack Obama put it crisply. In the midst of his 2008 campaign, he told a Columbia University audience that "Our campaign from the beginning has been about changing government." The goal, he said, was to "transform Washington" and "make government cool again."[25]

Despite the rising presidential rhetoric in support of public service, the government has struggled to attract the high quality of recruits it needs.[26] The very complexity of the personnel process can create a roadblock. As the National Advisory Council on the Public Service found, "the Federal government now has a confused and incomplete patchwork of recruiting programs. Potential applicants for Federal employment are discouraged by a perplexing and overly complicated process." In addition, "Too often, there is no link between the recruiting initiatives and the hiring process."[27] Indeed, the director of the federal Office of Personnel Management concluded that it was little wonder that potential government employees were confused by a process that is "intellectually confusing, procedurally nightmarish, inaccessible to students, and very difficult to administer."[28] A study conducted by Carolyn Ban and Norma Riccucci for the Winter Commission on the state and local public service likewise found that "probably the most important thing that state and local governments can do to improve the efficiency of their workforce is to improve the quality of the people they hire."[29]

Opportunities for public service continue to be available throughout government, but the Clinton administration's downsizing and the RIFs in many state and local governments have further discouraged many individuals from seeking government careers. At the federal level, moreover, the combination of downsizing and limits on the number of new positions has led to a gradual aging of the workforce. An analysis by the CBO found that the average age of federal employees had grown substantially. In December 2005, one-fourth of the government's salaried employees had reached the minimum retirement age of 55. One in ten employees could immediately retire with a full pension. The federal government is gray and getting grayer—and overall the federal government's employees are older than private-sector workers (see Figure 8.3). Its strategic planners worry increasingly about how best to manage the transition from retiring baby boomers to younger employees.[30]

EMPLOYEE RIGHTS AND OBLIGATIONS

The norm of equity calls for similar treatment for people in similar situations. It plays a part in each of the key elements of the civil service system: open, competitive examinations; the merit principle; equal pay for equal work within the government; comparability of civil servants' pay

FIGURE 8.3	Age Distribution of Federal vs. Private Sector Employees

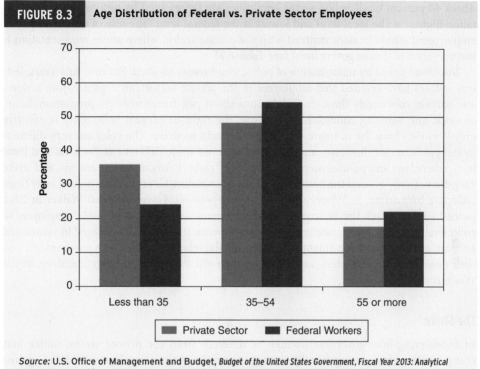

Source: U.S. Office of Management and Budget, *Budget of the United States Government, Fiscal Year 2013: Analytical Perspectives*, http://www.whitehouse.gov/sites/default/files/omb/performance/chapter11-2013.pdf.

Notes: Federal workers exclude the military and Postal Service, but include all other Federal workers in the Executive Branch. Private sector workers exclude the self-employed. Neither category includes state and local government workers. This analysis is limited to full-time, full-year workers, i.e. those with at least 1,500 annual hours of work.

with private enterprise's pay rates for the same levels of work; and nondiscrimination on the basis of political party, race, national origin, religion, sex, age, or physical disability.

Equity between public and private employees involves issues that extend well beyond pay-rate comparability. Civil service systems have long held that public employees should not be burdened with constraints on their public and private behavior as citizens and human beings beyond those borne by private employees unless such constraints are required by the special nature of government itself. Here our concerns are the right of government employees to organize and bargain collectively through labor unions, their right to privacy, and their right to engage actively in politics.

Unionization and Collective Bargaining

American governments must reckon with a major rise in **unionization** of public employees and an increased use of **collective bargaining** to determine conditions of employment.[31]

About 40 percent of all public-sector employees are represented by unions, with representation highest at the local level and lowest at the federal level. The role of unions in public employment stands in stark contrast with the private sector, where union representation is just one-sixth of that in government (see Table 8.3).

The issues posed by unionization of public employees run deep. For over fifty years, federal statutes have ensured that employees in the private sector can organize, join unions, and bargain collectively through their unions about pay, fringe benefits, promotion, hours of work, and working conditions. Of course, the right to bargain collectively is effective only if unions have the ultimate weapon of the right to strike. The rules are very different in the public sector, however, and the rules are even more different at the state and local level, where laws and policies on public employees' rights to organize, join unions, and strike vary dramatically around the nation. Some states, including Georgia, have moved away from collective bargaining. In Wisconsin, the state's Republican Governor Scott Walker in 2011 pushed a bill through the Wisconsin legislature removing the right of public employees to collectively bargain. Many state and local governments, moreover, are engaged in substantial reforms, and that process is further transforming the relationship between governments and their employees. Nevertheless, key issues on the right to strike and bargain endure, as the Wisconsin story illustrates.

The Strike

In considering how governments may be different from the private sector, notice first that governments do not generally concede the right of their employees to strike against the sovereign state. The reason for this reservation has to do with the critical nature of many governmental services. Citizens would consider it intolerable if they suddenly found themselves without police and fire protection, air traffic control, schools, and garbage collection. And while Americans might not notice it immediately if the employees of the State, Treasury, or Defense Departments went on strike, the implications could be equally momentous.

TABLE 8.3	Union Membership	
	Percentage union members	**Percentage represented by unions**
Private sector	6.6	7.3
Federal government	26.9	31.4
State government	31.3	34.9
Local government	41.7	45.2

Source: U.S. Bureau of Labor Statistics, "Table 3. Union Affiliation of Employed Wage and Salary Workers by Occupation and Industry," http://www.bls.gov/news.release/union2.t03.htm.

Note: Data are for 2012.

But this rationale becomes strained when it is applied to less vital governmental services, such as cataloguers at the public library or assistants in a federal research lab. Yet no simple rule can sharply distinguish among the occupations of public employees in terms of the tolerability of strikes. A 1977 strike by only 2,500 cleaners and handymen forced New York City's 960 public schools to hold only half-day sessions for their more than 1 million pupils and deprived half a million of them, mostly from poor families, of free hot lunches.[32] In Philadelphia, transit police officers have the right to strike (and they exercised it in 2008), but city police officers do not.

Theory may not matter, however. Public employees do strike, and government officials usually decide that resorting to the courts is not a promising method in getting employees back to work. Firing the strikers,

Teachers in Chicago's public schools, the third-largest district in the country, went on strike at the beginning of the 2012 school year for better compensation and job security.

as President Reagan did to the 11,000 air traffic controllers in 1981, leads to a long process—over many years in the case of the Federal Aviation Administration (FAA)—of recruiting and training a new staff. Meanwhile, the government risks having a public function poorly performed. But even when the government denies employees the right to strike, that prohibition does not prevent employees from resorting to job actions that can tie public administration in knots. A "sick-in" by schoolteachers can shut down the schools even while the teachers receive sick-leave pay. When air traffic controllers "work to the rule" (strictly adhering to prescribed procedures), they can cripple the flow of landings and takeoffs under the guise of enforcing every safety regulation to the letter. A "slowdown" by postal clerks can build up mountains of unsorted and undelivered mail. Teaching assistants at state universities can grade final exams but refuse to turn the grades over to the registrar, leaving thousands of seniors without the credits they need to graduate.

Who Are the Bargainers?

The second difference is that the civil service system itself, along with budget decisions by elected policymakers, sets the basic conditions of work. As a result, no executive official can bargain over many of the issues about which the union is concerned. Managers cannot agree to pay increases or fundamental changes in working conditions. Since the main decisions are political, often the most that the unions can do is to build their political strength, which turns them into interest group lobbyists—a very different role from that of unions in the private sector. The president of the largest federal union says, "We've got no choice except to try to put pressure on enough congressmen and senators to see things our way. That's our bargaining table."[33]

Faced with this prospect, the executive negotiator may give in too readily to union demands. Union members and their families have substantial voting strength in many legislators' districts and wards; those in local governments may actually be able to determine mayoral elections. The unions' voting strength, lobbying skill, and collective bargaining tactics reinforce one another. In addition, the public is often so angered by the loss of police, trash collection, or school services during a strike or slowdown that it puts pressure on government officials for a speedy settlement of the dispute. Public employee unions, of course, do not get all that they ask for, because government bargainers know that citizens dislike settlements that substantially raise taxes or that pay public employees more than others in the community who are doing comparable work. For the most part, government bargainers try to balance between protecting the merit principle and the civil service system and avoiding bargaining away government's ability to determine public policies and improve administrative performance.

There are two important lessons here. First, the civil service system and the supervisory arrangements it creates are one thing; labor-management relations often are quite different. At state and local as well as federal levels, the result frequently is a dual personnel system.[34] Second, despite the frequently large gaps between top officials and frontline managers, between management and labor, and between supervisors and subordinates, many managers are coming to recognize the need for fresh alliances. One private-sector executive's conclusion speaks loudly to the public sector as well: "We have lots of team efforts with union involvement. The biggest lesson we have learned is that we are all in the same boat and we need to work together."[35]

The Scope of Issues

Finally, government differs from private enterprise in the scope of issues on which employees and their unions want to, or are able to, bargain. The line between employees' own conditions of work and the government's policies and programs seems a clear one—the former being the stuff of collective bargaining, the latter the responsibility of legislative bodies and political executives. But public employee unions have blurred the line. If a union blocks a mayor's effort to staff police patrol cars with one officer instead of two, or if it prevents reducing the number of firefighters on a fire truck, that may simply reflect the concern that all unions have about workers' safety and the loss of jobs. But what if the mayor wants to shift firefighting companies at nighttime from the depopulated business districts to the most populous and fire-prone areas of the city? Should the size of school classes or the content of school programs be determined by government-union bargaining? Should the size of payments to welfare clients, or the location of welfare centers, be so determined? All these issues have in fact been the subjects of negotiation and strikes.[36]

In the federal government, the scope of negotiable issues is restricted. Bargaining cannot concern matters that are the subject of any law or government-wide rule or regulation, or any agency rule or regulation for which "a compelling need" exists (the Federal Labor Relations Authority [FLRA] settles disputes over compelling need). Further, the Civil Service Reform Act of 1978 (which established the FLRA) preserves the authority of agency management officials "to determine the mission, budget, organization, number of employees, and internal security practices" of their agencies; to hire, assign, lay off, and retain employees; to remove or otherwise discipline employees; and to assign work and determine the personnel by which agency operations shall be conducted. The procedures for exercise of such authority are negotiable, however, as are grievance procedures for adversely affected employees.[37] And, curiously, an agency may choose to bargain about "the numbers, types, and grades of employees or positions assigned to any organizational subdivision, work project, or tour of duty, or on the technology, methods, and means of performing work."[38]

What, given the statutory restrictions, do agencies and unions bargain about? So far, it has been mostly about the assignment and scheduling of work (overtime, workweek definition, temporary assignments, shift hours, work breaks, meal periods), grievance and other procedures, safety, employee counseling, technological displacement, and the color of wall paint. In comparison to the private sector and to state and local governments, the federal bargaining table is a meager one: many highly significant issues relating to pay, job security, promotions, and fringe benefits that are accepted as negotiable in the private sector are precluded from bargaining at the federal level. On many issues, federal statutes accord unions the right to be consulted—but consultation is not bargaining.

In recent years, public employee unions have nervously eyed government officials who have battled the unions. President George W. Bush worked to limit the collective bargaining rights of employees in the new Department of Homeland Security. Many federal managers believe that unions have grown too powerful. FAA managers, for example, have complained that they have great difficulty in scheduling work shifts because union provisions allow air traffic controllers to come to work early or stay late; this practice allows them to accumulate credit hours, which they can use flexibly at a later time. At the Centers for Medicare and Medicaid Services, negotiations at one point became so tense that a union official said simply, "It's a war."[39] In some states, like Wisconsin, that war spilled out into open conflict involving tens of thousands of demonstrators in the state capitol and an open revolt of Democratic state senators, who left the state rather than vote on a plan to strip public employee unions of most of their bargaining rights.

The Right to Privacy

The rise of drug abuse and the increasing awareness of AIDS in the 1980s provoked new confrontations between government and its employees. In 1986 President Reagan signed an Executive Order requiring federal employees to refrain from the use of illegal drugs and declaring persons who use illegal drugs unsuitable for federal employment.[40] He authorized each agency to test any applicant for illegal drug use and, most important, directed federal agencies to "establish a program to test for the use of illegal drugs by employees in sensitive positions." Such positions include more than the term suggests. Among those affected are employees in positions designated sensitive by their agency, employees with access to classified information, presidential appointees, law enforcement officers, and employees in "other positions that the agency head determines involve law enforcement, national security, the protection of life and property, public health or safety, or other functions requiring a high degree of trust and confidence." In 2004 the federal government extended the testing to include hair, saliva, and sweat samples. However, while many employees are required to submit to these tests, only about one-fourth of federal employees work in jobs covered by these tests.[41] Local governments have also instituted mandatory urinalysis for police, firefighters, schoolteachers, and other employees.

Employee unions oppose mandatory testing of urine for evidence of illegal drug use, if inclusive or random—without, therefore, reasonable grounds for suspicion of an individual employee—as an invasion of privacy and a violation of the Fourth Amendment's protection against unreasonable searches and seizures. In 1989, however, by a 5-4 vote the Supreme Court, while agreeing on the applicability of the Fourth Amendment, held reasonable the U.S. Customs Service's inclusive drug testing of newly hired and transferred employees whose duties included direct interception of drugs or carrying of firearms.[42] Though granting the government's "compelling interest in protecting truly sensitive information," the Court deferred ruling on the reasonableness of testing those handling classified information, pending a lower court's inquiry into why baggage handlers, messengers, lawyers, and accountants were included in the testing.

AIDS testing also invokes the issue of privacy. The standard blood test identifies persons who have HIV antibodies, but that does not mean that they have AIDS or will get it,[43] and the danger of their infecting others is limited to sexual relations and intermixture of blood (as when drug users inject with needles used by others). The U.S. Foreign Service began in 1987 to test its job applicants, officers, and their dependents for the AIDS virus, rejecting any applicants testing positive for HIV antibodies and restricting any persons in service abroad—the concerns being both adequacy of medical facilities at some foreign posts and foreign governments' attitudes toward receiving official representatives who have or may develop AIDS.[44]

Political Activity

Public employees, of course, are citizens and have basic rights. But how should employees' own political values and rights to free speech connect with their responsibilities to administer the law without political favoritism? The 2013 IRS scandal, in which investigators found that federal workers were subjecting conservative groups to additional scrutiny—provoked enormous outrage. And then further investigation showed that liberal groups received additional checks as well. Just what standards should shape the political rights of employees and protect citizens from political bias in the administration of the law?

The Hatch Act

To deal with these issues at the federal level, Congress in 1939 adopted "An Act to Prevent Pernicious Political Activities," usually called the **Hatch Act** after its sponsor, Sen. Carl Hatch of New Mexico. The key provision applicable to federal employees reads as follows:

> No officer or employee in the executive branch of the Federal Government, or any agency or department thereof, shall take part in political management or political campaigns. All such persons shall retain the right to vote as they may choose and to express their opinions on all political subjects.[45]

The act's restrictions extend to virtually all employees who are not in policymaking positions, whether in the merit system or not.[46]

From 1940 to 1974, the Hatch Act's ban on political activity extended to state and local appointive officers and employees engaged primarily in any activity wholly or partly financed by federal loans or grants. In 1974, Congress shrank the ban to cover only candidacy for office in a partisan election and use of official authority or influence to affect others' voting or political contributions. The act was further amended in 1993 to allow most employees of the federal government to be more involved in political campaigns. Federal employees therefore have the right to be candidates for office, but only in nonpartisan elections. They can vote and assist in voter registration drives. As Box 8.1 shows, they can make political contributions and express opinions about political issues. (However, some federal employees, including those working for the CIA, the FBI, and the Secret Service, have greater limits on their political activity.) State government and local government employees are allowed a broader range of activities, with fewer restrictions (see Box 8.2). In general, government officials cannot run for office in a partisan election, campaign while on the job, or use their position to influence an election.

Patronage Restrictions

Three Supreme Court decisions have directly tested the constitutionality of requiring party membership or support for retention of government employment (in two cases) or for appointment, promotion, or transfer (in another case). In *Elrod v. Burns* (1976),[47] Elrod, a Democrat, succeeded the Republican sheriff of Cook County, Illinois (Chicago's county), and proceeded, as was the custom, to dismiss Burns and other non–civil service employees (save those who joined the new sheriff's party or obtained sponsorship from a leader of that party). The Court's plurality opinion condemned such patronage dismissals of non–civil service employees in nonpolicymaking positions as a violation of First Amendment rights of freedom of belief and association (which are protected against both the federal government and, through the Fourteenth Amendment, state and local governments). A concurring opinion answered "no" to the question "whether a non-policymaking, nonconfidential government employee can be discharged from a job that he is satisfactorily performing upon the sole ground of his political beliefs."

BOX 8.1	**Hatch Act Rights and Restrictions for Federal Government Employees**

Federal and D.C. employees *may*

- be candidates for public office in nonpartisan elections
- register and vote as they choose
- assist in voter registration drives
- express opinions about candidates and issues
- contribute money to political organizations
- attend political fundraising functions
- attend and be active at political rallies and meetings
- join and be active members of political parties or clubs
- sign nominating petitions
- campaign for or against referendum questions, constitutional amendments, municipal ordinances

(Continued)

(Continued)

- campaign for or against candidates in partisan elections
- make campaign speeches for candidates in partisan elections
- distribute campaign literature in partisan elections
- hold office in political clubs or parties

Federal and D.C. employees *may not*

- use official authority or influence to interfere with an election
- solicit or discourage political activity by anyone with business before their agency

- solicit or receive political contributions (may be done in certain limited situations by federal labor or other employee organizations)
- be candidates for public office in partisan elections
- engage in political activity while
  - on duty
  - in a government office
  - wearing an official uniform
  - using a government vehicle
- wear partisan political buttons on duty

Source: U.S. Office of Special Counsel, http://www.osc.gov/hatchact.htm.

BOX 8.2	**Hatch Act Rights and Restrictions for State and Local Government Employees**

State and local employees *may*

- run for public office in nonpartisan elections
- campaign for and hold office in political clubs and organizations
- actively campaign for candidates for public office in partisan and nonpartisan elections
- contribute money to political organizations and attend political fundraising functions

Covered state and local employees *may not*

- be candidates for public office in partisan elections
- use official authority or influence to interfere with or affect the results of an election or nomination
- directly or indirectly coerce contributions from subordinates in support of a political party or candidate

Source: U.S. Office of Special Counsel, http://www.osc.gov/hatchact.htm.

In *Branti v. Finkel* (1980),[48] Branti, a Democrat, succeeded Finkel, a Republican, as public defender in Rockland County, New York, and sought to dismiss Finkel and other Republican assistant public defenders. The Supreme Court, turning away from the question of a position's policymaking or confidential character, held that the issue was whether party affiliation is an appropriate requirement for the effective performance of the position's duties. It said that in this instance it was not and ruled against the attempted dismissal.[49]

In *Rutan v. Republican Party of Illinois* (1990),[50] the Republican governor of Illinois imposed a hiring freeze in 1980 on the approximately 60,000 positions under his control and permitted exceptions only with his express permission. Rutan and her fellow litigants, "low-level employees" in the Court's words, charged that the governor had used the freeze and exceptions to operate a political patronage system, which, in their cases, denied the plaintiffs' appointments, promotions, and transfers because they had not worked for or supported the Republican Party.[51] "Unless these patronage practices are narrowly tailored to further vital government interests," said the Court, "we must conclude that they impermissibly encroach on First Amendment freedoms." Citing the *Elrod* and *Branti* cases, the Court dismissed claims that the patronage practices furthered the government's interest in securing loyal and effective employees. At upper levels of government, however, "A government's interest in securing employees who will loyally implement its policies can be adequately served by choosing or dismissing certain high-level employees on the basis of their political views."

These three decisions, covering not just dismissals but also appointments, promotions, and transfers, outlaw the patronage system at all levels of government except for high-level, policymaking positions where party membership or support is deemed an appropriate requirement for effective performance of duties. This dramatic development has mainly affected local governments and some state governments. But political bosses and officials do not lack ways to pursue their interests even under civil service systems. The most common tactics are choosing loyalists as civil service commissioners and underfinancing the commission so that registers of eligibles are allowed to expire and new examinations are postponed for months or years; in such cases, "temporary" noncompetitive appointments are then possible, and they tend to go to party supporters.

Revolving-Door Restrictions

Most governments also restrict activities of employees after they leave government service, for two reasons. First, the restrictions seek to prevent government officials from using their positions to set themselves up in lucrative jobs after their government employment. Many higher-level officials have the power to award contracts, and it would be tempting to use that power to steer contracts to a company and then jump to that company in a high-paying position to manage the work. Second, the restrictions seek to prevent government officials from joining a company and then using their vast network of government contracts to pull business to their new employer.

For example, in 2004 Boeing was fighting to win a large contract for 767 aircraft, which would be transformed into tankers to replace the Air Force's aging KC-135 models. The company's principal competition was Airbus, a European consortium that was the only other builder capable of producing a long-range tanker. The Air Force's second-highest civilian in charge of procurement, Darleen Druyun, was jailed for a deal she made: she favored Boeing in the competition and negotiated a new job with Boeing after she left the federal government. She received a nine-month prison sentence, plus seven months in-home (or halfway house) detention, a $5,000 fine, and orders to complete 150 hours of community service.

In her plea agreement, Druyun confessed that, as "a parting gift" to her new employer, she had supported a higher price than the deal required and that she had shared data about one of Boeing's competitors with the company. She also had favored Boeing on a $4 billion avionics contract, as well as on a $100 million NATO contract in 2002, and she had pushed for a $412 million settlement with Boeing on a contract dispute between the company and the government in 2000. As a further incentive, Druyun's daughter and son-in-law had been Boeing employees either at the time of or shortly after each of those deals.[52] Congressional heat, including attacks from Sen. John McCain (R-Ariz.), led the Air Force to call for a fresh competition for the contract. In 2008, the Air Force awarded the contract to Airbus, but GAO found that the Air Force had bungled the contract review, and the project went back to the drawing board yet again. In 2011, the Pentagon finally decided to grant the contract to Boeing.

Over the years, GAO carefully examined the issue of "the revolving door." In an analysis of 2,435 officials who had previously served in the government, it found

> There are acknowledged benefits to employing former government officials for both DOD [Department of Defense] and defense contractors; for example, former DOD officials bring with them the knowledge and skills in acquisition practices they have developed at DOD which also benefit DOD when communicating with these contractor personnel. However, a major concern with post-government employment has been that senior military and civilian officials and acquisition officials working for defense contractors immediately after leaving DOD could lead to conflicts of interest and affect public confidence in the government.[53]

Rules to prevent such problems vary with the level of government and typically are very complex. In general, however, former officials are permanently barred from joining a company and dealing with their former employer on issues for which they had direct responsibility. Most levels of governments impose "cooling-off periods," ranging from six months to several years, during which they may not contact their former employer on government issues. Despite the rules, GAO found that many former military officials had, in fact, worked on contracts related to their former work and some had even worked on the same contracts for which they had responsibility at the Pentagon.[54]

The revolving-door regulations are very complicated. Former employees often have a hard time deciphering the rules without hiring an attorney for guidance. There are many stories of individuals who turn down government jobs because of the restrictions they face on leaving public service. No one, of course, wants to allow government employees to trade on their service to line their own pockets. On the other hand, everyone wants the government to hire the most capable employees for the work to be done. The enduring challenge is determining how best to find the balance.

CONCLUSION

Getting high-quality workers is one of the most important issues in public administration. Indeed, perhaps the biggest lesson from the private sector for government management is that people are the most important resource, and that government's work depends on the quality of the government's employees. Because government employees exercise great power on behalf of the public, there is a strong public interest in ensuring that neither favoritism nor employees' own political values creep into administration. Discovering the best way to make that happen has long been the driving force of the government's civil service system.

The civil service *system* is actually a series of interlocking *subsystems*: one for position classification, one for staffing, and one for compensation. These subsystems are complex, largely because of the competing values the government seeks to balance. The rules that have grown up around the subsystems also help explain why so many of government's other problems regularly recur—from an impersonal style to a preoccupation with red tape. Even the most important goals, such as equity and merit, reinforce these tendencies. Indeed, as Patricia W. Ingraham pointed out, the system's "problems highlight the difficulties created by the long-term emphasis on *administering* procedures, rather than *managing* people and programs."[55]

The civil service system is complex because it brings together the basic challenges of the administrative process. It's about *effectiveness,* because the quality of government's people shapes the quality of its work. It's about *politics,* because it must balance the competing demands for employee's freedom and the need to protect the system from political favoritism. And it's about *accountability,* because the public rightly expects that they will get fair and impartial service from those entrusted with government's work. Balancing these values, however, has been very difficult for a very long time, because as a GAO study put it, "Federal employees have often been viewed as costs to be cut rather than as assets to be valued."[56]

If there's anything about which virtually everyone agrees, it's that the government's civil service system is broken. Conservatives believe it creates inflexibility and inefficiency. Liberals believe it undercuts government's responsiveness. Nearly everyone agrees that civil service rules hinder the performance of public programs. Looking ahead, everyone knows that with large numbers of baby boomers retiring from government, the need to improve the civil service system will only increase if government is to work well.

That led the Obama administration to make hiring reform a top priority. In 2010, OPM Director John Berry said,

> Hiring process reform isn't the most exciting topic, but it's extremely important, because it affects everything government does. Yet for far too long, our HR systems have been a hindrance. We have great workers in government now in spite of the hiring process, not because of it. As they retire, it's tough to replace them when it takes five months on average to hire someone. Or when there are 40 steps to the process and 19 signatures.[57]

The administration switched from complex applications, which included a dreaded KSA—a "knowledge, skills, and abilities" essay—to an application with just a resume and a cover letter. Hiring managers can see all the qualified applicants, instead of just the three applicants rated top by the complex screening process. The screening process will be streamlined, and hiring managers will have more control over filling jobs in their agencies. Berry made clear that "The merit principles are sacrosanct, and these reforms will honor them," including the commitment to veterans' preference. The focus, he said, "is about simplicity, flexibility, and efficiency," to "substantially reduce the time and aggravation it takes to find and hire the best."[58]

Despite the Obama reforms, the underlying puzzle came into sharper focus: how best to identify the skills that the government most needs and how to build them into government. In the midst of the contentious 2010 midterm elections, *Washington Post* writer Steven Pearlstein argued:

You can't expect to support and finance political candidates who preach that government is menacing and wasteful, that public employees are incompetent and corrupt, that taxes are always too high and destroy jobs, and then turn around and expect that the government will respond to your demands to hold down the cost of health care, or fund basic research, or provide good schools, efficient courts and reliable transportation systems.[59]

We turn to those puzzles in the next chapter.

CASE 8.1

Who Is More Efficient—Government Workers or Private Contractors?

Everyone knows that the private sector is more efficient than the public sector. A major case for privatizing public work, its proponents say, is that the private sector can do it better, cheaper, and smarter.

But is "everyone" right? Not if they look at the experience of Chesapeake, Virginia. In 1995 the city council told the public works director to get bids from private companies for collecting trash in the city's "Western Branch," the area collected on Mondays. The public works department responded with a "managed competition" model. "The bottom line cost to the citizens was the most important consideration," explained Thomas Westbrook, the department's assistant director.[1]

The city hired a private consultant to manage the competition process. Four bids for the job were received. The winner? As Bill Davis, the city's purchasing director, announced, "the proposal submitted by the city's public works department, solid waste division, was the most responsive and responsible offer and represents the least expensive and most advantageous situation for the city."[2]

In short, the public sector out-competed the private sector. How did this happen? Facing

the heat of competition, the city's solid waste division found a way to change its waste-collection process: instead of using two different trucks, staffed by two different crews, to collect overflow garbage and yard waste, it could use a single truck with a single crew and with its capacity split between the two loads. Had it not been for the competition, the department's officials might not have devised this method, which contributed to a 39 percent savings over the previous arrangement. Facing the potential loss of their jobs, however, city workers came up with an innovative approach.

"We felt that we were as cheap as private industry and we wanted to be able to bid on that service as well," Westbrook explained.[3] His employees did so—and Westbrook was right.

In this effective bidding process, Chesapeake followed a model established by Phoenix, Arizona, which has been contracting out public services since 1979. In the first twenty years of the process, Phoenix city officials estimate that they saved more than $30 million. In six garbage-collection auctions, the city department won three of the competitions, and in those it did not win, it placed second. Between 1979 and

1998, the cost of collecting a ton of garbage in Phoenix fell from $67.88 to $41.96, a 38 percent decrease. Moreover, analysts have determined that Phoenix's costs are less than those of similar cities.[4]

Phoenix established basic ground rules for all the competitors:

1. *Reserve rule*. Wanting to ensure that the city department remained viable in case service problems arose with the private contractors, Phoenix would not allow more than half of its households to be served by private contractors.
2. *Previous experience*. Bidders had to present evidence of garbage collection work in similarly sized areas.
3. *Bonding*. Private bidders had to post a bond to guarantee that they would complete the work.
4. *Insurance*. Private contractors had to carry liability insurance in case their vehicles and workers caused property damage or injury.
5. *Medical benefits*. The city required private contractors to provide medical insurance that matched what city workers received.
6. *Displaced city workers*. Private contractors were required to offer employment to any city workers who lost their jobs as a result of the competition.
7. *Fleet restrictions*. Competitors could not use their vehicles for other purposes, and garbage pickup was not allowed on Wednesdays and Saturdays.

When some private competitors chafed under these restrictions, city workers countered that private contractors should have to play by the same rules that the city observed. Accepting the ground rules would make it harder for those private companies to low-ball bids, especially by not funding basic benefits to employees and by using equipment for other purposes. Indeed,

public employees fought against any competition strategy that would allow private companies to win by providing their employees with fewer fringe benefits, in part because city employees believed that would be unfair and in part because they feared that it might increase pressure to lower their own benefits. Everyone agreed that competition helped lower costs, but determining how best to create a level playing field proved a deceptively difficult problem.

Analysts concluded that these cases demonstrate that the problem with governmental efficiency isn't government itself—or the people who work for it. Rather, it is the set of restrictions that limit government's flexibility and the lack of incentives to improve their productivity. Create a strong incentive—such as the potential loss of jobs—and city workers can produce remarkable efficiencies. Level the playing field, and they can even win out over the private sector. Private competitors countered that they could provide even cheaper service at lower cost if the city were to change its ground rules.

Beyond the procedural disputes, however, there's a surprising nugget of truth to be found in this mixed experience. What "everyone" knows—that the private sector is more efficient than the public sector—isn't true. Armed with the right incentives, government can outcompete the private sector.

Questions to Consider

1. What factors account for the cost savings in Chesapeake, Virginia, and Phoenix, Arizona?
2. Are there broader lessons that come from their experiences?
3. Should such competitions be extended to more cities? To more services? To more levels of government?

4. Are there public functions that should *not* be contracted out? Where would you draw the line?

5. Consider *who* does the public's work. How much does it matter if those providing public services are not public employees? Is there a value in having public employees provide public services? And, if so, how can we keep their work accountable, efficient, and effective?

NOTES

1. Rob Shapard, "Collection: City's Managed Competition Model Tops Private Sector," *Waste Age,* June 1, 1997, http://wasteage.com/mag/waste_collection_citys_managed.
2. Ibid.
3. Ibid.
4. Robert Franciosi, "Garbage In, Garbage Out: An Examination of Private/Public Competition by the City of Phoenix," January 1, 1998, http://goldwaterinstitute.org/article/garbage-garbage-out-examination-privatepublic-competition-city-phoenix.

CASE 8.2

Federal Furloughs: Government Employees Suffer from Budget Battles

"Everyone's bracing for the impact," said Army Master Sergeant Trey Corrales. He wasn't talking about a fear his plane would crash. He had just listened to a speech by Defense Secretary Charles Hagel, who warned the troops and their civilian Department of Defense partners that more budget cuts and furloughs were coming.[1] (Furloughs are days when employees may not work and are not paid.) Members of the armed forces were exempt from the furloughs but civilian support workers, who provide everything from health care to equipment supply, took the cuts.

The good news was that the initial forecast of twenty-two furlough days had been reduced to eleven days in 2013 and then reduced again to six days as the department found new ways to stretch its tight budget. The bad news was that when the furlough days began in July, civilian workers lost a day's pay every week, the equivalent of a 20 percent pay cut for every week with a furlough day. The worse news, Hagel said, was that a failure by Congress to pass a new budget

and restore the cuts imposed by sequestration, before the October 1 start of the new fiscal year, could lead to more budget reductions, layoffs of civilian workers, more furlough days, and more reductions in services by civilian support workers for the armed forces. Troops had already had extra pay for deployments to some danger spots eliminated. Training missions had been eliminated, and even the Navy's famous Blue Angels flight demonstration team had been grounded. When the rest of the nation celebrated Independence Day, fireworks on many military bases were eliminated in 2013.

One research manager at the Navy's air station in Jacksonville told Hagel, "I'm sure you realize how disruptive the furlough is to our productivity. So I'm hoping we're not going to do it again next year." Hagel's sober reply was that "there will be further cuts in personnel, make no mistake about it," if Congress failed to restore the cuts. "I don't have any choice." He sadly concluded, "There's no good news."[2]

In fact, Deputy Defense Secretary Ash Carter said there is "the possibility that this does become the new normal and that our budget is simply cut and stays low for a period of time." Carter told participants at the Aspen Security Forum in Colorado that furloughs are a "miserable way to treat people." In looking ahead to the new fiscal year, however, he said that more furloughs coupled with layoffs could continue in the next fiscal year.[3]

The furloughs were a bizarre side-product of the sequestration into which the federal government fell in early 2013. The original plan was to create budgetary consequences so severe that they would force the president and members of Congress to the bargaining table. However, those on the right found that they were getting—automatically—large cuts in government spending. Those on the left, including the president, found that they could not retreat from an automatic trigger to which they had agreed. In the end, there was no political means of escape, so the sequestration kicked in. The once-unimaginable cuts were automatic, affected all parts of the federal government except a handful of entitlements like Social Security and a small number of programs like veterans benefits, and were to be imposed uniformly down to the program and operational level. (Exemptions were later added for meat inspectors and air traffic controllers, after fears that the food processing and airline industries would be crippled by the furloughs.) Managers had no discretion about shuffling their budgets to produce the same level of savings. So from park rangers in national parks to staffers supporting members of the military on their bases, the hammer fell—hard, but uniformly.

For so many federal employees, however, the problem wasn't only that the furloughs came. It was that the number of furlough days and their timing was so unpredictable. That made it hard for families to plan everything from vacations to payments for college tuition, and it made it difficult for the government to manage its operations.

Questions to Consider

1. What do you think of the strategy of using sequestration and furloughs as a strategy to manage budget cuts? Some analysts say it forces the government to make the hard cuts it's been avoiding for a long time. Others say that the across-the-board cuts bear no resemblance to mission and are the worst way to manage budget cuts.

2. How would you treat this situation if you were a manager overseeing employees who were subject to these furloughs and cuts?

3. How would you approach the problem of reducing the federal budget? Everyone agrees that spending cuts are needed. What kind of strategy could build enough political support to obtain the needed reductions?

NOTES

1. "Pentagon Chief Can't Offer Hope in Budget Cuts," *USA Today*, July 22, 2013, http://www.usatoday.com/story/news/nation/2013/07/21/defense-cuts/2573881.
2. Ibid.
3. Leada Gore, "Pentagon Says Sequestration and Furloughs Could Be Its 'New Normal,'" *All Alabama*, July 22, 2013, http://blog.al.com/wire/2013/07/pentagon_says_sequestration_an.html.

CASE 8.3

Keeping Volunteers Out of the Library? Battling the Teachers Union in Bridgewater, Massachusetts

In the middle of a hotly contested gubernatorial campaign in Massachusetts, Republican candidate Charlie Baker stopped in Bridgewater for a press conference. He was outraged that the local teachers union in this town south of Boston was trying to stop the use of volunteers in school libraries. "There are many examples of teachers unions making decisions based on the interests of adults rather than the kids." He continued, "It's outrageous that the union leadership is trying to block the students from the library."[1]

Baker found support from Merry Boegner, a mother of two preschoolers, who supported the candidate's position. "I think it's disgraceful," she argued. "We're in economic times where we need to be creative. We do the same at home with our families. Here, you have people willing to help out, and you don't want it."[2]

No volunteers in the library? No one to help kids find the joy of reading and to provide extra support in tough budget times?

Union officials explained that the story was much more complicated than the candidate's hot rhetoric suggested. As the local budget crisis worsened, the school district reduced the number of middle school librarians in Bridgewater and in neighboring Raynham. The money they saved went into hiring more teachers to reduce class size as more students flooded the schools. To keep the libraries open, the district recruited volunteers. The teachers union objected that volunteers were taking the place of paid teachers—and couldn't possibly provide high-quality service.

The president of the union, Anita Newman, told a reporter, "You're putting unqualified people into the library who are not certified." She explained, "We don't want to ruffle feathers, but you're responsible for the children. We don't use volunteers for recess or lunch either." For the union, the question was simple. "I love volunteers," she said, "but when they take the place of a teacher—and a librarian is a teacher—that's a violation of the contract."[3]

For Baker, it was a matter of raw politics. He charged the teachers union with attacking him at every campaign stop. They're afraid that, if he wins, "it won't be business as usual" in the state capital. The union, usually aligned with the Democrats in Boston, knew that "All bets are off in January" if he won.[4]

"I was hoping this wouldn't become a tempest in a teapot, but it did," Newman sadly concluded.

Questions to Consider

1. Unions work hard to protect the jobs of their members, so their opposition to the use of volunteer librarians is understandable. But do you think the school district, faced with tight budgets, made the right call in shifting paid librarian positions to the classroom and using volunteers to keep the libraries open?

2. Does the use of volunteer, uncertified librarians put the education of middle school children at jeopardy?

3. The majority of union members now work for government, as traditional trade unions have lost manufacturing jobs and unions have successfully organized more government workplaces. Do you think that the spread of public employee unions—focused on promoting job security, good working conditions, and generous benefits—is a good thing? Or do you think that the rise of public employee unions unwisely restricts the ability of elected government officials to make policy decisions that are responsive to voters' wishes?

NOTES

1. Christine Legere, "Baker Criticizes Teachers' Union for Objecting to Library Volunteers," *Boston Globe* October 12, 2010, http://www.boston.com/yourtown/budget blues/2010/10baker_criticizes_teachers_unio .html.
2. Ibid.
3. Ibid.
4. Elizabeth Moura, "Gov. Candidate Baker Weighs In on Bridgewater-Raynham Union Grievance" October 13, 2010, http://www.wickedlocal. com/raynham/news/education/x1767883977/ Gov-candidate-Baker-weighs-in-on-Bridgewater-Raynham-union-grievance.

KEY CONCEPTS

bump   202

buyouts   202

civil service system   194

collective bargaining   207

comparable worth   205

grade creep   196

Hatch Act   212

position classification   194

reductions in force (RIFs)   202

unionization   207

FOR FURTHER READING

Ingraham, Patricia Wallace. *The Foundation of Merit: Public Service in American Democracy.* Baltimore: Johns Hopkins University Press, 1995.

Johnson, Ronald N., and Gary D. Libecap. *The Federal Civil Service System and the Problem of Bureaucracy.* Chicago: University of Chicago Press, 1994.

Mosher, Frederick C. *Democracy and the Public Service.* 2d ed. New York: Oxford University Press, 1982.

National Commission on the Public Service (the Volcker Commission). *Urgent Business for America: Revitalizing the Federal Government for the 21st Century,* January 2003. http://ourpublicservice.org/OPS/ publications/viewcontentdetails.php?id=92.

Perry, James L., and Ann Marie Thomson. *Civic Service: What Difference Does It Make?* Armonk, N.Y.: M. E. Sharpe, 2004.

SUGGESTED WEBSITES

The U.S. Census Bureau's "Public Employment and Payroll Data," **www.census.gov/govs/apes,** is an excellent source of comparative data on public employees at the federal, state, and local levels. At the federal level, the Office of Personnel Management's "Federal Employment

Statistics," especially "The Fact Book," is a useful guide; see **www.opm.gov/feddata**.

Labor practices vary greatly from state to state; some prohibit collective bargaining, while others allow government employees a limited right to strike. The Legal Information Institute at Cornell University compiles state laws, and its website provides a source for exploring state-by-state variations; see **www.law.cornell.edu/wex/table_labor**.

In recent years, more information about working for government, including available positions and (in some cases) applications, has moved online. The federal government's source for job openings is USAJobs, **www.usajobs.gov**. Many state and local governments have similar systems. Pennsylvania, for example, has an integrated website that lists private- and public-sector jobs (at all levels of government); see **www.pa.gov**.

The National Academy of Public Administration periodically issues reports on the role and function of the civil service; NAPA's studies can be found at **www.napawash.org**.

The Government Accountability Office, at **www.gao.gov,** consistently produces some of the most thorough analysis of human capital issues.

The Partnership for Public Service examines the policy issues in building a high-performing government workforce. Its studies and analyses can be found at **www.ourpublicservice.org**.

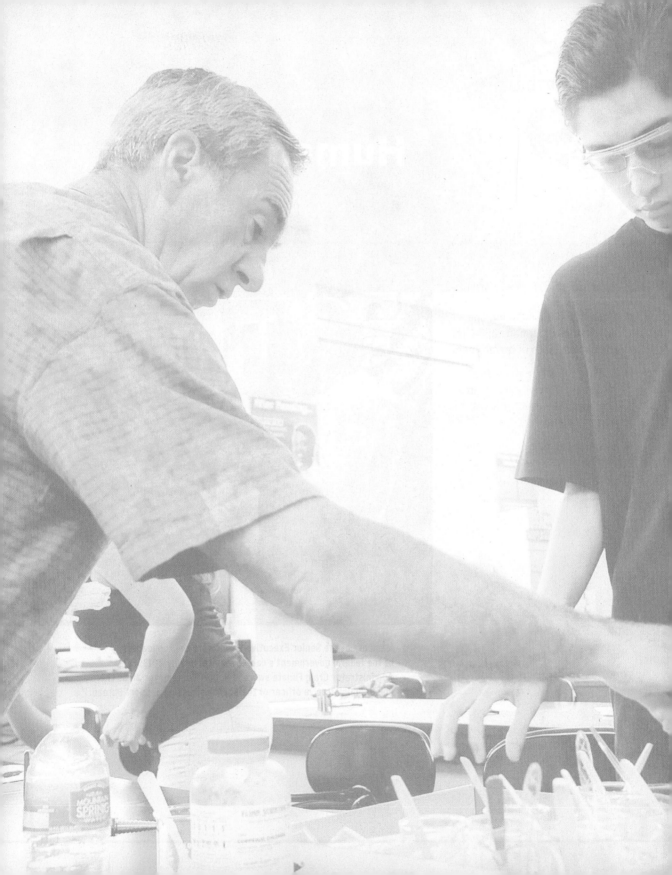

Human Capital

- Understand the meaning and importance of human capital for the performance of government

- Explore the alternatives for reforming the civil service and improving the government's human capital

- Examine the role of leadership in the public service

Members of the Senior Executive Service are the top leaders of the federal government's career service. In July 2013, FEMA Administrator Craig Fugate swore in Robert Waltemeyer Jr. as the chief administrative officer of the agency's Mission Support Bureau.

IF THE QUALITY OF GOVERNMENT DEPENDS ON THE QUALITY of the people who work for it, how good of a job is government doing in hiring skilled workers? This is the issue of **human capital:** to recruit and retain the employees the government needs to do its work and to ensure that they produce strong and effective governmental programs. Following its own review in 2003, the Government Accountability Office (GAO) concluded that "today's federal human capital strategies are not yet appropriately constituted to meet current and emerging challenges or to drive the needed transformation across the government." But, GAO concluded, "federal employees are not the problem." The real problem "is a set of policies that are viewed by many as outdated, overregulated, and not strategic."[1] Put differently, the government's human capital system is in disrepair—it is struggling to identify the workers it needs, to recruit them into government service, and to create a system in which they can perform at the highest level on behalf of the nation's citizens.

Much of government depends not on a straight function of turning inputs into outputs but on leveraging the activity of a vast and complex network of partners, in both the for-profit and nonprofit sectors. Government managers need to know what they need to do, how best to do it, how well they have accomplished results, and how most effectively to build partnerships. In short, they need to *know* perhaps more than they need to *do.*

For society at large, experts have increasingly pointed to the rise of a "knowledge society," as management expert Peter Drucker explains:

> Knowledge workers, even though only a large minority of the work force, already give the emerging knowledge society its character, its leadership, its central challenges and its social profile. They may not be the *ruling* class of the knowledge society, but they already are its *leading* class.[2]

This description of the knowledge economy is even more true for government, whose work increasingly depends on managing information and leveraging partners in the private and nonprofit sectors as well as in other government agencies. Indeed, many of the issues the later chapters examine on implementation and regulation revolve around tracking information and using it to improve performance. In this chapter, we explore the emerging issue of human capital, efforts to transform the civil service system, and strategies for strengthening leadership at the top of the bureaucracy.

THE HUMAN CAPITAL CHALLENGE

In January 2001, GAO named human capital management as a high-risk area facing the entire government—and it's been on the list ever since. The failure to build human capital, GAO worried, courted failure in the government's performance.

Building Human Capital

The challenge of building human capital revolves around four issues in particular.[3]

Leadership

The development of human capital begins at the top, with organizational leaders who focus on continuously improving the organization and building a workforce with the capacity to achieve the organization's goals. In part, this requires top managers to give sustained attention to management. Big policy issues—from scandals to political battles and new legislative proposals to congressional oversight hearings—often drive out a manager's focus on administrative issues. But whenever the urgent (as indeed these policy issues are) drives out the important (especially a long-term focus on organizational performance), governmental organizations risk spending their time fighting brush fires instead of accomplishing their overall missions.

For example, the Department of Homeland Security (DHS), created in 2002 to bring together more than twenty agencies and over 170,000 federal employees, presents a daunting administrative challenge. The department's secretary and top officials face a bewildering flood of terrorist warnings, intelligence analyses, logistical problems, and bureaucratic battles. Congress insists on regular briefings, and the secretary by necessity must invest a great deal of energy and time in working with the heads of other agencies charged with important pieces of the homeland security function, including the secretaries of defense and state and the heads of the FBI and the CIA. It is very easy for these issues to become all-consuming, but if the big policy questions consume the leadership, there may well be little time and no senior officials left to deal with the critical long-term task of bringing the department's vast bureaucratic empire together into a smoothly functioning operation. The risk is that the department's top officials will busy themselves with policy puzzles but find they do not have the capacity to implement them effectively.

But not only is the job of managing human capital difficult; it is also prolonged. Deep organizational change takes sustained effort over time—five to seven years or more, according to the private sector's experience. Yet high-level political appointees serve, on average, less than three years.[4] That pattern of transience at the top leaves much of the task of long-term transformation in the hands of senior career officials, but, as we will see later in this chapter, that part of the government's workforce is aging and many of the most experienced managers are nearing retirement. Leadership, therefore, requires not only sustained attention to management but also careful attention to the problem of building the next generation of leaders.[5]

Strategic Human Capital Planning

While government planning often gets a bad name, it is impossible for government to solve its human capital issues without taking a longer-term view of changing missions and needed capacity. Many government agencies, at all levels, face big turnover in their staffing. And as Generation X and the Millennials replace Baby Boomers, big challenges in the culture of government agencies lie ahead. The rise of Gen X, for example, has already brought fundamental changes in the way government agencies connect electronically with citizens. As today's college students move into the workforce, even bigger changes will follow, from the use of technology to debates about the role of government.[6] In the past, many government workers saw public employment as a lifetime career. Gen X and Millennial workers seem to show far less attachment to their employers, and that adds another layer to the challenge.

Acquiring, Developing, and Retaining Talent

Of course, government agencies are not the only organizations seeking to operate effectively in the knowledge society. Private and nonprofit organizations, in the United States and around the world, are competing for the highly skilled workers needed for these tasks. Although there are many advantages to working for the government—from fringe benefits to the rewards that come from serving the public—in many cases government workers can find similar positions in the private sector, and many of these private-sector jobs involve work under the general umbrella of government rules. The government thus needs to compete in hiring top talent—and it needs to work hard to keep its best employees committed to public service. Indeed, as Kay Coles James, director of the Office of Personnel Management (OPM), argued in 2004, "We have no problem attracting people." The crisis, she concluded, "is in the hiring process"—getting interested individuals in the door, as we saw in Chapter 8, is often the biggest problem.[7]

The Food and Drug Administration (FDA) has had great difficulty in retaining skilled scientists, even as drug companies have increased their own research and development of complex new drugs. If it is to protect consumers' health and safety, the FDA needs to ensure that its staff members know as much as the scientists developing the new drugs. Otherwise, government will lack the muscle to make an independent judgment of whether new pharmaceuticals are safe and effective. To tackle this problem, the FDA has developed new tactics, including retention bonuses for its most valued employees.

The problem of ensuring an adequate supply of skilled workers is common throughout government. In the Department of Housing and Urban Development (HUD), half of the staff members responsible for monitoring the performance of the contractors managing government housing programs were found to have no training in contract management. Even worse, HUD's procurement officials did not know of the gap.[8]

Underlying the search for talent is ensuring that talented workers can put their training to work. Surveys reveal substantial variations in how empowered workers feel to do their jobs. A 2013 survey, for example, found that women felt less comfortable in disclosing violations of laws. Women were more likely to believe that "arbitrary action, personal favoritism and coercion were tolerated." Women were less satisfied than men with their agency's efforts toward diversity. Employees with disabilities had less favorable views toward their workplaces than those without disabilities.[9]

The U.S. Department of Veterans Affairs matched job coaches with military veterans to help prepare them for the job market at this 2012 job fair in Washington, D.C.

Results-Oriented Culture

Too often, as we saw in the previous chapter, government personnel processes become ends in themselves: forms to be filled and rules to be followed, regardless of how these processes contribute to the bureaucracy's ability to accomplish its mission. Those very processes can, in fact, make it difficult to achieve the mission. In contrast, a focus on the agency's mission—on getting results—can make it easier to devise an effective personnel system. In the aftermath of the September 11, 2001, attacks, for example, the FBI discovered that the mismatch of rules and missions hindered the bureau's effectiveness. To resolve this problem, top FBI officials reorganized the bureau's structure to match its mission and worked to match the personnel system to the new priorities.

As American governments at all levels develop more aggressive performance management systems, it becomes easier to use those systems to drive the personnel system—and to reshape the personnel system to support the mission. Other nations have been pursuing just such strategies. In Canada, the province of Ontario has redefined its system for measuring employee performance to capture how well its employees contribute to the organization's goals. A similar overhaul has occurred in the Tax Office in Australia. These governments have created a "line of sight" performance management system, designed "to clearly demonstrate how an individual's performance contributes to the overall goals of the organization as well as to broader government-wide priorities."[10] The idea is simple: measure each employee's performance, and connect that employee's work to the work of the organization. Strengthening the incentives for each employee improves the ability of the organization to accomplish its mission.

Such an approach, of course, is both complex and difficult, but many analysts have concluded that this approach ought to be the foundation for reform in the United States.[11] As part of its broader reform effort, Barack Obama's administration launched a major performance improvement effort that focused on

- using performance information to lead, learn, and improve outcomes;
- communicating performance coherently and concisely for better results and transparency; and
- strengthening problem-solving networks, inside and outside government, to improve outcomes and performance management practices.

That effort, the administration said, would produce "unrelenting attention to achieve the ambitious, near-term performance goals" that agency leaders themselves identified as top-priority objectives.[12]

Government Reforms

OPM, the Office of Management and Budget (OMB), and the GAO have all launched major human capital efforts. OPM has published human capital standards; see Box 9.1, which charts the connections between agency missions, human capital, program performance, and government's accountability. Former Comptroller General David M. Walker concluded, "Strategic management of human capital should emphasize that people are the key to the success of our government transformation effort. As such, they should be treated more like assets instead of liabilities."[13] The Obama administration's reforms in performance and civil service advanced these notions one more step.

BOX 9.1 | **Human Capital Standards**

- **Strategic Alignment:** connecting the mission and objectives with strategic plans and budgets
- **Leadership and Knowledge Management:** effectively leading employees to sustain a learning environment focused on continuous improvement
- **Results-Oriented Performance Culture:** defining goals and providing incentives

- for employees to seek high levels of performance
- **Talent Management:** identifying the skills that the agency needs, defining the gap between existing skills and those needed, and developing a strategy for closing the gap
- **Accountability:** using a data-driven performance system to ensure results

Source: U.S. Office of Personnel Management, "Human Capital Management," http://www.opm.gov/policy-data-oversight/human-capital-management.

This strong convergence of rhetoric and ideas has begun to have an impact. During the Clinton administration, OPM wiped away two of the most notorious symbols of the troubled personnel system. Accompanied (literally) by a fife and drum corps, OPM director James King dumped the *Federal Personnel Manual* into the trash. This multivolume set of rules contained 10,000 pages of rules—including 900 pages of instructions for filling out just one federal form. As King explained, "It is written in such gobbledygook that it takes a team of Washington's finest attorneys to understand what is required to hire, fire, classify and reward employees."[14] The job of writing rules was instead turned over to federal agencies.

The Clinton administration followed up that theatrical gesture by eliminating the much-hated SF-171, the federal government's standard résumé form which, when completed, often stretched six feet or more. It was replaced by a computerized system and by acceptance of more standard résumés. With the death of knowledge, skills, and abilities essays in the Obama administration, the movement toward simplicity in the application process took another big step. Many state and local governments likewise have embraced the need for a strong human capital strategy as part of their efforts to build a government for the twenty-first century.

NEW FLEXIBILITY FOR THE PERSONNEL SYSTEM

In the late 1990s, however, new and more aggressive flexibilities began creeping into the personnel systems at all levels of government. Each was designed to link employee performance with agency missions and to enhance the ability of the government to do its job.

At all levels of government, managers complain that the personnel system has too many layers, with too many subcategories, which makes it difficult to classify employees and even more difficult to manage employees effectively. Because the nature of the job defines the personnel classification and the classification defines who can do the job, managers have a hard time moving employees to where they are most needed or into the jobs in which they might be able to produce the best results. For example, a 1997 survey of state government personnel managers found that they believed that their states had far too many job titles. The average state reported 1,802 titles that the personnel managers had to track, yet most of these titles covered very few employees—an average of just twenty-four each—which created groupings too small for broad policy. Moreover, the classification and pay systems were very old, averaging twenty-three years since their inception in the mid-1970s.[15] Government's functions and strategies had changed considerably in the meantime, but the personnel system had not.

Broadbanding collapses the typically large number of job categories in most government personnel systems into a far smaller number. The new categories tend to capture broad occupational families, with fewer pay grades and broader ranges within each pay grade. The system has several advantages:

- *Flexibility.* The supervisor has far greater flexibility in assigning workers to tasks; as new tasks emerge, employees can be shifted around the workplace without confronting the traditional barriers that constrain the existing system.
- *Career development.* Employees have more room for moving up the system and more opportunity for shifting horizontally into related jobs.
- *Linking pay to skills.* The system can also make it easier to link employees' pay to their skills and performance, as part of a reengineered human capital system.

However, the system also brings the following risks:

- *Downgrading positions without downgrading the work.* With additional flexibility, managers may be tempted to shift work from higher-skilled to lower-skilled workers. In health care programs, for example, the new flexibility might make it possible to transfer patient care from skilled professional staff to relatively less trained workers. Critics worry that this could lead to "de-skilling" the workforce.
- *Potential for abuse.* The current system limits managers' discretion, which prevents managers from easily shifting employees to different jobs or new assignments. Critics worry that the new flexibility could create the possibility of abuse.
- *Poor performance and stress.* Employees could find themselves facing a broader range of duties, and if their tasks were to change too often or stretch too far into unfamiliar territory, they could become stressed or begin to perform at a low level. Critics worry that this new pressure could leave employees worse off.
- *Failure to reward increased productivity.* Broadbanding often accompanies other performance improvement efforts, including decreases in staff and demands for increases in productivity. If employees do more with less, critics worry, they may not reap the benefits for the efficiencies the systems gain.[16]

At the federal level, broadbanding has not advanced far past the test stage. A number of federal agencies, including several Army facilities, an Air Force facility, and the Department of Commerce, have experimented with the strategy. The Navy's China Lake weapons center, the first of the broadbanding demonstration projects, permanently moved to a flexible broadband system after top officials concluded that performance had improved, supervisors found the system easier to manage, and employee satisfaction with pay and performance management had increased. The federal government rolled back an effort to apply broad-banding to the defense intelligence system, and intelligence units throughout the government scrambled to rebuild the personnel system without sacrificing the focus on performance that was its essential element.

Departmental Flexibilities

Many reformers have agreed on the need for an even more fundamental reform of the federal civil service system, but they disagree on how best to pursue it. Some reformers despaired of enacting a broad-based reform that would apply to the entire federal government after the power of public employee unions and a lack of congressional interest in such sweeping change paralyzed the effort. Faced with tough management problems, Congress has allowed some agencies exemptions from portions of the civil service law. But some reformers have worried that a series of ad hoc reforms would produce widespread inconsistency in federal personnel standards. Paul Volcker, the former Federal Reserve Board chairman who headed a series of civil service reform commissions, said that he sensed "something of a thread of incoherence" in the efforts of these agencies.[17] They struggled between doing what could be done—at the risk of undermining more than a century of uniform civil service policies—and seeking a broader reform—at the risk of inviting political conflicts that would make it impossible to do anything.

When the air traffic controllers went on strike in 1981, President Ronald Reagan determined that they had broken the law and he fired them; for years afterward, the FAA struggled to rebuild the system. In 1996, however, Congress approved an agency-wide reform granting top managers more flexibility. The law gave the FAA a broadband pay system, requirements for more frequent feedback on employee performance and a linking of performance with pay, better workforce planning, and a competitive hiring practice that bypassed the federal government's central system. The FAA initially clashed with its unions to establish these reforms, and GAO concluded that the FAA had not collected enough data to measure the success of its effort. Employees reported mixed reactions to the new system.[18]

In 1998, following intensive hearings that produced charges of widespread mismanagement, Congress gave similar personnel flexibility to the Internal Revenue Service (IRS). Its new system produced more progress than the one at the FAA, but IRS managers quickly discovered that real

An air traffic controller works at New York's LaGuardia Airport, in one of the nation's most crowded air spaces. Recruiting new controllers to replace retiring workers is one of the air traffic control system's biggest challenges.

reform takes a long time. Of the IRS broadbanding effort, Ron Sanders, the agency's chief human resources officer, explained, "The essence of pay banding is pay for performance. That means you've got to have some way of credibly measuring that performance."[19] That need required both transforming the internal culture and devising new mechanisms for assessing the quality of employees' work. But these IRS personnel reforms did not—and, indeed, could not—solve the problems that had first prompted Congress to act.

The agency had faced an avalanche of embarrassing congressional hearings, reports of abuse of taxpayers, and inadequate customer service. Many of these charges turned out, on later investigation, to be unfounded; others hinged on the basic dilemma of IRS's mission: balancing satisfaction of taxpayers with collection of taxes they do not want to pay—and finding a way to keep IRS employees happy and productive in the process of accomplishing this tradeoff. As the IRS worked hard on serving taxpayers better, the inevitable happened: charges soon began to surface that the agency was not collecting all of the taxes owed. Then, as it began shifting more emphasis toward collection, it inevitably devoted less energy to taxpayer satisfaction. The agency's personnel reforms could not resolve this dilemma. But observers did agree that the IRS reforms offered a possible model for the rest of the government.

This debate over agency-based flexibility fell right into the middle of the 2002 debate over creating a new Department of Homeland Security (DHS). President Bush opposed the congressional campaign for the department until, faced with strong evidence that information flows throughout the government had been seriously flawed before the September 11, 2001, attacks, he announced that he, too, favored creation of the department. The price for his support, however, was a waiver of many of the government's civil service rules. "The new secretary of Homeland Security must have the freedom and the flexibility, to be able to get the right people in the right jobs at the right time so we can hold people accountable," Bush argued in July 2002.[20] He pressed for substantial flexibility in the so-called **Title 5** requirements, which are contained in Title 5 of the U.S. Code: the classic standards for hiring and firing, the preferences for veterans in recruitment, the prohibitions against nepotism, the protections for whistleblowers, and the other requirements that had accumulated over more than a century of legislation and administrative rules. Congressional Democrats, fearful that Bush was using the debate to try to break public employee unions (many of which traditionally supported Democrats), fought the civil service waivers throughout the summer and fall. In the November 2002 midterm elections, however, Republicans won surprising victories over Democratic congressional candidates, and the party took control of both houses of Congress. The Democrats quickly conceded the battle, and Congress approved the new department. (See Box 9.2 for a comparison of the traditional civil service provisions and proposals for change in the new DHS.)

The creation of DHS framed some of the biggest steps away from the traditional civil service system. Indeed, Bush administration officials even proposed that similar flexibility be extended to the entire Department of Defense. However, congressional Democrats stalled that proposal and fought hard against the DHS strategy. In 2008, Congress prohibited DHS from spending any more to implement the new system, and that prohibition effectively killed the plan, and Obama's Secretary of Defense Robert Gates announced that the department would end its performance-pay system. But the controversy sharpened the debate about the

---

BOX 9.2	**Proposed Civil Service Rules for the Department of Homeland Security**

Provisions maintained	**Provisions not maintained**
Merit system principles	Employee appeal rights
Whistleblower protection	"Rule of three" hiring rule
Basic employment rules (e.g., veterans'	Performance appraisal system
preference)	Position classification
Senior Executive Service	Pay rates and systems
Reduction-in-force procedures	Labor-management relations
Training rules	Adverse action procedures
Incentive awards	Appeal rights
Personnel demonstration authority	
Payroll administration	
Travel rules	
Special allowances (e.g., for overseas duty)	
Attendance and leave standards	
Antidiscrimination	
Political activity limits	
Gift limits	
Drug-use policy	
Work life and safety services	
Injury compensation	
Insurance and retirement benefits	

Source: Brian Friel, "Homeland Security Leaders Win Broad Power over Civil Service Rules," *Government Executive*, November 21, 2002, http://www.govexec.com/dailyfed/1102/112102b1.htm.

---

future of the civil service system, and about whether reforms could—or should—proceed agency by agency or through a comprehensive, government-wide effort. And it focused the most basic question of all: what is the role and meaning of the nineteenth century merit system in the twenty-first century?

Rethinking the Meaning of Merit

Over the past two decades, three states—Texas, Georgia, and Florida—have taken even bigger steps toward escaping the bounds of the current civil service system. They took the advice of Walter Broadnax, former director of the New York State civil service system and long-time analyst of the process, who, in frustration at the system's constraints, said simply, "Blow it up."[21] These three states followed just that course.

The Texas legislature led the way in 1985 by abolishing the Texas Merit Council, a body that did not have control over all the state's employees but did oversee ten agencies' compliance with federal law. Deciding to eliminate the council, the state legislature delegated responsibility for complying with federal civil service standards to the state agencies themselves. The agencies, in turn, were given complete flexibility in setting hiring and firing procedures for their employees. The state government, for example, cannot calculate how long it takes to hire new employees, since the agencies follow their own rules and the state does not keep centralized statistics. Indeed, Texas is the only state without a central personnel office.

Georgia followed in 1996 with an even more radical reform, which Republican Governor Zell Miller made a centerpiece of his effort to transform government management. When the state set up its civil service system in the 1940s, he said, creating "a professional workforce that was free of political cronyism" was important. But, he contended,

> too often in government, we pass laws to fix particular problems of the moment, and then we allow half a century to roll by without ever following up to see what the long-term consequences have been. Folks, the truth of the matter is that a solution in 1943 is a problem in 1996. The problem is governmental paralysis, because despite its name, our present Merit System is not about merit. It offers no reward to good workers. It only provides cover for bad workers.[22]

Miller won overwhelming support for his plan to abolish the state's merit system. Employees hired after July 1, 1996, would serve at will, which meant that they had no civil service protection and could be fired without benefit of the standard civil service procedures. The new employees would receive the same benefits as employees currently in the system, but they would not accrue seniority rights, so, in case of reductions in force, they could not protect their jobs by "bumping" less senior employees (as described in the previous chapter). They would have no formal rights of appeal of disciplinary actions or performance assessments; managers could promote, demote, transfer, or fire employees as they saw fit. The legislature also abolished the traditional grade-and-step process that set employees' wages.

Despite the worries of many advocates of the traditional civil service, Georgia's new system has been remarkably free of tales of abuse. Investigative reporters found little expansion of patronage; in fact, they determined that patronage in Georgia was little different than in states with tough civil service laws. Different employees doing similar jobs might receive different pay, which would not have occurred in the old system. And managers found that they had lost the ability to blame the system for being unable to respond to requests. As one senior state official put it, the buck stops with managers, who have to shoulder responsibility for their decisions.[23] The 2008 Government Performance Project (GPP) survey of state government management capacity found the state at the cutting edge. "Georgia continues to push the envelope in workforce and human capital planning."[24]

In 2001 Florida made three fundamental changes in its civil service system. First, supervisors became **at-will employees**—top officials could hire and fire them without having to deal with civil service protections. Second, the state collapsed its existing pay structure into a broadband system. Finally, with a handful of exceptions for police officers, firefighters, and nurses, the state eliminated seniority protections for state employees. As journalist Jonathan Walters explained, "What lawmakers in Florida seemed to have decided was that if it's not possible to eliminate civil service coverage for all state employees outright, then the best thing to do was to drastically reengineer what that coverage amounts to."[25] The state continued to push ahead without a strategic workforce plan, however, and the GPP found

The federal General Services Administration offers a variety of training programs, both to help private-sector companies selling goods and services to the federal government and to help federal employees develop their skills in areas like contracts and technology, in order to better service their private-sector partners.

the state drifting into growing trouble. Florida outsourced more of its administrative work and made one-fifth of its workforce into at-will employees (that is, they could be fired at the will of their supervisors). Turnover rose, and the state's capacity to get its work done shrank.[26]

What effect did these reforms have? There has been little evidence in any of the three states of widespread abuse, either through hiring substandard workers or political interference in the hiring process. Few lawsuits alleging discrimination or other violations of the law have arisen. The basic principles for which the civil service system had been created a century before remained intact. Managers simply found it easier to manage: they had more flexibility and could act more quickly, and they had an easier time firing poor performers and, when necessary, shrinking the size of the government workforce.

What would happen if such reforms were to be instituted in other states with stronger traditions of political patronage would be hard to guess. As in the federal system, establishing good performance measurement systems proved difficult, and none of the states systematically assessed the impact of the reforms—with the devolution of responsibility came a hands-off policy on collecting data. But it is clear that, faced with a tension between the restrictions of the current civil service system and the needs of adapting government to fast-changing realities, more state and local governments will be exploring flexible personnel systems.[27]

Virginia's state government, in many ways, has become the national model. The GPP found that

> The commonwealth has a strategic plan for management of human resources (HR) that identifies current and future needs and is linked to the human capital plan. Virginia has readily available comprehensive data about its current and future workforce needs that it uses to make decisions involving human capital management. The commonwealth has evaluated and updated its classification, compensation and management systems and implemented emergency workforce planning.

Virginia developed innovative approaches to recruiting new employees, including a strategy to give state service a special cachet and a contract with a private company to recruit foreign-born nurses to fill high-demand positions. The state has broadband pay ranges and flexible fringe benefits, along with a generous pay-for-performance system. Training and development are high priorities.[28] The state found that making human capital development paid off with higher performance for taxpayers and better jobs for state employees.

More broadly, throughout the states fundamental changes are emerging to many of the civil service system's oldest features. Florida's at-will system has expanded to Georgia and Indiana. In Arizona, new employees must agree to "uncovered" status, forgoing traditional civil service protections. North Carolina has expanded the number of employees exempt from civil service requirements, and Tennessee has eliminated "bumping." As North Carolina Governor Pat McCrory put it, "I've got a $20 billion operation I've got to run, and you can't run it with your managers' and your executives' hands tied."[29] There is no agreement on the best civil service system for the twenty-first century—but there is a strong consensus that the current system is a poor match for today's governance challenges.

LEADERSHIP IN THE PUBLIC SERVICE

At the core of all of these reforms is a central concept: high performance in public agencies depends on leadership by top officials. No system for hiring, firing, promoting, and rewarding employees—whether it is a civil service system or not—can work without strong and sustained direction. Building and maintaining human capital begins, as GAO pointed out, with leadership.

Just as the government has grappled with how best to nurture its rank-and-file employees, it has long struggled with how best to recruit and reward its top leaders. In this section, we focus on leadership in the federal government. State and local governments often follow the same general pattern, but they can also present enormous variations.

Every modern government deals with the leadership task by creating a mix of political and administrative officials at the top. The fundamental puzzle is how to set that mix: political officials provide a larger measure of responsiveness, while career administrators bring a larger measure of professional competence. Methods for establishing the mix vary greatly. In Britain, a change of parties brings only about 120 members of Parliament into the executive part of the government, with such titles as minister, junior minister, and parliamentary secretary. In France, the government of the day has only 100 to 150 politicians, mostly ministers, secretaries of state, and their staff aides. In Germany, the strictly political echelon is thin—about 40 members, including ministers and parliamentary secretaries. Denmark has perhaps the thinnest layer of political officials of any major democracy: the minister of each agency is a political official, but all officials below that level are careerists. The American federal government, of course, stands at the opposite extreme.

Political Leadership

In the American executive branch there are over 3,000 political positions, of which about 1,500 are at the higher levels.[30] Of these, approximately 1,000 are leadership positions, including cabinet secretaries, administrators of agencies such as NASA and the Small Business Administration, ambassadors to foreign nations, and regulatory positions in agencies such as the Federal Trade Commission and the Securities and Exchange Commission.[31] By any measure, the United States has a far larger number of political officials at the top of the bureaucracy than other Western democracies. Moreover, the number of executives at the top of the federal bureaucracy has steadily been increasing over the past forty years.

Why does the United States stand out? One explanation is that some presidents—notably Richard Nixon, Jimmy Carter, and Ronald Reagan—have entered office on campaigns vilifying "the bureaucracy" and, believing their own rhetoric, concluded that only a small army of their own selection could ensure agencies' responsiveness to presidential policy priorities.[32] Even presidents who have expressed more confidence in government—including Bill Clinton and both presidents Bush—find that political appointments can help build a trusted cadre of officials throughout the government.

More basically, however, the American separation of powers, in contrast to European systems, leaves the president less in command of administrative agencies than are European executives, who have more administrative freedom. In parliamentary systems, leaders can count on legislative support because their party or coalition has the most votes. The U.S. president, in contrast, faces a Congress that engages in active oversight and intervention in administrative agencies' affairs, and the president often confronts a situation in which one or both houses are under the opposite party's control. In addition, as Terry Moe has argued, the mismatch between the public's extravagant expectations of a president's performance and the limited resources available for satisfying those expectations makes the president seize on the tools readily at hand, namely politicization of appointments and centralization in the White House.[33]

No one doubts the need for having a layer of political positions and, immediately below that layer, for mixing political appointees and careerists. It is widely agreed that a president or department head needs people who share the same policy orientation; who will advocate the chosen policies to congressional committees, interest groups, and the public; who can serve as their superiors' loyal agents in bringing the permanent bureaucracy into effective service of those policies; and who have their superiors' confidence. The leader also needs officials who are expendable—who can readily be removed when they lose the president's or department head's confidence, resist policy directives, or become liabilities because they have antagonized relevant congressional committees or interest groups.[34] The question for debate is how deep into the bureaucracy this political appointment process should go.

As Paul Light, a leading scholar of the presidential appointments process, found in an important study of senior officials, the federal government has steadily "thickened" as the number of political appointees has risen. There are, Light discovered, "more layers of leaders" and "more leaders at each layer." The result has been an important transformation in government:

> In the 1950s, the federal bureaucracy looked like a relatively flat bureaucratic pyramid, with few senior executives, a somewhat larger number of middle managers, and a very large number of frontline employees. By the 1970s, it was beginning to look like a circus tent, with a growing corps of senior political and career managers, a sizable bulge of middle managers and professionals, and a shrinking number of frontline employees.
>
> In the 1980s and 1990s, the configuration began to resemble a pentagon, with even more political and career executives at the top and almost equal numbers of many middle-level and frontline employees.[35]

In his survey, Light found fifty-two potential managerial layers of government from top to bottom in the federal government. Some positions are held by political appointees; others are occupied by careerists. Not all departments have every position: only the Department of Energy, for example, has a principal associate deputy undersecretary. Moreover, the government is getting even thicker: Light also discovered that in 2004 there were sixty-four different categories of supporting positions (chief of staff to the secretary, deputy chief of staff to the secretary, chief of staff to the undersecretary, and so on); that number was up from fifty-one in 1998 and thirty-three in 1992.[36]

Even amid the recent enthusiasm for downsizing the federal government, presidents have shown little inclination to reduce the number of layers or, especially, the number of political appointees who fill them. Every position is an opportunity to reward a valued campaign aide or a generous contributor. But the increase of governmental layers weakens accountability by making it harder to assign clear responsibility for results.

Recruitment

Filling those positions is one of the most daunting problems facing a new president. After the election, a new president has only about ten weeks to assemble the team that will take over the executive branch on inauguration day. The president must rely heavily on top campaign staff to handle the flood of candidacies self-generated or proposed by political and interest group patrons. Campaign staff members are rarely qualified for the shift of focus from campaigning to governing; the qualifications required for specific positions are poorly understood and often poorly match those of the chosen candidates.[37] After inauguration, the task shifts to the White House personnel office, and haste gives way to delay. By November of his first year, George H. W. Bush had not nominated candidates for 27 percent of departmental and other agency positions requiring Senate confirmation—a higher percentage than in the four preceding major transitions.[38] As Paul Light observed, "It now takes as long, on average, to get an appointee into office as it does to have a child."[39] It took the Obama administration more than a year to fill even 80 percent of its top politically appointed positions in the agencies.

The recruitment of political executives is so difficult that one must marvel that it works as well as it does. It succeeds best in the selection of cabinet members, a matter to which the president-elect gives personal attention. Most cabinet members have had federal government experience.[40] They are often generalists with prior service in other cabinet posts, at the subcabinet level, in Congress, or in the White House. Some have served at the state and local level, especially those named to cabinet posts for such departments as Health and Human Services (HHS) and Transportation, which have a heavy state and local government connection. They are likely to be qualified for the processes of advocacy, negotiation, and compromise that dominate governmental policymaking, especially if they are lawyers, though this skill set is less likely to be found with corporate executives and academics, and not at all with ideologues.[41]

The vast number of appointments below the cabinet level poses the real problem, making it virtually impossible for the president-elect (later, the president) to give the selections personal attention. Therefore, the president is dependent at first on the campaign staff and then on the personnel office at the White House. An initial impulse of some incoming presidents is to delegate to cabinet members the selection of their subordinates, but after the inauguration, subcabinet appointments are generally cleared or initiated in the White House personnel office.

Most political executives have solid educational backgrounds, and many have subject-matter knowledge relevant to their particular responsibilities. But there are two important problems. First, many political appointees have suffered from lack of experience in the federal executive branch; former appointees without such prior experience express regret at how poorly prepared they were for the Washington setting of interest groups, congressional committees, and White House staff; the goldfish-bowl exposure to the media; the budget process; and the permanent bureaucracy. A few appointees have even revealed defective appreciation of the Constitution, faithful execution of the laws, and the public service code of ethics. The contrast with Britain is striking. There the political officials are drawn from Parliament. A new cabinet typically consists of individuals who in opposition were members of a "shadow cabinet," each specializing in the affairs of a particular ministry. Often the ministers have had experience in one or more earlier governments when their party was in power.

The second problem is that many political appointees arrive at their positions without extensive management experience.[42] Many come from law firms, university faculties, research institute staffs, interest group organizations, and congressional members' offices and committees; such experience scarcely prepares them to run a bureau of 5,000 employees, let alone to operate effectively in one of the cabinet departments. In fact, the largest governmental organization Barack Obama had run before becoming president was his Senate office; Senate staffs average thirty-four persons. Recruits from business are more likely to have experience in large-scale management—although when Reagan appointed more businesspersons (a fifth of all his appointees) than any president since Eisenhower, his appointees did not exhibit significantly better performance. In 2008, G. Edward DeSeve laid out a set of competencies that political executives need to do their job, but progress in implementing these remained fleeting.[43]

Turnover

Political appointees serve only briefly in their posts. For decades, the median length of service for presidential appointees has been little more than two years; a third stayed a year and a half or less.[44] This rapid-fire **turnover** creates a host of problems, the most important of which is what Max Stier calls "continuity of focus."[45]

First, many presidential appointees leave after they have barely learned their jobs and adapted to the Washington environment; analysts widely agree that appointees need at least a year to become productive performers in their government posts. Some, moreover, are aware that the second year may be their last; to initiate and see results from new projects, they will prefer those that are short range, even though significant achievements in the public interest require emphasis on long-range outcomes. Executives who do not pay attention to the likelihood they will not be in the position very long may invest energy in substantial undertakings, but the job of carrying them through will be passed on to their successors, who may well push them aside to make way for a new set of priorities. An administration loses sustained focus through such a stop-and-go or go-and-stop process. One career civil servant, who became an assistant secretary of commerce, reported his experience this way:

> I don't know how many assistant secretaries I have helped break in. . . . And there is always a propensity for a new guy to come in and discover the wheel all over again. And then you have the classic case of a political officer who is going to make a name for himself, and therefore he is going to identify one golden chalice he is going after, and he will take the whole goddam energy of an organization to go after that golden chalice. He leaves after eighteen months, a new guy comes in, and his golden chalice is over here. "Hey guys, everybody, this way."[46]

Turnover at the cabinet level has similar costs. At the Department of Labor, the GAO reported, the then-serving secretary "has demonstrated the strong leadership needed for a well-managed Organization, and his management system established a sound framework for strategic planning and management." Nevertheless, of nearly 200 Labor Department managers polled about this official's efficient system, "about 92 percent believed it should remain despite top-level turnover, whereas only about 35 percent believed it would."[47] Below the cabinet and assistant secretaries, the phenomenon repeats itself: in the decade ending in 1987, the Social Security Administration had seven commissioners or acting commissioners. As the GAO found, "These short tenures, along with commissioners' differing priorities and management approaches, resulted in frequent changes of direction, diminished accountability, and little long-term operational planning."[48]

Second, despite frequent talk of a president's or department head's "team," rapid turnover undermines teamwork. In a department, the set of top executives is constantly changing, as the timing of individual departures is usually set by each official's choice. More broadly, because so many policies and programs involve interdepartmental collaboration, their shaping and constancy depend on interdepartmental networks of political executives sharing concerns with particular policy areas. Such networks, as Hugh Heclo has observed, require "relationships of confidence and trust."[49] But the chemistry of these interpersonal relations develops only over time; the subtraction and addition of new elements can upset the developed formula.

Third, civil servants' incentives to obey political superiors tend to fray when those superiors who are here today are likely to be gone tomorrow. Some high careerists patiently tutor one after another political executive to speed the learning process. But others, if in charge of bureaus and programs, mount defenses to minimize damage by ill-prepared and very temporary political executives.[50] Indeed, hardened top career officials have learned that there are two ways of embarrassing a new political appointee. One, they say, is to do nothing the new boss wants, on the assumption that the appointee will not be around long enough to notice. The other is to do *everything* the new boss wants, on the assumption that the appointee will quickly learn to depend more on the career staff to avoid the inevitable political problems that come from charging ahead too quickly.

Fourth, the high rate of turnover means that staffing the administration never really ends. Departures constantly create vacancies that need filling, which produces both problems and opportunities. A major problem is the many months, and sometimes years, required to recruit, nominate, and obtain Senate confirmation of successors to the vacant posts. On the eve of Reagan's second inauguration, HHS lacked three assistant secretaries, a general counsel, and two commissioners. Its Social Security Administration in early 1985 had an acting commissioner (who had served thus for sixteen months) and three acting deputy commissioners (two having served nineteen months).[51] At the beginning of 1986, one-sixth of the 176 cabinet department positions that required presidential nomination and Senate confirmation were either vacant or occupied by persons designated as only "acting" in their positions.[52] During the first years of the George W. Bush administration, the Presidential Appointee Initiative tracked appointments and charted a constant lack of leadership at the top. When a position is vacant or held by a temporary designee, fresh initiatives are rarely taken, on the grounds that those should be left for the properly appointed successor. Thus, to the red-and-green traffic light symbols of stop-and-go administration is added a yellow light for the long pause in filling vacancies.

In 1998, Congress passed the Vacancies Reform Act, which required agencies to report to Congress and the GAO on vacant positions requiring Senate confirmation. The law also limited the service of acting administrators to 210 days. Many agencies, however, proved slow in reporting vacancies and sometimes did not report them at all. Many acting administrators served for longer than the 210-day limit.[53]

Finally, during the last year or eighteen months of a presidency there is likely to be a substantial exodus of political appointees, many intent on capitalizing on their government experience by obtaining remunerative employment in the private sector. As a presidency winds down, restaffing can be exceedingly difficult, as few qualified persons will take public office for a predictably brief period. Moreover, no president wants to risk a contentious confirmation battle when launching a reelection campaign. Both problems can lead to weak leadership—or no leadership—in the waning months of an administration.

This constellation of issues posed special problems for the Department of Homeland Security. Turnover in the department in 2005 was 8.4 percent, twice the government-wide average. Among airport screeners, attrition was more than 14 percent. As FEMA, an agency within the department, struggled to respond to Hurricane Katrina in 2005, it had 500 vacancies, and acting administrators headed eight of its ten regions—including the region overseeing Louisiana. Basic problems of staffing and leading federal agencies continued to pose big problems of performance. The result? In a survey by the Partnership for Public Service, DHS placed thirty-first out of thirty-three agencies.[54]

How Many Are Too Many?

There has been an ongoing debate over whether the growing number of political appointees is a good thing for the administrative process. Political appointees are needed, it is argued, to ensure that the permanent bureaucracy faithfully serves the chief executive, adapting to a new administration's policy priorities regardless of how much change they may require. But two important questions remain: (1) How many political appointees are needed to achieve the objective? (2) At what point does the number of such appointees become so large as to frustrate the objective?

There are no precise answers to these questions, but political appointees themselves have proposed some formulations. President Nixon's top political recruiter wrote:

> The solution to problems of rigidity and resistance to change in government is not to increase the number of appointive positions at the top, as so many politicians are wont to do. . . . An optimum balance between the number of career and noncareer appointments . . . should be struck in favor of fewer political appointees, not more. In many cases, the effectiveness of an agency would be improved and political appointments would be reduced by roughly 25 percent if line positions beneath the assistant secretary level were reserved for career officials.[55]

The Volcker Commission, which included fifteen former top political appointees, recommended in 1989 that "the growth in recent years in the number of presidential appointees, whether those subject to Senate confirmation, noncareer senior executives, or personal and confidential assistants, should be curtailed. . . . The commission is confident that a substantial cut is possible, and believes a cut from the current 3,000 to no more than 2,000 is a reasonable target." On the second question, the commission observed that

> excessive numbers of political appointees serving relatively brief periods may undermine the president's ability to govern, insulating the administration from needed dispassionate advice and institutional memory. The mere size of the political turnover almost guarantees management gaps and discontinuities, while the best of the career professionals will leave government if they do not have challenging opportunities at the sub-cabinet level.[56]

If the answers seem so clear, why has it been so hard to translate them into reality? For two reasons: because Congress must act to transform political appointments to career staff and because presidents claim that they need these positions to steer the administration.

Gen X Comes to Government

Governing magazine's Rob Gurwitt tweaked his readers with an article in May 2013. Generation X is checking in to government's decision-making circles. Who are they? Born between the early 1960s and the early 1980s, they sit in the uneasy space between the aging Baby Boomers (born between 1946 and 1964), Generation Y (born between the early 1980s and early 2000s—most of the readers of this book), and the Millennials (who will be reading the next edition).

And what difference is Gen X making? Gurwitt found that they don't tend to show up for public meetings. Instead, they participate in online forums. They promote heavy reliance on information technology, transparency of information, and more access to data. They want to play an active role and not just listen to public officials. They are focused on families and schools and parks. And because they came of age in an era of gridlock, they are skeptical about big institutions, in both government and the private sector.

And if you're from Gen Y or the Millennial generation, they will be your bosses, as the Baby Boomers retire and they take the top jobs. What difference do you think this will make for the way big organizations—especially government organizations—will work?

As for the Millennials, Ron Fournier points to an even deeper distrust in government and public officials. They want to change Washington. But how will they be able to do it, Fournier asks, if they hate it?

Source: Rob Gurwitt, "How Gen X Is Shaping Government," *Governing*, May 2013, http://www.governing .com/topics/mgmt/gov-how-generation-x-shaping-government.html; Rob Fournier, "The Outsiders: How Can Millennials Change Washington If They Hate It?" *The Atlantic*, August 26, 2013, http://www.theatlantic.com/ politics/archive/2013/08/the-outsiders-how-can-millennials-change-washington-if-they-hate-it/278920.

CAREER LEADERSHIP

No matter how strong or problematic the bureaucracy's political leadership, effective performance depends on strong leadership from the bureaucracy's top career officials. Indeed, these executives serve as the critical shock absorber in the administrative system, connecting the expert bureaucracy with elected officials and ensuring that elected officials' policy is transmitted through the bureaucracy.

At the cornerstone of the Civil Service Reform Act of 1978 was the creation of the Senior Executive Service (SES), which was designed to provide this career leadership. The SES absorbed most of the previously GS-16 to GS-18 career and noncareer positions, together with some executive-level positions filled by the president without Senate confirmation. It consists of about 7,700 employees, mostly career officials but including 575 presidential appointees.

The 1978 reform act aimed at giving agency heads greater flexibility in assigning members of this cadre among positions and tasks. Under the old system, the position occupied (tenure, grade, and salary) determined a level GS-16 to GS-18 career official's status. Under the civil service rules, the agency could dislodge the incumbent (apart from position abolition, firing, or forced resignation) only by promotion, demotion, or transfer to a position at the same grade and matching his or her qualifications. It was often difficult to find a position for which a bureau chief or other high careerist had the requisite qualifications, let alone a position that was vacant or could be made so. Substituting an SES system of rank-in-person (with the salary set by the individual's qualifications) for the old one of rank-in-position (with the salary set by the requirements of the position) promised to remedy this problem. Even more important has been the definition of "executive core qualifications," which lists five skills that senior executives should possess:

- ECQ 1: Leading Change
- ECQ 2: Leading People
- ECQ 3: Results Driven
- ECQ 4: Business Acumen
- ECQ 5: Building Coalitions

Operation

In addition to this new flexibility in staffing, reformers believed that the senior levels of the government would be stronger if top officials could assemble their own management teams. Instead of encouraging long-term tunnel vision among executives who rose within their agencies and stayed there, the idea was to create a flexible cadre of skilled managers who could lend their expertise to government management.

Reassignment, Performance Appraisal, and Removal

Politically appointed agency executives have in the past been frustrated by the difficulty of moving top careerists from positions in which they were ineffective to positions in which they either would do better or at least would no longer be weak links in the chain of an important program's management. The reform act removed this difficulty, for SES members have no right to particular assignments. A noncareerist can be reassigned to any general position in the agency for which he or she is qualified. So, too, can a career appointee, after a four-month waiting period.

Each agency is required to establish performance appraisal systems and to set performance requirements for each senior executive in consultation with him or her. Appraisal of individual performance is by performance review boards, which, however, have only recommendatory functions. Each executive is to be judged on both individual performance and the organization's performance. With the advent of a government-wide performance system through the Government Performance and Results Act (which Chapter 11 explores), executives are assessed also on their contribution to their agencies' goals.

Issues

Although reformers intended the SES to be the cornerstone of the Civil Service Reform Act, in practice its operations have never been smooth. As a National Academy of Public Administration (NAPA) study found in 2002, "The world has changed dramatically since the SES was established in 1978, but the underlying support structures have not evolved with it. Demands on senior leadership have increased due to changes in international ramifications, and an all-embracing customer orientation." That gap has grown even larger since NAPA's 2002 report. The structure and workings of the SES system create a series of problems, both in managing federal programs and in building strong relationships with political officials.[57]

Rapid Turnover of Political Appointees

The SES is intended as the system's shock absorber, but the short tenure of political appointees—a little more than two years—creates constant shocks for the SES to absorb. When new political appointees arrive, there often is a settling-in period characterized by mutual distrust between the appointees and SES officials. And, typically, there is no succession plan or other strategy to bridge these recurring gaps between top policymakers and agency administration.

Specialization versus Generalization

The intent of the reform act was to create a cadre of skilled generalists. In fact, the members of the SES have tended to be highly specialized, and there has been relatively little lateral movement among agencies and departments. When SES members have attempted to exert leadership, it has been "neither visibly valued nor directly sought," NAPA found. The result is a series of stovepipe patterns among the SES members, with narrow functional thinking that makes it more difficult to create energetic leadership or broad coordination among related problems. It also makes it difficult for SES members to shift to new positions where their skills may best be used.

Proliferation of Top-Level Systems

Another of the reform act's ideas was to create a single cadre of top officials, but since 1978 many new leadership systems have evolved, especially to help solve the many problems of paying, attracting, and retaining good managers. The proliferation of new systems has made it even harder to manage the SES in integrated fashion.

Compression of Performance Ratings and Pay

The legislation created a pay system designed to recognize and reward top performers. There are two kinds of awards: performance awards, for superior performance in the previous year; and presidential rank awards, for consistent and long-term excellence. However, Congress and a series of presidential administrations have been reluctant to fund the systems—especially bonus systems—adequately. And, in practice, the rewards systems have never worked well.

In performance assessments of top managers, there has been a tendency to rate most managers highly, which has in turn qualified many of them for rewards intended only for the very best performers. An analysis in 2004 found that almost two-thirds of civilian federal employees received bonuses in fiscal year 2002. Within the SES in 2002, 75 percent of the service's members were rated at the very top level of the evaluation system. Although both the Office of the Secretary of Defense (OSD) and the Social Security Administration used three-level rating systems, all but one of the OSD officials and every one of the Social Security managers received top-level ratings.

Such ratings compression is largely the product of complex pressures on each agency's managers. After giving 99 percent of its SES members a top rating in 2001, the Department of Energy resolved to toughen up the system, and its supervisors awarded the top rating to just 18 percent of SES members the next year.[58] But this well-intentioned determination to make distinctions puts the government's personnel managers in a bind: most of the government's SES members probably are superior performers, but if everyone is ranked at the top, the rankings have little meaning. If officials tighten up the system, however, low rankings can discourage SES members, especially if there are no strong incentives connected with the ratings.

Moreover, much of the debate depends on the assumption that bonuses would enhance the performance of government's employees. Evidence from the private sector, however, does not support the enthusiasm that often accompanies the public-sector debate. A survey in 2004 found that 83 percent of companies using some kind of pay-for-performance system concluded that the approach was either somewhat successful or not working at all. In part, the low success rate was because top company officials had a difficult time clearly communicating goals to employees and measuring how well employees met those goals; in part, it was because companies do not always set good goals. Pay-for-performance systems sometimes do work, especially when the companies set clear goals and employees feel motivated—but those companies are in a minority.[59]

The result of these problems has been pay compression at the top—sometimes salaries of supervisors are the same as those two and even three levels below—and little support for providing performance-based incentives. Pay is only one incentive for performance, but when pay is compressed, it can discourage managers by signaling that performance does not matter. Interviews with SES members consistently signal that this is a crucial problem.

Lack of Attention to the Human Capital Problem

The government's top officials have paid relatively little attention to the need for excellence in the top levels of the career staff. Leadership from these top careerists is crucial. Indeed, as NAPA found:

> In the United States and abroad, governments and private sector firms have learned that identifying and developing executive talent are some of the most important functions that an organization can undertake. It should not be an afterthought, done once important policy issues are addressed.[60]

Too often, nurturing of top talent is not even an afterthought. The federal government has simply not paid much attention to the problem.

As part of the broader effort in the federal government to develop human capital, OPM, OMB, and GAO are working aggressively on these issues. For example, OPM has developed a more aggressive performance measurement system designed to link employees' performance with the performance of their agencies. On the other side, it has aggressively sought to reduce the tendency for most SES members to receive the highest level of evaluation. At the core, however, the basic problems remain. The large number of political appointees creates continuing friction with the career bureaucracy. The SES has never fully evolved into the "shock absorber" system that its framers intended. In part, this is because SES managers have never become the generalist cadre first envisioned, tending instead to remain within the agencies in which they built their careers and displaying little horizontal movement. In part, it is because the performance measurement and incentive systems have never fully developed. These forces tend to reinforce each other—and to frustrate the SES's ability to solve the problems for which it was created.

The human capital quandary runs deep. If we accept departing careerists' views at face value, we then come full circle, back to the issue of how to recruit political appointees who have executive ability and other qualifications for their positions and how to keep them while they learn their jobs and achieve full effectiveness.

Twelve state governments have introduced executive personnel systems of varying comparability to the SES. However, a careful assessment of them concludes that they have neither added to the attractiveness of a career in government nor been consequential in heightening the mobility of executives or their executive development.[61]

THE PROBLEM OF TOP-LEVEL LEADERSHIP

Despite recurring attempts to reform the system, the problem of leadership at the very top of the bureaucracy remains one of government's most important and difficult problems. At the core is a dilemma that is hard to break. Elliot Richardson, who headed four cabinet departments at different points of his career, summed it up this way:

> The trouble is that all too many [new] political appointees . . . suspect . . . that senior civil servants lie awake at night scheming to sabotage the President's agenda and devising plans to promote their own. Having worked with most of the career services under five administrations, I can attest that this is not true. . . .
>
> Almost any job at the deputy assistant secretary level . . . is more responsible and has wider impact on the national interest than most senior corporate positions. . . .
>
> I have many friends who once held responsible but not necessarily prominent roles in government and who now occupy prestigious and well-paid positions in the private sector—some of them very prestigious and very well-paid. Not one finds his present occupation as rewarding as his government service. . . . Society treats public servants, together with teachers, ministers, and the practitioners of certain other honorable but low-paid callings, as the beneficiaries of a high level of psychic income. But the psychic income of public service is being steadily eroded.[62]

At the end of Ronald Reagan's second term, C. William Verity, his secretary of commerce, formerly chief executive officer of a large steel company, added,

> I had always felt that Government people were not motivated, because in industry you have various incentives where you can motivate people, and that perhaps Government people didn't work so hard because they weren't so highly motivated. Well, I was dead wrong.
>
> I find that in this department there are a tremendous cadre of professionals, highly motivated not by financial incentives but to serve their country. It's as simple as that.[63]

A proper balance between financial and psychic incomes in the higher public service varies roughly by rank. Attracting cabinet members is not a serious problem: most are well off and at an age when family responsibilities are not pressing, and they welcome high public status and the prospect of posthumous life in history books as a suitable culmination of successful careers. None of these conditions apply, however, to most of the potential candidates for noncareer, subcabinet posts—who are, in fact, a diverse group. Consider, first, the individuals accepting presidential appointments. Most suffer salary cuts in accepting a federal appointment. We know that people of high quality decline presidential appointments for financial reasons, forcing the White House to turn to less preferred candidates.

Consider, second, the SES picture. Both noncareer candidates and career members are younger, their children are likely to be at or approaching college with its high tuition costs, and, for many, the government positions are at a level carrying only slight prestige. Yet such relatively young political appointees, whose primarily private-sector careers are still in the making, are likely to benefit from the government experience (notably in special fields such as taxation and antitrust law), the embellishment of their biographical résumés, and improved eligibility for higher governmental appointments in the future, when their party again wins the presidency. Some political SES members, of course, will in fact earn higher pay in the executive branch than in the think tanks, small advocacy organizations, and congressional staffs from which many come. Nonetheless, as one study concluded, "inadequate salaries are a barrier to recruiting from among one group of especially desirable candidates for government service: those highly trained technicians and midcareer managers whose expertise, energy, and creativity [have] been amply demonstrated in the private sector."[64]

There has been a steady stream of commissions on top-level salaries over the past generation, and every one of them has concluded that top federal officials are critically underpaid. The one reporting in December 1988 found that "the level of salaries of high federal officials are now only about 65–70 percent in constant dollars of what their 1969 salaries were for the same positions."[65] The other commissions produced similar results.

Many citizens express dismay at the salaries paid public officials. Imbued with the egalitarian spirit of democracy, and sensitive to the disparity between their own incomes and those of high officials, they show little patience with arguments that government needs a fair share of the best educated and most skilled managers and professional specialists. They do not easily accept that this fair share must come from an elite pool whose members need incentives for high performance. Yet without some way of solving this problem, citizens will not get the level of performance they expect—and, indeed, deserve—as value for the taxes they pay.

THE CHANGING WORKFORCE

Special challenges are arising from the new workers about to enter government—and all workplaces. Raised on the Internet and technology and immersed in information unlike any previous generation, the emerging workforce presents very different human capital challenges. We know that a talent war for the top achievers in this new generation has already broken out, and we know that bringing this new Internet-driven generation into the workforce at a time when older workers have very different norms will pose some big challenges.

How is the new generation different? It is distinctive—and large, even larger than the Baby Boomers who have dominated American society for the last generation. Analysts have identified eight norms that shape their lives:

1. *Freedom*: setting priorities, especially to focus on time with family and friends
2. *Customization*: flexibility in jobs, benefits, and working conditions, with a preference for positions that will allow them the most choice
3. *Scrutinizers*: an instinct for quick, comparative analysis, especially about competing job opportunities
4. *Integrity*: a search for employers with a commitment to high ethical values
5. *Collaboration*: an expectation of collaboration on what to do and how to do it
6. *Entertainment*: a search for jobs that are fun and rewarding
7. *Speed*: a focus on speedy communication, including quick feedback on performance and rapid professional growth within the organization
8. *Innovation*: work hard to devise new ideas and devices to fit their needs and solve their problems[66]

The result, a government report suggests, is a new generation shaped by very different events and driven by fundamentally different values (see Table 9.1). The result, government's human capital managers believe, will require the government to transform itself into a workplace with more flexible work schedules (including the ability to carry time over from week to week), more flexibility in workplaces (including telecommuting), and more flexibility in the work environment (including making the job more fun). Government is not alone in facing these challenges, but if it cannot adapt at least as fast as other employers, it's likely to fall behind in the quest for the new generation's best workers—and the quality of the work done for the American people will inevitably suffer. Perhaps most fundamentally, government needs to rise to the challenge of matching its human capital system, based for generations on the idea of a career workforce, with a new generation of workers whose members don't assume they'll work for a single organization throughout their careers.

CONCLUSION

Several matters should be clear by this time. First, the small percentage of federal employees who constitute the higher public service are of crucial importance. These are the managers of major federal programs; the advisers and often the decision makers on large policy questions; the interagency negotiators; the spokespersons for and bargainers with the Executive Office of the President, congressional committees, interest groups, and the general public;

TABLE 9.1	Understanding the Generations through Life-Defining Events			
	Greatest Generation	**Baby Boomers**	**Gen-X**	**Millennials or Net-Gen**
Age	Retired	Nearing retirement	Mid-life	Early career
Population	75 million	78 million	45 million	80 million
Key Characteristics	Pragmatic	Value-driven	Cynical	Tech-savvy and diverse
	Conservative	Priority on self-actualization	Media-savvy	Media-saturated
	Conformists		Individualistic	Fluid lifestyle
Defining Events	Great Depression	Berlin Wall up	Berlin Wall falls	Columbine, Virginia Tech shootings
	World War II	JFK, MLK, RFK shot	*Challenger*	Oklahoma City and September 11, 2001
	Korean War	Watergate	O.J. Simpson	Wars in Iraq and Afghanistan
		Vietnam	First Gulf War	Corporate scandals
Key Values	Accountability	Fulfillment	Freedom	Diversity
	Tradition	Indulgence	Reality	Flexibility
	Stability	Balance	Self-reliance	Empowerment
		Equality	Work-life balance	Service-oriented

Source: Chief Information Officers Council, *Netgeneration: Preparing for Change in the Federal Information Technology Workforce* (Washington, D.C.: Chief Information Officers Council, 2010), 45, table 6-1, http://www.govexec.com/pdfs/042310ah1.pdf.

and the agents of the current administration who, in trying to induce civil servants to follow the election returns, carry much of the responsibility for ensuring democratic control of the bureaucracy.

Second, the number of political appointments at the top of the bureaucracy in the United States is far larger than in other countries.

Third, the top career officials are a highly specialized and high-performing group. However, recruiting and retaining them—and providing incentives for superior performance—is an enduring problem that a series of reforms have not succeeded in solving.

Fourth, the careers of political appointees are short and those of careerists are long. This disparity makes for an uncomfortable relationship, one in which political superiors operate within a brief time frame, initiating enterprises they will not see through to completion, or restricting themselves to short-run ventures for which they can get credit. Careerists, operating within an extended time frame, have a memory of what has worked and not worked in the past, an awareness of the long lead time from genesis of a program to its maturation, and an institutional loyalty and interpersonal network within agency and government that are uncharacteristic of most of the strangers recruited for political posts. Government is like a repertory theater whose regular cast was there before and remains during and after the visit of each celebrity imported to star in plum lead roles for a short run.

Fifth, although strong support remains for protecting the civil service system from political interference, frustration is growing with the restrictions that have accumulated in the system over time. Reformers are eager to provide managers with more flexibility, but every reform raises twin problems: fears that the changes will uproot the nation's long and deep commitment to politically neutral administration, and worries that the reforms will not go far enough in ensuring government grows its capacity to meet big, tough problems.

Sixth, generational changes are bringing deep and sharp issues to which the government must adopt new and innovative approaches. These will rank among the biggest human capital challenges the government has faced in a very long time.

Seventh, these are deep, enduring, and critical issues. In his 2008 book *A Government Ill Executed*, Paul C. Light tracks the fundamental puzzles back to the debate between Thomas Jefferson and Alexander Hamilton on the nature of the American republic. Light found that although much of government works well, human capital problems cripple its ability to rise to fundamental challenges. He concludes that "the federal service is suffering its greatest crisis since it was founded in the first moments of the republic . . . running out of energy [and] unable to faithfully execute all the laws."[67] Only a fundamental and sweeping reform, Light argues, can help government rise to the challenges it faces. Solving government's most important and fundamental problems depends on resolution of these issues of human capital management—and on linking them to the broader puzzles of governmental decision making and implementation. Human capital is not an isolated topic in itself but one that is intimately connected to government's capacity to do what must be done. The next chapter turns to the issues raised in that connection of doing what must be done.

CASE 9.1

The Brain Train: Planning for the Coming Federal Retirement Boom

A careful study in 2013 by the Partnership for Public Service and the private consulting firm McKinsey & Company laid out a stark challenge. In the next five years, they estimated, two-thirds of the federal government's senior executives would be likely to retire. With government's problems growing, "The need for savvy, well-trained government leaders to fill executive positions will only become more acute." That, they pointed out, was a huge challenge, but "it also presents an opportunity to take a deliberate approach to developing talent and equipping future executives with the skills they will need." But that in turn frames the big challenge: "What exactly are agencies doing to ensure they have a healthy pipeline of leaders?"[1]

For years, human capital analysts had predicted a retirement boom, and for years it didn't seem to materialize. Some outsiders suspected that a weak economy, coupled with the stock market collapse, encouraged many employees to stay on the job until the situation improved. As the report appeared, however, there were two trends that seemed to suggest the retirement boom was likely to begin. The age distribution of the federal government was getting older; employees might delay their retirement, but they were going to take it at *some* point. Moreover, the trend toward retirement was growing. In 2009, 5.8 percent of the members of the federal government's senior executive service retired. By 2012, the number had grown to 8.3 percent. The retirement boom had come—and the challenge for restocking the government's brain train had begun.

The Partnership/McKinsey report laid out four big worries as the government prepared for this transition.[2]

1. "Each agency is responsible for preparing its own talent for executive positions, with little central oversight or accountability." The federal government is a vastly complicated place, of course, and no single strategy could fit every agency. The Office of Personnel Management, moreover, has provided assistance to agencies on executive development and shares best practices with agency leaders. Nevertheless, "No federal entity holds agencies accountable for developing potential executives who can become government-wide assets. There's no standardized approach for preparing executives for the SES— and because every agency independently develops its executive pipeline, quality varies markedly and little attention is given to government-wide needs."

2. "Many federal agencies have strong elements of SES talent development in place, but these elements are seldom part of a cohesive strategy." Many employees took part in coaching, mentoring, and advanced education, but they "often are disconnected from one another rather than functioning as parts of a cohesive strategy." There are few checks to see whether the skills in which executives were trained are the skills that government needs." As one individual interviewed for the report pointed out, "There are people who were hired 20 years ago that have skills we don't need anymore."

3. "Many senior agency leaders pay insufficient attention to executive development." The report concluded that many senior agency leaders simply pay little attention to how best to identify, prepare, and retain the best executives. Political appointees have many demands on their time, and they often have very short time horizons. The result, the report concluded, was a "disconnect" between the talent the agency needed and the processes in place to produce it.

4. "Agencies show a strong preference for a pipeline of internal talent." It's not surprising that agencies prefer to promote from within, but that strategy hinders the opportunity to bring fresh skills and perspectives from other agencies. Not only do most senior leaders pay little attention to the problem—they tend to solve it in ways that reinforce existing patterns.

It was time, the report concluded, to pay serious attention to this issue. The collision of the retirement boom and the patterns of human capital development demanded action.

Questions to Consider

1. If you were the head of the Office of Personnel Management, what steps would you take to address this issue?

2. As someone who has carefully studied the importance of human capital, what overall strategy do you think would be most useful in creating a long-term strategy, not only for filling the vacancies coming in the next few years but also in preparing younger workers for the senior executive service?

3. What steps would be most attractive to you as you consider the possibility of becoming a senior executive in the federal government at the height of your career?

NOTES

1. Partnership for Public Service and McKinsey & Company, *Building the Leadership Bench: Developing a Talent Pipeline for the Senior Executive Service* (Washington, D.C.: July 2013), 5, http://r20.rs6.net/tn.jsp?e=001v_sUtLmyjPCASX9jAoxQoL7Yo4OkyAYy-BL9yIfTdIMZVXc3Lkcv3G7UdTqd2pGWFczpTKAaGL-GJurOpbkrpkg9lxI-Au__HgUa6IDMi2fwuRhAxOC_ryJtb6Mqy4OsOin-_xXjDXhQUXzTg8FGL83WBi-o96Fal7kmzzMPRo8ycNLbO7gegz2Q==.

2. Ibid., 7–9.

CASE 9.2

Reining in the Unions? State Employees Targeted in Wisconsin, Ohio, and Beyond

Shortly before taking office as Wisconsin governor in 2011, Scott Walker fired a warning shot toward state employees. With multi-billion-dollar deficits looming, Walker said, "We can no longer live in a society where the public employees are the haves and taxpayers who foot the bills are the have-nots." He went on, "The bottom line is that we are going to look at every legal means we have to try to put that balance more on the side of taxpayers."[1] Walker, a Republican, proposed taking away the right of government employees to collectively bargain over contracts and working conditions and making it much harder for unions to collect dues to support their operations.

He wasn't alone. In Ohio, Governor John Kasich proposed an end to the ability of child-care and home-care workers to unionize and to ban strikes by teachers. "If they want to strike, they should be fired," Kasich said. "They've got good jobs, they've got high pay, they get good benefits, a great retirement. What are they striking for?"[2]

Elsewhere, attacks on public employee unions surfaced in Indiana, Maine, and Missouri. Even in California, with a Democratic governor, union power came under tough scrutiny. "We will have to look at our system of pensions and how to ensure that they are transparent and actuarially sound and fair—fair to the workers and fair to the taxpayers," Governor Jerry Brown said. The AFL-CIO warned that this was part of a national battle to wipe unions out by eliminating their ability to collect dues from everyone in a bargaining unit. If each employee had to opt in to allow union dues to be used for political purposes, "it will cut them off at their knees" because the move would starve unions of the cash on which they relied.[3]

The political motivation was clear. Public employee unions had long been strong supporters of Democratic candidates, including at the state and local levels. Many Republican governors had to fight against union campaigns to win election, so their interest in disabling the unions was understandable. The *New York Times* estimated that unions had invested more than $200 million in campaigns against Republican candidates.[4] But the issue goes much deeper. Following the Great Recession, which started in 2008, many taxpayers resented the job security, pay increases, and generous pensions that many state and local government employees received, even as these employees had to dig ever deeper into their own pockets to pay for them. Republicans—and some Democrats—asked whether government employees had become a privileged class of workers protected from the economic downturns that had savaged so many private-sector workers.

Moreover, even as some analysts argued that the economy has begun staggering back to its feet, state and local budgets remained deep in red ink. Unlike the federal government, which can borrow money to pay its bills, state and local governments must balance their budgets. In the early stages of the downturn, state officials had already used up most of the easy options to make do with less and economize, and began moving to harder and harder decisions. As states looked into projections about future budgets, one item that loomed especially large was the share of state and local government spending accounted for by employee salaries and especially fringe benefits, including pensions. In many states, state and local government employees were entitled to a fixed monthly pension, called a "defined benefit" plan, based on their salary and years of service. Most of the private sector had long ago moved away from such plans to "defined contribution" plans, in which individuals invested their own money sometimes along with a company contribution, and the monthly payment was determined by the performance of the investments. In the stock market crash of 2008, many individuals watched their retirement savings shrink. Those who had defined benefit plans, on the other hand, didn't have to worry.

In future years, however, analysts have projected that state and local governments will have increasing difficulty in meeting their pension obligations. The Government Accountability Office estimates that state and local governments have hundreds of billions of dollars in unfunded pension obligations (commitments to pay pensions to employees without having enough money in place).[5] New governors—Republicans and Democrats alike—have come into office and have had to confront these tough long-term projections. Many have concluded that they will not be able to balance their budgets without fundamentally restructuring their pension systems, perhaps by moving future employees to defined contribution systems and perhaps by reducing defined benefit programs for all employees. Public employee unions, of course, immediately objected to such plans, fearing that they would undermine one of the most important benefits they had negotiated for their workers. Some Republicans savored the opportunity for a fight against a group that had bankrolled their electoral opposition.

Nowhere was that battle more intense than in Wisconsin. For decades, the state's labor unions had invested heavily in issue ads during political campaigns. Business groups raised their own funds to counter-attack, in what had become an escalating arms race. Governor Walker's proposals to restrict the unions' power were, in part, to help the state deal with its enormous budget deficit. Restrictions on fringe benefits for state employees, and requirements that employees contribute more to their health and retirement plans, would help the state stem the flood of red ink. The proposal went further, however, in limiting the unions' ability to raise money from members and the length of time for which the unions could bargain over working conditions. All of the state's Democratic senators fled to Illinois, which denied Republicans the quorum they needed to pass the measure—until the Republicans found a parliamentary measure that permitted a vote without a quorum. With the Democrats hiding out across the border, the Republicans pushed the bill through the legislature and the governor signed it, before the Democrats could react.

As the smoke settled after the fire, long-time political analyst Mordecai Lee sadly wrote, "While ideology and energy are welcome in Wisconsin politics, I can't help but think that the politics of political destruction are not."[6] Wisconsin's struggle over the future of public employee unions helped stoke other blazes around the nation. Public employee union leaders said they were determined not to give in. Those seeking to weaken their power were just as determined to use the budget battles to redefine the unions' role—in both public administration and the nation's politics. Governor Walker beat the drive to recall him. The protests continued, with a daily "Solidarity Sing-along" at the Capitol. One protester, Steven Bray, was arrested a half dozen times—but he vowed to keep coming back to sing.[7]

Questions to Consider

1. Do you think that public employees ought to have the right to organize and be represented by unions? Do you believe that they ought to be able to bargain over the full range of issues—pay, fringe benefits, working conditions? Should they have the ability to strike to support their demands? Do you think there should be limits on which employees can organize and what steps they can take?

2. Public employee unions have long argued that their members don't always receive the highest pay, and that their efforts at negotiating better benefits have helped them win the fringe benefits that have created a quality workforce. A new breed of politician has argued that the nation can no longer afford these benefits and that public employees shouldn't receive better protection or benefits than other workers. How do you weigh this battle?

3. What do you think about the role that public employee unions play in elections? Should they be allowed to assess dues on their members and use the money to support individual candidates? Even if that risks having to work for elected officials whom they opposed?

4. A critical future issue is the role of public employee pensions. Should the public employee pension system be restructured to move public employees to defined contribution plans? How should this work, to be fair to employees who have spent their entire careers working for a pension and who wouldn't have time to build up their own individual savings plan to replace a government pension? The longer the transition to a new pension plan, of course, the longer it would take for state officials to realize budget savings from the change.

NOTES

1. Steven Greenhouse, "Strained States Turning to Laws to Curb Labor Unions," *New York Times,* January 3, 2011, http://www.nytimes.com/2011/01/04/business/04labor.html?pagewanted=all.
2. Ibid.
3. Ibid.
4. Ibid.
5. U.S. Government Accountability Office, *Government Pension Plans: Governance Practices and Long-term Investment Strategies Have Evolved Gradually as Plans Take on Increased Investment Risk,* GAO-10-754 (Washington, D.C.: Government Printing Office, 2010), http://www.gao.gov/new.items/d10754.pdf.
6. Mordecai Lee, "Welcome to Thunderdome Politics," *Milwaukee Journal-Sentinel,* March 12, 2011, http://www.jsonline.com/news/opinion/117830143.html.
7. Martin Mikkelson, "Two Years On, Protesters Still Fighting Wisconsin Governor," *National Public Radio,* September 12, 2013, http://www.npr.org/2013/09/12/221084521/two-years-on-protesters-still-fighting-wisconsin-governor?sc=17&f=1001.

Who You Gonna Call? It's One Man Who Decides Who Gets How Much from the BP Oil Spill Compensation Fund

When America faces an impossible job, who does the president call? For a series of tough tasks, it was the phone of Kenneth Feinberg that rang.

After the September 11, 2001, terrorist attacks, for example, Congress created a fund to compensate the families of the nearly 3,000 people killed. That was a strong and generous national gesture. But how much should each family receive? One approach would have been to divvy the money up, with each family receiving the same amount. Some of those killed, however, were very high-level executives whose families had homes, educational expenses, and other expenses that depended on that income. Some of those killed earned close to the minimum wage. Some were very young; others were at or past retirement age. Was it fair to give everyone the same amount? Congress decided no—but left it up to the Bush administration to figure out how to divide the money fairly. President Bush put Kenneth Feinberg in charge.

That was an effort to put a small bandage on a gaping national wound. However, the 2010 BP oil spill dwarfed the number directly affected by the September 11, 2001, attacks. As the oil flowed across the Gulf, many, many thousands of Gulf residents, some boat captains, others oysterman and shrimpers, others hotel and restaurant operators, lost their livelihoods for weeks or months, and some worried whether they would ever be able to regain their lives. BP put $20 billion in a compensation fund. But how to distribute the cash?

Those who believed they were injured had two choices. They could take their chances by filing suit in court, knowing that they were relatively small players up against one of the world's largest companies. Or they could make their case to Feinberg and accept what he believed was just. As Feinberg told the CBS newsmagazine show *60 Minutes,* "It's a free country. If you wanna come into the fund, with all the benefits of the fund, come on in. You're welcome. We'll give you a fair shake. We'll process your claim. We'll pay you what you're due. If you don't like what we're paying you, if you think we're nickel and diming you, if you think we're not being fair, opt out and go the other route [to court with a civil suit]." He had been down that road before, he explained. "Now, in 9/11, 97 percent of all eligible claimants entered the fund. Only 94 people out of 3,000 decided to litigate."[1]

His decisions for the September 11 fund involved payments to victims' families that, at the core, involved setting a value on human life. For the BP spill, the payments required Feinberg to determine the long-run impact on individuals' livelihoods. How many oysters in the future simply won't be there to be harvested? How many hotels and restaurants might suffer permanent economic damage because of the lost business? How many boat captains might have to look for new ways of making a living?

"What these fishermen and others want to see are checks and compensation," he told *60 Minutes*. The average for each claim, in the first months of the program, had been $5,000, for six months of damages, one audience member at a public meeting pointed out. "And that, sir, is nothing to brag about." Morley Safer, the *60 Minutes* correspondent, noted, "They really go after you." Feinberg replied, "They do. They do, but it goes with the territory." He continued, "I mean, you go in there expecting that you're gonna receive that criticism. And woe be unto you if you hide. That is a mistake. You cannot hide."

It was a tough process—an emergency payment, for six months to help those affected meet short-term needs, followed by a final settlement. Feinberg found himself in the middle of constant, raucous town meetings, facing furious Gulf residents who had lost money and, in some cases, their livelihoods, from the BP spill. BP executives and representatives weren't there; he was, and he bore the brunt of their anger. His job was to listen, take it, weigh their claims, and make awards he believed were fair—awards that, in many cases, were less than residents thought they deserved.

"Do you believe what he's telling you?" Safer asked a group of fishermen.

One replied, "Absolutely not." Another said, "I think he's just another attorney talking his talk."

Safer replied, "But don't you think his record in dealing with 9/11 was an honest job?"

"To be honest with you, I could care less about 9/11," one said. "I care about the oil spill. And I could care less about anyone else's claims. I care about my claim. That's it."

Questions to Consider

1. What do you think of this policy—creating a fund to compensate individuals for losses from major national incidents, and then giving the power to decide compensation to one person, armed with a small staff?

2. What kind of person would you hire to perform such a function? Feinberg is not a permanent government employee. Rather, he's been appointed by the government as "special master" for the September 11, 2001, victims compensation fund and as administrator for the BP compensation fund. This is a great deal of power to place in the hands of a single person. Do you think this is a good move?

3. Feinberg's background is as an attorney specially trained in mediation. He's taught extensively in law schools ranging from Columbia and Georgetown to Penn and Virginia. We're likely to encounter more mega-issues like September 11, 2001, and the BP oil spill that require the government to deal with tough compensation decisions. One of the tasks of public administration is to grow smart leaders who can do hard jobs in predictably high-quality ways. In fact, public administration exists to make sure we don't have to trust to chance in trying to do hard things well. What recommendations would you have for improving our chances for having top government leaders for important jobs like this one?

NOTE

1. "BP's Victims Fund: Kenneth Feinberg's Tough Task," *60 Minutes,* October 3, 2010, http://www.cbsnews.com/stories/2010/09/30/60minutes/main6915445.shtml?tag=contentMain;contentBody.

KEY CONCEPTS

at-will employees   236

broadbanding   232

human capital   227

Title 5   234

turnover   242

FOR FURTHER READING

DeSeve, G. Edward. *The Presidential Appointee's Handbook.* Washington, D.C.: Brookings Institution Press, 2008.

General Accounting Office (now the Government Accountability Office). *High-Risk Series: Strategic Human Capital Management,* GAO-03-120. Washington, D.C.: GAO, 2003.

Heclo, Hugh. *A Government of Strangers: Executive Politics in Washington.* Washington, D.C.: Brookings Institution, 1972.

Ingraham, Patricia W. "Striving for Balance: Reforms in Human Resource Management." In *Handbook of Comparative Administration,* edited by Laurence Lynn Jr. and Christopher Pollitt. Oxford: Oxford University Press, forthcoming.

Light, Paul C. *A Government Ill Executed: The Decline of Federal Service and How to Reverse It.* Cambridge, Mass.: Harvard University Press, 2008.

Light, Paul C. *Thickening Government: Federal Hierarchy and the Diffusion of Accountability.* Washington, D.C.: Brookings Institution, 1995.

Moe, Terry M. "The Politicized Presidency." In *The New Direction in American Politics,* edited by John E. Chubb and Paul E. Peterson, 235–271. Washington, D.C.: Brookings Institution, 1985.

Nathan, Richard P. *The Administrative Presidency.* New York: Wiley, 1983.

Radin, Beryl A. *The Accountable Juggler: The Art of Leadership in a Federal Agency.* Washington, D.C.: CQ Press, 2002.

Selden, Sally Coleman. *Human Capital: Tools and Strategies for the Public Sector.* Washington, D.C.: CQ Press, 2009.

SUGGESTED WEBSITES

The Government Accountability Office has carefully examined the problem of managing human capital for a long time; see its work **www.gao.gov.** In addition, the Office of Personnel Management, **www.opm.gov,** is an important source for both data and analysis of the human capital issue. For independent studies of human capital in government, see the work of the National Academy of Public Administration, **www.napawash.org**.

MAKING AND IMPLEMENTING GOVERNMENT DECISIONS

If organizational structure is the basic building block of administration, decision making is the central administrative act. However, organizational theorists have long disagreed about how *best* to make administrative decisions—and *which* decisions are best. This section probes the competing theories of decision making and applies those theories to the most important of all administrative decisions: the budget. In any public administration, most decisions are hollow without money to back them up.

Making good decisions, however, is not enough, because decisions are not self-executing. They require skillful management by effective managers if the bold promises embodied in public policy are not to end in disappointment. This section concludes by examining how to translate decisions into implementation.

CHAPTER

10

CHAPTER OBJECTIVES

- Understand the role of information and values in decision making

- Explore rationality as the foundation of decision making, in theory and practice

- Examine bargaining and other alternatives to rationality in decision making

- Probe the limits on decision making and where existing theories fall short

Decision Making

Former Newark mayor Cory Booker won a huge audience on his Twitter account—more than 1.4 million followers. In 2012 he took up a Twitter challenge to live on food stamps for a week. During blizzards, he tweeted from the cab of a city snowplow. He used this at-the-front approach to service delivery to win a 2013 race for a seat in the U.S. Senate.

MOST EARLY STUDENTS OF PUBLIC ADMINISTRATION concentrated on how to design an organization's structure so that it would function as efficiently as possible. Luther Gulick's classic formulation, discussed in Chapter 4, defined basic principles for administrators to use in organizing agencies. In 1945, however, Herbert A. Simon posed a very different approach. He contended that "a theory of administration should be concerned with the processes of decision as well as with the processes of action." In fact, Simon argued,

> The task of "deciding" pervades the entire administrative organization quite as much as does the task of "doing"—indeed, it is integrally tied up with the latter. A general theory of organization that will insure correct decision-making must include principles of organization that will include correct decision-making, just as it must include principles that will insure effective action.[1]

Simon thus established decision making as *the* central element, and it is impossible to understand administration without understanding administrative decision making.

In most of public administration, there is no single decision that defines action. Rather, administrative action occurs seamlessly from top to bottom in an organization, with important decisions made at each step. The job of administering governmental policy means that administrators along the way must determine what the policy is and what their role is to bring it to life. Decision making is the quintessential administrative act: as Simon pointed out, doing is impossible without deciding.

The study of administrative decision making, however, has often been full of conflict, and many theories fight for prominence. Moreover, each of these theories carries heavy baggage: descriptive elements—detailing how decision making typically *does* work; and normative elements—prescribing how decision making *should* work. Weighed down with these opposing burdens, no decision-making approach predominates. Each one, however, provides useful techniques for making decisions and describes the fundamental problems that theory must answer. This chapter first examines the basic problems that decision-making theories must answer. Then it probes competing approaches to decision making. The chapter concludes with an exploration of the enduring problems that plague decision making and those who attempt to develop good descriptions and prescriptions.

BASIC PROBLEMS

Every approach to administrative decision making must tackle two issues. First, what information can decision makers use in reaching their judgments? Information is the basic raw material of decisions, and decision makers must acquire, weigh, and act on the data they collect. Second, how do political values affect decisions? The sheer complexity of public problems and the overwhelming volume of information force decision makers to simplify the context shaping their decisions. This inevitable simplification is the product of political values. Moreover, for a decision to stick, it must win enough support to prevent others from seeking to overturn it. Building support means finding a common base of values among those who could sustain the decision. Both information and values constantly intermingle as administrators seek to make decisions and as theorists seek to develop arguments about how the process does—and ought to—work.

Information

If decision making is the central administrative act, information is the lifeblood of decision making. Decisions, of course, can be made at whim or on the basis of strong opinions. An administrator who believes that overdevelopment harms the environment or that all basic scientific research is useful, regardless of how much it costs, may be tempted to make decisions accordingly. Common knowledge, instinct, and bias can drive even the most complex of decisions.[2] In fact, public administrators are hired not for their bias but for their expertise, as Max Weber long ago pointed out.[3]

The importance of good information to effective public administration cannot be overestimated, but its fundamental role creates a dilemma. On the one hand, it is often deceptively difficult to uncover useful information and channel it to relevant decision makers. On the other hand, knowledge brings power, and it is hard for the nonexpert to control experts. This is, of course, a reprise of the classic public administration struggle between neutral competence and political accountability, but nowhere in public administration is this struggle sharper than in the administrative decision-making process.[4]

The problem is that information rarely is an abstract truth. More typically, information is a matter of interpreting reality. No one ever knows everything, and never does everyone know the same things. Acquiring information is often expensive, and some participants are advantaged because they have greater resources. Moreover, participants sometimes have a vested interest in keeping information hidden from others. In short, as Deborah A. Stone points out, "Because politics is driven by how people interpret information, much political activity is an effort to control interpretations."[5] Two aspects of information thus critically affect decision making: who has what information and how they and others choose to interpret the information they have.

Values

"Most important decision puzzles are so complicated that it is impossible to analyze them completely," Robert D. Behn and James W. Vaupel argue. Furthermore, they contend, "Decisions depend upon judgments—judgments about the nature of the dilemma, the probabilities of events, and the desirability of consequences. Decision making is inherently subjective."[6] Any process that includes some questions but not others, estimates the chances of different outcomes, and, especially, weighs some outcomes as better than others is a value-laden process. Therefore, decision-making theories must face the question of how best to make such value judgments.

Furthermore, no public policy decision, no matter how expertly reached, can endure if it does not command political support.[7] As Francis E. Rourke points out, political support for administrative decisions can come from higher levels of the executive branch, from Congress, or from the public.[8] Public support typically comes from two sources: an agency's decisions may enjoy a favorable opinion among the general public—what Rourke calls an agency's "mass public"—or they may draw support from its "attentive publics"—groups that have a "salient interest in the agency." These two forms of support are not exclusive, and many agencies actively cultivate both.[9] NASA, for example, works hard to promote the allure of space flight among the general public, while it labors to build support among its contractors for recurring battles on Capitol Hill over financing for its expensive programs.

As important as broad support is, political support from an agency's attentive publics typically is much more crucial. Few private citizens have the resources or the time to follow or comprehend the intricate detail and complex trail that most public policy decisions follow. In most decisions, only those who have the strongest interest are willing to devote the time and money needed to understand and influence the issues. This means, of course, that most difficult administrative decisions are reached within a relatively closed world dominated by those with common and intense interests.[10]

The relatively greater importance of strong support from narrow interests carries with it another dilemma for administrative decision makers: seeking the support of an agency's attentive publics risks sacrificing the broader interests of the general public. In contrast, decision makers who cultivate only mass public support risk offending powerful interests, which may then use their influence to exact a heavy price. In short, every administrative decision maker needs to win political support for decisions, but how that support is won can raise important problems. Few public decisions are ever stable, because the forces that support them change constantly. Most decisions involve carving out boundaries—what is acceptable and what is not, how much is enough and how much is too much. Such boundary setting is, in Stone's words, an "inherently unstable" process in which "boundaries are border wars waiting to happen."[11]

The complexity of decision making in bureaucracy has led to many different approaches. In this chapter, we explore four of them, and we examine how each one deals with the fundamental problems of information and values: (1) the rational approach, which seeks to maximize efficiency; (2) the **bargaining approach**, which seeks to maximize political support; (3) the **participative decision-making approach**, which seeks to improve decisions by intimately involving those affected by them; and (4) the **public-choice approach**, which attempts to substitute market-like forces for other incentives that, its supporters argue, distort decisions.

RATIONAL DECISION MAKING

Rational decision making, which is perhaps the classic approach, builds on the work of microeconomists (who seek to explain the behavior of individuals and firms) and holds efficiency as the highest value. Proponents of this school argue that the goal of any activity, including governmental programs, is to get the biggest return for any investment. Simply put, they seek to get the most bang for the buck.

The rational method fundamentally rests on the systems theory approach described in Chapter 4. The decision maker structures the decision-making problem as a system that processes inputs to produce outputs, and then seeks to produce the most output for a given level of inputs—or, alternatively, to determine the minimum amount of inputs needed to produce a given amount of output. In short, the decision maker seeks to maximize efficiency.

The systems approach is so simple, its logic so overpowering, that it is easy to understand how it has become a classic. After all, we speak of "computer systems," which are hunks and slivers of silicon, wires, and plastic that process inputs (such as letters typed into a keyboard) into outputs (such as letters, reports, and books like this one). Computer analysts strive to improve the system: to make computers work more quickly or more cheaply or do things that could not be done before.

Basic Steps

The rational decision-making approach follows five basic steps:

1. *Define goals.* The rational approach starts with a description of a problem to be solved and an output goal to be achieved. For example, a policy analyst might seek to determine the best way to reduce automobile accident deaths by 10 percent or to reduce air pollution below dangerous limits. This goal orientation is very different from conventional ways of thinking about governmental programs, which focus on activity measures, such as the number of Social Security checks mailed and the miles of highway built. The systems approach concentrates instead on most effectively producing desired outputs. The goals come to analysts through the legislative process.

2. *Identify alternatives.* Once the decision maker has determined the goal, the analyst tries to identify the different ways the goal can be achieved. In the search, the key is to think innovatively about new options that others might never have tried or even considered.

3. *Calculate the consequences.* The analyst then weighs the alternatives by measuring the costs and benefits of each one. In the strictest form of such analyses, in fact, every cost and benefit is translated into dollar terms. Furthermore, the analyst also considers indirect benefits and costs—often called **externalities** or **spillovers**—that relate to other goals. For example, a highway route that is best in terms of the stated transportation goal may destroy parks and increase downtown traffic congestion.

4. *Decide.* Once the analysis is finished, the decision maker chooses the alternative with the most favorable balance of benefits to costs.

5. *Begin again.* Systems analysis is not a once-and-done process. Instead, analysts see it as an iterative process: a project provides feedback—new information about what works and what does not, as well as consequences (intended and not) of a decision—which then helps the analyst redefine the problem, set new goals, and begin the process again. By continually working to fine-tune the system by learning from past mistakes, systems analysis, in theory, helps decision makers move ever closer to the best decisions.

Although the rational approach may seem abstract, it has the appeal of common sense: any sensible person will choose the most rational (and efficient) route to his or her goal. Who, after all, wants to be irrational?[12]

Ripped
from the Headlines...

The Battle over the Speed Limit

In mid-2013, Illinois Governor Pat Quinn faced a tough decision. Should he sign a bill that would increase the speed limit on the state's interstate highways from 65 to 70 miles per hour? In 1974, as gas prices soared, the federal government established a national speed limit of 55 mph, on the theory that slower speeds would save gas. That limit was wildly unpopular and, after the energy crisis eased, the feds gave the states the power to set their own speed limits. Since then, states across the nation inched up their limits. The highest speed limit in the country? A stretch of road between San Antonio and Austin, at a blazing 85 mph.

Advocates of higher speed limits said they had studies that showed higher limits did not increase the number of accidents. The Governors Highway Safety Administration countered that higher speed limits made the accidents that did occur more serious. Many drivers liked the higher speeds. Interests representing the trucking industry pushed especially hard for higher speeds—trucks moving faster can deliver more goods more quickly, and that's more money in the pockets of drivers and truck companies. Some engineers said that many highways could safely carry vehicles at the higher speed, but that the design of some highways—and high congestion in urban areas—made a case for lower speeds.

Governor Quinn faced a great deal of uncertainty about his decision. He also faced fierce political counter-pressures. There was no decision that would satisfy everyone. What would a rational decision look like for him? An incremental decision? A satisficed decision? Is there any way to make a good decision without balancing political values? In fact, what does "good" look like in this case?

Source: Adapted from http://www.governing.com/blogs/view/gov-states-legislature-continue-to-raise-speed-limits.html

Example: The Planning-Programming-Budgeting System

Because of its logic, the rational approach has many followers. However, as the classic case of the **Planning-Programming-Budgeting System (PPBS)** shows, the straightforward logic of rational decision making has many variations in practice. Furthermore, the considerable difficulties of *doing* systems analysis can also be its undoing.

In 1961 Secretary of Defense Robert McNamara introduced PPBS in the Pentagon.[13] The technique involved three phases: (1) planning, in which top-level managers developed five-year strategies for defense activities; (2) programming, in which the strategies were transformed into detailed descriptions of the department's needs, including which weapons systems had to be purchased on what schedule; and (3) budgeting, in which officials transformed the program into year-by-year budget requests. The basic idea was to link the annual budgetary process with long-range plans instead of making haphazard requests. Furthermore, each branch of the service was to budget by program instead of by organizational unit. The Pentagon, for example, would decide whether the nation's strategic needs required a new jet fighter and, if so, what capabilities it ought to have. Program budgeting, McNamara hoped, would drive down the cost of buying weapons systems by reducing competition among the services for their own individually tailored weapons systems.

President Johnson was so pleased with the results in the Department of Defense (DOD) that he extended the technique in 1965 to almost all federal civilian departments and agencies. Each agency submitted its budget to the Bureau of the Budget (now the Office of Management and Budget) by program.[14] The program budgets were, in turn, supported by massive memoranda that considered "all relevant outputs, costs, and financing needs" as well as "the benefits and costs of alternative approaches" to solving problems. Each agency also prepared a five-year projection of its future programs and financial requirements. The plans, however, were often "lengthy wish lists of what the agencies would like to spend on their programs if no fiscal constraints were imposed." The connection between PPBS paperwork and what agencies actually planned to do was often amorphous. Since Congress continued to run its appropriations process the old way, the link between PPBS and congressional decisions was fuzzy indeed.[15]

Instead of integrating and improving presidential and congressional decisions on the budget, PPBS produced its own paperwork domain. PPBS finally collapsed under the burden, and in June 1971 the federal government's PPBS ended, as the Office of Management and Budget ceased requiring that agencies submit PPBS documents with their conventional budget requests.[16]

In terms of its original objectives, PPBS was a failure. It never transformed the base of government planning or linked budgets—government's inputs—to its outputs. In foreign governments and nearly all state and local governments that have tried the system, it has produced similar results.[17] Part of PPBS's failure came from budgeters' inability to cope with the system's analytical burdens. More fundamentally, it failed because of a critical design flaw: PPBS's designers left Congress out of the system, and PPBS staffers "refused to reveal to Congress the studies and information produced by the PPB system . . . [though] without information of this kind, the ability of Congress to even ask the right questions concerning program performance is seriously impaired."[18]

Moreover, although PPBS was solely an instrument of the executive branch, even that limited environment was neglected. PPBS designers were inadequately prepared to neutralize bureaucratic resistance. Any innovation produces such resistance, but PPBS staffers seemed arrogant to many other government officials. Lower organizational units were upset that PPBS appeared to rob them of authority (centralizing it instead in agency heads and the Bureau of the Budget), that it shifted analytical work from agency staffs knowledgeable about an agency's policy area to PPBS technicians skilled in quantifying but unacquainted with the agency's policy area, and that it required an enormous amount of paperwork without discernible impact on decision making.

Nevertheless, PPBS's results were substantial. It brought into the government a number of able analysts, many of whom remained.[19] It acquainted a large number of top executives and career civil servants with a new style of discourse, one that emphasizes clarification of objectives, generation of alternative ways of serving the objectives, and quantification of benefits and costs where such measurement is appropriate. Multiyear projections of program costs are now transmitted to Congress as a regular part of the budgetary process. The approach has even spilled over into repeated efforts to apply cost-benefit analysis to other government strategies, such as regulation.

The Pentagon, moreover, still actively operates a modified PPBS. Defense officials continue to develop long-range plans, translate those plans into programs, and develop the programs into budgets. The way the process works has varied considerably by administration: Republicans have tended to vest more authority with the individual services, while Democratic administrations have pulled more authority to the defense secretary. Despite the longevity of the process, however, PPBS results continue to be disappointing. Lawrence J. Korb, former assistant secretary of defense, argues that during the Reagan administration, top officials' approach to PPBS "contributed to a near collapse of rational budgeting in DOD and helped undermine the consensus in this country for a buildup. Indeed, when [Defense Secretary Caspar] Weinberger departed the Pentagon in late 1987, the budgeting process was in near chaos." Korb contends that defense planning had "almost no impact on the process," that programming meetings had far too many participants to make meaningful decisions, and that previous decisions never drove final budget decisions.[20] This tale contains important nuggets of truth. The instinct toward rationality is irresistible, yet rationality is impossible to fully achieve. Efforts to seek it never go away, and the dilemma sets the stage for the next try.

Appraisal

Because the rational approach to decision making seems so straightforward, it has a large following. Even the most cynical critics of PPBS could scarcely argue against improving the way the federal government formulates its goals and how to achieve them. Still, the rational approach must struggle with several serious problems, dealing with both information and values.

Information

The pure systems approach requires an extraordinary amount of information. Decision makers must consider all alternatives to achieving a policy goal, which, of course, is impossible because no one's wit is equal to a complete search of possibilities. In fact, to some systems-approach critics, the impossibility of a truly comprehensive analysis itself renders the approach useless. As Charles E. Lindblom, perhaps the method's strongest critic, argues: "Men have always wanted to fly. Was the ambition to undertake unaided flight, devoid of any strategy for achieving it, ever a useful norm or ideal? . . . Achieving impossible feats of synopsis [comprehensive analysis] is a bootless, unproductive ideal."[21] Moreover, by trying to do the impossible, Lindblom worries, "they fall into worse patterns of analysis and decision." Even the cost, in time, energy, and money, of a nearly comprehensive search is extremely high, and the decision maker driven by comprehensiveness can never be sure what has been left out. The goal itself is impossible, the gaps are rarely defined, and the result is an uncharted gap in the analysis whose effects are unknown.[22]

In real life, of course, no one ever tries to be completely comprehensive. Decision makers instead simplify the process: (1) they screen out the silly options and restrict themselves to a few major alternatives, and (2) they stop searching for options when they come upon a satisfactory alternative, even though further search might turn up a better one. James G. March and Herbert A. Simon have called this approach **satisficing**.[23]

Both roads—searching for comprehensive analysis and settling for satisficing—do not go very far, for two reasons. First, most of the calculations required for translating benefits and costs into dollars and cents require value judgments: how much worth should be accorded a life, a child's happiness, a scenic view from the highway, or a pleasing architectural design? Economists in fact have developed mechanisms for pricing even such difficult things as the value of a human life.[24] The very attempt to weigh the value of different items, however, often leads to extremely difficult (and sometimes bizarre) judgments. As Lewis M. Branscomb writes,

> Despite the well-publicized conflict between economic and ecological interests, our appreciation for environmental impact and technology assessment is unique in the world. Where else would (i) a $600-million hydroelectric dam be held up to protect an endangered 3-inch freshwater fish called the snail darter, (ii) a unique butterfly enjoy priority at the end of the main runway of the Los Angeles International Airport, and (iii) the sexual aspirations of a clam threaten the construction of a nuclear power station in New Hampshire?[25]

Second, how much searching should we do to satisfice? To study some alternatives and not others is to make a value judgment, yet value-free analysis is the goal of rational decision making. Rational analysts thus return to the same dilemma between doing their best to guess what alternatives others might have had in mind and imposing their own values on the array of alternatives. We can never know all we need to know, and even if we could, we could not process all the information to produce truly rational decisions. This dilemma contributed to the decade-long war in Iraq. The conclusion by intelligence analysts that Saddam Hussein had weapons of mass destruction (WMDs) and was likely to use them was part of the rationale for going to war in Iraq. Only after the war had been underway for many months did the United States discover that there were no WMDs and that the conclusion was a massive intelligence failure. Underlying values of the Bush administration, in the aftermath of the September 11, 2001, attacks, helped provide the impetus for the war and for filling in gaps in the intelligence analysis. The decision of the Bush administration to launch the war frames the role of values in decision making.

Values

The systems approach depends on a clear statement of goals. Without such a statement, the approach quite simply cannot work. The classic literature on rational decision making, however, has little to say about who sets the goals. Instead, the theory presumes that some decision maker will define the objective in the precise form needed for rational decision makers at lower levels to proceed with their tasks. Yet Congress's statements of objectives often lack clarity and consistency, Congress would fight the president if the president attempted to set comprehensive goals, and the executive branch agencies usually get caught between the two. This uncertainty, in turn, leaves the rational decision makers with two choices: to make their own best guess about what Congress, for example, may have intended in passing a law (and risk being told they are wrong when, as is likely, someone disagrees) or to apply subjective values to define the goals (and risk undercutting the very objectivity at the core of systems analysis). Legislators at the state and local levels behave precisely in the same manner.

The American political system constantly formulates and reformulates goals as political majorities shift, as the effectiveness of various interest groups waxes and wanes, as population changes, and as new technologies and new information alter the shape of problems and our capacity to deal with them. The art of assembling majority support, among voters and legislators, for each program typically requires fuzzy goals and vague language. The more precisely objectives are defined, the easier it is for competing parties to disagree with them.

The rational, efficiency-minded approach often works very well for small-scale and technical issues, on which agreement over goals is relatively easy. Should a local government buy or lease its police cars? Which paving material will last the longest? What kinds of snow-removal equipment should a city buy? On larger questions, however, the constitutional separation of powers, political realities, bureaucratic dynamics, and rapidity of change in world and domestic conditions give little hope of finding a way to define goals clearly. What is the best solution if there is disagreement over what the problem is?

Efficiency, of course, is not the *only* goal we seek. Equality, for example, is often a central objective in public programs. In fact, the economist Arthur M. Okun calls the job of balancing equality and efficiency "the big tradeoff": "We can't have our cake of market efficiency and share it equally."[26] Another economist, Murray Weidenbaum, who served in the Ronald Reagan administration as chairman of the Council of Economic Advisers, goes even further, observing that

> it is possible to develop government investment projects which meet the efficiency criterion (that is, the total benefits exceed the total costs) but which fail to meet the simplest standards of equity. . . . Unfortunately, there has been a tendency on the part of some economists to dismiss such "distributional" questions as subjective and political, and hence not within the proper concern of economic analysis.[27]

The rational approach thus has great attraction because it offers an elegant prescription for how the best decisions can be made. In describing the practical policy world, however, it falls short. Its advocates, in fact, often follow rational techniques only as long as those techniques help them achieve their own political ends. Moreover, even in the abstract, rational techniques do not tell decision makers where to draw the line short of the impossible task of comprehensiveness. Nor do these techniques solve the fundamental question of *whose* values will be used to perform the analysis. Indeed, agreement on goals, as the bargaining approach contends, is the central problem of decision making.

Strategic Planning

Despite the difficulty of pursuing rational decision making, some governments have nevertheless decided to pursue a strategic, comprehensive approach. For example, the state of Oregon began in the late 1980s to create a strategic vision for its citizens' quality of life; it defined hundreds of benchmarks and began tracking the state's progress in achieving them, through a series of reports. The Commonwealth of Virginia took an even more systematic approach by creating a Council on Virginia's Future, a body headed by the governor and including legislative and community leaders. The council articulated a statewide long-term vision, including where the state wanted to be in economic growth and educational attainment, and it set up forty measures for assessing progress; finally, the council linked these goals to the performance of state agencies as a way of holding them accountable for results. Even some local governments, such as York County in southern Pennsylvania, have devised strategies that identify community goals and the plans for achieving them.

For all the reasons that had undermined previous comprehensive planning efforts, some critics suggested that such strategic planning exercises were likely to do little more than employ consultants and create meaningless debate. Despite the high obstacles, governments nonetheless seem committed to continuing the effort. They appear to see some value in having the conversation and in elevating the debate beyond the usual day-to-day struggles over budgets to the larger purposes for which the money is being spent. None are likely to be fully successful. However, it is a testimony to the enduring power of the *idea* of comprehensive planning that so many governments continue so vigorously to try to accomplish it.

BARGAINING

Chapter 4 noted the pluralistic approach to administrative organization, and Chapter 6 treated the alliances that sometimes develop among an agency, its related congressional committees, and its clientele interest groups. These issues demonstrate how decision making involves conflict, negotiation, persuasion, and individuals with stakes in particular policies and decisions.

The bargaining approach to decision making builds on these concepts to develop a different view of rationality. The approach's proponents, such as Charles E. Lindblom, argue that it is paradoxically most rational to conduct a limited analysis and then to bargain over a decision that can attract political support. Lindblom offers a simple prescription for the analysis of public decisions: **incrementalism**.[28] It is best, he says, to limit that analysis to a few alternatives instead of trying to judge them all; to weigh one's values along with the evidence instead of holding them separate, as the rational approach would suggest; and to concentrate on the immediate problems to be solved rather than the broader goals to be achieved. The great goals are almost always beyond reach, especially in the short run, and problems presented in smaller chunks are easier to define, diagnose, and solve. Furthermore, it is easier to build support for a series of incremental changes from the current situation and to correct any errors that might creep in. Decision making is thus essentially value laden.[29] Conflicts are the rule and officials cannot resolve them by rational analysis. Instead, **partisan mutual adjustment**—the pulling and hauling among decision makers with different views—offers the best hope for the best decisions, supporters of the bargaining approach contend.[30] Bargaining is often relatively unstructured, as the classic case of the Cuban missile crisis illustrates.

Example: The Cuban Missile Crisis

In October 1962 the United States came to the brink of nuclear war with the Soviet Union. American intelligence aircraft discovered that the Soviets had built missile bases in Cuba from which they could have launched nuclear strikes against New York, Washington, D.C., and other important East Coast targets. American experts estimated that the resulting war would kill 100 million Americans, more than that number of Russians, and millions more Europeans. President John F. Kennedy's advisers worried about why the Soviets had placed the missiles in Cuba to begin with and how they could convince the Soviets to remove the weapons.

The White House launched a public relations offensive against the Soviets, in which Adlai Stevenson, U.S. ambassador to the United Nations, dramatically revealed reconnaissance photos of the bases, demanded an explanation from the Soviet ambassador, and promised to wait for an answer "until hell froze over." The president's advisers developed several alternatives to deal with the crisis: military officials planned an attack on the missile bases to wipe them out before they could become fully operational; other advisers suggested a naval blockade to turn back further shipments of the missiles and to give the Soviets a chance to dismantle the missiles before hostilities began. Meanwhile, the administration conducted quiet back-channel diplomacy to try to uncover the Soviet Union's motives and to attempt to defuse the crisis.

President Kennedy decided on the blockade, and the nation waited anxiously to see if Soviet freighters bound for Havana would turn around; when they first stopped short of the blockade line and then returned to Soviet ports, tensions eased. Soviet premier Nikita S. Khrushchev agreed to remove the missiles and never again to deploy such weapons in Cuba. Kennedy in return promised not to invade Cuba and to remove the American missiles in Turkey that had worried the Soviets. After thirteen October days of high tension, the crisis ended.[31]

Graham Allison, who studied the crisis, argues that the events could be understood from three different perspectives. First, in what he christened Model I, the Cuban missile crisis could be analyzed from a traditional, rational-actor approach: both the United States and the Soviet Union had unified national positions that guided each side's decisions. Second, he advanced Model II, based on organizational processes: decisions could be understood by analyzing the standard operating procedures of the bureaucracies on both sides. Finally, he proposed Model III, identified as the bureaucratic-politics perspective: decisions could be understood as "a *resultant* of various bargaining games among players in the national government." By examining "the perceptions, motivations, positions, power, and maneuvers of the players," one could understand a decision.[32]

This bargaining model does help to illuminate the missile crisis. President Kennedy, for example, was vulnerable because of the failure of the American-supported Bay of Pigs invasion by Cuban exiles trying to overthrow Cuban leader Fidel Castro in April 1961. Americans had come to believe that communist domination of Cuba constituted a serious threat to

American security, and the failure of that invasion attempt made Kennedy seem indecisive. As a consequence, when faced with the discovery of missiles in Cuba, his administration had to act forcefully. The options of doing nothing or taking a diplomatic approach therefore lost ground to the prospect of a military response.

Kennedy initially favored what some advisers called a "surgical" air strike, designed to take out the missile launchers without doing more widespread damage. Other participants, however, including Defense Secretary Robert McNamara, worried deeply that even a limited attack might immediately escalate beyond either side's control into a full nuclear war. The president's brother, Attorney General Robert Kennedy, pointedly asked whether the president, if he launched a surprise attack, would become known as an American Tojo—the Japanese strategist who had planned the raid on Pearl Harbor. In fact, as Allison points out, "after these arguments had been stated so strongly, the president scarcely could have followed his initial preference without seeming to become what RFK had condemned."[33]

Three of the president's closest advisers—Robert Kennedy, McNamara, and presidential counselor Theodore Sorensen—teamed up to press for the blockade. Meanwhile, military advisers, CIA chief John McCone, and Secretary of State Dean Rusk argued in favor of the air strike, but their position weakened when one of the participants of the crisis group asked how the Soviets would likely respond. The best guess was that the Soviets would strike at American missile bases in Turkey, which would, under the NATO treaty, compel the United States to attack the Soviet Union. No one found that alternative appealing. Finally, military planners began to argue that a surgical air strike was impossible and that, to be effective, any military action against the missile launchers would have to be accompanied by a broad-scale attack against all Cuban military installations and, in all likelihood, an invasion of Cuba.

The ultimate decision to establish a blockade, along with the other key decisions of the crisis, thus can be viewed as the result of a bargaining process among the key players in Kennedy's crisis staff. Decisions are, in reality, complex arenas in which decision makers must resolve uncertainties and conflicting preferences. As Allison concludes, "What moves the chess pieces is not simply the reasons that support a course of action, or the routines of organizations that enact an alternative, but the power and skill of proponents and opponents of the action in question."[34] Decisions thus are viewed as the product of bargains. In the bargaining game, the perspective of each player is shaped by the player's position: "where you stand depends on where you sit," as the saying goes.[35] Who wins depends on who has the strongest hand and who bargains most effectively.[36]

Appraisal

The bargaining approach has drawn withering fire from its critics, especially among proponents of the rational approach.

Information

Critics contend that the bargaining approach is dangerously incomplete and risks depriving decision makers of important information.[37] The political process, they contend, can be counted on to present decision makers with political opinions, but it is far less useful in identifying which alternatives are likely to be the most efficient. The result, critics suggest, is that scarce resources can be wasted. When money is tight, bargaining over public programs might produce common ground only by spreading money among the combatants. One economist, Charles Schultze, acknowledged that "it may, indeed, be necessary to guard against the naïveté of the systems analyst who ignores political constraints and believes that efficiency alone produces virtue." But in taking aim at the incrementalists, he concludes, "it is equally necessary to guard against the naïveté of the decision maker who ignores resource constraints and believes that virtue alone produces efficiency."[38] It is possible, Schultze argues, to take account of political realities while doing systems analysis.

Lindblom replies that systems analysis cannot be done and argues that his decision-making approach is indeed analysis; he merely suggests that limited, successive comparison of alternatives is more successful than attempts at comprehensiveness. The bargaining approach, however, does not really tell the analyst just how comprehensive to be and how much analysis to do. How large should an increment be? How many alternatives should a decision maker consider? The only answer is a circular one: the increments should be small enough and the alternatives few enough to produce political consensus. A decision maker knows that the approach is right if a consensus forms and wrong if it does not. While this formula may offer a useful description of many decisions, it provides a weak guide for officials trying to design a decision-making process.

Values

The bargaining approach is obviously at its strongest in describing how decisions are made and, in particular, how decision makers build political support for their judgments. Indeed, incrementalism grows directly out of enduring American traditions of participation in politics as well as more recent theories of pluralism. Its foundation in this participatory and pluralistic heritage gives the bargaining approach extra appeal.

Nevertheless, the role of special interests in decision making varies substantially in the government. In some agencies, such as the Department of Agriculture or the Social Security Administration, relatively broad interests pay careful attention to decisions such as farm price supports or retirement benefits; interest group pressure is intermittent but occasionally intense. In other agencies, such as the Departments

As tensions with the Soviet Union escalated in 1962, President John F. Kennedy met with his brother, Attorney General Robert F. Kennedy, on the portico outside the Oval Office. The government's decision-making strategies during that month's Cuban missile crisis became a much-studied case of how—and how not—to frame governmental policy.

of State and Defense, the range of interests is narrower, and public attention is much less intense. For the most part, the partisans at work are those with a direct stake in the decisions, such as military contractors, Defense Department officials, and representatives of other parts of the government. The players and their roles in the bargaining process thus are likely to vary greatly by the type of agency and the nature of its programs. The value of the bargaining approach in resolving decision-making conflicts is likely to vary accordingly.

Furthermore, it is often difficult to bargain out differences. When issues are complicated and the interests narrow, it is easy for broader public interests to be submerged. Intense attentive publics can wield heavy influence over decisions before the general public even knows that a major decision is to be made. Well-financed special interests, furthermore, have a large advantage over an agency's general public: they can play a role in framing the decision to begin with, in producing analyses to influence the decision, and in gaining the ears of decision makers at crucial times. Their intimate familiarity with the issues and the decision makers gives them a strategic advantage that members of the general public can rarely match.

In contrast, especially in foreign policy and national security issues, the range of participants can be very limited, and the possibility of bargaining typically evaporates. Indeed, during the Reagan administration, a small group of White House officials conducted a clandestine policy of selling arms to Iran to win the release of American hostages in the Middle East—a policy developed outside regular State and Defense Department channels and without the benefit of expert advice. In many foreign policy cases, top decision makers often work above the alternatives produced by staff at lower levels.[39]

Bargaining thus provides a useful description of how many, but not all, administrative decisions are made. Just as with the rational approach, however, there are important normative problems with bargaining, particularly because not everyone is represented equally around the table, and some interests may not even be invited. Nevertheless, the approach is important for its assertion of the importance of values in decision making and for its stark contrast with the rational model.

PARTICIPATIVE DECISION MAKING

Beyond incrementalism is another approach founded even more directly on political democracy: participative decision making, which calls at the most general level for participation by those who will be affected by the decisions. That generality, however, leaves two ambiguities.

First, what does *participation* mean? It may mean being consulted for advice by someone who has power to make a decision, or it may mean sharing decision-making power, as when those affected vote on a proposed decision and their vote settles whether the proposal is adopted or rejected. Second, just who should be entitled to participate in decision making? Claims to such status can be made by four groups: (1) the employees of the organization making the decision; (2) the persons whom the organization serves or regulates (the clientele); (3) the taxpayers whose pocketbooks the decision will affect; and (4) the whole public, or at least the voting public, of the country. These participants are potentially in conflict: the course of action that any of these groups may recommend can vary sharply from what any other group might choose.

On the surface, the value of such participation seems obvious. Who could object to having the decision-making process enlightened by the views of those who have to live with the decision? The problem, of course, is that each group invokes "democracy" as its battle cry—sometimes to the exclusion of all other claimants. Furthermore, when one group gains leverage on a decision, such influence often comes only at a cost to other groups. For example, the poor, especially those in inner-city neighborhoods, have for decades sought a greater voice in the programs serving them. Residents of middle-class neighborhoods similarly demand a say about new projects, school closings, and other governmental initiatives that seem boons or threats to their quality of life. Often, in fact, the demand for such participation leads to the **NIMBY phenomenon**: strong pressures to keep potentially objectionable programs "not in my backyard." Federal statutes and administrative regulations require local community or neighborhood participation in decisions about community development, antipoverty programs, community mental health centers, and other programs. Meanwhile, a host of nongovernmental organizations—most of them newly created for the purpose—have been delegated responsibilities for administering governmental programs. For example, Congress created the Prospective Payment Advisory Commission to advise the Health Care Financing Administration on rates hospitals should be paid for Medicare cases; medical professionals dominate the commission, so physicians have a voice in what the federal government pays them. In a number of large cities, likewise, the board of education has decentralized power to elected neighborhood councils. Sometimes decision makers see a reverse side of NIMBY: powerful arguments against closing neighborhood fire stations and schools, even if shrinking populations leave neighborhoods with more fire stations than they need and schools with many empty desks.

New techniques for participation evolved so quickly from the 1960s to the 1980s that many have supposed that clientele participation in decision making is a novel idea. In fact, American public administration has had long and rich experience with consultation and shared decisions, especially at the local level. These arrangements have not always been successful, and fewer frustrations would arise if new ventures toward participatory democracy and grassroots decentralization took account of the hazards so well marked out by experience.

Example: The Federal Level

Federal agencies have long used advisory committees of private citizens in the decision-making process. Most important among these have been industry advisory committees, which have a painful history of troubles over representativeness, secrecy, conflicts of interest, profiteering on privileged information, temptations to violate antitrust laws, and displacement of responsible government officials as the real decision makers.

The high-water mark of these industry advisory committees came early in the New Deal when the National Recovery Administration relied heavily on trade associations, first, for the drafting of the nearly 500 codes of fair competition controlling the production and prices of as many industries, and second, for selection of members of the code authorities to which enforcement powers were delegated.[40] During World War II, industry advisory committees proliferated—the War Production Board had a thousand of them, and the Office of

Price Administration some 650—and at national and regional levels joint industry-labor-government boards were given decisional power in labor disputes.[41] In the 1950s, the Business Advisory Council of the Department of Commerce attracted so much criticism as a privileged big-business channel of influence on administration policy that it was reconstituted as a private organization.[42] Dogging this history of industry advisory committees has been the risk that the government's assembling of representatives of an industry will validate Adam Smith's dictum: "People of the same trade seldom meet together, even for merriment and diversion, but the conversation ends in a conspiracy against the public, or in some contrivance to raise prices."[43]

A second major area of clientele participation through national advisory committees has to do with the allocation of funds for scientific research, including the awarding of research grants and contracts to individual scientists and institutions. The National Science Foundation, the National Institutes of Health, and other research-supporting agencies rely heavily on peer review by committees of scientists in the specialized fields. Here again, issues of representativeness, insiders' advantages, and unconscious bias have been raised about clientele participation.[44] During the Carter administration, the number of federal advisory committees was cut by 30 percent, to 816, but critics continued to complain that secrecy afflicted the committees.[45] In 2001 environmentalists made just that charge about a task force headed by Vice President Dick Cheney, which produced the Bush administration's energy policy.

Example: The Local Level

Over the past sixty years, a variety of national programs have promoted decentralized, grassroots participation by their clients. A few programs, in fact, involve all of their clients, rather than just representative councils and committees. For example, compulsory marketing quotas and marketing orders for several agricultural commodities can be instituted only by a two-thirds favorable vote in a referendum of all growers of that commodity.[46]

More commonly, federal agencies have relied on local committees whose part-time members were intended to be representative of their communities or neighborhoods. In some programs the local committees were appointed by the president or a federal agency after consultation with the governor, local government officials, or the agency's own field agents. This was true of the 5,500 War Price and Rationing Boards established in World War II by the Office of Price Administration (OPA). And it was true of the some 4,000 local Selective Service Boards that administered the draft during the Vietnam War. Though appointive, each board was meant to be "representative of the community as a whole" (OPA) or "composed of friends and neighbors of the registrant it classifies" (Selective Service).[47]

Farmers and Cattle Ranchers

The administration of agricultural programs is among the oldest forms of local participation in decision making for federal programs. In a participatory system that is literally from the grassroots, farmers since 1933 have been elected to serve on committees in 3,000 counties. Members of the three-member committees are chosen either directly by the county's farmers

★★★ Advisory Neighborhood Commission 3D
A.U., Foxhall, Kent, New Mexico/Cathedral, Palisades, Spring Valley, & Wesley Heights

HOME　　AGENDAS　　ISSUES　　MINUTES　　RESOURCES　　COMMISSIONERS

ANC3D Events

- Regular Meeting
  Wed. 6 Nov. 2013 (7:00 pm - 9:00 pm)
- Regular Meeting
  Wed. 4 Dec. 2013 (7:00 pm - 9:00 pm)

Show Full Calendar

Officers

Chair: Penny Pagano
Vice Chair: Gayle Trotter
Secretary: Joe Wisniewski
Treasurer: Rory Slatko

Commissioners

Find Your ANC SMD

3D01 Kent Slowinski
3D02 Tom M. Smith
3D03 Nan S. Wells
3D04 Stu Ross

Welcome to Advisory Neighborhood Commission 3D

The 1976 Home Rule Charter provides for Advisory Neighborhood Commissions (ANC). ANC3D represents A.U., Foxhall, Kent, New Mexico/Cathedral, Palisades, Spring Valley and Wesley Heights, in Ward Three. It is one of 37

In many communities, like Washington, D.C., advisory councils work on issues affecting their neighborhoods. These local governments consider a variety of policies and programs, like parking, trash collection, zoning, and street improvements.

or indirectly by the members of community committees. A county committee exercises real power: it "is ultimately responsible for program and administrative policies and decisions at the county level."[48] It establishes individual farms' acreage allotments and marketing quotas for some commodities, administers crop-support loans, provides disaster payments, and supervises government-owned commodity storage facilities. Choosing committee members is often difficult—a problem that spills over into other national programs. In one year's election, for example, the turnout nationally was only 23 percent, and in six major farming states the turnout ranged from 5 to 8 percent.[49] In half the communities of one Illinois county, there were more candidates than voters!

The grazing boards in the West, elected by local stockmen and ranch owners who grazed their cattle on prairie lands, are reminders that clientele participation can magnify self-interest at the expense of public interest and, indeed, of other special interests. These boards effectively made most of the decisions on issuing permits for grazing on public lands, and, as Grant McConnell pointed out, the most influential ranchers have dominated the boards. Participation in district elections has been low, averaging less than 10 percent in Oregon and Idaho, and the committees have been dominated by the same powerful ranchers for a long time. As a result, "the general [public] interest in conservation of the soil has, on occasion at least, suffered from the pattern of power deriving from the autonomous systems of government of these lands."[50]

City Dwellers

Urban America has wrestled with the same problems without any attentiveness to the lessons of the rural experience. A series of federal programs that began in the mid-1960s required communities to establish citizen committees to help determine how the money should be spent. The mandates began with the 1964 Economic Opportunity Act, which required each local community action program in the War on Poverty to be "developed, conducted, and administered with the maximum feasible participation of the areas and members of the groups served." The 1966 Model Cities Act required that any local plan for rebuilding and revitalizing slum or blighted neighborhoods must provide for "widespread citizen participation" from those neighborhoods. In 1974 the Housing and Community Development Act (which superseded the Model Cities Act, among others) required that any local government applying for community development funds offer "satisfactory assurances" that it had provided citizens with "adequate" information, had held public hearings to learn citizens' views, and had provided citizens with a chance to shape the application. If you think the quoted congressional phrases are imprecise, you are right: what is maximum, or widespread, or adequate participation was left an open question, which led to brutal battles over infusing each term with a specific meaning.

Or consider education. There are approximately 16,000 local school boards around the country. As the movement to improve basic education gained steam in the mid-1980s, however, critics began to look seriously at the boards. "The system isn't working, and the reason it isn't working is that the stakes that have become the focus for most of the boards are the jobs involved, not what is happening in the schools and with the kids," said New York City Board of Education president Robert Wagner Jr. In fact, one *New York Times* headline announced, "School Boards Found Failing to Meet Goals," and its reporter concluded that the school district system was little more than a collection of "political clubhouses."[51] Turnout for school board elections in the city was consistently less than 10 percent, while patronage loomed over educational issues.[52] As part of a major 2002 reform the city changed the system to one with thirty-two Community District Education Councils, and each council has an advisory board composed of nine parents, two area residents, and a high school senior (who serves without a vote).

Internet-based methods for encouraging collaboration have broadened the opportunities for participation. Many governments have created blogs, and the web has made it easy to create quick, if unscientific, online polls through tools like SurveyMonkey. Twitter and Facebook have quickly become governmental

Students at a Denver elementary school made signs to protest cuts in funding for local schools. Reductions in spending led teachers and students to furlough days, in an effort to save money.

institutions, as public officials worked to keep up with the torrent of virtual communication. More traditional neighborhood forums, like actual town hall meetings, continue to flourish. Nearly everyone finds these processes valuable, and nearly everyone has a way to participate in some form or another. The lasting question is what impact universal participation has on decision making—and how this participation might improve the quality of the decisions made.

Appraisal

Since the mid-1970s, as complaints about decentralization have grown and as budgets have gotten tighter, the trend gradually has been to centralize control and put more decision-making responsibility in the hands of elected officials. This trend underlines the recurring dilemmas of participative decision making.

Information

One of the biggest advantages offered by participative approaches is the wealth of information they provide. Few insights into the management of public programs are better than those of the persons who must administer them, and few observers of any program's effects have keener insights than the citizens most affected by them. The very wealth of this information is a problem, however, because it typically flows to decision makers as a large, undifferentiated mass, with no easy clues about which information is most important. Too much information can sometimes be as bad as too little, and that can encourage decision makers to fall back on their preconceptions and see only what they want to see.

Values

In sorting through the vast amount of information that the participative approach produces, decision makers must also confront important value questions. The approach spawns these recurring dilemmas:

1. *Self-interest versus no interest:* whether to serve a narrow clientele dedicated to protection of its own self-interest or a broad, mixed clientele with a less keen interest in the policy
2. *Too much versus too little representation:* whether to allow direct participation in decision making by all members of the clientele who wish to participate—at the risk of assembling an impossibly large group to deal with—or direct participation only by those who get appointed or elected to committees, councils, or boards that are officially assumed to represent the clientele—but that may not be very representative
3. *Too much versus too little power:* whether to give formal or informal power to citizens for making governmental decisions—raising the problem of who looks out for the public interest—or have them simply provide advice (and demands) to public administrators who weigh those views with other considerations and make the actual decisions—but who may not take that advice seriously

The choices are hard, but they carry important implications for responsive and effective policymaking. On the one hand, participative decision making has led to new public access to governmental decisions and to the creation of a new cadre of civic leaders. On the other hand, the system has created some avenues of patronage and new officials seeking to protect their own positions. The record is mixed.[53]

PUBLIC CHOICE

Some microeconomists have developed a different theory to explain how public agencies make decisions, hence the name *public choice*.[54] Public-choice theory spins off the rational approach described in Chapter 4, beginning with the bedrock of all economics: the assumption that human beings are rational and seek to maximize whatever is important to them. The most rational thing, according to the theory, is to promote one's self-interest. Whether choosing where to live or what car to buy, these economists argue, individuals attempt to maximize their utility: the value they derive from their decisions. In the private sector, this makes individuals and corporations competitive and leads to the most efficient distribution of resources.

Public-choice theory argues that public officials, like all other individuals, are self-interested, which leads them to avoid risk and to promote their careers. These objectives, in turn, mean that they seek to enlarge their programs and increase their budgets. As a result, public-choice economists argue, an organization full of self-interested bureaucrats is likely to produce bigger government that is both inefficient and prone to operating against the public's interest.[55] Bureaucrats' pursuit of their own self-interest, they contend, helps explain the often disappointing performance of American government.

This inference has led proponents of the public-choice school to argue that, wherever possible, government functions ought to be turned over to the private sector. From the Japanese government's sale of that nation's largest airline to Mexico's divestiture of 250 government-owned corporations, governments around the world have followed the public-choice prescription in privatizing public services. In fact, Japan has moved even further to a decade-long privatization of its postal system. Where this proves impossible, for either practical or political reasons, public-choice proponents contend that public functions ought to be contracted out to the private sector. The contracting process, they assert, simulates private-sector competition and dilutes the influence of government bureaucrats.[56] As Stuart Butler, one of the movement's strongest voices, put it, **privatization** is a kind of "political guerrilla warfare" that directs demand away from government provision of services and reduces the demand for budget growth.[57]

Example: Banks and Bubbles

The public-choice approach has also led to innovative regulatory strategies. Rather than have government issue rules that require any industry that creates pollution to reduce impurities below a fixed ceiling, regulators can create incentives for industries to reduce pollution more efficiently. The Environmental Protection Agency, for example, set pollution standards allowing companies that reduced their pollution below prescribed levels to "bank" their pollution savings for use in future expansion. Other companies, since 1979, have been allowed to establish a "bubble" around all their facilities in a given area and then find the cheapest way to reduce overall pollution within that area, rather than having to deal with individual rules applying to each polluting facility. In both pollution banking and bubbles, the strategy is to allow each company's assessment of its self-interest to promote the overall goal of reducing pollution.

In 1980, for example, the first bubble plan approved saved an electric utility $27 million when it switched from high-sulfur coal to low-sulfur coal at one plant and switched to natural gas from low-sulfur coal at another. The plan not only saved substantial money but also reduced overall emissions. DuPont engineers, furthermore, estimated that a regional bubble for the company's operations could produce an 85 percent reduction in pollution for $14.6 million in costs, whereas if the company were to reduce each source of pollution by 85 percent, it would have cost more than seven times—$91 million—more.[58] Such bubble plans have significantly reduced emissions for some pollutants and have created an actual commodities market for pollution on the Chicago Board of Trade.[59] In the 2008 presidential election, both John McCain and Barack Obama put forth similar strategies for a national effort to reduce greenhouse gases, but hyper-partisan gridlock has made it hard to advance that initiative in Congress.

Appraisal

The public-choice approach to decision making attacks governmental programs with a simple diagnosis—that the self-interest of government officials produces inefficient programs—and with a simple prescription—to turn over as many public programs as possible to the private sector and, when that is impossible, to mimic private-sector competition within the government. The approach, however, leaves significant questions of both information and values unanswered.

Information

The attraction of the public-choice approach lies in its embrace of the market. Market-like competition, whether actually in the market or in market-based mechanisms such as contracts, its proponents believe, maximizes efficiency. Decision makers are driven to seek the right information and make the best decisions; if they do not do so, others will outcompete and overtake them, and they will lose their jobs. The power of this logic rests on the basic characterization of the bureaucrat as a rational human being: the administrator will single-mindedly pursue goals of immediate utility to him or her—personal power, security, and income.

It is hard to argue that any individual does not look to enhance his or her position. Nevertheless, Steven Kelman contends, this account of the operation of the political process is a terrible caricature of reality:

> It ignores the ability of ideas to defeat interests, and the role that public spirit plays in motivating the behavior of participants in the political process. The "public choice" argument is far worse than simply descriptively inaccurate. Achieving good public policy, I believe, requires . . . a norm of public spiritedness in the political action—a view that people should not simply be selfish in their political behavior. . . . The public choice school is part of the assault on this norm.[60]

It is difficult to accept the notion that in administering governmental programs, government bureaucrats are driven so hard to maximize their own utility that more publicly oriented objectives slip out of sight. Thus, the theory's very simplicity may well be its undoing. Are bureaucratic officials really so single-minded of purpose that there is no room for pride in performance, for striving to meet the goals of legislation, for a sense of public service in the public interest?

As we saw in Chapter 8, many top administrators could doubtless double or triple their salaries in the private sector, but a sense of devotion to the public good keeps them working in the public sector. An approach to the public service that starts with a cynical view of public servants is dangerously flawed, especially when used as a prescription for managing governmental programs. Moreover, as former chairman of the president's Council of Economic Advisers Murray Weidenbaum contends, some economists have a tendency to dismiss difficult questions as "subjective and political" and thus to define them as outside the proper sphere of rational analysis of efficiency.[61]

The public-choice movement's great attraction is its parsimonious explanation of government problems, which dovetails neatly with the antigovernment feeling that has grown up in the aftermath of Watergate, under the conservative philosophy championed by the Reagan administration, and amid the reforms led by the George W. Bush administration. Moreover, it offers a neat solution: replace the decisions of government bureaucrats with the allegedly self-correcting influence of the market. Markets, it is argued, eliminate the need for a conscious search for decision-making information, since the self-interested motivations of the participants ensure that relevant data are available. The very parsimony of the explanation, however, greatly oversimplifies the much more interesting problems with which public managers must deal and feeds an unhealthy cynicism about government and the public service. Furthermore, the approach greatly underestimates the tremendous power of public ideas: the concept that some things are good for all of us and that decision makers seek to achieve those things.[62]

Values

The market analogy, furthermore, suggests that both the goals and the motives of the private sector are identical to those of the public sector. Arguments for privatization, however, sometimes muddle together two very different issues: what government should do and how government should do it. Most fundamentally, privatization is an argument about how the government does things, not what it ought to do.

That distinction, in turn, underlines an important question: what functions are, at their core, public—for which government has the basic responsibility? As I noted earlier, efficiency is not the only goal of public programs; pursuing other important goals, such as equality, typically means making difficult tradeoffs. The deepest debates are usually about ends—what should or should not be public functions—and the public-choice movement's focus on means thus begs the most crucial point. Some programs are intrinsically public, which means that there is, quite simply, a *public* interest in public administration.[63]

Even if we focus solely on means, the public-choice approach is still unsatisfying. Public-choice proponents typically assume that the self-regulating features of the market will solve any problems plaguing public programs. Instruments are not neutral, however, and the long history of government contracts, as well as more recent horror stories in the newspapers, offer ample proof that this is not so.[64]

One point is very simple yet often overlooked: contracts do not administer themselves. Moreover, relying on contracts often replaces one set of values with another. If directly administered governmental programs are plagued by self-interested bureaucrats, contracted-out programs must deal with self-interested proxies, each of which is seeking to maximize its own utility, sometimes at the government's expense. And because contracts must themselves be administered to ensure high accountability and performance, the role of government administrators may be different, but it does not disappear. As Eli Freedman, Connecticut commissioner of administration, persuasively argued, "You can't contract away responsibility to manage."[65] As any defense official facing harsh questions about overpriced weapons could tell you, contracting out does not eliminate the government's basic responsibilities; it only changes them. (Chapter 12 discusses this issue more fully.)

The public-choice argument thus leads paradoxically to an important point: there is an irreducible governmental role in shaping government. At the same time, the line between the public and private spheres is not very distinct. The public-choice prescription, therefore, is on the surface an appealing one, but a close examination reveals that it is based on an overly simplistic understanding of government administration. The model is, in fact, more useful for the problems it raises than for the answers it provides.

LIMITS ON DECISION MAKING

From this discussion, it is clear that no one approach offers a solution to the problems of making administrative decisions. Each approach has its own special virtues and its own idiosyncratic problems. Every approach, though, shares the fundamental complication that administrative decisions, after all, are made by collections of human beings, each of whom operates in a large organization full of complex pressures, contradictory information, and diverse advice. Even the theories of satisficing and incrementalism do not fully take account of the psychological environment in which government executives must operate. James Webb, who served for eight years as a NASA administrator, put the problem well:

> Executives within . . . a large-scale endeavor . . . have to work under unusual circumstances and in unusual ways. . . . The executive trained only in . . . traditional principles, able to operate only in accord with them and uncomfortable in their absence, would be of little use and could expect little satisfaction in a large complex endeavor. So too would the executive who has to be psychologically coddled in the fashion that the participative school of management advocates.
>
> In the large-scale endeavor the man himself must also be unusual; he must be knowledgeable in sound management doctrine and practice, but able to do a job without an exact definition of what it is or how it should be done; a man who can work effectively when lines of command crisscross and move in several directions rather than straight up and down; one who can work effectively in an unstable environment and can live with uncertainty and a high degree of personal insecurity; one willing to work for less of a monetary reward than he could insist on elsewhere; one who can blend public and private interests in organized participation for the benefit of both.[66]

Two social psychologists, Irving Janis and Leon Mann, put the point more poignantly. They see the human being "not as a cold fish but as a warm-blooded mammal," one "beset by conflict, doubts, and worry, struggling with incongruous longings, antipathies, and loyalties, and seeking relief by procrastination, rationalizing, or denying responsibility for his own choices."[67] All approaches to decision making share problems: the enormous uncertainty surrounding complex issues, bureaucratic pathologies that distort and block the flow of important information, and recurrent crises that deny the luxury of lengthy consideration.

Uncertainty

It is easy to underestimate how difficult it is for decision makers to know what results their decisions will produce, or even to get good information about what the current state of the world is. Congress, for example, has charged the Federal Reserve with making monetary policy, but it is deceptively difficult even to decide just what "money" is.[68] The Fed has developed various measures of money—including cash, checking accounts, savings accounts, and long-term certificates of deposit—but these measures have been changed over the years as Americans' banking practices have changed. To make things worse, the supply of money is really only an estimate, subject to constant revision.

Other important economic statistics share the same problems. It often takes months to get good numbers on the growth of the economy or the rate of inflation; what initially seemed to be good months can sometimes become bad months as more data emerge. Furthermore, it is sometimes hard to interpret the numbers: is high economic growth, for instance, a sign of a healthy economy or of an inflationary trend that is starting to take off? There are lots of numbers, but Fed officials constantly struggle to obtain good, reliable, up-to-date information about the true state of the economy. Even worse, there are very few reliable models about what figures from the past may signal for the economy's future. And even if Fed officials could determine the health of the economy and where it is headed, it is even more difficult to determine how—and when—best to use its tools to steer the economy in a different direction. Moreover, even before the meltdown of the home mortgage market in 2007 and 2008, some analysts had predicted the impending collapse. Determining what to do, who should do it, and when to act, however, proved impossible—until the collapse forced the regulators' hands.

With increasing frequency, in areas ranging from space exploration to homeland security, from new telephone technologies to the risk of new diseases, decision makers must tackle issues on the edge of current knowledge, where experts disagree and the road ahead is uncertain. Indeed, risk is the first cousin to uncertainty, and the cost of being wrong can sometimes be catastrophic (as, for instance, in judging the risk of exposure to known cancer-causing chemicals).[69] Apart from political pressures, this uncertainty makes any one approach to decision making an inadequate guide—and the risk all the more hazardous because many decisions, once made, are irreversible and offer no opportunity for the feedback and correction assumed in both the rational and bargaining approaches.

Despite uncertainty, decision makers ultimately must make decisions, from which there is no going back. That, in fact, is the lesson of Julius Caesar at the Rubicon River. Roman law forbade him from bringing his army back into Rome, for the Romans knew that armed emperors would be impossible to resist, and the Rubicon was the boundary. But as Caesar returned to Rome after a successful military campaign in 49 B.C., he decided to challenge the law and Rome's rulers. Once he crossed the boundary, the Rubicon River, with his army, conflict was inevitable. As Plutarch writes:

> [Caesar] wavered much in his mind . . . often changed his opinion one way and the other . . . discussed the matter with his friends who were about him . . . computing how many calamities his passing that river would bring upon mankind and what relation of it would be transmitted to posterity. At last, in a sort of passion, casting aside calculation, and abandoning himself to what might come, and using the proverb frequently in their mouths who enter upon dangerous and bold attempts, "The die is cast," with these words he took the river.[70]

In an age in which a detection system may incorrectly report an enemy's launching of an atomic attack, the few minutes afforded for decision on whether to launch a counterattack permit little computation and calculation, yet the decision is irreversible. The die will have been cast.

Many decisions less momentous for the world are irreversible, or substantially so: drafting an individual into military service and assignment to a war zone, withholding of a license to practice a profession or operate a business, denial of a loan to prevent bankruptcy of a business or farm, refusal of a pardon to a prisoner scheduled for execution. Decisions often have a stubborn finality for those who suffer loss or risk of life and for those whose livelihoods are impaired. A decision maker doesn't know what results a decision will produce, and the burden of uncertainty weighs all the heavier on decisions that are irreversible.

Information Pathologies

The very structure of bureaucracy, furthermore, can distort the flow of information as it moves upward through the organization. Not all information collected at the bottom, of course, can be passed along to officials at the top—they would quickly become overwhelmed and uncertain about what is actually happening—and therefore, information must be condensed at each bureaucratic level. The process of condensation, however, often leads to filtering. Public officials, not surprisingly, tend to pass along the good news and suppress the bad. At best, this tendency can distort the information flow; at worst, it can completely block early warnings about emerging problems. Furthermore, the official's own professional training can attune him or her more to some kinds of information than others. An engineer, even one who has assumed a general managerial position, still may attend more carefully to engineering problems than to others that might be more pressing.[71]

Sometimes these information pathologies create continuing, nagging problems. In the Peace Corps, one former official discovered, "Training was usually inadequate in language, culture, and technical skills. Volunteers were selected who were not suited to their assignments." But upper-level officials were usually in the dark about this problem, he explained, because lower-level officials often worked "to prevent information, particularly of an unpleasant character, from rising to the top of the agency, where it may produce results unpleasant to the lower ranks."[72]

Sometimes these pathologies cause disasters. On the night before NASA's launch of the space shuttle *Challenger* in January 1986, for example, engineers for one NASA contractor argued furiously that the cold weather predicted for the launch site the next morning could be dangerous. Mid-level NASA managers rejected the advice and refused to pass it on to top launch officials. The engineers, however, proved tragically good prophets, and the shuttle exploded 73 seconds into the flight. Officials with the responsibility for giving the "go" for the launch did not learn about the worries the engineers had expressed that night until the investigation into the disaster began.[73] When the *Columbia* disintegrated on reentry in 2003, officials later discovered that similar worries expressed by engineers had never been communicated to top agency officials.[74]

Decision makers obviously cannot make good decisions without the right information, so they often create devices to avoid the pathologies. They can rely on outside sources, ranging from newspapers to advice from external experts. They can apply a counter-bias, using their past knowledge about information sources to judge the reliability of the facts they receive. They can bypass hierarchical levels and go right to the source; some management experts, in fact, advocate "management by walking around," getting the manager out from behind the desk and onto the front lines to avoid the "nobody ever tells me anything" problem.[75] They can develop precoded forms that avoid distortion as the forms move up through the ranks.[76] Many governmental forms and much red tape, in fact, are designed precisely to prevent uncertainty from creeping into the process ("what information should I pass along?") even if it adds additional headaches to the lives of administrators and citizens.

Nevertheless, attempts to rid the information chain of these pathologies can, paradoxically, create new problems:

- Improvements in incoming information may clog internal channels of information.
- Increasing the amount of information flow to decision makers and attempting to eliminate the fragmented features of decision making may simply overload top officials.
- Greater clarity and detail in the wording of decisions may overwhelm implementing officials.[77]

These paradoxes paint a disturbing but very real picture. Administrators are scarcely defenseless, however, because the problem often is not having too little information but having too much—and then trying to sort through it all to find the right combination of facts on which to make decisions. In fact, top NASA officials had been informed earlier of the problem that caused the *Challenger* disaster, "but always in a way that didn't communicate the seriousness of the problem," a House committee found.[78] Later, the same lack of urgency surfaced again to claim a second shuttle. The key to resolving such problems of information management is redundancy: creating multiple sources of feedback that allow decision makers to blend competing pieces of information together into a more coherent picture—without wasting scarce resources on too much redundant information. Determining how much is just right is one of the hardest tasks that decision makers must face.

Crisis

Crises often precipitate decisions. The deaths of 119 men in a 1951 mine explosion and of 78 men in a 1968 mine explosion led to passage of national coal mine safety acts in 1952 and 1969. Catastrophic floods have time after time broken logjams that had obstructed major changes in national flood-control policy.[79] A 1979 accident in a Pennsylvania nuclear reactor, Three Mile Island, imperiling the population for miles around, stimulated a fundamental reconsideration of governmental policy toward the nuclear power industry. The 2011 crisis at Japan's nuclear reactors rekindled all those debates. The *Challenger* explosion speeded up redesign of the booster rocket and produced plans for a new emergency escape system, while the *Columbia* accident led to new launch procedures and improvements of many parts of the space shuttle. And Superstorm Sandy's horrific assault in late 2012 on the northeast prompted a fundamental rethinking of the nation's infrastructure and its zoning policies in flood plains.[80]

In addition to upsetting the normal sequences of decision making, crises increase the difficulty of many potential strategies: the comprehensive analyses that rational decision making requires, the trial and error of bargaining, the consultation of participative decision making, and the reliance on the private sector of public choice. Crises accentuate the problems of uncertainty, especially in areas of technological complexity. Most important, they underline an issue of decision making in the public sector not well considered in most approaches: in the end, the public official is responsible for ascertaining and ensuring the public interest—a task that always proves difficult.

Crises can be managed. In the private sector, the manufacturers of Tylenol were widely hailed for their aggressive action in dealing with the poisoning of their capsules in 1982. Furthermore, Irving L. Janis argues, "vigilant problem solving" can reduce the risks of crises, as managers aggressively seek to formulate the problem, collect available information, reformulate the situation, and frame the best options.[81] When Governor Richard Thornburgh of Pennsylvania faced the potential of a nuclear disaster during the Three Mile Island nuclear power plant crisis in 1979, he had to follow precisely these steps in finding his way. Nevertheless, the sudden appearance of the unexpected coupled with high risk for wrong decisions poses enormous problems for decision makers.

CONCLUSION

We have examined several approaches to administrative decision making: rational analysis, bargaining, participative, and public choice. Though in some measure all these approaches have been put into practice, they all are expressions of theories—full of assumptions—which have tended to harden into dogmas. They also offer, as Table 10.1 shows, a wide range of tactics for dealing with the lasting problems of information and values.

The approaches share, in varying degrees, certain basic defects. This chapter discussed some oversights, especially uncertainty, information pathologies, and crisis, but there are others, such as how a problem or a need for a decision is discovered, formulated, and put on the agenda (most approaches start with a known and stated problem or need). Furthermore, nondecision—the decision not to decide or the avoidance of an issue altogether, whether

TABLE 10.1	Approaches to Decision Making	
Approach	**Information**	**Values**
Rational	Collect comprehensive information to maximize rationality	Are assumed
Bargaining	Limited	Are struggled over
Participative	Acquired through those affected by decision	Focus on clients' values
Public choice	Use self-policing forces of the market	Use self-interest of players

conscious or unconscious—often has consequences as great as those of a decision itself. When senior Bush administration officials received the President's Daily Brief on August 6, 2001, that warned, "Bin Laden Determined to Strike in U.S.," no one took action. The brief was unclear about how or when, and it wasn't clear from the brief what the administration could or should do. But this was a case where a nondecision had powerful consequences just a month later.

More basic are two problematic tendencies. First, each approach tends to focus on a single value, as is evident in economists' eagerness to increase efficiency through systems analysis, incrementalists' dedication to maximizing participation, participative managers' commitment to full public voice in decisions, and public choice adherents' reverence for the virtues of private-sector competition. These are all important values, however, which means that an approach single-mindedly focused on only one of them is inadequate for the complex reality of the political world.

The second shared tendency is the failure to understand what is required to make an approach succeed. Sometimes, as in systems analysis, the conditions may not exist in the real world, and the theorists do not explain very well how to adapt their approaches to reality. Often, however, the adaptations may need to be so substantial that the approach will be drained of its essential character. For example, attempts to adapt the rational decision-making approach by taking account of the elusiveness of policy goals, the shortage of sufficient quantitative data in many analytic areas, the distortion risked in converting qualitative goals or accomplishments into measurable terms, and the behavior of members of Congress may lead to so truncated a version of the rational approach that it is less useful than, say, the more reality-oriented incremental approach.

It is possible, of course, to identify which approaches work best on which problems.[82] The rational approach, for example, tends to work better for issues with clear objectives, quantitative measures, and minimal political pressures. However, even if we can somehow determine which approaches best fit which problems—itself a very tall order—we are left with the puzzle of how to put these different tactical systems to work as a coherent whole.

Those puzzles come into the sharpest focus in the budgetary process, which we examine in the next chapter. As the government's system-wide decision-making process, budgeting raises the difficult issues of how best to deal with the conflicting pressures toward comprehensive planning and incremental politics that lie at the core of decision making. Theorists and public officials alike have long struggled to manage an elusive marriage between the two so as to capture the value of each while avoiding the flaws of both.

CASE 10.1

Baltimore Battles the Banks

In 2012, Baltimore Mayor Stephanie Rawlings-Blake publicly savaged international bankers for taking money out of the pockets of city residents. The bankers, she told reporters, "are pretty much playing fast and loose with the people they are meant to protect." She added, "We are not afraid of a fight."

How did a mayor of a medium-sized city end up dueling with giant banks like Barclays, Bank of America, Citigroup, HSBC, JPMorgan Chase, and UBS? Like many state and local governments, Baltimore invested its cash in complex financial instruments, including interest-rate swaps. Rawlings-Blake and other litigants in a federal lawsuit charged that the banks set interest rates artificially low, which cut governments' investment returns and led to bigger spending cuts. No politician likes to slash programs or raise taxes. Every politician hates to discover they had to do so more than might have been necessary.

Because many state and local governments borrow at floating rates, investment returns can be highly unpredictable. So to smooth out the highs and lows, financial managers trade the floating bonds for fixed-rate investments. Most of the rates for floating bonds and swaps are pegged to "Libor," the London Interbank Offered Rate. Insiders know it as BBA Libor (for British Bankers' Association Libor), the product of a daily survey among bankers about the rates banks can get in the London market at 11 a.m.

every business day, across a range of maturities. They toss out the highest and lowest rates, and the average of what's left determines the interest rates that just about everyone pays for just about everything. In fact, anyone can follow the results on Twitter: @BBALIBOR.

This is rather arcane stuff, but it worked well through gentlemen's agreements for decades until July 2012. In both the United States and the United Kingdom, government regulators found that traders working for one of London's most respected banks, Barclays, had been playing Libor games by misrepresenting the rates. Soon government regulators in Canada and Switzerland joined in the investigation, which spread to 16 banks, including Bank of America, Citigroup, and JPMorgan Chase in the United States. Fallout quickly ensued when Barclays' high-flying chairman Marcus Agius was forced to resign.

The regulators probed whether the banks had colluded to keep interest rates artificially low, in part to make money on trades and in part to convey the impression that, even in the financial meltdown, they remained solid companies. (The riskier the company, the higher the rates it would have to pay. So lower rates both helped banks play the market better and signaled a rosy corporate picture.)

That takes us back to Baltimore and a quickly growing list of state and local governments filing legal action. Their claim: By artificially driving

Libor down, the banks cheated them out of enormous investment returns at a time when their budgets were already badly damaged from the Great Recession and when every dollar of investment income was a dollar of services that didn't have to be cut.

The Libor scandal has exploded across the global financial scene. It's already cost the jobs of top bankers and has dragged many of the world's leading banks into a very harsh spotlight, just as they were trying to make the case for the return of financial stability. Mad-as-hell government officials, who concluded they slashed spending more than was necessary, are seeking compensation and retribution. Moreover, many state and local investment officials holding bonds with variable rates converted them to interest-rate swaps to stabilize their returns, but now they can't get out of them because in many cases the penalties are too high. So not only are their investment returns lower than they should be—they're stuck with them.

Perhaps most fundamentally, the foundations of much they had taken for granted have been shaken. It turns out that the key benchmark for most interest rates around the world was Libor, and that Libor wasn't the actual rates bankers charged but estimates that could be gamed. As blogger Darwin Bond-Graham sharply put it, "Libor was always a club of powerful banks inventing the price of money," and with Agius's resignation, the workings of that club came under investigation, including the threat of criminal rate-fixing charges. According to one government official, "It's hard to imagine a bigger case than Libor."

That all leads to two final questions. First, why didn't the feds step in sooner to help protect state and local governments? The Treasury had detected the problem a few years earlier and even managed to extract a $450 million settlement from Barclays. Some state and local officials have complained that federal regulators were not riding shotgun for them.

Second, how much of the problem came from state and local investment officials putting money into instruments whose risks they didn't really understand? As Jeffrey Gibbs, director of special investigations for Pennsylvania's auditor general, put it, swaps, derivatives, and other complex financial instruments are typically understood only by the people who sell them. It's another searing lesson of the risks of governing in a globalized world, with state and local leaders forced to navigate through seas they can't control and sometimes can't even see.

Questions to Consider

1. What lessons does Baltimore's Libor experience teach? What would you advise the mayor of your community about how to make decisions on such investments?

2. An important question about modern budgeting and complex financial instruments is the last point: only the people who sell them (and, sometimes, not even the salespersons) understand the important questions. A time-honored piece of investment advice is that investors should never put their money in something they don't understand. But is that realistic in today's global marketplace? If you have a savings account in your bank, do you really know where the money is going? How much information do you need to make good decisions?

3. What do you think you have to know to be a good steward of the public's money? How should a government build adequate capacity in its own agencies to ensure it manages the public's money well?

Note: This case comes from my column in *Governing* (October 2012), http://www.governing.com/columns/potomac-chronicle/col-global-libor-scandal-cost-states-localities-millions.html.

CASE 10.2

Pay to Spray? Fire Protection and the Free Rider Problem in South Fulton, Tennessee

Gene Cranick was devastated as he poked through the remains of his house. His grandson Lance had been clearing out trash and burning it in a barrel near the home. Lance went inside to take a shower and when he came back outside he found a shed in flames. His garden hose couldn't keep up with the spreading fire, which soon reached the house. The family lost everything, including three dogs and a cat and a lifetime's belongings.

The rural town of South Fulton, Tennessee, had a fire department. In fact, the fire department arrived at the scene—and watched as the home burned down. The town imposes an annual $75 fire protection fee, commonly known as "pay to spray," for citizens like Cranick who live outside the South Fulton city limits and who rely on South Fulton's fire department. "I just forgot to pay my $75," Gene Cranick explained later. "I did it last year, the year before. . . . It slipped my mind." The firefighters arrived when his neighbor, who had paid the fee, called 911. The trucks sprayed down the fence line separating the homes but refused to put out the fire at Cranick's house. As Jeff Vowell, South Fulton's city manager, later explained, "We have to follow the rules and the ordinances set forth to us, and that's exactly what we did."[1]

Cranick's neighbor had pleaded with the fire department to train the hoses next door. They begged firefighters to help the family, and Cranick offered to pay whatever it would cost for help. The firefighters responded that it was simply too late. The policy, in place for more than two decades, was clear: pay, in advance, to spray. "Anybody that's not inside the city limits of South Fulton, it's a service we offer. Either they accept it or they don't," South Fulton Mayor David Crocker said.[2]

The sad case led to a national debate over the decision of the firefighters to stand by and watch the home burn. Jacqueline Byers, at the National Association of Counties, explained, "If the city starts fighting fires in the homes of people outside the city who don't pay, why would anyone pay?"[3] It's a classic free rider problem, some experts said: allow others to pay the cost of municipal services, and then use the services when they're needed. But the president of the International Association of Fire Fighters said the policy was "incredibly irresponsible." He argued, "Professional, career firefighters shouldn't be forced to check a list before running out the door to see which homeowners have paid up." Instead, "They get in their trucks and go."[4]

Conservative commentator Glenn Beck said that the argument will go "nowhere if you go onto 'compassion, compassion, compassion, compassion.'" The fee, he said, is "to pay for the fire department to have people employed to put the fire out." He concluded that to use fire services without paying the fee "would be sponging off your neighbor's $75."[5] But another conservative commentator, Daniel Foster, countered with this argument: "I have no problem with this kind of opt-in government in principle—especially in rural areas where individual need for governmental services and available infrastructure vary so widely. But forget the politics: what moral theory allows these firefighters (admittedly acting under orders) to watch this house burn to the ground when 1) they have already responded to the scene; 2) they have the means to stop it ready at hand; 3) they have a reasonable expectation to be compensated for their trouble?"[6]

Questions to Consider

1. Do you believe that the firefighters should have used their equipment to put out the fire, even though local policy explicitly told them not to?

2. Should Cranick have been able to pay on the spot for service, so the firefighters could save his house?

3. Do you think that a policy to opt-in for governmental programs—to pay in advance for basic municipal services—is a good one? Do you think there are some services where such a policy is appropriate and some where it is not? Consider, for example, a range of basic services including fire protection, police protection, garbage pickup, snow plowing, road repair, parks, recreation, and local schools. Are some services different from others—and, if so, how would you differentiate between them?

4. If local ordinances set clear policies for local administrators, under what circumstances might it be proper for these administrators to step over the policies? It must have been hard for the firefighters to watch a family grieve as all their possessions went up in flames. Then there is the free rider problem: if someone can plead their case in a crisis, why shouldn't everyone rely on their neighbors to pay for the cost of providing the service? Would it ever be permissible to go against policy in the case of need?

Notes

1. Bradley Blackburn, "Family Misses Fee, Firefighters Let House Burn," *ABC News,* October 6, 2010, http://abcnews.go.com/m/story?id=11806407.

2. "No Pay, No Spray: Firefighters Let Home Burn," *NBC,* October 6, 2010, No Pay, No Spray: Firefighters Let Home Burn.

3. Blackburn, "Family Misses Fee."

4. "No Pay, No Spray."

5. Evann Gastaldo, "Glenn Beck: Firefighters Right to Let Home Burn," *Newser,* October 6, 2010, http://www.newser.com/story/102300/glenn-beck-firefighters-right-to-let-home-burn.html.

6. Daniel Foster, "Pay-to-Spray Firefighters Watch as Home Burns," *National Review,* October 4, 2010, http://www.nationalreview.com/corner/248649/pay-spray-firefighters-watch-home-burns-daniel-foster.

CASE 10.3

Tweeting to the Rescue? How the Mayor of Newark Used Social Media to Improve Public Service Delivery

Some newswriters christened the 2010 Christmas weekend blizzard the Great Tsnownami or Snowmageddon. As nearly two feet of snow buried New York in deep drifts, in one of the five worst storms ever to hit the metropolitan region, thousands of flights were canceled and Amtrak was stalled for two days. Dozens of ambulances became stuck in drifts and even heavy front-loaders had to be tugged out of clogged city streets.

Local newspapers complained about the pace of snow removal. The website of the *New York Daily News* ran a photo of the Staten Island home of John Doherty, the sanitation commissioner.

"Does your street look like this?" the website asked. That street, the *Daily News* said, "was plowed clean," but "the dead-end streets on either side of his block remained a snow-choked winter blunderland."[1]

New York Mayor Michael Bloomberg acknowledged that "many New Yorkers are suffering serious hardships." He also said, however, "The world has not come to an end." In fact, "The city is going fine. Broadway shows were full last night. There are lots of tourists here enjoying themselves. I think that the message is that the city goes on." A *New York Times* writer thought wryly of Bloomberg's comment as he was looking at two men trying to push a Cadillac Escalade out of a Brooklyn snowbank, with the smell of burning rubber from spinning tires in the air. Were they thinking of taking in a Broadway play, the writer asked? One of the men trying to free the Escalade was incredulous. "Take in a play?" he asked. "What does the mayor suggest? Walking?" Times Square, after all, was a ten-mile hike or a half-hour drive, even in good traffic without snow.[2]

Across the Hudson River, Newark Mayor Cory Booker was camped on Twitter (http://twitter.com/corybooker) and was putting his own shoulder to the shovel. One woman said she was stuck and needed to get to a medical procedure. "I will dig you out. Where are you?" he Tweeted. One Twitter follower worried about how Booker's back was holding up. "Thanks 4 asking, back killing me," he responded. "Breakfast: Advil and Diet Coke."

Booker assured residents he was personally on the case. Two days after the storm ended, he Tweeted, "Stepping off streets for hour or so 2 take a meeting I couldn't cancel. We still have dozens of trucks & 100s of workers out clearing snow." When he got out of the meeting, he told a worried resident, "I'm on my way to Treamont Ave now to help dig your mom out." Then a Tweet arrived:

"don't forget brunswick street by astor." He was quickly back in touch. "Thanks for the heads up. I'm sending a crew. It will be there in a bit." From a worried resident, about Booker's trademark look: "Saw u out there on S Orange. Put a hat on that head. Us baldies can't be going commando out there." The reply: "No need I've got a hot head."

Snow removal has a long history of causing officials heartburn, both political and administrative. Chicago Mayor Michael Bilandic lost a primary election in 1979 because, most local political analysts believed, local voters punished him for failing to respond quickly enough to a major blizzard. In 1969, another New York blizzard so politically crippled Mayor John Lindsay that he never recovered. When he visited Queens, residents scorned him. "You should be ashamed of yourself," screamed one angry woman. Another said, "Get away, you bum."[3]

Booker was determined to avoid that fate. A Tweet arrived: "quitman/spruce need plowing. noone has touch those streets—becoming dangerous." He shot back, "We r on it. DM me ur # if u want 2 talk."

Questions to Consider

1. Compare the two strategies: Bloomberg and Booker. Consider the differences in scale between the two cities. Think about the differences in communication. Which do you believe was most effective?

2. How has the rise of social media, like Twitter and Facebook, changed the decision-making landscape, both in how officials make decisions and how they are *seen* to make decisions? How do social media affect the way accountability for public decisions might work?

3. Voters and citizens expect good results from their public officials. They expect to hold them accountable for their decisions and, as the Chicago and New York examples show, they can do so at the ballot box. On the other hand, is there a risk in a decision maker becoming too personally identified with individual actions on the front lines? Is there a risk that having a mayor shovel out the car of one resident himself might take him away from command decisions that affect opening up the streets for everyone? How should decision makers sort out the question of who makes which decisions?

Notes

1. Edgar Sandoval and Larry Mcshane, "Sanitation Boss John Doherty's Street Plowed Clean, But Nearby Streets Remain Winter Blunderland," *New York Daily News,* December 29, 2010, http://www.nydailynews.com/ny_local/2010/12/29/2010-12-29_a_madhouse_out_there_but_not_for_boss.html.
2. Michael Powell, "For A Snow-Crippled City, A Morsel of Humble Pie from the Mayor," *New York Times,* December 28, 2010, http://www.nytimes.com/2010/12/29/nyregion/29about.html.
3. Sewall Chan, "Remembering a Snowstorm That Paralyzed the City," *New York Times,* February 10, 2009, http://cityroom.blogs.nytimes.com/2009/02/10/remembering-a-snowstorm-that-paralyzed-the-city.

KEY CONCEPTS

bargaining approach   265

externalities   266

incrementalism   272

NIMBY phenomenon   277

participative decision-making approach   265

partisan mutual adjustment   272

Planning-Programming-Budgeting System (PPBS)   267

privatization   282

public-choice approach   265

rational decision making   265

satisficing   270

spillovers   266

FOR FURTHER READING

Allison, Graham T. *Essence of Decision: Explaining the Cuban Missile Crisis.* Boston: Little, Brown, 1971.

Cohen, Michael, James March, and Johan Olsen. "A Garbage Can Model of Organizational Choice." *Administrative Science Quarterly* 17 (March 1972): 1-25.

Downs, Anthony. *An Economic Theory of Democracy.* New York: Harper and Row, 1957.

Etzioni, Amitai. "Mixed Scanning: A Third Approach to Decision-Making." *Public Administration Review* 27 (December 1967): 385-392.

Lindblom, Charles E. "The Science of 'Muddling Through.'" *Public Administration Review* 19 (Spring 1959): 79-88.

Simon, Herbert A. *Administrative Behavior: A Study of Decision-Making Processes in Administrative Organization.* 3rd ed. New York: Free Press, 1945, 1976.

SUGGESTED WEBSITES

The study and practice of decision making has produced a vast array of approaches to this important and complex field. Many areas of public policy have developed new methods of decision making, for instance, in the environmental arena (see the Global Development Research Center, **www.gdrc.org/decision**). In health care, many practitioners have argued for an approach to the field that is based far more on the application of evidence, including work at websites like **www.evidencebased.net**. Moreover, the Federal Executive Institute's training programs for the federal government's top managers contains a wide-ranging collection of courses on decision making (see **www.leadership.opm.gov**).

The Society for Judgment and Decision Making has prepared a useful website, which contains links to a wide spectrum of work in the field (see **www.sjdm.org/links.html**). In addition, the *International Journal of Information Technology and Decision Making*, **www.worldscinet.com/ijitdm/ijitdm.shtml**, regularly reviews cutting-edge thinking on the subject.

CHAPTER

11

Budgeting

CHAPTER OBJECTIVES

- Understand the twin roles of budgeting: steering the economy and making political choices

- Chart the steps in the budgetary process

- Explore the challenges to budgeting

- Compare federal versus state and local government budgeting

Air travelers across the country were furious in 2013 when furloughs of air traffic controllers slowed down traffic at airports across the country, including here in Atlanta. The Federal Aviation Administration won an exemption from the sequestration, but many other federal employees were furloughed throughout the rest of the fiscal year.

IF DECISION MAKING IS THE CENTRAL ADMINISTRATIVE ACT, budgeting is the fundamental administrative decision. Bold rhetoric is important, but ideas are nothing without the money to back them up. Budgets both set and embody the basic priorities. To know what an organization—or a government—truly values, look at how the money is spent. Likewise, to change an organization's priorities, change the budget. According to an old saying, attributed to many insiders, "Grab them by their budgets, and their hearts and minds will follow." Most of the big battles in government—and in public administration—sooner or later become budgeting battles. That, in turn, makes budget making perhaps the most central political act in public administration.

Budget decisions are both important and political because they frame the focus on three central questions that have recurred throughout history.[1]

First, *what should government do?* Budgeting is, at its core, the fundamental decision about the use of scarce resources from the people. There are always more good ideas than there is money to fund them. Just how big should government be? Which public programs most deserve the public's support: highways or health care, weapons or welfare? Budgetary politics is enmeshed in perpetual conflict because it involves the toughest, most central questions that societies must answer.

Second, *who in government should decide these questions?* Throughout the history of the United States, the balance of financial power has shifted between the national and subnational governments, and between the legislature and the executive. The budgetary arena has been the continuing forum for broad policy disputes and pitched battles over not only who should benefit from governmental programs but also who should decide the fate of those programs. Charting the *who* of budgets also provides a strong guide to sources of real governmental power.

Finally, *how should citizens and public officials make these decisions?* In 1940 political scientist V. O. Key Jr. framed the classic problem: "On what basis shall it be decided to allocate *x* dollars to activity A instead of activity B?"[2] Budgeting is about scarcity, and there are always more claims on budget dollars than there is money to spend. Budget makers always face the challenge of deciding which claims are funded—and which are not. In part, this is a question is about process. In part, it is about analysis and what defines the best way of making decisions, as we saw in Chapter 10. In part, it is about politics and the battles over the public's money. And in part, it is about basic values about how decisions should be made. In fact, note how often the word *should* appears in discussions about budgeting. That provides a hint about the big value debates that are never far from any budgetary discussion.

This chapter explores these questions in sorting out the functions and processes of budgeting. It begins with an examination of the far-reaching economic and political roles of the budget. It continues by probing the basic parts of the budgetary process: budget making, budget appropriation, and budget execution. Finally, it concludes by reviewing the relationship between budgetary politics and public administration. State and local governments vary tremendously in the way they budget and account for their money, and trying to describe the full range of their practices would fill another book this size. So this chapter will focus heavily on the federal government's budget strategies and tactics to explore the basic issues that stretch across the budgetary issues for all governments.

THE BUDGET'S TWIN ROLES

All budgets are about financial decisions. At the federal level, the budget plays an additional role, because of how the budget shapes the national economy. Because these decisions affect the allocation of resources among competing claimants, the budget has important political effects as well. After exploring these broad economic features, we'll turn to the issues affecting budgets at the federal, state, and local levels.

The Economic Role

The very size of the government's financial activity inevitably makes it a strong player in the national economy.[3] That role is reciprocal: the budget has enormous impact on the economy, and the economy plays a strong role in shaping the budget. That leads, not surprisingly, to the conclusion that because the budget *can* be used to steer the economy, it *should* do so.

The Budget's Effect on the Economy

Let's start with the basics. Governments do their accounting by their budget calendar, known as the **fiscal year.** They can run a **surplus** (where revenues exceed expenditures) or a **deficit** (where expenditures exceed revenues). Governments can borrow money in the short term and repay it in the long term. This is **debt.** At the federal level, the government borrows money to finance deficits, and the accumulated deficits over time produce the **national debt.** Federal surpluses have been relatively rare, so most of the debate hinges on the role of deficits and the management of the national debt. At the state and local level, both constitutional restrictions and good economic practice require balanced budgets. State and local governments borrow money—that is, they incur debt—but the basic principle is that they ought to borrow money over the long term only to pay for items that have long lives, and borrow money only for the life of the project. For example, if a state wants to build a bridge that will last twenty-five years, it would borrow money by issuing a twenty-five-year bond. If a local government wants to buy a new school building that will last twenty years, it would issue a twenty-year bond. Sound practice, and in many cases the law, prohibit state and local governments from borrowing money for long periods to fund short-term expenses, like salaries and program expenses.

At least since the Great Depression in the 1930s, economists and government officials have recognized that government taxation and spending, known as **fiscal policy,** affect the economy. (The word *fiscal* is Old French in origin and appears to have roots in the Latin word for "treasury" or "basket," terms which, put together, sum up the topic well.) British economist John Maynard Keynes argued that government can—and should—use the budget to steer the economy: to boost employment, to cut inflation, to improve the nation's balance of trade abroad, and to keep the value of the dollar secure.[4] That theory has grown into the cornerstone of macroeconomics and the study of the broad interactions between government's economic activity and the behavior of the economy. Belief in the power of fiscal policy to steer the economy reached its zenith with the Kennedy tax cut, passed in 1964 after John F. Kennedy's assassination to spur economic growth.[5] Since then, presidents and economists alike have tangled over the relationship between taxes, spending, and the economy, and what combination would produce the best long-run economic growth.

Economists have long recognized that the economy goes through cycles of growth and recession. Keynesian economics preaches that the government can use its taxing and spending powers to moderate those cycles, to offset the dangers of both too-rapid growth (inflation) and recession (unemployment). The theory suggests that in good times, the government ought to run a surplus to keep the economy from expanding too quickly; in bad times, it should run a deficit to keep the economy from becoming sluggish. Because state and local budgets must be balanced, and because no individual state or local budget is big enough to steer the national economy, this is a tool exclusive to the federal budget. And it inevitably creates temptations to use the budget's steering forces for political advantage.[6]

Although the basic Keynesian model retains a strong hold on economists and budgeters, in practice it has lost most of its power. The federal government has fallen into an overwhelming pattern of deficits; since 1973, the federal budget has been in surplus only four times, between 1998 and 2001. In fact, as Figure 11.1 shows, deficits have been the rule for most of our recent history. Using the budget to steer the economy requires making decisions that can shift the

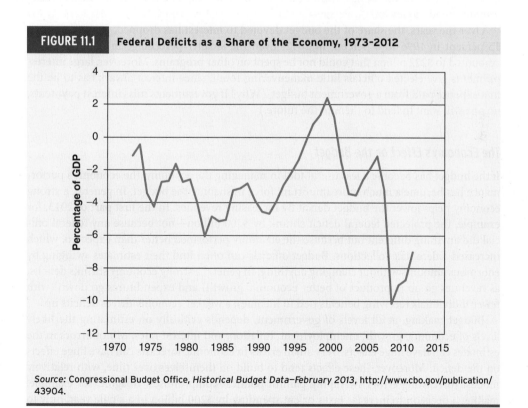

FIGURE 11.1   **Federal Deficits as a Share of the Economy, 1973-2012**

Source: Congressional Budget Office, *Historical Budget Data–February 2013*, http://www.cbo.gov/publication/43904.

budget from surplus to deficit and back again; the overwhelming sea of red ink has the budget's engines stuck in one direction, constantly pumping stimulus into the economy. That, in turn, has left most of the work of steering the economy to the Federal Reserve, which has used its power to manage interest rates and the money supply (called **monetary policy**).[7] As deficits have become a near-permanent condition of fiscal policy, the Fed and its monetary policy have become the only game in town. In fact, when the collapse of the financial markets crippled the national—and the global—economy in 2008, it was the Fed and its central bank partners around the world that provided most of the tools to cushion the fall.

Most economists agree that continued huge deficits are unsupportable. The more money the government borrows, the less there is left for private investment (and thus to feed future growth). They argue that big deficits over the long run make inflation worse than it would otherwise be. They contend that large deficits would tie the federal government's hands in fighting future recessions, since there would be limited ability to increase spending and thus stimulate the economy. Finally, they conclude that deficits over the long run would worsen the nation's international trading position by eroding the value of the dollar. In the short run, deficits can help the government negotiate through difficult economic problems, but budget deficits over the long run are dangerous. The larger the deficit, the more the federal budget must be devoted simply to paying interest. The more money paid in interest, the less money that is available for the things, from new roads to new weapons, that public officials really want to spend money on.

Over the years, the share of the budget devoted to interest has dropped, from more than 15 percent in 1996 to 6 percent in 2012. Even the smaller percentage in 2012, however, amounted to $222 billion that could not be spent on other programs. Moreover, large interest payments give elected officials little maneuvering room, since interest always has to be the first expense paid from a government budget. (Why? If governments miss interest payments, no one will want to lend to them in the future.)

The Economy's Effect on the Budget

If the budget has become a less useful tool in managing the economy, the economy's performance has become a much more important force in shaping the budget. In general, a strong economy helps lower the budget deficit by increasing revenues. In the first part of 2013, for example, the projected federal deficit shrank by $200 billion—not because any federal official did anything different but because the economy performed better than expected, which increased federal tax collections. Budget officials can often find their estimates swinging by enormous amounts without changing anything. In general a strong economy shrinks deficits, as revenues go up (a product of better economic growth) and expenditures go down (with fewer individuals receiving benefits tied to income); a weaker economy drives deficits up.

Budget making, at all levels of government, depends critically on estimating the likely levels of economic growth, unemployment, inflation, and interest rates. Minor errors in the estimates can have huge effects. Very small errors in economic forecasts can have huge effects on the deficit. Moreover, these effects tend to build on themselves over time, with relatively modest forecasting errors swamping painful political compromises. Imagine, for example, making a decision to increase taxes or cut spending by $200 billion in a single year, only to have changes in the economy swamp these decisions. That in turn tempts budget analysts to choose economic forecasts that makes their job easier. As Rudolph G. Penner, former head of the Congressional Budget Office, and Alan J. Abramson, explain,

> Changing a deficit estimate by $10 billion by changing an economic forecast is a minor statistical event. Changing policies sufficiently to alter a deficit estimate by $10 billion is a significant political event. This asymmetry creates an enormous temptation to achieve a given target deficit reduction by adopting optimistic economic assumptions rather than by cutting programs or raising taxes.[8]

That can make it possible for deficits to shrink or even evaporate in the long run. It also helps explain why that hopeful long-run day never seems to arrive. As former Citicorp President Walter Wriston put it, "A government budget deficit is the intersection of two wild guesses [on expenditures and revenues] a year from now."[9]

These crosscurrents—the effect of the budget on the economy and the effect of the economy on the budget—have taken on greater importance through the years. The federal budget is far greater than the sum of the government's expenditures and revenues: it is a statement of the government's relationship with the rest of the economy and of political officials' attempts to influence economic performance. The crosscurrents have, in addition, affected the way the budget is made. The technique and politics of forecasting have taken on a far larger role, and this in turn has opened a new arena in which fundamental budget battles are fought. Finally, the crosscurrents have enhanced the role of the staff members who run the computer models that produce the economic estimates.[10]

The Political Development of the Budgetary Process

Budgeting is, of course, much more than an economic decision about how to allocate citizens' wealth among governmental programs. Budgeting embodies fundamental political choices, both about values—which programs get funded and which do not—and institutions, especially the relative sway of the legislative and executive branches of government.

Forecasts of low economic growth, or even a recession, can prove especially difficult for policymakers. A slow economy drives up spending, shrinks tax revenue, and increases the deficit. It is little wonder, therefore, that top officials shy away from forecasts of a slow economy, because they make budgeting even more painful. In the Carter administration, Alfred Kahn, adviser on inflation and later chairman of the Council on Wage and Price Stability, got into trouble with the president's political advisers for talking too much about the risks of a recession. He continued to insist on speaking his mind, but he changed his language. In briefings, he substituted the word "banana" for "recession" and discussed the risk that the economy might encounter a banana. For politicians, as Clinton political strategist James Carville was fond of pointing out, "It's the economy, stupid." The economy always has enormous political implications for political campaigns—and big effects on the budget. It's little wonder that the economics and politics of the budget are so closely intertwined.

First Steps

Americans have always distrusted public officials' dealing with their money. The Boston Tea Party was about the king's effort to tax the colonists. When the new country came to life, there were big debates about how best to organize the country's financial operations. Although there was little question that the State and War departments would each be headed by a single secretary, Congress considered putting the Treasury under the control of a board (so that no single person could become too powerful) and keeping the board under its own tight control (so that the legislative branch could closely oversee how the executive spent money). Although the Constitution clearly granted the executive branch the power to wage war and make treaties, it gave Congress the power to coin money, levy taxes, and appropriate money. The Constitution explicitly requires that all tax measures originate in the House of Representatives, the body that the founders believed would be the "people's house," to make sure that citizens had a voice in their own taxation. Ever since, budgetary politics has been a forum for sharp competition between the president and Congress.[11] Two different national banks collapsed under populist pressure—and the Internal Revenue Service has long been one of Americans' least favorite agencies.

For America's first century, federal budgeting was mostly a congressional function. The so-called budget submitted to Congress by the executive branch, in fact, was little more than the Treasury Department's assembly of agency and departmental requests. Congress was the central force in budgeting.

The Rise of Presidential Power

At the beginning of the twentieth century, the Progressive movement increased citizens' concern about the management of government at all levels. Budgetary reform swept state and local government as part of the broader trend toward strengthened executive powers.[12] By the end of World War I, the congressionally dominated system had proved inadequate for managing the federal government's vastly expanded fiscal functions, and the budget-reform movement launched in the states and cities bubbled up to the federal level.

The culmination of this movement was passage in 1921 of the Budget and Accounting Act, which revolutionized federal budgeting. For the first time, the president was to submit an annual budget to Congress. A Bureau of the Budget was created in the Treasury Department (and later moved to the president's own executive office) to assemble and adjust, if necessary, the department's requests to conform to the president's program.[13] Meanwhile, the Treasury Department's auditing functions were transferred to Congress's new General Accounting Office (GAO, which was renamed the Government Accountability Office in 2004). By gaining the authority to produce their own budget, presidents acquired leverage over both the executive branch departments and agencies—which first had to bargain with the president before having their requests sent to Congress—and Congress itself, because the document submitted by the president would frame the terms of debate.

The 1921 act thus divided the traditional budget functions into areas of executive and legislative supremacy: budget preparation and execution in the executive branch, budget appropriation and post-audit in the legislative branch, and shared executive-legislative authority over budget control.[14] The division has always been sloppy, but the act nevertheless put the president into a position of preeminence not previously known.

from the Headlines...

Do Rising Sea Levels Threaten Cities?

Superstorm Sandy's 2012 assault on the northeastern United States sent shudders down the spines of local planners. With roads, bridges, water, sewer, and even New York City's fabled subway system crippled, did the region face more superstorms in the future?

A paper in the *Proceedings of the National Academy of Sciences* painted a bleak picture: climate change, said author Benjamin Strauss, threatened the stability of more than 1,400 towns and cities—including New Orleans, Miami, Atlantic City, and Virginia Beach—up the coast. Carbon emissions to date, he warned, will put parts of 316 cities underwater. A continuation of current patterns of global warming could threaten an additional 1,100 cities, which could find themselves under water at high tide.

Of course, not all scientists agree with Strauss, and even some scientists who have concluded that the threat is real worry that looking so far down the road could distract planners in local governments who need to make decisions in the next few decades. But Sandy's ravage made the issue inescapable. The future is uncertain, but some of the implications, thanks to Sandy, are already clear. Some of the long-term effects are difficult to predict, but waiting until they're clear could make it impossible to react in time. Some decisions require national—and global—action, but local officials can make some decisions that could help their own communities. What should local government officials do now? How can they best ensure the welfare of their citizens in the face of uncertainty?

Source: Wendy Koch, "Study: Sea-level Rise Threatens 1,400 U.S. Cities," *USA Today,* July 29, 2013, http://www.usatoday.com/story/news/nation/2013/07/29/sea-level-rise-cities-towns/2593727.

Moreover, the growing pressure of the federal deficit steadily enhanced the power of the president and budget makers, especially within the executive branch. The budgetary process produced strange twists and turns, sometimes with the budget makers' own peculiar vocabulary and complex recordkeeping. As the budgetary process limped along, the short-term bargains that kept it alive required central oversight within the executive branch of each agency's spending patterns, and performing that task in turn enhanced the role of the Office of Management and Budget (OMB), which grew out of the president's Bureau of the Budget.[15]

The Budget and Accounting Act of 1921 proved a significant advance in presidential power—in many ways, it marked the emergence of the modern presidency. It was the beginning of fifty years of steadily growing presidential dominance over Congress in the budgetary process. While Congress has tried, especially since the mid-1970s, to regain its earlier preeminence in the budgetary process, the president has held the upper hand over most of the years since.[16] These struggles between the branches have played themselves out in the arenas of budget making, budget appropriation, and budget execution. (Chapter 14 deals with a related part of the budgetary process, post-audit and performance measurement.)

BUDGET MAKING

We now turn to the basic steps for budgets at all levels of government. The first step is preparation of the budget: a set of spending and revenue plans combined in a single document.[17] While the details vary around the country, the process typically includes both top-down and bottom-up features.[18]

Budgeting: Top-Down

A government's budget is not simply a collection of agencies' spending requests. Instead, each government's executive—whether mayor, city manager, county administrator, governor, or president—sets broad targets for overall spending and revenues. These broad targets are the product of estimates made by the executive's budget staff: how expected changes in the economy will affect revenues and expenditures (will the economy's growth bring more tax collection, or will its slump put higher demands on welfare?); how demographic changes are likely to affect existing programs (will more school-age children require the school board to hire more teachers?); and how major planned program changes will affect spending (how much money will be required to launch a new defense system?).[19]

 Budget preparation is virtually nonstop, with the process pegged to the start of the fiscal year. (At the federal level, the fiscal year begins on October 1. Most state and local governments have a July 1 start for their fiscal years.) Well before the beginning of the fiscal year, economic forecasters estimate the revenue that will likely be available. They also calculate the likely costs of decisions made in the past, such as a multiyear legislation (a five-year job training program that might be in year two) and automatic programs (such as spending for Social Security and Medicare, which are based on formulas including the number of eligible individuals and the likely cost of the services). This produces a three-part package of spending, revenue, and economic estimates, which form the basis for the executive's initial decisions. These decisions produce targets that go out to agency heads, who then break down the targets into subtargets for their operating units. Budget proposals, including requests for new money for new programs, then flow back up the chain to the budget director, with final appeals going to the executive in the weeks before the budget is officially submitted to the legislature (Congress, state legislature, county board, or city council) for review and action.

Preparing the federal budget thus begins nearly a full year before the finished document is submitted to Congress, more than a year and a half before the fiscal year begins, and two and a half years before the fiscal year's end. Getting the numbers right requires an especially good crystal ball—and it makes constant tinkering inevitable. At any given time, administrators must deal with three different sets of figures: executing the current fiscal year's budget, defending the next year's requests before the legislature, and making budget estimates for the year after that. Any year's budget battle is thus actually part of interlocking skirmishes that stretch over many years.[20]

Budgeting: Bottom-Up

The top-down snapshot is the big picture, full of worries about the size of the budget deficit, the budget's role in macroeconomic policy, and large-scale policy changes such as the introduction of new defense systems, new schools, or new highways. From the point of view of lower-level administrators, however, the picture is much different.

The central theory (both descriptively and prescriptively) of bottom-up budgeting is incrementalism, originally put forth by Aaron Wildavsky. It builds on the theory of incremental decision making explored in Chapter 10, and it captures the twin threads of the theory: incrementalism, he argues, is both the best description of how budgeting works and the best prescription for how it *should* work. How much should an agency official request in the budget preparation process? How should it answer V. O. Key's basic question about how resources are to be allocated? Wildavsky's answer was that officials do, and should, begin with their budget base and ask for a "fair share" increase. "The base is the general expectation among the participants that programs will be carried on at close to the going level of expenditures," Wildavsky explained. The increments are relatively small increases over the existing base that reflect the agency's share of changes in the budgetary pie.[21]

In budgeting, incrementalism thus has two important implications. First, no one really considers every amount for every item in the budget. The package is too big for anyone to examine everything, so it is far easier and, Wildavsky argues, more rational to focus on *changes*. Second, the political battles focus on the size of an agency's increment—and of the increment's size compared with those received by other agencies. Budgeting is a battle fought on the margins, with the sharpest struggles focused on changes in the distribution of the government's pie.

Incremental theory, both as a description of how budgeting operates and as a primer on how agency officials should behave, has dominated the budgeting debate since the first publication of Wildavsky's work in 1966.[22] Many theorists have taken sharp issue with his view, for three reasons. First, incremental budgeting begins with the budget base, but the definition of that concept is anything but clear. It can be the current estimate of spending in the previous year, although that estimate constantly changes as legislators act on the budget and agencies carry out their programs. It can be the cost of continuing current activities at the same level, which includes increases for inflation and population shifts and decreases for improved productivity. Finally, it can be a spending level set by law, which often can be a different amount from the first two.

Second, budget experts do not always make changes from the existing level of spending in small increments. On average, budgeting does appear incremental, but the averages hide the rich politics of budgeting: aggressive program managers seeking to build budgets, budget officials seeking to keep a ceiling on total spending, and executives and their staffs seeking to pursue new initiatives.[23] Big changes sometimes do occur. In the turbulent weeks after the September 11, 2001, terrorist attacks, the Bush administration led an effort to federalize all airport screeners in a single, massive shift of responsibility from the private sector.

Third, the real focus of budgetary politics is not changes in *agencies'* budgets but changes in their *programs'* budgets. At the agency level, budgets and politics are usually rather stable. "Yet within departmental and agency boundaries (and occasionally between them . . .), there is a constant struggle by program directors, lobbyists, congressmen, state and local politicians, and White House personnel to fund new ideas and to continue the funding of old ones," analysts conclude. The competitive success of alternative programs, not changes in the budgets of agencies, occupies budget makers, and in that arena it is the power of the policy entrepreneurs who can build the strongest political case for their ideas that makes the difference.[24]

In short, the incrementalism model has many shortcomings, from areas such as fair-share increases to the budget base. It nevertheless continues to have a very powerful force on budgeting. Most budgeters tend to think about their budgets as a search for increases over their base. Most reporters focus on those debates. And there's a powerful momentum in the system toward the model, even if it doesn't always capture budgeting reality. Despite its weaknesses, incrementalism tends to capture the way most people think about budgeting—how it works and even how it *ought* to work.

Attempts to Reform Incrementalism

Especially since the mid-1960s, chief executives have experimented with different budget reform techniques to secure greater control over budget preparation. Most notable was Lyndon Johnson's Planning-Programming-Budgeting System (PPBS), which Chapter 10 discussed. During the Nixon administration, OMB attempted a different strategy, **management by objectives (MBO)**, which was intended to strengthen the ability of managers to manage. Agency heads and their principal executives would fix on quantified objectives to be attained in the coming year and then break down each objective into targets for achievement in, say, each quarter year; this process would then be repeated in turn for each subordinate. MBO had a mixed record: in some departments and bureaus it made a significant contribution; in many others it failed and was quickly abandoned. As with PPBS, there has been "a noticeable disenchantment with MBO as a panacea in the government."[25]

When Jimmy Carter took office in 1977, he brought with him the **zero-base budgeting (ZBB)** approach that he had used as governor of Georgia. ZBB was an assault on incrementalism from a different perspective, but it was not, despite the name, budgeting from a zero base. Instead, budgeters began from a certain level of spending (say, 80 percent of current expenditures); they then assembled "decision packages" (consisting of different ways of increasing the level of services) and then ranked them. In this way, decision makers could set priorities for spending increases.[26] ZBB seemed attractive at first, but it encouraged agency budget makers to play games with the process (for instance, by ranking very low a project they knew would never be cut, in the hope that they could win funding for other programs at the same time). These tactics, combined with ZBB's paperwork burden, led to a short life at the federal level. At the state and local levels, however, many governments continued to find the process a helpful one for making choices within their smaller budgets.[27]

Since then, executives have tried a variety of performance-based tools to get greater leverage over the budgetary process. Bill Clinton had his **National Performance Review**, which managers used to devise strategies for improving government operations while setting top-down targets for reducing the number of government employees. George W. Bush instituted a new **Program Assessment Rating Tool (PART)** and sought to integrate measures of agency performance with budgetary decisions. Barack Obama used a more decentralized management agenda designed to improve the cross-boundary management of government programs. Similar strategies have emerged at the state and local levels of government. But from this remarkable cauldron of innovation, two conclusions have emerged. First, every chief executive now feels obliged to launch a major reform in analysis and management to improve control over the budget. Second, few of these reforms endure, because they rarely give executives real leverage over decisions that are inevitably political.

The Rise of the Uncontrollables

Even more important, more government spending has become dictated by past policy decisions, especially at the federal level. At the federal level, budgeters encounter the stark reality of **uncontrollable expenditures,** which are dictated by mandatory formulas for programs like Social Security and Medicare. As Figure 11.2 shows, discretionary spending—the share of the budget not locked in by these mandatory formulas or by interest in the debt—fell from 67 percent in 1962 to 36 percent in 2012. At the same time, mandatory spending (including entitlement programs, like Social Security and Medicare, where recipients are entitled to benefits by law) grew from 32 percent to 63 percent. Even with "discretionary" programs, however, government officials often have little real discretion. Having signed contracts for new weapons systems, defense planners don't want to walk away from their investment. It wouldn't be easy to shut down federal prisons and national parks, and no one wants to send the armed forces home without pay. In any given year, the share of the budget over which the

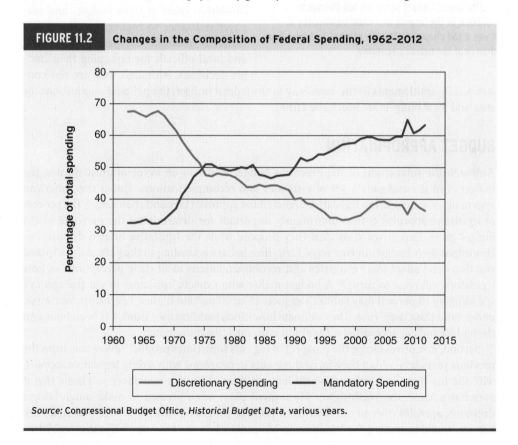

| **FIGURE 11.2** | **Changes in the Composition of Federal Spending, 1962–2012** |

Source: Congressional Budget Office, *Historical Budget Data,* various years.

Economic decline and continuing budget problems led Detroit to declare bankruptcy in 2013, in the largest municipal bankruptcy in American history. It was a sad chapter in the life of what had once been one of the biggest drivers of the nation's economy.

president and Congress have any real control is thus very, very small. It's little wonder, therefore, that as controllable spending has shrunk, budgetary politics has become more intense. When members of Congress tried to make good on the Tea Party movement's pledge to slash spending in 2011, debates raged about cutting funding for National Public Radio and reducing the pay of federal workers.

State and local governments do not tend to measure uncontrollables as explicitly as the federal government does. But many state governments find that formula-based spending for many programs, from aid to local schools to money for highways, takes up a growing share of their budgets. Moreover, years of tight budgets and taxpayer resistance to higher taxes have dramatically reduced the flexibility of state and local officials for reshaping their budget decisions. Although they are not constrained by entitlements in the same way as the federal budget, the political implications for state and local budgets are much the same.

BUDGET APPROPRIATION

Although the submission of the executive budget is always an event of great theater, the budget is in the end only a set of estimates and recommendations. Under the American system of government, the legislative branch must approve taxes and spending.[28] The process of legislative approval is thus enormously important for determining the outcome of the budget game. Executives know that they propose while the legislative branch disposes, so they adjust their budgets in two ways. First, they behave according to the **rule of anticipated reactions** and adapt their estimates and recommendations to fit their perceptions of how legislators will react to them.[29] A budget maker who expects legislators to cut the agency's spending by 10 percent may submit a request 15 or 20 percent higher. Legislators, of course, understand this classic ruse. They estimate how much padding they think has been built into the budget and cut accordingly. The result is an intricate chess match.

Second, executives facing the prospect of big cuts sometimes propose severe cuts from the previous year's levels—but they focus those cuts in programs with strong legislative support, with the bet that the legislators won't dare cut them. This is a maneuver so classic that it even has a name: the **Washington Monument ploy**: when pressed to make tough budget decisions, agencies offer to cut their most popular programs (which, for the National Park Service, would be closing the Washington Monument), in the full knowledge that legislators will never allow such cuts to take effect (see Case Study 11.2 for the background on the Washington Monument ploy and for a recent example of how budgeters use it). The executive may also propose new taxes to bring the budget into balance, and then leave to legislators the tough decision to reject the taxes or risk a deficit.[30] Veteran budgeters have a long catalog of games they've become especially skilled at playing.

Congressional Budget Decisions

With the Congressional Budget Act of 1974, Congress launched major reforms of the budget process.[31] The act shifted the start of the fiscal year from July 1 to October 1 to give Congress more time to complete its work on the budget. It also mandated that the president each year present a "current services budget" projection: an estimate of the cost of continuing in the new fiscal year all the previous year's programs, at the same level and without policy changes. Members of Congress thus hoped to separate debate over program changes from proposals for continuation of existing programs—that is, to force the president to identify increments, and decrements, in the budget. The act also created new budget committees in each house and instituted a three-part legislative process to accompany them:

1. *Setting the totals.* For the first time, Congress obligated itself to prepare a **legislative budget**: an estimate of total expenditures and revenues—and thus of the deficit. To do the job, the 1974 act established a new Committee on the Budget in each house. Early each year, each congressional committee reports to the budget committee of its respective chamber about the cost of bills it anticipates passing. Each house's budget committee then revises these requests and combines them into a single resolution that sets estimates of revenues and ceilings on expenditures. Supporting this work was the creation of the Congressional Budget Office, to provide staff support and a counterweight to the president's Office of Management and Budget.

2. *Authorizing programs.* Next, the subject-area committees create **authorizations** for programs under their purview. These authorizations, approved by both houses of Congress and signed by the president, can be for one year (including much of the government's routine operations); for several years (including many defense programs); or for permanent programs (including Social Security), which remain in effect until the basic law is changed. These authorizations set ceilings on the money that Congress can spend on programs or, in the case of permanent authorizations, define the standards by which benefits are to be paid.

3. *Appropriating money.* While authorizations create the programs, **appropriations** provide the money to fund them. Congress can authorize a program without providing any appropriations for it, and it often authorizes higher spending than can be covered by the appropriations it is willing to provide. The reverse, of course, does not happen, since appropriations cannot exceed the original authorization. Like authorizations, appropriations can last for varying lengths of time. The appropriations committees in each house decide how much money should actually be spent by recommending **budget authority.**

This three-step process, however, does not precisely define the items that get the most attention: how much revenue the government actually collects, the money it actually spends, and the level of the deficit (which is the amount by which spending exceeds revenues). Revenues and spending depend heavily not only on Congress's authorizations and appropriations, but also on the level of spending in automatic programs like entitlements as well as the state of the economy and how fast administrators can spend money (which sometimes proves far harder than one might imagine, given the complexity of government's processes). So to get a fix on the deficit, congressional analysts must produce estimates of revenues as well as how much money the government will actually spend, which is known as **outlays.**

As Figure 11.3 shows, estimating outlays (and, therefore, the deficit) is a complicated process: analysts must determine how much budget authority from past years will be used in a given fiscal year, how much new budget authority will be created and spent, how much previous budget authority will expire at the end of its time limit, and how much budget authority will be carried over into subsequent years. For some uncontrollable spending, such as Medicare, the outlays depend on how many people get sick and what kinds of treatment they require. Outlays can vary according to the rate of unemployment or the progress in building a new fighter at an aircraft plant or how many natural disasters strike. Thus, no matter how close a watch Congress keeps on its books, it has only a loose rein on outlays in any given year. Hard-fought congressional deficit battles, which revolve around budget authority

---

FIGURE 11.3   **Relationship of Budget Authority to Outlays for 2014**

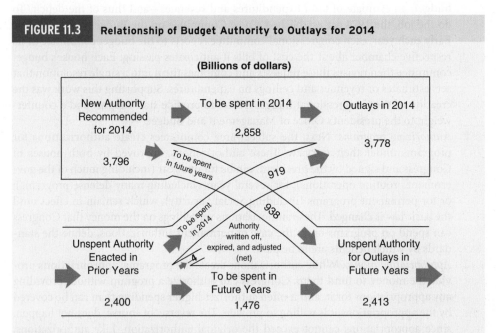

(Billions of dollars)

New Authority Recommended for 2014	To be spent in 2014	Outlays in 2014
3,796	2,858	3,778

To be spent in future years

919

938

To be spent in 2014

Unspent Authority Enacted in Prior Years	Authority written off, expired, and adjusted (net)	Unspent Authority for Outlays in Future Years
2,400	To be spent in Future Years 1,476	2,413

Source: U.S. Office of Management and Budget, *Budget of the United States Government: Fiscal Year 2014, Analytical Perspectives* (Washington, D.C.: OMB, 2014), 130, http://www.whitehouse.gov/sites/default/files/omb/budget/fy2014/assets/spec.pdf.

levels, can be undone when outlay totals do not cooperate—if, for example, economic growth proves sluggish, interest rates rise, or unemployment surges.

Bumps in the Federal Budget Process

The 1974 federal congressional budget reforms have struggled since the beginning, but in recent years the challenges have grown to the breaking point. First, more of the budget is classified, and this **black budget** does not receive the same oversight as other kinds of federal spending. As one aviation policy analyst put it, "The Pentagon's 'black' budget for secret programs is a riddle wrapped in a mystery inside an enigma, taped up in a Wheaties box and locked in a safe that has then been built into a bridge abutment adjacent to the one containing the mortal remains of Jimmy Hoffa," the union leader who mysteriously disappeared in 1975.[32] The only people in government who know what or how much is in this black budget cannot tell, and the size and scale of these secret projects are hidden from all but a handful of members of Congress. Some projects have secret code names, such as "Tractor Rose" or "Retract Larch," while others are funded by vague appropriations that do not describe what the money buys. The black budget hides the size of the Central Intelligence Agency's budget, estimated at $40 billion, and there is no way to tell how much the government spends for its spy satellites, intelligence gathering, and research and development of top-secret weapons programs. One estimate put the Defense Department's black budget at $57.8 billion in fiscal year 2011, with billions more hidden in other agencies.[33] The Clinton administration used the black budget to pay for spy satellites, and the second Bush administration expanded it to support its so-called war on terrorism as well as the wars in Afghanistan and Iraq. The entire process, one author wrote, has long been plagued by a "bewildering babble of classified code words and nicknames" that made effective spending control impossible.[34] Officials who work in the programs often sport embroidered patches. One for "Project Zipper" shows a smiling face with sunglasses and a zipped mouth and the motto "We make threats not promises." Another has a mushroom on a dark background—mushrooms are grown in the dark—and the motto *Semper en Obscurus* (always in the dark). A third quotes the first-century Roman emperor Caligula with *Oderint Dum Metuant,* which means "let them hate so long as they fear."[35] The growing size of the black budget pulls more defense and intelligence spending out of regular review through the congressional budget process. Following Edward Snowden's leak in 2013 of an enormous quantity of classified information, including reports on the black budget itself, the entire process came under much tougher scrutiny.

Second, although the shift in the start of the federal fiscal year from July 1 to October 1 was designed to give Congress more time to finish its work, Congress has fallen further and further behind in its schedule. As noted budget expert Philip G. Joyce has found, Congress managed to get its work done on time just three times since 1977 (in fiscal years 1989, 1995, and 1997).[36] When Congress can't complete its work,

Officials who work on classified black budget programs within the Department of Defense sometimes wear embroidered arm patches, like the one pictured here.

it has resorted to passing **continuing resolutions,** which allow the government to continue operating until Congress passes a budget—or another continuing resolution. Sometimes (as in 1979) Congress has operated the entire year on a single continuing resolution. At other times, it has passed a flurry of continuing resolutions, with the record at 21 in 2001, Joyce found. Congress sometimes has failed to pass a continuing resolution, and since 1980 that has had draconian consequences. That year, Attorney General Benjamin Civiletti took a tough view on Article I, Section 9 of the Constitution, which states that "No Money shall be drawn from the Treasury, but in Consequence of Appropriations Made by Law." In practice, that meant that if appropriations expire, no federal agency can spend money. As Joyce has pointed out, "the consequences of failed budgets became much more real after 1980."[37] For example, fierce battles between the Clinton administration and Republican House Speaker Newt Gingrich led to a five-day shutdown in November 1995, followed by a twenty-one-day shutdown stretching from late December 1995 through early January 1996, which was then capped by an epic blizzard that further crippled the capital. During such shutdowns, essential employees (like air traffic controllers and federal prison guards) can continue to work, but other employees must go home—and not even touch their government-issued smartphones.

Third, in an effort to force a budget agreement, Congress in 2011 invoked a process called **sequestration**. In 1985, Congress passed the Gramm-Rudman-Hollings Deficit Reduction Act, named after the three Senators who sponsored it. It was intended to increase budgetary discipline. Under the budget process, Congress passed an overall budget resolution, setting a target for spending, and then individual appropriations bills. If the appropriations bills exceeded the amount that Congress agreed to in the overall resolution, then automatic spending cuts would kick in to bring spending back to the total in the resolution. No one really expected the automatic cuts would take place—it was aimed at creating political leverage—and many parts of the budget, including Social Security, were not subject to the automatic cuts. The idea was to create a device whose implications were so unthinkable that it would increase congressional discipline. And, for years, Congress managed to steer around sequestration's consequences.

Until 2013, that is. In August 2011, the federal government hit the ceiling on the debt that Congress authorized it to issue. (A reminder: the debt is the total of past deficits, and the federal government borrows money from investors, at home and abroad, to finance it. But the debt is issued for fixed periods, and the debt limit prevented the federal government for borrowing new money to keep finances afloat.) Barack Obama and the Republican Congress struggled for days over a "grand bargain" to bring down the deficit in the long run, but they could not reach a deal. They decided instead on a mixed plan: an increase in the debt ceiling, agreement to keep the government going through a continuing resolution through the end of 2012, and a loaded gun to force warring Democrats and Republicans to the table: a sequestration that would force automatic across-the-board cuts covering almost all the federal government, except a handful of programs like Social Security and veterans care. The plan was simply this: create consequences so dire, with deep cuts in programs that Republicans and Democrats supported, that failure to reach agreement would be unthinkable.

Except that the unthinkable happened. As the December 31, 2012, deadline approached, Congress and the White House found itself deadlocked. They stretched the deadline one more time until early March but, in the end, couldn't agree on a deficit-reduction plan. The sequestration kicked in, with automatic cuts in both defense and domestic programs as well

Due to the lapse in federal government funding, this website is not available.

After funding has been restored, please allow some time for this website to
become available again.

For information about available government services, visit usa.gov

To view U.S. Department of Agriculture Agency Contingency plans, visit: http://www.whitehouse.gov/omb/contingency-plans

Message from the President to U.S. Government Employees

When the Congress and President Obama failed to agree on a plan to fund the federal government in 2013, many parts of the federal government shut down. Some agencies, like the Department of Agriculture, simply had their websites go blank.

as days off without pay, called **furloughs** for many federal employees. Several cuts, for inspectors in meat-processing facilities and for air traffic controllers, did prove so dire that lobbyists appealed to Congress for relief, and these programs received exemptions from the sequestration. For most of the rest of government, however, deep cuts came, with two big consequences. One was the cuts themselves. From federally funded Meals on Wheels programs, which provided food for the elderly, to guides who gave tours of the White House, the sequestration brought real reductions in service. The other was the uncertainty that the process created. It took a very long time for top executive branch officials to determine how best to implement the sequestration, more time for agency-level officials to transmit the guidance to their employees, and more months for the cuts to kick in. The White House had issued dire warnings about the harm sequestration would bring, but a *Washington Post* story concluded, "They said the sequester would be scary. Mostly, they were wrong."[38] Republican conservatives discovered that they were able to impose larger cuts than they had imagined, but the executive director of the National Head Start Association called the process a "meat cleaver."[39]

But that was only the first phase of what became perhaps the biggest constitutional crisis of recent times. Congress and the Obama administration maneuvered through the spring and summer of 2013 with a continuing resolution. On October 1, however, that short-term spending authority expired and, without appropriations to keep the federal government running, much of it shut down. "Essential" federal employees, like air-traffic controllers, border patrol agents, the Secret Service, and the Capitol Police were told to continue to come to work. Other employees, including employees at the Environmental Protection Agency, NASA, and the Library of Congress stayed home, and they were told they could not use their government-issued Blackberries or check their government email accounts. As the shutdown developed, the definition of who was "essential" changed. At first, the Pentagon announced that the armed forces football teams could not play, but a later ruling held that the games could go on as scheduled. Most of the Pentagon's civilian workers were originally told to stay home, but part way through the shutdown they were told they were essential enough they could come to work.

Several headline-grabbing stories soon demonstrated the tensions of the government shutdown. Three days into the shutdown, the Secret Service and the Capitol Police found themselves in a tense car chase. A dental hygienist from Stamford, Connecticut, tried to ram her car into barriers protecting the White House, struck a Secret Service agent, and then raced her car at speeds of 80 miles per hour down Pennsylvania Avenue to the Capitol. She led federal officers on a wild chase around the building until they cornered her car against a barricade and the shot her when she tried to bolt from the car. Nervous members of Congress were caught inside the Capitol as the building was locked down. In guarding the White House and Capitol, the Secret Service and Capitol Police were surely essential employees—and they put their lives on the line even though they weren't being paid. Meanwhile, hundreds of miles above them, the International Space Station was circling with two American astronauts on board. Not only were they not being paid, Karen Nyberg and Mike Hopkins couldn't share what they saw with Americans below because NASA's website was dark because of the shutdown. They sent back some remarkable photos, but they had to use their personal Twitter accounts.[40] (The NASA and contractor workers ensuring their safety, of course, were "essential.")

The shutdown ricocheted around the nation and around the world. Visitors to the American cemetery in France, where soldiers stormed the Normandy beaches during World War II, discovered that the gate was locked and the American flag wasn't flying. The scenic roads through the Great Smoky Mountains National Park in Tennessee were closed, at the peak autumn foliage season. The state government, along with two county governments that had seen tourist income evaporate, provided their own funds of their own to get the park reopened. In New York, the state government paid to reopen the Statue of Liberty. The families of four soldiers killed in action in Afghanistan were told that the government could not pay for their funerals or provide death benefits, until the Pentagon worked out a deal with the Fisher House Foundation to make the payments until the government could reimburse them later. As the shutdown stretched on into a second week, such stories continued to accumulate. Public disgust, directed especially at members of Congress, soared.

Conservative Republicans in the House of Representatives insisted they would not vote to fund the government unless the agreement defunded the money needed to pay for Obamacare, the president's signature health care reform. The White House and congressional Democrats refused. They pointed out that Congress has passed the program, the president had easily won reelection afterwards, and the Supreme Court had upheld its constitutionality. Democrats bet that public opposition to the shutdown would force the Republicans to back down. Two weeks into the shutdown, a second crisis emerged. On October 17, the Treasury would not have enough money to fund the federal government's debt, and experts warned that defaulting on those obligations would cause financial chaos. Members of Congress had set the expiration of the continuing resolution on purpose, with each side calculating that the deadline would give them an advantage. The October 17 deadline to raise the debt ceiling made the stakes even higher. The debt of the United States government has long been considered by investors to be the safest in the world, and financiers had long assumed that no matter what else happened the federal government could be counted on to repay the money it borrowed. That turned up the heat even higher as the debt deadline approached.

Conservative "Tea Party" Republicans in the House refused to budge, and many openly speculated that the government could maneuver around the debt ceiling by selectively paying some bills and not others. Both government and private-sector financial managers replied that was impossible. International investors got increasingly nervous, and the Chinese news agency used the impasse to suggest "it is perhaps a good time for the befuddled world to start considering building a de-Americanized world."[41] House Speaker John Boehner (R-Ohio) tried to put together a deal that his party could support but it crumbled, leaving the government in shutdown and at the edge of default. Senate leaders Harry Reid (D-Nev.) and Mitch McConnell (R-Ken.) finally reached a last-minute agreement to fund the government for three months, extend the debt ceiling, create a committee to work out a long-term deal, and provide back pay to federal employees. The White House said it would sign the deal, the Senate quickly passed it, and House Democrats joined with enough House Republicans to make it law. The agreement reopened the government on October 17 after a 16-day shutdown, averted an even bigger crisis but, as so often proved the case, Congress postponed discussion of the big issues about the nation's long-term financial stability yet again.

The battle even more deeply split an already polarized federal government. Congressional Republicans were in disarray. Sen. McConnell said that, for his fellow Republicans, the shutdown was like the kick of a mule. There wouldn't be another shutdown, because "I think we have fully now acquainted our new members with what a losing strategy that is." He warned his colleagues, "There is no education in the second kick of a mule."[42] President Obama chided the Republicans and said they have to "understand that how business is done in this town has to change,"[43] but no one had a plan to escape the ongoing brinksmanship.

The fierce politics of the shutdown reminded us, yet again, that tough politics inevitably surrounds big decisions—and few decisions are bigger than those about taxing and spending. The issues of substance driving the politics were surprising, however. Although conservative Republicans decided to make Obamacare their line in the sand, senior Republican leaders quietly warned them there was no chance the White House would budge on that signature issue. Meanwhile, the conservatives' preoccupation with defunding the plan distracted them and the media from the immense problems that surrounded the launch of Obamacare on the same day the government shut down, and they missed a big chance to wound the president. Behind these health care battles, however, there was one overriding truth: the disputes that shut the government down had very little to do with the big questions of entitlement spending and taxes that were central to the ongoing deficit debate.

The shutdown also seriously damaged the congressional budget process, and close observers wondered if the federal budget process had broken down completely. Lurching from one crisis to the next, with funding supplied through short-term continuing resolutions, was making it ever more difficult for federal managers to plan anything. Federal managers were spending an inordinate amount of time trying to understand and cope with the uncertainties, for their own paychecks and for the operations they were responsible for managing. The real decisions on the budget were becoming increasingly disconnected from the formal process of submitting, debating, and approving the budget, and the short-term battles were increasingly separate from the fundamental long-term budgetary issues. Critics complained that the budgetary process was no longer accountable to the public—or to anyone else, for that matter. Even the most optimistic Washington observers concluded that budgeting had run amok.

One analyst warned of a budgetary "ice age"—with the process locked in "a frozen mass of spending priorities that no one has really chosen and that no one really likes."[44] Proposals surfaced to reform the budget, including creating a budget that would last two years instead of one and passing a constitutional amendment to require a balanced budget. None of the procedural fixes, however, offered much hope for resolving what, at their core, were political problems. In 1987, Sen. Mark O. Hatfield (R-Ore.) captured the problem with an analysis that still rings true: "We are not going to work our way out of federal deficit difficulties with procedural gimmicks. There is nothing wrong with our present system if we summon the will to make it work. And if we do not have will, no new procedures will work any better." Carol G. Cox, president of the Committee for a Responsible Federal Budget, agreed: "These are not economic problems. They are not analytical problems. They are political problems."[45]

Of course, budget battles between the president and Congress are as old as the Republic, but the battles have unquestionably become more fierce since the mid-1960s. Divided party control of the executive and legislative branches accounts for some of the conflict. So too does the rise of entitlements, which focus more political attention on a smaller share of the budget. Even more fundamentally, the nation is in the midst of profound debate about how big government ought to be and what it ought to do. These big questions shape the process and the politics of the federal budgetary process.

BUDGET EXECUTION

Once the executive and legislature agree on a budget, the challenge falls to the executive to, well, execute the spending plan. The authority derives fundamentally from the Constitution, and the president's constitutional obligation to "take Care that the Laws are faithfully executed." While the importance of this stage of the budgetary process might seem self-evident, Allen Schick has noted that executive practices are a "dark continent" of budgeting.[46] The budget execution process is a delicate balance between ensuring that a program's legislative goals are served and providing adequate flexibility for administrators to do their work.

For legislators, it's a dual problem: making sure that executive branch officials do not exceed their authority to spend money and making sure that they implement the programs that legislators have approved. Either problem—doing more than the legislature approved or not doing all that the legislature expects—proves enormously frustrating to legislators.

Presidents from Franklin D. Roosevelt to Lyndon B. Johnson had claimed and exercised authority to **impound**: the refusal by the president to spend money appropriated by Congress. Richard Nixon was especially aggressive in asserting the impoundment power and, as Louis Fisher, the leading authority on impoundment, put it, Nixon's actions "were unprecedented in their scope and severity."[47] Congress responded by drafting statutes more narrowly, to deprive the president and agency heads of discretion in implementing programs. Congress now increasingly votes "The Secretary shall . . . ," instead of the traditional "The Secretary is authorized to. . . ." As the impoundment strategy receded, presidential signing statements arose to replace it, especially in the George W. Bush administration, as we will see in Chapter 14.

A critical piece of budget execution is management control, and "follow the money" is its basic commandment. The flow of money throughout the bureaucracy provides a valuable tool for controlling the implementation of governmental programs, and it provides important leverage on administrators' activities.[48] First, the money trail demonstrates who is doing what. It is very difficult for administrators to do much without spending any money. The flow of cash doesn't tell us much about the quality of an agency's work, but it does tell us whether work is taking place. The same is true for the activities of contractors and grantees who produce much of government's work.

Second, by controlling the flow of money, the executive can control the direction and pace of governmental activity. Managers sometimes presume that everyone within an organization is working toward the same goal, only to be surprised later by employees' actions that are grossly out of line with the organization's goals. The flow of money is important symbolically because it signals the goals an organization considers important. It is important managerially because it helps to secure a match between the broader goals of the organization and the individual goals of workers.

Finally, the flow of money is important for reporting and evaluating an agency's performance. It can help managers to identify the "hot spots" that need attention, either because a unit is spending too much money too quickly or, paradoxically, because it is spending too little. More broadly, it provides important raw materials for program evaluation. By measuring what the money goes for, managers can take a first step toward determining a program's, and thus an agency's, efficiency and effectiveness.

"With rare exceptions," Robert N. Anthony and David W. Young explain, "a management control system is built around a financial structure."[49] This structure, in turn, is constructed with the building blocks of accounts—for functions or agencies, for subunits within those functions or agencies, and on to the individual components of an agency. In most governmental accounting systems—federal, state, and local—every expenditure is tagged with an account number. Account number 3-45983-6803, for example, might identify precisely the source and use of the money: the first 3 might mean that the money comes from a particular funding source, such as an excise tax on gasoline; the 45983 might mean that the money is allocated to the field unit in charge of repairing roads in the southern part of the state; and the 6803 might mean that the money is going to purchase asphalt patching material. Thus, by means of computers, government managers can monitor the status of all their activities, separated into whatever components they desire, and link them back to the appropriation that authorized the activity.

Weak accounting systems have sometimes cost the government millions of dollars. GAO, for example, discovered that eighteen federal agencies paid 25 percent of their bills late, costing the government millions of dollars in penalties. Another 25 percent of the bills were paid too early, which meant that the government often had to borrow money, costing it $350 million annually in interest. The Department of Defense, meanwhile, could not account for over $600 million that foreign customers had forwarded for the purchase of weapons. Many agency accounting systems are "antiquated," GAO concluded. "As a result, billions of dollars are not being adequately accounted for, managed or financially controlled."[50]

Different governments operate by different systems, but they all rely on management control systems built on accounts.[51] While the intricacies of such fund accounting often seem boring to those worrying over broad legislative-executive conflicts and the politics of deficit reduction, they provide the ultimate control on the government's money. Management control gives executive branch officials important information about the behavior of those who implement governmental policies, both within and outside government. Through routine auditing functions, it provides the mechanism for discovering problems and correcting them before they become large. Most important, effective management control provides important leverage over the activities of government officials, contractors, and grantees, and thus improves the chances for effective and efficient provision of public services.

One especially intriguing initiative to improve the connection between budgeting and results, inputs and outputs, is the movement in federal, state, and local governments toward performance management. Governments at all levels have increasingly introduced results-oriented management, built around strategic planning, to define more carefully an organization's goals; performance measurement, to develop clear indicators of program outcomes; and the development of new management systems, especially information and human resource systems, to support the broader movement. Such cities as Sunnyvale, California, have moved to focus management more on results—such as the condition of local parks. Oregon launched a long-term effort to define state goals, from success in school to the cleanliness of the environment, and to measure the state's performance against these goals.[52]

Congress passed the Government Performance and Results Act in 1993, and expanded it in 2011, to require all federal agencies to prepare annual performance plans and to report annually on the agencies' actual performance. These reforms mirrored even more far-reaching strategies launched in Great Britain, Australia, and New Zealand. (We return to this and other performance-based techniques in later chapters.) The reforms have had sweeping implications. They require radically different skills and approaches for government managers, who must focus much more on outputs (such as program outcomes) instead of inputs (such as the budget). The information they produce offers greater potential leverage for such central management agencies as OMB. Indeed, OMB was one of the Government Performance and Results Act's most enthusiastic supporters.

The evidence both from the American states and from abroad is that performance management is extremely difficult to develop and use. It imposes daunting measurement and management problems. Moreover, legislators have frequently made limited use at best of the great volumes of information such processes produce, in part because finding consensus on what goals ought to be measured is difficult, and in part because legislators often focus much more on attacking problems by passing laws and appropriating money than on overseeing results (as Chapter 13 discusses). Nevertheless, the evidence from both foreign and American experiments is that managers often have found results-oriented management useful in focusing agency staff on high-priority goals and for surviving in the increasingly stringent fiscal environment in which they find themselves. The federal government's effort, however, is the largest such experiment in the world, and observers are looking carefully at whether it will offer real promise or will go the way of such previous reforms as PPBS, MBO, and ZBB.[53]

BUDGETING FOR STATE AND LOCAL GOVERNMENTS

There are as many strategies for state and local government budgeting as there are state and local budgets. But they do share several common features. First, unlike the federal budget, state and local governments must balance their budgets. The federal government can print money and engage in long-term borrowing to cover its operating deficits. State and local governments cannot. If they suffer a temporary shortage, they can slide deficits over into the next fiscal year, dip into rainy day funds, or engage in short-term borrowing, but they cannot engage in the long-term patterns of debt that shape so much of federal budgeting.

Second, state and local governments draw fundamental distinctions between their operating budget (to cover the cost of day-to-day functions) and **capital budgets** (to cover the cost of long-term expenses for equipment and facilities). Although GAO has long campaigned to create a capital budget for the federal government, state and local governments have used them for generations. In general, state and local governments borrow to fund capital expenditures. The basic principle of capital budgeting is that the term of the loan ought to match the life of the equipment or facility. A state or local government might issue a twenty-year bond to pay for a sewage treatment plant expected to last two decades or a ten-year bond for a new fire engine. Taxes pay for operating expenses, like the salaries of firefighters and police officers.

Third, in some states, like Wisconsin, state activities continue automatically at the same level if the legislature and the governor cannot agree on a new budget before the start of a new fiscal year. But in most states, failing to pass a budget means that the authority to spend money expires and shutdowns, from closing state campgrounds to laying off employees, is both fiscal reality and political theater. In the recent economic downturn, many state and local government employees found themselves subject to furloughs as their governments

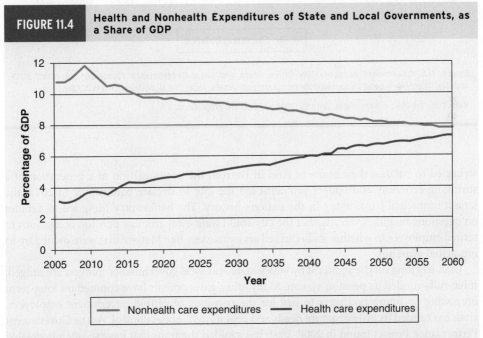

| FIGURE 11.4 | Health and Nonhealth Expenditures of State and Local Governments, as a Share of GDP |

Source: U.S. Government Accountability Office, *State and Local Governments' Fiscal Outlook* (April 2013 update), http://www.gao.gov/special.pubs/longterm/pdfs/state_local_fiscal_outlook_charts2013apr.pdf.

Note: Data for 2012 are estimates; data for 2013 to 2060 are projections.

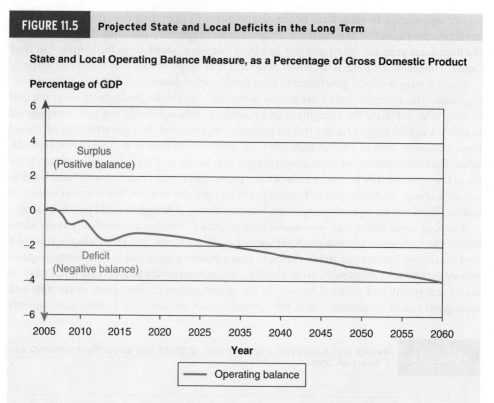

FIGURE 11.5   Projected State and Local Deficits in the Long Term

State and Local Operating Balance Measure, as a Percentage of Gross Domestic Product

Source: U.S. Government Accountability Office, *State and Local Governments' Fiscal Outlook* (April 2013 update), http://www.gao.gov/special.pubs/longterm/pdfs/state_local_fiscal_outlook_charts2013apr.pdf.

Note: Data for 2012 are estimates; data for 2013 to 2060 are projections.

struggled to balance their budgets. And in Detroit, the accumulation of a generation of a shrinking economy and budget problems led the city to declare bankruptcy in 2013, the largest municipal bankruptcy in the nation's history. The bankruptcy filing led to debates on questions ranging from whether the city could walk away from its pension obligations to retired employees to whether it should sell art by masters like Matisse that were owned by its municipal museum.

Utah has long set the standard by which state and local governments' budgets are judged. It has fully funded its pension system. Many other governments have counted on long-term borrowing or future taxpayers to pay for the pensions of retired government employees. Utah has funded its infrastructure needs and kept its debt under control. As the Government Performance Project found in 2008, Utah has avoided the traps that have so often bedeviled other states.

However, the long-term fiscal picture for state and local governments raises many of the same big questions facing the federal budget. Health care expenditures are rising rapidly and, GAO projects, will equal all other state expenditures by 2060 (see Figure 11.4). The rise of these expenditures, coupled with the ongoing struggle of state and local governments to modernize their tax systems to fit the twenty-first century economy, threatens to drive their budgets deeper into the red in the coming years (see Figure 11.5). These challenges will strain their budgets—and their budgetary policies and politics.

CONCLUSION

Few things capture the central issues of the politics of the administrative process better than budgeting: the effect of government taxing and spending on the economy, the effect of the economy on the budget, and the use of the budgetary arena for fighting out (if not always resolving) battles between the legislative and executive branches. Budgeting is the arena that most fundamentally shapes public policy decisions. By putting dollars together with often ambitious, and sometimes conflicting, goals, policymakers provide the resources needed to bring programs to life. While the budgetary process varies greatly at all levels of government, the basic issues remain. Nothing is more important than V.O. Key's basic question: "On what basis shall it be decided to allocate x dollars to activity A instead of activity B?"

The decision-making models discussed in Chapter 10 laid out the basic issues. This chapter demonstrates, however, that decisions reached and formalized at one stage of a multistage process may be superseded and reshaped by decisions made at later stages, by elected officials and administrators alike. The decision-making process, then, is considerably more complex than is suggested by theories focused on how one person or one organizational unit makes choices among alternatives at a single point in time. In fact, many such processes operate simultaneously in government, sometimes at cross-purposes. But nothing is more basic than the allocation of financial resources to support government activities.

The next question, of course, is how the administrative process acts on those decisions: how it adapts, refines, and sometimes even reshapes the results of the legislative-executive contests. That is the process we call implementation, to which we turn in the next chapter.

CASE 11.1

Going Black: The United States' "Black Budget" Intelligence Operations

The movie "Zero Dark Thirty" won an Oscar for its portrayal of the daring raid on terrorist mastermind Osama bin Laden in 2011. The movie peels back just a bit of the secret intelligence world that made the raid possible. But the reality is a far larger and more sophisticated world than most Americans—in fact, most members of Congress—realized. For example, as SEAL Team Six was on the ground, they had help from incredibly sophisticated satellites overhead that picked up intelligence as the commandos broke into the compound. Before the SEAL team hit the ground, the federal National Reconnaissance Office had collected more than 387 high-resolution images of the compound, and a special outfit called the Tailored Access Operations group installed spyware and tracking devices on phones and computers used inside the al Qaeda network. A special stealth drone, the RQ-170, flew over Pakistan to pick up information. All this helped intelligence analysts determine they had zeroed in on their target. Afterwards, managers managed to dig up an extra $2.5 million in money for overtime and extra computers to sift through all the intelligence that the SEALs brought out with them on their helicopters.[1]

All this came out of the federal government's "black budget," hidden in super-secret compartments of the national security budget. Only a handful of members of Congress know the details of what's inside the "black" part of the defense budget and, until very recently, almost no one outside the intelligence community even knew how large it was. Until, that is, former National Security Agency analyst Edward Snowden leaked top-secret documents to *The Washington Post* and Britain's *Guardian* newspapers. From those materials came a first-ever portrait of the government's clandestine world.

As Figure 11.6 shows, the "black" budget is $52.6 billion in fiscal year 2013, with the CIA receiving the largest share. Close behind are the National Security Agency, which intercepts

foreign electronic signals to analyze intelligence, and the National Reconnaissance Office, which operates reconnaissance satellites. Two smaller operations round out the top 5 of the "black" world: the National Geospatial-Intelligence Program, which develops imagery and mapping, and the General Defense Intelligence Program, which assesses foreign intelligence and capabilities. Together these 5 agencies account for over 85% of total "black" budget spending.

And who works inside this secret world? The leaked documents reveal that the intelligence community has almost 84,000 civilian employees, in the United States and abroad (with the CIA accounting for the largest share, at more than 21,000). Military officials account for 23,400 employees, two-thirds of whom are in the National Security Agency. And as Figure 11.7 shows, about 17% of the total, 21,800, are full-time contractors—like Edward Snowden (who worked for the NSA in Hawaii, after receiving his security clearance after a review by employees working under contract).

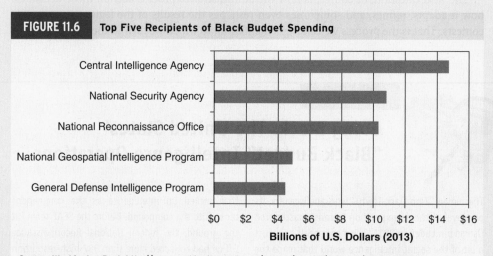

FIGURE 11.6   Top Five Recipients of Black Budget Spending

Billions of U.S. Dollars (2013)

Source: Washington Post, http://www.washingtonpost.com/wp-srv/special/national/black-budget.

Note: The top 5 recipients amount to approximately $45.1 billion of a total $52.6 billion (about 85.7%) in black budget spending. The remaining recipients include the Department of Justice, Office of Director of National Intelligence, Specialized Reconnaisance Programs, Department of Defense Foreign Counter-Intelligence Program, Department of Homeland Security, and Department of Energy.

| **FIGURE 11.7** | **Employees in the Intelligence Community** |

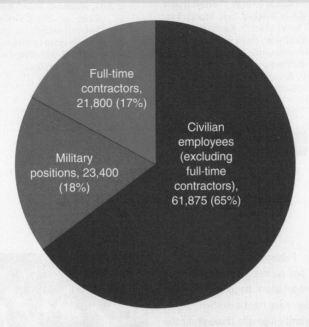

Source: Washington Post, http://www.washingtonpost.com/wp-srv/special/national/black-budget.

The bin Laden raid is only part of the huge "black" world. In 2011, the *Post* learned, the intelligence community undertook 231 offensive cybersecurity operations. In an operation under the code name GENIE, American exerts hacked into foreign computers to allow the government to monitor their operations and control them from afar. Special targets were China, Iran, North Korea, and Russia, the top-secret documents said. And in an elite operation known as "the ROC" (short for the Remote Operations Center), elite NSA hackers ran a sophisticated effort to discover and exploit defenses in foreign computers.[2]

These "black" operations might not make for the blockbuster drama of a midnight raid by Navy SEALs. But that raid wouldn't have been possible without these "black" operatives—and the operatives define a vast new part of the nation's intelligence operations that had been largely invisible before Edward Snowden leaked the documents.

Questions to Consider

1. Are you surprised by the dimensions of the "black budget" and the people paid by it? What, if anything, surprises you most?

2. Consider the issues of accountability. Given the competing demands for transparency and oversight, do you believe that the "black budget" is sufficiently accountable?

3. Now consider the future of cybersecurity and "black ops" programs. They're sure to increase, as pressures mount about information security and terrorism. No intelligence official will want to manage programs through the pages of the *Washington Post* or the *Guardian*. What would you recommend for the future of budgeting for these programs?

NOTES

1. Craig Whitlock and Barton Gellman, "To Hunt Osama bin Laden, Satellites Watched Over Abbottabad, Pakistan, and Navy SEALs," *Washington Post* (August 29, 2013), at http://www.washingtonpost.com/world/national-security/to-hunt-osama-bin-laden-satellites-watched-over-abbottabad-pakistan-and-navy-seals/2013/08/29/8d32c1d6-10d5-11e3-b4cb-fd7ce041d814_story.html?wpisrc=al_national

2. Barton Gellman and Ellen Nakashima, "U.S. Spy Agencies Mounted 231 Offensive Cyber-Operations in 2011, Documents Show," *Washington Post* (August 30, 2013), at http://www.washingtonpost.com/world/national-security/us-spy-agencies-mounted-231-offensive-cyber-operations-in-2011-documents-show/2013/08/30/d090a6ae-119e-11e3-b4cb-fd7ce041d814_story.html

CASE 11.2

From the Front Lines of Budgeting: Funding SEPTA

As a Southeastern Pennsylvania Transportation Authority (SEPTA) bus passed Independence Hall in Philadelphia, negotiators haggled over how best to support the mass transit system. SEPTA daily carried half a million people throughout the region.

For years, customers of Philadelphia's mass-transit system could hardly get through their daily commute without bumping into a sign advertising the system's motto: "We're getting there." Disgruntled commuters asked, "When?"

Cynics couldn't help but point out a double meaning: "We're getting there" was meant to suggest progress, but it also implied that SEPTA[1] had a long, long way to go. Full buses often drove right past impatient commuters waiting at the stops. Long delays left trolley riders fuming. Fares continued to rise, and patrons continued to complain about the service.

By many measures, SEPTA's troubles shouldn't even have existed. Philadelphia has one of the nation's best mass-transit systems, due in large part to its long history and its prime location along the busy New York–Washington corridor. In contrast to cities such as Washington, D.C., that

In Philadelphia in June 2008, a striking transit police officer distributed flyers to pedestrians shortly after his union declared a strike against SEPTA, the regional transportation authority. The prospect of inadequate security in the city's subway system led to a quick settlement.

have squeezed their mass-transit lines into already fast-growing suburbs, Philadelphia's suburbs grew up along preexisting mass-transit routes. Despite those advantages, SEPTA has faced chronic budget deficits, and those deficits in turn have created bigger and bigger service problems.

Toward the end of 2004, the system faced a $62 million budget deficit, which SEPTA officials said could lead to a 25 percent fare hike, a 20 percent reduction in service (including the elimination of all weekend service), and a cut of 1,400 jobs. One plan even raised the possibility of boosting the $2 fare to $3, which would have resulted in one of the highest fares in the nation. "This is the worst crisis to face SEPTA in its 36-year history," system chairman Pasquale T. Deon Sr. said. SEPTA's general manager, Faye Moore, added, "The impact of these measures on the lives of our customers, businesses in the region, as well as my fellow SEPTA employees, would be devastating."[2]

In November of that year, the system's budget woes exploded into a statewide issue. SEPTA organized busloads of riders, system managers, and union members for a bus trip to the state capitol in Harrisburg to lobby for state help. These activists pleaded with the governor for aid, and they warned state legislators of the economic crisis that would befall the region if the aid did not arrive in time.

Those who followed Pennsylvania politics recognized that a SEPTA budget crisis was a recurring drama. Every two years, as its budget came up for debate in the state legislature, SEPTA presented a forecast full of red ink. Every two years, it warned riders and employees that, without more state support, the system would face big cutbacks. Every two years, the state provided additional support. And then, by the next year, the whole process began again.

The recurring budget crises made some state officials, both Democrats and Republicans, suspect that the threats of service cuts were SEPTA's version of the "Washington Monument ploy." This was a strategy invented by George B. Hartzog, who directed the National Park Service during the Nixon years. In 1969, the administration cut the service's budget. Hartzog responded by closing all national parks, including the Washington Monument and Grand Canyon, for two days each week. "It was unheard of," he recalled later. "Even my own staff thought I was crazy."[3] He complied with the letter of the policy but created such a political storm that Congress and the administration soon restored the funding. Other leaders copied his lesson and responded to threats of budget cuts by offering up cuts that were politically unacceptable. But it also made policymakers cynical and suspicious, for it became difficult to tell which problems were real and which were just clever budget tricks. In SEPTA's case, a spokesperson for House Majority Leader Samuel H. Smith suggested that "SEPTA creates these budgets to create a crisis."

But the head of the Pennsylvania Public Transit Association, Michael Imbrogno, insisted that the 2004 crisis was real. The implications, he warned, could stretch from Philadelphia to Pittsburgh, which had the state's other large mass-transit system, and from there to "nearly all the systems, including community services that impact senior citizens, the disabled and transit-dependent workers."[4] The system's advocates contended that the spillover effects on the state's economy would be huge, since so many people without cars relied on the system and that, without a good system, traffic in key transportation corridors would become hopelessly clogged. The chairman of the SEPTA board put it more bluntly, warning that if the agency did not get state help, "The ship is really going down this time."[5]

Whether real or manufactured, SEPTA's critics concluded, the transit system's perpetual crisis was in large part a symptom of deeply rooted management problems. Providing more aid each year gave the system no incentive to fix them. If the state caved in again, they warned, SEPTA would only learn once again just how well its budget strategy worked.

For their part, SEPTA officials claimed that the deepening budget problems were a symptom of the state's failure to provide a firm foundation for the system's financial operations. They never knew how the budget battles would come out, so they could never plan ahead. Because the state provided inadequate support, these officials argued, they had little choice but to divert funds intended to build the system's future to pay for this year's emergency maintenance. As a result, they were forced to delay maintenance that needed to be done and to squeeze riders with higher fares, less service, and more unpredictable trains and buses and trolleys.

SEPTA officials argued that the problem could be fixed once and for all if the state would provide a predictable flow of revenue to the system from a dedicated funding stream (that is, a revenue source whose proceeds would flow automatically to SEPTA). They suggested that a higher gasoline tax would do the trick: it would keep money within the transportation system, it would nudge the cost of gas higher and thus create incentives for riders to switch to more fuel-efficient mass transit, it would get SEPTA out of the battle for other state revenues, and it would allow system officials to make long-term plans for a more reliable system.

Unfortunately, that proposal was not very popular in Harrisburg, where the Republicans who controlled both houses of the legislature were not eager to drive up the price of gasoline for their constituents and then ship the revenues off to Democratic Philadelphia. That city's legislators tried to build a broader coalition with the moderate Republicans who represented the suburbs around the city, but raising taxes was never an easy sell for them. The Philadelphia legislators also hoped for help from Governor Ed Rendell, a Democrat who had previously been mayor of Philadelphia, but he had no love for SEPTA, and other battles he needed to fight with the Republican legislators made him wary about engaging them on this front.

The Republicans, for their part, saw real value in the biennial fight to save SEPTA. It was a must-win issue for their Democratic colleagues from Philadelphia—and every must-win issue created opportunities to extract votes from them on other issues that mattered to legislators elsewhere in the state.

No one really wanted SEPTA to go down the drain—or even to eliminate weekend service—but no one was sure exactly how to fix its chronic problems. Meanwhile, keeping the budget game going worked, sometimes in subtle ways, for many of the players in the state budgetary process.

Questions to Consider

1. How does the "Washington Monument ploy" work? Do you believe it is likely to be an effective strategy? Will players in the process catch on after an agency has tried it once or twice?

2. How does the regular nature of SEPTA's budget battles affect its ability to plan and operate in the long term?

3. What lessons does the biennial budget game teach about the incentives for those who play it?

4. What options might policymakers consider for "fixing" SEPTA? What would you recommend?

NOTES

1. See the system's website: http://www.septa.org.
2. "SEPTA Proposes Drastic Actions to Deal with Deficit," press release, September 9, 2004, http://groups.yahoo.com/neo/groups/nwgreens/conversations/topics/176.
3. Matt Schudel, "George B. Hartzog, Jr., 88: Expanded Nation's Park System," *Washington Post*, July 6, 2008, C6.
4. "Fund a System in Need," editorial, *Philadelphia Inquirer*, November 11, 2004, A18.
5. Jere Downs, "SEPTA Details Proposed Cuts," *Philadelphia Inquirer*, November 12, 2004, B8.

Performing under Fire: Budget Constraints Force Fire Departments to Better Manage Resources

Jonathan Walters is a long-time journalist and a veteran firefighter. He's president of Ghent Fire Company Number One in upstate New York. He's a Class A interior-attack qualified firefighter, which means that if your home or building catches fire, he's trained to come inside and save you. He's been a volunteer for fifteen years in his fire company and, as he jokes, he's used "to things getting hot around me."[1]

He's also an expert on performance management in government. He worries about basic questions: "in the face of constrained budgets, is my fire company amassing and deploying resources in the smartest, most sophisticated way possible?" His conclusion, he says, "is that we in the fire service have a long way to go when it comes to using performance metrics to drive what we do. We like to talk about our annual run rate, response times, crew sizes, etc., but not about how many of our calls are real, or what they consist of, or how we performed once we got to the scene. As I tell my guys all the time, our image as local heroes isn't going to inoculate us forever from tough questions about what we cost versus what we do."[2]

Firefighters do have an image as local heroes. Which of us, after all, would stir from a sound sleep, leap onto a truck, and run into a burning building that could collapse around us? But as local budgets across the country suffered hard hits in the Great Recession, calls have come for wage give-backs and cuts in pensions. "Painting firefighters as something of a pampered class," he wrote, "would have been unheard of just a few years ago. Today, it's a widespread practice."[3] Lowell, Massachusetts, relies on mutual aid from surrounding communities in case of big fires. Baltimore firefighters faced the tough choice of five to eight furlough days—days off, without pay—or losing 100 positions. San Diego officials created "rolling brownouts," which closed firehouses on a rotating basis to save money. As Tom Wieczorek, director of the International City/County Management Association's Center for Public Safety Management noted, "It's one of the most challenging times I've ever seen."[4]

As local fire departments are facing these realities, they're also being forced to confront the nature of their work. In many communities, fire departments respond both to fires and to medical emergencies. In the typical community where the department handles both, 80 percent of the calls are for EMS and just 20 percent for fires. Many fire calls are for small fires or false alarms. In San Jose, a call for a medical emergency gets a response with a pumper and four firefighters. In Fargo, North Dakota, the chief says the department has moved away from that approach. Fire trucks are dispatched, says Chief Bruce Hoover, if "there's bleeding, breathing complications, or trauma." That, in turn, has "cut our run count back by 1,000 a year, and has kept apparatus and manpower in place for real emergencies."[5]

That step, however, is a big one for most local governments, where that shift would challenge long-standing practice. The alternative, Wieczorek says, could be far worse. "Don't get caught up in the hysteria trap of believing that if you pursue things like brownouts and budget cuts that children are going to die and senior citizens will burn up," he argued. "That might happen, but only if we keep doing business in the same old ways."[6]

Questions to Consider

1. What do you make of Walters's argument that fire departments need to move to better performance measures as a strategy for dealing with tight budgets?
2. If you agree with this approach, what barriers do you see standing in the way? What would you do to break these barriers? If you disagree, what alternatives would you suggest?
3. Consider Wieczorek's argument that the real threat to public safety lies not in restructuring fire departments but in failing to do so—and risking that tight budgets will lead

to larger and harder-to-manage budget cuts. Do you agree?

4. This is an issue that always provokes sharp public debate. How would you deal with citizens as such a debate literally catches fire?

NOTES

1. Jonathan Walters, "Firefighting through a Performance Management Lens," *Governing*, January 10, 2011, http://www.governing.com/blogs/view/Firefighting-Through-a-Performance-Management-Lens.html.
2. Ibid.
3. Jonathan Walters, "Firefighters Feel the Squeeze of Shrinking Budgets," *Governing*, January 2011, http://www.governing.com/topics/public-workforce/firefighters-feel-squeeze-shrinking-budgets.html.
4. Ibid.
5. Ibid.
6. Ibid.

KEY CONCEPTS

FOR FURTHER READING

Arnold, H. Douglas. *Congress and the Bureaucracy: A Theory of Influence.* New Haven, Conn.: Yale University Press, 1979.

Key, V. O., Jr. "The Lack of a Budgetary Theory." *American Political Science Review* 34 (December 1940): 1237–1240.

Rubin, Irene S. *The Politics of Public Budgeting.* 4th ed. New York: Chatham House, 2000.

Tufte, Edward R. *Political Control of the Economy.* Princeton, N.J.: Princeton University Press, 1978.

Webber, Carolyn, and Aaron Wildavsky. *A History of Taxation and Expenditures in the Western World.* New York: Simon and Schuster, 1986.

Wildavsky, Aaron, and Naomi Caiden. *The New Politics of the Budgetary Process.* 5th ed. New York: Pearson/Longman, 2004.

SUGGESTED WEBSITES

A rich amount of information about the federal budget is available on the Internet. An excellent place to start is the Office of Management and Budget (OMB) website, **www.whitehouse .gov/omb**, which contains each year's budget as proposed by the president, voluminous supporting information, and historical tables to track the budget's long-term trends. Several databases can be downloaded from this website into spreadsheet programs, which makes analysis and charting easy.

The Congressional Budget Office's website, **www.cbo.gov**, contains a wide variety of studies and analyses. In addition, its historical tables provide useful information that often break down government spending and income differently than OMB's data, which often can be useful in considering long-term trends, especially for entitlement, discretionary, and uncontrollable spending.

The president's Council of Economic Advisers publishes analyses at **www.white house.gov/cea**, as does the Board of Governors of the Federal Reserve at **www.federalreserve.gov**.

Implementation

- Understand the forces that contribute to success and failure in program implementation

- Explore the role of state and local governments and the private sector as partners in implementing government programs

- Examine the role of evaluation and information in improving program implementation

The release of classified documents by Edward J. Snowden in 2013 produced a startling insight into the scope of contracting in government. He was an employee of Booz Allen Hamilton, which had a major contract for the National Security Agency. He worked on Washington-based projects, but lived in Hawaii. His security clearance was processed by yet another government contractor on behalf of the U.S. Office of Personnel Management.

IN THE END, NOTHING IN PUBLIC ADMINISTRATION MATTERS more than results. Elected officials and agency managers can make decisions, but citizens expect they will get their tax dollar's worth from government. Even a casual look at the headlines shows how difficult the job is. There are frequent complaints about governmental performance, from overpriced spare parts for the Pentagon to failures in responding to major hurricanes, from the quality of local schools to drug rings in state prisons. It's an old issue, of course. More than 125 years ago, Woodrow Wilson—then a professor at Princeton University before his days as president—wrote that "it is getting harder to *run* a constitution than to frame one."[1] To Wilson's observation, add this: it is easier to *write* laws than to *execute* them.

Concerns about the execution of laws gave birth to a new field of study called **implementation**. Traditional public administration focused on government agencies as the basic unit of analysis, seeking to understand the way that bureaus operated. Implementation studies, by contrast, concentrate on programs and the results the programs produce. Implementation analysts use many of the traditional approaches of public administration, but by shifting the focus from the agency to the program, they hope to discover why program performance so often seems disappointing. More important, they seek to determine what can be done to manage programs better.

Every citizen—and taxpayer—is entitled to ask straightforward questions about the administration of governmental programs. Which programs are successful and should be continued? Which are failures and should be ended? What changes make the most difference in improving the efficiency and responsiveness of governmental programs? Which of these changes can be made by program administrators themselves, and which require action by elected legislators or executives?

The questions are straightforward, but straightforward answers are hard to come by. It is hard even to define what success and failure are, let alone to learn how to achieve success while avoiding failure. This chapter explores the rocky terrain of implementation in several ways: by considering how to judge a program's success or failure; by studying the special implementation problems of administering governmental programs through the American intergovernmental system, as well as through private contractors; and, finally, by examining case studies that demonstrate that failure is not inevitable—and that success requires great skill in both politics and administration.

JUDGING PROGRAM SUCCESS AND FAILURE

This process called implementation can be a bit confusing: isn't the entire public administration field about the management of government programs, and thus about implementation? In broad terms, the answer, of course, is yes. As long as people have been engaged in the administration of government, from the earliest days of human civilization, they have been worried about implementation. The book of Exodus in the Bible says that Moses shattered the first version of the Ten Commandments because, as he came down from the mountain, he discovered that his people were already violating the new rules they had agreed to.

However, the study of implementation as a discrete process in administration is more recent. In 1973 Jeffrey L. Pressman and Aaron B. Wildavsky sparked great interest in the process—or, as their subtitle, one of the longest and greatest in literary history, put it: *How*

Great Expectations in Washington Are Dashed in Oakland; Or, Why It's Amazing that Federal Programs Work at All, This Being a Saga of the Economic Development Administration as Told by Two Sympathetic Observers Who Seek to Build Morals on a Foundation of Ruined Hopes.[2] Their worry: too many programs start with bold objectives, but disappointment soon creeps in.

The study of implementation differs from more traditional approaches to public administration because it focuses narrowly on the "*interaction* between the setting of goals and the actions geared to achieving them," as Pressman and Wildavsky noted. In short, implementation analysis concentrates on the *results* of administrative action, not just on its *process*. As their clever subtitle implies, Pressman and Wildavsky turned to the subject because of their observation that a program's performance so often did not match its promise. The reason, they suggest, was that the "seamless web" of programs tends to become very complex—and the greater the complexity, they believe, the greater the chance of failure. Students of implementation see policymaking and policy execution as a web in which each strand depends on all the others.[3]

The studies that followed Pressman and Wildavsky echo their pessimism about the implementation process. One such study concludes, "Domestic programs virtually never achieve all that is expected of them."[4] Others see the process as "an uphill battle from start to finish."[5] Some scholars of implementation look on themselves as physicians seeking to diagnose the many diseases afflicting governmental programs.[6] The field is the very embodiment of Murphy's Law: "If anything can go wrong, it will." Indeed, the presumption of failure seems endemic to the study of implementation.[7] It is mostly a collection of programs gone wrong.

There is a fundamental problem in an approach focusing on failed programs. While failures of government performance so often seem epidemic, two facts must be kept in mind. First, successes rarely attract attention. Newspapers never feature banner headlines declaring "Mail Delivered Yet Again Today," "Thousands of Flights Land Safely Because of Air Traffic Control System," or "Rescue Squad Saves Life of Accident Victim." Of course, bad news deserves attention, because taxpayers and policymakers alike deserve to know when programs fail and why. But it would be a mistake to use news coverage and the speeches of public officials as evidence of how well public programs work. Successes are ignored, and failures dominate the headlines. Second, from the daily runs of emergency medical technicians to the backwoods work of forest rangers, most governmental programs work pretty well most of the time. The trick is determining what works well, what does not, and how to transform the latter into the former.

What Are Success and Failure?

To judge whether a program has succeeded or failed, one needs to compare its results with its goals. Implementation analysis thus shares features of the rational decision-making model discussed in Chapter 10. This obvious comparison, however, is extremely difficult in practice because legislative objectives typically are unclear, often are many rather than one, and frequently change over time. In the Johnson administration's War on Poverty, for example, the law required local communities to provide "maximum feasible participation" for the poor in making spending decisions. This legal standard proved a classic in cognitive fuzziness;

according to a classic formulation by Daniel Patrick Moynihan, it produced only "maximum feasible misunderstanding."[8]

Another community development program provided federal grants to local governments, directing them to spend the money on programs that gave maximum feasible priority to programs assisting low- and moderate-income families, or aiding in the prevention of slums and blight, or meeting urgent community development needs.[9] The law, however, did not tell administrators just how strong a priority must be to pass the maximum feasibility test. Nor did it define *low- and moderate-income families*, so it was hard to tell precisely who was eligible. What constituted an urgent need was anything but clear. So the program found itself engulfed in constant controversy over its level of success, precisely because its objectives were so unworkably vague.

Passing a law in Congress means winning a majority of votes, and the path to coalition building usually is paved with compromises that render its meaning unclear. That means laws often include vague, even competing language, as the price of obtaining compromise. As a result, the law might not prove a very good measure for a program's success, and implementation can become a long-term struggle that reflects the conflicts at the core of a law's passage.[10] The debate about "success" and "failure" is often a continuation of the struggles that shaped the program to begin with.

Moreover, goals can change over time. In New Haven, Connecticut, for example, local officials created a youth employment program. The original goal was placing program participants in union jobs, but a slowdown in building construction made that difficult, so they broadened their goals to include nonunion placements. When they found that the sixteen-year-olds in the program were too young to work in some construction jobs, they recruited older participants than the program was first designed to recruit. And when the officials discovered that most participants lacked the high school degree that many apprenticeship programs required, the director of the program taught an evening General Educational Development class to help participants qualify for apprenticeships.[11]

Still, goals and objectives are critical for shaping the success or failure of governmental programs. Donald Rumsfeld, who had the distinction of serving twice as secretary of defense (for Presidents Gerald Ford and George W. Bush) and once as chief of staff (for President Ford), collected a series of axioms outlining the problem—he called them "Rumsfeld's Rules." On one hand: "If you get the objectives right, even a lieutenant can write the strategy," he quotes World War II General George Marshall as saying. He added an axiom of his own: "When you're skiing, if you're not falling you're not trying."[12] When objectives are clear, implementation is easy, but government often tackles the very hard problems that the private sector cannot or will not take on. Each painful step in the Iraq war demonstrated how hard it is to turn Rumsfeld's simple rules into effective government action. Government constantly risks falling down the slopes because it contends with some of society's slipperiest challenges.

The Evolution of Goals

Goals evolve through the implementation process because administrative reality is never easy to forecast. Unexpected events continually pop up and require administrators to adjust.

As one commentator put it, "One should expect that the expected can be prevented, but the unexpected should have been expected."[13] Goals also change because their definition is inextricably wrapped up in the ongoing political process. The complex system of American government, with its intricate balance of powers and intergovernmental relations, provides many different points of access to the political process. The substance of a policy can change at many points: laws must be interpreted and regulations written by administrators; those interpretations can be challenged in court by those who hold another view; intergovernmental and public-private mechanisms create the possibility of great variation in the way different individuals pursue the same program; and every decision can be challenged somewhere else. (Chapter 13 examines the regulatory issues.) Implementation is a continuing game in which every supposed failure or success sets the stage for the next conflict; those disappointed by the results of one stage of the policy process can always seek better luck around the next turn.[14] Indeed, implementation rarely is a linear start-to-finish process but often is a closed circle in which each event affects the next.

Implementation can thus be understood as the outcome of a continuing, dynamic, often turbulent process in which the many forces of American pluralism struggle to shape administrative action just as they fight over legislative, judicial, and executive decisions.[15] In fact, implementation is a highly interactive, interdependent process. The more the public and private sectors of American society are intertwined, the more all three levels of American federalism become linked. And the more legislative actions are challenged as agencies write regulations and the regulations are challenged in the courts, then the more implementation depends on a loosely coupled structure. The chain of implementation is not a hierarchical set of linkages structured by authority but, rather, a collection of organizations working—often loosely—to collaborate with each other. These continuing interactions shape and reshape policy implementation.[16]

If the standards for success and failure are so mushy, is there any clear standard for measuring how well a program works? The classical approach is to weigh a program's results against its legislative intent, but legislative language is a poor benchmark, with goals that are typically vague, multiple, and conflicting. Administrators have a legal and ethical obligation to pursue these goals as written, and the courts use legislative goals as standards by which to judge administrative action. That sets up an inevitable, always-lively battle. It also introduces two different kinds of discretion into the process: that of administrators, in divining what the legislature had in mind; and that of courts, in comparing administrators' interpretations with their own judgments about legislative intent.

Standards for Judging Results

In a legal sense, legislative intent supplies the standards for judging a program's success or failure. It does not provide an objective measure, since, as with Rorschach inkblot tests, everyone reads into the presumed legislative intent just what he or she wishes to see. To deal with this quandary, analysts often employ two additional measures for administrative action.

Economists have always argued that efficiency is a premier standard for judging action. Whatever a legislature's goals may have been, the public expects public programs to be run efficiently. What outputs are produced for a given level of inputs? Could a different administrative approach produce more outputs for the same level of inputs (or the same level of output for less input)? Invoking the efficiency standard gives one measure by which to judge implementation.

In addition, the public expects programs to be responsive: Does implementation reflect the popular will? And who represents that popular will—elected officials or those affected by a program? The problem, of course, is that strategies that emphasize efficiency often sacrifice responsiveness. It is costly, for example, to allow those affected by decisions to have a full chance to make their opinions heard. The problem of judging implementation is thus the broader problem of American government: although everyone holds the performance of governmental institutions to broad standards of efficiency and responsiveness, many have very different ideas about what these standards mean in individual cases. Furthermore, because a program's goals are almost always vague, judgments about whether a program succeeds or fails vary with the observer. Of course, people always prefer successes over failures, they want programs that are efficient rather than inefficient, and they want programs to achieve their goals. Even if one cannot agree on precisely what these terms mean, they set the language in which the implementation debate rages.

PROBLEMS OF PERFORMANCE

What factors most make the difference in implementation? Five issues tend to resurface: (1) uncertainty about how to reach a program's goals; (2) inadequate resources to get the job done; (3) organizational problems that interfere with an agency's handling of its programs; (4) uneven leadership in guiding bureaucracies through difficult issues; and (5) growing dependence on others, whether at other levels of government or in the private sector, through a complex of networked government.

Uncertainty

Difficult problems may have no known solutions—and tough problems tend to end up at government's doorstep. After all, the reason that many problems become governmental problems is that the private sector cannot, or will not, solve them. That realization often leads policymakers to embrace the merely plausible, the currently fashionable, or the most powerfully advocated program. One local official once described this to me as the "nifty idea, I'm for that!" approach to problem solving. Elliot Richardson, a member of President Richard Nixon's cabinet, wrote in more detail:

> Our impatience toward delays in curing social ills reinforces the "don't just stand there, do something" impulse. [This syndrome] encourages . . . the illusion that we know how to cure alcoholism, treat heroin addiction, and rehabilitate criminal offenders. In fact, we do not. The state of the art in these areas is about where the treatment of fevers was in George Washington's day.[17]

In fact, George Washington's wife Martha died of a fever. Washington himself was bled for a fever he contracted and the treatment contributed to his death. Fashion often shapes strategies, but the strategies very often build on uncertainty.

When policymakers attempt to eliminate poverty, to provide decent housing for every American family, to conquer cancer, to make the country's lakes and rivers fishable and swimmable, to ensure everyone's access to adequate health care, to make the streets safe, and to eliminate discrimination based on race, sex, national origin, age, and physical disability, they are expressing noble hopes that may be dashed because they have not learned how to actually accomplish these things. As the authors of a study of Medicaid put it, "idealists may frame laws; realists have to administer them."[18]

Even when the uncertainty is technological, formidable challenges often remain. The Soviet nuclear disaster in Chernobyl, near Kiev, in 1986 and the tragic disintegration in February 2003 of the space shuttle *Columbia* all too vividly demonstrate the tremendous difficulty of combining complex engineering tasks in never-before-attempted systems. Engineers designed Japanese nuclear reactors to survive a massive earthquake—which they did when a 9.0 temblor hit in March 2011. The resulting tsunami, however, swamped the seawalls protecting the reactors and knocked out the cooling systems. When the problem is social instead of technological, as with welfare programs, the uncertainty about how to deal with complexity is different, though just as troubling.

The difficulty is imperfect knowledge, particularly when the law directs an agency to solve a new problem or attack an old problem in a new (but unspecified) way. Moreover, administrators' sophistication is often no match for the imagination of average citizens, let alone the skilled specialist. Programs intended to reduce the oversupply of major agricultural crops have offered subsidies to farmers for taking some of their acreage out of production, but when the farmers choose their poorest-yield acres as the ones to lie fallow and step up the output of their remaining acres, the program's goals for curtailing production are not met. The ingenuity of taxpayers seeking loopholes in the Internal Revenue Service's voluminous regulations is legendary: even when the agency's administrators attempt to anticipate the "unanticipated" consequences of their actions, their judgment can never surpass the inventiveness of thousands, or millions, of clever attorneys, accountants, and other experts who make it their business to find loopholes and save their clients money.

Uncertainty thus often handicaps program implementation. Complex technologies, from space shuttles to nuclear reactors, from the Internet to electronic commerce, produce problems that are hard to predict. Interactions between people, and between citizens and their government, are even harder to forecast and influence: people often do not know what they want done, not just in government but in many aspects of an intricate society—and even when they do know, they often do not know how to do it. All these uncertainties can hurt the performance of governmental programs.

Inadequate Resources

The resources, in both budgets and skilled personnel, often aren't adequate to implement the ambitious programs created by legislatures. Cynics, of course, argue that government is full of unnecessary bureaucrats, but in fact there's often a large gap between government's capacity and the job to be done.

Going to the Cloud

For city officials in Nogales, Arizona, the challenge was how best to connect citizens and businesses to a wide range of services like getting licenses and permits, managing municipal assets, and taking care of the town's land. For example, the city has a large number of downtown buildings that are more than a century old. Preserving and restoring them has raised some tough questions of tracking paperwork and the steps in the restoration process. Nogales officials wanted to create a "one-stop shop" for helping developers navigate the steps required to get plans and permits approved.

The challenge? Nogales is a small city, with a population of just 20,948. With a small municipal staff, how could it trim the administrative costs and streamline the process? Nogales officials didn't have the money or expertise to develop a new information technology system, so they turned to Accela Automation, a cloud-based system that provided both sophisticated search and mapping features. Accela also gave citizens a way to make requests for municipal services and track the progress in solving their problems. In time, Nogales officials planned to roll these features out to Apple, Android, and Microsoft Windows devices, so that citizens and developers could connect with the city through their smartphones or iPads.

Program implementation has advanced a long way when small cities can connect their services to their citizens through the cloud, with smartphones talking to the municipal permit office. But the key to this is a private developer, who writes and deploys the app—and trusting the cloud for the safety and security of public records and private plans. Would *you* trust the cloud for mission-critical services in your town? What steps would you take to ensure that the new system is accountable?

Source: Adapted from Cities Take Licensing, Permit Services to the Cloud," GCN blog, July 25, 2013, http://gcn .com/blogs/pulse/2013/07/cloud-based-licenses-and-permits.aspx

Money

When he was secretary of the Department of Health, Education, and Welfare (later split into the Department of Health and Human Services and the Department of Education), Elliot Richardson discovered that the $100 million Congress had approved for a new elderly nutrition program would reach only 5 percent of those who were eligible, and the Community Health Program only 20 percent of the intended beneficiaries. When he asked his staff to estimate the cost in fiscal year 1972 of having all the department's programs reach every eligible person, they told him that the amount needed was $250 billion—more than the total federal budget at that time. He concluded that "all too often, new legislation merely publicizes a need without creating either the means or the resources for meeting it."[19]

Legislatures can and often do impose new duties on an agency, expand old programs, or require more elaborate procedures without increasing the agency's appropriations. Chief executives may lean hard on agency managers to give a single program top priority without considering the effects on the full range of the agency's obligations. State and local governments often find that the federal government requires them to meet national guide-lines without supplying the money to do so. In mid-1986, for example, officials in St. George, Utah, faced fines up to $25,000 per day for failing to meet federal clean water standards. A new sewage treatment plant they were planning would help the city meet the standards, and city officials had already spent $100,000 trying to qualify for a federal grant that would fund 75 percent of the plant's $13 million cost. At the same time, however, the Ronald Reagan administration was attempting to eliminate the grant program entirely. "We've been chas-ing after EPA [Environmental Protection Agency] dollars for years," said Larry Bulloch, St. George's public works director. "It's like a carrot on a string; we just never catch up with it."[20] The gap between a program's goals and its funding is often substantial—a problem that has grown with the federal deficit. When Congress passed the No Child Left Behind legisla-tion in 2001, it had widespread support, until school administrators contended that there wasn't enough funding to help them meet the act's ambitious performance goals.[21] Anti-crime programs often tend to fall short of their promise because there aren't enough cops to do the work, and the national registry of bridge safety lists many spans that fall short of standards without providing funds to fix them.

Staff

As Chapter 2 showed, the number of federal employees has lagged behind the growth of pop-ulation, federal expenditures, and programs to be administered. Even at state and local levels, governmental responsibilities have outpaced government employment. A staff too small for its responsibilities will be hard-pressed to interpret the statute, write and amend regulations, answer correspondence, confer with clientele organizations, disburse money to applicants for a program's benefits, and keep accounts on where the money has gone. Moreover, an understaffed organization will not assign enough of its personnel to monitoring a program's performance or detecting program abuse and fraud.

Organizational Problems

The department or agency in which a program is located has much to do with the program's odds of success. Some agencies have an open culture and are extremely friendly toward new programs, whereas others treat new ventures as unwanted children. Often, even when a pro-gram does find an inhospitable home, no existing department is likely to be more appropri-ate, or other factors prevent its being assigned a better location. In such cases, it is useful to know the hazards—and to know that they can be partially countered by protective measures. Three common organizational problems make the case.

First, it is risky to place regulatory responsibilities in an agency whose primary function is service. For instance, many states have regulatory bodies to control industrial activities, a setup which implies an actual (or potential) adversarial relationship between the government agency and the regulated industry. In contrast, promotion of industrial development and employment requires close, sympathetic collaboration between the agency and its clients. No single agency could serve both goals well.

Second, it is risky to place a program in an agency whose staff is unsympathetic to the program.[22] In the early years of the Reagan administration, for example, top EPA officials had a negative attitude toward government regulation of business, and many environmental programs suffered. Many critics blamed the move of the Federal Emergency Management Agency (FEMA) from independent status to part of the new Department of Homeland Security for its failure in 2005 to move more swiftly to deal with the many disasters that Hurricane Katrina produced. Furthermore, new programs need an imaginative and vigorous administrative staff and such vigor is not likely to come from an established old-line department whose civil servants have been there for years. Yet, as we know, the multiplication of government agencies creates new problems: more conflict between agencies, more need for coordination at the chief executive's level (whether president, governor, county administrator, or mayor), and more centralization of authority in the chief executive's staff.

Third, it is risky to assign closely *related* programs to *different* agencies. The program manager's strategy may then depend on the strategies and actions of his or her rivals, and bureaucratic objectives may tend to replace public policy objectives. In the competition for "customers," the manager may overserve or underregulate the clientele shared with other programs. Classic examples include the competition between the Army Corps of Engineers (in the Defense Department) and the Reclamation Service (in the Interior Department) to build dams, and local governments' shopping around among the four federal agencies (the Departments of Agriculture, Commerce, and Housing and Urban Development, as well as the EPA) that can make sewage treatment construction grants. In the regulatory arena, three federal agencies oversee banks: the Comptroller of the Currency (in the Treasury Department) as well as the Board of Governors of the Federal Reserve System and the Federal Deposit Insurance Corporation (both independent regulatory agencies). The result, said one Federal Reserve chairman, is "a jurisdictional tangle that boggles the mind" and fosters "competition in laxity, sometimes to relax constraints, sometimes to delay corrective measures. Agencies sometimes are played off against one another."[23] That tangle vastly complicated efforts in the late 1980s to solve the savings-and-loan crisis and created even worse problems in managing the recovery from the 2008 financial collapse.

Uneven Leadership

As Ralph Waldo Emerson put it, "an institution is the lengthened shadow of one man."[24] In the bureaucratic world, an exceptional administrator can make the difference in a program's success. For a generation, the Federal Bureau of Investigation was indeed the lengthened shadow of director J. Edgar Hoover. The early success of the Peace Corps owed much to the energetic leadership of Sargent Shriver, and James E. Webb managed NASA's remarkable drive to the moon in the 1960s. Tom Ridge guided the first uncertain steps of the federal government's homeland security operations. At the state and local levels, great leaders have often dominated individual agencies. Bureaucratic entrepreneurs have radically transformed government agencies with the force of their ideas and energy. [25]

As James Q. Wilson has pointed out, however, "the supply of able, experienced executives is not increasing nearly as fast as the number of problems being addressed by public policy." And, he continued,

> the government—at least publicly—seems to act as if the supply of able political executives were infinitely elastic, though people setting up new agencies will

often admit privately that they are so frustrated and appalled by the shortage of talent that the only wonder is why disaster is so long in coming.[26]

We often fall short of what we seek to accomplish because our government agencies fall short of the leadership talent they need.

Programs whose effectiveness depends on individual leaders tend to falter when their leaders depart. In April 1966, when the Commerce Department's Economic Development Administration (EDA), which had previously had a rural emphasis, moved into urban development with a $23 million public works showcase to relieve unemployment in Oakland, California, the change was led by Eugene P. Foley, characterized as "the enthusiastic, restless and imaginative Assistant Secretary of Commerce who heads EDA." Five months later, however, Foley resigned, and several key staff people soon left after Foley's departure. Without his leadership, the program fell back into the normal channels in Washington, where "its priority and singular importance diminished." As Pressman and Wildavsky report, "both Secretary of Commerce Connor and Foley's successor, Ross Davis, felt that the Oakland project was Foley's personal project; they did not share Foley's enthusiasm for a dramatic EDA push in urban areas." The program failed soon afterward.[27]

Networked Government

It's increasingly the case that no single organization can control any problem that really matters, and that every complex solution requires a complex, interrelated network.[28] In fact, "the dividing line between the federal government's sphere of operations and the rest of the economy has become increasingly blurred, if not eliminated," as economist Murray L. Weidenbaum put it.[29] On the one hand, government has taken an ever-increasing role in setting policy for the entire society, from providing subsistence for the poor to defining the terms of competition for industry. On the other hand, the government has come to rely ever more on third parties—other levels of government, nonprofit organizations, and private organizations—to execute programs. Implementation has thus become a complex business of managing interrelationships between government and the many proxies who carry out its programs.[30] The reasons are both managerial and political. It's impossible for any single organization to gather all the expertise needed to manage any complex problem. And spreading the responsibility for government's work also builds a stronger political network among individuals and organizations who benefit from government's money. But the more interrelated the public and private sectors have grown, the fuzzier the boundaries have become between what is public and what is private. That, in turn, has complicated the challenge of implementing programs efficiently, with strong accountability.

The fundamental problem is that different organizations have different purposes, and the people who work for them naturally pursue different goals. Whenever the government relies on a proxy to produce a service, it faces the task of trying to impose its goals on the often very different objectives of the proxy. The least problematic outcome that can result from such a process is conflict; the most problematic, a deflection of the government's goals toward those of its proxy. The two varieties of this proxy implementation strategy raise particular concerns within their separate spheres of operation: relations with different levels of government, and contracts with the private sector.

INTERGOVERNMENTAL RELATIONS

The national government delegates the implementation of many of its programs to state and local governments. This strategy enjoyed a remarkable growth in the 1960s, in particular, as the federal government sought to advance such values as decentralization, local self-government, and neighborhood power. While federal grants once flowed mostly to the states, the expansion of direct federal-local grants in the 1960s made local governments full and direct administrative partners in federal programs, and that trend has continued since.

But there's the rub. If intergovernmental programs advance state and local values, what becomes of the federal government's policy goals? And if state and local governments advance their goals in implementing federal programs, what becomes of the federal government's goals that created the programs? It's an ageless dilemma of American federalism.

In 2013, the IRS revealed that agents working in its Cincinnati field office had targeted applications for tax exemption from the Tea Party and gave those forms extra scrutiny. Protestors launched nationwide protests, including this one outside the U.S. Capitol, to complain about the agency's misuse of its power. The "Don't Tread on Me" flag dates from the nation's colonial times, when Americans raised it to signal their resolve in shedding British power.

Intergovernmental implementation strategies are of three sorts: (1) grant programs, in which a higher-level government pays lower-level governments to do what it wants done; (2) regulatory programs, sometimes tied to grants and sometimes not, which subtly force changes in governments' behavior; and (3) off-budget programs, such as tax expenditures and loan programs, that provide additional support for governmental goals.

Administration through Grant Programs

The federal government uses state and local governments as its administrative agents; as Martha Derthick has written, "the essence of the grant system is that it entails achievement of federal objectives by proxy."[31] The same can be said of state grants to local governments, which use local governments as administrative agents for state programs. At the high-water mark of federal aid to state and local governments in 1978, there were about 500 grant programs.[32] The Reagan administration began a major effort in the early 1980s to reduce grant spending and to consolidate programs; by 1986, the number of grant programs had dropped to 340, and 85 percent of federal spending was concentrated in only 25 programs.[33] Since then, federal spending for grants, especially grants to fund projects ranging from job training to urban renewal, have dropped sharply. At the state level, most grants go for aid to local schools.

Grant programs vary by their general function and by the way in which they are distributed.

Function

About half of all federal grants are, in reality, part of the complex system of government payments to individuals, through federal programs such as Medicaid and child nutrition, which are run by the state governments. In 1940, just over 25 percent of all federal grants were for payments to individuals. By 2018, the Office of Management and Budget estimates, that share will triple to more than 75 percent. Just 25 percent of federal grants are of the more traditional project grant. Federal grants for individuals have steadily soared, especially since the passage of Medicaid in 1965. Discretionary grants since the 1970s have been relatively stagnant (see Figure 12.1).

| FIGURE 12.1 | Federal Grants to State and Local Governments, 1940-2018 |

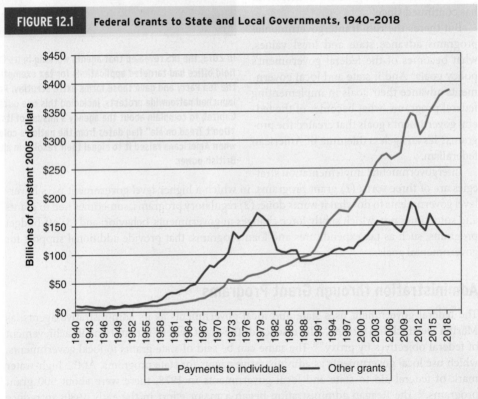

Source: Office of Management and Budget, *Budget of the United States Government, Fiscal Year 2014: Historical Tables*, Table 12.1, http://www.whitehouse.gov/omb/budget/historicals.

Note: Data for 2013-2018 are estimates.

Distribution

Federal funds may be distributed either by formula or by project. In **formula-based programs**, statistical procedures determine both who is eligible for money and how much they can receive. The rise of grants for payments to individuals (mostly Medicaid) has led to a rapid increase in formula-based aid. Distribution of funds by project is strikingly different: each state or local government meeting eligibility requirements may apply for a grant by describing in detail its proposed project, its capabilities for executing it, and the anticipated benefits to the public. The sponsoring federal agency then selects the projects that it will fund (within its budgetary limits). **Project-based programs** thus are competitions that will produce unhappy losers, and they have other problems as well: they impose heavy paperwork burdens on applicants, and they give broad discretion to federal administrators over who actually receives money. A less obvious advantage is that project-based programs permit concentration of limited federal money where the federal government thought that the money will do the most good.

The rise of formula-based programs and the relative decline of project grants has reduced, but not eliminated, the importance of **grantsmanship** in the federal aid system, where entrepreneurial local and state administrators exploit the project system for maximum funding.[34] As grantsmanship has declined, however, bargaining over formulas has increased, because grant formulas can be incredibly complex. Medicaid, in particular, involves a vast array of federal regulations and state choices that make it not one program but 51, with different versions in every state and the District of Columbia.

Administration through Regulation

The intergovernmental grant system is more than a device for transferring money. Each grant program brings with it a package of regulations and **mandates** that further spreads federal influence over state and local governmental activities. By reserving to the states any powers that are not otherwise given to the federal government, the Tenth Amendment to the Constitution prohibits the federal government from directly ordering states to engage in many activities. In the irresistible lure of grants, however, the federal government has found a way around this constitutional impediment: by making the money available, but subject to certain conditions, it can get state and local governments to do what they otherwise might not be inclined to do.[35]

Every program carries its own special rules. Potential Medicaid recipients must meet certain income guidelines, and federal highway funds can be spent only on certain kinds of projects. In addition, the federal government has promulgated a remarkable range of crosscutting rules that apply across the board, to all grant programs. Recipients must, of course, properly account for how they spend their money, but they must also survey the environmental effects of any program they plan, they must not discriminate in how the money is spent, they must preserve the historical aspects of federally funded projects, and they must make projects accessible to the disabled, among many other things.

Furthermore, state and local recipients must comply with **crossover sanctions**: failure to meet one program's standard can produce a punishment in another program. For example, during the energy crisis of the 1970s, Congress forbade the secretary of transportation from approving any highway construction project in a state posting a speed limit of more than 55 miles per hour. Since many states, especially in the West, had speed limits of 65 miles per hour on highways, they had the choice of lowering the limits or losing the money; the choice was obvious.[36] From automobile pollution inspection to a minimum drinking age of twenty-one, such crossover sanctions are a favorite instrument for inducing uniform national standards.

The federal government sometimes employs a mixed regulatory strategy, called **partial preemption**.[37] A federal agency sets standards that state and local governments must follow—for example, legislation mandating minimum water quality standards—and if the subnational government does not meet those standards, the federal government steps in to administer the program itself. Thus, in some states, a program will be run by a state or local official; in others, federal field officials will administer it. For example, the Occupational Safety and Health Administration itself conducts inspections and enforces regulations in thirty states while only approving and monitoring programs run by twenty state governments. The financial structure of such a mixed-level program can be equally complicated.

Attacking the mandates was easy; devising a solution was far tougher. Most reforms would not roll back existing mandates but would only make it harder to impose new ones. Estimating the costs of mandates before they are imposed, however, is an extremely difficult technical problem. Moreover, many interest groups find it far easier to organize in Washington to press for a uniform policy to be applied across the country than to fight fifty separate battles in the state capitals. Many businesses worried about trying to accommodate fifty separate sets of laws and standards may also find uniform standards, enacted in Washington, much more desirable.

Administration through Off-Budget Programs

In addition to grants (and their related regulations), the federal government uses a complex collection of off-budget strategies to advance its goals. For example, individuals are allowed to deduct local property tax payments from their federal taxable income, resulting in a boon both to taxpayers and to local governments. The deductions mean that the federal government shares some of the cost of the local tax and that any tax rate is less painful to taxpayers than it otherwise would be. Exclusions from the federal income tax provide another important form of aid: those who invest in state and local government bonds, for example, do not pay federal income tax on the interest they earn. The governments, therefore, do not have to pay as high an interest rate as they otherwise would, and the result is a substantial savings in interest costs.

The federal government also provides credit to state and local governments, making direct loans for such projects as rural development and college housing, while guaranteeing other loans made to state and local governments, as well as private lending for low-rent public housing and services. Implementation through such programs relies on the creation of incentives for both governments and citizens; whether supporting loans for college dormitories or giving special tax breaks for sports arenas, the federal government supplies the impetus for action and thus powerfully influences the implementation process.

Implementation Problems

Even though policymakers have used intergovernmental strategies during nearly all of American history, implementation problems persist. Three of them merit particular attention: inequity, fragmentation, and lax federal control.

Inequity

Where you live determines what you get so long as state and local governments have the option to participate or not in a grant program, to set standards of eligibility for the program, and to fix the level of benefits the program provides. Many state and local governments refused to participate in some federal programs—such as food stamps and Medicaid, which provide food and medical assistance to the poor—during their early years. The grant system thus can exacerbate existing differences in wealth among the states.[38]

Fragmentation

Societal problems rarely respect geographical or programmatic boundaries. Polluted water and dirty air flow across state boundaries. Many metropolitan areas contain over a hundred local governments; the Chicago area has over a thousand. National programs depend for program implementation on state and local governments, each of which has only a piece of a jigsaw puzzle. Furthermore, the multiplicity of federal aid programs—each with its own goals and rules, procedures and forms—creates a maze of great complexity. The rise of **block grants** has reduced some of this confusion, but less money has at the same time reduced grant recipients' ability to deal with the problems. It is scarcely surprising, therefore, that frustration, impasse, and inconsistency often result.

Lax Federal Control

Federal agencies issue numerous regulations and guidelines, and state and local officials complain about their proliferation. Paradoxically, federal control of state and local implementation is weak, and in block-grant programs, federal control is intentionally weak because broad discretion is a central federal goal. The federal government may require each state and local government to plan for the use of the grant and to report how the grant was allocated and spent, but it cannot question the money's uses unless the usage clearly violates the law or applicable regulations. Federal agencies usually impose a large number of *procedural* requirements, but they usually exercise only weak control over the *substance* of state and local decision making and the actual achievement of the program's objectives. The principal sanction for performance problems is withholding a grant—a draconian measure that is rarely invoked—but federal officials otherwise have relatively little leverage. "In our federal system," as Michael Reagan has noted, "no national government can dismiss a state government official."[39]

Even if the federal government were to develop a good reporting system on the use of funds and effective sanctions for poor performance, it still would be difficult to determine what results the grants produced. Because dollars are dollars, one interchangeable with another, a state's or city's money that would have been spent in one program may be replaced with a federal grant, and the freed funds used instead to reduce taxes or increase services in other areas. In effect, the grant extended for one purpose has instead expanded services in another, a problem known as **fungibility**. Thus the uses and effects of federal funding often cannot be fully assessed.

The same issue holds for state governments, which spend a large share of their tax dollars on grants to local governments. State governments provide about a third of local budgets, on average, mostly for local schools but also for a variety of other purposes.[40] All of the issues this chapter has explored about federal grants to state and local governments apply to state grants to local governments as well—along with one more: given the enormous variety of patterns in the state-local relationship, state aid takes on remarkably complex forms and is hard to categorize. Over the years, however, local governments have come to depend on these transfers and, as state budgets have gotten tighter, intergovernmental tensions have grown.

A Cornerstone of Implementation

Intergovernmental administration of government programs has become a central cornerstone of implementation. The system is exceptionally complex, but state and local governments are natural, if sometimes reluctant, administrative partners in federal programs. By relying on them the federal government promotes the principles of responsive self-government that date from the nation's earliest days.[41] After all, the federal government is the creation of the states, and we've chosen to call ourselves the *united states* in the continent of America. The intergovernmental system often strains under the weight of its burdens, and it's struggled with budget cuts, but the strategy of shared responsibility through federalism is here to stay.

CONTRACTING

Contracting in America is older than American government itself. As commander of the Continental army, George Washington constantly struggled with his private suppliers, who schemed to make a quick profit at the expense of his soldiers.[42] Contracting issues, in fact, go back thousands of years. Julius Caesar had his own troubles in dealing with the private merchants on which he relied for supplies during his foreign campaigns.

Contracting now stretches into virtually every nook and cranny of American government. Governments have long relied on for-profit contractors to build roads. Minneapolis hired a private organization to manage its schools and linked its pay to performance on educational goals. Florida privatized its child welfare program. The city of Los Angeles decided to contract out the management of its convention facility. The Texas Department of Transportation moved most of its information technology workers to a private company, in a search for greater productivity. Most state governments rely on their counties to administer social service programs, and many of these programs are administered through nonprofit organizations that serve as contractors. It's hard to find any area of government at any level that has not joined the march to greater contracting out.

The federal government obtains a substantial amount of goods and services for its operations through contracts with private companies, research institutions, and individual consultants. In fiscal 2011, federal spending on contracts totaled $535 billion, about 15 percent of all federal spending.[43] The Department of Defense accounted for most of the contracting, followed by the Departments of Energy, Health and Human Services, and NASA. Aggressive efforts to rein in contracting during the Obama administration produced a substantial slowdown from the growth of federal contracting that had characterized federal spending for decades, and the administration celebrated "this bending of the procurement spending curve."[44]

Despite this slowdown, the federal government contracts out for a remarkable range of activities. Traditionally, contracts have dealt with such needs as the purchase of supplies and equipment and the lease of buildings, but now contractors also provide

During America's campaigns in both Iraq and Afghanistan, there was more than one contractor for every soldier.

research and development of everything from new weapons systems to new treatments for bioterrorism. Contractors do much of the work of the space program; indeed, 90 percent of NASA's budget goes to contracts. Contracting has spread far into the defense and intelligence services, including what P. W. Singer calls the rise of a new "privatized military industry" in which hundreds of companies, thousands of employees, and billions of dollars work to support the armed forces.[45] When the United States invaded Iraq in 2003, contractors provided most of the logistical support, from trucking in gasoline to cooking the meals. The contractors trained the Iraqi police force and guarded military convoys. When American administrator Paul Bremer traveled around Iraq, he flew in a helicopter operated by a private security company, which also provided his personal bodyguards. And in 2004, when investigators learned that American soldiers had been caught on camera torturing Iraqi prisoners, they also discovered that the prison personnel included security officers and interrogators who were private contractor employees. In the end, there were as many contractor employees as soldiers in Iraq. As Singer concluded,

> the problem is that not all those involved were U.S. soldiers. While the military has established structures to investigate, prosecute and punish soldiers who commit crimes, the legal status of contractors in war zones is murky. Soldiers are accountable to the military code of justice wherever they are located, but contractors are civilians—not part of the chain of command.[46]

Contractors were an integral part of the wars in Iraq and Afghanistan, to the point that there was one contractor for every soldier in the battlefield (see Table 12.1). The contractors provided a vast range of services, from transportation of fuel and ammunition to cafeteria and maintenance. That contrasts sharply with the strategy for World War II, where there

TABLE 12.1	Presence of Contractor Personnel during U.S. Military Operations		
	Estimated Personnel (Thousands)		
Conflict	**Contractor**[a]	**Military**	**Estimated Ratio of Contractor to Military Personnel**[a]
Revolutionary War	2	9	1 to 6
War of 1812	n.a.	38	n.a.
Mexican-American War	6	33	1 to 6
Civil War	200	1,000	1 to 5
Spanish-American War	n.a.	35	n.a.
World War I	85	2,000	1 to 24
World War II	734	5,400	1 to 7
Korea	156	393	1 to 2.5
Vietnam	70	359	1 to 5
Gulf War	9[b]	500	1 to 55[b]
Balkans	20	20	1 to 1
Iraq Theater as of Early 2008[c]	190	200	1 to 1

Source: U.S. Congressional Budget Office, *Contractors' Support of US Operations in Iraq* (Washington, D.C.: Congressional Budget Office, August 2008), 13, http://www.cbo.gov/ftpdocs/96xx/doc9688/08-12-IraqContractors.pdf.

Note: n.a. = not available.

a. For some conflicts, the estimated number of contractor personnel includes civilians employed by the U.S. government. However, because most civilians present during military operations are contractor personnel, the inclusion of government civilians should not significantly affect the calculated ratio of contractor personnel to military personnel.

b. The government of Saudi Arabia provided significant amounts of products and services during Operations Desert Shield and Desert Storm. Personnel associated with those provisions are not included in the data or the ratio.

c. For this study, the Congressional Budget Office considers the following countries to be part of the Iraq theater: Iraq, Bahrain, Jordan, Kuwait, Oman, Qatar, Saudi Arabia, Turkey, and the United Arab Emirates.

were seven soldiers for every contractor. Digging more deeply into history, however, reveals a big surprise. America has *always* relied on contractors when waging war. The Revolutionary War wasn't that different from the Korean War or the war in Vietnam. Why contractors? They provide valuable support, enhance the government's flexibility, and allow the military to deploy more of its forces to battle instead of holding them back for support. The use of contractors, however, sometimes comes with considerable risks. In 2010, a Senate committee discovered that contractors hired to provide security for American forces in Afghanistan were, in some cases, secretly members of the Taliban, the very group that the soldiers were deployed in Afghanistan to root out.[47]

Advantages

Contracting out has several important advantages, including efficiency and flexibility.

Cost Reduction

To many of its proponents, the greatest advantage of contracting is saving money. During the Reagan administration, a presidential commission concluded that "privatization" of many goods and services would improve them and that it would be better to have government "provide services without producing them"—that is, by contracting out.[48] In fact, the commission's chairman, J. Peter Grace, concluded that "one of the major inefficiencies in government is that it tries to do everything." Although estimates of cost savings usually vary wildly, most analysts agree that contracting can save money.

Special Expertise

Contracts enable the government to obtain the services of outside specialists. An agency may not have workers with the needed skills, or those it has with those skills may be fully occupied with their regular duties. For some assignments, the most competent specialists may be found outside government either because the pay is better or because they favor the work environment in universities, research institutes, and private companies.

Reducing Red Tape

Contracting also tends to bypass the bureaucratic syndrome that handicaps large government agencies: the very bureaucratic rules designed to promote fairness, competence, and accountability can prevent quick and effective action on problems. An independent organization can assemble an integrated team to study multidimensional problems; within government, such efforts often encounter all the difficulties of interbureau and interdepartmental coordination. Many projects, fur-  thermore, are short term in nature, and a contract (with a built-in termination date) avoids the problem of setting up permanent bureaucratic units for temporary problems.

Additional Flexibility

Contracting is often attractive because contractors' staff members are not counted as government employees and are not subject to regulations governing the civil service. When budget constraints put ceilings on agency size, and when elected officials are leery of appearing to support the unpopular government bureaucracy, policymakers can minimize bureaucratic growth by contracting out. Government's reach thus can be extended without increasing its employment rolls. And because contractors are not subject to many government regulations, especially in the hiring, firing, and pay rates of staff, many government managers welcome the opportunity to contract out.

Problems

Contracting out can also pose problems, some of them the mirror images of the supposed advantages. Most of the problems come down to two questions: How can contractors be selected and their performance controlled so that the government's objectives are achieved? How can contractors preserve their independence in the face of controls that the government attempts to impose? In short, contracting confronts the same issue of control versus autonomy that arose in the consideration of grant programs.

Choice of Contractors

The organizations with which the government contracts for goods and services are a varied lot. Some are operated for profit, while others (such as universities) are nonprofit organizations. Some contractors take on the government's work as only a fraction of their total activity; others are wholly dependent on government contracts; many that have other income, including universities as well as private firms, find government contract income indispensable to their survival. The theory of contracting is that opening government programs up to competitive bids invites competition among contractors that will drive prices down and keep quality up. Nevertheless, many federal contracts, especially smaller ones, are not awarded through competition: one-third of federal contract dollars are awarded noncompetitively.[49]

Large contracts are sometimes so complicated that few potential providers can assemble the expertise needed to do the job. One of the richest contracts in federal government history, a $4.5 billion competition for a new government telephone system, drew sustained interest from only two groups of bidders—and the contract was so complicated that even AT&T did not tackle the project on its own.[50] Even where there is competition, the government often cannot take full advantage of it. For example, because only two American companies are equipped to build submarines, the Pentagon believes that it is in the national interest to keep both companies in the business, so it often splits or alternates contract awards to ensure that both companies survive. Boeing found itself enmeshed in a major scandal in 2002 and 2003 because the Pentagon tried to direct a big contract for new air-refueling tankers to the company—and away from its major European competitor, Airbus Industries—although critics, including Sen. John McCain (R-Ariz.), charged that the planes might not be needed, were overpriced, and might not be the best suited to the job.[51]

Though the evidence is mixed, the contracting system appears to reward entrepreneurship more than demonstrated competence.[52] Large firms receive new contracts and extensions of old ones despite expensive past failures, lack of staff qualified for the particular projects, and conflicts of interest. Sometimes a sponsoring agency shows partiality to a firm that is sympathetic to the program, is unlikely to criticize its implementation, enjoys past connections with key agency personnel, or is in a position to facilitate their future careers.

Overspecification

Government contracting, especially for weapons, tends to prescribe "ultra" features to out-perform any potential threat or surpass any potential problem. Government naturally wants the best, especially for its fighting men and women, but the procurement bureaucracy has a knack for "goldplating" specifications.[53] In *The Pentagon and the Art of War*, Edward N. Luttwak argued that this problem is the result of overmanagement caused by an oversupply of senior military officers, which produces "the ultimate case of too many cooks in one kitchen—or rather, of kitchens greatly enlarged to accommodate more cooks around fewer pots."[54] In military weapons, furthermore, contractors must follow a complex collection of military specifications that prescribe in elaborate detail just how the equipment must perform. The specifications for one military aircraft ranged over 24,000 documents, one of which, for electronic parts, referred to 235 other documents, which in turn referred to 1,374 more, of which half were more than ten years old. To follow the rules precisely meant installing obsolete components into frontline equipment.[55]

Not surprisingly, as problems change over the life of the contract, so too do contracts' goals—which makes the problem of measuring results against objectives ever more complex. Overspecification of the details of a contract can limit the flexibility of government managers and contractors alike, drive up the cost, and lengthen the time needed to produce the goods; it can also enhance "specification creep," whereby more and more requirements get built into the contract. Of course, too few specifications can produce goods that cannot perform in the harsh environments that government goods—especially military hardware—sometimes face. In the absence of a clear financial bottom line, an attitude of "better safe than sorry" often leads to overspecification.

Underperformance

The American Federation of State, County, and Municipal Employees (AFSCME), worried that the growth of contracting would eliminate the jobs of government employees who were union members, compiled an extensive catalog of contract abuses. AFSCME found, for example, that 30 percent of school lunch "meal packs" served by contractors were deficient in basic nutrients:

> It would appear that a child eating these meal packs—especially with the usual amount of plate waste—would not be receiving iron and Vitamin A in adequate amounts. Here, it is essentially critical to remember that iron deficiency anemia is the most common of our [nutritional] deficiency diseases.

Of thirty-four meals served by one contractor, fourteen were hamburgers, "variously adorned," and eight were hot dogs. Children were served vegetables only six times in a two-month period.[56]

The Government Accountability Office (GAO) surveyed contracts issued by the General Services Administration (GSA) over three years and found that the government had awarded more than $1 billion in contracts to vendors who repeatedly had failed to meet contract specifications and delivery schedules. Despite the problems, "GSA has continued to do business with repeat poor performing vendors." GAO found two reasons for this laxity. First, GSA's managers often had little good information on vendors' past performance; managers could not avoid poor vendors if they did not know who they were. Second, GSA had not always emphasized product quality in making decisions. "Poor performance on GSA supply contracts has been a long-standing problem," GAO concluded.[57]

Overregulation

Contractors face a bewildering array of regulations with which they must comply. It is not unusual for the attachments to a small contract simply listing all these rules to be longer than the stipulations of the contract itself. So in addition to having to deliver goods and services that often are tailor-made to the government's specifications, contractors also must comply with a host of procedural standards, from financial recordkeeping to hiring principles, that can often prove expensive and time consuming.

Sanctions

Government officials supervising private contractors confront the same problem in imposing sanctions as do their colleagues overseeing federal grants: cutting off the contract is often more trouble than it is worth and, in the meantime, deprives government of the goods or services it needs. When the space shuttle *Challenger* exploded because of a defect in its solid rocket booster, NASA had no other supplier it could turn to. Punishing the contractor, Morton Thiokol, by canceling the booster contract would have grounded the shuttle for years until a new contractor geared up its operations. Even in the provision of more routine services, such as garbage collection, governments often have relatively few contractors among which to choose.

Corruption

The awarding of valuable contracts has always tempted the unscrupulous to make a quick profit at the government's expense. As the AFSCME study put it, "Government contracting and corruption are old friends."[58] Corruption in state and local contracts has a rich history, as contractors have long paid government officials kickbacks and bribes to win contracts, and contractors have colluded among themselves to fix bids and thus share the government's contract bounty. In New York State, for example, ten road construction companies were indicted for bid rigging: arranging among themselves who would bid how much on which contracts, thus boosting their profits on more than $100 million in contracts over eight years.[59] More recently, the fuzzier lines between the public and private sectors have increased conflict-of-interest problems, in which government employees steer business to firms that have been in the past—or may be in the future—their business connections. Of the enormous growth in what some experts call this "new patronage," one Washington interest group official noted, "The opportunities for misbehavior have increased tremendously as governments have gone to contracting out" as a way to save money.[60] "You make more money rigging bids than robbing banks—more than you could dealing drugs," one federal attorney explained.[61]

Nor are contracting scandals limited to state and local governments. During the Reagan administration, Wedtech, a small Bronx, New York–based tool-and-die manufacturer, used every device at its disposal to acquire more than $200 million in government contracts. The company admitted that it had forged more than $6 million in invoices submitted to the federal government for payment, and, federal prosecutors charged, the company's officials had used their friendship with top administration officials, including presidential counselor and later Attorney General Edwin Meese, to win contracts. The company eventually went out of business, but not before sixteen people connected with the scandal had been indicted, ranging from former White House aide Lyn Nofziger, to a member of Congress, Rep. Mario Biaggi (D-N.Y.), to the New York regional administrator for the Small Business Administration.[62]

It would be tempting to leap to the cynical conclusion that such corruption is epidemic in government contracting, but, of course, it is not. Most contractors are honest and hardworking, and most government officials struggle to get the most for the public's tax dollar. The recurring lessons of corruption in contracting, however, emphasize two broader lessons about implementation through contracting. First, contracting is not an automatic, easy solution to the problems of implementing programs directly through government agencies; instead, it replaces one set of administrative problems with another. Second, to be managed well, contracting requires a sophisticated collection of different administrative tools, which need to be tailored to the special implementation problems of contracting.[63] Also, it requires incorruptible and highly competent government officials to manage the contracts.

Inherently Governmental Functions

Basic governmental policy requires that the government itself make the basic decisions that are fundamental to the public interest, what federal regulations call "inherently governmental functions."[64] Federal regulations, for example, prohibit the government from contracting out the prosecution of criminal cases, the command of the armed forces, the conduct of foreign relations, and the decisions about agency policy and budgets. The dividing line separating these functions and activities that can be contracted out, however, is anything but clear. In 2013, intelligence analyst Edward Snowden stunned Americans—and most of the rest of the world—by revealing that the secret National Security Agency was monitoring vast amounts of telephone and email communication in the search for clues about possible terrorist plots. Insiders were not surprised. The activities were reviewed by select members of Congress and approved by a special, secret federal Foreign Intelligence Surveillance Court. Investigations revealed that Snowden himself was not working for the NSA but for a private contractor, Booz Allen Hamilton. He had a top-level security clearance to do the work, and a private contractor did the background check that produced the clearance. That is, a private contractor reviewed the qualifications of another private contractor to have access to private communications of American citizens. In fact, of the nearly five million Americans who held "top secret" security clearances, more than 20 percent worked for private contractors.[65] Everything about this story seemed completely legal, except for Snowden's decision to disclose highly classified information. But the under-story raised profound questions about the role of private contractors in some of the most sensitive issues in American public administration.

THE IMPORTANCE OF FEEDBACK

Getting good results depends on the ability of managers to obtain feedback on how well their subordinates are performing and what results the program is producing. The problem, as Herbert Kaufman puts it, is this: "When managers die and go to heaven, they may find themselves in charge of organizations in which subordinates invariably, cheerfully, and fully do as they are bid. Not here on earth."[66] There often is a mismatch between goals and results—much of the implementation literature is based on this notion, as illustrated by Pressman and Wildavsky's plaintive subtitle, *How Great Expectations in Washington Are Dashed in Oakland.*[67]

Furthermore, managers often have a very difficult time discovering the bad news. As Chapter 10 showed, numerous bureaucratic pathologies block and distort the flow of information, especially about problems, from the bottom of an organization (or from outside proxies) to the top. In late 1988, for example, top officials from the Department of Energy and from its predecessor, the Atomic Energy Commission, denied ever having been told that there were serious safety problems at the department's Savannah River nuclear power plant. The highest officials apparently were unaware that there had been a partial meltdown at the plant in 1970, among thirty other accidents.[68]

Administrative Feedback

Such information blockages pose critical problems for implementers. It is unreasonable to expect any manager to get things right the first time, since difficulties inevitably crop up. Indeed, the crucial problem in implementation is not avoiding problems but detecting and solving them, and solving problems is obviously impossible if managers cannot discover them. Therefore, good implementers must develop strategies for obtaining feedback.

Some feedback comes through routine administrative monitoring. Kaufman, for example, identifies five major sources of information about implementation: (1) the trail of paper that programs generate, which can provide valuable clues about performance; (2) personal inspection, which gets supervisors out from behind their desks to see what is happening in the field; (3) personal contacts outside the agency, which can help administrators bypass internal information problems; (4) investigations, which allow administrators to probe individual problems; and (5) centralized data collection, which can provide early warning about problems.

Unexpected sources of information can also provide valuable feedback. Citizens' complaints can hint at problems lower in the bureaucracy. Reports by the news media, such as the 1988 *New York Times* investigation of the Department of Energy's nuclear power plant problems, can help bring important data to the surface. Disaffected employees, often called whistleblowers, can sometimes produce explosive surprises.[69] For example, the federal False Claims Act, passed in 1863 to penalize contractors who were cheating the army, entitles the government to three times the amount of any overcharges or fraudulent claims—and the person who brings the charge to light is entitled to a reward of 15 to 25 percent of the government's takings. The prospect of a multimillion dollar bounty has prompted some employees and former employees of defense contractors to come forward with evidence against their bosses.[70]

Formal Program Evaluation

Unsystematic feedback, no matter how useful, leaves large gaps. Managers therefore often develop formal systems of evaluation to provide regular, high-quality feedback. "With objective information on the outcomes of programs, wise decisions can be made on budget allocations and program planning. Programs that yield good results will be expanded; those that make poor showings will be abandoned or drastically modified," as Carol H. Weiss argues.[71] Faced with the inevitable paradox of too much or too little information, officials seek regular and reliable feedback through formal evaluation strategies.

Formal evaluation has obvious advantages. Managers can design their program evaluations to test precisely what they want and to obtain just the information they need. Moreover, compared with the rest of policy research, the methodology for conducting evaluation research is well accepted and effective.[72] Balancing the potential for such careful experimentation, however, is the risk that, when finished, the research will simply collect dust. Careful program evaluation requires controlled experiments and lengthy tests. The political world sometimes cannot tolerate the controls, such as having some groups receive the program while others do not, because most public programs are perceived as benefits, and it is hard to deprive some of the potential advantages for experimental purposes. Furthermore, the long time required to conduct careful research means that results sometimes emerge years after initial interest in new programs—and perhaps years after policy decisions were made. Managers sometimes respond by conducting quick-and-dirty studies that provide useful, if not always fully scientifically valid, feedback. They can also design evaluation strategies that feed more directly into management decisions.[73] But even if evaluations do not directly affect program decisions, they often do affect the intellectual debate over programs by shaping the ideas that structure future decisions. The key, Majone argues, is "to develop methods of assessment that emphasize learning and adaptation rather than expressing summary judgments of pass or fail."[74] Evaluations can be expensive, and policy analysis is often the first area cut when budget reductions loom. But a clear-headed look at whether programs produce solid results is a fundamental building block of good administrative leadership.

Results-Based Management

Many state and local governments have created quick-response information systems to measure success and failure. Unlike other performance systems, which take long-term perspectives to evaluate the overall performance of governmental programs, these systems seek to give managers real-time feedback.

Soon after taking office in 1994, New York mayor Rudolph Giuliani committed his administration to reducing crime in the city. His police commissioner, William Bratton, announced that he would seek to reduce crime by 40 percent in three years—a target three times higher than the city's improvement over the previous three years—and he devolved substantial operating decisions to the city's precinct commanders. To help them focus their actions, he then launched a major results-based management system, christened CompStat. A special unit produced weekly reports on crime in each precinct; Bratton and his senior staff made these reports the focus of twice-per-week staff meetings. The centerpiece of these sessions was an array of three eight-by-eight-foot screens, which mapped crime patterns on precinct-based street grids. This geographic information system (GIS) provided an instant snapshot of where crime was occurring, including whether patterns were emerging. If, for example, the GIS showed that a cluster of robberies had occurred in a particular neighborhood over the previous week, the precinct commander could devise a strategy for deploying police officers to break that pattern.

In the past, crime statistics had often appeared months later and had little to do with setting patrol patterns. In contrast, the rapid-response potential of CompStat, coupled with the GIS, gave Bratton and his staff the ability to track where problems were occurring and to shift police strategy very quickly. It also gave the staff timely information about the performance of precinct commanders. CompStat thus helped reinforce the crime-control strategy of the department's top officials, and crime statistics fell dramatically—by 12 percent overall, compared with a 1.1 percent decline nationwide.[75] NYPD has continued to use the CompStat system aggressively, and the program has led to further dramatic declines in crime. Some critics have suggested that complaints about police misconduct rose at the same time, perhaps because the new police strategy encouraged police officers to be more aggressive. Nevertheless, it was impossible to escape the fact that the results-based management approach had led to a dramatic decline in crime.

Many state and local governments have adopted similar performance systems. Baltimore, for example, developed an aggressive effort to measure the ongoing performance of all city programs and to feed the information into regular meetings between the mayor and top city officials. Called CitiStat, the system shifted analysis from the broad-scale long-term analysis of PPBS (planning-programming-budgeting system) and previous analytical budget systems to a focus on weekly turnaround of information about key indicators. CitiStat transferred these indicators to maps of the city, and the mayor and his top officials used these maps to measure performance, to administer programs, and ultimately to make budgetary decisions. Then-Mayor Martin O'Malley (he was later elected Maryland governor and took the system statewide) outlined four basic tenets of the approach:

- accurate and timely intelligence
- effective tactics and strategies
- rapid deployment of resources
- relentless follow-up and assessment[76]

For example, city officials tracked the location of fires to identify whether the arson prevention task force was effective, monitored the trail of the city's cleanup program, and evaluated efforts to rub out rats. Other GIS displays showed the status of solid waste problems, graffiti cleanup, and filled potholes. Like many other cities, Baltimore also created a separate 311 call center, which allowed citizens to telephone city officials to report nonemergency problems and to get information about city services. Baltimore created extensive mapping capabilities on its website (www.baltimorecity.gov/Government/AgenciesDepartments/CitiStat.aspx) to allow citizens to track the progress of 311 calls as well as other city services.

CitiStat represents a new strategy for producing better information about the results of governmental programs and coupling them to budgetary decisions. Baltimore officials have supplemented CitiStat with CitiTrack, a central call system to help solve citizen problems.

Citizens can dial the 311 number and use CitiTrack to connect with the agency that handles the problem. The city not only uses CitiTrack to help streamline citizens' interaction with government but also feeds the complaints back into CitiStat as evidence of what problems are popping up where. New York City created a broad and data-rich City-wide Performance Reporting Tool (CPR, for short; www.nyc.gov/html/ops/cpr/html/home/home.shtml), which revolutionized the way the city collected and managed data on the performance of its programs.

When O'Malley was elected Maryland governor, he took the system with him and expanded it to a new system to reduce pollution in the Chesapeake Bay. This BayStat system provides monitoring of the Bay's health, as well as ongoing tracking of the government programs designed to scrub pollution from its waters. The system produces a regular report card (see Case 7.3 for a sample report card and more discussion of this program) and tracks pollution sources around the Bay's shoreline.

Other states, especially Utah, Virginia, and Washington, have led high-level efforts to strengthen information technology and e-government in improving service delivery. Former Virginia governor Mark Warner, for example, championed consolidation of the state's vast technology systems into a single new agency that has integrated the state's e-mail systems and funneled more than $1 billion in purchases through the new online procurement system, eVA.[77] Citizens are relying increasingly on e-mail to contact state legislators, and legislators are distributing e-newsletters to their constituents. These "stat" systems, Robert Behn has found, are becoming increasingly widespread and important in helping managers manage.[78]

These innovative efforts reflect yet again two of the big issues this chapter has examined. First, to make the technology systems work, governments have relied increasingly on private contractors, and that reliance has increased the need to manage these contractors well, because system design problems have sometimes proved costly. Second, the technological issues sometimes pale by comparison to the old and established problems of managing complex organizations. As Texas's chief information officer, Carolyn Purcell, argued, "The complexity is in the relationships, not really in the technology itself."[79]

FROM FAILURE TO SUCCESS

Overall, however, the story of implementation all too often is not a happy one. One study by the World Bank found that nearly a quarter of all World Bank projects failed, and that in construction and high-tech projects the failure rate sometimes rises to 60 percent. Things go wrong, the authors found, because a program might have been poorly designed, had weak top-level support, encountered bottlenecks, and didn't have feedback hard-wired in to help managers learn.[80]

However, the World Bank team—Jody Zall Kusek, Marelize Gorgens Prestidge, and Billy C. Hamilton—argue that five simple rules can greatly improve the odds of success:[81]

1. *Make it about the how.* Figuring out what managers are trying to accomplish, how much the program will cost, and who is in charge of doing what are essential first steps.
2. *Keep your champions close but your critics closer.* The World Bank team learned their lesson from *The Godfather Part II,* when Michael Corleone shared this wisdom with the members of his Mafia family. Some have attributed the quote to the Chinese general

Sun Tzu or the Italian philosopher Niccolò Machiavelli, but the point is clear: managing stakeholders, both friends and opponents, is critical to maintaining political support for moving forward.

3. *Informed networks matter; work with them.* No one organization can control everything it touches. Both the formal and informal networks connected with a program can play a powerful role in shaping success.

4. *Unclog the pipes.* Success often comes from anticipating problems before they happen and acting quickly to sweep bottlenecks away.

5. *Build the ship as it sails.* No one gets everything right the first time, and it's impossible to anticipate and solve all problems in advance. Effective programs build in a system to learn from problems, even failures. They build from a small scale, learn where the problems lie, and move to scale once managers know how best to solve or avoid the problems that lurk around the corner.

Too often, there's a sense of dread that surrounds government management because of the expectation that programs will fail. The World Bank team has seen plenty of failure. But they underline a very important point: failure isn't inevitable, and charting the right steps can vastly shrink the odds of problems and greatly enhance the chances for success.

CONCLUSION

The perspective on implementation is thus a mixed one, full of hype, hope, and despair. Three considerations may partially shift the balance toward hope.

First, many problems we label implementation actually reflect far larger administrative issues. What we call failure may be the product of goals that policymakers do not agree on and results that they do not like. If true implementation is separated out and defined as "program operations," then many alleged failures turn out not to be breakdowns in the actual process of implementation but the consequence of poor policy choices, impossibly high hopes announced at a program's conception, or misjudgments in legislative prescription of implementation strategies. Sometimes, indeed, the more efficient the implementation of a bad policy, a poor program, or a legislatively mandated faulty strategy, the more conspicuous will be the failure. So-called implementation failures thus often reflect deep and enduring problems in other parts of the policy process.

Second, our principal focus has been on implementation by American governments. But wallowing in government failure stories can make it easy to forget that the private sector's record is scarcely clean. Anyone who has ever worked for a private organization can vouch for substantial waste of materials, inefficient ways of processing paperwork, and problems of bureaucracy that match those of the public sector. Millions of automobiles have been recalled for defects, drugs have been introduced and later found to cause fatal injuries and serious birth defects, computers break down, and other problems in workmanship, services, and materials abound. This catalog of missteps is not meant to compound our misery by suggesting that nothing works anywhere but to emphasize that poor performance is not a purely public-sector problem. In fact, most of the outrageous fraud, waste, and abuse stories about government itself have involved private organizations trying to take advantage of public programs.

Finally, many implementation problems arise out of the increasing complexity of American society rather than from any failing in government itself. The more the boundaries blur—between the public and private sectors, among federal, state, and local governments—the more dependent programs become on the interrelationship of all of these organizations and the more difficult it is to achieve true success.

These mitigating considerations do not mean that implementation by American governments is what it should be. On the contrary, the evidence shows not only that implementation is often unsatisfactory but also that its improvement has been neglected—by Congress, by the president, by operating agencies, and by the research community. Improving performance requires correcting that neglect.[82]

CASE 12.1

Crashing to Earth: Obama's Signature Health Insurance Program Stumbles

In late September 2013, Sen. Ted Cruz (R-Tex.) was determined to bring back the great tradition of the filibuster, when members of the Senate would talk on the floor for endless hours to delay consideration of an issue they opposed. For Cruz, the issue was President Barack Obama's signature health insurance program, the Affordable Care Act which was also commonly referred to as "Obamacare." The program required all Americans to sign up for health insurance if they didn't already have it, and Cruz was determined to shut down the federal government, if necessary, to stop the launch of the program on October 1, 2013. And talk he did, for 21 hours straight, complete with a reading of Dr. Seuss's *Green Eggs and Ham* and an impression of Darth Vader from *Star Wars*. He failed to stop funding for Obamacare, but his speech helped galvanize Republican opposition to the program. True to their threats, they refused to continue funding the government if the funding included money for the president's program. And that led to a limited shutdown of the federal government on October 1.

But in one of the biggest ironies in American history, the program actually started up just as much of the rest of the government shut down. Obamacare launched with funding independent of the annual congressional appropriations so it was unaffected by the shutdown, and the Democrats gleefully watched Republicans take the heat for closing many government operations—except for the very one they aimed at. Political pressures rose, with the public blaming Republicans most for the shutdown. As the country neared the ceiling on the national debt on October 17, congressional Republicans caved in. They agreed to reopen the government without defunding Obamacare, and the Democrats celebrated.

For the most part, Obamacare wasn't government-funded health care. It wasn't even government-funded health insurance. It was a government-created marketplace, called an "exchange," where citizens could shop among private health insurance plans and decide what to buy. Citizens who already had health insurance didn't need to do anything. Citizens without health insurance were required to buy it, with escalating penalties over time if they did not; the poor were aided by federal subsidies to help them afford the insurance. Democrats looked forward to signing up millions of uninsured Americans, and locking in support from happy consumers so Republicans could never uproot the program.

For citizens, the exchange was really a website, Healthcare.gov, where they could shop and sign up for coverage. In the first days of October, there were early signs the website wasn't working well. Some consumers complained that they couldn't access the site, that it crashed, or that it lost their personal information after they began entering it. Administration officials pointed to the technical glitches as a sign of the program's success. It was so popular, they said, that huge demand crashed the site. "Americans are excited to look at their options for health coverage, with record demand in the first days of the marketplaces," said an administration release announcing that there would soon be fixes to the information technology problems.[1]

But the reports of problems escalated—that the website was crashing or was simply unavailable, and that it would fail to capture the information that citizens entered. As soon as the government shutdown ended, reporters began turning to the website story, and they found complaints wherever they looked. At its launch, the site featured a smiling woman who seemed thrilled to be signing up for health insurance. As the problems mounted, the government took down her picture and replaced it with four icons suggesting ways to sign up: computer, phone, an in-person visit with a counselor (called a "navigator"), and an old-fashioned paper form.

The administration brought in Jeff Zients, former acting director of the Office of Management and Budget, to troubleshoot the site, and Zients promised quick action. "We're confident by the end of November, HealthCare.gov will be smooth for a vast majority of users," he said.[2] The website gradually became more reliable and reports began surfacing of citizens who had successfully signed up for coverage, but progress was slow.

As the website improved, however, many citizens who held existing insurance policies began to receive notices that their policies were being cancelled. Estimates of the number of citizens who would lose existing policies ran into the millions. That produced outrage, since one of the bedrock promises of Obamacare had been "if you like your plan, you can keep it." In fact, he said

it at least 34 times, in some version, during the debate on the bill's passage and in the months that followed.[3] Obama was forced to apologize, saying "I am sorry that they, you know, are finding themselves in this situation, based on assurances they got from me." He reassured Americans that "I've assigned my team to see what we can do to close some of the holes and gaps in the law."[4] And he pointed out that the insurance most Americans would get under his plan would be better than the insurance it replaced. Republicans seized on the problem as evidence that they were right from the beginning: that Obamacare was a bad idea that should be repealed or defunded. One critic labeled it a sample of the "half-baked liberalism that has been popular among many Democrats for several decades."[5]

As investigating reporters started digging, the problems tumbled out. In the law, the states had primary responsibility for the exchanges and the websites, and the federal site was a fallback for states that could not—or would not—participate. Many Republican governors decided they wanted nothing to do with Obamacare, and some other governors decided it would be easier to let the feds figure out how to launch the program. So instead of Healthcare.gov covering just a handful of states, it was ultimately responsible at the program's launch for citizens in 36 states. That, in turn, made the job far larger than the administration originally anticipated.

Building the information system also proved very complicated—more complex, one state health official said, than the Manhattan Project, the program that was responsible for the first atomic bomb in the 1940s.[6] The information technology managers had to pull together information from insurance companies, provide citizens a chance to submit their own personal information, create computer matches for the options available for citizens with certain characteristics in each state, calculate the subsidy that lower-income citizens would receive under the program, allow citizens to shop for coverage, and then sign up. That was a very large number of simultaneously moving parts, and many of the pieces came together just in the last weeks before the October 1 launch.

That left very little time for careful testing—and no time at all to stress-test the system as a whole under the demand of millions of citizens expected to visit the Healthcare.gov site. By mid-November, the first numbers emerged on how many citizens managed to navigate the system—fewer than 27,000 people, of the perhaps 40 million uninsured, signed up under the federal government's portion of the program.[7] The signup period stretched until March 31, 2014, and administration officials had always expected that most individuals would sign up close to the finish line. The administration had been hoping for a first-month signup of ten times that size. The low numbers embarrassed the administration and reinforced the sense of chaos surrounding the program.

The website issues revealed deeper implementation problems. The federal government itself didn't build the website. Rather, the feds built a large private network of at least 47 different contractors to construct different parts of the system, according to a survey conducted by the Sunlight Foundation. The collection included some consulting giants, like Booz Allen Hamilton and Deloitte, a relatively unknown company called CGI Federal, which relied on contracts for almost all its business, and even a private university, George Washington University.[8] The feds had no effective "systems integrator" to supervise the effort and to pull the pieces together, so it was little wonder that, while individual pieces seemed to work well enough, the system failed when launched as a whole. And, to insulate what was essentially a startup venture from political scrutiny, the Obama administration pushed much of the work out from the Department of Health and Human Services into one of its small and relatively little-known agencies, the Centers for Medicare and Medicaid Services (CMS). CMS manages the two giant programs that compose its name, but its officials had no experience in managing a startup or in leveraging private insurance companies.

Obama's popularity slid through the debacle to the lowest point to date in his administration, and with more citizens disapproving than approving of his job performance. He suffered especially among independents, who had been so important to his reelection in 2012.[9] Democrats and Republicans fiercely debated whether the problems were the natural growing pains of a large and complex new program or a sign of a fatal overreach. Former President Bill Clinton said "we're better off with this law than without it," but House Speaker John Boehner (R-Oh.) countered "that Americans were misled when they were promised that they could keep their coverage under President Obama's health care law. The entire health care law is a train wreck that needs to go."[10] This certainly wasn't the start Obama had been hoping for in the program he intended to be his most important legacy.

Questions to Consider

1. Do you think that the Obamacare problems in October 2013 were simply the result of launching a very complicated program? Or were they the result of a serious overreach by the Obama administration? Think about the administrative implications—not whether you believe that Obamacare is a good policy.

2. In retrospect, what steps do you think that the Obama administration should have taken, from the beginning, to avoid the problems it encountered?

3. How many of the problems came from the basic design of the program—that is, from policy making—and how many came from the way it worked—that is, from program implementation? What lessons do you see in this case for the links needed between policy making and implementation?

4. Step back and consider how the government communicates expectations to citizens. Policy makers want to claim credit for big

ideas. But the bigger the idea, the harder it is to pull off. The government could promise less and exceed expectations—or make big promises and risk falling short. The government could also tell citizens that big change is hard and will take time to produce big results. How should policy makers deal with the challenge of communicating about big ideas and hard problems?

NOTES

1 CBS News, "Obamacare Website Goes Down for Repairs" (October 4, 2013), http://www.cbsnews.com/8301-201_162-57606175/

2 Jason Millman, "Jeff Zients: HealthCare.gov working by end of November," *Politico* (October 25, 2013). http://www.politico.com/story/2013/10/jeff-zients-healthcaregov-working-by-end-of-november-98850.html#ixzz2k0CK5oGo

3 Politifact.com, "Sorting Out the Real Story on 'If You Like Your Plan, You Can KeepIit'" (November 6, 2013), http://www.politifact.com/truth-o-meter/article/2013/nov/06/sorting-out-truth-if-you-your-plan-you-can-keep/

4 Juliet Eilperin, "President Obama Apologizes to Americans Who Are Losing Their Health Insurance," *Washington Post* (November 7, 2013), http://www.washingtonpost.com/politics/president-obama-apologizes-to-americans-who-are-losing-their-health-insurance/2013/11/07/2306818e-4803-11e3-a196-3544a03c2351_story.html

5 Julian Zelizer, "Obamacare and the failure of half-baked liberalism," *CNN Opinion* (November 11, 2013), http://www.cnn.com/2013/11/11/opinion/zelizer-obamacare-liberalism/

6 Interview with the author.

7 William Branigin, Sarah Kliff and Sandhya Somashekhar, "Administration: 106,000 enrolled in health insurance in first month of HealthCare.gov," Washington Post (November 13, 2013), http://www.washingtonpost.com/politics/house-committee-hears-from-technology-officials-on-health-care-exchanges/2013/11/13/91d0bc5a-4c6e-11e3-9890-a1e0997fb0c0_story.html?hpid=z1

8 Bill Allison, "Good Enough for Government Work? The Contractors Building Obamacare," *Sunlight Foundation* (October 9, 2013), http://reporting.sunlightfoundation.com/2013/aca-contractors/

9 David Lauter, "Obama's Approval Ratings Continue to Slide, New Poll Shows," *Los Angeles Times* (November 8, 2013), http://www.latimes.com/nation/politics/politicsnow/la-pn-obama-approval-ratings-slide-20131108,0,1519711.story#axzz2kRulymTo

10 Juliet Eilperin, "Bill Clinton Identifies 3 Big Problems with the Obamacare Rollout," *Washington Post* (November 12, 2013), http://www.washingtonpost.com/blogs/post-politics/wp/2013/11/12/bill-clinton-identifies-3-big-problems-with-the-obamacare-rollout/?hpid=z3

CASE 12.2

Can You See Me Now? Local Officials Grumble at New Federal Road Sign Requirements

On top of everything else you can blame aging Baby Boomers for, add millions of dollars for new street signs. The Federal Highway Administration (FHWA) has issued new regulations on street signs. Gone are old signs with street names in ALL CAPS. In are street signs in Upper and Lower Case. Why? Experts say that the mixed lettering is easier to read.

"As drivers get older, we want to make sure they're able to read the signs," explained FHWA administrator Victor Mendez. "Research shows that older drivers are better able to read signs when they're written in both capital and small letters. It's really driven by safety."[1] In addition, new FHWA regulations (http://mutcd.fhwa.dot.gov)

require communities to make their road signs easier to see at night, making them more reflective so drivers can see stop, yield, and railroad crossing signs better.

"I think it's ridiculous," complained Milwaukee Alderman Bob Donovan. His city will have to spend $1.4 million to meet the new sign standards. "Our street signs have worked perfectly well for 100 years or more. I think it's just the federal government run amok. If they don't have far more important things to deal with, they're not doing their job." In Canyon, Texas, the cost to the town would be nearly 2,000 signs at $100 each. City manager Randy Criswell said he had aging parents: "They think this is silly."[2] Critics pointed out that the feds require the new signs—but aren't providing any money to pay for them.

The regulations are very detailed. If a community installs a sign so the speed limit can be changed, the light-emitting diodes on the sign must be white.[3] Wisconsin signmakers can't use a picture of a lake to signify the exit to get to the lake.[4] In Washington State, the agency said communities couldn't use signs whose bottoms were too low (two feet instead of five feet above ground level).[5]

Then there's the answer to a question from the assistant township engineer in Wayne Township, New Jersey. The Federal Highway Administration tells him that the standard for signs warning of curves ahead is:

> In advance of horizontal curves on freeways, on expressways, and on roadways . . . that are functionally classified as arterials or collectors, horizontal alignment warning signs shall be used . . . based on the speed differential between the roadway's posted or statutory speed limit of 85th-percentile speed, whichever is higher, or the prevailing speed on the approach to the curve, and the horizontal curve's advisory speed.[6]

That, at least, was what the federal agency wrote in an attempt to clarify the policy.

Questions to Consider

1. What do you make of the criticisms from local officials of the new federal road sign requirements? Do you think that the federal government was going too far? Or are the regulations an attempt to make sure that older drivers—a group that is getting larger in number every day—can more easily see the signs on the road?

2. What's the case for allowing local officials to design their own signs, free from federal supervision and interference? What's the case for ensuring national standards for signs everywhere in the country?

3. Consider the last explanation of federal standards for warning sides of a curve ahead. Does it make sense to you? (Hint: the idea is that wherever drivers are in the country, they ought to get about the same warning of which way the road is going, and that the faster that they are driving, the farther in advance they ought to get a warning. The trick is how to translate that idea into placing the sign—and how to compensate for the fact that drivers don't always travel at the speed limit.)

NOTES

1. Larry Capeland, "ALL CAPS? Not OK on Road Signs, Federal Government Says," *USA Today,* October 21, 2010, http://www.usatoday.com/news/nation/2010-10-21-road-signs-all-caps-lowercase_N.htm.
2. Ibid.
3. http://mutcd.fhwa.dot.gov/resources/interpretations/pdf2_09_3.pdf.
4. http://mutcd.fhwa.dot.gov/resources/interpretations/pdf2_646.pdf.
5. http://mutcd.fhwa.dot.gov/resources/interpretations/pdf/2_660.pdf.
6. http://mutcd.fhwa.dot.gov/resources/intrepretations/pdf/2_09_2.pdf.

Whooping Cough Epidemic in Washington: The Importance of Public Health

A century ago, whooping cough spread dread across the country, causing more than 5,000 deaths a year. But after scientists discovered that the pertussis bacteria caused the awful respiratory disease, with its characteristic "whoop" sound, researchers produced an enormously effective vaccine. Then they went a step further and combined that vaccine and the antibodies to diphtheria and tetanus into a single shot (DPT), putting an end to the three diseases that had terrorized kids for decades.

But by the 1970s, parents were growing increasingly suspicious of the DPT vaccine, particularly that it was causing brain damage, including encephalopathy, a condition that can produce personality changes, tremors, and seizures. After a 1982 NBC documentary won an Emmy Award for its tale of children said to be injured by the vaccine, an anti-vaccination epidemic was born, spurred further by a 1998 study that suggested the measles, mumps, and rubella vaccine caused autism. (In 2010, that study was retracted by the journal that had published it.)

Today, untold thousands of children have never received these vaccinations. As a result, the dreaded diseases of the early 1900s are making a comeback. In May 2013, Washington state public health officials declared a health emergency as whooping cough galloped across the state. In just the first month, the disease infected more than 2,500 Washingtonians, with children ages ten to thirteen hit especially hard. Other states, including California and Wisconsin,

have had outbreaks as well, but in Washington the infection rose to an epidemic.

How could a disease we thought we had licked have spread so fast? Part of the explanation comes from Washington parents who took advantage of a new law allowing them to opt out of vaccinations for their kids. Another part comes as a result of a new DPT vaccine designed in the 1990s to cause fewer side effects, but which declined in effectiveness over time, leaving adults with lower levels of protection.

Perhaps the biggest part of the problem, however, comes from underinvestment in public health. Financially strapped states, including Washington, have been struggling to support programs to immunize kids, advertise the benefits of the dreaded shots, track the spread of diseases of all kinds, and manage the consequences. Becky Neff, a registered nurse in Skagit County, along the Puget Sound near the Canadian border, told a reporter, "It's the largest epidemic I've ever seen." How large? No one really knows, she explained, because the county has just two nurses compiling disease reports, compared with five just a few years ago. The nurses who are left "don't have time to call and say who's positive and negative."

The economic downturn has left a trail of debris in its wake, and public health has been especially hard hit. Rhode Island's free breast and cervical cancer screening programs have been suspended. In Washtenaw County, Michigan, budget cuts forced the government to suspend new enrollment in a health coverage program for low-income residents who didn't qualify for Medicaid. In the last two years, the local public health workforce has dropped 15 percent, according to the National Association of County and City Health Officials.

Public health workers are usually the last noticed of the first responders. The public tends to dismiss them as disease-counters and shot-givers—until killer tomatoes strike (with a salmonella outbreak in 2008) or anthrax threatens (after the 9/11 terrorist attacks).

The recent whooping cough outbreak shows how fast disease can spread. The 1918 Spanish flu pandemic, which killed more than fifty million people around the world, showed just how serious that can be. And in today's super-linked world, any disease anywhere can deposit itself on anyone's doorstep in just hours. In fact, just one airplane passenger from Hong Kong brought severe acute respiratory syndrome (SARS) to Toronto in 2003. The resulting outbreak virtually shut the city down and killed forty-four people.

The Washington whooping cough emergency, fortunately, didn't rise to that scale. But it does raise two very worrisome points. First, disinvesting in public health now can pose serious consequences down the road. Whether we can accurately count the number of preteens struggling with whooping cough might not seem like a big deal, but if we suddenly have to track and manage the spread of a SARS-like disease, the lack of capacity would aggravate a grade-A crisis.

Second, if nervous parents push opt-out provisions on state policymakers, and if individual states loosen the requirements for vaccinations and other public health strategies, the individual decisions can quickly create far broader ripples. Many public health programs rely on the inelegantly named "herd" strategy. If almost everyone is immunized, a single whooping cough victim can easily be isolated. If large numbers of kids haven't been vaccinated, or if vaccines for their parents begin to wear off, one cough can quickly spread across the population.

Individual parents' decisions about vaccinating their kids might seem limited to their own families, but nothing could be further from the truth. It's no exaggeration to say that such parental decisions, sanctioned by individual states and repeated many times over, can have national consequences. Couple that with budget cuts at the heart of the nation's public health capacity. We see evidence everywhere of the huge consequences of the Great Recession, but Washington's whooping cough outbreak shows an important break in our first-response lines of defense.

Questions to Consider

1. How strong a stand should public health officials play in encouraging parents to vaccinate their children against whooping cough? Should aggressive regulations, like banning children from school, be part of the strategy?

2. What should be the public role of public health workers? What media briefing would you design in such a case?

3. What does this case say about the broader problem of homeland security, especially creating enough capacity in public health to deal with possible problems? Should the government invest more in state and local public health officials? How should they make that tradeoff?

Note: This case was taken from my column in *Governing*, August 2012, http://www.governing.com/columns/potomac-chronicle/col-whooping-cough-comeback-raises-troubling-questions.html.

KEY CONCEPTS

FOR FURTHER READING

Derthick, Martha. *New Towns In-Town.* Washington, D.C.: Urban Institute, 1972.

Hogwood, Brian H., and B. Guy Peters. *The Pathology of Public Policy.* Oxford: Clarendon Press, 1985.

Kusek, Jody Zall, Marelize Goergens Prestidge, and Billy C. Hamilton. *Fail-Safe Management: Five Rules to Avoid Project Failure.* Washington, D.C.: World Bank, 2013.

Mead, Lawrence M. *Government Matters: Welfare Reform in Wisconsin.* Princeton, N.J.: Princeton University Press, 2004.

Pressman, Jeffrey L., and Aaron B. Wildavsky. *Implementation.* Berkeley: University of California Press, 1973.

Wholey, Joseph S., Harry P. Hatry, and Kathryn E. Newcomer, eds. *Handbook of Practical Program Evaluation.* San Francisco: Jossey-Bass, 1994.

Wilson, James Q. *Bureaucracy: What Government Agencies Do and Why They Do It.* New York: Basic Books, 1989.

SUGGESTED WEBSITES

The Internet is full of the new initiatives in the area of program implementation. For New York City's performance management system, see **www.nyc.gov/html/ops/cpr/html/home/home .shtml**. Information about Baltimore's CitiStat program can be found at **www.baltimorecity .gov/Government/AgenciesDepartments/ CitiStat.aspx**.

For case studies on implementation problems, see the report of the study committee that investigated the *Columbia* space shuttle accident, **www.nasa.gov/columbia/home/ index.html**; the special report on emergency response in New York on the morning of September 11, 2001, **www.nyc.gov/html/fdny/ html/mck_report/index.shtml**; and the report of the Arlington County September 11, 2001, response at the Pentagon, **www.co.arlington .va.us/Departments/Fire/edu/about/ FireEduAboutAfterReport.aspx**.

PART

V

ADMINISTRATION IN A
DEMOCRACY

Establishing bureaucracy in a democracy creates two sets of issues. As we saw in Chapter 1, not only do we want to see programs managed efficiently and effectively, but we also want the process and the results to be responsive and accountable. And as we have seen throughout the book, the quest for accountability and effectiveness is, at its core, a political act. This section examines the dynamics of bureaucracy's relationship with the larger political and economic system, especially the exercise of administrative power through regulation. We also examine the methods that legislatures can use in controlling the way administrators exercise the power delegated to them.

The core of administrative ethics in the public sector lies in balancing the competing goals of efficiency and accountability. We want administrators to be efficient and accountable, but crosscutting political forces make it hard to achieve either goal, let alone accomplish both. We conclude the book by revisiting where we started: with a careful look at how the competing forces of accountability, effectiveness, and politics affect administration in a democracy.

CHAPTER

13

- ■ Understand the role of regulation in public administration

- ■ Explore the kinds of regulation

- ■ Examine the steps in regulatory procedure

- ■ Probe the ways in which regulators are held accountable

Regulation and the Courts

As the New York Yankees finished their 2008 baseball season, a new stadium rose next door. For nostalgic fans, it was a difficult transition. Babe Ruth had christened the old stadium with a home run on its opening day in 1923. The new stadium promised luxury boxes and a martini bar.

MAJOR LEAGUE BASEBALL HELD ITS 2008 ALL-STAR GAME at venerable Yankee Stadium. As baseball Commissioner Bud Selig explained, "When you think of Yankee Stadium, it is the most famous cathedral in baseball, and, I think, the most famous stadium in the world." And the 2008 season was also the stadium's last, "So we really believe that this is the way we can honor the cathedral that has meant so much to this sport for so long."[1] Baseball fans everywhere knew it as "the house that Ruth built," an enduring homage to one of the game's most famous sluggers and a tribute to legions of fans who cheered on the championships. But it was also a reminder to Yankees' fans of the culture shock coming their way. As a new stadium rose next door, officials were planning the demolition of the old relic and conversion of the site into a park.

During the new stadium's construction, however, city officials discovered a big problem. Local government regulations required a check on the quality of the concrete poured in construction projects—faulty concrete could cause buildings to collapse. At the stadium and at other projects in New York City, including the new building rising at the World Trade Center, city investigators found that a private company, Testwell Laboratories, had not properly completed required tests on the concrete and then falsely certified more thorough tests. When asked why a company might not conduct required tests, an official explained, "I guess it keeps your overhead and costs down if you don't actually do the tests."[2] That, of course, does nothing to ensure the safety of the building.

Tough concrete standards are important. After all, the collapse of part of the concrete ceiling in Boston's "Big Dig" tunnel killed a driver in July 2006. To get the job done, the regulatory chain was complex: the city wrote the rules, and it hired a private contractor to check on whether other private contractors were complying with the standards. As we saw in Chapter 11, layers of contractors are part of the implementation process. They are just as essential to government regulation. Regulation, of course, is a core element of government's work. It defines how government officials exercise their discretion, and how private companies connect with the public, from the safety of the foods we eat to the security of our bank deposits. Decisions might be the central governmental act, and budgets provide what administrators need to carry out those decisions, but regulations are the central nervous system of government.

REGULATION AS A FOUNDATION FOR GOVERNMENT'S WORK

Government regulation defines *how* government administrators do their work. It translates complex tax laws into the forms that taxpayers love to hate, and it sets the rules that keep planes safely in the air. Regulations specify the size of reflectors on bicycle wheels and ensure the accessibility of public buildings. Rules both empower and limit government employees. They define how far government administrators can push into the lives of ordinary citizens, and thereby restrict their freedom; they limit how far government administrators can push their control, and thereby protect citizens. Government regulates the vitamin pills we take and the therapeutic claims that go on our toothpaste tubes. It controls the safety of our prescription drugs and of our cars. It oversees the maintenance of airplanes and buses and sets the standards for highway guardrails and interstate buses. It is literally impossible to get out of bed in the morning without encountering a government regulation, since the government regulates the bedding on which we sleep and, famously, the tags on the pillows on which we rest our heads. (It *is* legal to cut away the tags on pillows—but only consumers can use the scissors, after they take the pillows home. The tags protect consumers by providing information about what materials are inside the pillow but which the consumer can't see.) If public administration revolves around the balance of power and accountability, regulation defines how public administrators balance individual freedom and government control.

Some government regulation exists to promote public health and safety. There are rules restricting the sale of tobacco and requiring warning labels on packages. There is consumer information on prescription drugs and even more information supplied to doctors. In 1997, the Food and Drug Administration (FDA) ordered the popular diet pill Fen-Phen (short for the combination of fenfluramine and phentermine) be taken off the market because of evidence that it had caused fatal side effects. Applying for a credit card or a student loan brings pages of disclosure information; in recent years, government has continually revised the rules to provide more protection while making the disclosures easier to read.

Three issues are central to this work. One is the *source of regulatory authority*: the law vests administrative discretion in agencies, and it specifies how that discretion can be exercised. A second is the *amount of resources* that legislatures and the executive make available to the agencies for performance of their regulatory responsibilities: regardless of what the law or regulations say, administrators cannot enforce the rules unless they have the resources—people, computers, and travel funds, among others—to do so. An ageless part of the regulatory game is to write a law but handcuff the regulation, especially by denying agencies the resources they need to manage the rules. A third feature is *regulatory procedure*: the interplay between responsibility for regulating private behavior and the rules that the legislature, the chief executive, and the courts establish to govern the behavior of regulating agencies and employees. These three issues form the core of this chapter.

Government regulations range broadly. At one extreme are speed limits and stoplights, which govern ordinary behavior in daily life. At the other extreme are fundamental restrictions on liberty, and sometimes government intrusion into individual privacy. An individual cannot practice medicine or law without a state license; some states regulate hairdressers and dog groomers as well. In most cities, local governments set the fares that taxicab drivers can charge. In New York State, dentists battled state rules over who could regulate the state's dentists and what role the regulators can play. Many citizens were surprised to learn in 2013 the scope of the National Security Agency's surveillance of phone calls and email traffic. To truly understand government—and even more fundamentally, to truly understand public administration—one must understand government regulation.

The Roots of Regulation

Regulation goes back millennia. The Ten Commandments, after all, were part of God's compact with the Israelites after their release from pharaoh's bondage. In the United States, regulation goes back to the beginning of the nation. The Constitution in 1789 gave Congress the power "to promote the progress of science and useful arts by securing for limited times to authors and inventors the exclusive right to their respective writings and discoveries."[3] This book is protected against plagiarism by a certificate issued by the U.S. Copyright Office, which administers a statute based on that provision. But this same constitutional grant of power has had far broader impact. In 1988, administering a statute under the same clause, the Patent and Trademark Office awarded the world's first animal-invention patent to Harvard University, whose scientists had transformed a mouse through genetic manipulation.[4]

Just *how far* government's regulatory power should go, of course, is a fundamental question of government. In this book, we focus on *how* the executive branch administers regulation. But the nonstop *how far* political controversy inevitably spills over into the *how* question. Regulation is grounded in law, but it's shaped by politics.[5]

The public certainly has mixed feelings about regulation. Many critics complain that government regulation of business usually does more harm than good, that there are too many government regulations, and that too many rules make too little sense.[6] Yet most people do not favor rolling back government regulations that protect their workplace, safeguard the environment in their neighborhood, ensure the safety of the airplanes on which they fly, or set standards for the security of their bank accounts. Individuals do not like the idea of a big government interfering in their freedom, but they clearly expect government to protect them from danger, even if that means interfering in someone else's freedom. Indeed, the standard reaction to problems ranging from plane crashes to poisoned food is to interview government regulators. Why, reporters ask, did government fail to prevent the problem from happening, even if the problem was the result of mistakes made by private companies?

Regulation is inevitably a matter of balancing its costs with its benefits, but it's just as much a matter of determining *who* pays the costs and *who* receives the benefits. America's approach to regulation is unique, David Vogel finds, because of both the way the process works and the level of the conflict it creates:

> The American system of regulation is distinctive in the degree of oversight exercised by the judiciary and the national legislature, in the formality of its rulemaking and enforcement process, in its reliance on prosecution, in the amount of information made available to the public, and in the extent of the opportunities provided for participation by nonindustry constituencies. . . . The restrictions the United States has placed on corporate conduct affecting public health, safety, and amenity are at least as strict as and in many cases stricter than those adopted by other capitalist nations. As a result, in no other nation have the relations between the regulated and the regulators been so consistently strained.[7]

THE JOB OF REGULATION

Regulatory agencies vary in the kinds of regulation they administer.[8] Administrators are typically more expert in the issues than the legislators who write the laws and the courts who interpret them, but all three branches of government play major roles in regulation.

Kinds of Regulations

Government regulation is of two kinds: economic and social. The expansion of **economic regulation** began in the states, but in the federal government it dates from 1887, when the Interstate Commerce Commission was established to regulate the railroads.[9] It was the dominant form of regulation until the 1960s. Economic regulation has two characteristics. First, it has long sought to ensure competition by preventing monopolies and unfair methods of competition (including deception of consumers); these **antitrust laws** embrace all industries where such evils may appear and are administered by the Justice Department and the Federal Trade Commission. Second, in the effort to ensure fair and quality markets, the federal government has regulated the following aspects of economic activity: (1) entry to a business (by issuance or denial of "certificates of convenience and necessity," which are licenses to do business and serve certain routes or areas); (2) prices (by fixing maximum and, in some cases, minimum rates to be charged); (3) safety; and (4) standards of service.

At both the state and the federal levels, government has typically lodged responsibility in independent regulatory commissions. These bodies tend to be separate from cabinet agencies and headed by boards. In most cases, the law ensures a balance on the boards between the political parties (although the party in power can often appoint the chair and secure a majority of commission votes). Each commission regulates a single industry or handful of industries, such as public utilities (gas, water, electric, and telephone companies), taxicabs, and airlines. The single-industry focus gives the regulatory commission special expertise, but it also increases the chance that the commission will fall under the domination of the industry it is supposed to regulate. Analysts have long worried about the **capture** of regulators by the organizations they regulate.[10] As oil was spewing from BP's well in the Gulf of Mexico, for example, critics charged that the chief regulator, the Minerals Management Service, had not paid enough attention to safety issues because it was preoccupied with helping oil producers expand production.

Social regulation began growing in importance early in the twentieth century, through restrictions on child labor and drugs, and then expanded enormously in the 1960s and 1970s. It focuses on the quality of life by seeking to safeguard the environment, protect workers' health and safety, ensure the safety and quality of consumer products, and prohibit discrimination on grounds of race, color, sex, age, or disability. Responsibility for achieving social regulation is mostly lodged not in independent commissions but in bureaus within departments or, as with the U.S. Environmental Protection Agency (EPA), in an independent agency with a single leader instead of a board. The jurisdictions of these bureaus and agencies are not confined to single industries but cover all industries where threats to health, safety, fair employment, and the environment may occur. Although social regulation is addressed to the quality of life rather than to economic imperfections of the market, it can also have substantial market effects—by reducing a business firm's freedom to act purely in its own self-interest and, more important, by often increasing costs.

Defense of the government's power of intervention rests on the economic concept of externalities, sometimes called spillover effects (discussed in Chapter 10). If a paper mill discharges pollutants into a river, downstream communities must pay the costs of cleaning up the river or purifying their intake to assure safe drinking water for their citizens, while downstream swimmers, fishermen, and boaters pay the price in pleasures forgone. The polluting practice reduces manufacturing costs and so is rational behavior for the company, but the secondary costs—financial, aesthetic, and health-related—exported to people downstream are high. Economists would compare the manufacturer's savings to the downstream costs, and would justify regulatory action to return the costs to the polluter if the value of the benefits accrued downstream were high enough. Thus, government could make an economic case for forcing the paper mill to internalize the externalities.[11]

Economic regulation and social regulation are not two sides of a single coin. In the political world, at least, they are two quite distinct coins. Although retreating from extensive regulation of trucking, airlines, telecommunication, and financial services,[12] the Jimmy Carter and even Ronald Reagan administrations placed more elaborate protections on the environment, workers' health and safety, and consumers' products. The underlying politics were complex: economists of both liberal and conservative stripes succeeded in convincing both the president and members of Congress that economic deregulation would promote lower prices, better services, and stronger consumer choice. Meanwhile, however, the consumer and environmental movements were growing, building pressure for stronger social regulation.

There are very different political and administrative implications for economic and social regulation. In economic regulation, the regulatory agency often must consider just how much a stronger regulation might hinder market competition and increase costs. Local taxi commissions, for example, regularly debate whether they should mandate how clean a taxi should be, how the taxis are maintained, and whether taxi drivers must accept credit cards. Taxi companies often fight back on each of these rules by arguing that they would increase their costs—and the fares they must charge customers. How best to balance quality service with low fares is a central issue for local taxi commissions.

On the other hand, social regulatory agencies must often act to enforce strong, nonnegotiable standards. For example, the law requires the FDA to act immediately when a food or drug on the market is found to cause death or serious disease—and the procedural niceties must follow, rather than precede, an order to remove the product from store shelves. Sometimes regulatory action simply demands disclosure of information, such as the law requiring the labeling of health hazards on cigarette labels, or the EPA's standards for companies' disclosure of toxic materials they release into the environment. Regulated industries often fight back against proposed rules, but sometimes they actually welcome them. A single federal rule can replace a confusing collection of state and local standards. Tough rules can sometimes reassure customers and, thus, protect a company's sales.

Government agencies have many techniques for measuring a company's compliance with regulations. Some rules set technical standards, such as installing a guard around moving machine parts or installing bicycle reflectors of a certain size. Others set performance standards, such

In most communities, government regulations dictate what fares taxi drivers can charge, where they can take passengers, and even how clean their cabs have to be. In New York City, the regulations also cover where taxis can pick up and drop off their passengers.

as an allowable level of pollution a facility can release. The company can then choose the method it prefers to reach the goal. The federal government has gone even further by creating a regulatory market to regulate some pollutants. In the effort to reduce acid rain, companies can buy and sell the *right to pollute* on the Chicago Board of Trade, in yet another case in which one private company—the Board of Trade—assists the government in the regulation of other companies. This system gives companies economic incentives to reduce their emissions, with the strongest incentives for the companies that can do so most cheaply. As a result, pollution has been dramatically reduced, acid rain levels have declined, and companies have won the flexibility to determine how best to reach the legislative goal.[13]

In addition to market incentives, regulatory information provides other pressures on companies' behavior. Crash tests by the federal government's National Highway Traffic Safety Administration and by private groups such as the Insurance Institute for Highway Safety have created strong inducements for automobile manufacturers to build safer cars. Federal research on medical errors has led to consumer scorecards of hospitals. Government inspections of nursing homes and restaurants often lead either to adverse publicity for poor performers or to certificates of approval that high performers can proudly hang on their walls.[14] Other agencies rely on companies' self-reporting of workers' accidents and health impairments, although owners' incentives for accurate reporting in this area are slight.[15]

State and Local Regulations

Regulation is also a major activity of state and local governments, such as New York City's efforts to ensure that concrete for the city's construction is safe and its campaign to force fast-food restaurants to list the nutritional information of the items they sell. Their regulatory work is of two kinds. One is substantially autonomous of the national government. State governments have created public utility commissions to control intrastate rates and services, banking departments to regulate state-chartered banks, and "lemon laws" to impose disclosure and warranty requirements on used-car dealers, as well as minimum-wage and antidiscrimination laws, bottle-deposit and recycling laws, and health and safety laws and regulations that cover a wide range of enterprises—from factory conditions to nursing homes to restaurants and bars to farmers' use of pesticides. Some states impose a five-cent deposit on recyclable beverage containers; in Michigan, it's ten cents. The states, not the federal government, regulate insurance companies, even though many insurance companies operate nationally. Local governments also regulate broadly, sharing in the assurance of health and safety protections and the honesty of weights and measures (such as grocery scales and gas pumps). They administer land-use zoning, which seeks to control the location, structural features, and uses of buildings.

About 800 occupations are regulated in the United States. Some, such as attorneys, physicians, pharmacists, barbers, cosmetologists, and real estate agents, are regulated in every state.[16] Over half the states regulate funeral directors, chauffeurs, plumbers, and hearing-aid dealers, to cite only a few. Typically, licensing laws, which restrict entry to the professions and some other occupations, derive from lobbying by professional associations, which want to keep the number of competitors down and their prices up. They are often administered by substantially autonomous licensing boards whose members are effectively nominated by the associations. Though rationalized as social regulation, necessary to protect the health and safety of consumers of such services, the licensing systems actually tend to produce economic regulation, limiting competition by restricting entry.

The second regulatory role of state and local governments is administration of national regulatory programs.[17] Congress has the power to preempt much state regulatory activity, displacing it with programs executed directly by federal officials. But in many cases it has chosen the alternative of partial preemption (see Chapter 12).[18] In such fields as environmental protection, occupational safety and health, meat and poultry inspection, and energy regulation, "partial preemption centralizes policy formulation, but it shares policy implementation with the states."[19] Under this arrangement, the national government decides on regulatory standards, and each state government may choose either to administer those prescribed standards or to create and administer its own standards, provided they are at least as stringent as those of the federal government. If a state fits neither situation, the appropriate national agency directly administers its national program within the state. In fact, a state may switch around. In mid-1987, California terminated its occupational safety and health enforcement program, thereby shifting that regulatory function to direct national administration by the Department of Labor's Occupational Safety and Health Administration (OSHA). Two years later, however, California was seeking OSHA's permission to reinstitute its own program, including resumption of enforcement responsibility.

Partial preemption is now a prominent part of the regulatory system, allowing some adaptation to local circumstances and letting individual state governments choose their roles in a regulatory system. It has the advantage of permitting a state to adopt more rigorous standards than those of the national laws and regulations, which would not be possible under full national preemption. It has the disadvantage shared by all farming-out of the implementation of national policies—the weakness of federal sanctions against third-party noncompliance with national directives.[20]

In some cases, moreover, state governments set the standard that other states and even the federal government will eventually follow. California was the first state to require the installation in cars of catalytic converters, which reduce air pollution. No automaker could afford to ignore the huge California market or to build cars just for sale in California, so the catalytic converter soon became a national standard. Even though the George W. Bush administration had backed away from worldwide standards on global warming, California in 2002 passed a bill requiring that all cars sold in the state after 2009 meet tough standards for greenhouse gases, the carbon-based emissions that scientists believe promote global warming. This legislation produced a long battle with the Bush administration. Yet again, automakers could not ignore the California market, so the state's action helped nudge regulatory policy in a direction toward which the Bush administration did not want to go. In 2008, the Bush administration rejected California's policy, and both sides headed off to the federal courts.

Local governments, of course, issue regulations of their own. Most communities create zoning laws to determine where buildings can be constructed and how their owners can use them. Housing construction is impossible without water and sewage permits, and decisions about where to put water and sewer lines are the closest thing many communities have to an overall economic development plan. Some communities have even set their own minimum wages.

Statutory Mandates

Economic regulation and social regulation differ sharply in the content of legislative mandates. At both national and state levels, the economic regulation statutes have vested broad discretion in regulatory agencies: licenses to enter a business field are to be issued to serve "the public interest, convenience, or necessity," and fixed rates are to be "just and reasonable." The Federal Trade Commission is charged to eliminate "unfair methods of competition" and "deceptive practices."

Congress's social regulation statutes often contain broad phrases as well. EPA is empowered to promulgate such regulations for treatment and disposal of "hazardous wastes . . . as may be necessary to protect human health and the environment." The secretary of labor is directed "to the extent feasible" to eliminate worker exposure to toxic substances capable of causing health impairment. The Consumer Products Safety Commission is required "to protect the public against unreasonable risks of injury associated with consumer products." But sometimes the standards are remarkably detailed. The most famous specific provision is the Delaney Clause of the Food, Drug, and Cosmetic Act, which, following general requirements that the FDA approve only substances that are safe, provides that no food additive, color additive, or drug for food animals "shall be deemed to be safe if it is found to induce cancer when ingested by man or animal, or . . . after tests which are appropriate for the evaluation of the safety of [noningested] additives, to induce cancer in man and animal."[21] The clause's plain meaning is that once an additive has been found to induce cancer in animals, the FDA must ban it despite any finding that humans who ingest or apply the additive face no significant risk—and regardless of costs to manufacturers and merchants. Although the FDA has tried to chip away at the absolute standard—for example, when human risk is rated at one in a million or less—courts have insisted on strict compliance with the statute.[22]

It has always been hard to know just how to deal with the scientific uncertainty and political pressures around such regulatory issues. In 1970 the FDA banned cyclamate, an artificial sweetener, because researchers found that it caused cancer in animals. Saccharin replaced it, but researchers determined that this chemical also caused cancer in animals, although critics complained that the researchers had subjected the animals to enormous doses. Under the law, the FDA had no choice but to remove saccharin from the market, but dieters and diabetics pressured Congress to prevent the ban from taking place, pointing out that they had lost cyclamate and that there were no other good alternatives on the market. The lawmakers stepped in to permit the continued sale of saccharin (in products such as Sweet 'N Low), provided that the packaging carried a warning about the potential risks. Research continued, and in 2000 saccharin was removed from the list of chemicals causing cancer in humans. Congress promptly legislated the removal of the warning notice, although there was no dispute that saccharin caused cancer in animals. The question was how much risk this caused for humans, and whether humans were likely to ingest enough to raise their risks significantly. The scientific debate continued; the legal battle had ended.

The same issues spill over into environmental policy. For example, some statutes name specific air and water pollutants on which EPA must act. The most innovative practice is congressional setting of deadlines for agency accomplishment of statutory objectives. In the 1960s, chemical runoffs into streams often killed fish by the thousands and acid mixed with rain spread pollution even into isolated lakes. A 1969 incident in Cleveland, Ohio, drew national attention—an oil slick on the city's Cuyahoga River caught fire and caused tens of thousands of dollars of damage, especially to bridges overhead. The specter of a burning river drove home the need for fundamental changes to the nation's pollution control policies. The 1972 amendments to the Federal Water Pollution Control Act, more popularly known as the Clean Water Act, directed that navigable waters were to become fishable and swimmable by 1983 and that all discharge of pollutants into navigable waters was to be eliminated by 1985; the "best practicable" control technologies were to be in place by 1977 and the "best available" technologies by 1983—phrases that substantially limited EPA's ability to consider the cost to the regulated interests. In 1984 Congress set over two dozen specific statutory deadlines for EPA regulation of the management and disposal of currently generated hazardous waste.[23] In all, the laws for EPA contain thirty-eight mandatory deadlines for issuance of rules and regulations, and thirty-six deadlines for studies, guidelines, and reports.[24] Though many deadlines have been extended by Congress, their action-forcing is law until amendment occurs, and so they offer a peg on which environmental and other groups can hang a court case against the agency. They also serve as a spur to action, even when achievement falls short of meeting a deadline.

Expertise

Over time, the concentration of regulatory agencies on a limited agenda of concerns builds great experience with what works and what does not. Indeed, it can be difficult to match the level of expertise that the regulators have—which, however, is not all to the good. A specialized agency may develop a myopia that blinds it to the relation of its initiatives to those already taken or being contemplated by other agencies. Over time, the agency's professional focus may harden its commitment to a single way of achieving statutory goals and to one set of procedures for obtaining input from affected interests. Such commitment may be powerfully reinforced by the agency's most influential clientele—whether a regulated interest, a public interest group, or a professional association—which has gotten used to the traditional approach and learned how to benefit from it.

The expertise of regulatory agencies is an important assumption, not least because courts have long cited it as a reason for deferring to the agencies' judgments. It is a valid assumption for most agencies' staffs. The largest regulatory agency, the EPA, has about 18,000 employees, distributed among offices concerned with regulating air pollution, water pollution, solid waste, hazardous waste, toxic substances, radiation, and pesticides, together with others occupied with policy analysis, research, enforcement, and other legal matters. Scientists, engineers, economists, lawyers, and other professional specialists abound. The dynamics of intra-agency conflict among these specialists tend to counteract the danger of adherence to a time-established orthodoxy of approach.[25] State governments, however, have often contested EPA's rules and, in some cases, have pushed environmental rules much farther than EPA.

When Congress knows what it wants, it wants it sooner rather than later. But in most social regulation, this urgency rarely takes account of the uncertainties of science and technology. What we do not know can hurt us, and in many regulatory programs, experts lack firm knowledge of causes, consequences, and remedies. Part of the problem is time: there are scores, sometimes hundreds, of suspected pollutants in the air and water, and of cancer-causing and other unhealthful and unsafe elements in the workplace; not all can be researched and their threats appraised within a few years. Often the scientific community lacks answers. Similarly, the technologies for eliminating or lessening known threats may be elusive, while newly developed technologies make earlier decisions obsolete.

Cost-benefit analysis has come to play a large role in regulatory programs—an effect that is largely attributable to the increased influence of economists in the government and recent administrations' commitment to reducing regulatory burdens on industry. But it has taken on a strongly ideological flavor as well, with the Reagan and Bush administrations energetically seeking to promote the strategy. Their assumptions have been that government has too many regulations and that too many of the existing regulations do not produce benefits that exceed their costs. Forcing regulations to meet the cost-benefit standard, they believe, will result in fewer and less intrusive regulations.

At the core of this effort is an appeal to a basic proposition: that a proposed government regulation should result in greater benefits than costs. On its face, this proposition is a striving for certainty. Some statutes require consideration of costs; others rate some evils so great that they should be eliminated or reduced regardless of cost. The calculations are quantitative, but some costs and especially some benefits are difficult to express in dollar terms. What is the value of an unspoiled national park or forest; of a Grand Canyon view free of noisy, low-flying airplanes; of fishable and swimmable streams; of nondiscriminatory employment?[26]

Translation of these values into dollar figures becomes what Supreme Court Justice Oliver Wendell Holmes called, in another connection, "delusive exactitude," but it has a powerful impact on public policy. In July 2008, EPA quietly changed the value of a human life. Each of us might well believe we are priceless, but government regulators routinely set a dollar value on human lives. They then use that value to determine whether imposing new regulations is cost-effective, since policymakers have long held that the cost of regulations should not exceed their benefits. EPA had previously used a value of $8.04 million for each human life, but top officials decided to cut that value to $7.22 million. That is still a lot of money, but the lower value makes it that much harder to make an economic case for tougher federal rules: the benefits of a new government regulation would have to be that much greater to make the rules worthwhile.

For example, the Consumer Product Safety Commission (CPSC) faced a decision on whether to make mattresses less flammable. One proposal would require the industry to pay an extra $343 in manufacturing costs, but CPSC analysts expected the change to save 270 people. The agency used a value of a human life of $5 million, which produced a benefit of $1.3 billion. That big margin for benefits over costs, agency officials concluded, made the new rule economically sensible.[27] Most people get uncomfortable with such calculations, but government has to use *some* standard for deciding which rules make sense and which ones do not. If policymakers do not explicitly set a value on human life, implicit judgments about what regulations are worthwhile will be made anyway. If the value is explicit, citizens and policymakers can debate it. But that does not make the debate any easier—and making the value explicit often draws fierce attack, as was the case with EPA's 2008 decision, because critics believed EPA was using the change to block new regulations.

Indeed, in a powerful critique of the application of cost-benefit analysis to government regulation, Frank Ackerman and Lisa Heinzerling contend,

There is no reason to think that the right answers will emerge from the strange process of assigning dollar values to human life, human health, and nature itself, and then crunching the numbers. Indeed, in pursuing this approach, formal cost-benefit analysis often hurts more than it helps: it muddies rather than clarifies fundamental clashes about values. By proceeding as if its assumptions are scientific and by speaking a language all its own, economic analysis too easily conceals the basic human questions that lie at its heart and excludes the voices of people untrained in the field. Again and again, economic theory gives us opaque and technical reasons to do the obviously wrong thing.[28]

Risk assessment has taken its place alongside cost-benefit analysis as a presumably expert approach to regulation. We all are constantly exposed to risks: some risks are more serious than others, and some persons are more exposed than others, yet some risks are a necessary cost of progress, even of progress toward greater safety.[29] Which risks should government try to eliminate or diminish and which should it leave unregulated? As with cost-benefit analysis, measurements and tradeoffs are supposed to provide answers. Adequate reporting systems should tell us which industries and occupations have the highest rates of worker injuries and deaths, how many children are strangled by crib toys or hurt by lawn darts. With ingenuity, we can compare risks, suggesting, for example, that (1) traveling the same route by automobile as by a scheduled airline increases the likelihood of death by a factor of seventy and (2) death is equally probable from one chest X-ray, a thousand-mile scheduled air flight, and living for fifty years within five miles of a nuclear reactor. A nagging problem, though, is that the public's perception of relative degrees of risk often does not fit the risk assessments by agencies' expert staffs. The agendas of both the EPA and the Consumer Product Safety Commission have given priority to citizens' concerns rather than to their staffs' top risk-rated concerns.[30]

Many citizens have distorted perceptions of risk: one airline accident killing 200 people will get far more attention, from journalists and government regulators alike, than 300 traffic accidents across the country that kill twice as many people. More people have been killed by traditional power plants than by nuclear plants, but the potentially catastrophic nature of nuclear accidents attracts far more concern. A major issue that surfaced after the devastation that Hurricane Katrina inflicted on New Orleans was that many homeowners had not purchased flood insurance because they believed they did not need it or could not afford it. Following Superstorm Sandy's assault of the northeast in 2012, many homeowners found their homes destroyed, but some found they could not rebuild because standards for elevating the home to prevent another catastrophe proved more than they could afford. Risk is in part a matter of statistics, but it is also a matter of perception—and perception shapes the political strategy for dealing with regulatory problems.

Regulatory agencies, regardless of their expertise, find themselves caught between detailed statutory mandates, including often unrealistic deadlines for action, and the uncertainties stemming from inadequate scientific, technological, and economic knowledge. Agencies face heavy pressures to consider benefits, costs, and risks, yet political pressure can force them away from such technical standards. Progress may be possible, but failure to meet expectations is virtually certain. Congress's response tends to be an odd mix of greater specification of mandates and postponement of previously mandated deadlines.

In August 2010, salmonella contaminated the eggs sold in supermarkets in several states. Consumers called on the federal government to issue tighter regulations to protect food safety.

REGULATORY PROCEDURE

The Fifth and Fourteenth Amendments to the Constitution prohibit the national government and the states (including their local governments) from depriving any person of life, liberty, or property without due process of law. These amendments, along with an enormous body of case law interpreting them, frame what government regulations can do and the procedures government officials must follow in implementing regulations. These constitutional prohibitions have long been interpreted to treat corporations as "persons" and to construe deprivation of property as including denial of the opportunity to earn a fair return from prudent management of the property. Historically, the courts have applied these provisions in two ways. One is the obvious approach of requiring fair procedures before taking a depriving action. The other, used against statutes as well as regulatory orders, is not procedural but substantive: a deprivation of property or of a fair return on it must in itself be "reasonable" in the eyes of the courts—a test that has often been failed when conservative judges consider progressive legislation and rate-fixing orders of regulatory commissions. The courts have largely abandoned this directly substantive approach, though sometimes achieving it camouflaged as a procedural question.[31] In the case of regulatory administration, the courts usually avoid reference to the constitutional amendments. Instead, they either accept statutorily prescribed procedures as adequate (fair to citizens and consistent with legal requirements) or add requirements they deem necessary to preserve constitutional guarantees and their own powers.

At the federal level, prescriptions for rulemaking are found in two sources. One is the Administrative Procedure Act of 1946 (APA), as amended by the Freedom of Information Act and the Government in the Sunshine Act.[32] The other is the organic statute establishing an agency and assigning its functions, together with other statutes on individual programs. The two sources are intertwined, as some APA provisions depend on what agency-specific statutes actually say.[33] State and local governments typically operate under their own similar standards.

These standards have led to two basic regulatory approaches by administrative agencies. One is **administrative rulemaking**, in which the agency sets forth broad standards that apply to all persons and organizations meeting certain guidelines; for example, the Department of Transportation might spell out the standards for reflectors on bicycles or the lights on eighteen-wheel trucks. The other is **adjudication**, in which administrative law judges within the agencies hear individual cases; over time, these cases accumulate into a body of rules that individuals and organizations must follow. Because administrative rulemaking is far more prevalent and has become far more important in shaping regulatory policy, this chapter concentrates on that approach here.

Administrative Rulemaking

The core of administrative rulemaking lies in Congress's delegation of power to administrators. Such delegation of legislative powers to administrative agencies is an accepted feature of the American political system, but it was not always so. The Constitution says, "All legislative Powers herein granted shall be vested in a Congress of the United States." In 1935 the Supreme Court held two New Deal measures unconstitutional as violative of this provision. Neither before nor since, though, has the Court nullified a statute for this reason.[34] Since then, congressional delegation of power has only increased in importance as government's job has become more broad and complex.

If much administrative power comes from congressional delegation, how should administrators exercise it, especially in the regulatory arena? Most regulatory proceedings are informal, advancing through the following steps: (1) publication of a notice of proposed rulemaking in the *Federal Register,* which is the daily journal containing all rules and notices affecting the public;[35] (2) an interval to give interested parties an opportunity to submit written comments; and (3) after consideration of the relevant material presented, publication of the final rule, together with an explanation of the basis and purpose of the rule. In rulemaking, the APA does not require oral hearings or opportunities for cross-examination of witnesses (which are key elements of adjudicative procedure), unless an agency's particular statutes prescribe them (see Figure 13.1).

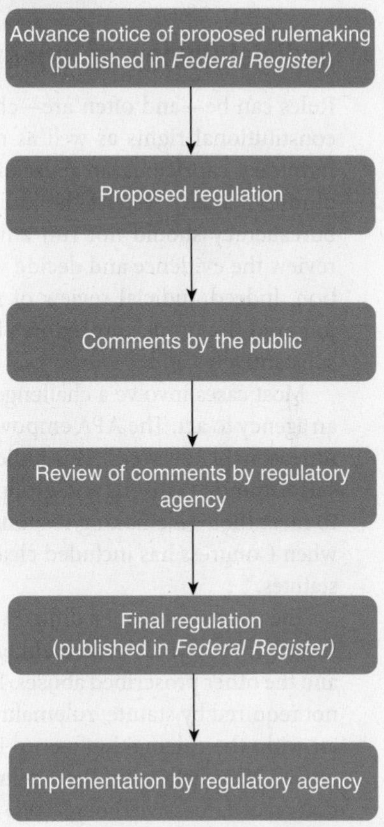

Agencies' extensive use of rulemaking is a relatively recent development. In the past, most economic regulatory agencies tended to proceed on a case-by-case basis of adjudication. Critics contended that such regulation failed to build more general policies on which the industry could rely and that, because of changes in commission membership, policies sometimes proved inconsistent over time. In contrast, social regulation agencies, facing known evils that needed prompt correction throughout society—such as cancer-causing asbestos in the workplace, schools, and other public places—could not address these problems at the creeping pace of case-by-case actions, so they chose instead to regulate through general rules.

FIGURE 13.1   Federal Regulatory Process

- Advance notice of proposed rulemaking (published in *Federal Register*)
- Proposed regulation
- Comments by the public
- Review of comments by regulatory agency
- Final regulation (published in *Federal Register*)
- Implementation by regulatory agency

It was expected that voluntary compliance would achieve the principal objectives, and the formal case-by-case method could be limited to cases alleging violation of the rules.

Judicial Review of Rulemaking

Rules can be—and often are—challenged in court. The courts are charged with protecting constitutional rights as well as reviewing agencies' actions to determine whether they are "arbitrary, capricious, an abuse of discretion, or otherwise not in accordance with law." These phrases actually restrict the judicial review of rules, because they manifest a concern that bureaucracy should not run amok—a very different standard from inviting the courts to review the evidence and decide whether an agency was factually correct in issuing a regulation. Indeed, judicial review of regulation tends to revolve around whether agencies have followed the proper procedures in issuing their rules, not whether the rules themselves are substantively valid.

Most cases involve a challenge to an agency's action, but parties can also file suit to force an agency to act. The APA empowers a court to "compel agency action unlawfully withheld or unreasonably delayed." This judicial latitude has enabled consumers, environmentalists, and safety-minded citizens and groups to use courts to bring pressure on foot-dragging agencies to meet their rulemaking responsibilities. The opportunity for court action arises especially when Congress has included clear mandates and set calendar deadlines in program-specific statutes.[36]

The courts confront a difficult problem in reviewing informal rules. They need, they say, a record of the agency's rulemaking to have something to review—even to test for arbitrariness and the other proscribed abuses. Because oral hearing and cross-examination of witnesses are not required by statute, rulemaking fails to produce the kind of record that courts are familiar with; the rulemaking record instead consists of the mass of written comments received, often a huge collection that includes both significant and trivial contributions. Courts want that record, massive though it is, and they also want to know how the agency reacted to each "significant" objection to the proposed rule. The result is a considerable burden on a regulatory process that is intended to be informal; the burden to build a record for the court goes well beyond the agency's obligation to provide a concise general statement of the basis and purpose of a rule. Once they have the record of evidence, the courts are tempted to regard agency failure to deal satisfactorily with one or another significant objection as a sign of arbitrariness. Their range of tolerance is then likely to vary, depending on whether a court does or does not choose to emphasize, and defer to, the expertise of the regulatory agency.

COURTS' REGULATION OF THE REGULATORS

Courts regulate the regulatory system in many ways. Often, they arbitrate appeals from agency rules and specific decisions. At other times, they deal with suits filed against agencies to require the issuance of rules mandated or implied in statutes. Sometimes, an agency sues a company, seeking to punish noncompliance with a rule or order by obtaining a court order requiring compliance. Apart from these agency-involvement suits are suits between private parties in which a corporation as defendant is charged with violation of a statute or rule.

Consider a set of simultaneous cases—all within the metropolitan area of New York City—involving the regulation of asbestos (a harmful air pollutant that can cause cancer and lung disease, though the effects may not appear for many years). In November 1987 about two hundred employees sued the Consolidated Edison Company, seeking millions of dollars in damages because of asbestos exposure. In January 1988 the EPA filed a civil suit against Consolidated Edison, seeking civil penalties of over $1 million and a court order requiring the company's full compliance with the Clean Air Act; the violations charged were failure to follow prescribed asbestos-removal procedures and failure to inform EPA fully and promptly of the removal operations. A few days earlier, the government had filed a criminal suit against officials of twenty-three companies removing asbestos materials; they were charged with bribing a federal inspector to overlook violations of federal regulations.[37] Here are three suits—a civil suit for damages brought by private citizens, a civil suit brought by the government, and a criminal suit brought by the government. None is an appeal from an agency, though all relate to EPA and its regulations.

Amid the legal questions about regulation, one is paramount: who has **standing to sue** under what circumstances? That legal question, in turn, suggests a practical question: who can afford the costs of litigation?

Access to the Courts

Doctrines governing the right to sue have changed over time. Many laws governing particular programs provide an opportunity for judicial review of agency actions. In addition, the Administrative Procedure Act of 1946 offers a blanket authorization: "A person suffering legal wrong because of agency action, or adversely affected or aggrieved by agency action within the meaning of a relevant statute, is entitled to judicial review thereof." This apparently wide-open invitation is qualified, however, for it does not apply if "(1) statutes preclude judicial review; or (2) agency action is committed to agency discretion by law." Nor does it apply to persons who, though unhappy about an agency decision, are held not to have suffered a "legal wrong." Until 1989, Congress made the Veterans Administration's denial of claims under the Veterans' Benefit Act unreviewable by the federal courts. In sum, despite generous judicial interpretations of the main provision of the APA, access for aggrieved persons is not so broad as it seems at first reading.

Class-Action Suits

Recourse to a class-action suit has proved important in cases involving a number of citizens, most of whom have suffered so small a monetary loss that it is not worthwhile for each individual to hire a lawyer for representation in legal proceedings, though the damage to the whole class of affected individuals (and the profit to a corporation) may amount to millions of dollars. A **class action** is a private lawsuit for money damages, usually brought against a private person or corporation. Though the active plaintiff is typically only one or a few of the persons damaged—who are presumably sufficiently indignant and well off to afford the lawyer—the suit is brought on behalf of all the affected individuals. Class-action suits are relevant here because the plaintiffs often claim damages on the grounds that the defendant has violated statutes or rules. A class-action suit, therefore, may complement government agencies' efforts to enforce the law or, indeed, substitute for such efforts when agencies neglect their responsibilities. As in other kinds of damage suits (automobile injury cases, for example), the defendant often prefers to settle out of court rather than risk the court's (especially a jury's) making of a generous award. Defendant corporations are inclined to regard class-action suits as "legalized blackmail," but they and others in the same business are also likely to mend their ways so as to conform to statutes and avoid future class-action suits.

In the early 1970s, class-action suits were gaining popularity as a way for otherwise help-less citizens to deter and redress corporate damage to their interests. They also indirectly spurred agencies to enforce statutes designed to protect those interests.In 1974, however, a Supreme Court decision held that the plaintiff could not seek damages for himself and the other 6 million persons in his "class" unless he first notified all of the more than two million persons whose names were known.[38] Giving this notice would have cost him $225,000, though his own damage claim was for only $70. Faced with such a notification require-ment, few will venture a class-action suit, even though its claims may rest on violations of antitrust and security statutes (as in this case) or of other laws protective of the pub-lic. In 1988 an appeals court required the National Wildlife Federation, in challenging the Interior Department's strip-mining regulations, to spend tens of thousands of dollars obtaining 1,300 pages of affidavits from its members to establish standing.[39]

In this area, as in some others, the courts' decisions are inconsistent. The most dramatic class-action suit was brought against seven corporations on behalf of over 15,000 named per-sons who had severe illnesses or whose children suffered birth defects that they claimed had resulted from exposure to a herbicide, Agent Orange, that had been used by the army during the Vietnam War. In 1985 the case ended with what, to that date, was the largest tort-case settlement in history: $180 million plus interest.[40]

In 1998, however, an even bigger settlement was reached. Years earlier, the Mississippi attorney general had begun a long legal campaign against the tobacco companies, seeking to recover damages to the state and its taxpayers that, he said, had been caused by smoking. This legal action snowballed into an action eventually involving all the states, promising to pay them an estimated $246 billion over twenty-five years and imposing new restrictions on the advertising of tobacco products. By cleverly claiming standing to sue the tobacco companies on the grounds of their need to recover Medicaid costs incurred in the treatment of smokers, the states won an enormous settlement and forced a major change in tobacco companies' business practices. Martha Derthick, however, raises serious questions about whether this entrepreneurial litigation circumvented constitutional practice by inserting executive-branch officials in a province of policymaking that should have been left to the legislature.[41]

Private Attorneys General

Individuals and organizations may cast themselves in the role of **private attorneys general**, filing suit not for money damages but to compel a government agency or a corporation to do or cease doing something that affects a major public interest or group—the environment, consumers, and the like. This issue has become more important because the courts have become more liberal in granting standing to sue.

To have standing to sue, the traditional rule is that the plaintiff must show that a so-called legal wrong is involved—that is, he or she must plausibly claim to have individually suffered a wrong protected against by the Constitution, legal statutes, or the common law. The APA, which acknowledges this traditional rule, extends standing to any person "adversely affected or aggrieved within the meaning of a relevant statute." Interpretation of this provision was liberalized in the 1960s and early 1970s, to recognize that the adverse effect or grievance might be recreational, environmental, or aesthetic, rather than only economic or physical.[42] Agency-specific legislation, beginning in the 1970s, has often specified that any person may sue administrators for taking unauthorized action or for failing to perform nondiscretionary duties (such as those mandated by law). And in the liberalization period, the courts often found an implied, even if not statutory, right to redress.

Tort Liability of Governments and Officials

A **tort action** is a civil suit seeking monetary damages for harm allegedly done to the plaintiff by the defendant. The majority of tort actions in America arise out of automobile accidents, but they also are used extensively against manufacturers of products claimed to be dangerous or detrimental to users' health and against employers of workers exposed to hazardous conditions. From 1976 to 1986, asbestos suits accounted for 60 percent of the growth in product-liability tort cases in federal courts.[43] Suits relating to product liability and working conditions supplement or substitute for governments' direct regulation.

The tort liability of governments and their officials has evolved through a tangled history and it will continue to evolve.[44] Summarized simplistically, the federal and state governments cannot be sued for torts without their consent; this principle derives from English law, which long held that "the king can do no wrong" and could not be sued without his consent. However, government employees can be sued: schoolteachers, policemen, and FBI and narcotics agents are frequent targets of tort suits.

Governments can waive their sovereign immunity by consenting to be sued. The Federal Torts Claims Act of 1946 provided a partial waiver, permitting a damage suit against the government for personal injury, death, or property damage caused by the "negligent or wrongful act or omission" of any federal employee acting within the scope of his or her employment.[45] However, the statutory qualifications and exceptions severely narrow this apparent waiver. Most notably, the government is not liable for an act or omission when the government employee is "exercising due care, in the execution of a statute or regulation, whether or not such statute or regulation be valid," or when he or she is performing or failing to perform "a discretionary function or duty on the part of a federal agency or an employee . . . whether or not the discretion involved be abused." Other significant limitations are (1) that the government is liable only to the extent that a private individual would be liable under the relevant state's law (though some government actions have no private counterpart) and (2) that the government is not liable for interest prior to judgment or for punitive damages (as distinguished from merely compensatory damages), for both of which a private defendant might be liable.

In the 1960s, courts accorded federal officials absolute immunity from tort actions when performing duties committed by law to their control or supervision.[46] In the 1970s, the Supreme Court made a sharp turn, holding officials liable for violation of constitutional rights if they knew or reasonably should have known that they were violating them.[47] It is presumed that an official should know the rights protected by the Constitution, although the presumption has been criticized on grounds that every such right has been and continues to be interpreted through court decisions, which an official cannot be expected to have mastered. In 1988 the Supreme Court held that federal employees could be held personally liable for damages caused by negligent performance or omission of nondiscretionary conduct (such as, in this case, negligence in handling and storing hazardous material). Congress responded by passing a statute that makes the government, rather than the employee, the defendant in such suits.[48]

State governments, under the Eleventh Amendment, are immune from damage suits in federal courts, but local governments are not immune. State and local officials are liable under an 1871 act that provides: "Every person who, under color of any statute [or] regulation . . . of any State, subjects . . . any citizen . . . to the deprivation of any rights, privileges, or immunities secured by the Constitution and laws, shall be liable to the party injured in an action at law."[49] This provision is known as Section 1983 (from its location in the *U.S. Code of Federal Regulations*). Beginning in 1961, the federal courts experienced a great increase in Section 1983 tort actions, consistent with the Supreme Court's narrowing of officials' defenses. The principal defense is now lack of knowledge or presumptive knowledge of relevant provisions of the Constitution and laws.

Tort law's evolution cannot be understood without considering the dilemma expressed in many court opinions. On the one hand are citizens' rights to receive monetary compensation for damages done them by overzealous, negligent, or malicious government officials and employees—plus the promise of deterrence that such court victories will exert on other bureaucrats. On the other hand is the need for prompt and effective administrative action in executing laws and regulations—a need that entails considerable scope for discretionary judgment. The deterrent effect can be considered a virtue, but it also invites officials to avoid risks and even disobey superiors' orders (for such orders are no shield against personal liability); the result could be a serious weakening of the administrative system and of its responsibility for achieving legislative objectives.

The solution to the courts' dilemma, it appears, is abandonment of the immunity of governments from torts and the substantial freeing of officials and employees from personal liability. That solution, however, implies that agencies will have administrative systems strong enough to control the behavior of subordinate officials and employees. Readers of this book may have doubts about how easy it might be to create such a rigorous environment, given the great hierarchical distance between agency heads and "street-level bureaucrats"[50] as well as the huge expansion in delegation of discretionary powers.[51]

Ripped
from the Headlines...

POLITICS

Is the Oversight of Electronic Surveillance Full of Politics?

The judges in America's most secret court were furious with suggestions that they were simply political pawns in a bigger battle. In 2013 when Edward Snowden leaked massive amounts of classified information to newspapers in Great Britain and the United States, federal officials reassured members of the public that Congress oversaw the data collection—and that before any data-gathering effort could be launched, it had to be approved by a special court: the Foreign Intelligence Surveillance Court (FISC). Eleven judges took turns reviewing the government's requests for information, and no data could be collected—from emails, telephones, or web-surfing—without approval by one of the judges.

Critics of the government's data collection, however, complained that the FISC was little more than a rubber stamp. During George W. Bush's administration, for example, the government made 14,353 electronic surveillance requests, and just 9 were denied. In the Obama administration's first four years, there were 6,556 requests with 1 denied. Some civil libertarians asked: what kind of oversight was that? They pointed out that the court operated in an unusual fashion—there is only one side presenting the case, with no one representing the argument *against* granting the government's request for surveillance.

The court's defenders pointed out that the statistics presented do not account for requests that the government withdrew following tough questions by the judges. Moreover, the judges' review also led to changes in the government's surveillance strategy. One official with close knowledge of the court's operations said, "The court is a neutral party, not a collaborator or arm of the government." But the official acknowledged that "the information out there now leaves people wondering why the court endorsed these programs." It's a case, pure and simple, of judicial review of administrative activities. Critics asked tough questions, however: Is the oversight by a court, whose operations are by necessity conducted in secret, enough to provide careful oversight of the administrative actions? Or did the courts simply provide political cover? Officials in the intelligence community and in the FISC strenuously argued that the process was tough and free from political pressure, but because of the secrecy of its operations they could not marshal the facts to make their case.

Source: Carol D. Leonnig, Ellen Nakashima, and Barton Gellman, "Secret-Court Judges Upset at Portrayal of 'Collaboration' with Government," *Washington Post*, June 29, 2013, http://www.washingtonpost.com/politics/secret-court-judges-upset-at-portrayal-of-collaboration-with-government/2013/06/29/ed73fb68-e01b-11e2-b94a-452948b95ca8_story.html?hpid=z2; "The Foreign Intelligence Surveillance Court," *Washington Post*, June 7, 2013, http://www.washingtonpost.com/politics/the-foreign-intelligence-surveillance-court/2013/06/07/4700b382-cfec-11e2-8845-d970ccb04497_graphic.html.

Systems and Values

The question of access to the courts leads to a more fundamental issue: How interventionist should courts be in reviewing regulatory agencies' policymaking and enforcement activities? How aggressively should the courts themselves work to open the doors for judicial redress of grievances? These questions raise two issues: (1) the difference between the judicial system and the administrative system in which regulatory agencies operate and (2) the array of public values that everyone—citizens and policymakers alike—want to see in the regulation of private affairs. How one balances these considerations has much to do with the balance between the regulatory agencies and the courts.

The Judicial and Administrative Systems

In regulatory administration, courts and agencies make strange partners. The two institutions have different traditions and are staffed with very different kinds of people.[52] Courts are passive; they depend on parties to bring cases before them. Because of that passivity and because their jurisdiction is broad, they hear cases in sequence, with no discernible connection; most of these cases are unrelated to governmental regulation. With few exceptions (the federal district and appeals courts in the District of Columbia), the judges have expertise neither in regulation generally nor in particular regulatory programs, and they lack expert supporting staffs, so they must rely instead on evidence and analysis offered by lawyers for the two sides.

The most significant characteristic of judicial involvement in the regulatory field is a court's focus on the single case before it. Long-standing judicial practice holds that courts must decide only on the basis of the case before it and the court's interpretation of how the law affects that case. Courts cannot, on their own, reach beyond the case to make broader law. For regulation, this means that the issue is the reasonableness of a single agency's decision, made at a single point in time and affecting a single individual, corporation, or group. The court's judgment fits in a setting of legal doctrine and precedents, but it largely ignores how the particular agency's decision fits with the agency's full responsibility for achieving program objectives with limited funds and staff. Instead, a court may require the agency to respond to the particular case before it, without considering how this requirement may subtract from the resources supporting the agency's other programs.

By contrast, most agencies are *active*—each one develops an agenda of priorities that balances its resources against relative opportunities for a significant impact. An agency makes decisions through time, linking each one with others to create coherence both in technical foundations and in program effectiveness. Within that agenda and continuity of focus, its staff gathers facts, analyzes problems, and consults with interested persons and organizations, all as a basis for framing regulatory rules and orders. In sharp contrast to the courts, agencies specialize in their assigned subjects, and they have career staffs expert in economics, science, and engineering, as well as in law. Except for agency lawyers, the judges and agency staff members march to different drummers.[53] It would be a wonder if the two sides kept in step—and they rarely do.

Two strategies have emerged to accommodate these differences.[54] First, the courts have pressed the agencies to widen the participation of interested citizens and groups in the formulation of rules, and, though less clearly, the courts have widened access to judicial redress for such interested parties.[55] Second, the courts have tended to "make law," attributing intentions to Congress that are not apparent in the language of statutes.[56] The agencies generally regard both of these strategies as helpful: increased participation has favored environmental and other public interest groups whose efforts support the agencies' missions; and in giving statutory weight to program activities not clearly specified in statutes, the courts have expanded the jurisdictions of the agencies. Shep Melnick reports, "While complaining about some decisions, EPA officials generally credit the courts with improving the agency's competence and programs."[57] Reconciliation of the two systems has also advanced because of what Jerry Mashaw characterizes as the Supreme Court's "significant retrenchment from its procedurally interventionist posture in the early 1970s."[58]

Values: Conflict or Harmony?

Regulatory administration revolves around three basic values: procedural fairness, substantive correctness of decisions, and achievement of public policy goals. Everyone agrees that the process leading up to agency issuance (or nonissuance) of a rule or individual order should be fair. But it is tempting for courts to say, "Why can't administrative agencies be more like us?" The question applies principally to agencies' adjudicative procedures, though courts have often wished that administrators would behave more like the courts in their regulatory functions as well. In fact, the APA and many agency-specific statutes, as we have seen, support the courts' view, requiring notice, oral hearings, and cross-examination of witnesses. To be sure, these procedures are less rigorous in the rulemaking setting than in ordinary court cases, but they are, nonetheless, enough alike that lawyers play the leading roles, paperwork mounts, and tactics of delay are practiced by companies facing regulatory action. Despite these similarities, however, the trend in regulation is away from formal toward informal rulemaking—away from the procedures that are more judicial and toward those that the courts find troublesome.

The second value is not procedural, but substantive: the correctness of the decision reached. Theoretically, what the system should ensure is a correct decision, and if the agency does not make one, the court should. But neither agency nor court can ensure that a decision is correct, because scientific and technological uncertainties plague policy issues, and even when there is relative clarity on the technical issues, different political judgments can muddy any sense about which decision is the right one. Both the agency subsystem and the court system provide opportunities for appeal to higher levels, but even in the judicial branch there is no certainty that the highest court's decision will be correct. The possibility of appeal can often simply create new arenas for political interests to continue—and to try to change— policy debates. At best, the courts can hope to limit error to a low, but not zero, tolerance level. Judges' self-restraint, reinforced by deference to agency expertise, permits agency discretion to operate in accord with this objective.

Of course, many issues turn out to be such a mixture of fact and law that a court cannot decide the legal question without also deciding a factual question. Appellate courts have historically often capitalized on this mixed focus to substitute their judgment for that of lower courts, by treating as a question of law whether the evidence was sufficient to support the lower court's decision. Appellate court doctrines have varied on whether they were merely looking to determine if there was "substantial" evidence on the winning side to warrant the decision, or whether they were completely second-guessing the lower court by weighing the evidence on both sides; in the latter case, disagreement about the preponderance of evidence can lead to overturning the lower court's decision. In reviewing agency decisions, the courts have applied the substantial-evidence test, but they take "a hard look."

The third value is achievement of public policy objectives. Here lurks a danger that two very different institutions—judicial and administrative—will find their traditional modes of operation at loggerheads. Excessive formalization of procedure can tie administrative regulation in knots—causing delay, absorbing budgetary and staff resources, increasing red tape, and inviting passivity in agency pursuit of policy goals. Some agencies react to the risk of judicial reversal by adopting even more cumbersome procedures than courts are likely to demand; others seek to demonstrate the evidence behind a decision with massive accumulations of documents. Even in rulemaking, the courts' insistence that an agency respond to every significant objection filed by individuals, groups, and companies imposes a burden that is likely to be exaggerated by agencies' uncertainty as to which objections the courts may deem significant. Meantime, the agency is charged by Congress with implementing programs fully and expeditiously—an assignment whose shortfalls may expose the agency to congressional retribution.

The administrative tasks of some agencies are enormous, and their huge burden makes court-like procedures inappropriate. In the new Department of Homeland Security, which is charged with reviewing applications for immigration and naturalization, the backlog of cases in 2004 was more than six million and growing. As T. Alexander Aleinikoff concluded, "If the process is not improved, millions of people will continue to wait many years for naturalization and immigration benefits to which they are entitled as a matter of law."[59] A hidden side effect of this backlog was that Homeland Security officials were lagging behind the effort to determine whether any of those on the list might be members of terrorist sleeper cells, quietly preparing for a new attack.

The three values of regulatory administration—fair procedures, sound decisions, and policy achievement—are interlinked and in conflict. Each is important in its own right, but to elevate one over the others is to invite trouble. Fairness in regulatory procedure may be enough to reassure everyone, including the courts, about the correctness of the decision reached. Relaxation of the expectation that regulatory procedures mimic that of courts may promote effective implementation of policy objectives. In the end, the courts have tended to reconcile these issues through the doctrine of judicial deferral to agencies' expertise, but this is not an ideal formula, as courts will differ on how much deferral is appropriate, how expert agencies really are, and whether in a particular decision the claim of expertise covers other issues on which the courts might weigh in. It is little wonder, then, that the courts' relationship with regulators continues to evolve.

REGULATION OF THE REGULATORS

Presidents seek to control regulatory agencies, insisting that the agencies are part of the executive branch and thus must be accountable to the president. Otherwise, goes the argument, their policymaking, via rules and regulations under broad delegations from Congress, would flout the American democratic system of government. This argument rests on three concepts (all familiar from earlier chapters of this book): (1) the need for coordination, lest agencies contradict or duplicate one another; (2) the need for consistency with the president's policy agenda, lest one executive function conflict with another; and (3) the need for economy and efficiency, lest the president's budgetary and policy agenda be undermined by the cost of federal regulations.

Especially since the Reagan administration, presidents have been working hard to exert greater control over government regulation. Republican presidents—Ronald Reagan and both Presidents Bush—have tried to use cost-benefit regulation and the Office of Management and Budget (OMB) review of draft regulations to rein in the number and cost of federal regulations. The Reagan administration was the first to require that agencies prepare and submit to OMB for review a cost-benefit analysis of each proposed major rule and that, to the extent permitted by law, the agency not act unless benefits exceed costs to society, net benefits are at a maximum, and among alternative approaches the one with the least net cost to society is chosen. No agency may publish a notice of proposed rulemaking until the OMB review is completed, nor may it publish a final rule until the OMB director has communicated any views and the agency has responded. Moreover, each agency is required annually to prepare and submit to OMB a regulatory program detailing every significant agency regulatory action (later defined as a "rule") "planned or underway," explaining, among other things, how they are consistent "with the Administration's policies and priorities." Any proposed regulatory action not included in the earlier regulatory program or materially different from an action described in that program must be submitted to the OMB for review and, except for cases of statutory or judicial deadlines and emergency situations, must be deferred until completion of that review. In the case of both the regulatory program and proposed actions later contemplated, the OMB director may return agency submissions for reconsideration.[60]

The George W. Bush administration in 2003 expanded this review through OMB Circular A-4, which requires stringent economic review of regulations before they can take effect. OMB's circular makes the case in two ways: "The motivation is to (1) learn if the benefits of an action are likely to justify the costs or (2) discover which of various possible alternatives would be the most cost-effective."[61] But even the Clinton administration worked hard through OMB to manage better the flow of federal regulations. In general, recent presidents have wanted to integrate regulatory policy more tightly into the overall thrust of their management efforts. And some presidents have tried to use these techniques to restrict regulations for ideological reasons. In both cases, it is a sign of pushing government regulation from a quasi-judicial arena to policy control more like that presidents seek in other parts of the executive branch.

The regulatory management process has thus provoked much friction.[62] The OMB has gained review authority not only over the final stages of rulemaking but also over such early stages as initiation of research studies meant to contribute to agency consideration of whether to start rulemaking proceedings.[63] Delays of months and years have characterized some reviews. The small review staff, in the OMB's Office of Information and Regulatory Affairs, consists of persons trained in economics, business administration, and law, who are often young and with scant prior knowledge of the agency programs they oversee; understandably, agencies' expert staffs have chafed at the sometimes nitpicking objections and the revisions OMB imposes. OMB has consulted industry representatives (a practice sharply reduced by the George H. W. Bush administration) and communicated with agency officials, often by telephone, without such contacts or their substance being reflected in the rulemaking record. These criticisms escalated during the George W. Bush administration, in which several high-ranking officials resigned because of their disagreement with the administration's regulatory policies. For example, Eric V. Schaeffer, director of EPA's Office of Regulatory Enforcement, complained in his letter of resignation that "we seem about to snatch defeat from the jaws of victory. We are in the 9th month of a '90 day review' to reexamine the law, and fighting a White House that seems determined to weaken the rules we are trying to enforce."[64]

The focus is on rulemaking. For better or worse, many people view the actions of regulatory agencies as part of the president's executive function, and they expect the president to manage the flow of federal regulations. For presidents seeking to demonstrate their control over the bureaucracy, efforts to rein in the regulators have been irresistible. In principle, no one wants regulations whose costs vastly exceed their benefits. But it is much easier to measure—and display—costs than it is to assess benefits. Moreover, many benefits of government regulations come in the form of saving lives and improving the health and safety of individuals. It is economically possible to make estimates about such values. Indeed, in the aftermath of the September 11, 2001, attacks, one official found himself charged with setting the level of payment to each of the families who had lost a loved one in the attacks—and calculating those payments according to the economic value of each life lost. But what is economically possible often becomes politically difficult. Explicit discussions about the values of health and safety bring many citizens and policymakers into genuinely uncomfortable territory.

That discomfort factor implicitly biases such analysis: a focus on the things easier to measure—the costs—and a tendency to slide past the more difficult puzzles—especially the benefits. Such bias, in turn, makes it easier to make the case against regulations, which fits the interest of conservative Republicans in slowing the flood of regulations. Their opponents, however, have pointed to the inherently imprecise nature of the analysis as one of the reasons why government regulates, "to demand and produce legal protections for health and the environment," as Ackerman and Heinzerling argue. Indeed, they conclude, "we must give up the idea, reassuring to many, that there is, somewhere, a precise mathematical formula waiting to solve our problems for us."[65] The debate between precision and measurement, more and less regulation, is at its core about values: about government's role and how best to pursue it.

CONCLUSION

Regulation of the behavior of private individuals and corporations to protect others from harm is a central responsibility of government. The scope and methods of such regulation are disputed issues of public policy. However those issues are resolved, there is no doubt that some discretion must be vested in regulatory agencies and that discretion is subject to abuse. Legislatures, courts, and chief executives all seek to reduce opportunities for such abuse, but, in using this control authority, they often seek to advance their own policy preferences or to impose regulatory procedures that, intentionally or not, impede regulatory effectiveness.

The balance between effective and ineffective regulation shifts from time to time, largely reflecting public opinion, elections, and appointments and attitudes of administrators and judges. As we move deeper into the twenty-first century, signs of a shift toward effective regulation are visible, most clearly in the field of environmental protection and workers' health and safety. Yet signs of success have hardly protected regulatory agencies from political attack.

Administrative discretion is tolerable only when not misused, and therein lies a major problem. One distinguished scholar of the legal aspects of public administration, Phillip Cooper, puts it this way:

> Just how we ensure that the public interest is served and that administrative power is not abused is the problem of administrative responsibility. . . . [While] the formal legal constraints have received the most attention . . . there is a risk that excessive concern with avoiding suits will cause us to ignore many aspects of the responsibility question of equal or greater significance.[66]

The next chapter addresses those very important aspects.

CASE 13.1

"The Dude" and Seattle's Police: Conflicting Marijuana Policies

Has The Dude, the pot-smoking character played by Jeff Bridges in the film *The Big Lebowski*, become Seattle's new poster child? In December 2012, using small quantities of marijuana became legal in Washington state, and the Seattle Police Department (SPD) responded by posting Bridges' picture on its website with the caption, "The Dude abides, and says 'take it inside.'"

Under the referendum passed by voters in November, state residents can possess small amounts of pot, but not in public. The SPD's advice: "Under state law, you may responsibly get baked, order some pizzas and enjoy a 'Lord of the Rings' marathon in the privacy of your home, if you want to."

Breckenridge, Colorado, might have beaten them to it. For years, newspaper reporters have long referred to the town as "The Amsterdam of the Rockies," where some residents quietly encouraged tourists to come for "our great outdoor beauty—and then relax with a joint at the end of the day." Now, residents in Colorado have also joined with Washington, voting to legalize the possession of small quantities of pot.

But if voters in Colorado and Washington decriminalized the possession of marijuana, federal law remains clear and inflexible. National drug policy still classifies pot as a Schedule I drug, along with heroin, ecstasy, and LSD, with "no currently accepted medical use in the United States" and "a high potential for abuse." That has left the Obama administration nothing but tough choices: invoking federal preemption and taking a tough enforcement stand, which would anger many members of the base that just returned the president to the White House; doing absolutely nothing; or artfully threading their way through the dilemma of strong state support for decisions that are in opposition to national policy.

Even Amsterdam has struggled with this tension. The Dutch capital is home to hundreds of "coffee shops," where customers can legally enjoy both java and ganja. In fact, tourist officials estimate that 35 percent of all visitors to Amsterdam stop by a coffee shop. However, the center-right Dutch government in May banned the purchase of pot without a "wietpas" or weed pass, a membership in the coffee shops that is only available to residents. "The objective is to combat the nuisance and crime associated with coffee shops and the trade in drugs," Prime Minister Mark Rutte explained.

The government's crackdown stirred a huge backlash. Amsterdam Mayor Eberhard van der Laan said the ban could push the marijuana trade from the coffee shops into the back alleys, as tourists "swarm all over the city looking for drugs." He said, "This would lead to more robberies, quarrels about fake drugs and no control of the quality of the drugs on the market—everything we have worked toward would be lost to misery."

Ultimately, the Dutch national government found a crack to squeeze through. It insisted on maintaining its policy but left implementation in the hands of local officials. Amsterdam's mayor quickly signaled that he wouldn't be enforcing the ban. The coffee shops were back in smoke-filled business. Lady Gaga celebrated during an Amsterdam concert by smoking a spliff onstage she called "wondrous."

But the national government hadn't finished. In November, it proposed a new ban on "skunk" pot, which contains more than 15 percent of THC (tetrahydrocannabinol, the magic in marijuana). The Dutch justice minister said it was a "hard drug" that created dangerous addiction. The coffee shop industry countered that this could also lead to more danger and crime—"Weak weed in the coffee shops, strong weed on the streets," as a spokesman put it. Tourists would spill back into dangerous back alleys looking for the more potent high that the coffee shops could no longer provide.

For governments everywhere, toking up has raised some exceptionally tough issues. How far can national governments go in enforcing laws out of sync with local officials? How can local officials slide around national policies so they stay in sync with their citizens? In the Netherlands, as in most countries, the battle plays out among governments that are all part of the same (more or less) governmental system. Neighboring governments in France and Germany insisted they would keep their pot bans in place, and the Danish government refused a request from Copenhagen's city council to experiment with Amsterdam-style deregulation. In the Czech Republic, Portugal, and Switzerland, the national governments have taken a more Breckenridge-like position. In all these cases, national policy rules the day—to the degree that national officials can deal with intransigent local officials and the habits of their citizens.

In the United States, federalism puts an emphasis on local enforcement of laws. The dilemma comes when local laws—and practice—differ with national laws. Seattle's police dealt with this problem by suggesting users not "flagrantly roll up a mega-spliff and light up in the middle of the street," and instead manage their munchies in the quiet of their own homes. But the Obama administration has to find a road that doesn't abandon federal law when state voters decide they oppose it.

Governing everywhere is much more about finding a common ground between policy goals and different levels—and charting a road to reconcile what officials want and what citizens will actually do. Our system of federalism, as always, adds a special twist.

Questions to Consider

1. Seattle's police department took an unusual step in embracing a pot-smoking movie

character to talk to the city's citizens about enforcing the new marijuana law. What do you think about this approach?

2. Local officials, in the United States and abroad, have struggled over how best to balance enforcement of the law and effectiveness of results. Tough enforcement can sometimes drive illicit activity into back alleys and cause even bigger problems. Tolerating a certain level of illegal activities can shrink that problem, but risk signaling that the police are not serious about enforcing the law. How would you set this balance?

3. Do you think it's a concern that law enforcement on issues like marijuana in the United States can vary from jurisdiction to jurisdiction? If so, what should we do about it? If not, are there some issues on which enforcement *should* be uniform?

Note: This case comes from my column in *Governing* (February 2013), http://www.governing.com/columns/potomac-chronicle/col-marijuana-laws-conflict-worldwide.html.

CASE 13.2

SCOTUS and Below: Comparing the U.S. Supreme Court and Lower Federal Courts' Contribution to Public Administration

The first Monday of October brings the start of another term of the U.S. Supreme Court. When fans of new Supreme Court Justice Elena Kagan looked on the start of the 2010–2011 session, they celebrated. Liberals hoped that Kagan would offer a counterbalance to the rightward tilt of Chief Justice John Roberts's Court. Conservatives committed to working even harder to hold a 5–4 edge on the big issues facing the Court.

In most media coverage about the federal judiciary, the Supreme Court of the United States (SCOTUS, for short) captures the big headlines. President Obama and Chief Justice Roberts engaged in an icy stare-down during Obama's State of the Union address, and big battles over the future of the judiciary continued to simmer.

But while SCOTUS gets most of the ink, the lower courts do most of the judiciary's work. In 2008–2009, SCOTUS heard 87 cases. One step down, the Federal Courts of Appeals dealt with 57,740 cases. Federal District Courts, the first level of the federal system, handled 276,397

civil cases and 76,655 criminal cases. The odds that SCOTUS will decide a case first filed with a district court is tiny—less than 3 in 10,000, so the lower courts are the last stop for most issues.

In the process, the lower courts are making their own landmark rulings. For example, U.S. District Judge Martin Feldman halted the Interior Department's 2010 moratorium on offshore drilling in the Gulf of Mexico. Feldman held that the moratorium was far too broad. He ruled that the feds couldn't shut down all the wells because one rig failed, and "no one ever fully knows why." Oil producers—and the Gulf workers on their payrolls—celebrated while the Obama administration hastily redrafted its response to the gooey fallout from BP's *Deepwater Horizon* drilling disaster.

Judge Susan R. Bolton blocked Arizona's tough new immigration law, which required police to investigate the status of every person they detained. That, she said, would increase "the intrusion of police presence into the lives of legally present aliens (and even United States citizens), who will necessarily be swept up" by the policy. Bolton found that the Arizona law conflicted with the federal government's laws and policies. Her ruling broadcast a warning to other states considering similar laws.

Judge Vaughn Walker struck down California's Proposition 8, which banned same-sex marriages. In his opinion, Walker wrote that "Proposition 8 fails to advance any rational basis in singling out gay men and lesbians for denial of a marriage license." California Governor Arnold Schwarzenegger applauded the decision, but legal observers wondered whether proponents of same-sex marriage would be able to find five votes if the case reached SCOTUS. Schwarzenegger was partially right—when the Court decided the case in 2013, it ruled 5–4 that the state's ban was illegal as it was drawn, but the Court stopped short of ruling that same-sex couples could marry.

We all know about the separation of powers from our high school civics and college public administration courses. We learned that the Framers gave the courts independent power because they didn't fully trust democratic rule. When monumental decisions like those discussed here come down, however, they always strike like lightning bolts at the center of the typical battles between elected legislators and executives.

And we all know that the judiciary is independent of politics. But the lightning bolts are always political—they are launched by judges who bring to each case their own reading of the Constitution and the law, and the judges were put in place by elected officials who hoped that those readings were the right ones.

Before Obama, Republicans held the White House for twenty-eight of the previous forty years, and their lifetime appointments of federal judges have made a deep mark on the federal bench. Obama's election sent shivers through those who closely follow the federal lower courts, for they knew that Obama would have a large number of appointments to make. One judge, J. Harvie Wilkinson III of the Fourth Circuit Court of Appeals, appointed by President Reagan to a circuit viewed as the nation's most conservative, warned in a *Washington Post* op-ed in January 2009 that Obama's election would bring a "takeover" of the lower courts. In the Senate, some Republican senators have been sitting on Obama's nominations for the lower courts to try to prevent this from happening.

In one recent study, Washington attorney Eric R. Haren wrote that conservatives held the majority on most of the dozen federal courts of appeals, but he argued that "these courts are up for grabs, and Obama's impact on them could be sweeping." Some analysts have concluded that Obama had already tipped two appellate courts to a majority appointed by Democrats. That could bring an impact even larger and more lasting than whatever will happen on SCOTUS.

Huge policy battles with deep implications continue to brew in the states. We surely haven't seen the last of cases on issues like offshore drilling, immigration, and same-sex marriage. With the lower courts the last stop for more than 99 percent of all cases, whoever shapes the judiciary beyond SCOTUS could well make that his or her most quiet but lasting legacy.

Questions to Consider

1. Compare the roles of the U.S. Supreme Court and the lower federal courts. How would you assess their relative contributions to public administration?

2. Suppose you wanted to maximize your impact on policy and administration. Where would you invest most of your energy? (Trick question: You'd want to focus on both the Supreme Court and lower courts, but weigh how to balance the headline-grabbing potential of the Supreme Court with the fact that the lower courts decide most of the judicial questions.)

Note: This comes from my column in *Governing* (October 2010), http://www.governing.com/columns/potomac-chronicle/why-states-localities-are-watching-lower-federal- courts.html.

Profile in ICE? Local Officials Opt Out of Federal Program They Worry Could Lead to Racial Profiling

Arlington County, Virginia, found itself in a scrap with the U.S. Immigration and Customs Enforcement agency (ICE, for short). Local officials opted out of a federal program that requires police to send the fingerprints of those arrested to ICE for a check against the FBI database and against Homeland Security records.

In Arlington, officials worried that the information would be used for racial profiling. J. Walter Trejeada, a member of the County Board, pointed out that one-fourth of the county's residents were born outside the United States and that one-third of the residents were multiracial. Bringing the federal immigration database together with the local arrest records, he feared, could lead to a dangerous blurring of responsibilities. John Morton, director of ICE, countered that local officials simply weren't responsible for federal policy. "No one in the Department of Corrections, no one in Arlington County, no one in the other jurisdictions in Virginia is being asked to enforce federal immigration law."[1]

The battle erupted out of requirements in the federal Secure Communities program, administered by ICE. The program's website noted that

ICE is committed to protecting civil rights and civil liberties, and is serious about responding to complaints or allegations of racial profiling as a result of Secure Communities. Individuals and organizations should report allegations of racial profiling, due process violations or other violations of civil rights or civil liberties related to the use of this capability.[2]

But critics wondered if trading fingerprints was really advancing homeland security. One study concluded that "DHS's track record on prioritizing violent criminals is far from stellar, leaving much doubt about ICE's compliance with the stated intentions of the Secure Communities program."[3]

In New York, demonstrators picketed the governor's New York City office. "We were basically asking Governor Paterson to rescind the agreement involving S-Comm. The program is going to further terrorize our community and tear our families apart," Manisha Vaze, a representative of Families for Freedom, argued. "I think it's important that people know that the name Secure Communities does the opposite of what its name implies. It is masked as something that will benefit our community when in reality people don't know what the program is all about . . . mass deportation." A spokesman for ICE countered, "People are going to be arrested regardless." He defended the program by arguing that it was whether an individual committed a crime, and not his or her appearance, that prompted the program. "Of course you don't expect to be arrested because of how you look, whether it's Asian, Hispanic, Indian or whatever. If you commit a crime then you can start to worry. S-Comm will simply provide more tools to find out arrestees' criminal and immigration histories."[4]

In Virginia, Attorney General Ken Cuccinelli welcomed the program as an important tool in crime prevention and homeland security. He pointed out that state law requires local governments to submit fingerprints to the state police, who in turn check them with the FBI database. "It's not a situation where Arlington's fingerprints can be treated differently," he argued.[5]

Questions to Consider

1. Map the regulatory chain for this program. Who's involved, and who's doing what?
2. Do you believe that communities ought to have the right to opt out of such national programs? If they can do so, can a national program truly be national? If you don't believe they should be able to do so, is there any place to draw the line in federal rules on local policing?
3. One of the issues prompting the Safe Communities program was the painful lesson taught by the September 11, 2001, terrorist attacks. One of the hijackers was stopped by a police officer for a routine traffic check, but the hijacker didn't trigger any alarms. The Safe Communities program applies only

to people who were arrested, but federal policymakers were haunted by the possibility that a local government might have a potential terrorist in jail but fail to connect the dots with the federal FBI and immigration databases before an attack. Does the program make sense in this context?

NOTES

1. Dena Potter, "ICE: No Opt-Out for Program Checking Legal Status," *Associated Press,* October 8, 2010, http://www.utsandiego.com/news/2010/Oct/08/ice-no-opt-out-for-program-checking-legal-status.
2. See http://www.ice.gov/about/offices/enforcement-removal-operations/secure-communities.
3. Immigration Policy Center, *The Secure Communities Program: Unanswered Questions and Continuing Concerns* (November 4, 2010), http://www.immigrationpolicy.org/special-reports/secure-communities-program-unanswered-questions-and-continuing-concerns.
4. Daysi Calavia-Lopez, "Rally against the Secure Communities Program," *Queens Courier,* December 22, 2010, http://queenscourier.com/2010/rally-against-the-secure-communities-program-10908.
5. Potter, "ICE."

KEY CONCEPTS

adjudication   382

administrative rulemaking   382

antitrust laws   374

capture   374

class action   385

cost-benefit analysis   380

economic regulation   373

private attorneys general   386

risk assessment   381

social regulation   374

standing to sue   385

tort action   387

FOR FURTHER READING

Ackerman, Frank, and Lisa Heinzerling.
Priceless: On Knowing the Price of Everything and the Value of Nothing. New York: New Press, 2004.

Bardach, Eugene, and Robert A. Kagan.
Going by the Book: The Problem of Regulatory Unreasonableness.
A Twentieth Century Fund Report.

Philadelphia: Temple University Press, 1982.

Cooper, Phillip J. *Governing by Contract: Challenges and Opportunities for Public Managers.* Washington, D.C.: CQ Press, 2002.

Derthick, Martha A. *Up in Smoke: From Legislation to Litigation in Tobacco Politics.* 2nd ed. Washington, D.C.: CQ Press, 2005.

Howard, Phillip K. *The Death of Common Sense.* New York: Random House, 1994.

Skowronek, Stephen. *Building a New American State: The Expansion of National Administrative Capacities, 1877–1920.* New York: Cambridge University Press, 1982.

Wilson, James Q., ed. *The Politics of Regulation.* New York: Basic Books, 1980.

SUGGESTED WEBSITES

The issues of government regulation provide rich puzzles for Internet-based research. Many complex public policy questions have played out through studies and analyses, which can easily be found through web search engines.

The federal government's catalog of regulations can be found at the website for the *Code of Federal Regulations,* **www.gpoaccess .gov/cfr/index.html.** Daily changes to federal regulations are published in the *Federal Register,* **www.gpoaccess.gov/fr/index.html**.

The National Academy of Public Administration has conducted an exhaustive study of federal clean air regulations. See *A Breath of Fresh Air: Reviving the New Source Review Program* (Washington, D.C.: NAPA,

2003), **http://www.ntis.gov/search/product .aspx?ABBR=PB2003106653**. In addition, the Government Accountability Office, **www.gao .gov**, regularly reviews regulatory issues through its studies.

Moreover, many government regulatory agencies have their own websites, which are invaluable for tracking policy issues. See, for example, the website for the National Highway Traffic Safety Administration, **www.nhtsa .gov**, for information about the safety of cars and trucks; the Food and Drug Administration, **www.fda.gov**, for the safety of prescription and over-the-counter drugs; and the Environmental Protection Agency, **www.epa.gov**, for clean air and water regulations.

Administrative Accountability, Effectiveness, and Politics

CHAPTER OBJECTIVES

- Understand the role of public administration in an environment of separation of powers

- Explore the role and function of legislative oversight of administration

- Examine the implications of performance information to promote accountability

- Take a final look at the challenges for accountability in modern public administration

President George W. Bush and Defense Secretary Donald H. Rumsfeld found themselves immersed in a fierce national debate over the interrogation techniques used during the Iraq war, especially at Abu Ghraib prison.

AS REPORTS SWIRLED ABOUT OF THE ABUSE OF SUSPECTED TERRORISTS at the Abu Ghraib prison facility during the war in Iraq, an international debate erupted. Was the use of torture ever justified? If the military had custody of a prisoner who might have knowledge of a pending terrorist attack—for example, if one of the September 11, 2001, hijackers had been captured before that fateful morning—would interrogators be justified in using any means at their disposal, no matter how distasteful, to extract information that could save hundreds or thousands of lives? Is torture unlikely to produce useful information? Most fundamentally, is it the kind of thing in which American democracy ought to engage, under any circumstances at any time?

The torture debate was as sharp a question about the role of executive power as the nation has ever seen. What standards should the executive branch follow? If the executive decided to use torture, what limits could—and should—Congress set? And how could Congress enforce these limits? Could—and should—the courts supervise such practices? The debate quickly sharpened not only into one of moral justice and military effectiveness but also into the separation of powers. It was a central puzzle in the role of executive power: how to use it effectively, how to hold it accountable, and how to navigate the deep political issues that always lie at the core of important administrative decisions.

In 2006, the debate came to a head. Congress passed a bill that made torture illegal. President George W. Bush signed it, and the prohibition against torture became law. As he signed the law, however, the president also issued a **signing statement** that contained the administration's interpretation of the law and how it would be enforced. The signing statement read, in part, that "The executive branch shall construe [the law] in a manner consistent with the constitutional authority of the President . . . as Commander in Chief." The approach, Bush contended, "will assist in achieving the shared objective of the Congress and the President . . . of protecting the American people from further terrorist attacks."

But what did this signing statement mean? A Bush administration official reassured observers that "We are not going to allow this law" and "We consider ourselves bound by the prohibition on cruel, unusual, and degrading treatment." The official added a reservation, however. "Of course the president has the obligation to follow this law, [but] he also has the obligation to defend and protect the country as commander in chief, and he will have to square those two responsibilities in each case." If the responsibilities came into conflict, the official left no doubt that President Bush was willing to use torture if he believed it necessary for national defense. A New York University law professor who specialized in executive power, David Golove, was more blunt:

> The signing statement is saying "I will only comply with this law when I want to, and if something arises in the war on terrorism where I think it's important to engage in cruel, inhuman, and degrading conduct, I have the authority to do so and nothing in the law is going to stop me"[1]

The phenomenon of signing statements was largely unknown to the public until a series of articles by the *Boston Globe*'s Charlie Savage, a sharp reporter with a keen eye for important issues. In April 2006, he wrote a long story that pointed to more than 750 signing statements that the Bush administration had signed. In these cases, ranging from affirmative action to immigration, the administration asserted its executive power to push aside laws if the president concluded it was essential for pursuing the executive function.[2] Savage's reporting rocked the political debate and won him the 2007 Pulitzer Prize. Just what effect did these signing statements actually have on executive branch behavior? The Government Accountability Office (GAO) found that federal officials did not execute the law as written in at least nine cases.[3] Savage found that an adviser to Vice President Dick Cheney routinely scanned legislation for provisions that might challenge executive power and on which the president might issue a signing statement.[4] The debate spilled over into the 2008 presidential campaign, when reporters pressed both John McCain and Barack Obama on whether they would follow a similar course. The two candidates, who both were legislators, pledged to avoid using signing statements to reverse congressional action. On taking office, however, although President Obama issued fewer signing statements than his predecessor, he did not give up the practice, and he also used executive orders and other steps to bypass increasingly nasty relationships with congressional Republicans.

There is little meaning to governmental policy without administration, and that makes administration an ongoing focus of tensions between political powers. Policymakers make policy by delegating its execution to administrators. They expect effective results. Administrators administer by making decisions, and decision making requires the application of values. Values are inherently political—as is the product of administrative action. That frames the central and enduring issue of the politics of the administrative process: balancing executive power with political accountability. And as in all truly important things in American democracy, the answer requires balancing competing values.

THE SEPARATION OF POWERS

The classical view of the policy process draws a line between the legislative and executive branches: the legislature makes policy and the executive branch implements it. In reality, the roles are far more complex and the lines much more blurred. In much of the American system, the Constitution creates elaborate checks and balances, not just a separation of powers—which means that political responsibility is shared. Furthermore, as one scholar of congressional oversight has pointed out, "oversight is in many respects a continuation of preenactment politics."[5] The political battles that surround lawmaking continue to play out in the administrative process. Political forces that lose in the legislature often try to regain the advantage as administrators take over, and the forces that win the early battle must continue to struggle to make sure they retain their edge. Laws must be translated into rules; rules must be supported by budgets. And in the richly textured system of American federalism, few decisions rest at a single level of government.[6] That quickly focuses the question of political control of administration on the role of legislative oversight. Much of the analysis about legislative oversight focuses on Congress, but most of the issues apply just as sharply to oversight by state legislators, county boards, and city councils.

The Paradox of Oversight

At the core of legislative oversight is a profound paradox: although much of what Congress does is oversight, in one form or another, the activity tends to rank low among congressional priorities. Nevertheless, oversight is essential to effective administration because, as Chapter 12 discussed, policy has little meaning except in its implementation.

As one panel of experts has pointed out, "oversight permeates the activities of Congress."[7] Many congressional actions involve some form of supervision of administrative actions, from the enactment of laws and budgets to committee hearings to program reviews by congressional staff agencies, such as the GAO and the Congressional Budget Office. Variations in the level of oversight can be quite remarkable, from investigation of a program's overall performance to probes of the most detailed of program activities. In 1987 the Senate attached eighty-six amendments to a bill authorizing the State Department's budget; policy questions addressed in the amendments ranged from the Chinese government's treatment of Tibetan monks to traffic tie-ups caused by long, honking motorcades for foreign dignitaries in Washington.[8] Nothing the federal government does lies beyond the reach of legislative oversight.

In fact, critics have blamed congressional micromanagement for problems in many defense systems. In 1985, for example, the Pentagon submitted 24,000 pages of documentation to Congress in order to comply with 458 different reporting requirements established in previous legislation. The number of these reports, Defense officials estimated, increased 1,000 percent in the decade and a half after 1970.[9] Such a penchant for particulars, moreover, imposes a heavy burden on top administrative officials. Former secretaries of state Henry Kissinger and Cyrus Vance, for example, have complained: "Surely there are better ways for the executive and legislative branches to consult than having the secretaries of state and defense spend more than a quarter of their time on repetitive congressional testimony."[10] As the federal government tried to strengthen its homeland security system in the aftermath of September 11, 2001, investigators found that many of the worst problems originated in the Immigration and Naturalization Service, which, they discovered, was allowing too many security breaches and struggling to cope with a rising paperwork backlog. One critic felt that congressional micromanagement had caused many of the agency's problems; what Congress most needed to do, the expert concluded, was to make up its mind and then get out of the way.[11]

Despite the enormous power that oversight can bring, oversight usually is a low priority for legislators. Routine oversight does little to enhance a member's reputation back in the district. Instead, passing legislation, taking stands on issues, and tending to constituents' needs through casework dominate members' attention.[12] There rarely are regular procedures for conducting oversight.[13] Members are typically more interested in shaping the immediate future than in investigating what has gone wrong in the past, unless past events prove so scandalous that an investigation will win wide publicity and be embarrassing to the opposition party. The level of oversight, in fact, often seems most attuned to the odds of attracting television cameras. An old joke in Washington is that the most dangerous place on Capitol Hill is between a member of Congress and a television camera. Immigration hearings rarely attract much public or media attention, but a 2010 immigration hearing featuring celebrity comedian Stephen Colbert packed the congressional hearing room and led to committee members sparring for the limelight.

Much oversight involves difficult and detailed issues, and this kind of detailed work is unlikely to engage legislators' interest. Legislators, of course, care deeply about details—making things right for individual constituents is the cornerstone of casework. Constituents often want help in getting Social Security and disability benefits, Medicare reimbursements, admission to a veterans' hospital, emergency home leave from military service, or a flag that flew over the Capitol. Members of Congress know that constituents care a lot about such requests, and they devote great energy to meeting them. The same is true for state legislators, even if the calls for help come from constituents trying to sort out their federal Social Security checks. They've learned that they get credit for helping solve a problem, even if it's not dealing with a state program. Suggesting that an unhappy constituent check with a federal agency would miss the chance for credit and would likely bring blame. Legislators also pay a great deal of attention to fighting for projects in their districts—roads, dams, job training programs, and money for schools.

This frames the paradox of oversight: while nearly all legislative activities are a form of oversight, the kinds of activities in which legislators are most likely to be involved are least likely to provide good information about administrative problems. Big problems can promise big headlines, and that can draw legislators' interest. When there's a chance to embarrass executives of the opposite party, the taste for oversight grows.[14] Most of the time, however, oversight is likely to be unsystematic, sporadic, episodic, erratic, haphazard, ad hoc, and based on a crisis.[15] Long-term improvement of implementation requires systematic, sustained attention. Legislative incentives often run at cross-purposes to what improved implementation requires.

Mathew D. McCubbins and Thomas Schwartz have christened this approach the **fire alarm** style of oversight, in which members of Congress respond to complaints as they arise—as opposed to **police patrol** oversight, in which they conduct routine patrols at their own initiative. These analysts argue that fire-alarm oversight "serves congressmen's interests at little cost" and that it produces oversight that is much more effective: through periodic interventions sparked by apparent problems, members of Congress can more clearly define the goals they have in mind. Moreover, they contend, responding to problems as they arise is much more likely to detect troubles than is maintaining a regular police-patrol style.[16] This argument is much debated. At the least, however, oversight is a much more subtle process than the formal checks-and-balances system might suggest.

The Purposes of Oversight

Even if it is intermittent and ad hoc, oversight nevertheless serves a number of important purposes for legislators.[17]

- *Assurance that administrators follow legislative intent.* Legislators naturally wish to ensure that administrators' actions are consistent with what legislators intended in passing legislation. That intent is sometimes hard to determine, of course, because legislation is notoriously imprecise; often, in fact, legislators do not know what they want until they see what they get. In these cases, oversight provides an opportunity for communicating more clearly, if often informally, to administrators just what results legislators expect.
- *Investigation of instances of fraud, waste, and abuse.* This unholy trinity is a frequent target of legislative investigations. From stories of overpriced hammers purchased by

the Pentagon to suggestions of irregularities by contractors serving Native American reservations to problems with the parking authority, allegations of inefficiencies and illegalities frequently fuel the kind of press attention that draws legislators, which often sparks oversight.

■ *Collection of information.* Since many programs must be reauthorized, oversight gives legislators and their staffs the opportunity to obtain basic data that will help them determine how laws ought to be changed and which new laws should be enacted.

■ *Evaluation of program effectiveness.* Oversight can also provide legislators with information about how well a program is performing. This information can help legislators determine how best to improve an agency's effectiveness.

■ *Protection of legislative prerogatives.* Legislators also sometimes use oversight to protect what they view as their constitutional rights and privileges from encroachment by the executive branch. The checks-and-balances system often breeds boundary-line disputes, and oversight gives legislators an opportunity to defend their points of view.

■ *Personal advocacy.* Oversight frequently gives legislators their own "bully pulpits" from which to advance programs of interest and to attract publicity. Some legislators have built their reputations by championing particular causes, while others have used televised hearings to promote their careers.

■ *Reversal of unpopular actions.* Finally, oversight provides members with leverage to force agencies to reverse unpopular decisions. Through veiled threats and direct confrontation, legislators can signal administrators about what activities are unacceptable and what can be done to address members' concerns.

Legislative oversight occurs through several channels, which this chapter investigates. We will focus especially on the work of Congress, which provides a model for how many state and local legislators operate. We will examine (1) the work of committees and their staffs, (2) program reviews conducted by the GAO, and (3) performance-based information. All three channels revolve around the flow of information.

COMMITTEE OVERSIGHT OF ADMINISTRATION

Even more than is the case with its legislative work, Congress depends heavily on its committees for monitoring administrative agencies and their implementation of programs. Indeed, the connection between congressional committees and administrative agencies is one of the most important in government.[18] The old saying "Congress at work is Congress in committee" applies especially to the executive-legislative relationship. Committee members write the legislation and fund the programs that bureaucrats must implement; the bureaucrats' decisions affect the members' abilities to claim credit for governmental action. It is an exchange relationship: "The ability of each to attain his goals is at least partially dependent on the actions of the other," R. Douglas Arnold writes.[19]

Legislators have powerful sanctions in their arsenal, but their use of these tools varies. Some committees engage more frequently in oversight, especially those watching over agencies that must receive annual appropriations; some committees are far tougher in approving budgets

The Urge to Bypass Congress

Barack Obama spent most of his presidency dueling with a Republican Congress determined to stop his initiatives, from Obamacare to his choices for executive-branch appointments. Obama's supporters pointed out that he won election—twice—and had a mandate from citizens. Republicans countered that they were not about to roll over for policies they didn't believe in.

In the summer of 2011, his frustration about Washington gridlock boiled over. In a speech to a major Hispanic organization, he said he'd like to "bypass Congress and change the laws on my own." He knew, of course, he didn't have that unilateral power, but his advisers quietly were working on strategies, ranging from temporary appointments of executive-branch officials to executive orders, to advance his agenda. Republicans fired back that they would not stand for any increase in executive power. The battle ended in a major impasse in August 2011, when the president and Congress failed to agree on a long-term solution to the budget. Standard and Poors, one of the largest bond-rating firms, downgraded the United States debt for the first time in history and suggested that the future prognosis was uncertain. Financial markets, at home and abroad, were worried. A senior Australian official quietly and soberly told me, "This is how great empires fall."

Has the American separation-of-powers system, enshrined in our Constitution, reached the breaking point? Accountability is one of our nation's bedrock principles, but has it hamstrung our government's ability to function efficiently? Is our Constitution a solid base on which to make decisions in the twenty-first century? Or do you believe that it provides a framework to force—eventually—a consensus on strategies to govern the nation, within a framework of accountability?

Source: "Obama: 'I'd Like to Bypass Congress and Change the Rules on My Own,'" *Fox Nation,* http://nation.foxnews.com/president-obama/2011/07/25/obama-id-bypass-congress-and-change-rules-my-own.

than others. Furthermore, some committees tend to be largely populated by members whose goal is constituency service, and, in providing that service, bureaucrats can gain powerful allies. When a committee has a broad national agenda, such as education or labor, instead of a narrow constituency focus, however, oversight may be harsher.[20] Nevertheless, "committees in both houses tend to give more attention to investigations of broad policy questions than to inquiries into agency implementation of programs."[21]

Varieties of Committee Review

Three sets of standing committees have responsibility for **legislative review** (the official term for legislative oversight): the regular legislative committees (usually known as

authorizing committees, because they prepare the laws that authorize programs); the **appropriations committees**; and committees on government operations.

Authorizing committees can initiate, review, and report out bills and resolutions in particular subject-matter areas (such as labor, commerce, education, and foreign affairs). Each has the oversight responsibility to review the administration of laws within its jurisdiction. While some legislative committees have conducted extensive oversight, the overall tendency is for these subject-area committees to concentrate more on the passage of new laws than on reviewing the execution of existing ones. Further decreasing the frequency of oversight here is the growth in the number of programs receiving permanent authorizations (discussed in Chapter 11); when program managers do not need to appear regularly to request continuation of their programs, the likelihood of oversight diminishes. Some committees are also moving toward longer reauthorizations to help reduce their workload, which has further reduced the opportunities for oversight.[22] Furthermore, some legislative committees (and subcommittees) are so favorably disposed toward the agencies and programs under their purview that they are not eager to initiate penetrating inquiries into possible administrative mismanagement or program ineffectiveness.

Appropriations committees have the most impressive credentials for control of administration: prestige, broad scope, power, and competence. Appropriations Committee members, and especially their staffs, typically command a knowledge of agencies and programs rivaling that of career administrators and surpassing that of political executives. Yet Congress cannot rely mainly on the appropriations committees for the oversight function, because the members of these committees are already heavily burdened by their primary responsibility: they operate under the time pressure of the annual appropriations process, and their focus is on dollar figures and incremental changes from the previous year. The House Appropriations Committee's oversight, a staff member has said, is wide but not deep, whereas legislative committees' oversight is deep but not wide.[23] Moreover, with the rise of the omnibus acts and reconciliation measures discussed in Chapter 11, the influence of the appropriations committees, on both budgeting and congressional oversight, has decreased. The committees have responded by adding more riders and earmarks—detailed requirements about how money appropriated for individual programs can be used—but, in general, the effectiveness of oversight by the appropriations committees remains mixed.

The Senate Committee on Homeland Security and Government Affairs and the House Committee on Oversight and Government Reform have the broadest responsibility and strongest powers for overseeing administrative activities. (After September 11, 2001, Congress rolled the new homeland security mission into governmental affairs to create a more unified look at governmental operations.) Since the early 1800s, Congress has used such committees to go beyond the usual grasp of legislative and appropriations committees. They are *the* oversight committees of Congress, and their jurisdiction is not constrained by the usual departmental or committee boundaries.[24]

While their potential for effective oversight is great, these committees have traditionally ranked relatively low in prestige.[25] One consequence is that the committees' members focus their primary interest elsewhere: members serve on multiple committees, and their other committee assignments often offer more of what they need for reelection. The oversight committees rarely have adopted any strategy to guide their work in monitoring administrative agencies, and the subject-area committees have jealously guarded their jurisdictions from review. When investigations promise big headlines, other committees are quick to seize the agenda. Both houses' oversight committees have been highly selective and episodic in the choice of the administrative activities to be reviewed, generally reflecting their own specific areas of legislative jurisdiction (e.g., executive reorganization, intergovernmental relations), reacting to public scandals, or registering the special concerns of leading committee members. They rarely have been able to pursue sustained investigations, however, because they receive only modest funding.[26] When major issues surface, such as the conduct of the second Bush administration's war in Iraq or decisions about licensing a new drug, the authorizing committees tend to take center stage.

Oversight and Redundancy

The problem of legislative control, at all levels of government, is clearly not a shortage of committees with oversight responsibilities and opportunities. Indeed, the multiplicity of committees and the overlaps among their jurisdictions provide many different avenues for legislative influence on administrative activities. In Congress, the increasingly decentralized system has expanded the points of access and the number of hearings, but "it has at the same time weakened the ability of Congress to conduct serious oversight and administrative control." The growing complexity of administrative activities, the difficulty of developing good information about program performance, and the counterbalancing power of interest groups all combine to lessen Congress's direct leverage over the executive branch.[27] As experts debated the creation of the new Department of Homeland Security in 2002, congressional scholar Norman J. Ornstein counted thirteen House and Senate committees with at least some jurisdiction over the issue, and there were more than sixty subcommittees sharing jurisdiction—for a total of eighty-eight committees and subcommittees in all.[28] After September 11, 2001, anyone who could assert jurisdiction over a piece of the action did so. For top officials at the Department of Homeland Security, the situation is even worse. More than 80 congressional committees and subcommittees oversee the department's vast operations. The drive from the department's temporary headquarters in far northwest Washington to Capitol Hill is a tortuous one through the capital's clogged traffic. Constant congressional hearings, which are essential for accountability, make it hard to get work done.

Redundancy has magnified, not solved, Congress's oversight problem. Changes in the budget process have duplicated the number of reviews to which agencies are subjected and have blurred the responsibilities of each committee. As one Georgetown University study on defense oversight argued, "redundancy in the congressional review process seriously aggravates the oversight problem." The redundant steps mean that "Congress rarely takes conclusive action on any issue," as a Senate Armed Services Committee staff report concluded.[29] One estimate is that assistant secretaries must spend as much as 40 percent of their time preparing for congressional testimony and responding to inquiries by members of Congress.[30] Thus, congressional committee structures and operating rules hinder rather than help in the oversight of administration. The multiplicity of committees overseeing the Department of Homeland Security led to constant complaints by senior officials, who said they needed to spend so much time tending their congressional relationships that they had little time left for their work. In 2008, Stephen R. Heifetz, the department's deputy assistant secretary for policy development, argued that "Congress should step back, streamline the number of committees with responsibility for homeland security—and give us room to do our job."[31] Congressional committees might reply that there was nothing more important in doing the job than ensuring accountability to Congress.

Congress's ability to monitor administrative activities effectively depends on its access to information, most of it generated in the executive branch. On the one hand, there are significant barriers to obtaining information about what is happening in the executive branch; on the other hand, legislators typically are awash in data. Effective oversight requires separating the truly useful information from the huge volumes of paper that flood Washington—as well as state capitals and city halls. Distilling the key issues from the mass of detailed data evokes the classic problem of trying "to distinguish the forest from the trees."

Barriers to Information Flow

Since Congress depends heavily on outside forces for the information needed to drive oversight, barriers in the way of the flow of information have a huge impact on the quality of oversight. Several kinds of barriers, both institutional and political, can effectively impede this information flow.

Secrecy

Secrecy, particularly in the conduct of foreign affairs, the planning of military strategy and tactics, and the pursuit of intelligence activities, is the most formidable barrier.[32] Few would argue that these matters should be carried on in full view of the public or, for that matter, of the 535 members of Congress. The problem is that under the guise of national security, it is possible for administrators to classify any documents they choose as "top secret," "secret," or "confidential." Classification, once done, is difficult to undo, however trivial or improper the reasons for its having been done. During World War II, for example, documents often received security classifications  simply because that sped their delivery to government offices. In the Defense Department, newspaper clippings have been stamped "secret," and a memorandum urging less use of the top secret classification was itself classified top secret.[33]

Forty years after the end of World War II, the Tower Commission, investigating the Reagan administration's elaborate plan to sell arms to Iran to secure the release of Americans held hostage there, and then to divert the arms-sales profits to aid the Contras in Nicaragua, concluded that "concern for preserving the secrecy of the initiative provided an excuse for abandoning sound process."[34] Congressional investigators, furthermore, found that secrecy concerns enormously complicated their probe. When administrative officials argued the need for flexibility in conducting foreign relations and said they had planned to notify Congress after the hostages were released, Sen. William S. Cohen (R-Maine) acknowledged that the president needs flexibility but warned, "flexibility is too often taken as license, and then after the fact it's rationalized as a constitutional power that cannot be diluted or diminished by congressional action." He concluded, "comity is important, but it has to run in two directions on Pennsylvania Avenue."[35] Almost fifteen years later, members of Congress

Gen. Keith B. Alexander, director of the National Security Agency and head of the U.S. Cyber Command, faced tough questions from congressional investigators in 2013. Following the leak of secrets through British and American newspapers by an NSA contractor, members of Congress probed the scope of the agency's surveillance of Americans' telephone and Internet communications.

continued to complain that they had not received timely information from the Pentagon about problems with the war in Iraq, especially about abusive treatment of Iraqi prisoners by American soldiers. Sen. Carl Levin (D-Mich.) sternly admonished Defense Secretary Donald Rumsfeld in 2004 that consultation with Congress "is not supposed to be an option but a long-standing and fundamental responsibility" of administration officials.[36]

The problem of excessive security classification has two dimensions. One is the denial to Congress of information that in fact has no valid claim to secrecy or confidentiality. The other is the withholding from Congress of information that, though secret or confidential, is essential to congressional decision making and oversight with respect to the nation's foreign relations, military posture, and intelligence gathering. The typical solution proposed for this problem has been furnishing classified information to only a selected few committees (usually the House and Senate Intelligence Committees) in executive session, to only the chairpersons and ranking minority members of such committees, or to only their pro-Pentagon members. However, the disclosure that high Reagan administration officials had been secretly using the proceeds from their arms sales to Iran to fund the White House's Central American program revealed how inadequate such a solution often is. So, too, does the growing share of the Pentagon budget that is devoted to the so-called black—that is, secret—programs that are hidden from all but select members of Congress (discussed in Chapter 11). When news broke of the National Security Agency's widespread screening of Americans' communications, many citizens—and many members of Congress—were outraged. But both the Bush and Obama administrations had kept select members of Congress informed on the details, and there was no suggestion that the NSA had acted illegally. There was legislative oversight, but it did not involve most members of Congress.

Executive Privilege

A second barrier to the flow of information is **executive privilege**—a prerogative never mentioned in the Constitution but now asserted to be inherent in the president's powers. Presidents have claimed that this immunity from compulsion to disclose information is akin to the legal doctrine of "privileged communications," such as those between husband and wife, doctor and patient, attorney and client, and priest and parishioner. In the government, the doctrine has most powerfully been invoked to protect the confidentiality of oral and written communication between the president and White House aides, especially during the Nixon administration's Watergate affair. The question of executive privilege has continued to resurface ever since, however, constricting the ability of courts and Congress to elicit information in incidents ranging from Bill Clinton's appearance before a grand jury investigating his personal conduct in office to George W. Bush's testimony before a commission investigating the September 11, 2001, attacks. Executive privilege was the core of George W. Bush's case for the use of signing statements. Senior Bush aide Karl Rove claimed executive privilege as a defense against testifying before Congress on the leak of the identity of the name of a CIA spy to the media.

Administrative Confidentiality

A third, but lower, barrier to legislative access to information is **administrative confidentiality**, which covers two distinct practices. One is the protection of private information: individuals' tax returns, completed census forms, possibly derogatory personal details collected in investigative agencies' files, and businesses concerns' trade secrets and financial data. Such information is normally collected by government agencies under pledges of confidentiality, and the administrators often resist committee demands for such records. They argue, with considerable force, that abuse of confidentiality could impair the government's ability to obtain full and accurate information.

The other claim to administrative confidentiality relates to drafts, memoranda, and other internal records bearing on policies and decisions that may or may not be under serious consideration. Agencies' concern is that premature disclosure of such internal records may lead to distorted publicity and public misunderstanding—many memoranda by subordinate staff members make suggestions that will in fact be rejected at higher levels, but newspaper headlines drawn from them could give the impression that the agency is about to adopt the suggestion. Equally important (and paralleling the argument for executive privilege at the presidential level), the possibility that they will have to defend their memoranda before congressional committees may inhibit those on whom a department head relies for imaginative ideas and frank advice. Congressional committees and their staffs are nevertheless often eager to share in the shaping of agency policies, partly because once announced, such policies are difficult to reverse.[37]

Finding the Balance

Secrecy, executive privilege, and administrative confidentiality are all embroiled in disputes that essentially pit the separation of powers against the checks-and-balances system. There remain moral, prudential, and practical considerations that need to be balanced against these institutional concerns, weighing in favor of restoration of a freer flow of information. On one side are citizens' stake in the confidentiality of personal information in government files, the president's and department heads' need for candid advice from their immediate assistants, the effects of disclosure of preliminary proposals, and the special need for secrecy in matters affecting defense and the conduct of foreign affairs. On the other side are the often deplorable results of official activities cloaked in secrecy; the people's right to know so that they can participate in democratic government; Congress's oversight responsibilities as creator, authorizer, and financier of agencies and their programs; and its role as investigator and exposer of corrupt, illegal, and unethical behavior in the executive branch. With so many constitutional, moral, prudential, and pragmatic considerations in conflict, no formula, however complex, can provide a solution to this dilemma of administrative accountability.

Staffing to Stem the Tide

Congress is buried in paradox: it struggles to obtain some important but sensitive information, but it is also overwhelmed with information from administrative agencies. A large amount comes in the form of regular reports—annual, quarterly, monthly—that their authorizing statutes require. This tidal wave of information, in fact, is mainly of Congress's own making. The Pentagon reports cited earlier are only one sign of Congress's increasing insistence that administrative agencies provide regular reports on their activities as well as answer detailed intermittent inquiries. The Environmental Protection Agency, for example, must respond to more than 4,000 letters per year from Congress requesting information.[38] In addition, "elaborate public relations programs in some agencies blanket congressional committees with more—and often irrelevant—'information' than they can possibly handle, befogging issues and distorting facts in the process."[39] Congress's informational problem stems, in part, from a deliberate agency strategy of communications overkill, but, more commonly, it reflects the lack of fit between congressional interests and the way that information is organized and summarized in administrative agencies. The increasingly scientific and technological character of many fields of governmental activity has further complicated the problem.[40]

For years, Congress dealt with the problem of information overload by vastly increasing the size of its own staff. In a move mirrored in state legislatures around the country, it attempted to close its expertise gap with the executive branch by taking three steps: increasing the personal staffs of members, hiring more staff for committees, and strengthening the three staff agencies that serve Congress (the Congressional Research Service, the Congressional Budget Office, and the GAO, discussed below).[41] "Committee staffs grew when it became apparent that even specialized committee members needed help if Congress was to get the information required for making informed decisions," Michael J. Malbin argues. "Without its staff, Congress would quickly become the prisoner of its outside sources of information in the executive branch and interest groups."[42]

In fact, from 1965 to 2009, these congressional staffs doubled in size, while executive-branch employment rose only slightly (see Figure 14.1). As part of their takeover of Congress in 1995, the Republicans significantly cut the congressional staff as a symbol of their commitment to shrinking government, but the staffing levels quickly recovered. By global standards, Congress's staff is large indeed; the second most heavily staffed legislature in the world, Canada's parliament, had a staff just one-tenth as large.[43]

These staffs have helped members of Congress devote more time to casework for constituents. When a constituent writes to complain about a slow Social Security check, malfeasance by local grant recipients, or even allegedly abusive treatment by a relative's commanding

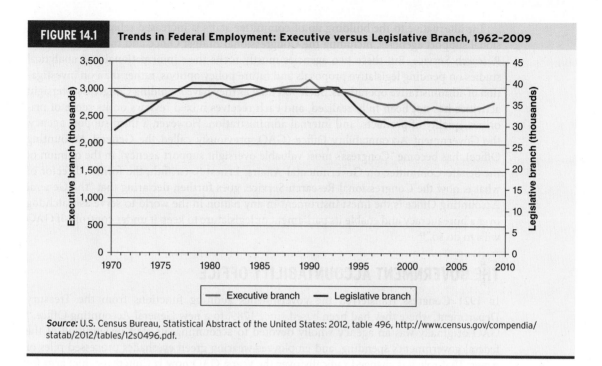

FIGURE 14.1   Trends in Federal Employment: Executive versus Legislative Branch, 1962-2009

Source: U.S. Census Bureau, *Statistical Abstract of the United States: 2012*, table 496, http://www.census.gov/compendia/statab/2012/tables/12s0496.pdf.

officer in the military, the letter is assigned to a worker in a member's office. Congressional mail receives special treatment in government offices; special, brightly colored "buck slips" are usually stapled to the first page of the letters to make sure they get to the top of the action list. Most agencies require quick turnaround times for responses, and they maintain congressional liaison units that monitor responses, to ensure that quick and accurate replies are sent.

Members of Congress and administrators take such letters very seriously, because no one wants to seem indifferent to constituents. There is evidence, however, that such referrals often are not very effective at solving the problems, "since they are usually handled at the same level of the agency (often by the same official) where the complaint arose in the first place." Furthermore, because the complaints are random and extremely detailed, they rarely provide good evidence for broad administrative oversight issues. Occasionally, patterns of complaints or particularly unusual issues may surface, but evidence of wrongdoing does not often emerge through such casework.[44]

No one seriously supposes that a committee can or should match the expertise of the administrative agencies under its jurisdiction. Even a moderate expansion of committee staffs could mean multiplication of little congressional bureaucracies, each requiring direction and coordination by the committee or its chair—responsibilities for which members of Congress have little time and, often, little talent. In the absence of such control, staff members have been known to go off on their own, harassing agency officials and, in effect, participating in agency decision making. Such staff members purport to be representing their committees but in fact may be representing only themselves.

The alternative to the building up of committee staffs is increased reliance on congressional support agencies, including the Congressional Budget Office and the Congressional Research Service. But these two agencies mostly focus their informational and analytical studies on pending legislative proposals and future policy options, rather than on investigation of administrative operations. Such potential as they have for aiding Congress's oversight activities has not been fully realized, and each receives mixed reviews on its sense of priorities, quality of products, and internal administration. However, a third support agency, the Government Accountability Office (GAO, previously called the General Accounting Office), has become "Congress's most valuable oversight support agency" in the opinion of the Senate Committee on Governmental Affairs. Ernest S. Griffith, the former director of what is now the Congressional Research Service, goes further, declaring that "the General Accounting Office is the finest instrument in any nation in the world to serve as watchdog over a bureaucracy and enable its parliament or legislature to keep it under control—if GAO wills to do so."[45]

THE GOVERNMENT ACCOUNTABILITY OFFICE

In 1921 Congress transferred the government's auditing functions from the Treasury Department, where they had been based since 1789, to a new General Accounting Office.[46] GAO originally was an agency wholly devoted to accounting: its staff reviewed all of the federal government's spending, and employees wearing green eyeshades processed piles of paper. That role has changed radically over the years; GAO now is Congress's chief arm for examining the performance of governmental programs—and that evolution was recognized with the change in the agency's name.

The comptroller general of the United States, who heads GAO, is appointed by the president subject to Senate confirmation. Because Congress wanted to ensure that GAO was protected from interference by the executive branch, the comptroller general holds a fifteen-year term (the longest in the government, except for the lifetime appointment of federal judges) and can be removed only by a joint resolution of Congress or by impeachment.

GAO performs functions with both executive and legislative roots: its legislative branch duties include auditing the expenditures of executive branch agencies; its executive branch duties involve approving agencies' payments and settling their accounts. This ambiguous position has been a source of continuing controversy. When the Competition in Contracting Act of 1984 gave GAO the power to halt a contract under dispute, President Ronald Reagan objected to this power, and Attorney General William French Smith instructed executive branch agencies not to comply with the provision. A federal district judge ruled Smith's action illegal, and Congress backed up the decision by withholding all funds from the attorney general's office until he agreed to go along with the law; Smith's successor, Edwin Meese III, eventually backed down. Meanwhile, a federal appeals court agreed with Congress, holding that GAO was a "hybrid agency" that could exercise such executive functions as reviewing contracts before their execution.

In 1986, however, the Supreme Court held, in *Bowsher v. Synar,* that the comptroller general was an agent of Congress and so could not constitutionally exercise executive budget-cutting powers.[47] Thus, GAO is a hybrid whose constitutional position is a vague one. Much of its work revolves around the detailed examination of individual programs, although during the first George W. Bush administration GAO sued Vice President Cheney in an attempt to force him to reveal the names of those with whom his special energy task force had consulted. GAO lost that suit, but its work sparked objections from others in Washington and fueled a continuing controversy over corporate influence on the Bush administration's policies.

An Era of Detailed Control

Two major provisions in the 1921 Budget and Accounting Act's definition of GAO's powers created the basis for much of this friction.[48] One reads: "The Comptroller General shall prescribe the forms, systems, and procedure for . . . accounting in the several departments and establishments, and for the administrative examination of fiscal officers' accounts and claims against the United States." This meant that the government's accounting systems could be designed primarily with GAO's preferences in mind and without attention to the accounting needs of the operating departments, the Treasury Department, and the budget bureau. GAO's external-control needs could be met at the expense of the executive branch's internal-control needs.

The 1921 act's second major provision reads as follows: "All claims and demands whatever by the Government of the United States or against it, and all accounts whatever in which the Government of the United States is concerned, either as debtor or creditor, shall be settled and adjusted in the General Accounting Office." This appeared to mean (and was so interpreted by the first comptroller general, John R. McCarl) that no financial transaction of the government could legally be completed until specifically approved by GAO. Agency officials continued to spend money for goods and services, but the vouchers for all transactions were transported from all over the world to Washington for review by the GAO; if it disapproved any expenditure, the public official who had approved the expenditure would, by law, be personally responsible for the difference.[49] The risk of such personal liability was so threatening that spending officers often asked GAO for advance opinions, and GAO increasingly preaudited expenditures before they were made. As a result, GAO not only delayed actions but became less an after-the-fact auditor than an active participant in the very transactions it was supposed to audit later.

For the first fifteen years, Comptroller General McCarl cherished his role as "watchdog of the Treasury"—he usually interpreted grants of spending power narrowly and statutory restrictions broadly. *Interpreted* is the key word here, and one that is often overlooked in discussions of external control. Statutory provisions, as observed earlier, are often open to varying interpretations, and their meaning depends on who has the last word.[50] Lawyers from an agency and the Treasury might interpret a provision one way and, in case of doubt, obtain an official opinion from the attorney general. The comptroller general, however, did not accept the attorney general's rulings as binding. If GAO disallowed an expenditure as "contrary to law," the ruling would stand unless the executive branch carried the dispute to court. Thus, giving the last word to an external-control official can—and, in this case, did—open opportunities for hamstringing of programs with which that official—here, the comptroller general—is unsympathetic.[51]

Reorientation

Remarkable changes have taken place in recent decades. Although GAO still has power to, and does, audit some individual transactions, it has come to emphasize the strengthening of agencies' internal audit and control systems, whose effectiveness relieves GAO of the need to audit every transaction. Instead, it can concentrate on programs that are important in financial terms and those that have provoked criticism or congressional interest. GAO, in short, has moved from cost accounting to program auditing, from examining the money trail to measuring program performance. Its reports on cost overruns in weapons procurement have often created sensations, but in more routine audits of agencies, GAO uses statistical sampling and other strategies to test the effectiveness of internal control systems, thus again removing itself from the burden of second-guessing every transaction. GAO has also begun identifying and tracking "high-risk programs," federal activities that have an unusually high threat for waste, fraud, and abuse. Most audits are done on site—that is, in the agencies and their field offices—so freight-car loads of vouchers need no longer be shipped to GAO in Washington. These and other changes have reduced GAO staff numbers from 15,000 in 1946 to 3,300 today.

GAO has moved far toward becoming an all-purpose, external-control agent. Former comptroller general Elmer B. Staats observed that governmental auditing "no longer is a function concerned primarily with financial operations. Instead, governmental auditing now is also concerned with whether governmental organizations are achieving the purpose for which programs are authorized and funds are made available, are doing so economically and efficiently, and are complying with applicable laws and regulations."[52] Legislation enacted during the 1970s emphasized that GAO "shall review and evaluate the *results* of Government programs and activities."[53] GAO's reviews are remarkable for both their detail and their variety, as a sample of report titles shows:

- "Women in the Military: Impact of Proposed Legislation to Open More Combat Support Positions and Units to Women"
- "File Sharing Program: Users of Peer-to-Peer Networks Can Readily Access Child Pornography"
- "Highways: How State Agencies Adopt New Pavement Technologies"
- "Seafood Safety: Seriousness of Problems and Efforts to Protect Customers"
- "Contract Management: DOD Needs Measures for Small Business Subcontracting Program and Better Data on Foreign Subcontracts"
- "AIDS Education: Reaching Populations at Higher Risk"
- "Reserve Forces: Observations on Recent National Guard Use in Overseas and Homeland Missions and Future Challenges"

After the past several presidential elections, moreover, GAO has released a transition series, providing advice to members of Congress and newly elected presidents on topics ranging from the budget deficit and the public service to NASA and national defense. It also produces reports on the high-risk programs especially susceptible to waste and abuse. Those reports have had great impact.[54]

As a direct congressional agent exercising delegated control authority over administrative agencies, GAO occupies a powerful position. In addition, it has a substantial, skilled investigative and analytical staff that aids congressional committees in their oversight of agency performance and sometimes conducts reviews on its own initiative.

GAO has two handicaps that make it hard for the agency to focus public attention on its work.[55] The first is its "green eyeshade" image, but the staff pattern has been shifting toward recruitment of business and public administration specialists, economists and other social scientists, engineers, and computer and information specialists. The lingering image problem led Comptroller General David M. Walker to win approval of the agency's name change from "accounting" to "accountability" in 2004.

The second handicap is the time required to investigate and audit programs. This stems largely from GAO's commitment to accuracy, thoroughness, and objectivity, but the result is that its reports often lack timeliness for Congress's agenda. Nevertheless, GAO's reports—and their handy "highlights" page that summarize key findings—are staples at congressional hearings and in news reports of governmental activities. In the 1980s, GAO's computer experts provided much of the data used to track down the secret financial transfers used by Reagan aide Oliver North to channel arms-sale profits to Central American guerrillas. GAO's influence, moreover, has spilled over into the states, where many legislatures have established their own "mini-GAOs" to conduct evaluations of state programs.

State and Local Legislative Control

Although GAO is the unquestioned master of legislative staff agencies, many state governments have similar bodies. They often have arcane titles, such as the Virginia Joint Legislative Audit and Review Commission, California's State Joint Legislative Audit Committee, and Wisconsin's Joint Committee on Audit, but their work is just as important and far-reaching. State legislators share the same information mismatch with their federal legislative colleagues, since administrators have far more expertise at their disposal. In the states where legislative service is part time, the problem is even worse. These state-level versions of GAO are typically small but highly professional, and their work often makes headlines.

In local governments, legislators (members of city councils and county boards) rarely have a separate GAO-style staff. They tend to rely on their own staffs. In small communities, such support is often meager, but in larger communities, legislators often have personal staffs that rival those of members of Congress.

PERFORMANCE-BASED INFORMATION

A final form of congressional control of administration is performance-based information. In 1993 Congress passed the **Government Performance and Results Act (GPRA)**, which required all federal agencies to produce strategic plans and to measure their success in achieving those goals. GPRA was exceptionally ambitious: it committed the government to measuring its outcomes within a very short time—just seven years. In short, Congress required the federal government to go further and faster than other governments around the world, such as that of New Zealand, which had ventured down the performance management road.[56] In 2010, Congress significantly expanded the act by prescribing a tighter connection between plans, programs, and performance reports; more frequent reporting of results; and more aggressive strategic planning by federal agencies.[57] The Obama administration reinforced this focus on information-based performance through its Performance.gov website, which presented a substantial amount of information on government operations.

For example, the Department of Education's Federal Student Aid Program laid out its goals and indicators to assess how well it was achieving those goals (see Table 14.1). The Department of Education ranked among the most effective government agencies in meeting the challenges of the new GPRA system, but all federal agencies worked hard to produce the reports required by the legislation, evolving five different measures:

- *Outputs:* the goods and services provided
- *Efficiency:* the price for the goods and services
- *Customer service:* citizen satisfaction with the goods and services
- *Quality:* the value of the goods and services
- *Outcome:* the social impact of the goods and services

GAO found that managers increasingly developed performance measures in each of these areas. "Ten years after enactment, GPRA's requirements have laid a solid foundation of results-oriented agency planning, measurement, and reporting," GAO concluded. Moreover, "Performance planning and measurement have slowly yet increasingly been part of agencies' culture."[58]

But as has long been the case with new strategies that put heavy reliance on planning and measurement, GPRA has faced major challenges. The advance of GPRA's techniques has depended heavily on the commitment of top managers: where there has been strong leadership, GPRA has advanced; progress has been halting where top leaders have not used it as a tool. Moreover, in many agencies, the information has been collected but not used. This point, of course, connects to the last: if top leaders are not committed to the process and see little value in it, they are unlikely to use the information, even if Congress requires them to collect it.

Most of all, GPRA's progress has depended on Congress itself—and Congress's interest in performance information. Top federal managers have been concerned about "the reluctance of Congress to use performance information when making decisions, especially appropriations decisions," according to a GAO survey. The evidence is that Congress is making far more use of this information than in the program's early days—and to a significantly greater extent than cynics would have predicted. However, one unsurprising conclusion has emerged: "the information presented and its presentation must meet the needs of the user," Congress. GAO found that the more Congress has been involved as a partner in defining agency goals and in shaping the presentation of the data, the more members of Congress and their staffs tend to use the data.[59]

GPRA has significantly changed the fabric of congressional oversight. By requiring agencies to prepare performance reports, Congress has increased the amount and quality of information. It has forced agency managers to pay far more attention to the goals they are trying to achieve and to demonstrate that they are producing results. It has heightened Congress's own

TABLE 14.1	Performance Results for Federal Student Aid, 2012		
Performance Metrics	**FY 2012 Target**	**FY 2012 Actual**	**Result**
Strategic Goal A: *Provide superior service and information to students and borrowers.*			
% of first-time FAFSA filers among high school seniors	>=52%	54.0%	Met
% of first-time FAFSA filers aged 19-24 among those in population that are high school graduates, no college	>=27%	28.4%	Met
% of first-time FAFSA filers among workforce aged 25+, high school graduates, no college	>=3.6%	3.7%	Met
% of first-time FAFSA filers among low-income students	>=57%	63.1%	Met
Customer satisfaction score (ACSI)	78	78.5	Met
Strategic Goal B: *Work to ensure that all participants in the system of funding postsecondary education serve the interests of students, from policy to delivery.*			
Ease of doing business school survey (1-100 Scale)	>=72	74	Met
Percent of borrowers>90 days delinquent	<=10%	9.5%	Met
Strategic Goal C: *Develop efficient processes and effective capabilities that are among the best in the public and private sectors.*			
Aid delivery costs per application	$10.90	$10.85	Met
Loan servicing costs per borrower	$19.64	$18.94	Met
Strategic Goal D: *Ensure program integrity and safeguard taxpayers' interests.*			
Improper Payment rate	Set baseline	Pell Grant 2.10% Direct Loan 0.58% FFEL 1.93%	Met
Direct Loan default rate	<=11.3%	9.6%	Met
Collection rate	Set baseline	$31.90	Met
Strategic Goal E: *Strengthen FSA's performance culture and become one of the best places to work in the federal government.*			
FSA Morale Index (Subset of questions from government-wide view point survey) - % of positive responses to survey (does not include neutral responses)	58%	–	N/A

Source: U.S. Department of Education, Federal Student Aid Annual Report 2012, http://www2.ed.gov/about/reports/annual/2012report/fsa-report.pdf, pp. 44–45.

Note: Explanation of the following notations:

"Met" means that the performance result met or exceeded the target.

"Not Met" means that the performance result did not meet the target.

"N/A" means that the performance result is not applicable because the performance metric was not developed, the performance metric was not implemented, or the required data were not available in time for inclusion.

attention to agency management and to oversight. And, in ways that are perhaps surprising, it has promoted a conversation between agency managers, members of Congress, and congressional committee staffs about what goals the programs are seeking. Given the ambiguity that often surrounds the creation of federal programs, this is no mean feat. The problem, however, is that neither Congress nor the agencies *use* the information very often to improve the results of federal programs.

The ultimate goal of linking presidential budgeting, congressional oversight, and agency management remains a distant goal, however. One skilled observer of the process concluded:

> As a result of the PART [Program Assessment Rating Tool, George W. Bush's performance reform], GPRA and the residual effects of the previous acronyms, federal managers are paying more attention to the results of their programs. But the idea of "performance budgeting," in which program effectiveness is directly linked to spending decisions, is one grail that will likely remain far out of reach.[60]

When the Obama administration took office, it quietly slid away from the PART process, but it developed a far-reaching approach to performance management throughout the government.

The long history of analytical techniques to improve government management suggests several lessons. One is that many acronym-based changes—from PPB (planning-programming-budgeting) through MBO (management by objectives) and ZBB (zero-base budgeting) to PART—rarely last long after the president who created them leaves office. Another is that Congress, always eager to protect its own prerogatives, has rarely bought into these presidential agendas. But GPRA is different in at least this one important respect: Congress itself established its steps and requires agencies to submit annual reports. That transition underlined the fact that performance management, in one form or another, is increasingly central to federal government accountability.

More fundamentally, however, the bold promises of performance improvement through better performance management have fallen short. As Donald Moynihan found in *The Dynamics of Performance Management,* government has invested a great deal of energy to increase the amount of information collected.[61] The effective use of performance management has often fallen short, because agency leaders have not always embraced it, measurement systems have often conflicted with deeply embedded organizational culture, and broader outcomes have not always been linked with performance management systems.

The struggle of performance management is one of the profound ironies of public administration. The basics—define goals, measure results, use information to improve performance—seems so self-evident that creating and improving performance management has become one of the bedrocks of executive management. After all, as the most famous saying of performance management puts it, "what gets measured gets done." No self-respecting executive can any longer advance a mature strategy without embracing metrics. No less a figure than Microsoft's Bill Gates argued:

> I have been struck again and again by how important measurement is to improving the human condition. You can achieve amazing progress if you set a clear

goal and find a measure that will drive progress toward the goal. . . . This may seem pretty basic, but it is amazing how often it is not done and how hard it is to get right.[62]

There are two profound truths in Gates's observation. One is how central measurement has become in modern management. The other is how hard it is to get it right. In the public sector, we can add a third truth: while political punishment for administrative failures can be quick and fierce, and President George W. Bush discovered in 2005 when FEMA flailed in helping New Orleans recover from Hurricane Katrina, there is often little political reward for good performance. Americans expect their government to perform well—after all, they pay high taxes and expect strong government. The challenge for performance management is linking measures with results. That is a tall order for administrators, all the more because so often elected officials see little political support for embracing Bill Gates's conclusion.

AN ASSESSMENT OF LEGISLATIVE CONTROL

Legislative control of administration is based on the sound proposition that legislators as well as executives have a legitimate concern with seeing to it "that the laws be faithfully executed." Legislators can by law fix the objectives and methods of implementing the programs they authorize, determine the funding of each program, and organize and reorganize agencies. They can limit the life span of program authorizations and appropriations. Through committees and accountability offices, such as GAO, they can make their own investigations of agency performance. The circle is completed by legislative alteration of enabling statutes, appropriations, and organizations so as to make agencies' future performance conform more closely to congressional intent.

As Christopher H. Foreman Jr. has observed, following a study of congressional oversight of regulatory policies:

> Oversight emerges as a sometimes painful, inevitably self-interested process of consultation and second-guessing that reasonably well keeps administration sensitive to the concerns of persons and groups affected by or attentive to regulatory policy. As a system for monitoring agency decision making and adherence to approved procedure—that is, as a set of mechanisms for enforcing accountability regarding agency behavior and policy choice—oversight succeeds.

While the process is often confusing, with muddled jurisdictional boundaries and uncertain leverage, the whole entourage comprises "an intricate and impressive system of screens or 'fire alarms.'"[63] It is a system that defies easy description or rational organization, but the intricate relationships nevertheless provide an impressive range of information and leverage, both formal and informal, for legislative influence on administrative activities. It is also a system in which members of Congress can transmit signals—sometimes blunt, sometimes subtle—about their expectations of administrators' actions.

We have discovered two major problems. One is that Congress—as well as legislatures at other levels—has often proven to have limited interest and modest capacity for oversight.[64]

Its oversight efforts are at best intermittent, and sustained congressional attention to major administrative issues is rare. Information-based reforms, such as GPRA, offer potential, but the basic problems are deeply rooted.

The other problem is the danger that legislators (especially in committees and subcommittees) will intrude excessively into the executive function, sometimes to promote their own self-interest.[65] Legislators should not—for reasons of both constitutional comity and administrative efficiency—so confuse their roles as to become, in effect, co-administrators of agencies and programs. A long-time chairman of the House Naval Affairs Committee, for example, was dubbed "the Secretary of the Navy," for his tireless interest in the Navy's activities. The involvement of judges in administration raises similar issues, as we saw in the previous chapter.

HOW DOES ACCOUNTABILITY WORK?

The central problem of public administration, as discussed in Chapter 1, is how to give administrators enough power to accomplish the work that policymakers want done, without having them exercise that power in a way that threatens democracy and liberty. Accountability, at its core, is *who is responsible to whom for what, through what means.* It is a relationship more than a process. It is dynamic rather than static. And it is the most important question of public administration.

Systems for holding public administrators accountable have at least four elements: voluntary compliance, standard setting, monitoring, and sanctions.

The foundation of accountability is *voluntary compliance.* Even though people are not saints, people most of the time voluntarily comply with most of the significant constraints on their behavior. They do so for a variety of reasons, ranging from moral standards to indifferent acquiescence to self-interest. As Max Weber stressed, they often do so because they believe in the legitimacy of the system of authority. Were it unrealistic to rely on substantial voluntary compliance, the scope and intensity of control systems would be unbearable.

The second element, *standard setting*—crafting rules to guide administrative discretion—accomplishes several things. It tells administrators what they are supposed to do (and what behavior they will be punished for). Some standards are obvious: few people need to be told that stealing is wrong, although petty theft—from pilfering government office supplies to using government photocopy machines to duplicate favorite recipes—is common. At the other extreme, some standards are so complicated that no one can know all of the rules that apply to their actions: the question of how—and how much—to pay government's contractors fills thick manuals. Frontline administrators rarely understand all the rules, and they rely on agency lawyers, procurement specialists, and masters of accounting regulations to raise a red flag about potential problems. Observing the standards, however, can become mechanical and trivial; nearly everyone has had experience in dealing with administrators so obsessed with rules and forms that the basic mission of public service becomes lost. The key to effective administration lies in ensuring that attention to the details does not undermine effective pursuit of the broader policy.

Third, an effective accountability system must *monitor* whether the standards are met. Sometimes that happens in advance—an administrator may need to get an action approved in advance. Some state governments, for example, require advance approval of all administrative rules before they become effective. Sometimes, before it becomes final, an action must "incubate"—lie in a congressional committee—for, say, sixty days, during which time committee members may (or may not) seek to persuade the agency to abort the action. Other forms of monitoring call for reviewing actions already completed. For example, monitors often conduct post-audits of financial transactions and review the error rate in payments to welfare clients; the auditors can criticize any improprieties they find and demand that the administrative agency mend its ways in the future. The newer forms of performance monitoring—including the Office of Management and Budget's performance management systems, the Government Performance and Results Act, and Baltimore's CitiStat (discussed in Chapters 11 and 12)—provide government officials with quick feedback about policy impacts.

Should policymakers use monitoring to identify, prevent, or correct all possible errors?[66] It is tempting to answer yes, but, in fact, that can make programs more expensive and less effective. An effort by the Internal Revenue Service to wring out every last nickel of taxes owed by every citizen would cost far more (in the time of revenue agents) than it would collect, and in the process, the heavy-handed approach would infuriate taxpayers. So, instead, overseers selectively review administrators' actions, often in response to complaints by citizens, members of the press, congressional committees, or employees.[67] They may use sampling—by examining, say, every fifth case or by reviewing all of an agency's units' cases in one out of five years; the sampling process shifts the focus from correcting individual errors to identifying those agencies or units that have so poor a pattern of actions that they need fundamental change. Or they may concentrate on areas (such as the awarding of government contracts or the operation of lottery programs) that might be especially prone to problems, or on programs in which government officials (such as inspectors, social workers, police officers, and other "street-level bureaucrats") frequently must make quick decisions or exercise broad discretion, which present special problems of accountability.

Finally, to be credible, an accountability system needs the ability to impose *sanctions*; if overseers find problems, there must be consequences. The delicate task here is to devise sanctions strong enough to be taken seriously by administrators but not so strong as to disrupt an agency's mission. They cannot be so punitive as to be impossible to enforce or so repressive as to require an impossible burden of proof. Sanctions can sometimes be too tough, as when a federal agency offends Congress and Congress responds with a sharp budget cut, forcing the curtailment of important public services. Sometimes sanctions may be too mild or too poorly directed to serve as adequate punishment or deterrent, as when a congressional investigation produces only a critical report—but no change in law or budget—so the agency may simply ignore the proceeding.

Accountability is thus a matter of balancing internal norms with external processes. The external processes can be within the agency or from oversight bodies in both the executive and legislative branches. If the nation's founders created a separation-of-powers system to restrain government's power, American public administration has over time evolved a complex and layered system for holding administrators accountable.

The process relies on two principles to make this layered accountability system work. One is *independence*: making each control agency autonomous and insulated from those

Gina Gray, public information officer at Arlington National Cemetery, was fired for disagreeing with the restrictions placed on the media's coverage of the burials of soldiers killed in Iraq and Afghanistan. The case touched off a national debate on the responsibilities of government administrators to balance the privacy of families with freedom of the press.

individuals and forces that might corrupt or restrain it. Independence helps ensure integrity by insulating it from the cross-pressures that often engulf elected institutions. For example, Congress's principal control agency, GAO, is designed to be independent of the executive departments and is separate from Congress's own day-to-day work. The other answer is *redundancy*: multiplying the control agencies and overlapping their functions.[68] If one control agency misses a problem, having other control agencies with overlapping jurisdictions can increase the chances of catching it. Furthermore, competition among control agencies may stimulate energy in all of them. Inspectors general are likely to be more vigilant because they know that GAO, the Office of Management and Budget, and congressional watchdog committees may catch anything they miss—and possibly embarrass them for having missed it.

Redundancy, of course, can itself be a problem. On the one hand, multiple control agencies can make conflicting demands. For example, until the 1950s, GAO, the Treasury Department, and the Bureau of the Budget separately prescribed the kinds of information that agencies' accounting systems had to produce. On the other hand, when several control agencies have jurisdiction over an especially troublesome case, each may await another's move—and in the end, nothing may happen. Finally, redundancy has one very obvious drawback: duplication of oversight is expensive, and at some point the costs may overwhelm the advantages produced. The trick lies in getting the watchdogs to bark loudly enough to alert policymakers to problems but not so obsessively that they become a distracting nuisance.

Consider the case of Gina Gray, appointed by the Pentagon as public affairs director of Arlington National Cemetery in early 2008. She discovered that top Department of Defense officials were imposing limits on media coverage of the burial of soldiers killed in Iraq. After poking through the regulations, she found no regulation against media coverage. If families approved the coverage, she allowed it. But just ten days into the job, she found that a senior cemetery official moved the media fifty yards from the service, which made it impossible for reporters to hear or photograph the service. Her supervisors took away her BlackBerry, demoted her, and ultimately fired her. "Had I not put my foot down, had I just gone along with it and not said regulations were being violated, I'm sure I'd still be there," Gray told a *Washington Post* reporter. "It's about doing the right thing."[69]

The "right thing," of course, was precisely what the issue was about. Who should make policy? What obligations do government officials have in following it? What should they do if they believe that the decisions of their supervisors violate policy or ethical standards? In a close call, should the decisions of supervisors or an official's internal norms rule? Gray decided that the rules did not forbid media coverage of the funerals and she was fired for her stand. In her termination letter, her supervisor said she had "been disrespectful to me as your supervisor and failed to act in an inappropriate manner." It was an unusual typo—a double negative that created profound irony. The *Washington Post* reporter concluded, "Only at Arlington National Cemetery could it be considered a firing offense to act appropriately."[70]

CONCLUSION: ETHICS AND THE PUBLIC SERVICE

No matter how many layers of accountability policymakers build, the responsiveness and effectiveness of public administration depend ultimately on the ethics of individual public administrators. One implication of Michael Lipsky's theory of street-level bureaucrats, mentioned in Chapter 13, is that many administrators operate far from the view of elected officials and top policymakers. They have broad discretion on how they do their jobs, they have a big impact on the lives of citizens, and there are few watchdogs on hand to catch misdeeds. Roving television news helicopters might occasionally catch an unusual event, and investigative reporters are always on the prowl for a good story. The inescapable fact, however, is that the quality—as well as accountability—of the administrative system depends critically on the decisions that individual administrators make and the values they hold in making them.

Debates flourish over whether ethics can be taught. Researchers into child development constantly remind us that the values of most children are formed by the age of three. Moreover, debates constantly swirl over whether ethics can be reliably enforced. No amount of oversight can fully control the uncountable numbers of individual decisions that administrators make every day to make public administration work.

The surest course to an ethical public administration is a careful balance. It requires a balance between the individual values of public administrators and the professional training they bring to the job. It requires a balance between the cultures of their agencies and the oversight of external forces. Most of all, it requires a strong relationship between public administrators and the citizens to whom they ultimately are responsible, for the effective use of public power and for the responsible protection of individual freedom.

CASE 14.1

The Department of Expectation Management

At a conference not long ago of homeland security experts from both the private sector and government, one of the participants said we needed a new government agency: the "Department of Expectation Management." The comment got big laughs from the audience—and some knowing smiles that suggested it wasn't such a bad idea. For many of the members of the audience, managing expectations was an enormous part of their lives. People don't think much about homeland security, they confided, unless something happens—a terrorist stages an attack, a tornado strikes a town, a hurricane floods a city—and then citizens expect instant and effective action.

Of course, the problem of managing expectations stretches much further than homeland security. One analyst joked that the perfect local bus service is one that picks up residents at their home, takes them directly to where they want to go, and costs a dollar. When it snows, citizens expect that their street will see the plow first. And for anyone who's taken ill, the wait for an ambulance can feel like an eternity as the siren gets louder.

Part of public administration is delivering high-quality services to citizens at a low cost. Just as much a part of public administration is defining what "high-quality" and "low" mean. Most public administrators, if they can quietly confide their own dreams, would wish for a

Department of Expectation Management to help them.

Questions to Consider

1. Suppose you were appointed to head the mythical, magical Department of Expectation Management for your community. How would you approach your job? What steps would you take? Do you think you could succeed?
2. What does the discussion at the conference tell you about the puzzles of public administration—and the jobs of public administrators?
3. How much do you think that public administrators ought to care about what the public expects? After all, it might be impossible to meet the public's expectations, no matter what they do. And some would argue that it's the job of public administrators to administer the law—nothing more, nothing less—and that it's the job of elected officials to deal with what the public wants.

CASE 14.2

Scary Words: Governments Must Start "Doing More with Less"

Ronald Reagan famously said, "The nine most terrifying words in the English language are: I'm from the government and I'm here to help." The words are so famous that, decades later, it's possible to buy t-shirts with the words proudly displayed.

But columnist Bill Bott says there are four words even scarier: "Doing more with less." No

saying, he argued, "strikes fear into the work place like 'doing more with less' because we all know what we're really saying is you are about to get a whole lot less." For government employees, it means "A whole lot less people, a whole lot less money, a whole lot less support, and a whole lot less enthusiasm for doing the work we love."[1]

The saying has been around for a long time. Vice President Al Gore used it to champion his "reinventing government" movement. The idea was simple: provide incentives for government workers to be more productive; government can produce more and better services while saving taxpayers money. In practice, the idea proved terribly hard to achieve. It was easy to cut programs to save money. It was possible to invest strategically to make service better. But it proved very, very hard to make government work better *and* cost less at the same time.

Bott has hope. It begins, he argues, with a change of philosophy. He says that "we need to lose the words accountability, blame and fault. We need to stop thinking of errors as a people mistake, or a mistake at all. An error is simply what happens when something didn't go down the quickest path the first time." Cut down hand-offs of officials-to-officials-to-more-officials and focus on results, Bott says. Then cut down the time that citizens have to spend in line transacting business with government. The key, he says, is to "reduce the number of handoffs and subsequent CYA measures." By doing this, he said that the State of Washington's Department of Social and Health Services cut down waiting times for visits from three to four weeks to five to forty-five minutes. The average time to process benefits shrank from fourteen to eighteen days to four to eight days, with increased accuracy. That allowed the department to deal with a 40 percent increase in customer demand while absorbing a 24 percent budget cut.

That scenario might not fit Reagan's quip. But Bott suggests that citizens are in no mood for fewer services, and government has little choice but to improve its productivity if it is to meet the challenge of twenty-first-century government.

Questions to Consider

1. What do you think about the "doing more with less" line? Does it capture the reality of twenty-first-century government?
2. Which do you think fits public perception better: Reagan's quip or Gore's motto?
3. Now consider Bott's argument to move away from accountability, which suggests the effort to identify and root out error, and to move toward a system that focuses squarely on trying to streamline the process, to learn from mistakes, and to focus government more on serving citizens better. Is that a better meaning for accountability? Or are there things that this approach might miss?

NOTES

1. Bill Bott, "The Scariest Four Words in Government," *Governing*, October 25, 2010, http://www.govern ing.com/blogs/public-great/Scariest-Four-Words-in-Government.html.

CASE 14.3

Will We Drink to That? The Florida Board of Education's War on Chocolate Milk

As he prepared to take over as Florida's agriculture commissioner, Adam Putnam stopped a budding statewide movement. Over several years, Florida's Board of Education had championed efforts to take chocolate milk off school lunch menus.[1]

For kids, the dispute had already produced a big battle. The state had eliminated sugared sodas and cut down on desserts. The next target was chocolate milk. The problem, nutritionists said, wasn't the flavor—it was the extra sugar that came with it. Vanilla- and strawberry-flavored milk each had 30 grams of sugar in an eight-ounce serving. Regular milk has just 13 grams. The American Heart Association recommends that children aged four to eight limit their sugar intake to 12 grams of sugar per day.

Most kids remember chocolate milk from their grade school days. Some of us enjoyed it during kindergarten snack breaks. But officials like state Board of Education member John Padget took a close look at the nutrition guidelines and concluded that the chocolate milk had to go.

Putnam called a time-out to give analysts at the state Department of Agriculture and Consumer Services time to consult with officials from the state Department of Education. Critics charged that Putnam was trying to pull the decision out from the Education Department and into the Agriculture Department because industry lobbyists thought they'd get a better hearing there. Putnam denied that there was any industry pressure. He described it as "Let's hit the pause button, and let's begin a new type of conversation and an unprecedented collaboration between the source of our food and one of the biggest providers of children's food—that being the school system." At the bottom, many political analysts suspected, was an effort to move the management of school lunches from the Education Department to the Agriculture Department. That shift, some critics said, was Putnam's move to satisfy the dairy industry, which had contributed to his campaign. According to some sources, only New Jersey and Texas has a similar structure.

The decision had big implications. In the 2010 school year, just the four largest school districts spent a total of $13 million on flavored milk, as students consumed 49 million half-pints of chocolate milk.

Some experts argued that the state ought to go far past chocolate milk to look at other items on school menus that had lots of sugar. Salad dressings, for example, often contain added sugar. Lora Gilbert, head of Orange County's cafeterias, concluded, "Rather than center on one food, really it's the whole diet you have to look at."

Questions to Consider

1. Do you think that government and its administrative agencies ought to get involved with the decision of which products to regulate?
2. The main mission of the Education Department is to produce a high-quality education for Florida's students. The main mission of the Agriculture Department is to promote agriculture and food safety. Which do you think would be the better home for resolving this question? Do you think it makes a difference which agency handles the question?
3. What implications does this debate have for accountability in government? There are crosscutting issues, multiple stakeholders, competing goals, and many government players. What is the public interest question in providing chocolate milk to school children? How should we sort it out?

NOTE

1. Denise-Marie Balona, "Next Agriculture Chief Stops State's Push to Bar Flavored Milk in Schools," *Orlando Sentinel*, December 25, 2010, http://www.orlandosentinel.com/health/os-fla-schools-ban-chocolate-milk--20101225,0,678391.story.

KEY CONCEPTS

administrative confidentiality   413

appropriations committees   409

authorizing committees   409

executive privilege   412

fire alarm   406

Government Performance and Results
Act (GPRA)   419

legislative review   408

police patrol   406

signing statement   403

FOR FURTHER READING

Aberbach, Joel D. *Keeping a Watchful Eye: The Politics of Congressional Oversight.* Washington, D.C.: Brookings Institution Press, 1990.

Arnold, R. Douglas. *Congress and the Bureaucracy: A Theory of Influence.* New Haven, Conn.: Yale University Press, 1979.

Behn, Robert D. *The PerformanceStat Potential: A Leadership Strategy for Producing Results.* Washington, D.C.: Brookings Institution Press, 2014.

Dodd, Lawrence C., and Richard L. Schott. *Congress and the Administrative State.* New York: Wiley, 1979.

Foreman, Christopher H., Jr. *Signals from the Hill: Congressional Oversight and the Challenge of Social Regulation.* New Haven, Conn.: Yale University Press, 1988.

Heclo, Hugh. "Issue Networks and the Executive Establishment." In *The New Political System,* ed. Anthony King. Washington, D.C.: American Enterprise Institute, 1978, 87-124.

Mayhew, David R. *Congress: The Electoral Connection.* New Haven, Conn.: Yale University Press, 1974.

Mosher, Frederick C. *The GAO: The Quest for Accountability in American Government.* Boulder, Colo.: Westview Press, 1979.

Scher, Seymour. "Conditions for Legislative Control." *Journal of Politics* 25 (August 1963): 526-551.

SUGGESTED WEBSITES

Each federal agency annually publishes the reports required by the Government Performance and Results Act; the reports are available on the agencies' websites. For example, the reports for the Department of Defense can be found at **www.defenselink.mil/comptroller/par**. For the Food and Drug Administration, the report can be found here: **www.fda.gov/ope/gpra/gpraext.htm**.

The Government Accountability Office website, **www.gao.gov**, is a treasure trove of reports on the performance of government agencies.

Finally, the Office of Management and Budget website (**www.whitehouse.gov/omb**) contains a great deal of useful information on the performance of government agencies, including the reports OMB requires in support of the annual budgetary process.

Notes

1. Accountability

1. Douglas A. Blackmon, Vanessa O'Connell, Alexandra Berzon, and Ana Campoy, "There Was 'Nobody in Charge,'" *Wall Street Journal* (May 27, 2010), http://online.wsj.com/article/SB10001424052748704113504575264721101985024.html.

2. "Embattled BP Chief: I Want My Life Back," *The Times* (London, May 31, 2010), http://www.thetimes.co.uk/tto/news/article2534734.ece.

3. Bobby Jindal, "Obama's Woes and Big Government," CNN.com (May 24, 2013), http://www.cnn.com/2013/05/24/opinion/jindal-obama-big-government/index.html.

4. Sewell Chan, "Remembering a Snowstorm that Paralyzed the City," *New York Times* (February 10, 2009), http://cityroom.blogs.nytimes.com/2009/02/10/remembering-a-snowstorm-that-paralyzed-the-city.

5. Peter Self, *Administrative Theories and Politics* (London: Allen and Unwin, 1972), 277–278. (Emphasis in original.)

6. Juvenal, *Satires,* line 347. Our free translation communicates more immediately and less ambiguously than the standard translations, such as "Who will be guarding the guards?" "Who is to keep guard over the guards?" and "Who will watch the warders"—particularly as Juvenal describes distrusting the guards of a harem.

7. "The need for operative ideas on how to make accountability a reality under modern conditions is urgent, but it must be admitted that there is a remarkable dearth of such ideas despite great dissatisfaction with the present state of affairs and with the older . . . notions of accountability." *The Dilemma of Accountability in Modern Government,* ed. Bruce L. R. Smith and D. C. Hague (New York: St. Martin's, 1971), 28.

8. Ben Zimmer, "The Epithet Nader Made Respectable," *Wall Street Journal* (July 12, 2013), http://online.wsj.com/article/SB10001424127887323368704578596083294221030.html.

9. Joseph R. Strayer, *On the Medieval Origins of the Modern State* (Princeton: Princeton University Press, 1970).

10. David Clark, "The Many Meanings of the Rule of Law," *Law, Capitalism, and Power in Asia: The Rule of Law and Legal Institutions,* ed. Kanishka Jayasuriya (Oxford: Routledge, 1999), 28–43.

11. Barry R. Weingast, "The Political Foundations of Democracy and the Rule of Law," *American Political Science Review* 91, no. 2 (1997): 245–263; and Judith N. Shklar, "Political Theory and the Rule of Law," in *The Rule of Law: Ideal or Ideology,* ed. Allan C. Hutchinson and Patrick Moynihan (Toronto: Carswell, 1987), 1–16.

12. Guillermo O'Donnell, "Why the Rule of Law Matters," *Journal of Democracy* 15, no. 4 (2004): 32–46.

13. Woodrow Wilson, "The Study of Administration," *Political Science Quarterly* 2 (June 1887): 220.

14. Frank J. Goodnow, *Politics and Administration* (New York: Russell and Russell, 1900).

15. John M. Gaus, "Trends in the Theory of Public Administration," *Public Administration Review* 10 (1950): 168.

16. John M. Gaus, "The Responsibility of Public Administration," in *Frontiers of Public Administration*, ed. John M. Gaus, Leonard D. White, and Marshall E. Dimock (Chicago: University of Chicago Press, 1936), 27.

17. Ibid., 31.

18. See H. George Frederickson, "The Repositioning of American Public Administration," *PS: Political Science & Politics* (December 1999): 701–711; and David H. Rosenbloom, "Whose Bureaucracy Is This, Anyway? Congress's 1946 Answer," *PS: Political Science & Politics* (December 2001): 773–777.

19. Carl J. Friedrich, "Public Policy and the Nature of Administrative Responsibility," in *Public Policy*, ed. Carl J. Friedrich and E. S. Mason (Cambridge: Harvard University Press, 1940), 3–24; and Herman Finer "Administrative Responsibility in Democratic Government," *Public Administration Review* no. 1 (1941): 355–350.

20. Gaus, "The Responsibility of Public Administration," 37.

21. Smith and Hague, *Dilemma of Accountability*, 29.

22. "$16 Muffin Included Coffee, Tea, Event Space," *Politifact* (October 4, 2011), http://www.politifact.com/truth-o-meter/statements/2011/oct/04/bill-oreilly/16-muffin-included-coffee-tea-event-space.

23. We should not be interpreted as going so far as one scholar: "Bureaucrats ought not determine which of several competing demands they should follow, nor should they themselves 'scale down' impossibly high expectations. They should, however, refuse to be 'passed the buck,' and they should encourage higher authorities to make proper decisions." And "Bureaucrats incur responsibilities to make sure that policy makers provide the resources necessary to their policy tasks." John P. Burke, *Bureaucratic Responsibility* (Baltimore: Johns Hopkins University Press, 1988), 51, 82.

24. Albert O. Hirschman, *Exit, Voice, and Loyalty: Responses to Decline in Firms,* *Organizations, and States* (Cambridge, Mass.: Harvard University Press, 1970).

25. Ethical breakdowns in the 1980s partly account for growth of the literature about governmental ethics. See John A. Rohr, *Ethics for Bureaucrats: An Essay on Law and Values,* 2d ed. (New York: Marcel Dekker, 1989); James S. Bowman and Frederick A. Elliston, eds., *Ethics, Government, and Public Policy: A Reference Guide* (Westport, Conn.: Greenwood Press, 1988); and Robert N. Roberts, *White House Ethics: The History of the Politics of Conflict of Interest Regulation* (Westport, Conn.: Greenwood Press, 1988).

26. G. Calvin Mackenzie, "'If You Want to Play, You've Got to Pay': Ethics Regulation and the Presidential Appointments System, 1964–1984," in *The In-and-Outers: Presidential Appointees and Transient Government in Washington,* ed. G. Calvin Mackenzie (Baltimore: Johns Hopkins University Press, 1987), 77.

27. Michael A. Nutter, Inaugural Address, January 7, 2008, http://media.philly.com/documents/NutterInauguralSpeechFinal.pdf.

28. Preamble to the Constitution of the United States.

29. "Remarks to the Members of the Senior Executive Service," January 26, 1989, *Weekly Compilation of Presidential Documents* 25 (Washington, D.C.: Government Printing Office, 1989), 117–119.

30. "Q&A: Obama Talks with Rick Stengel," *Time* (November 29, 2007), http://content.time.com/time/magazine/article/0,9171,1689228,00.html.

2. What Government Does— and How it Does It

1. Dwight Waldo, *The Administrative State: A Study of the Political Theory of American Public Administration* (New York: Ronald Press, 1948).

2. See, for example, *A Centennial History of the American Administrative State,* ed. Ralph

Clark Chandler (New York: Free Press, 1987); John A. Rohr, *To Run a Constitution: The Legitimacy of the Administrative State* (Lawrence: University Press of Kansas, 1986); Lawrence C. Dodd and Richard L. Schott, *Congress and the Administrative State* (New York: Wiley, 1979); Emmette S. Redford, *Democracy and the Administrative State* (New York: Oxford University Press, 1969); and David H. Rosenbloom, *Building a Legislative-Centered Public Administration: Congress and the Administrative State, 1946–1999* (Tuscaloosa: University of Alabama Press, 2000).

3. Paul C. Light, *The True Size of Government* (Washington, DC: Brookings Institution, 1999).

4. U.S. Bureau of the Census; U.S. Office of Management and Budget, *Budget of the United States Government: Historical Tables*.

5. Social Security Administration, "Social Security Basic Facts" (February 7, 2013), http://www.ssa.gov/pressoffice/basicfact.htm.

6. *Wall Street Journal,* March 17, 1989, A1.

7. Philip Shenon, "Chilean Fruit Pulled from Shelves as U.S. Widens Inquiry on Poison," *New York Times,* March 15, 1989, http://www.nytimes.com/1989/03/15/us/chilean-fruit-pulled-from-shelves-as-us-widens-inquiry-on-poison.html.

8. Fire Department of the City of New York, "Citywide Performance Indicators" (2012), http://www.nyc.gov/html/fdny/pdf/stats/2012/fire/cw/fire_cwsum_cy12.pdf.

9. Port of Los Angeles, "Facts and Figures," http://www.portoflosangeles.org/about/facts.asp.

10. Christopher C. Hood, *The Tools of Government* (Chatham, N.J.: Chatham House, 1983), 2.

11. See Donald F. Kettl, *The Next Government of the United States: Why Our Institutions Fail Us and How to Fix Them* (New York: Norton, 2009), 109–110.

12. See Donald F. Kettl, *Government by Proxy: (Mis?)Managing Federal Programs* (Washington, D.C.: CQ Press, 1988); and Lester M. Salamon, ed., *Beyond Privatization: The Tools of Government Action* (Washington, D.C.: Urban Institute, 1989).

13. Moshe Schwartz and Jennifer Church, *Department of Defense's Use of Contractors to Support Military Operations: Background, Analysis, and Issues for Congress* (Washington, D.C.: Congressional Research Service, May 17, 2013), http://www.fas.org/sgp/crs/natsec/R43074.pdf.

14. Donald Haider, "Grants as a Tool of Public Policy," in Salamon, *Beyond Privatization,* 93.

15. U.S. Office of Management and Budget, *Budget of the United States Government, Fiscal Year 2014: Special Analyses,* Table 16–1.

16. For a review of tax expenditures, see Stanley S. Surrey and Paul R. McDaniel, *Tax Expenditures* (Cambridge, Mass.: Harvard University Press, 1985); John F. Witte, *The Politics and Development of the Federal Income Tax* (Madison: University of Wisconsin Press, 1985); and Paul R. McDaniel, "Tax Expenditures as Tools of Government Action," in Salamon, *Beyond Privatization,* 167–196.

17. Lester M. Salamon, "Rethinking Public Management: Third-Party Government and the Changing Forms of Government Action," *Public Policy* 29 (Summer 1981): 260.

18. Ted Kolderie, "The Two Different Concepts of Privatization," *Public Administration Review* 46 (July–August 1986): 285–291.

19. Pew Research Center for People and the Press, "Public Trust in Government: 1958–2013" (January 31, 2013), http://www.people-press.org/2013/01/31/trust-in-government-interactive.

20. CBS News, "Poll: 80% of Americans Unhappy with Washington" (March 26, 2013), http://www.cbsnews.com/8301-250_162-57576433/poll-80-of-americans-unhappy-with-washington.

21. Dan Balz, "Republicans Ride the Tea Party Tiger," *Washington Post* (September 15, 2007), http://www.washingtonpost.com/wp-dyn/content/article/2010/09/15/AR2010091503387.html?hpid=topnews&sid=ST2010091503606

3. What is Public Administration?

1. Honoré de Balzac, *Les Employés*. English translations carry various titles (e.g., *The Civil Service, Bureaucracy,* and *The Government Clerks*).

2. These and other meanings of the term *bureaucracy* are fully analyzed in Martin Albrow, *Bureaucracy* (New York: Holt, Rinehart and Winston, 1971).

3. Nikolai I. Ryzhkov, speaking to the seventeenth Communist Party Congress, quoted in Philip Taubman, "Soviet Premier, in Congress Talk, Criticizes Economy," *New York Times,* March 4, 1986; Zhao Ziyang (later named general secretary of China's Communist Party), quoted in Edward A. Gargan, "More Change Due in China's Economy," *New York Times,* October 26, 1987.

4. For example, see Donald F. Kettl, *The Global Public Management Revolution: A Report on the Transformation of Governance* (Washington, D.C.: Brookings Institution, 2000).

5. For a well-documented and well-argued case explaining and defending bureaucracy, see Charles T. Goodsell, *The Case for Bureaucracy: A Public Administration Polemic,* 4th ed. (Washington, D.C.: CQ Press, 2004).

6. For a thorough exploration of the definitional problem, see Andrew Dunsire, *Administration: The Word and the Science* (New York: Wiley, 1973).

7. Dwight Waldo, *The Study of Public Administration* (Garden City, N.Y.: Doubleday, 1955), 5–6; and Herbert A. Simon, *Administrative Behavior* (New York: Macmillan, 1947; 3d ed., New York: Free Press, 1976), 72–73. Ascertaining what the goals are and relating rational action to them is a difficult problem, recognized by both Waldo and Simon, as is determining the nonrational dimension of human behavior.

8. For a review of these arguments, see Harold F. Gortner, Julianne Mahler, and Jeanne Bell Nicholson, *Organization Theory: A Public Perspective* (Chicago: Dorsey Press, 1987), 16; and Gary L. Wamsley and Mayer N. Zald, *The Political Economy of Public Organizations: A Critique and Approach to the Study of Public Administration* (Bloomington: Indiana University Press, 1973), 4.

9. Douglas Yates Jr., *The Politics of Management* (San Francisco: Jossey-Bass, 1985), 7.

10. Barry Bozeman, *All Organizations Are Public: Bridging Public and Private Organization Theories* (San Francisco: Jossey-Bass, 1987), 83–85.

11. William A. Robson, "The Managing of Organizations," *Public Administration* (London) 44 (Autumn 1966): 276.

12. Dwight Waldo, *The Enterprise of Public Administration: A Summary View* (Novato, Calif.: Chandler and Sharp, 1980), 164. Compare Bozeman, *All Organizations Are Public,* 5; and Hal G. Rainey, Robert W. Backoff, and Charles H. Levine, "Comparing Public and Private Organizations," *Public Administration Review* 36 (March–April 1976): 234.

13. See Graham T. Allison Jr., "Public and Private Management: Are They Fundamentally Alike in All Unimportant Respects?" in *Current Issues in Public Administration,* 3d ed., ed. Frederick S. Lane (New York: St. Martin's, 1986), 184–200.

14. Some theorists, for example, argue that the distinction is based on who benefits; public agencies are those whose prime beneficiary is the public. See Peter M. Blau and W. Richard Scott, *Formal Organizations: A Comparative Approach* (San Francisco: Chandler, 1962), 42–43. Others have argued that they are distinctive because of who owns and funds them; public agencies are those "owned" by the state. See Wamsley and Zald, *Political Economy of Public Organizations,* 8.

15. Gortner, Mahler, and Nicholson, *Organization Theory,* 26.

16. Steven Kelman, presentation to Seventeenth Intergovernmental Audit Forum (Philadelphia: May 22, 2008).

17. These distinctions are based on comparisons developed by John T. Dunlop

and summarized in Allison, "Public and Private Management," 17–18. See also Ralph Clark Chandler, "Epilogue," in Ralph Clark Chandler, ed., *Centennial History* (New York: Free Press, 1987), 580–586; and Rainey, Backoff, and Levine, "Comparing Public and Private Organizations."

18. Anthony Downs, *Inside Bureaucracy* (Boston: Little, Brown, 1967), 30.

19. Arthur Okun, *Equality and Efficiency: The Big Tradeoff* (Washington, D.C.: Brookings Institution, 1975).

20. See Marver H. Bernstein, *The Job of the Federal Government Executive* (Washington, D.C.: Brookings Institution, 1958), 26–28; and James W. Fesler et al., *Industrial Mobilization for War* (Washington, D.C.: Government Printing Office, 1947), 971–972. The "goldfish-bowl" phenomenon applies specifically to the United States, rather than to public administration everywhere. See Harold L. Wilensky, *Organizational Intelligence* (New York: Basic Books, 1967), 116–118.

21. U.S. Code 31, § 1341.

22. There are, of course, requirements for private officials and their organizations to comply with governmental standards. But, in general, the point applies: in the private sector, officials and their organizations are free to follow their own judgment except as the law applies.

23. Wallace Sayre, "The Unhappy Bureaucrats: Views Ironic, Helpful, Indignant," *Public Administration Review* 10 (Summer 1958): 245.

24. See *Revitalizing Federal Management: Managers and Their Overburdened Systems: A Panel Report* (Washington, D.C.: National Academy of Public Administration, 1983); and *Urgent Business for America: Revitalizing the Federal Government for the 21st Century* (Washington, D.C.: National Commission on the Public Service, 2003), http://www.brookings.edu/events/2003/01/07governance.

25. For example, see Anne M. Khademian, *Working with Culture: How the Job Gets Done in Public Programs* (Washington, D.C.: CQ Press, 2002).

26. For the variety of approaches, see *Public Administration: The State of the Discipline,* ed. Naomi B. Lynn and Aaron Wildavsky (Chatham, N.J.: Chatham House, 1990); and Chandler, *Centennial History.*

27. Dwight Waldo, "Politics and Administration: On Thinking about a Complex Relationship," in Chandler, *Centennial History,* 89–112, at 96–104.

28. See Frank J. Goodnow, *Politics and Administration* (New York: Macmillan, 1900). Wilson is discussed later in this chapter.

29. Nicholas Henry, "The Emergence of Public Administration as a Field of Study," in Chandler, *Centennial History,* 37–85. See also *American Public Administration: Past, Present, and Future,* ed. Frederick C. Mosher (Tuscaloosa: University of Alabama Press, 1975).

30. Luther Gulick, "Time and Public Administration," *Public Administration Review* 47 (January–February 1987): 115–119.

31. Carl J. Friedrich, *Man and His Government* (New York: McGraw-Hill, 1963), 464–483. The remarkable and lasting innovations in British and French administrative institutions and methods in the twelfth to fourteenth centuries are treated in James W. Fesler, "The Presence of the Administrative Past," in *American Public Administration: Patterns of the Past,* ed. James W. Fesler (Washington, D.C.: American Society for Public Administration, 1982), 1–27, at 3–16. A comprehensive administrative history, much broader than its title, is Carolyn Webber and Aaron Wildavsky, *A History of Taxation and Expenditure in the Western World* (New York: Simon and Schuster, 1986).

32. Alexis de Tocqueville, *Democracy in America* (New York: Knopf, 1945), 1:211–212; paperback ed. (New York: Vintage Books, 1954), 1:219–220.

33. All quotations of Woodrow Wilson are from his "The Study of Administration," *Political Science Quarterly* 2 (June 1887), as reprinted in *Political Quarterly* 56

(December 1941): 481–506. As the first scholarly article urging attention to public administration, Wilson's treatise is often described as "seminal"; however, the article was not widely read until its reprinting in 1941. For a full canvass of Wilson's significance, see *Politics and Administration: Woodrow Wilson and American Public Administration,* ed. Jack Rabin and James S. Bowman (New York: Marcel Dekker, 1984); and Daniel W. Martin, "The Fading Legacy of Woodrow Wilson," *Public Administration Review* 48 (March–April 1988): 631–636.

34. Fesler, *American Public Administration.* An excellent starting point is Stephen Skowronek, *Building a New American State: The Expansion of National Administrative Capacities, 1877–1920* (New York: Cambridge University Press, 1982).

35. Christopher Pollitt, *Time, Policy, Management: Governing with the Past* (Oxford: Oxford University Press, 2008), 2.

36. The list is not exhaustive. See James G. March, "How We Talk and How We Act: Administrative Theory and Administrative Life," in *Leadership and Organization Culture: New Perspectives on Administrative Theory and Practice,* ed. Thomas J. Sergiovanni and John E. Corbally (Urbana: University of Illinois Press, 1984, 1986), 18–35, esp. 21.

37. For a broad critique, see Charles Perrow, *Complex Organizations,* 3d ed. (New York: Random House, 1986).

38. The concept of overlays is presented in John M. Pfiffner and Frank R. Sherwood, *Administrative Organization* (Englewood Cliffs, N.J.: Prentice Hall, 1960), 16–32. They propose a basic sheet portraying the formal structure of authority, with five overlays: sociometric ("contacts people have with each other because of personal attraction"); functional (arising out of "the relationships created by technical experts" and the authority they exercise "because of their superior knowledge and skills"); decisional; power; and communication.

4. Organizational Theory

1. For an exceptionally thoughtful review of organizational theory, see H. George Frederickson and Kevin B. Smith, *Public Administration Theory Primer* (Boulder, Colo.: Westview Press, 2003).

2. Daniel Katz and Robert L. Kahn, *The Social Psychology of Organizations,* 2d ed. (New York: Wiley, 1978), 188, 196. Note, however, the caveat: "Role expectations are by no means restricted to the job description as it might be given by the head of the organization or prepared by some specialist in personnel, although these individuals are likely to be influential members of the role set of many persons in the organization" (p. 190).

3. This description merely lays the groundwork for the structural approach to governmental administration. For more substantial analysis of the complex issue of authority, see, for example, Carl J. Friedrich, *Man and His Government* (New York: McGraw-Hill, 1963); and Charles E. Lindblom, *Politics and Markets* (New York: Basic Books, 1977), 17–32.

4. Luther Gulick, "Notes on the Theory of Organization," in *Papers on the Science of Administration,* ed. Luther Gulick and L. Urwick (New York: Institute of Public Administration, 1937), 1–45. For an attack on that essay, see Herbert Simon, *Administrative Behavior* (New York: Macmillan, 1947, and later editions), 20–44. For reviews of the controversy, see Alan A. Altshuler, "The Study of Administration," in *The Politics of the Federal Bureaucracy,* 2d ed., ed. Alan A. Altshuler and Norman C. Thomas (New York: Harper and Row, 1977), 2–17; Vincent Ostrom, *The Intellectual Crisis in Public Administration* (Tuscaloosa: University of Alabama Press, 1973), 36–47; Brian R. Fry, *Mastering Public Administration: From Max Weber to Dwight Waldo* (Chatham, N.J.: Chatham House, 1989), 73–97; and Thomas H. Hammond, "In Defense of Luther Gulick's 'Notes on the Theory of Organization,'" *Public Administration* (London) 58 (Summer 1990).

5. Gulick, "Notes on the Theory of Organization," 31.

6. Weber's views became accessible to American readers through two translations of portions of his works, which appeared in 1946 and 1947 and were reprinted in the following paperback editions: *From Max Weber: Essays in Sociology*, trans. and ed. H. H. Gerth and C. Wright Mills (New York: Oxford University Press, 1958); and *The Theory of Social and Economic Organization*, trans. A. M. Henderson and Talcott Parsons (New York: Free Press, 1964).

7. Weber, *Theory of Social and Economic Organization*, 328.

8. Weber, *From Max Weber*, 209.

9. Weber, *Theory of Social and Economic Organization*, 330.

10. Ibid., 337.

11. Weber, *From Max Weber*, 196–197.

12. Ibid., 228.

13. See Talcott Parsons's introduction to Weber, *Theory of Social and Economic Organization*, 56, 58–60n.

14. Systems theory and its organizational derivatives are more fully treated in Katz and Kahn, *Social Psychology of Organizations*, 17–34; and Chadwick J. Haberstroh, "Organization Design and Systems Analysis," in *Handbook of Organizations*, ed. James G. March (Chicago: Rand McNally, 1965), 1171–1211.

15. For a trenchant argument that an organization's survival is the lucky result of natural selection processes rather than of efforts to achieve that objective, see Herbert Kaufman, *Time, Chance, and Organizations: Natural Selection in a Perilous Environment* (Chatham, N.J.: Chatham House, 1985).

16. Sir Eric (later Lord) Ashby, *Technology and the Academics* (New York: Macmillan, 1958), 67–68.

17. President-elect Nixon, announcing his choice of cabinet members, quoted in *Congressional Quarterly Weekly Report* 26 (December 13, 1968): 3263.

18. President Nixon's Message to Congress, March 25, 1971, in Office of Management and Budget, Executive Office of the President, *Papers Relating to the President's Departmental Reorganization Program* (Washington, D.C.: Government Printing Office, March 1971), 7.

19. *United States Government Manual 1973/74* (Washington, D.C.: Government Printing Office, 1973), 94.

20. USDA Performance and Accountability Report for FY2003, http://www.usda.gov/ocfo/usdarpt/pdf/par04.pdf.

21. Systems theories vary in attentiveness to authority. For a work that does incorporate authority and its hierarchical structuring in a systems framework, see Katz and Kahn, *Social Psychology of Organizations*, esp. 199–222.

22. Frederick Winslow Taylor, *The Principles of Scientific Management* (New York: Harper and Brothers, 1911; Mineola, N.Y.: Dover, 1998). See Fry, *Mastering Public Administration*, 47–72.

23. Taylor, *Principles of Scientific Management*, 28.

24. An early canvass of this literature is in James G. March and Herbert Simon, *Organizations* (New York: Wiley, 1957), although it is puzzling that the findings were not brought to bear on the book's later concerns with organizational structure and processes.

25. For reports of the research and reappraisals of the findings, see George C. Homans, *The Human Group* (New York: Harcourt Brace Jovanovich, 1950); and H. M. Persons, "What Happened at Hawthorne?" *Science* 183 (March 8, 1974): 922–932.

26. "Group members tend to feel better satisfied under moderate degrees of structure than under overly structured or totally unstructured situations. But they prefer too much structure over none at all. Groups tend to be more productive and more cohesive in structured rather than unstructured situations. Formal structure does not necessarily block satisfaction of needs for autonomy and self-actualization. Some degree of structure is necessary for the satisfaction of follower needs." Bernard M. Bass, *Stogdill's Handbook of Leadership: A Survey of Theory and*

Research, rev. and exp. ed. (New York: Free Press, 1981), 588–589.

27. Edwin A. Locke, "The Nature and Causes of Job Satisfaction," in *Handbook of Industrial and Organizational Psychology,* ed. Marvin D. Dunnette (Chicago: Rand McNally, 1976), 1297–1349, at 1332. As Locke points out, the human relationists' causal arrow may point the wrong way; that is, high productivity may be a cause of high satisfaction.

28. Chris Argyris, "Being Human and Being Organized," *Transaction* 2 (July 1964): 5. See also his "Some Limits of Rational Man Organization Theory," *Public Administration Review* 33 (May–June 1973): 253–267, esp. 253–254, 263–265.

29. For a full description and critique of the human relations model, see Charles Perrow, *Complex Organizations,* 3d ed. (New York: Random House, 1986), 79–118. See also H. Roy Kaplan and Curt Tausky, "Humanism in Organizations: A Critical Appraisal," *Public Administration Review* 37 (March–April 1977): 171–180.

30. Douglas McGregor, *The Human Side of Enterprise* (New York: McGraw-Hill, 1960), 33–57.

31. Lawrence B. Mohr, *Explaining Organizational Behavior: The Limits and Possibilities of Theory and Research* (San Francisco: Jossey-Bass, 1982), 125–153; and Bass, *Stogdill's Handbook of Leadership*, passim.

32. Abraham H. Maslow, "The Superior Person," *Transaction* 1 (May 1964): 12–13. For a major test of "the participation hypothesis" in public administration, see *Government Reorganizations: Cases and Commentary,* ed. Frederick C. Mosher (Indianapolis: Bobbs-Merrill, 1967).

33. Bass, *Stogdill's Handbook of Leadership,* 560–565.

34. Among the many writings illustrative of the pluralistic approach to public administration, three classics are David B. Truman, *The Governmental Process,* 2d ed. (New York: Knopf, 1971), esp. 395–478; J. Leiper Freeman, *The Political Process: Executive Bureau–Legislative Committee Relations,* rev. ed. (New York: Random House, 1965); and Francis E. Rourke, *Bureaucracy, Politics, and Public Policy,* 3d ed. (Boston: Little, Brown, 1984).

35. Rourke, *Bureaucracy, Politics, and Public Policy.* See also Carl E. Van Horn, William T. Gormley Jr., and Donald C. Baumer, *Politics and Public Policy,* 3d ed. (Washington, D.C.: CQ Press, 2001).

36. A good introduction is J. Steven Ott, *The Organizational Culture Perspective* (Chicago: Dorsey Press, 1989). See also Edgar H. Schein, *Organizational Culture and Leadership* (San Francisco: Jossey-Bass, 1987); Michel Crozier, *The Bureaucratic Phenomenon* (Chicago: University of Chicago Press, 1964); and Anne Khademian, *Working with Culture: The Way the Job Gets Done in Public Programs* (Washington, D.C.: CQ Press, 2002).

37. Spatial relations are rarely treated in the literature. For a valuable exception, see Frederick C. Mosher, *A Tale of Two Agencies: A Comparative Analysis of the General Accounting Office and the Office of Management and Budget* (Baton Rouge: Louisiana State University Press, 1984), 87–98. The whole book usefully contrasts the organizational cultures of the two agencies.

38. Harold Seidman and Robert Gilmour, *Politics, Position, and Power: From the Positive to the Regulatory State,* 4th ed. (New York: Oxford University Press, 1986), 167. See pages 166–194, on "The Executive Establishment, Culture and Personality."

39. Donald F. Kettl, *Leadership at the Fed* (New Haven: Yale University Press, 1986). The dominance issue is treated at pages 30–32 and 85–88.

40. Herbert Kaufman, *The Forest Ranger: A Study in Administrative Behavior* (Baltimore: Johns Hopkins University Press, 1960).

41. National Aeronautics and Space Administration, *Assessment and Plan for Organizational Culture Change at NASA* (Washington, D.C.: NASA, 2004), 4.

42. Warren E. Leary, "Better Communication Is NASA's Next Frontier," *New York Times* (April 14, 2004), A22.

43. Frederick C. Mosher, "The Changing Responsibilities and Tactics of the Federal Government," in *American Public Administration: Patterns of the Past*, ed. James W. Fesler (Washington, D.C.: American Society for Public Administration, 1982), 198–212, quoted passage at 201. See also Lester M. Salamon, "Rethinking Public Management: Third-Party Government and the Changing Forms of Government Action," *Public Policy* 29 (Summer 1981): 259–278; and Lester H. Salamon, ed., *The Tools of Government: A Guide to the New Governance* (New York: Oxford University Press, 2002).

44. See, for example, Howard Aldrich and David A. Whettan, "Organization-Sets, Action-Sets, and Networks: Making the Most of Simplicity," in *Handbook of Organizational Design,* vol. 1, *Adapting Organizations to Their Environments,* ed. Paul C. Nystrom and William H. Starbuck (New York: Oxford University Press, 1981), 385–408; W. W. Powell, "Neither Market nor Hierarchy: Network Forms of Organization," in *Research in Organizational Behavior,* ed. B. Staw and L. L. Cummings (Greenwich, Conn.: JAI Press, 1990), 295–336; Robert Agranoff, "Human Services Integration: Past and Present Challenges in Public Administration," *Public Administration Review* 51 (1991): 533–542; H. Brinton Milward and Keith G. Provan, "Services Integration and Outcome Effectiveness: An Empirical Test of an Implicit Theory," paper presented at the annual conference of the Association for Public Policy Analysis and Management, 1993; Fritz W. Scharpf, "Coordination in Hierarchies and Networks," in *Games in Hierarchies and Networks: Analytical and Empirical Approaches to the Study of Governance and Institutions,* ed. Fritz W. Scharpf (Boulder, Colo.: Westview Press, 1993), 125–165; and Eugene Bardach, "Generic Models in the Study of Public Management," paper presented at the annual conference of the Association for Public Policy Analysis and Management, 1993.

45. Eugene Bardach, "But Can Networks Produce?" paper prepared for the conference on "Network Analysis and Innovations in Public Programs," La Follette Institute of Public Affairs, University of Wisconsin–Madison, 1994, 2.

46. Rosemary O'Leary, Lisa Blomgren Bingham, and Catherine Gerard, guest eds., "Special Issue on Collaborative Public Management," *Public Administration Review* 66 (2007); and Stephen Goldsmith and Donald F. Kettl, eds., *The Power of Networks: Keys to High-Performance Government* (Washington, D.C.: Brookings Institution Press, 2009).

47. The section that follows is adapted from Donald F. Kettl, *The Transformation of Governance: Public Administration for the 21st Century* (Baltimore: Johns Hopkins University Press, 2002), 88–90.

48. See Harrison C. White, "Agency as Control," in *Principals and Agents: The Structure of Business,* ed. John W. Pratt and Richard J. Zeckhauser (Boston: Harvard Business School Press, 1985), 187–212.

49. See Ronald H. Coase, "The Nature of the Firm," *Economica* 4 (1937): 386–405; and Oliver E. Williamson, *Markets and Hierarchies: Analysis and Antitrust Implications* (New York: Free Press, 1975).

50. See B. Dan Wood and Richard W. Waterman, "The Dynamics of Political Control of the Bureaucracy," *American Political Science Review* 85 (1991): 801–828.

51. Charles Perrow, "Economic Theories of Organization," *Theory and Society* 15 (1986): 41.

52. Terry M. Moe, "The New Economics of Organization," *American Journal of Political Science* 28 (1984): 739–777; and "An Assessment of the Positive Theory of 'Congressional Dominance,'" *Legislative Studies Quarterly* 12 (1987): 475–520.

53. For a comprehensive review of theories we have discussed—and many more that reinforce the impression of disparity—see Jeffrey Pfeffer, "Organizations and Organization Theory," in *Handbook of Social Psychology,* vol. 1, ed. Gardner Lindzey and Elliot Aronson (New York: Random House, 1985), 379–435.

5. The Executive Branch

1. Rufus E. Miles, "The Origin and Meaning of Miles' Law," *Public Administration Review* 38 (September–October 1978): 399–403.

2. Harold Seidman, *Politics, Position, and Power: The Dynamics of Federal Organization* (New York: Oxford University Press, 1998), 142.

3. California Performance Review, *Form Follows Function*, 2004, chap. 1, http://cpr .ca.gov/cpr_report/pdf/Vol_2_FormFolFun ct.pdf.

4. The War Department is treated here as the antecedent of the Department of Defense, established in 1949; the War Department included naval concerns until establishment of the Navy Department in 1798.

5. Three of these six departments were substantially conversions to departmental status of the previously established Federal Security Agency (1939), Housing and Home Finance Agency (1947), and Veterans Administration (1930). For the latest two departmental creations, see Beryl A. Radin and Willis D. Hawley, *The Politics of Federal Reorganization: Creating the U.S. Department of Education* (New York: Pergamon Press, 1988); Terrel H. Bell (first secretary of education), *The Thirteenth Man: A Reagan Cabinet Memoir* (New York: Free Press/Macmillan, 1987); and *Evaluation of Proposals to Establish a Department of Veterans Affairs* (Washington, D.C.: National Academy of Public Administration, 1988).

6. See "The Independent Status of the Regulatory Commissions," in U.S. Senate Committee on Governmental Affairs, *Study on Federal Regulation,* vol. 5, *Regulatory Organization* (Washington, D.C.: Government Printing Office, 1977), 25–81.

7. Donald F. Kettl, *Leadership at the Fed* (New Haven: Yale University Press, 1986), 1.

8. William E. Brigman, "The Executive Branch and the Independent Regulatory Agencies," *Presidential Studies Quarterly* 11 (Spring 1981): 244–261; and David M. Welborn, *Governance of Federal Regulatory Agencies* (Knoxville: University of Tennessee Press, 1977).

9. The chairman appoints and supervises the staff, distributes the workload, and allocates funds. Often several fellow commissioners are patronage appointees, content to follow the chairman's lead. For a disheartening assessment of the quality of appointments from 1949 to 1974 (especially to the Federal Communications Commission and the Federal Trade Commission), see U.S. Senate Committee on Commerce, *Appointments to the Regulatory Agencies* (Washington, D.C.: Government Printing Office, 1976).

10. Tennessee Valley Authority, "A Short History of the TVA," http://www.tva.gov/ abouttva/history.htm.

11. Because no accepted definition of government corporations exists, counts differ. The figures cited are respectively from Ronald C. Moe, *Administering Public Functions at the Margin of Government: The Case of Federal Corporations,* Report No. 83–236 GOV, processed (Washington, D.C.: Congressional Research Service, December 1, 1983); and General Accounting Office, *Congress Should Consider Revising Basic Corporate Control Laws* (Washington, D.C.: Government Printing Office, 1983). Both reports are valuable reviews of the status and problems of government corporations.

12. For organizational history to 1922, see Lloyd M. Short, *The Development of National Administrative Organization in the United States* (Baltimore: Johns Hopkins University Press, 1923).

13. See Walter Isaacson, *Benjamin Franklin: An American Life* (New York: Simon and Schuster, 2003).

14. The contrasting problems of the functional and areal systems are explored and contrasted in James W. Fesler, "The Basic Theoretical Question: How to Relate Area and Function," in *The Administration of the New Federalism,* ed. Leigh E. Grosenick (Washington, D.C.: American Society for Public Administration, 1973), 4–14.

15. In France, as elsewhere, functional pressures by central departments force departures from the model, followed periodically by efforts to reestablish the model's purity.

16. For a vivid account, see "Turf Wars in the Federal Bureaucracy," *Newsweek,* April 10, 1989, 24–26. For much of the 1980s, coordination of the war on drugs was under the National Drug Enforcement Policy Board, but it was ineffective in dealing with interagency disputes. A drug "czar" was appointed in 1989.

17. See Donald F. Kettl, *System under Stress: Homeland Security and American Politics* (Washington, D.C.: CQ Press, 2004); and The Century Foundation, *The Department of Homeland Security's First-Year Report Card* (New York: Century Foundation, 2004).

18. The general problem is reviewed in James W. Fesler, *Area and Administration* (Tuscaloosa: University of Alabama Press, 1949, 1964).

19. U.S. Constitution, Art. 2; *Myers v. United States,* 272 U.S. 52 (1926), as modified for quasi-judicial officers by *Humphrey's Executor* (1935) and by *Weiner v. United States,* 357 U.S. 349 (1958).

20. Molly Ivins, *Shrub: The Short but Happy Political Life of George W. Bush* (New York: Vintage Books, 2000).

21. See Peri E. Arnold, *Making the Managerial Presidency: Comprehensive Reorganization Planning, 1905–1980* (Princeton, N.J.: Princeton University Press, 1986), 361–364; and, more generally, Richard P. Nathan, *The Administrative Presidency* (New York: Wiley, 1983); and Colin Campbell, *Managing the Presidency: Carter, Reagan, and the Search for Executive Harmony* (Pittsburgh: University of Pittsburgh Press, 1986).

22. *Leadership in Jeopardy: The Fraying of the Presidential Appointments System* (Washington, D.C.: National Academy of Public Administration, 1985), 4–5.

23. Kareem Fahim and Colin Moynihan, "An Emergency Call Brings So Much Help a Scuffle Breaks Out," *New York Times,* September 3, 2005, B1.

24. President's Committee on Administrative Management, *Report with Special Studies* (Washington, D.C.: Government Printing Office, 1937), 40.

25. Herbert Emmerich, *Federal Organization and Administrative Management* (Tuscaloosa: University of Alabama Press, 1971), 199; and U.S. Bureau of the Census, *Statistical Abstract of the United States,* various years. Here and later in this section, official data are presented; however, their accuracy has often been questioned. For the varying counts, see John Hart, *The Presidential Branch,* 2d ed. (Chatham, N.J.: Chatham House, 1995), 42–46, 112–125; Gary King and Lyn Ragsdale, *The Elusive Executive* (Washington, D.C.: CQ Press, 1990), Tables 4.1 and 4.2; Office of Personnel Management, *Employment and Trends;* and Office of Administration, Executive Office of the President, "Aggregate Report on Personnel Pursuant to Title 3," *U.S. Code of Federal Regulations,* sec. 113 (annual), processed.

26. General Accounting Office, *Personnel Practices: Detailing of Federal Employees to the White House* (Washington, D.C.: Government Printing Office, July 1987); and *Personnel Practices: Federal Employees Detailed from DOD to the White House* (Washington, D.C.: Government Printing Office, March 1988).

27. Thomas E. Cronin, "The Swelling of the Presidency: Can Anyone Reverse the Tide?" in *American Government: Readings and Cases,* 9th ed., ed. Peter Woll (Boston: Little, Brown, 1984), 345–360.

28. President's Committee on Administrative Management, *Report with Special Studies,* 5.

29. Samuel Kernell, "The Creed and Reality of Modern White House Management," in *Chief of Staff: Twenty-Five Years of Managing the Presidency,* ed. Samuel Kernell and Samuel L. Popkin (Berkeley: University of California Press, 1986), 193–222.

30. For a full and admiring description of the White House staff, see Bradley H. Patterson Jr., *The Ring of Power: The White House Staff and Its Expanding Role in Government* (New York: Basic Books, 1988).

31. Greg Schneiders, "My Turn: Goodbye to All That," *Newsweek*, September 24, 1979, 23. Cf. "Even when working a seventy-hour week the President does not see most of his White House Office staff, or most of his Cabinet." Carter devoted a third of his time to seeing senior staff members and a sixth to seeing cabinet and other officials. Richard Rose, *The Postmodern President: The White House Meets the World* (Chatham, N.J.: Chatham House, 1988), 151–152.

32. Samuel Kernell, "The Evolution of the White House Staff," in *Can the Government Govern?* ed. John E. Chubb and Paul E. Peterson (Washington, D.C.: Brookings Institution Press, 1989), 235.

33. The best comprehensive review of the OMB is U.S. Senate Committee on Governmental Affairs, *Office of Management and Budget: Evolving Roles and Future Issues,* 99th Cong., 2d. sess., February 1986, S. Rpt. 99–134 (Washington, D.C.: Government Printing Office, 1986). For OMB's and the Budget Bureau's history, see also Larry Berman, *The Office of Management and Budget and the Presidency, 1921–1979* (Princeton, N.J.: Princeton University Press, 1979); and Frederick C. Mosher, *A Tale of Two Agencies: A Comparative Analysis of the General Accounting Office and the Office of Management and Budget* (Baton Rouge: Louisiana State University Press, 1984).

34. Hugh Heclo, "OMB and the Presidency— The Problem of 'Neutral Competence,'" *Public Interest* 38 (Winter 1975): 80–98.

35. This will seem unimportant only to those who have not observed the frequency with which "new" ideas are enthusiastically advanced and acted on by newly recruited high officials who are unaware that the same idea, or a near analog, was earlier introduced and failed.

36. Hugh Heclo, *A Government of Strangers: Executive Politics in Washington* (Washington, D.C.: Brookings Institution, 1977), 80–81.

37. See David A. Stockman, *The Triumph of Politics: The Inside Story of the Reagan Revolution* (New York: Harper and Row,

1986; paperback ed., New York: Avon Books, 1987).

38. Ronald C. Moe, "Assessment of Organizational Policy and Planning Function in OMB," in U.S. Senate Committee on Governmental Affairs, *Office of Management and Budget,* 147–167, at 163. See also General Accounting Office, *Managing the Government: Revised Approach Could Improve OMB's Effectiveness* (Washington, D.C.: Government Printing Office, 1989).

39. *Revitalizing Federal Management: Managers and Their Overburdened Systems* (Washington, D.C.: National Academy of Public Administration, 1983), 10–13.

40. 50 U.S. Code 401. Reorganization Plan No. 4 of 1949 placed the NSC in the Executive Office of the President.

41. Attendance was expanded by President Reagan to include the attorney general, the secretary of the treasury, the director of OMB, and the chief delegate to the United Nations.

42. For details on the interagency committee structure and national security advisers' conceptions of their role before and after the Iran-Contra scandal of 1985–1986, see Robert C. McFarlane, Richard Saunders, and Thomas C. Shull, "The National Security Council: Organization for Policy Making," in *The Presidency and National Security Policy,* ed. R. Gordon Hoxie et al. (New York: Center for the Study of the Presidency, 1984), 261–273; and Colin L. Powell, "The NSC System in the Last Two Years of the Reagan Administration," in *The Presidency in Transition,* ed. James P. Pfiffner, R. Gordon Hoxie, et al. (New York: Center for the Study of the Presidency, 1989), 204–218. (McFarlane and Powell were national security advisers.) The first Bush administration simplified the interagency committee structure; see Bernard Weinraub, "Bush Backs Plan to Enhance Role of Security Staff," *New York Times,* February 2, 1989.

43. Bert Rockman, "America's Departments of State: Irregular and Regular Syndromes of

Policy Making," *American Political Science Review* 75 (December 1981): 911–927.

44. The NSC staff's organizational status is ambiguous. Fifteen staff members are special assistants to the president, thus bringing them within the White House Office. Nine of these assistants head staff units (e.g., Asian Affairs, African Affairs, Defense Policy, Intelligence Programs). *The Capital Source* (Spring 1996): 11–12.

45. Keith Schneider, "North's Record: A Wide Role in a Host of Sensitive Projects," *New York Times,* January 3, 1987.

46. See, for example, Perri 6, *E-Governance: Styles of Political Judgment in the Information Age Polity* (New York: Palgrave, 2004); Jane E. Fountain, *Building the Virtual State: Information Technology and Institutional Change* (Washington, D.C.: Brookings Institution, 2001); and Organization for Economic Co-operation and Development, *The E-Government Imperative* (Paris: OECD, 2003).

47. Kathryn Zickuhr and Aaron Smith, *Digital Differences* (Washington, DC: Pew Research Center's Internet & American Life Project, April 13, 2012), http://www.pewinternet.org/~/media//Files/Reports/2012/PIP_Digital_differences_041312.pdf.

48. Fountain, *Building the Virtual State*, 205–206.

49. John B. Horrigan, *How Americans Get in Touch with Government* (Washington, D.C.: Pew Internet and American Life Project, 2004), http://www.pewinternet.org/Reports/2004/How-Americans-Get-in-Touch-With-Government.aspx.

6. Organization Problems

1. Verne Kopytoff, "Move over Mr. Mayor, Cities Are Getting Chief Innovation Officers," *Fortune/CNNMoney*, May 22, 2013, http://management.fortune.cnn.com/2013/05/22/move-over-mrmayor-cities-are-getting-chief-innovation-officers.

2. U.S. Environmental Protection Agency, "Food Recovery Challenge," http://www.epa.gov/smm/foodrecovery.

3. Jack H. Knott and Gary J. Miller, *Reforming Bureaucracy: The Politics of Institutional Choice* (Englewood Cliffs, N.J.: Prentice Hall, 1987), 274.

4. Herbert Kaufman, "Emerging Doctrines of Public Administration," *American Political Science Review* 50 (December 1956): 1059–1073. He assigns the relative dominance of these doctrines historically in this sequence: representativeness, neutral competence, and executive leadership.

5. Todd S. Purdom, "Scuba Feud Pits Idled Bravest against Prideful Finest," *New York Times,* May 5, 1988; and Ari L. Goldman, "New Rules Set for Handling Emergencies," *New York Times,* July 5, 1990.

6. For an analysis, see National Commission on Terrorist Attacks upon the United States, *The 9/11 Commission Report* (New York: Norton, 2004), chap. 9.

7. Federal Regulation Study Team, *Federal Energy Regulation: An Organizational Study* (Washington, D.C.: Government Printing Office, April 1974), appendix D, D1–D2.

8. Ibid., D2.

9. E. S. Turner, *The Court of St. James's* (London: Michael Joseph, 1959), 305–306.

10. *United States Government Organization Manual, 1977–1978,* 312.

11. The concept of core activities is akin to the concept of organizational essence in Morton H. Halperin, *Bureaucratic Politics and Foreign Policy* (Washington, D.C.: Brookings Institution, 1974), 28–40. Halperin soundly argues that an organization must vigorously protect its organizational core or essence.

12. See Allen Schick, "The Coordination Option," in *Federal Reorganization: What Have We Learned?,* ed. Peter Szanton (Chatham, N.J.: Chatham House, 1981), 85–113, esp. 95–99.

13. For details on interagency strife in narcotics control, see W. John Moore, "No Quick Fix," *National Journal* 20 (November 21, 1987): 2954–2959; and "Turf Wars in the Federal Bureaucracy," *Newsweek,* April 20, 1989, 4–6.

14. 102 U.S. Statutes 4181. The czar is formally the director of National Drug Control Policy.

15. Sandra Panem, *The AIDS Bureaucracy* (Cambridge, Mass.: Harvard University Press, 1988).

16. See Jean Blondel, *The Organization of Governments: A Comparative Analysis of Government Structures* (Beverly Hills, Calif.: Sage, 1982).

17. *Commission on the Organization of the Government for the Conduct of Foreign Policy, Report* (Washington, D.C.: Government Printing Office, 1975), 32–33. (Emphasis in original.)

18. Robert T. Golembiewski, *Organizing Men and Power: Patterns of Behavior and Line-Staff Models* (Chicago: Rand McNally, 1967), 62. Pages 60–89 provide the definitive analysis of the tensions between line and staff-auxiliary-control activities.

19. For major critiques of the neutral competence approach, see Knott and Miller, *Reforming Bureaucracy*; and *Organizing Governance and Governing Organizations*, ed. Colin Campbell and B. Guy Peters (Pittsburgh: University of Pittsburgh Press, 1988). See also Harold Seidman and Robert Gilmour, *Politics, Position, and Power: From the Positive to the Regulatory State*, 4th ed. (New York: Oxford University Press, 1986); James G. March and Johan P. Olsen, "Organizing Political Life: What Administrative Reorganization Tells Us about Government," *American Political Science Review* 77 (June 1983): 281–296; and Terry M. Moe, "The Politics of Bureaucratic Structure," in *Can the Government Govern?*, ed. John E. Chubb and Paul E. Peterson (Washington, D.C.: Brookings Institution, 1989), 267–329.

20. "Remarks by the President in State of the Union Address" (January 25, 2011), http://www.whitehouse.gov/the-press-office/2011/01/25/remarks-president-state-union-address.

21. *Immigration and Naturalization Service v. Chadha*, 462 U.S. 919 (1983). See Barbara Hinkson Craig, *Chadha: The Story of an Epic Constitutional Struggle* (New York: Oxford University Press, 1988; paperback ed., Berkeley: University of California Press, 1990).

22. 98 U.S. Statutes 3192 (November 8, 1984). The president cannot use this method to propose creating a new agency outside a department or existing agency.

23. See Peri E. Arnold, *Making the Managerial Presidency: Comprehensive Reorganization Planning, 1905–1980* (Princeton, N.J.: Princeton University Press, 1986).

24. Others, however, led to later reforms. See James W. Fesler, "The Brownlow Committee Fifty Years Later," *Public Administration Review* 47 (July–August 1987): 291–296.

25. See Ronald C. Moe, *The Hoover Commissions Revisited* (Boulder, Colo.: Westview, 1982).

26. Herbert Emmerich, *Federal Organization and Administrative Management* (Tuscaloosa: University of Alabama Press, 1971), 127.

27. Office of Management and Budget, *Papers Relating to the President's Departmental Reorganization Program, March 1971* (Washington, D.C.: Government Printing Office, 1971). See also the revised edition of February 1972.

28. Frustrated by Congress's failure to act, Nixon set out in 1973 to do by fiat what Congress would not let him do by law: four cabinet members were additionally given White House posts as counselors to the president, each with powers over the existing departments in the fields of the proposed departments. In May 1973, with Watergate unraveling, Nixon abandoned this scheme of "supersecretaries."

29. The major success claimed was reform of the civil service, but this was mostly nonorganizational.

30. Reagan supported creation of the Department of Veterans Affairs, but its success in Congress was already assured.

31. The success of Reagan's strategy is assessed in *The Reagan Legacy: Promise and Performance*, ed. Charles O. Jones (Chatham, N.J.: Chatham House, 1988), esp. chaps. 1 and 4.

32. James K. Conant, "In the Shadow of Wilson and Brownlow: Executive Branch Reorganization in the States, 1965 to 1987," *Public Administration Review* 48 (September–October 1988): 892–902. One state, Iowa, reorganized in 1985–1986.

33. March and Olsen, "Organizing Political Life," 288, 292.

34. See Herbert Kaufman, *The Limits of Organizational Change* (Montgomery: University of Alabama Press, 1971); and *Are Government Organizations Immortal?* (Washington, D.C.: Brookings Institution, 1976).

35. For a classic analysis of the expansive tendencies, see Matthew Holden Jr., "'Imperialism' in Bureaucracy," *American Political Science Review* 60 (December 1966): 943–951.

36. Craig W. Thomas, "Reorganizing Public Organizations: Alternatives, Objectives, and Evidence," *Journal of Public Administration and Theory* 3 (1993): 457–486.

7. Administrative Reform

1. Portions of this chapter were originally presented at a conference in Brisbane, Australia, sponsored by the Australian Fulbright Symposium on Public Sector Reform. The conference, "New Ideas, Better Government," was held June 23–24, 1994, and was organized by the Griffith University Centre for Australian Public Sector Management. We are grateful to the conference organizers, Glyn Davis and Patrick Weller, for their support of the research and for their permission to use the material developed for the conference in this chapter.

2. Organization for Economic Co-operation and Development, *Government of the Future* (Paris: OECD, 2001), 15.

3. *A Pledge to America* (2010), 6, http://pledge.gop.gov/resources/library/documents/pledge/a-pledge-to-america.pdf.

4. Roy Bahl, *Financing State and Local Governments in the 1980s* (New York: Oxford University Press, 1984), 184–185.

5. Irene Rubin, *The Politics of Public Budgeting: Getting and Spending, Borrowing and Balancing*, 2d ed. (Chatham, N.J.: Chatham House, 1993), 51–52.

6. J. Richard Aronson and John Hilley, *Financing State and Local Governments*, 4th ed. (Washington, D.C.: Brookings Institution, 1986), 223–224.

7. Ciruli Associates, "Coloradans Support TABOR Amendment Limits on Taxes and Government Spending," February 19, 2003, http://www.ciruli.com/polls/tabor03.htm.

8. See Bahl, *Financing State and Local Government*.

9. E. S. Savas, *Privatizing the Public Sector: How to Shrink Government* (Chatham, N.J.: Chatham House, 1982), 16–17.

10. President's Private Sector Survey on Cost Control (Grace Commission), *A Report to the President* (Washington, D.C.: Government Printing Office, 1984), II-1.

11. Charles Goodsell, "The Grace Commission: Seeking Efficiency for the Whole People," *Public Administration Review* 44 (May–June 1984): 196–204.

12. David Osborne and Ted Gaebler, *Reinventing Government: How the Entrepreneurial Spirit Is Transforming the Public Sector, from Schoolhouse to Statehouse, City Hall to the Pentagon* (Reading, Mass.: Addison-Wesley, 1993).

13. Al Gore, *From Red Tape to Results: Creating a Government that Works Better and Costs Less* (Washington, D.C.: Government Printing Office, 1993), iii–iv.

14. General Accounting Office, *Federal Employment: The Results to Date of the Fiscal Year 1994 Buyouts at Non-Defense Agencies*, GGD-94-214, September 1994.

15. Osborne and Gaebler, *Reinventing Government*.

16. William Niskanen, *Bureaucracy and Representative Government* (Chicago: Aldine Atherton, 1971); Savas, *Privatizing the Public Sector*; and Andrè Blais and Stèphane Dion, *The Budget-Maximizing Bureaucrat: Appraisals and Evidence* (Pittsburgh: University of Pittsburgh Press, 1991).

17. General Accounting Office, *High Risk Series: An Update,* GAO-01–263, January 2002, 73.

18. Donald F. Kettl, *Sharing Power: Public Governance and Private Markets* (Washington, D.C.: Brookings Institution, 1993).

19. Statement of Kathleen King, U.S. Government Accountability Office, Medicare: CMS Has Addressed Some Implementation Problems from Round 1 of the Durable Medical Equipment Competitive Bidding Program for the Round 1 Rebid, GAO-10–1057T, September 15, 2010, http://www.gao.gov/new.items/d101057t.pdf.

20. Michael Hammer and James Champy, *Reengineering the Corporation: A Manifesto for Business Revolution* (New York: Harper Business, 1993).

21. Jerry Mechling, "Reengineering Part of Your Game Plan? A Guide for Public Managers," *Governing* 7 (February 1994): 41–52; Russell M. Linden, *Seamless Government: A Practical Guide to Re-Engineering in the Public Sector* (San Francisco: Jossey-Bass, 1994); and Sharon L. Caudle, *Reengineering for Results* (Washington, D.C.: National Academy of Public Administration, 1994).

22. Hammer and Champy, *Reengineering the Corporation*, 2, 3.

23. Ibid., 47–49.

24. Mechling, "Reengineering Part of Your Game Plan?"

25. General Accounting Office, Management Reforms: Examples of Public and Private Innovations to Improve Service Delivery, AIMD/GGD-94–9, 1994, 37–38.

26. H. George Frederickson, "Painting Bull's Eyes around Bullet Holes," *Governing* 5 (October 1992): 13.

27. Ronald C. Moe, Edward Davis, Frederick Pauls, and Harold Relyca, *Analysis of the Budget and Management Proposals in the Report of the National Performance Review* (Washington, D.C.: Congressional Research Service, September 1993, photocopied), 4.

28. Henri Fayol, *General and Industrial Management* (London: Pitman and Sons, 1925).

29. L. Urwick, "The Function of Administration," in *Papers on the Science of Administration,* ed. Luther Gulick and L. Urwick (New York: Institute of Public Administration, 1937), 124.

30. Luther Gulick, "The Theory of Organization," in ibid., 25.

31. Michael M. Harmon and Richard T. Mayer, *Organization Theory for Public Administration* (Boston: Little, Brown, 1986), 42–47.

32. James Q. Wilson, *Bureaucracy: What Government Agencies Do and Why They Do It* (New York: Basic Books, 1989), 163.

33. For an excellent survey, see James L. Perry, ed., *Handbook of Public Administration* (San Francisco: Jossey-Bass, 1989).

34. Hammer and Champy, *Reengineering the Corporation*, 6.

35. See the findings of the Government Performance Project. For example, consider the findings of the 2001 GPP survey of state performance, offered in *Governing* (February 2001), http://governing.com/gpp/2001/gp1intro.htm.

36. See W. Edwards Deming, *Out of Crisis* (Cambridge, Mass.: Massachusetts Institute of Technology Center for Advanced Engineering Study, 1986); and Rafael Aguayo, *Dr. Deming: The American Who Taught the Japanese about Quality* (New York: Simon and Schuster, 1990).

37. Aguayo, *Dr. Deming,* 19.

38. Bill Creech, *The Five Pillars of TQM: How to Make Total Quality Management Work for You* (New York: Dutton, 1994), 27, 54.

39. Steven Cohen and Ronald Brand, *Total Quality Management in Government: A Practical Guide for the Real World* (San Francisco: Jossey-Bass, 1993).

40. Creech, *Five Pillars,* 78.

41. Cohen and Brand, *Total Quality Management in Government,* 175–197.

42. Ibid., 197.

43. Peter M. Senge, *The Fifth Discipline: The Art and Practice of the Learning Organization* (New York: Doubleday, 1990); and Donald F. Kettl, "Learning Organizations and Managing the Unknown," in *New Paradigms for Government: Issues for the Changing Public Service,* ed. Patricia W. Ingraham and

Barbara S. Romzek (San Francisco: Jossey-Bass, 1994), 19–40.

44. H. Metcalf and L. Urwick, *Dynamic Administration: The Collected Papers of Mary Parker Follett* (New York: Harper & Brothers, 1942).

45. Abraham Maslow, "A Theory of Human Motivation," *Psychological Review* 50 (July 1943): 370–396.

46. See, for example, Michael Barzelay with Babak J. Armajani, *Breaking Through Bureaucracy: A New Vision for Managing in Government* (Berkeley: University of California Press, 1992); and Harry P. Hatry and John J. Kirlin, *An Assessment of the Oregon Benchmarks: A Report to the Oregon Progress Board* (June 1994, photocopied).

47. Quoted in Megan Hupp, "OMB Seeks Focus on Useful Performance Data," *Government Executive* (October 13, 2010), http://www .govexec.com/dailyfed/1010/101310h1.htm.

48. Jeffrey D. Zients, "Memorandum for the Senior Executive Service" (September 10, 2010), http://www.whitehouse.gov/sites/ default/files/omb/memoranda/2010/Account ableGovernmentInitiative_09142010.pdf.

49. For two excellent surveys of administrative issues around the world, see Randall Baker, ed., *Comparative Public Management: Putting U.S. Public Policy and Implementation in Context* (New York: Praeger, 1994); and B. Guy Peters, *The Future of Governing: Four Emerging Models,* 2d ed., rev. (Lawrence: University of Kansas Press, 2001). The Organization of Economic Co-operation and Development also publishes regular updates on reforms in public administration; see http://www.oecd.org/topic/0,2686, en_2649_37405_1_1_1_1_37405,00.html.

50. An important commentary on reform in the developing world is Allen Schick, "Why Most Developing Countries Should not Try New Zealand Reforms," *World Bank Research Observer* 13 (February 1998): 123–131.

51. For a broad discussion, see Peter Aucoin, "Administrative Reform in Public Management: Paradigms, Principles, Paradoxes and Pendulums," *Governance* 3

(1990), 115–137; and Christopher Pollitt and Geert Bouckaert, *Public Management Reform: A Comparative Analysis—New Public Management, Governance, and the Neo-Weberian State* (Oxford: Oxford University Press, 2011).

52. See Donald F. Kettl and John J. DiIulio Jr., eds., *Inside the Reinvention Machine: Appraising the National Performance Review* (Washington, D.C.: Brookings Institution, 1995).

53. Allen Schick, *The Spirit of Reform: Managing the New Zealand State Sector in a Time of Change* (Wellington, N.Z.: State Services Commission, 1996).

54. Office of Management and Budget, *The President's Management Agenda: Fiscal Year 2002* (Washington, D.C.: Government Printing Office, 2001), 3.

8. The Civil Service

1. Associated Press dispatch, *New Haven Register,* July 18, 1969; and 5 U.S. Code of Federal Regulations, 5546, 5547.

2. See Megan Garber, "Apollo 11's Astronauts Received an $8 Per Diem for the Mission to the Moon," *The Atlantic,* August 28, 2012, http://www.govexec .com/technology/2012/08/apollo-11s-as- tronauts-received-8-diem-mission- moon/57698/?oref=govexec_today_nl.

3. Statement of David M. Walker, Human Capital: Taking Steps to Meet Current and Emerging Human Capital Challenges, GAO-01-965T, July 17, 2001, 1.

4. Jonathan Walters, *Life after Civil Service Reform: The Texas, Georgia, and Florida Experiences* (Washington, D.C.: IBM Endowment for the Business of Government, 2002), 7.

5. David Osborne and Ted Gaebler, *Reinventing Government* (Reading, Mass.: Addison-Wesley, 1992).

6. Max Cacas, "OPM Hosts CHCO Hiring Reforms Summit Today," *Federal News Radio,* May 12, 2010, http://www.federal- newsradio.com/?nid=35&sid=1954833.

7. 5 U.S. Code of Federal Regulations 3304(a). The substance and much of the language date from the Pendleton Civil Service Act of 1883.

8. U.S. Merit Systems Protection Board, *Federal Appointment Authorities: Cutting through the Confusion* (Washington, D.C.: MSPB, 2008), http://www.mspb.gov/netsearch/view docs.aspx?docnumber=350930&version=3 51511&application=ACROBAT.

9. Brittany R. Ballenstedt, "MSPB: Competitive Hiring on the Decline," *Government Executive,* July 29, 2008, http://www.govexec .com/story_page.cfm?articleid=40577& dcn=e_gvet.

10. Organization for Economic Co-operation and Development, *Fostering Diversity in the Public Service* (2009), 5, http://www.oecd .org/dataoecd/44/21/44860884.pdf.

11. See David Weisman, *Common Characteristics of the Government* (2011), 21, http://www .opm.gov/policy-data-oversight/data-analy sis-documentation/federal-employment- reports/common-characteristics-of-the- government/ccog.pdf.

12. Bureau of Labor Statistics, "Table 3. Total Separation Levels and Rates by Industry and Region, Seasonally Adjusted," http:// www.bls.gov/news.release/jolts.t03.htm.

13. Kellie Lunney, "Survey: Feds Have It Good Compared to Private Sector Workers," *Government Executive,* December 10, 2012, http://www.govexec.com/pay-benefits/ 2012/12/survey-feds-have-it-good-compared -private-sector-workers/60054.

14. Stephen Losey, "Officials Sound the Alarm over Recruitment, Retention," *Federal Times,* March 20, 2013, http://www.federal times.com/article/20130320/PERSONNEL02/ 303200004/Officials-sound-alarm-over- retention-recruitment.

15. One study found that clerk-typists and sec- retaries, with small pay gaps compared to private salaries, had high quit rates, while chemists, accountants, and engineers, with large pay gaps, had low quit rates. General Accounting Office, *Federal Workforce: Pay, Recruitment, and Retention of Federal Employees* (Washington, D.C.: Government

Printing Office, 1987), 2–3. For more comprehensive occupational analysis of voluntary separations, see Congressional Budget Office, *Employee Turnover in the Federal Government* (Washington, D.C.: Government Printing Office, 1986), 6–8.

16. For a comparison of government and pri- vate-sector employees' evaluation of a num- ber of such job features, see Michael P. Smith and Steven L. Nock, "Social Class and the Quality of Work Life in Public and Private Organizations," *Journal of Social Issues* 30 (1980): 59–75; and Barry Bozeman, *All Organizations Are Public: Bridging Public and Private Organizational Theories* (San Francisco: Jossey-Bass, 1987), 15–23. Federal workers' appraisals are surveyed in Merit Systems Protection Board, *Federal Personnel Policies and Practices: Perspectives from the Workplace* (Washington, D.C.: Government Printing Office, 1987).

17. Congressional Budget Office, "Comparing the Compensation of Federal and Private- Sector Employees," January 30, 2012, http:// www.cbo.gov/publication/42921.

18. James Sherk, *Inflated Federal Pay: How Americans Are Overtaxed to Overpay the Civil Service,* Report CDA10-05 (Washington, D.C.: Heritage Foundation, 2010), http:// thf_media.s3.amazonaws.com/2010/pdf/ CDA10-05.pdf.

19. U.S. Office of Management and Budget, *Budget of the United States Government, Fiscal Year 2014: Analytical Perspectives* (Washington, D.C.: OMB, 2013), 107, http:// www.whitehouse.gov/sites/default/files/ omb/budget/fy2014/assets/spec.pdf.

20. See http://www.federalnewsradio.com/pdfs/ house_oversight_gs_system.pdf.

21. Terry W. Culler, "Most Federal Workers Need Only Be Competent," *Wall Street Journal,* May 21, 1986.

22. The leading case, that of Washington State, is assessed in Peter T. Kilborn, "Wage Gap between Sexes Is Cut in Test, but at a Price," *New York Times,* May 31, 1990. For Minnesota and Oregon, see Sara M. Evans and Barbara J. Nelson, *Comparable*

Worth and the Paradox of Technocratic Reform (Chicago: University of Chicago Press, 1989). See also Joan Acker, *Doing Comparable Worth: Gender, Class, and Pay Equity* (Philadelphia: Temple University Press, 1989); Steven R. Rhoads, *Incomparable Worth: Pay Equity Meets the Market* (New York: Cambridge University Press, 1993); Elaine Sorensen, *Comparable Worth: Is It a Worthy Policy?* (Princeton, N.J.: Princeton University Press, 1994); and Michael W. McCann, *Rights at Work: Pay Equity Reform and the Politics of Legal Mobilization* (Chicago: University of Chicago Press, 1994).

23. June Ellenoff O'Neill, "Comparable Worth," in *The Concise Encyclopedia of Economics*, http://www.econlib.org/library/Enc1/ComparableWorth.html.

24. George H. W. Bush, statement issued October 5, 1988; and "Remarks of the President to the Career Members of the Senior Executive Service," January 26, 1989. Reprinted in *Bureaucrat* 18 (Spring 1989): 3.

25. Ben Smith, "Obama Plans To 'Make Government Cool Again,'" *Politico*, September 11, 2008, http://www.politico.com/blogs/bensmith/0908/Obama_plans_to_make_government_cool_again.html.

26. See Merit Systems Protection Board, *Attracting College Graduates to the Federal Government: A View of College Recruiting* (Washington, D.C.: Government Printing Office, 1988); *Leadership for America Report*, 3–4, 24; and *Task Force Reports*, 84–88.

27. National Advisory Council on the Public Service, *Ensuring the Highest Quality National Public Service* (Washington, D.C.: National Advisory Council on the Public Service, 1993), 20.

28. Constance Horner, OPM director, as quoted in Judith Havemann, "U.S. Plans New System for Hiring," *Washington Post*, June 23, 1988. Ms. Horner announced a new student recruitment program, but its realization depended on its appeal to her successor under the Bush administration. See Office of Personnel Management, "New Program to Fill GS-5 and GS-7 Entry-Level Jobs," June 23, 1988, processed.

29. Carolyn Ban and Norma Riccucci, "Personnel Systems and Labor Relations: Steps toward a Quiet Revitalization," in *Revitalizing State and Local Public Service: Strengthening Performance, Accountability, and Citizen Confidence*, ed. Frank J. Thompson (San Francisco: Jossey-Bass, 1993), 83.

30. Congressional Budget Office, *Characteristics and Pay of Federal Civilian Employees* (Washington, D.C.: CBO, March 2007), 8, http://www.cbo.gov/ftpdocs/78xx/doc7874/03-15-Federal_Personnel.pdf.

31. For a thorough coverage of the issues, see Richard B. Freeman and Casey Ichniowski, eds., *When Public Sector Workers Organize* (Chicago: University of Chicago Press, 1988).

32. Leonard Buder, "Walkout Is Hobbling Schools in New York," *New York Times*, February 24, 1977.

33. Quoted in Frank Swoboda, "AFGE's Optimistic Organizer," *Washington Post*, January 21, 1988.

34. Joel M. Douglas, "State Civil Service and Collective Bargaining Systems," *Public Administration Review* 52 (January–February 1992): 162–171.

35. Quoted in National Academy of Public Administration, *Leading People in Change: Empowerment, Commitment, Accountability* (Washington, D.C.: NAPA, 1993), 10.

36. Ibid., 89–111; and Steven M. Goldschmidt and Leland E. Stuart, "The Extent and Impact of Educational Policy Bargaining," *Industrial and Labor Relations Review* 39 (April 1986): 350–360.

37. For the Federal Labor Relations Authority's interpretations of "compelling need" and "procedures," see Sar Levitan and Alexandra Noden, *Working for the Sovereign: Employee Relations in the Federal Government* (Baltimore: Johns Hopkins University Press, 1983), 36–40; and annual reports of the FLRA.

38. 5 U.S. Code, Part III, Subpart F, Chapter 71, Subchapter I, Section 7106.

39. Brian Friel, "Labor Pains," *Government Executive,* October 1, 2002, http://www.govexec.com/magazine/2002/10/labor-pains/12518/ .

40. Executive Order 12564, September 15, 1986. For its implementation, see General Accounting Office, *Drug Testing: Federal Agency Plans for Testing Employees* (Washington, D.C.: Government Printing Office, 1989); and *Drug Testing: Action by Certain Agencies When Employees Test Positive for Illegal Drugs* (Washington, D.C.: Government Printing Office, 1990).

41. Amelia Gruber, "New Policy Would Broaden Drug-Testing Methods," *Government Executive,* April 6, 2004, http://www.govexec.com/dailyfed/0404/040604a1.htm.

42. *National Treasury Employees v. Von Raab,* 109 S. Ct. 1384 (1989).

43. The relationship between the presence of HIV antibodies and the likelihood of having AIDS is a matter of dispute. For technical discussion, see "The Cause of AIDS," *Science* 242 (November 18, 1988): 997–998.

44. Richard L. Berke, "State Department to Begin AIDS Testing," *New York Times,* November 29, 1986.

45. 5 U.S. Code of Federal Regulations 7324–7327. For specifically permissible activities and prohibited activities, see 5 U.S. Code of Federal Regulations 733.111 to 733.122. Exceptions to the ban exist (1) for nonpartisan elections and with regard to questions (such as constitutional amendments and referenda) not specifically identified with a national or state political party and (2) in certain local communities near Washington, D.C., and elsewhere (designated by OPM) where federal employees are a majority of voters. OPM restricts activity in such communities' partisan elections to candidacy as, or advocacy or opposition to, an independent candidate.

46. Those free of the restrictions are the president and vice president, aides paid from appropriations for the president's office, heads and assistant heads of executive departments, and officers who are appointed by the president, by and with the advice and consent of the Senate, and who determine policies to be pursued by the United States.

47. 427 U.S. 347 (1976).

48. 445 U.S. 507 (1980).

49. For a criticism of the two cases, see Kenneth J. Meier, "Ode to Patronage: A Critical Analysis of Two Recent Supreme Court Decisions," *Public Administration Review* 41 (September–October 1981): 558–563.

50. 497 U.S. 62 (1990); and Linda Greenhouse, "Court Widens Curb on Patronage in Jobs for Most Public Workers," *New York Times,* June 22, 1990.

51. In contrast, the City of Chicago's Democratic administration substantially ended its patronage hiring system when it settled federal court suits by signing a consent decree. For an excellent review, see Anne Freedman, "Doing Battle with the Patronage Army: Politics, Courts, and Personnel Administration in Chicago," *Public Administration Review* 48 (September–October 1988): 847–859.

52. George Cahlink, "Ex-Procurement Chief Gets Jail Time," *Government Executive,* October 1, 2004, http://www.govexec.com/dailyfed/1004/100104g1.htm. The plea agreement can be found at this link.

53. Government Accountability Office, *Defense Contracting: Post-Government Employment of Former DOD Officials Needs Greater Transparency,* Report GAO-08-485 (2008), 6.

54. Ibid.

55. Patricia Wallace Ingraham, *The Foundation of Merit: Public Service in American Democracy* (Baltimore: Johns Hopkins University Press, 1995), 74. Emphasis in original.

56. Government Accountability Office, *High-Risk Series: Strategic Human Capital Management,* Report GAO-03-120 (2003), 7.

57. John Berry, "Launch of Hiring Reform Initiative," May 11, 2010, http://www.opm.gov/news/speeches-remarks/launch-of-hiring-reform-initiative.

58. Ibid.

59. Steven Pearlstein, "Can Business Afford Jim DeMint?" *Washington Post,* September 29, 2010, http://www.washingtonpost.com/wp-dyn/content/article/2010/09/28/AR2010092806308.html.

9. Human Capital

1. General Accounting Office, *High-Risk Series: Strategic Human Capital Management,* GAO-03-120 (Washington, D.C.: Government Printing Office, 2003), 3–4. For a broad examination of the issues, see Jonathan D. Breul and Nicole Willenz Gardner, eds., *Human Capital 2004* (Lanham, Md.: Rowman and Littlefield, 2004).

2. Peter Drucker, "Knowledge Work and Knowledge Society: The Social Transformations of This Century," *1994 Godkin Lecture* (Cambridge, Mass.: John F. Kennedy School of Government, Harvard University, 1994).

3. GAO, *High-Risk Series,* 8–21.

4. Ibid., 10.

5. For a discussion of these issues, see Donna D. Beecher, "The Next Wave of Civil Service Reform," *Public Personnel Management* 32 (Winter 2003): 457–474.

6. Rob Gurwitt, "How Generation X Is Shaping Government," *Governing,* May 2013, http://www.governing.com/topics/mgmt/gov-how-generation-x-shaping-government.html.

7. David McGlinchey, "Unwieldy Hiring Process Can Be Fixed, Top Personnel Official Says," *Government Executive,* June 8, 2004, http://www.govexec.com/dailyfed/0604/060804d1.htm. See also General Accounting Office, *Human Capital: Status of Efforts to Improve Federal Hiring,* Report, GAO-04-796T (Washington, D.C.: Government Printing Office, 2004).

8. General Accounting Office, *HUD Management: Actions Needed to Improve Acquisitions Management,* GAO-03-157 (Washington, D.C.: Government Printing Office, 2002).

9. Partnership for Public Service, "Best Places to Work in the Federal Government: Analysis—Diversity and Inclusion" (2013), http://www.govexec.com/media/gbc/docs/pdfs_edit/071113cc4.pdf.

10. General Accounting Office, *Results-Oriented Cultures: Insights for U.S. Agencies from Other Countries' Performance Management Initiatives,* GAO-02-862 (Washington, D.C.: Government Printing Office, 2002), 4.

11. For an excellent analysis of human resource reform, see Patricia W. Ingraham, "Striving for Balance: Reforms in Human Resource Management," in *Handbook of Comparative Administration,* ed. Laurence Lynn Jr. and Christopher Pollitt (Oxford: Oxford University Press, forthcoming).

12. Shelley Metzenbaum, "Performance Improvement Guidance: Management Responsibilities and Government Performance and Results Act Documents," *Memorandum for Executive Departments and Agencies* (June 25, 2010), http://www.whitehouse.gov/sites/default/files/omb/assets/memoranda_2010/m10-24.pdf.

13. Keynote address by David M. Walker, "Comptroller General of the United States, Joint Financial Management Improvement Program," 32nd Annual Financial Management Conference (March 11, 2003), http://www.gao.gov/cghome/jfmip32.pdf.

14. Stephen Barr, "OPM Turns over 10,000 New Leaves," *Washington Post,* January 28, 1994, A21.

15. American Federation of State, County, and Municipal Employees, "Broadbanding" (Spring 1997), http://www.afscmestaff.org/cbr/cbr297_1.htm.

16. Ibid.

17. Quoted in Stephen Barr, "Is Road to Chaos Paved with 'Ad Hoc' Reform?" *Washington Post,* February 22, 2004, C2.

18. General Accounting Office, *FAA's Reform Effort Requires a More Strategic Approach,* GAO-03-156 (Washington, D.C.: Government Printing Office, 2003).

19. Eric Yoder, "The IRS Hopes to Hit Paydirt," *Government Executive,* April 1, 2001, http://www.govexec.com/features/0401/0401s1s3.htm.

20. Keith Koffler and Mark Wegner, "Bush Urges Waiver of Civil Service Rules in Homeland Department," *Government Executive,* July 22, 2002, http://www.gov-exec.com/dailyfed/0702/072202cd1.htm.

21. Quoted in Jonathan Walters, *Life after Civil Service Reform: The Texas, Georgia, and Florida Experiences* (Washington, D.C.: IBM Endowment for the Business of Government, 2002), 7. The discussion that follows draws heavily on Walters's analysis of the civil service reforms in these three states.

22. Ibid., 22.

23. Ibid., 28.

24. See http://www.pewstates.org/states/georgia-328017.

25. Ibid., 30.

26. See http://www.pewstates.org/states/florida-328016.

27. For a broad assessment, see Jerrell D. Coggburn, "Personnel Deregulation: Exploring Differences in the American States," *Journal of Public Administration Research and Theory* 11 (2000): 223–244; Sally Coleman Selden, Patricia Wallace Ingraham, and Willow Jacobson, "Human Resource Practices in State Government: Findings from a National Survey," *Public Administration Review* 61 (September–October 2002), 598–607; and J. Edward Kellough and Sally Coleman Selden, "The Reinvention of Public Personnel Administration: An Analysis of the Diffusion of Personnel Management Reforms in the States," *Public Administration Review* 63 (March–April 2003): 165–176.

28. See http://www.pewstates.org/states/virginia-328052.

29. Melissa Maynard, "States Overhaul Civil Service Rules," *Stateline,* August 27, 2013, http://www.pewstates.org/projects/stateline/headlines/states-overhaul-civil-service-rules-85899500482.

30. I have interpreted "higher levels" strictly (i.e., at Executive Schedule levels, in the Senior Executive Service, at GS-16 to GS-18, or serving in the White House, or serving as ambassadors and ministers). About 1,650 persons are political appointees under Schedule C ("positions of a confidential or policy-determining character") at the GS-15 level and below; as noted earlier, about 1,000 of them are at GS-13 to GS-15 levels.

31. The Presidential Appointee Initiative, *A Survivor's Guide for Presidential Nominees* (Washington, D.C.: Brookings Institution, 2000), http://www.brookings.edu/research/papers/2000/11/15governance.

32. On Nixon and Reagan, see Richard P. Nathan, *The Administrative Presidency* (New York: Wiley, 1983).

33. Terry M. Moe, "The Politicized Presidency," in *The New Direction in American Politics,* ed. John E. Chubb and Paul E. Peterson (Washington, D.C.: Brookings Institution, 1985), 235–271.

34. Expendability is impaired when, as is often the case, a political appointee is the darling of a congressional committee, interest group, or both.

35. Paul C. Light, "How Thick Is Government?" *American Enterprise* 5 (November–December 1994): 60–61. See also the book based on his study, *Thickening Government: Federal Hierarchy and the Diffusion of Accountability* (Washington, D.C.: Brookings Institution Press, 1995).

36. Paul C. Light, "Fact Sheet on the Continued Thickening of Government," July 23, 2003, http://www.brookings.edu/research/papers/2004/07/23governance-light.

37. For qualifications needed to perform well in one set of political posts, see John H. Trattner, *The Prune Book: The 100 Toughest Management and Policy-Making Jobs in Washington* (Lanham, Md.: Madison Books, 1988).

38. G. Calvin Mackenzie, "Appointing Mr. (or Ms.) Right," *Government Executive* 22 (April 1990): 30–35; the transitions exclude Johnson's and Ford's rises from the vice presidency. Cf. Burt Solomon, "Bush's Laggard Appointment Pace . . . May Not Matter All That Much," *National Journal* 21

(December 2, 1989): 2952–2953. Through 1989 and often beyond, the Consumer Products Safety Commission lacked a quorum; only four of eighteen top Energy Department officials were in place, as was true of six of eleven assistant secretaries of Labor; the Census Bureau's director had not been appointed, although the 1990 census was soon to start; and in Health and Human Services the headships of the National Institutes of Health, Food and Drug Administration, and Health Care Financing Administration were unfilled.

39. Quoted in Christopher Lee, "Bush Slow to Fill Top Federal Posts," *Washington Post,* October 18, 2002, A35.

40. From 1953 to 1976, 55 percent of the initial appointees and 85 percent of appointees had had such experience. James J. Best, "Presidential Cabinet Appointments: 1953–1976," *Presidential Studies Quarterly* 11 (Winter 1981): 62–66.

41. This and later paragraphs draw on James W. Fesler, "Politics, Policy, and Bureaucracy at the Top," *Annals of the American Academy of Political and Social Science* 466 (March 1983): 23–41, and sources cited there.

42. For informative analyses of political officials who had such capability, see Jameson W. Doig and Erwin C. Hargrove, eds., *Leadership and Innovation: A Biographical Perspective on Entrepreneurs in Government* (Baltimore: Johns Hopkins University Press, 1987).

43. G. Edward DeSeve, *The Presidential Appointee's Handbook* (Washington, D.C.: Brookings Institution Press, 2008).

44. *Leadership in Jeopardy: The Fraying of the Presidential Appointments System* (Washington, D.C.: National Academy of Public Administration, 1985), 4–5. Regulatory commissioners, who have fixed terms and are removable only "for cause," are excluded from the figures we use. The figures measure tenure in specific positions; appointees' median service within the same agency was 3 years, and within the government 4.3 years.

45. Charles S. Clark, "Low Morale at DHS Linked to Heavy Turnover, Weak Training," *Government Executive,* March 22, 2012, http://www.govexec.com/defense/2012/03/low-morale-dhs-linked-heavy-turnover-weak-training/41549.

46. For details, see Linda L. Fisher, "Fifty Years of Presidential Appointments," in *The In-and-Outers: Presidential Appointees and Transient Government in Washington,* ed. G. Calvin Mackenzie (Baltimore: Johns Hopkins University Press, 1987), 21–26; Carl Brauer, "Tenure, Turnover, and Post-government Employment Trends of Presidential Appointees," in Mackenzie, *In-and-Outers,* 174–194; and Trattner, *Prune Book.* See also General Accounting Office, *Political Appointees: Turnover Rates in Executive Schedule Positions Requiring Senate Confirmation* GGD-94-115 FS (Washington, D.C.: Government Printing Office, 1994).

47. Robert Thalon Hall, quoted in Brauer, "Tenure, Turnover, and Post-government Employment," 178–179.

48. General Accounting Office, *Department of Labor: Assessment of Management Improvement Efforts* (Washington, D.C.: Government Printing Office, 1986).

49. General Accounting Office, *Social Security Administration: Stable Leadership and Better Management Needed to Improve Effectiveness* (Washington, D.C.: Government Printing Office, 1987), 3.

50. Hugh Heclo, *A Government of Strangers: Executive Politics in Washington* (Washington, D.C.: Brookings Institution, 1972), 158 and passim.

51. For an entertaining fictional account of the comparable interplay between a British minister and his ministry's permanent secretary, see *The Complete "Yes, Minister": The Diaries of a Cabinet Minister by the Right Hon. James Hacker MP,* ed. Jonathan Lynn and Anton Jay (Topsfield, Mass.: Salem House, 1987).

52. HHS (including SSA) data from Robert Pear, "Many Policy Jobs Vacant on Eve of

Second Term," *New York Times,* January 14, 1985. In 1987, when five Central American countries proposed a regional peace plan, the United States had ambassadors in only two of those countries; lesser-ranked diplomats represented the United States in the other three. Neil A. Lewis, "U.S. Envoys Told to Convey Doubt over Latin Plan," *New York Times,* August 18, 1987. The president's special envoy for Central America had also resigned.

53. U.S. General Accountability Office, *Federal Vacancies Reform Act: Key Elements for Agency Procedures for Complying with the Act,* GAO-03–806 (Washington, D.C.: Government Printing Office, 2003), http://www.gao.gov/new.items/d03806.pdf.

54. Clark, "Low Morale at DHS."

55. General Accounting Office, *Temporary Appointments: Extended Temporary Appointments to Positions Requiring Senate Confirmation* (Washington, D.C.: Government Printing Office, 1986), appendix 1.

56. Frederick V. Malek, *Washington's Hidden Tragedy* (New York: Macmillan, 1978), 102–103.

57. National Academy of Public Administration, *Strengthening Senior Leadership in the U.S. Government* (Washington, D.C.: 2002), 1–2.

58. See ibid., esp. 3–4.

59. David McGlinchey, "OPM Seeks 'Rigorous and Realistic' Executive Ratings," *Government Executive,* February 19, 2004, http://www.govexec.com/story_page.cfm?articleid=27701&printerfriendlyVers=1&.

60. Kathy Chu, "Employers See Lackluster Results Linking Salary to Performance," *Wall Street Journal,* June 15, 2004, D2. For analysis of the broader issues, see National Academy of Public Administration, *Recommending Performance-Based Federal Pay* (Washington, D.C.: National Academy of Public Administration, 2004).

61. Ibid., 4.

62. Frank P. Sherwood and Lee J. Breyer, "Executive Personnel Systems in the States," *Public Administration Review* 47 (September–October 1987): 410–416.

63. Elliot L. Richardson, "Civil Servants: Why Not the Best?" *Wall Street Journal,* November 20, 1987. In the Nixon period he was undersecretary of state and then headed the Health, Education, and Welfare, Defense, and Justice Departments; under Ford he was ambassador to the Court of St. James's and secretary of commerce; under Carter, he was ambassador-at-large.

64. John W. Macy, Bruce Adams, and J. Jackson Walters, *America's Unelected Government: Appointing the President's Team* (Cambridge, Mass.: Ballinger, 1983), 82.

65. *Fairness for Our Public Servants,* Report of the 1989 Commission on Executive, Legislative and Judicial Salaries (Washington, D.C.: Government Printing Office, 1988), 1, see chart 2.

66. See Don Tapscott, *Grown up Digital* (New York: McGraw-Hill, 2009); and Chief Information Officers Council, *Netgeneration: Preparing for Change in the Federal Information Technology Workforce* (Washington, D.C.: Chief Information Officers Council, 2010), 38–39, http://www.govexec.com/pdfs/042310ah1.pdf.

67. Paul C. Light, *A Government Ill Executed: The Decline of the Federal Service and How to Reverse It* (Cambridge, Mass.: Harvard University Press, 2008), 4.

10. Decision Making

1. Herbert A. Simon, *Administrative Behavior: A Study of Decision-Making Processes in Administrative Organization,* 3rd ed. (New York: Free Press, 1945, 1976). A few years earlier, Chester I. Barnard had also argued the importance of decision making; see *The Functions of the Executive* (Cambridge, Mass.: Harvard University Press, 1938). Simon's work, however, has proved more influential.

2. See, for example, Charles E. Lindblom and David K. Cohen, *Usable Knowledge: Social Science and Social Problem Solving* (New Haven, Conn.: Yale University Press, 1979).

3. Max Weber, "Bureaucracy," in *From Max Weber: Essays in Sociology,* trans. and ed. H. H. Gerth and C. Wright Mills (New York: Oxford University Press, 1946), 196–244. Francis E. Rourke discusses this point more generally in *Bureaucracy, Politics, and Public Policy,* 3rd ed. (Boston: Little, Brown, 1984).

4. See, for example, Don K. Price, "The Scientific Establishment," *Proceedings of the American Philosophical Society* 106 (June 1962): 235–245; and idem, *The Scientific Estate* (Cambridge, Mass.: Harvard University Press, 1965). The Congressional Research Service has assembled a useful collection of readings on the role of science in decision making. See House Committee on Science and Technology, *Expertise and Democratic Decision Making: A Reader,* Science Policy Study, Background Rpt. No. 7, prepared by the Congressional Research Service, 99th Cong., 2d sess., 1986.

5. Deborah A. Stone, *Policy Paradox and Political Reason* (Glenview, Ill.: Scott Foresman, 1988), 21.

6. Robert D. Behn and James W. Vaupel, *Quick Analysis for Busy Decision Makers* (New York: Basic Books, 1982), 19, 20.

7. See Charles O. Jones, *An Introduction to the Study of Public Policy,* 3rd ed. (Monterey, Calif.: Brooks/Cole, 1984), esp. chap. 6.

8. Rourke, *Bureaucracy, Politics, and Public Policy,* 49.

9. Ibid., 50.

10. This follows Hugh Heclo's argument in "Issue Networks and the Executive Establishment," in *The New American Political System,* ed. Anthony King (Washington, D.C.: American Enterprise Institute, 1978), 87–124.

11. Stone, *Policy Paradox and Political Reason,* 309.

12. Donald W. Taylor, "Decision Making and Problem Solving," in *Handbook of Organizations,* ed. James G. March (Chicago: Rand McNally, 1965), 70.

13. For sympathetic accounts of PPBS in the Department of Defense, written by those in charge of its application, see Charles J. Hitch, *Decision Making for Defense* (Berkeley: University of California Press, 1965); and Alain C. Enthoven and K. Wayne Smith, *How Much Is Enough? Shaping the Defense Program, 1961–1969* (New York: Harper and Row, 1971). Compare James R. Schlesinger, "Uses and Abuses of Analysis," in Senate Committee on Government Operations, *Planning, Programming, Budgeting: Inquiry,* 91st Cong., 2d sess., 1970, 125–136; and Blue Ribbon Defense Panel (Gilbert W. Fitzhugh, chair), *Report to the President and the Secretary of Defense on the Department of Defense* (Washington, D.C.: Government Printing Office, 1970), 112–118, which reports, "the PPBS does not contribute significantly to the decision-making process for consideration of programs which center on major weapons systems" (114).

14. Bureau of the Budget, *Bulletin No. 68–69,* April 12, 1968. All descriptive, but no evaluative quotations are from this text.

15. Jack W. Carlson (assistant director for program evaluation, Bureau of the Budget), "The Status and Next Steps for Planning, Programming, and Budgeting," in U.S. Congress, Joint Economic Committee, *The Analysis and Evaluation of Public Expenditures: The PPB System,* 91st Cong., 1st sess., 1969, 2: 613–634; and his testimony in U.S. Congress, Joint Economic Committee, *Economic Analysis and the Efficiency of Government,* Hearings, 91st Cong., 2d sess., 1970, Pt. 3, 694–706.

16. For the leading analysis of why PPBS failed, see Allen Schick, "A Death in the Bureaucracy: The Demise of Federal PPB," *Public Administration Review* 33 (March–April 1973): 146–156.

17. Allen Schick, *Budget Innovation in the States* (Washington, D.C.: Brookings Institution, 1971); Aaron Wildavsky, *Budgeting: A Comparative Theory of Budgetary Processes* (Boston: Little, Brown, 1975), 335–352; Jack Rabin, "State and Local PPBS," in *Public Budgeting and Finance,* 2nd ed., ed. Robert T. Golembiewski and Jack Rabin (Itasca, Ill.: Peacock, 1975), 427–447. The most searching critiques of PPBS's inherent

defects are in Aaron Wildavsky, *The New Politics of the Budgetary Process* (Glenview, Ill.: Scott Foresman, 1987), 416.-420; idem, *The Revolt against the Masses* (New York: Basic Books, 1971); and Leonard Merewitz and Stephen H. Sosnick, *The Budget's New Clothes: A Critique of Planning-Programming-Budgeting and Benefit-Cost Analysis* (Chicago: Markham, 1971). See also Ida R. Hoos, *Systems Analysis in Public Policy: A Critique* (Berkeley: University of California Press, 1972).

18. U.S. Congress, Joint Economic Committee, *Economic Analysis and the Efficiency of Government,* Report, 91st Cong., 2d sess., 9 February 1970, 9.

19. For an illuminating study of these and other analysts (mostly oriented to economics), see Arnold J. Meltsner, *Policy Analysts in the Bureaucracy* (Berkeley: University of California Press, 1976).

20. Lawrence J. Korb, "Ordeal of PPBS in the Pentagon," *Bureaucrat* 17 (Fall 1988): 19–21.

21. Charles E. Lindblom, "Still Muddling, Not Yet Through," *Public Administration Review* 39 (November–December 1979): 518. Lindblom himself has been subjected to vigorous counterattack.

22. To make matters worse, "rational decision makers" never use all the information they get, yet continue to seek even more. See Martha S. Feldman and James G. March, "Information in Organizations and Signal and Symbol," *Administrative Science Quarterly* 26 (1981): 171–186.

23. James G. March and Herbert A. Simon, *Organizations* (New York: Wiley, 1958), 140–141.

24. See Steven E. Rhoads, ed., *Valuing Life: Public Policy Dilemmas* (Boulder: Westview, 1980).

25. Lewis M. Branscomb, "Science in the White House: A New Start," *Science* 196 (May 20, 1977): 848–852. To protect the snail darters, a court injunction enforcing the Endangered Species Act held up an almost completed $120 million Tennessee Valley Authority (TVA) water project. *Tennessee Valley Authority v. Hill,* 437 U.S. 153 (1978). Congress then established a review commission to grant exemptions from the act, but the commission refused to exempt the TVA project. In 1979, Congress itself voted the exemption.

26. Arthur M. Okun, *Equality and Efficiency: The Big Tradeoff* (Washington, D.C.: Brookings Institution, 1975), 2.

27. Murray Weidenbaum, *The Modern Public Sector* (New York: Basic Books, 1969), 178.

28. The most persuasive and comprehensive descriptions and defenses of the incremental decision-making model are by Charles E. Lindblom. A good, brief statement is his "The Science of 'Muddling Through,'" *Public Administration Review* 19 (Spring 1959): 79–88. The model is further elaborated in *The Intelligence of Democracy: Decision Making through Mutual Adjustment* (New York: Free Press, 1965); *Politics and Markets: The World's Political-Economic Systems* (New York: Basic Books, 1977), 314–324; and *The Policy-Making Process,* 2nd ed. (Englewood Cliffs, N.J.: Prentice Hall, 1980). He responds to criticisms of the model in "Still Muddling, Not Yet Through."

29. The incremental approach, moreover, has not been limited to politics. For applications to business decision making, see James Brian Quinn, "Strategic Change: 'Logical Incrementalism,'" *Sloan Management Review* (Fall 1978): 7–21; "Strategic Goals: Process and Politics," *Sloan Management Review* (Fall 1977): 21–37; and "Managing Strategic Change," *Sloan Management Review* (Summer 1980): 3–20, in which Quinn promotes Lindblom's "muddling-through" approach.

30. The bargaining model has also spun off several related procedures, most notably the "garbage can" approach, in which participants dump problems and solutions into a garbage can; decisions are not made but rather "occur," in response to many ambiguous values and objectives. See Michael Cohen, James March, and Johan Olsen, "A Garbage Can Model of Organizational

Choice," *Administrative Science Quarterly* 17 (March 1972): 1–25.

31. Robert Kennedy's dramatic first-person memoir of the crisis, *Thirteen Days* (New York: Norton, 1969), provides a detailed description of the events. For an analytical version, see Graham T. Allison, *Essence of Decision: Explaining the Cuban Missile Crisis* (Boston: Little, Brown, 1971), from which the discussion that follows is drawn. In particular, see Chapter 6.

32. Allison, *Essence of Decision*, 6.

33. Ibid., 203.

34. Ibid., 145.

35. The aphorism, first discussed in Chapter 5, is credited to Rufus Miles and is often known as "Miles's Law." See Rufus E. Miles, "The Origin and Meaning of Miles' Law," *Public Administration Review* 38 (September–October 1978): 399–403. See also Allison, *Essence of Decision,* 176.

36. For another case study of bargaining in decision making, see the study by two *Wall Street Journal* reporters of the passage of the tax reform act of 1986: Jeffrey H. Birnbaum and Alan S. Murray, *Showdown at Gucci Gulch: Lawmaking, Lobbyists, and the Unlikely Triumph of Tax Reform* (New York: Random House, 1987).

37. See Charles L. Schultze, *The Politics and Economics of Public Spending* (Washington, D.C.: Brookings Institution, 1968).

38. Ibid., 76. (Emphasis in original.)

39. For a thoughtful treatment of this and related matters, see Alexander L. George, "The Case for Multiple Advocacy in Making Foreign Policy," *American Political Science Review* 66 (September 1972): 751–785; and his *Decision Making in Foreign Policy: The Effective Use of Information and Advice* (Boulder, Colo.: Westview, 1980).

40. Leonard S. Lyon and others, *The National Recovery Administration* (Washington, D.C.: Brookings Institution, 1935).

41. Edythe W. First, *Industry and Labor Advisory Committees in the National Defense Advisory Commission and the Office of Production Management, May 1940 to January 1942* (Washington, D.C.: Civilian Production Administration, 1946); selected portions appear in *Public Administration: Readings and Documents,* ed. Felix A. Nigro (New York: Holt, 1951), 406–426. See also Harvey C. Mansfield, *A Short History of OPA* (Washington, D.C.: Government Printing Office, 1948), 311; and Allan R. Richards, *War Labor Boards in the Field* (Chapel Hill: University of North Carolina Press, 1953).

42. Grant McConnell, *Private Power and American Democracy* (New York: Knopf, 1966), 276–279. For a more recent look at the role of interest groups in decision making, see Jeffrey M. Berry, *The Interest Group Society* (Boston: Little, Brown, 1984).

43. Adam Smith, *The Wealth of Nations,* Everyman's ed. (London: Dent, 1910), 1:117.

44. See National Academy of Sciences (Committee on the Utilization of Young Scientists and Engineers in Advisory Services to Government, National Research Council), The Science Committee, *Report* and (separately) *Appendixes* (Washington, D.C.: National Academy of Sciences, 1972); and Thane Gustafson, "The Controversy over Peer Review," *Science* 190 (December 12, 1975): 1060–1066.

45. "The President's War on Advisory Committees," *National Journal,* May 12, 1979, 800; U.S. Comptroller General, *Better Evaluations Needed to Weed Out Useless Federal Advisory Committees* (Washington, D.C.: General Accounting Office, 1977); Kit Gage and Samuel S. Epstein, "The Federal Advisory Committee System: An Assessment," *Environmental Law Reporter* 7 (February 1977): 50, 101–112; and Henry Steck, "Private Influence on Environmental Policy: The Case of the National Industrial Pollution Control Council," *Environmental Law Reporter* 5 (Winter 1975): 241–248.

46. An illuminating case study is Don F. Hadwiger and Ross B. Talbot, *Pressures and Protests: The Kennedy Farm Program and the Wheat Referendum of 1963* (San Francisco: Chandler, 1965).

47. Imogene H. Putnam, *Volunteers in OPA,* issued by Office of Price Administration, U.S. Office of Temporary Controls (Washington, D.C.: Government Printing Office, 1947); and James W. Davis and Kenneth M. Dolbeare, *Little Groups of Neighbors: The Selective Service System* (Chicago: Markham, 1968). Membership of OPA's local boards totaled 125,000; Selective Service Boards, 17,000.

48. Agricultural Stabilization and Conservation Service, *U.S. Department of Agriculture, Programs and Services* (Washington, D.C.: Information Division, Agricultural Stabilization and Conservation Service, 1977), 17. See also the service's *Farmer Committee Administration of Agricultural Programs* (Washington, D.C.: Agricultural Stabilization and Conservation Service, 1975).

49. U.S. Department of Agriculture, *Review of the Farmer Committee System: Report of the Study Committee* (Washington, D.C.: Agricultural Stabilization and Conservation Service, U.S. Department of Agriculture, 1962), Pt. 4, 132.

50. McConnell, *Private Power and American Democracy,* 207, 210–211.

51. *New York Times,* December 5, 1988, B1.

52. *New York Times,* December 16, 1986, B8.

53. The most comprehensive survey, covering 269 case studies of decentralization in urban areas, is Robert K. Yin and Douglas Yates, *Street-Level Governments* (Lexington, Mass.: Lexington Books, 1975). For private interest groups' participation in national and state administration, McConnell, *Private Power and American Democracy* is the classic source.

54. "Microeconomists" deal with decision making by individuals and organizations; "macroeconomists," in contrast, study the broad economy of society, including governmental finance.

55. For the roots of the theory, see Anthony Downs, *An Economic Theory of Democracy* (New York: Harper and Row, 1957); James M. Buchanan and Gordon Tullock, *The Calculus of Consent* (Ann Arbor: University of Michigan Press, 1962); Gordon Tullock, *The Politics of Bureaucracy* (Washington, D.C.: Public Affairs Press, 1965); Anthony Downs, *Inside Bureaucracy* (Boston: Little, Brown, 1967); and William A. Niskanen, *Bureaucracy and Representative Government* (Chicago: Aldine-Atherton, 1971).

56. For a discussion, see the "Symposium on Privatization," *International Review of Administrative Sciences* 54 (December 1988): 501–583.

57. Stuart Butler, *Privatizing Federal Spending* (New York: Universe Books, 1985), 58, 166.

58. This discussion draws on Steven E. Rhoads, *The Economist's View of the World: Government, Markets, and Public Policy* (Cambridge: Cambridge University Press, 1985), 44–50; and Joseph E. Stiglitz, *Economics of the Public Sector* (New York: Norton, 1986), chap. 8.

59. For a review of market approaches in air pollution programs, see National Academy of Public Administration, *A Breath of Fresh Air: Reviving the New Source Review Program* (Washington, D.C.: NAPA, 2003).

60. Steven Kelman, "'Public Choice' and Public Spirit," *Public Interest* 87 (Spring 1987): 81.

61. Weidenbaum, *Modern Public Sector,* 178. More broadly, compare Rhoads, *The Economist's View of the World.*

62. See Robert B. Reich, ed., *The Power of Public Ideas* (Cambridge, Mass.: Ballinger, 1988).

63. See Ted Kolderie, "The Two Different Concepts of Privatization," *Public Administration Review* 46 (July–August 1986): 285–291; Ronald C. Moe, "Exploring the Limits of Privatization," *Public Administration Review* 47 (November–December 1987): 453–460; and James W. Fesler, "The State and Its Study: The Whole and Its Parts," *PS* 21 (Fall 1988): 891–901.

64. The American Federation of State, County, and Municipal Employees, for example, compiled a lengthy collection of stories illustrating that privatization-as-contracting often breeds its own problems. American Federation of State, County, and Municipal Employees, *Passing the Bucks* (Washington, D.C.: AFSCME, 1983); and *When Public Services Go Private: Not Always Better, Not*

Always Honest, There May Be a Better Way (Washington, D.C.: AFSCME, 1987).

65. Speech to Spring Meeting, National Academy of Public Administration, Washington, D.C., June 6, 1986.

66. James E. Webb, *Space Age Management: The Large-Scale Approach* (New York: McGraw-Hill, 1969), 136–137.

67. Irving L. Janis and Leon Mann, *Decision Making: A Psychological Analysis of Conflict, Choice, and Commitment* (New York: Free Press, 1977), 15.

68. See Donald F. Kettl, *Leadership at the Fed* (New Haven, Conn.: Yale University Press, 1986), 7–8.

69. *Science* 236 (April 17, 1987): 267–300, contains a useful symposium on the problems of risk and uncertainty in public policy; see R. Wilson and E. A. C. Crouch, "Risk Assessment and Comparisons: An Introduction"; B. N. Ames, R. Magaw, and L. S. Gold, "Ranking Possible Carcinogenic Hazards"; P. Slovic, "Perception of Risk"; M. Russell and M. Gruber, "Risk Assessment in Environmental Policy Making"; L. B. Lave, "Health and Safety Risk Analyses: Information for Better Decisions"; and D. Okrent, "The Safety Goals of the U.S. Nuclear Regulatory Commission."

70. Plutarch, *The Lives of the Noble Grecians and Romans* (New York: Modern Library, n.d.), 874.

71. See Peter M. Blau and W. Richard Scott, *Formal Organizations* (San Francisco: Chandler, 1962); Tullock, *Politics of Bureaucracy*, 137–141; Downs, *Inside Bureaucracy*, chap. 10; Harold L. Wilensky, *Organizational Intelligence* (New York: Basic Books, 1967), chap. 3; and Brian W. Hogwood and B. Guy Peters, *The Pathology of Public Policy* (Oxford: Oxford University Press, 1985), chap. 4.

72. Charles Peters, "From Ouagadougou to Cape Canaveral: Why the Bad News Doesn't Travel Up," *Washington Monthly*, April 1986, 27.

73. See Presidential Commission on the Space Shuttle *Challenger* Accident [Rogers Commission], *Report to the President*

(Washington, D.C.: Government Printing Office, 1986).

74. See *Columbia* Accident Investigation Board, *Final Report* (2003), http://www.nasa.gov/columbia/home/CAIB_Vol1.html.

75. Thomas J. Peters and Robert H. Waterman Jr., *In Search of Excellence* (New York: Warner Books, 1982).

76. See Downs, *Inside Bureaucracy*, 118–127, for a discussion of anti-distortion factors.

77. Hogwood and Peters, *Pathology of Public Policy*, 85.

78. House Committee on Science and Technology, *Investigation of the* Challenger *Accident*, Report, 99th Cong., 2d sess., 1986, 172.

79. Senate Report No. 91–411, *Federal Coal Mine Health and Safety Act of 1969*, 91st Cong., 1st sess., September 17, 1969, 5–6; Henry C. Hart, "Crisis, Community, and Consent in Water Politics," *Law and Contemporary Problems* 22 (Summer 1957): 510–537.

80. All rational (in the broad sense) models assume that crisis decisions made under severe time pressures are usually worse than those affording more time for data assemblage, specialists' advice, and deliberation. For the view that "a 'hasty' decision made under pressure may on average be better than a less urgent one," see Wilensky, *Organizational Intelligence*, 75–77. A full treatment of decision-making behavior under stress of crisis and shortness of time is provided by Janis and Mann, *Decision Making*, 45–67.

81. Irving L. Janis, *Crucial Decisions: Leadership in Policymaking and Crisis Management* (New York: Free Press, 1989).

82. See Amitai Etzioni, "Mixed Scanning: A Third Approach to Decision-Making," *Public Administration Review* 27 (December 1967): 385–392

11. Budgeting

1. For a broad look at the history of budgeting, see Carolyn Webber and Aaron Wildavsky, *A History of Taxation and Expenditures in*

the Western World (New York: Simon and Schuster, 1986). On what questions a theory of budgeting must answer, see V. O. Key Jr., "The Lack of a Budgetary Theory," *American Political Science Review* 34 (December 1940): 1237–1240; and Verne Lewis, "Toward a Theory of Budgeting," *Public Administration Review* 12 (Winter 1952): 42–54.

2. Key, "Lack of a Budgetary Theory," 1237.

3. See, for example, Herbert Stein, *Governing the $5 Trillion Economy* (New York: Basic Books, 1989).

4. Keynes is best known for *The General Theory of Employment, Interest, and Money* (1936; repr. New York: Harcourt Brace Jovanovich, 1964). On compensatory economics in the Roosevelt administration, see Donald F. Kettl, "Marriner Eccles and Leadership in the Federal Reserve System," in *Leadership and Innovation: A Biographical Perspective on Entrepreneurs in Government,* ed. Jameson W. Doig and Erwin C. Hargrove (Baltimore: Johns Hopkins University Press, 1987), 318–342.

5. See Herbert Stein, *The Fiscal Revolution in America* (Chicago: University of Chicago Press, 1969); and James E. Alt and K. Alec Chrystal, *Political Economics* (Berkeley: University of California Press, 1983), 54–77.

6. See Edward R. Tufte, *Political Control of the Economy* (Princeton, N.J.: Princeton University Press, 1978).

7. The Federal Reserve operates through three principal policy tools: fixing reserve requirements that banks must hold against deposits (the higher the reserves required, the less money banks can lend out, and thus the higher interest rates become and the more economic growth is slowed); setting the discount rate (the rate at which the Fed lends to banks, which then affects interest rates across the nation); and managing open-market operations (in which the Fed purchases government securities to increase the money supply—thus lowering interest rates and fueling economic growth—and buys securities to decrease the money supply—thus raising interest rates and slowing economic growth).

. The classic treatment of the history of monetary policy is Milton Friedman and Anna Jacobson Schwartz, *A Monetary History of the United States, 1867–1960* (Princeton, N.J.: Princeton University Press, 1963). For a favorable account of the Volcker era, see Donald F. Kettl, *Leadership at the Fed* (New Haven, Conn.: Yale University Press, 1986), chap. 7. William Greider, in *Secrets of the Temple: How the Federal Reserve Runs the Country* (New York: Simon and Schuster, 1987), takes a far more critical view.

8. Rudolph G. Penner and Alan J. Abramson, *Broken Purse Strings: Congressional Budgeting, 1974–88* (Washington, D.C.: Urban Institute Press, 1989), 99.

9. *Wall Street Journal,* August 21, 1986, 22.

10. An excellent survey of the federal budget process is Allen Schick, *The Federal Budget: Politics, Policy, Process* (Washington, D.C.: Brookings Institution, 1995).

11. For a history of these issues, see Leonard D. White, *The Federalists* (New York: Macmillan, 1956), 116–127; Frederick C. Mosher, *A Tale of Two Agencies: A Comparative Analysis of the General Accounting Office and the Office of Management and Budget* (Baton Rouge: Louisiana State University Press, 1984), 13–34; and Jerry L. McCaffery, "The Development of Public Budgeting in the United States," in *A Centennial History of the American Administrative State,* ed. Ralph Clark Chandler (New York: Free Press, 1987), 345–377.

12. See William F. Willoughby, *The Movement for Budgetary Reform in the States* (New York: Appleton, 1918).

13. In the wake of the Brownlow Committee's report (1937), the Bureau of the Budget was transferred from the Treasury Department to the newly established Executive Office of the President.

14. Mosher, *Tale of Two Agencies,* 32.

15. See David G. Mathiasen, "The Evolution of OMB," *Public Budgeting and Finance* 8 (Autumn 1988): 3–14; and Peter M. Benda and Charles H. Levine, "Reagan and the Bureaucracy: The Bequest, the Promise, and

the Legacy," in *The Reagan Legacy: Promise and Performance,* ed. Charles O. Jones (Chatham, N.J.: Chatham House, 1988), 102–142.

16. See Howard E. Shuman, *Politics and the Budget: The Struggle between the President and the Congress* (Englewood Cliffs, N.J.: Prentice Hall, 1984).

17. The federal budget is a two-inch-thick volume, the size of a large city's telephone directory, printed on very thin paper with tiny type. The task of publishing such a huge volume of information, in the quantities needed by members of Congress, the press, and interested members of the general public, preoccupies the Government Printing Office for more than a month each year. Copies of the budget are available at nearly all college and university libraries, usually in the government documents section.

18. See Lance T. LeLoup, "From Microbudgeting to Macrobudgeting: Evolution in Theory and Practice," in *New Directions in Budget Theory,* ed. Irene S. Rubin (Albany: State University of New York Press, 1988), 19–42.

19. On forecasting, see, for example, Larry D. Schroeder, "Forecasting Revenues and Expenditures," in *Management Policies in Local Government Finance,* ed. J. Richard Aronson and Eli Schwartz (Washington, D.C.: International City Management Association, 1981), 66–90. On the problems of forecasting the federal budget, see "Uncertainty and Bias in Budget Projections," in Congressional Budget Office, *The Economic and Budget Outlook: An Update* (Washington, D.C.: Government Printing Office, 1987), 63–86.

20. R. Douglas Arnold argues, for example, that congressional decisions may be used "partly as rewards for past support, partly as payments for support during the current year, and partly to create a favorable climate for future years." Arnold, *Congress and the Bureaucracy: A Theory of Influence* (New Haven, Conn.: Yale University Press, 1979), 56.

21. Aaron Wildavsky, *The New Politics of the Budgetary Process* (Glenview, Ill.: Scott Foresman, 1988), 83.

22. Wildavsky's work received support at the federal level by Otto A. Davis, M. A. H. Dempster, and Aaron Wildavsky, "A Theory of the Budgetary Process," *American Political Science Review* 60 (September 1966): 529–547; and at the state level by Ira Sharkansky, "Agency Requests, Gubernatorial Support and Budget Success in State Legislatures," *American Political Science Review* 62 (December 1968): 1220–1231. In his later work, Wildavsky moved away from incrementalism. For a discussion, see Irene Rubin, "Aaron Wildavsky and the Demise of Incrementalism," *Public Administration Review* 49 (January–February 1989): 78–81.

23. Lance T. LeLoup and William B. Moreland, "Agency Strategies and Executive Review: The Hidden Politics of Budgeting," *Public Administration Review* 38 (May–June 1978): 232–239; see also Peter B. Natchez and Irwin C. Bupp, "Policy and Priority in the Budgetary Process," *American Political Science Review* 67 (September 1973): 951–963.

24. Natchez and Bupp, "Policy and Priority in the Budgetary Process," 956, and, more generally, 951–963. On the role of entrepreneurs in building support for their programs, see *Leadership and Innovation: A Biographical Perspective,* ed. Doig and Hargrove.

25. Frank P. Sherwood and William J. Page Jr., "MBO and Public Management," *Public Administration Review* 36 (January–February 1976): 11. The Office of Management and Budget agrees; see Clifford W. Graves and Stefan A. Halper, "Federal Program Evaluation: The Perspective from OMB," in Senate Committee on Government Operations, *Legislative Oversight and Program Evaluation,* committee print, 94th Cong., 2d sess., 1976, 266–267. The MBO experience is perceptively analyzed in James A. Swiss, "Implementing Federal Programs: Administrative Systems and Organization Effectiveness" (PhD diss., Yale University, 1976). See also Richard Rose, *Managing Presidential Objectives* (New York: Free Press, 1976).

26. Peter A. Pyrrh introduced the system at Texas Instruments and helped Carter install it in Georgia. See his *Zero-Base Budgeting:*

A Practical Tool for Evaluating Expenses (New York: Wiley, 1973). More broadly, see "Forum: ZBB Revisited," *Bureaucrat* 7 (Spring 1978): 3–70; Thomas P. Lauth, "Zero-Base Budgeting in Georgia State Government: Myth and Reality," *Public Administration Review* 38 (September–October 1978): 420–430; and George Samuel Minmier, *An Evaluation of the Zero-Base Budgeting System in Governmental Institutions* (Atlanta: School of Business Administration, Georgia State University, 1975), excerpted in Senate Committee on Government Operations, Subcommittee on Intergovernmental Relations, *Compendium of Materials on Zero-base Budgeting,* committee print, 95th Cong., 1st sess., 1977.

27. Stanley B. Botner discusses the spread of PPBS, MBO, and ZBB, among other tools, in "The Use of Budgeting/Management Tools by State Governments," *Public Administration Review* 45 (September–October 1985): 616–620.

28. For an analysis of how congressional and presidential policies have differed, see Mark S. Kamlet and David C. Mowery, "Influences on Executive and Congressional Budgetary Priorities, 1955–1981," *American Political Science Review* 81 (March 1987): 155–178.

29. Carl J. Friedrich, *Man and His Government* (New York: McGraw-Hill, 1963), 199–215.

30. For a catalog of the many strategies used in the budget game, see Wildavsky, *New Politics of the Budgetary Process,* 21–62.

31. *Congressional Budget and Impoundment Control Act of 1974,* Public Law 93-344, 88 Stat. 337. For an analysis of the act's effects on Congress, see Dennis S. Ippolito, *Congressional Spending* (Ithaca, N.Y.: Cornell University Press, 1981); and Allen Schick, *Congress and Money: Budgeting, Spending, and Taxes* (Washington, D.C.: Urban Institute Press, 1980).

32. Bill Sweetman, "Is There Too Much Secrecy?" *Aviation Week & Space Technology,* December 3, 2012, http://www.aviationweek.com/Article.aspx?id=/article-xml/AW_12_03_2012_p02-521102.xml.

33. Todd Harrison, *Analysis of the FY2011 Defense Budget* (Washington, D.C.: Center for Strategic and Budgetary Assessments, 2010), http://www.csbaonline.org/4Publications/PubLibrary/R.20100629.Analysis_of_the_FY/R.20100629.Analysis_of_the_FY.pdf.

34. David C. Morrison, "Truth Elusive in 'Black' Maze," *National Journal,* October 10, 1987, 2552.

35. William J. Broad, "Inside the Black Budget," *New York Times,* April 1, 2008, http://www.nytimes.com/2008/04/01/science/01patc.html?pagewanted=all&_r=0.

36. Philip G. Joyce, *The Costs of Budget Uncertainty: Analyzing the Impact of Late Appropriations* (Washington, D.C.: IBM Center for the Business of Government, 2012), 12, http://www.businessofgovernment.org/report/costs-budget-uncertainty-analyzing-impact-late-appropriations.

37. Ibid., 9.

38. David A. Fahrenthold and Lisa Rein, "They Said the Sequester Would Be Scary. Mostly, They Were Wrong," *Washington Post,* June 30, 2013, http://www.washingtonpost.com/politics/they-said-the-sequester-would-be-scary-mostly-they-were-wrong/2013/06/30/73bdbbfc-da7a-11e2-8ed8-7adf8eba6e9a_story.html.

39. "Sequester Has Caused Much Chaos," *Washington Post,* July 5, 2013, http://www.washingtonpost.com/opinions/sequester-has-caused-much-chaos/2013/07/04/5672c82a-e2be-11e2-8657-fdff0c195a79_story.html.

40. These photographs can be viewed at http://newswatch.nationalgeographic.com/2013/10/16/nasa-shutdown-unleashes-beautiful-astronaut-photos-on-twitter/.

41. Liu Chang, "Commentary: U.S. Fiscal Failure Warrants a De-Americanized World," *Xinhua News Service* (October 13, 2013), http://news.xinhuanet.com/english/indepth/2013-10/13/c_132794246.htm?utm_source=The+Sinocism+China+Newsletter&utm_campaign=725c8d2fea-Sinocism10_14_131&utm_medium

=email&utm_term=0_171f237867-725c8d2fea-24573061

42. NBCNews, "Congress: McConnell: No Need for a Second 'Mule Kick,'" (October 18, 2013), http://firstread.nbcnews.com/_news/2013/10/18/21023857-congress-mcconnell-no-need-for-a-second-mule-kick

43. Barack Obama, "Remarks by the President on the Reopening of the Government," (October 17, 2013), http://www.whitehouse.gov/the-press-office/2013/10/17/remarks-president-reopening-government

44. Jonathan Rauch, "The Fiscal Ice Age," *National Journal,* January 10, 1987, 58. For an appraisal of the process, see Donald F. Kettl, *Deficit Politics: The Search for Balance in American Politics,* 2nd ed. (New York: Longman, 2003); Wildavsky, *New Politics of the Budgetary Process*; Schick, *Congress and Money*; Allen Schick, ed., *Making Economic Policy in Congress* (Washington, D.C.: American Enterprise Institute, 1983); and Allen Schick, *The Capacity to Budget* (Washington, D.C.: Urban Institute Press, 1990).

45. Lawrence J. Haas, "If All Else Fails, Reform," *National Journal,* July 4, 1987, 1713.

46. House Committee on the Budget, *Congressional Control of Expenditures,* Report prepared by Allen Schick, committee print, 95th Cong., 1st sess., 1977, 126.

47. Louis Fisher, *Presidential Spending Power* (Princeton, N.J.: Princeton University Press, 1975), 176. See 147–201 for a detailed analysis of presidential impoundment. This chapter has drawn heavily on this account for the discussion.

48. This discussion draws on Robert N. Anthony and David W. Young, *Management Control in Nonprofit Organizations,* 4th ed. (Homewood, Ill.: Irwin, 1988), esp. 3–49.

49. Ibid., 21. (Emphasis in the original omitted.)

50. U.S. Comptroller General, *Financial Integrity Act: Continuing Efforts Needed to Improve Internal Control and Accounting Systems* (Washington, D.C.: General Accounting Office, 1987). See also these other GAO reports: *Financial Management: Examples of Weaknesses* (Washington, D.C.: GAO, 1988); and *Managing the Cost of Government: Building an Effective Financial Management Structure* (Washington, D.C.: GAO, 1985).

51. For an examination of these issues, see Leo Herbert, Larry N. Killough, and Alan Walter Steiss, *Governmental Accounting and Control* (Monterey, Calif.: Brooks/Cole, 1984); and Leon E. Hay, *Accounting for Governmental and Nonprofit Entities,* 8th ed. (Homewood, Ill.: Irwin, 1989).

52. For example, see Oregon Progress Board, *Oregon Benchmarks: Standards for Measuring Statewide Progress and Institutional Performance* (Salem: Oregon Progress Board, 1994).

53. See, for example, General Accounting Office, *Managing for Results: State Experiences Provide Insights for Federal Management Reforms,* GGD-95-22 (Washington, D.C.: GAO, 1994); and John J. DiIulio et al., *Performance Measures for the Criminal Justice System* (Washington, D.C.: Bureau of Justice Statistics, 1993).

12. Implementation

1. Woodrow Wilson, "The Study of Administration," *Political Science Quarterly* 2 (June 1887): 212.

2. Jeffrey L. Pressman and Aaron B. Wildavsky, *Implementation* (Berkeley: University of California Press, 1973). They cite their debt to an earlier work on implementation by Martha Derthick, *New Towns In-Town* (Washington, D.C.: Urban Institute, 1972).

3. Pressman and Wildavsky, *Implementation,* xv.

4. Randall B. Ripley and Grace A. Franklin, *Policy Implementation and Bureaucracy,* 2nd ed. (Chicago: Dorsey Press, 1986), 2.

5. Daniel A. Mazmanian and Paul A. Sabatier, *Implementation and Public Policy* (Glenview, Ill.: Scott Foresman, 1983), 277. See also Eugene Bardach, *The Implementation Game: What Happens after a Bill Becomes a Law* (Cambridge, Mass.: MIT Press, 1977).

6. Brian W. Hogwood and B. Guy Peters, *The Pathology of Public Policy* (Oxford: Clarendon Press, 1985).

7. For a spirited rebuttal to the literature of failure, see Sar A. Levitan and Robert Taggart, *The Promise of Greatness* (Cambridge, Mass.: Harvard University Press, 1976). See also Henry J. Aaron, *Politics and the Professors: The Great Society in Perspective* (Washington, D.C.: Brookings Institution, 1978); Robert H. Haveman, ed., *A Decade of Federal Antipoverty Programs: Achievements, Failures, and Lessons* (New York: Academic Press, 1977); and Malcolm L. Goggin, Ann O'M. Bowman, James P. Lester, and Laurence J. O'Toole, *Implementation Theory and Practice: Toward a Third Generation* (Glenview, Ill.: Scott Foresman/Little, Brown, 1990).

8. See Daniel P. Moynihan, *Maximum Feasible Misunderstanding: Community Action in the War on Poverty* (New York: Free Press, 1970).

9. Housing and Community Development Act of 1974, 88 U.S. Statute 633.

10. Ripley and Franklin, *Policy Implementation and Bureaucracy*, 22–23.

11. Martin A. Levin and Barbara Ferman, *The Political Hand: Policy Implementation and Youth Employment Programs* (New York: Pergamon Press, 1985), 72–73.

12. See Ross Douthat, "Rumsfeld's Rules Revisited," *The Atlantic*, September 1, 2004, http://www.theatlantic.com/magazine/archive/2004/09/rumsfeld-s-rules-revisited/303425. For an examination of these rules, see Jeffrey A. Krames, *The Rumsfeld Way: The Leadership Wisdom of a Battle-Hardened Maverick* (New York: McGraw-Hill, 2002).

13. Norman R. Augustine, *Augustine's Laws* (New York: Viking, 1986), 313.

14. Stephen Percy, *Disability, Civil Rights, and Public Policy: The Politics of Implementation* (Tuscaloosa: University of Alabama Press, 1990).

15. See Giandomenico Majone and Aaron Wildavsky, "Implementation as Evolution," in Jeffrey L. Pressman and Aaron Wildavsky, *Implementation*, 3rd ed. (Berkeley: University of California Press, 1984), 163–180.

16. Paul Berman, "The Study of Macro- and Micro-Implementation," *Public Policy* 26 (Spring 1978): 165.

17. Elliot Richardson, *The Creative Balance* (New York: Holt, Rinehart and Winston, 1976), 128.

18. Robert Stevens and Rosemary Stevens, *Welfare Medicine in America: A Study of Medicaid* (New York: Free Press, 1974), 73.

19. Richardson, *Creative Balance*, 130, 132–134.

20. W. John Moore, "Mandates without Money," *National Journal*, October 4, 1986, 2366.

21. Paul Manna, *Collision Course: Federal Education Policy Meets State and Local Realities* (Washington, D.C.: CQ Press, 2010).

22. See Mazmanian and Sabatier, *Implementation and Public Policy*, 24.

23. Quoted in Louis M. Kohlmeier, "Banking Reform Chances Grow Dimmer," *National Journal*, September 20, 1975, 1341.

24. Ralph Waldo Emerson, "Self-Reliance," in *Essays*, Emerson (Boston: Houghton Mifflin, 1865, 1876, 1883), 62.

25. See Jameson W. Doig and Erwin C. Hargrove, eds., *Leadership and Innovation* (Baltimore: Johns Hopkins University Press, 1987); John Kingdon, *Agendas, Alternatives, and Public Policies* (Boston: Little, Brown, 1984), 129–130; Eugene Bardach, *Implementation Game*, 274–275. See also Levin and Ferman, *Political Hand*, 5.

26. James Q. Wilson, "The Bureaucracy Problem," *Public Interest* 6 (Spring 1967): 7. See also his *Bureaucracy: What Government Agencies Do and Why They Do It* (New York: Basic Books, 1989).

27. Pressman and Wildavsky, *Implementation*, 1, 31, 48, 100. All quotations come from this source.

28. See Donald F. Kettl, *The Next Government of the United States: Why Our Institutions Fail Us and How to Fix Them* (New York: Norton, 2009).

29. Murray L. Weidenbaum, *The Modern Public Sector: New Ways of Doing the Government's Business* (New York: Basic Books, 1969), 4. See also Bruce L. R. Smith, "Changing Public-Private Sector Relations: A Look at the United States," *Annals of the American*

Academy of Political and Social Sciences 466 (March 1983): 149–164.

30. See Lester M. Salamon, "Rethinking Public Management: Third-Party Government and the Changing Forms of Government Action," *Public Policy* 29 (1981): 255–275; and Donald F. Kettl, *Government by Proxy: (Mis?)Managing Federal Programs* (Washington, D.C.: CQ Press, 1988).

31. Martha Derthick, *The Influence of Federal Grants: Public Assistance in Massachusetts* (Cambridge, Mass.: Harvard University Press, 1970), 197.

32. Advisory Commission on Intergovernmental Relations, *A Catalog of Federal Grant-in-Aid Programs to State and Local Governments: Grants Funded FY 1978* (Washington, D.C.: Government Printing Office, 1979).

33. Office of Management and Budget, *Budget, Fiscal Year 1988: Special Analyses*, H-25.

34. See General Accounting Office, *Fundamental Changes Are Needed in Federal Assistance to State and Local Governments* (Washington, D.C.: Government Printing Office, 1975), 12.

35. See, for example, Donald F. Kettl, *The Regulation of American Federalism* (Baltimore: Johns Hopkins University Press, 1987); Advisory Commission on Intergovernmental Relations, *Regulatory Federalism: Policy, Process, Impact and Reform* (Washington, D.C.: Government Printing Office, 1984); and Edward I. Koch, "The Mandate Millstone," *Public Interest* 61 (Fall 1980): 42–57.

36. Congress reversed itself in 1996 and allowed states to increase the speed limit back to 65 miles per hour.

37. For an examination, see Joseph F. Zimmerman, *Federal Preemption: The Silent Revolution* (Ames: Iowa State University Press, 1991).

38. See Martha Derthick, *Uncontrollable Spending for Social Services Grants* (Washington, D.C.: Brookings Institution, 1975).

39. Michael D. Reagan, "Accountability and Independence in Federal Grants-in-Aid," in *The New Political Economy: The Public Use of the Private Sector,* ed. Bruce L. R. Smith (New York: Wiley, 1975), 206.

40. Pew Charitable Trusts, American Cities Initiative, *The Local Squeeze: Falling Revenues and Growing Demand for Services Challenge Cities, Counties, and School Districts* (June 1, 2012), http://www.pew-states.org/research/reports/the-local-squeeze-85899388655.

41. Robert P. Stoker, *Reluctant Partners: Implementing Federal Policy* (Pittsburgh: University of Pittsburgh Press, 1991).

42. See John D. Hanrahan, *Government by Contract* (New York: Norton, 1983), esp. chap. 3.

43. Danny Werfel, Controller of the Office of Federal Financial Management, The White House, "Contracting Smarter, Saving More," February 24, 2012, http://www.whitehouse.gov/blog/2012/02/24/contracting-smarter-saving-more.

44. Ibid.

45. P. W. Singer, *Corporate Warriors: The Rise of the Privatized Military Industry* (Ithaca, N.Y.: Cornell University Press, 2003).

46. Peter W. Singer, "Beyond the Law," *Guardian,* May 3, 2004, http://www.guardian.co.uk/comment/story/0,3604,1208237,00.html.

47. James Risen, "Afghans Linked to the Taliban Guard U.S. Bases," *New York Times,* October 7, 2010, http://www.nytimes.com/2010/10/08/world/asia/08contractor.html?_r=2. See also Congressional Research Service, *Department of Defense Contractors in Iraq and Afghanistan: Background and Analysis* (Washington, D.C.: Congressional Research Service, 2010), http://www.fas.org/sgp/crs/natsec/R40764.pdf.

48. President's Private Sector Survey on Cost Control, *Report on Privatization* (Washington, D.C.: Government Printing Office, 1983), 1. Compare President's Commission on Privatization, *Privatization: Toward More Effective Government* (Washington, D.C.: Government Printing Office, 1988).

49. General Services Administration, Federal Procurement Data Center, *Federal Procurement Data System: Fiscal Year 1993*

(Washington, D.C.: Government Printing Office, 1994), 13.

50. Steve Coll and Judith Havemann, "Dispute Threatens U.S. Phone Contract," *Washington Post,* July 31, 1987, B1. See also Donald F. Kettl, *Sharing Power: Public Governance and Private Markets* (Washington, D.C.: Brookings Institution, 1993), chap. 4.

51. Amy Svitak, "Boeing Lobbying on Tankers Faces Critical Review on the Hill," *Government Executive,* September 2, 2003, http://www.govexec.com/dailyfed /0903/090203cd1.htm.

52. For scathing critiques, see Garry Brewer, *Politicians, Bureaucrats, and the* Consultant (New York: Basic Books, 1973); Daniel Guttman and Barry Wilner, *The Shadow Government: The Government's Multi-Billion-Dollar Giveaway of Its Decision-Making Powers to Private Management Consultants, "Experts," and Think Tanks* (New York: Pantheon, 1976); and John D. Hanrahan, *Government by Contract.* For a broad look at the evidence, see John D. Donahue, *The Privatization Decision: Public Ends, Private Means* (New York: Basic Books, 1989).

53. Senate Armed Services Committee, *Defense Organization: The Need for Change,* staff report, 99th Cong., 1st sess., 1985, 558. For one example, see Nick Kotz, *Wild Blue Yonder: Money, Politics, and the B-1 Bomber* (New York: Pantheon, 1988).

54. Edward R. Luttwak, *The Pentagon and the Art of War* (New York: Simon and Schuster, 1984), 184.

55. *New York Times,* June 15, 1986, sec. 3, 4.

56. American Federation of State, County, and Municipal Employees, *Passing the Bucks* (Washington, D.C.: AFSCME, 1983), 38.

57. General Accounting Office, *General Services Administration: Actions Needed to Stop Buying Supplies from Poor-Performing Vendors,* GGD-93–34 (January 1993), 2, 4.

58. AFSCME, *Passing the Bucks,* 69.

59. Selwyn Raab, "U.S. Indicts Ten Road Contractors on Bids," *New York Times,* June 26, 1987, B1.

60. W. John Moore, "Grass-Roots Graft," *National Journal,* August 1, 1987, 1963, 1966.

61. AFSCME, *Passing the Bucks,* 69–70.

62. Josh Barbanel, "Wedtech: Rise and Fall of a Well-Connected Bronx Company," *New York Times,* January 19, 1987, B1; George Lardner Jr., "Wedtech Going Out of Business," *Washington Post,* July 25, 1987, A5.

63. Effective contracting requires careful management. For a discussion of this problem, see John A. Rehfuss, *Contracting Out in Government: A Guide to Working with Outside Contractors to Supply Public Services* (San Francisco: Jossey-Bass, 1989).

64. Office of Management and Budget, Circular No. A-76, revised March 29, 1979.

65. Sean Reilly, "Report: 4.9 Million Feds, Contractors Hold Security Clearances," *Federal Times,* June 23, 2012, http://www.federaltimes.com/article/20120723/PERSONNEL01/307230002/Report-4-9-million-feds-contractors-hold-security-clearances.

66. Herbert Kaufman, *Administrative Feedback: Monitoring Subordinates' Behavior* (Washington, D.C.: Brookings Institution, 1973), 2.

67. Pressman and Wildavsky, *Implementation.*

68. Keith Schneider, "Ex-Nuclear Aides Deny Being Told of Plant Mishaps," *New York Times,* October 5, 1988, A26.

69. Kaufman, *Administrative Feedback,* chap. 3. See also Myron Peretz Glazer and Penina Migdal Glazer, *The Whistleblowers: Exposing Corruption in Government and Industry* (New York: Basic Books, 1989).

70. James Hirsch, "Singer Case Whistle-Blower Says Decision Was Difficult," *New York Times,* March 16, 1989, D1.

71. Carol H. Weiss, *Evaluation Research: Methods of Assessing Program Effectiveness* (Englewood Cliffs, N.J.: Prentice Hall, 1972), 2.

72. See, for example, ibid.; Donald T. Campbell and Julian C. Stanley, *Experimental and Quasi-Experimental Designs for Research* (Chicago: Rand McNally, 1966); and Joseph S. Wholey, Harry P. Hatry, and Kathryn E. Newcomer, eds., *Handbook of Practical Program Evaluation* (San Francisco: Jossey-Bass, 1994).

73. See Harry Hatry, Richard E. Winnie, and Donald M. Fisk, *Practical Program Evaluation for State and Local Governments,* 2nd ed. (Washington, D.C.: Urban Institute Press, 1981); and Joseph S. Wholey, Kathryn E. Newcomer, and Associates, *Improving Government Performance: Evaluation Strategies for Strengthening Public Agencies and Programs* (San Francisco: Jossey-Bass, 1989).

74. See Giandomenico Majone, "Policy Analysis and Public Deliberation," in *The Power of Public Ideas,* ed. Robert B. Reich (Cambridge, Mass.: Ballinger, 1988), 173.

75. An excellent summary of CompStat is *Assertive Policing, Plummeting Crime: The NYPD Takes on Crime,* C16–99–1530.0 (Cambridge, Mass.: Kennedy School of Government Case Program, Harvard University, 1999).

76. Baltimore CitiStat, http://www.baltimorecity.gov/Government/AgenciesDepartments/CitiStat.aspx.

77. See eVA: Virginia's Total e-Procurement Solution, http://www.eva.state.va.us.

78. Robert D. Behn, *The PerformanceStat Potential: A Leadership Strategy for Producing Results* (Washington, D.C.: Brookings Institution Press, 2014).

79. Quoted in Conradi, "Leadership, Process, and People."

80. Jody Zall Kusek, Marelize Gorgens Prestidge, and Billy C. Hamilton, *Fail-Safe Management: Five Rules to Avoid Project Failure* (Washington, D.C.: World Bank, 2013), 2.

81. Ibid., 10–11.

82. For one effort, see James D. Carroll, "Public Administration in the Third Century of the Constitution: Supply-Side Management, Privatization, or Public Investment?" *Public Administration Review* 47 (January–February 1987): 106–114.

13. Regulation and the Courts

1. Jack Curry, "Yankee Stadium Gets One Last All-Star Game," *New York Times,* February 1, 2007, http://www.nytimes.com/2007/02/01/sports/baseball/01base.html?_r=0.

2. William K. Rashbaum, "Company Hired to Test Concrete Faces Scrutiny," *New York Times,* June 21, 2008, http://www.nytimes.com/2008/06/21/nyregion/21concrete.html?scp=2&sq=concrete&st=nyt.

3. U.S. Constitution, Art. 1, § 8, cl. 8. The current statute permits "fair use" of copyrighted material; the term's reach is judicially determined in individual cases.

4. Keith Schneider, "Biotechnology Advances Make Life Hard for Patent Office," *New York Times,* April 17, 1988.

5. For a more developed analysis, see *The Politics of Regulation,* ed. James Q. Wilson (New York: Basic Books, 1980), 364–372.

6. See Philip K. Howard, *The Death of Common Sense* (New York: Random House, 1994).

7. David Vogel, *National Styles of Regulation: Environmental Policy in Great Britain and the United States* (Ithaca, N.Y.: Cornell University Press, 1986), 267.

8. The best guide to each regulatory agency's activities, including problems encountered, is the *Federal Regulatory Directory,* 11th ed. (Washington, D.C.: CQ Press, 2003). In particular, see the section on the regulatory process.

9. For the development of Interstate Commerce Commission railroad regulation to 1920, see Stephen Skowronek, *Building a New American State: The Expansion of National Administrative Capacities, 1877–1920* (New York: Cambridge University Press, 1982), 248–284.

10. The classic work on the capture phenomenon is Marver H. Bernstein, *Regulating Business by Independent Commission* (Princeton, N.J.: Princeton University Press, 1955).

11. Our treatment draws on Michael D. Reagan, *Regulation: The Politics of Policy* (Boston: Little, Brown, 1987), 38–40.

12. For an insightful account and analysis of the deregulation movement, see Martha Derthick and Paul Quirk, *The Politics of Deregulation* (Washington, D.C.: Brookings Institution, 1985).

13. See National Academy of Public Administration, *A Breath of Fresh Air: Reviving the*

New Source Review Program (Washington, D.C.: NAPA, 2003).

14. Regulatory inspectors' roles and performance are a major subject of Eugene Bardach and Robert A. Kagan, *Going by the Book: The Problem of Regulatory Unreasonableness*, a Twentieth Century Fund report (Philadelphia: Temple University Press, 1982).

15. See General Accounting Office, *Occupational Safety and Health: Assuring Accuracy in Employer Injury and Illness Records* (Washington, D.C.: Government Printing Office, 1988).

16. See Reagan, *Regulation*, 203–204; and Kenneth J. Meier, *Regulation: Politics, Bureaucracy, and Economics* (New York: St. Martin's Press, 1985), esp. 175–201, on occupational licensing.

17. See, especially, Reagan, *Regulation*, 178–202; Donald F. Kettl, *The Regulation of American Federalism* (Baton Rouge: Louisiana State University Press, 1983); and Advisory Commission on Intergovernmental Relations (ACIR), *Regulatory Federalism: Policy, Process, Impact and Reform* (Washington, D.C.: Government Printing Office, 1984).

18. ACIR, *Regulatory Federalism*, 9–10, 82–88.

19. Ibid., 82.

20. However, individuals claiming entitlement to benefits under federal statutes that a state fails to provide may sue to obtain the benefits for themselves and others with like entitlements. *Maine v. Thiboutot*, 448 U.S. 1 (1979).

21. 21 U.S. Code of Federal Regulations 348, 360b, 576.

22. *Public Citizen v. Young*, 831 F.2d [Federal Circuit Court for the District of Columbia, 1987], 1108. The FDA's revisionary efforts and the court's decision are fully treated in Richard A. Merrill, "FDA's Implementation of the Delaney Clause: Repudiation of Congressional Choice or Reasoned Adaptation to Scientific Progress?" *Yale Journal on Regulation* 5 (Winter 1988): 1–88.

23. Reagan, *Regulation*, 96–97.

24. Lee M. Thomas, EPA administrator, address to the National Academy of Public Administration, June 6, 1986. Compare, on EPA's and other agencies' deadlines, *Congressional Oversight of Regulatory Agencies: The Need to Strike a Balance and Focus on Performance* (Washington, D.C.: National Academy of Public Administration, 1988), 20.

25. See R. Shep Melnick, *Regulation and the Courts: The Case of the Clean Air Act* (Washington, D.C.: Brookings Institution, 1983), 38–43, 258–261; and William F. West, "The Growth of Internal Conflict in Administrative Regulation," *Public Administration Review* 48 (July–August 1988): 773–782.

26. For a detailed critique, see Reagan, *Regulation*, 123–131.

27. David A. Fahrenthold, "Cosmic Markdown: EPA Says Life Is Worth Less," *New York Times*, July 19, 2008, A1.

28. Frank Ackerman and Lisa Heinzerling, *Priceless: On Knowing the Price of Everything and the Value of Nothing* (New York: New Press, 2004), 9.

29. One of many provocative points made by Aaron Wildavsky, *Searching for Safety* (New Brunswick, N.J.: Transaction, 1988). The risk assessment literature is large. Entry to it and the issues may be pursued through ibid.; Charles Perrow, *Normal Accidents: Living with High-Risk Technologies* (New York: Basic Books, 1984); and Leroy C. Gould et al., *Perceptions of Technological Risks and Benefits* (New York: Russell Sage Foundation, 1988).

30. Peter Passell, "Life's Risks: Balancing Fear against Reality of Statistics," *New York Times*, May 8, 1989, and "Making a Risky Life Bearable: Better Data, Clearer Choices," *New York Times*, May 8 and 9, 1989; Adam Clymer, "Polls Show Contrasts in How Public and EPA View Environment," *New York Times*, May 22, 1989; and Cathy Marie Johnson, "New Agencies: What They Do and Why They Do It—The Case of the Consumer Product Safety Commission," paper prepared for the 84th annual meeting of the American Political Science Association, September 1–4, 1988.

31. For an argument that courts have moved to substantive review of regulatory agencies' actions, see Martin Shapiro, "The Supreme Court's 'Return' to Economic Regulation," in *Studies in American Political Development* (New Haven, Conn.: Yale University Press, 1986), 1:91–141; and idem, *Who Guards the Guardians? Judicial Control of Administration* (Athens: University of Georgia Press, 1988).

32. 5 U.S. Code of Federal Regulations, 551–559; and 702–706 (judicial review).

33. For example, the APA's adjudicative requirements apply only if the agency's statutes require that its cases must "be determined on the record after opportunity for an agency hearing."

34. For a review of the delegation issue's development, see Louis Fisher, *Conflicts between Congress and the President* (Princeton, N.J.: Princeton University Press, 1985), 99–139; and Theodore J. Lowi, *The End of Liberalism: The Second Republic of the United States*, 2nd ed. (New York: Norton, 1979)—the latter a spirited critique of "the end of the rule of law." We should note that courts tend to interpret narrowly a statute that otherwise would be vulnerable to the constitutional attack.

35. See Office of the Federal Register, National Archives and Records Administration, *The Federal Register: What It Is and How to Use It*, rev. ed. (Washington, D.C.: Government Printing Office, 1985).

36. For the problems associated with the "statutory duty" concept, see Martin Shapiro, *Who Guards the Guardians? Judicial Control of Administration* (Athens: University of Georgia Press, 1988), 115–124.

37. Leonard Buder, "U.S. Is Suing Con Edison over Asbestos," *New York Times*, January 8, 1988.

38. *Fisen v. Carlyle & Jacquelin*, 417 U.S. 156 (1974).

39. Rochelle L. Stanfield, "Out-Standing in Court," *National Journal* 20, February 13, 1988, 388–391. The case, *National Wildlife Federation v. Hodel* (earlier titled *In Re: Permanent Surface Mining Regulation Litigation*), was pending in the Federal Court of Appeals for the District of Columbia. The case had been in the courts since 1979.

40. See Peter H. Schuck, *Agent Orange on Trial: Mass Toxic Disasters in the Courts* (Cambridge, Mass.: Harvard University Press, 1986). In 1989 the Department of Veterans Affairs abided by, instead of appealing, a federal court decision that could result in government payments up to 35,000 veterans who claimed disabilities from Agent Orange. Charles Mohr, "U.S. Not Appealing Agent Orange Case," *New York Times*, May 12, 1989.

41. For an analysis of this story, see Martha A. Derthick, *Up in Smoke: From Legislation to Litigation in Tobacco Politics*, 2nd ed. (Washington, D.C.: CQ Press, 2005).

42. *Data Processing Service Organizations v. Camp*, 397 U.S. 150 (1970). This decision propounded the "zone of interests" doctrine: even if a plaintiff cannot tie his or her claimed injury directly to a particular statutory or constitutional provision, the suit may proceed if the plaintiff's interest is "arguably within the zone of interests to be protected or regulated by the statute or constitutional guarantee in question." Ibid., 151–152.

43. General Accounting Office, *Product Liability: Extent of "Litigation Explosion" in Federal Courts Questioned* (Washington, D.C.: Government Printing Office, 1988).

44. For the history, see Phillip J. Cooper, *Public Law and Public Administration*, 2nd ed. (Englewood Cliffs, N.J.: Prentice Hall, 1988), 363–389. An admirable review, with proposals for increasing governments' liability, is Peter H. Schuck, *Suing Government: Citizen Remedies for Official Wrongs* (New Haven, Conn.: Yale University Press, 1983). Our treatment draws extensively on this work and on Jerry L. Mashaw and Richard A. Merrill, *Administrative Law* (St. Paul, Minn.: West, 1992), 783–843. See also Jeremy Rabkin, "Where the Lines Have Held: Tort Claims against the Federal Government," in *New Directions in Liability Law: Proceedings*

of the Academy of Political Science 37, no. 1, ed. Walter Olson (New York: Academy of Political Science, 1988), 112–125.

45. 28 U.S. Code 1346, 2674, 2680. A 1974 amendment specified tort liability for assault, battery, false imprisonment, false arrest, abuse of process, and malicious prosecution by federal "investigative or law enforcement officials." Ibid., sec. 2680 (h).

46. The leading case is *Barr v. Matteo,* 360 U.S. 564 (1959).

47. *Bivens v. Six Unknown Named Agents of the Federal Bureau of Narcotics,* 403 U.S. 388 (1971), and *Wood v. Strickland,* 420 U.S. 308 (1975). Curiously, absolute immunity continues to protect judges, administrative law judges, and prosecutors from tort actions (though not from criminal prosecution). The Supreme Court's reasoning, seemingly serving the self-interest of its branch's members and associates, has been criticized as indistinguishable from the reasoning that would ensure executive officials' risk-free exercise of discretionary judgment.

48. *Westfall v. Erwin,* 108 Supreme Court Reporter 580 (1988). Federal Employee Liability and Tort Compensation Act, 102 U.S. Statutes 4563. The key question becomes whether the employee was acting "within the scope" of his or her official duties, not whether the duties were discretionary or nondiscretionary.

49. 42 U.S. Code 1983.

50. See Michael Lipsky, *Street-Level Bureaucracy: The Dilemmas of the Individual in Public Services* (New York: Russell Sage Foundation, 1980).

51. For an exploration of the issues of administrative law, see Phillip J. Cooper, *Governing by Contract: Challenges and Opportunities for Public Managers* (Washington, D.C.: CQ Press, 2002).

52. For further development of the contrasts, see Donald L. Horowitz, *The Courts and Social Policy* (Washington, D.C.: Brookings Institution, 1977).

53. So do agency lawyers and those in the Department of Justice, which claims (not always successfully) a monopoly of litigating

authority. For the conflicting attitudes, see Donald L. Horowitz, *The Jurocracy: Government Lawyers, Agency Programs, and Judicial Decisions* (Lexington, Mass.: Lexington Books, 1977). For agency lawyers' attributes and incentives, see Eve Spangler, *Lawyers for Hire* (New Haven: Yale University Press, 1986), 107–143.

54. See Phillip J. Cooper, "Conflict or Constructive Tension: The Changing Relationship of Judges and Administrators," *Public Administration Review* 45 (Special Issue, November 1985): 643–652.

55. The classic analysis of the courts' emphasis on wide participation in agency proceedings is Richard B. Stewart, "The Reformation of American Administrative Law," *Harvard Law Review* 88 (June 1975): 1667–1813.

56. The courts derive such intentions from the legislative history of a statute. For an argument that this has unhappily magnified the role of congressional subcommittees and their staffs, which compile the legislative history (reports, floor statements, and hearings), see R. Shep Melnick, "The Politics of Partnership," *Public Administration Review* 45 (Special Issue, November 1985): 651–660.

57. Melnick, *Regulation and the Courts,* 379. Melnick's book is an admirable review of the throes of developing policies in a court-monitored setting.

58. Jerry Mashaw, *Due Process in the Administrative State* (New Haven, Conn.: Yale University Press, 1985), 160–161. The shifting attitudes are well traced and appraised in this work. For greater detail, see Mashaw and Merrill, *Administrative Law.*

59. T. Alexander Aleinikoff, "Immigration," in *The Department of Homeland Security's First Year: A Report Card,* ed. Donald F. Kettl (Washington, D.C.: Brookings Institution, 2004), 94.

60. Executive Orders 12,291, 3 U.S. Code (1981 compilation), and 12, 498, ibid. (1985 compilation).

61. Office of Management and Budget Circular A-4, September 17, 2003, http://www .whitehouse.gov/omb/circulars_a004_a-4.

62. Major assessments are Morton Rosenberg, "Regulatory Management, in U.S. Senate Committee on Governmental Affairs," *Office of Management and Budget: Evolving Roles and Future Issues,* 98th Cong., 2d sess., Senate print 99–134 (February 1986), 185–233; *Presidential Management of Rulemaking in Regulatory Agencies: A Report by a Panel of the National Academy of Public Administration* (Washington, D.C.: National Academy of Public Administration, January 1987); and William J. Pielsticker, "Presidential Control of Administrative Rule Making: Its Potential and Its Limits," paper delivered at the 1988 annual meeting of the American Political Science Association, Washington, D.C., September 1–4, 1988. See also General Accounting Office, *Regulatory Review: Information on OMB's Review Process* (Washington, D.C.: Government Printing Office, 1989).

63. This is reinforced by OMB's power, under the Paperwork Act of 1980, to review and disapprove agencies' proposals to collect information. But the Supreme Court overturned OMB's use of the act to block agencies' regulations that require private parties such as employers to disclose information (e.g., exposure to hazardous substances) to other private parties such as employees. *Dole v. U.S. Steelworkers of America,* 110 Supreme Court Reporter 929 (1990).

64. "Text of Whitman Letter of Resignation," *CNN,* May 21, 2003, http://www.cnn .com/2003/ALLPOLITICS/05/21/whitman .letter/index.html.

65. Ackerman and Heinzerling, *Priceless,* 234.

66. Cooper, *Public Law and Public Administration,* 398–399.

14. Administrative Accountability, Effectiveness, and Politics

1. Charlie Savage, "Bush Could Bypass New Torture Ban," *Boston Globe,* January 4, 2006.

2. Charlie Savage, "Bush Challenges Hundreds of Laws," *Boston Globe,* April 30, 2006.

3. Statement of Gary L. Kepplinger, *Presidential Signing Statements: Agency Implementation of Selected Provisions of Law,* GAO-08–553T (Washington, DC: GAO, March 11, 2008).

4. Charlie Savage, "Cheney Aide Is Screening Legislation," *Boston Globe,* May 28, 2006.

5. Christopher H. Foreman Jr., *Signals from the Hill: Congressional Oversight and the Challenge of Social Regulation* (New Haven, Conn.: Yale University Press, 1988), 12. For a thorough and careful look at oversight, see Joel D. Aberbach, *Keeping a Watchful Eye: The Politics of Congressional Oversight* (Washington, D.C.: Brookings Institution Press, 1990).

6. See Richard E. Neustadt, "Politicians and Bureaucrats," in *The Congress and America's Future,* 2d ed., ed. David B. Truman (Englewood Cliffs, N.J.: Prentice Hall, 1973), 119. For a history of congressional-administrative relations, see James L. Sundquist, "Congress as Public Administrator," in *A Centennial History of American Public Administration,* ed. Ralph Clark Chandler (New York: Free Press, 1987), 261–289.

7. National Academy of Public Administration, *Congressional Oversight of Regulatory Agencies: The Need to Strike a Balance and Focus on Performance* (Washington, D.C.: NAPA, 1988), 1.

8. Nathaniel C. Nash, "Telling State Dept. How to Run Foreign Policy . . . ," *New York Times,* October 12, 1987.

9. J. Ronald Fox with James L. Field, *The Defense Management Challenge: Weapons Acquisition* (Boston: Harvard Business School Press, 1988), 76. See also David C. Hendrickson, *Reforming Defense: The State of American Civil-Military Relations* (Baltimore: Johns Hopkins University Press, 1988), 30–34. More broadly, see Louis Fisher, "Micromanagement by Congress: Reality and Mythology," in *The Fettered Presidency: Legal Constraints on the Executive Branch,* ed. L. Gordon Crovitz and Jeremy A. Rabkin (Washington, D.C.: American Enterprise Institute, 1989), 139–157.

10. Henry Kissinger and Cyrus Vance, "Bipartisan Objectives for American

Foreign Policy," *Foreign Affairs* 66 (Summer 1988): 901.

11. Siobhan Gorman, "Experts Say INS Restructuring Won't Solve Management Problems," *Government Executive,* May 3, 2002, http://www.govexec.com/dailyfed/05 02/050302nj4.htm.

12. See David R. Mayhew, *Congress: The Electoral Connection* (New Haven, Conn.: Yale University Press, 1974).

13. See Seymour Scher, "Conditions for Legislative Control," *Journal of Politics* 25 (August 1963): 526–551.

14. Ibid., 527.

15. These and similar terms are scattered throughout Senate Committee on Government Operations, *Study on Federal Regulation,* vol. 2, *Congressional Oversight of Regulatory Agencies,* committee print, 95th Cong., 1st sess., 1977. Despite the restrictive title, this volume is one of the best reviews of performance and problems of oversight of both regulatory and nonregulatory agencies by both the House and the Senate. See also NAPA, *Congressional Oversight of Regulatory Agencies,* which reached similar conclusions.

16. Mathew D. McCubbins and Thomas Schwartz, "Congressional Oversight Overlooked: Police Patrols versus Fire Alarms," *American Journal of Political Science* 28 (Fall 1984): 169, 172.

17. This list comes from NAPA, *Congressional Oversight of Regulatory Agencies*, 7–9.

18. See Hugh Heclo, "Issue Networks and the Executive Establishment," in *The New Political System,* ed. Anthony King (Washington, D.C.: American Enterprise Institute, 1978), 87–124.

19. R. Douglas Arnold, *Congress and the Bureaucracy: A Theory of Influence* (New Haven, Conn.: Yale University Press, 1979), 35.

20. Ibid., 67–68.

21. Lawrence C. Dodd and Richard L. Schott, *Congress and the Administrative State* (New York: Wiley, 1979), 170. More generally, see Morris S. Ogul, *Congress Oversees the Bureaucracy: Studies in Legislative*

Supervision (Pittsburgh, Pa.: University of Pittsburgh Press, 1976).

22. NAPA, *Congressional Oversight of Regulatory Agencies,* 9.

23. See Foreman, *Signals from the Hill,* chap. 4.

24. Dodd and Schott, *Congress and the Administrative State*, 166.

25. On the basis of members' shifts to and from other committees prior to 1973, the House Government Operations Committee ranked eighteenth in prestige among the twenty standing committees, and its Senate counterpart ranked thirteenth among the sixteen standing committees. See Leroy N. Rieselbach, *Congressional Politics* (New York: McGraw-Hill, 1973), 60–61n.

26. Dodd and Schott, *Congress and the Administrative State*, 168.

27. Ibid., 173–184.

28. Norman J. Ornstein, "Perspectives on House Reform of Homeland Security," testimony before the Subcommittee on Rules, Select Committee on Homeland Security, U.S. House of Representatives, May 19, 2003, http://www.aei.org/speech/foreign-and-defense-policy/perspectives-on-house-reform-of-homeland-security.

29. Senate Committee on Armed Services, Staff Report, *Defense Organization: The Need for Change,* committee print, 99th Cong., 1st sess., 1985, 581–582. The Georgetown University study is quoted in this report.

30. Thomas P. Murphy, "Political Executive Roles, Policymaking, and Interface with the Career Bureaucracy," *Bureaucrat* 6 (Summer 1977): 107.

31. Stephen R. Heifetz, "The Risk of Too Much Oversight," *New York Times,* July 21, 2008, http://www.nytimes.com/2008/07/21/opinion/21heifetz.html.

32. For one interest group's discussion of these issues, see Stephen L. Katz, *Government: Decisions without Democracy* (Washington, D.C.: People for the American Way, 1987).

33. Improper classification and other issues are reviewed in House Committee on Government Operations, *Executive Classification of Information . . . Third Report,* House Rpt. 93–221, 1973.

34. Summary of the board's findings by Edmund S. Muskie, in John Tower, Edmund Muskie, and Brent Scowcroft, *The Tower Commission Report* (New York: Bantam Books, 1987), xvii.

35. Christopher Madison, "Flexibility v. Congress's Right to Know," *National Journal,* July 4, 1987, 1727.

36. Pauline Jelinek, "Rumsfeld Apologizes for Iraq Prison Abuse," *Miami Herald,* May 7, 2004.

37. In 1972 both the Justice Department and the White House refused to furnish the draft of Executive Order 11753 (on classification of documents) to the House Committee on Government Operations, arguing that it was only a working draft; this occurred after a newspaper's disclosure of details of the draft. See House Committee on Government Operations, *Executive Classification of Information . . . Third Report,* 53.

38. NAPA, *Congressional Oversight of Regulatory Agencies,* 24.

39. Frederick C. Mosher and others, *Watergate: Its Implications for Responsible Government* (New York: Basic Books, 1974), 115.

40. Excellent treatments of earlier congressional efforts to cope with scientific and technological issues are Thomas P. Jahnige, "The Congressional Committee System and the Oversight Process: Congress and NASA," *Western Political Quarterly* 21 (June 1968): 227–239; and House Committee on Science and Aeronautics, Subcommittee on Science, Research, and Development, *Technological Information for Congress,* 92d Cong., 1st sess., 1971.

41. Francis E. Rourke, "Bureaucracy in the American Constitutional Order," *Political Science Quarterly* 102 (Summer 1978): 217–232.

42. Michael J. Malbin, *Unelected Representatives: Congressional Staff and the Future of Representative Government* (New York: Basic Books, 1979), 5. On the role of staffs in helping with congressional casework, see Morris P. Fiorina, *Congress: Keystone of the Washington Establishment* (New Haven, Conn.: Yale University Press, 1977). See also Harrison W. Fox and Susan Webb Hammond, *Congressional Staffs: The Invisible Force in American Lawmaking* (New York: Free Press, 1977).

43. Malbin, *Unelected Representatives,* 10.

44. Dodd and Schott, *Congress and the Administrative State,* 270–271.

45. Senate Committee on Government Operations, *Study on Federal Regulation,* 2:71; and Ernest S. Griffith, in Senate Commission on the Operation of the Senate, *Congressional Support Agencies,* committee print, 94th Cong., 2d sess., 1976, 126.

46. For a study of the history, development, and role of the General Accounting Office, see Frederick C. Mosher, *The GAO: The Quest for Accountability in American Government* (Boulder, Colo.: Westview, 1979).

47. See Louis Fisher, *The Politics of Shared Power: Congress and the Executive,* 2nd ed. (Washington, D.C.: CQ Press, 1987), 125–129; and *Bowsher v. Synar,* 106 S. Ct. 3181 (1986).

48. Budget and Accounting Act of 1921, Secs. 309, 305 (31 U.S. Code 49, 71).

49. These officials could then attempt to collect disallowed payments from the recipients; failing that, they might seek passage of congressional acts reimbursing them. In the 1940s, about a million federal employees paid almost $2 million annually to insurance companies to cover any liabilities for disallowed payments of public funds. Finally, in 1955, Congress authorized agencies themselves to purchase blanket surety bonds for their employees. See Senate Committee on Government Operations, *Financial Management in the Federal Government,* 92d Cong., 1st sess., 1971, 2:233–238.

50. Nicely illustrative of the point, as well as of auditors' petty tendency to question commonsense judgments of ambassadors and other officials, are the case studies in Gerald C. Schulsinger, *The General Accounting Office: Two Glimpses,* Inter-University Case No. 35 (Syracuse, N.Y.: Inter-University Case Program, 1956). For a full set of case studies illustrating past and current

practice, see *Cases in Accountability: The Work of the GAO,* ed. Erasmus H. Kloman (Boulder, Colo.: Westview, 1979).

51. See the classic study, Harvey C. Mansfield, *The Comptroller General* (New Haven, Conn.: Yale University Press, 1939).

52. General Accounting Office, *Standards for Audit of Governmental Organizations, Programs, Activities and Functions* (Washington, D.C.: Government Printing Office, 1973), 1.

53. Congressional Budget Act of 1974, 88. Stat. 326; 31 U.S. Code of Federal Regulations 1154. (Emphasis added.)

54. See Government Accountability Office, "High Risk List," http://www.gao.gov/highrisk/overview.

55.. These and other problems are treated by Joseph Pois and Ernest S. Griffith in Senate Commission on the Operation of the Senate, *Congressional Support Agencies,* 31–54, 126–133; Joseph Pois, "Trends in General Accounting Office Audits," and Ira Sharkansky, "The Politics of Auditing," in *The New Political Economy: The Public Use of the Private Sector,* ed. Bruce L. R. Smith (New York: Wiley, 1975), 245–318; and John T. Rourke, "The GAO: An Evolving Role," *Public Administration Review* 38 (September–October 1978): 453–457. A full history and analysis is Mosher, *The GAO.*

56.. For an exploration of other approaches to performance management, see Robert L. Cardy, *Performance Management: Concepts, Skills, and Exercises* (Armonk, N.Y.: M. E. Sharpe, 2004); and Paul R. Niven, *Balanced Scorecard: Step-by-Step for Government and Nonprofit Agencies* (New York: Wiley, 2003).

57. John M. Kamensky, "GPRA Modernization Act of 2010 Explained," http://www.business ofgovernment.org/blog/business-gover nment/gpra-modernization-act-2010-explained-part-1.

58. Statement of Patricia A. Dalton, General Accounting Office, *Results-Oriented Government: GPRA Has Established a Solid Foundation for Achieving Greater Results,* GAO-04–594T (Washington, D.C.: GAO, March 31, 2004), 3.

59. Ibid., 15.

60. Tom Shoop, "The Missing Link," *Government Executive,* April 1, 2004, http://www.govexec.com/magazine/magazine-outlook/2004/04/the-missing-link/16410.

61. Donald Moynihan, *The Dynamics of Performance Management: Constructing Information and Reform* (Washington, D.C.: Georgetown University Press, 2008).

62. "2013 Annual Letter from Bill Gates," http://annualletter.gatesfoundation.org/?loc=en#nav=section1&slide=0.

63. Foreman, *Signals from the Hill,* 6, 7. See also McCubbins and Schwartz, "Congressional Oversight Overlooked."

64. Complicating Congress's role is the era of divided government, with different parties in control of Congress and the presidency, for nearly all of the post-Vietnam period. See James L. Sundquist, "Needed: A Political Theory for the New Era of Coalition Government in the United States," *Political Science Quarterly* 103 (Winter 1988–1989): 613–635.

65. Judith E. Gruber, *Controlling Bureaucracies: Dilemmas in Democratic Governance* (Berkeley: University of California Press, 1987), 57.

66. See Chapter 12's discussion of "The Importance of Feedback."

67. For the prevalence and the inadequacy of this approach to internal control, see U.S. Comptroller General, *Federal Agencies Can and Should Do More to Combat Fraud in Government Programs* (Washington, D.C.: Government Printing Office, 1978); and Jerome B. McKinney and Michael Johnston, eds., *Fraud, Waste, and Abuse in Government: Causes, Consequences, and Cures* (Philadelphia: Institute for the Study of Human Issues, 1986).

68. The classic argument for redundancy in administrative organization and process is Martin Landau, "Redundancy, Rationality, and the Problem of Duplication and Overlap," *Public Administration Review* 29 (July–August 1969): 346–358.

69. Dana Milbank, "Putting Her Foot Down and Getting the Boot," *Washington Post,* July 10, 2008, A3.

70. Ibid.

Glossary of Key Concepts

accountability: the process of holding administrators responsible for their actions, especially their compliance with the law and their effectiveness in managing programs.

adjudication: one of two basic regulatory approaches used by administrative agencies wherein administrative law judges within agencies hear individual cases and develop a body of rules.

administrative confidentiality: privacy protections afforded by government to individuals and organizations; and restrictions of access to internal records collected by governmental organizations.

administrative responsibility: the process of holding specific individuals responsible, within the bureaucracy, for specific actions.

administrative rulemaking: one of two basic regulatory approaches used by administrative agencies wherein public managers write regulations that apply to all persons and organizations meeting certain guidelines.

administrative state: Dwight Waldo's term to describe the rising importance and power of bureaucracy in American democracy.

agencies: the generic term for public bureaucracies, which carry out public programs on behalf of policymakers.

agents: those who carry out policies on behalf of superiors (known as principals).

Antideficiency Act: the federal law that forbids government officials from spending money not specifically appropriated for a purpose. The act limits the discretion of administrators.

antitrust laws: legislation intended to promote free competition by eliminating the power of monopolies.

appropriations: legislation that commits money to be spent (compare authorizations).

appropriations committees: standing committees that manage the annual appropriations process.

areal (or prefectoral) system: an approach to government that structures its organizations by a particular geographic region.

assembled examination: a written test used principally to qualify individuals for lower levels of the civil service.

at-will employees: employees in an at-will employment system in which can be fired at the discretion of managers.

authority: the basic skeleton of bureaucracy, through which a government, an agency, or an individual is vested with the rightful power to make decisions within constitutionally defined limits with the expectation of widespread compliance.

authorizations: legislation that creates programs and puts a limit on the money to be spent managing them (compare appropriations).

authorizing committees: standing committees that can initiate, review, and report out bills and resolutions in particular subject-matter areas.

auxiliary staff: the staff of an agency that provides basic housekeeping functions, including management of the personnel and budgetary processes.

Balanced Budget and Emergency Deficit Control Act: an act sponsored by Sens. Phil Gramm, Warren Rudman, and Ernest Hollings, and passed in 1985, which set automatic spending cuts if Congress and the president could not agree on budget reductions. Its goal was to eliminate the federal deficit by 1990. Also known as the Gramm-Rudman Act.

bargaining approach: a method of making decisions in which parties negotiate their differences. This approach seeks to maximize political support.

black budget: the spending authorized for secret government activities.

block grants: a strategy of intergovernmental assistance that gives the recipient broad discretion in how the money may be used (compare categorical grants).

broadbanding: a civil service reform that replaces multiple levels of job categories ("bands") of the civil service system with fewer, wider categories that encompass more employees and more skills.

budget authority: legislative approval of programs and the ability to spend money, which must be supported by an appropriation.

bump: the practice whereby a higher-seniority government employee can force out a lower-seniority employee.

bureaucratic model: the traditional approach to bureaucracy, based on hierarchy and authority.

bureaucratic responsibility: the duty of public administrators, which is made up of two overlapping, and generally, but not always, compatible elements, accountability and ethical behavior.

bureaus: the basic building blocks of governmental organizations.

buyouts: offers of lump-sum payments to government employees in exchange for their agreement to retire from government service.

cabinet: the collection of administrative departments, as well as those additional offices that the chief executive (such as the president) raises to that rank.

capital budgets: the portion of the budget for items with long useful lives, like roads and fire trucks.

capture: the use of political influence by interest groups to shape the decisions of administrators.

categorical grants: a strategy of intergovernmental assistance that gives the recipient relatively narrow discretion in how the money may be used (compare block grants).

chain of command: the line of authority from top policymakers through the hierarchy, which is used to define who is responsible for doing what.

charismatic authority: an approach to authority that relies on the personal magnetism of the leader.

civil service system: the collection of rules and procedures that govern the employees who work in career positions in government.

class action: legal action taken by a small group of individuals on behalf of a far larger group of people who share the same complaint.

classical theory: typically refers to organizations that operate through hierarchies structured with authority.

clearance procedure: a method of cooperation among agencies that entails that an agency's proposed decisions in a subject-matter area be reviewed, whether for comment or for formal approval or veto, by other interested agencies.

closed-system theorists: an approach to systems theory that focuses on the internal workings of the system.

collective bargaining: negotiation by members of a union over employee rights and compensation.

comparable worth: the principle that individuals ought to receive equivalent pay for equivalent responsibilities.

compensatory economics: use of the budget to steer the economy.

continuing resolutions: Congressional actions that continue the level of spending after the fiscal year at its current level while Congress and the president negotiate the details of a new budget.

continuous improvement: a management strategy devoted to developing ongoing feedback about an organization's results to enhance its success.

contracting: legal arrangements in which a seller agrees to provide a good or service to a buyer for a mutually agreeable price. Government at all levels has increasingly relied on contracts with private sector experts and outside organizations for the delivery of public services.

contracts: legal agreement in which a seller agrees to provide a good or service to a buyer for a mutually agreeable price. Government has increasingly relied on contracts with private-sector experts and outside organizations for the delivery of public services.

control staff: the staff of an agency that helps top officials maintain a check on the behavior of other agency employees.

coordination: the process of orienting the activities of individuals and organizations so they are mutually supportive.

core staff: the staff of an agency that provides basic support to the agency's line activities.

cost-benefit analysis: a comparison of the expenditures required for a program with the gains it produces. An example is risk assessment.

crossover sanctions: punishments incurred in a program that were caused by failures to meet another program's standards.

customer service movement: a management strategy devoted to focusing an organization's efforts on improving the satisfaction of its "customers"—those who benefit from its goods and services.

debt: money borrowed by the government in the short term and repaid in the long term.

deferrals: the decision by executive-branch officials to postpone spending for a program (compare impoundment).

deficit: the excess of expenditures over revenues in any given fiscal year (compare surplus).

delegation: legislative assignment of power to administrators to implement public programs; and reliance on one level of government to accomplish the goals of another.

direct administration: the provision of government goods and services by government organizations themselves, as compared with indirect administration, in which goods and services are provided through grants, contracts, tax incentives, or other multi-organizational/multi-sectoral policy strategies.

direct delivery of services: the provision of public goods and services by government agencies themselves (compared with contracts and other tools of indirect government).

direct tools: instruments of government action through which government agencies themselves provide government goods and services.

downsizing: a focus on reducing the size and cost of government operations, especially through reductions in the workforce.

earmarks: decisions made by legislators and put into appropriations bills to fund narrow, particular projects (usually as "pork-barrel" spending).

economic regulation: the portion of public sector rulemaking that affects the behavior of private markets (compare social regulation).

efficiency: a measure of the level of inputs required to produce a given level of outputs.

e-government: a strategy of using information technology, especially the Internet and the World Wide Web, to make it easier for citizens to interact with government.

entitlements: governmental programs through which an individual is automatically guaranteed services—typically, a payment—because the individual meets requirements set in law.

ethical behavior: the adherence to moral standards and avoidance of even the appearance of unethical actions.

executive leadership: strategic direction provided by the top officials of an organization.

executive privilege: the claim by presidents that communication with aides is protected from outside scrutiny, including investigation by Congress.

exit: the decision by members of an organization to leave, especially because they disagree with policies and programs.

externalities: an economic term referring to indirect benefits and costs beyond the direct costs and benefits of a project. Also called spillovers.

federal grants: transfer of money from the federal government to state and local governments in pursuit of national objectives.

feedback loop: an element of systems theory that connects the outputs an organization produces to its inputs.

fire alarm oversight: a strategy of legislative oversight of bureaucracy based on instigation and response to crises and problems. Compare "police patrol oversight."

fiscal accountability: a method of accountability that focuses on the flow of money through an organization.

fiscal policy: decisions about government spending and taxing, and their effect on the economy's performance (compare monetary policy).

fiscal year: the government's budget year (starting October 1 for the federal government, July 1 for many state and local governments).

formal approach: a theory of bureaucracy that relies on a rigorous model of the relationships between actors, especially between principals and agents.

formula-based programs: intergovernmental grant programs in which the amount of the grant is determined by criteria defined by law.

function: the specific role or duty performed by a part of an organization.

fungibility: the ability of grant recipients to transfer the proceeds from a grant to cover the expenses of another activity.

furloughs: days off without pay for federal employees.

government by proxy: the rise of government's use of indirect tools of public action (including contracts, grants, regulations, and special tax provisions) to pursue public goals.

government-by-proxy approach: an approach to organizations that notes that government delegates authority to other governments, to private organizations, and to mixed public-private enterprises as well as within its own organizational structure.

government corporations: organizations that perform public functions but that are organized—and operate—like private companies, with a profit-and-loss bottom line (including Amtrak and the Federal Deposit Insurance Corporation).

Government Performance and Results Act (GPRA): legislation passed by Congress in 1993 that requires executive branch agencies to define their goals and measure their performance in achieving them.

grade creep: the tendency for agencies to increase over time the number of top administrative positions and to seek higher classifications for existing positions.

grantsmanship: the aggressive search for money from other sources of funds, especially the search by governments for aid from higher levels of government.

Hatch Act: federal legislation passed in 1939 restricting political activity by government employees. Also called "An Act to Prevent Pernicious Political Activities."

hierarchy: the relationship between levels of a bureaucracy.

human capital: an approach to management that focuses on identifying the skills employees need to accomplish an organization's work and in developing those skills to ensure that they produce strong and effective governmental programs.

human relations movement: an approach to organizations that holds that the relationships among individuals, especially in motivating employees, is the most important element of organizational theory. Also called the humanist approach.

humanist approach: a strategy of management that builds on interpersonal relationships and that relies on motivating individuals toward high performance.

implementation: the process of transforming policy goals into results.

impound: refusal by the president to spend money appropriated by Congress (compare deferrals).

incrementalism: a theory that decisions typically are—and should be—made in small steps, with the opportunity to make adjustments in between. This approach is the basis for bottom-up budgeting.

independent agencies: governmental organizations that exist separately from the cabinet departments.

indirect tools: the provision of public goods and services by nongovernmental partners (and partners outside the level of government creating a program), through instruments like grants, contracts, regulations, and special tax provisions.

inner cabinet: the Departments of State, Defense, Justice, and Treasury, which constitute the federal government's oldest functions and manage its most important missions.

inputs: the resources, especially money and employees, that organizations use in producing outputs.

interagency agreements: mutual understandings reached by several organizations, which detail the contributions each organization will make to a common goal.

interagency committees: committees that exist to promote collaboration between jointly occupied areas at the cabinet, subcabinet, and bureau levels.

iron triangle: a theory that suggests agency managers, congressional committees and subcommittees, and interest groups work closely to shape policy, and that their shared work is more important than other forces on the process.

layer cake federalism: a theory of intergovernmental relations that holds that the responsibilities of federal, state, and local governments can be cleanly separated, like the layers of a cake.

lead agency formula: a method of cooperation wherein one agency is designated to lead and attempt to coordinate all agencies' activities in a particular area.

legislative budget: fiscal policy decisions framed by the actions of the legislature, compared with budget recommendations made by the executive branch.

legislative review: the official term for legislative oversight.

line activities: those actions that contribute directly to the mission of an organization (compare staff activities). Also called operating activities.

line-item veto: authority granted to executives (principally governors) to strike individual items from legislation. Presidents have long asked for the same line-item veto power that governors enjoy.

loan programs: an indirect tool of government that seeks to fund public goals by making credit available to individuals and organizations, either by the government's making a direct loan or by the government guaranteeing the repayment of a loan made by a private organization.

management by objectives (MBO): a strategy in which managers chart quantitative objectives for a program to accomplish in the coming year, which in turn determines the budget required for the program.

mandates: requirements that must be met as a condition of aid.

marble cake federalism: the theory of intergovernmental relations that holds that the responsibilities of federal, state, and local governments cannot be cleanly separated and that, instead, they tend to mix and swirl like the colors of a marble cake.

monetary policy: decisions by the Federal Reserve on interest rates and the money supply, and their effect on the economy's performance (compare fiscal policy). ·

national debt: the net deficit that accumulates over time.

National Performance Review: used during the Clinton administration by managers to devise strategies for improving government operations while setting top-down targets for reducing the number of government employees.

National Security Council: an organization within the Executive Office of the President, established in 1947, to advise the president on matters of foreign and military policy.

network analysis: an approach to organizational theory that focuses on the relationships among organizations in sharing responsibility for programs.

neutral competence: the public administration principle that administrators ought to perform their jobs to the highest possible level, without political favoritism.

neutrality doctrine: the principle that public administrators ought to manage programs without political favoritism.

NIMBY phenomenon: the aversion of citizens for projects they perceive will have a direct negative effect on them and their local area (short for "not in my backyard").

nongovernmental organizations: nonprofit organizations, typically devoted to the social purposes of its members, which play an increasingly important role as front-line providers of governmentally funded services.

nonprofit: society's third sector, in addition to the public and private sectors. Some nonprofits charge fees, some receive grants and contracts from the public and private sectors, and others receive voluntary contributions; many operate under a combination of all three revenue sources. Nonprofits exist to serve social purposes, instead of making profits (like private organizations). They operate outside the public sector, but often help implement governmental goals.

Office of Management and Budget: an organization within the Executive Office of the President, to advise the president on budgetary and management policies. Initially established in 1921 in the Treasury Department, it came under the purview of the Executive Office in 1939.

Office of Policy Development: an organization within the Executive Office of the President, to advise the president on domestic policies.

open-system theorists: those who advocate an approach to systems theory that focuses on the relationship of the system with the environment.

organizational cultures: the ethos and philosophy that shape the behavior of individuals within an organization.

organizational structure: the arrangement of elements within an organization.

organizational theory: the collection of concepts that seeks to describe and predict the way that organizations—and the people within them—act.

outer cabinet: the remaining cabinet-level departments outside the inner cabinet.

outlays: expenditures that occur within any given fiscal year.

outputs: the goods and services that an organization produces.

oversight: review of the behavior of individuals within organizations, and organizations themselves, by those with authority over them. In public administration, the term is used most commonly to refer to the review of administrative acts by legislatures.

partial preemption: the decision by a higher level of government that, if a lower government does not meet predetermined standards, the higher level of government will step in and administer the program itself.

participative decision-making approach: a strategy of decision making that attempts to build support for decisions by including those affected in the decision-making process.

partisan mutual adjustment: a strategy of bargaining in which those involved in a decision (partisans) bargain out their differences (mutual adjustment).

performance management: a strategy to improve the results of governmental programs by focusing on evaluation of results.

performance measures: assessments of success, of organizations and individuals, in achieving the goals set for them.

Planning-Programming-Budgeting System (PPBS): a budgeting system first introduced in the federal government in the early 1960s, which seeks rational decisions through the identification of goals, developing those goals into programs, and translating the programs into a long-term budget plan.

pluralist approach: an approach to organizations that focuses on the interaction of political forces in shaping organizational behavior.

police patrol oversight: a strategy of legislative oversight of bureaucracy based on regular, routine reviews of administrative practice. Compare "fire alarm oversight"

policy-administration dichotomy: the separation of political decision making from administrative policy implementation.

policymaking: the process of defining the goals that public organizations are charged with seeking. Also referred to as policy formation.

politics-administration dichotomy: the notion, advanced by Woodrow Wilson in a famous 1887 article, that the tools for administering public policy can be separated from the politics of making it. It Is often used as the foundation for neutral competence, the idea that administrators need to have the capacity to administer programs, regardless of their political roots.

position classification: the identification of the specific knowledge a job requires, the job's level of difficulty, and the job's responsibilities.

principal-agent theory: a formal approach to organizations that focuses on the relationship between principals and agents.

principals: the superiors who shape the behavior of agents.

private attorneys general: role played by individuals or organizations in which a suit is filed not for money damages but to compel a government agency or a corporation to do or cease doing something that affects a major public interest or group.

Private Sector Survey on Cost Control: a commission appointed by President Ronald Reagan and chaired by industrialist J. Peter Grace, which focused on efforts to reduce the costs of government, especially by eliminating federal governmental programs and relying more on contracting out. Also called the Grace Commission.

privatization: a strategy for turning over public responsibilities to the private sector, either by selling public assets or transferring responsibility to the private sector, or by relying on private companies to supply a good or service through contracts.

process accountability: a method of accountability that focuses on how an organization pursues its objectives.

program accountability: a method of accountability that focuses on an organization's achievement of its policy objectives.

Program Assessment Rating Tool (PART): a budgeting system, developed during the George W. Bush administration, in which agency managers define their goals and measure their performance in meeting them.

Progressives: reformers who campaigned for stronger government regulation to protect citizens from private power and more public programs to improve the lives of ordinary Americans.

project-based programs: intergovernmental grant programs in which the amount of the grant is determined by the details of an approved project.

public administration: the process of translating public policies into results.

public bureaucracy: the organizations charged with public administration.

public-choice approach: a method of decision making that assumes individuals pursue their self-interest and derives propositions about their behavior—and the behavior of organizations—from this assumption. According to this approach, individuals are best motivated by market forces.

rational decision making: a method of decision making that seeks the most efficient solution for problems.

rational-legal authority: an element of traditional organizational theory that focuses on hierarchy and authority to accomplish an organization's goals.

red tape: a colloquial term for government regulations that tend to impose large costs with few benefits. The term comes from Civil War–era documents, which were tied up with red ribbons.

reductions in force (RIFs): involuntary layoff or termination of government employees.

reengineering: a strategy for improving an organization's results by transforming the organization's basic processes.

regulations: rules set by government to govern the behavior of individuals and organizations.

regulatory commissions: government organizations, typically independent agencies, whose function is to write and enforce rules governing private-sector behavior and whose policies are set by a multi-member board.

regulatory negotiation sessions: a strategy of bargaining in which all parties work out a mutually acceptable regulation and, in the process, greatly reduce the chances that the rule will be litigated.

reinventing government: the Clinton administration's strategy for producing "a government that works better and costs less."

representativeness: the degree to which the employees of a government agency, or of the government overall, reflect the demographic makeup of society at large.

rescissions: joint action by the president and Congress to take back budget authority.

risk assessment: a type of cost-benefit analysis that evaluates whether to regulate risks based on the tradeoffs between expenditures and gains.

rule of anticipated reactions: a strategy by executives to frame their budgetary requests according to how they believe legislators will react to them.

rule of law: the structure of legal process and precedent that frames agreed-upon strategies for resolving complex social, economic, and political problems.

satisficing: a strategy of decision making that seeks a satisfactory (not necessarily the best or most efficient) alternative.

scientific management movement: an approach to bureaucracy that seeks to improve performance by improving efficiency, especially in transforming inputs into outputs.

sensitivity training: an element of the human relations movement that seeks to make members of an organization more cognizant of the needs and incentives of their fellow organizational members.

signing statement: statement signed by the president that contains the administration's interpretation of a law and how it will be enforced.

social regulation: the portion of public sector rule-making that affects the health, safety, and well-being of citizens (compare economic regulation).

spillovers: a term from economics to describe effects of activities on those not directly involved in a market transaction. A factory, for example, might sell its products to buyers, but the pollution it produces is a cost that those living in surrounding areas might have to bear.

staff: the common term used to refer to the employees of an organization, not to be confused with staff activities. Sometimes also called pure-staff to distinguish from auxiliary and control staff.

staff activities: those actions (like personnel and budgeting) that support the mission of an organization (compare line activities).

stagflation: a simultaneous increase in inflation and decrease in economic growth, which stymied policymakers in the 1970s.

standing to sue: the legal right of an individual or organization to file a legal action.

structure: a formal arrangement among the people engaged in the organization's mission.

surplus: an excess of revenues over expenditures in any given fiscal year (compare deficit).

system boundaries: the border between a system and the rest of the environment.

system purpose: the function for which a system exists.

systems theory: an approach to organizations that focuses on how they translate inputs into outputs.

tax expenditures: special advantages in the tax code to create incentive for behavior the government wants to encourage. Tax expenditures include deductions (in which individuals can reduce their income by the amount of an expenditure, such as a home mortgage) and credits (in which individuals can reduce the tax due by the amount of an expenditure, such as payments for child care).

Taxpayer Bill of Rights (TABOR): Colorado's effort to reduce the growth of state government. The strategy has since been debated in other states as well.

throughputs: in systems theory, the process of transforming inputs into outputs.

Title 5: the classic standards for hiring and firing in the civil service.

tort action: a wrongful action, which causes damage or injury, for which individuals or organizations can file a civil suit.

total quality management (TQM): a strategy for improving an organization's results by focusing all of its processes and employees on the goal of increasing the value of the organization's work.

traditional authority: an orientation toward authority that relies on a belief in the sacredness of longstanding customs and that relies on the loyalty of individuals to someone who has become a leader in a long-established way.

transaction costs: the expenses, in time and money, incurred in how an organization conducts its operations.

transparent performance: an argument that the full disclosure of information about government's activities and the results of its programs will create strong incentives to achieve high levels of performance.

turnover: the rate at which employees leave an organization.

unassembled examination: a comprehensive résumé, detailing an applicant's education, training, and experience, which a personnel office uses to assess the applicant's qualifications for a position.

uncontrollable expenditures: outlays required by law, typically for formula-based payments to individuals such as social security. The expenditures are not strictly speaking uncontrollable; they can be changed by law, but such changes are difficult and frequently take a long time.

unionization: the effort by organized unions to increase their membership and bargaining power in government.

voice: the decision by members of an organization to remain within an organization and protest policies and programs with which they disagree.

Washington Monument ploy: a tactic used by administrators to shield themselves from budget cuts by threatening to eliminate their most popular programs (like tours of the Washington Monument) if legislators reduce appropriations.

whistleblowers: individuals who divulge details about the behavior of other members of their organization who might be in violation of the law.

zero-base budgeting (ZBB): a budget strategy that rejects incrementalism and asks administrators to analyze the implications of different packages of spending, from substantial reductions in current spending (the base) through significant increases.

Photo and Image Credits

Index

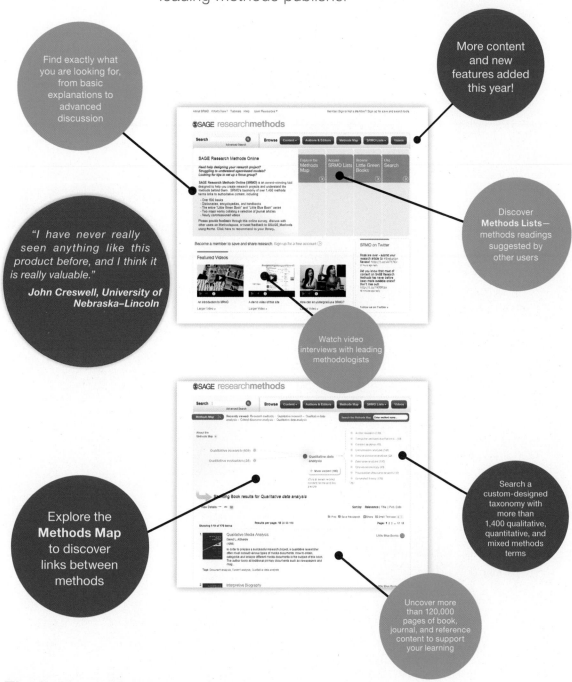

SAGE researchmethods

The essential online tool for researchers from the world's leading methods publisher

Find exactly what you are looking for, from basic explanations to advanced discussion

More content and new features added this year!

"I have never really seen anything like this product before, and I think it is really valuable."

John Creswell, University of Nebraska–Lincoln

Discover **Methods Lists**—methods readings suggested by other users

Watch video interviews with leading methodologists

Explore the **Methods Map** to discover links between methods

Search a custom-designed taxonomy with more than 1,400 qualitative, quantitative, and mixed methods terms

Uncover more than 120,000 pages of book, journal, and reference content to support your learning

Find out more at
www.sageresearchmethods.com